GREAT EVENTS
FROM
HISTORY II

GREAT EVENTS FROM HISTORY II

Business and Commerce Series

Volume 4
1967-1980

Edited by

FRANK N. MAGILL

SALEM PRESS

Pasadena, California   Englewood Cliffs, New Jersey

Library of Congress Cataloging-in-Publication Data
Great events from history II. Business and commerce series / edited by Frank N. Magill.
    p.   cm.
Includes bibliographical references and index.
   1. Economic history—20th century—Chronology.
   2. Business—History—20th century—Chronology.
   3. Commerce—History—20th century—Chronology.
I. Magill, Frank Northen, 1907-   . II. Title: Great events from history 2. Business and commerce series.
III. Title: Business and commerce series.
HC55.G68   1994
330.9—dc20
ISBN 0-89356-813-9 (set)   94-27299
ISBN 0-89356-817-1 (volume 4)   CIP

PRINTED IN THE UNITED STATES OF AMERICA

VOLUME IV

GREAT EVENTS
FROM
HISTORY II

AT&T IS ORDERED TO REDUCE CHARGES

Categories of event: Monopolies and cartels; consumer affairs
Time: July 5, 1967
Locale: Washington, D.C.

Suspicious accounting practices triggered an investigation of AT&T's activities that resulted in a $120 million reduction in charges for long-distance services

Principal personages:

ROSEL H. HYDE (1900-   ), the chairman of the Federal Communications Commission, 1966-1969

FREDERICK R. KAPPEL (1902-   ), the chairman and chief executive officer of American Telephone & Telegraph in 1967

EDWARD B. CROSLAND (1912-   ), a lobbyist for AT&T

BENJAMIN JAVITS (1894-1973), a major shareholder in AT&T

FRANK MORISSEY, a California public utility commissioner

Summary of Event

After the Communications Act of 1934, the telephone communications market slowly evolved from a pure monopoly to a competitive oligopoly, in which a few carriers compete to provide long-distance and international telephone services. Under the Communications Act, a common (or main) carrier such as American Telephone & Telegraph (AT&T) and its affiliated companies is compelled to make telephone services available to all customers at the same fees. A cornerstone for allowing AT&T to operate without competitive forces was that the government regarded the telecommunications industry as a natural monopoly. In a natural monopoly, a single firm can produce at a lower cost than can two or more firms in competition. Government regulation may then be appropriate to correct any problems caused by the lack of outside competition, such as high prices.

The Federal Communications Commission (FCC) has repeatedly stated that competition provides the best means for furthering the goals of the Communications Act, namely providing the public with efficient telecommunication services through adequate facilities at reasonable prices. The underlying rationale for the FCC's reasoning is that competition brings prices down to the level of costs, thereby eliminating all profits above a normal rate of return while promoting innovation and improved quality of products and services.

AT&T's confrontation with the government dates back to 1949, when a report on Bell system practices found them in violation of the Sherman Act, the main antitrust legislation of the United States. This report prompted the Justice Department to launch its first antitrust suit against the carrier. The Justice Department cited AT&T for maintaining a monopoly on the manufacture, distribution, and installation of telephones and related equipment. It forced AT&T to cut links with Western Electric, which manufactured telephone equipment. Under the court settlement, AT&T would not engage in any business other than common-carrier communications and therefore would be prevented from later entering areas such as computer software, hardware, office automation equipment, cable television, data processing, and electronic information publishing. Some of these areas did not yet exist, but the general restrictions covered them. At the same time, Western Electric was restricted to the manufacture of equipment used by the Bell system.

By the 1950's, the Bell system was under close watch for keeping telephone rates far above costs. The resulting profits caused other companies to raise the issue of antitrust violation. In 1956, the U.S. court of appeals reversed an FCC decision and ruled that Bell customers had the right to choose telephone equipment manufactured by companies other than Western Electric. The FCC had sided with AT&T, which had long contended that it could not provide telephone service except to customers with Western Electric equipment because it could not otherwise ensure safety or quality.

The origins of the FCC's first confrontation with AT&T can be traced to the California Public Utility Commission (CPUC), which on July 26, 1967, began an official probe of Pacific Telephone and Telegraph (PT&T) a Bell subsidiary. Throughout the 1940's and 1950's, PT&T had managed to receive authorizations for many of the rate increases it sought from the utility commission. These increases ensured a comfortable rate of return for PT&T that climbed gradually from 5.5 percent to 6.75 percent per year. The 1960's marked a new direction for the utility commission. Its economists found that the PT&T rate increases over the preceding years had been excessive. The CPUC internal study coincided with preparations by PT&T for a request for one of the largest rate increases ever.

The commission held public hearings on the issue for forty-nine days. It questioned PT&T's accounting practices, which inflated operating expenses and therefore understated the company's rate of return. The CPUC found that had PT&T adopted sound bookkeeping techniques, California telephone users would have saved more than $40 million per year. The findings led the commission on June 11, 1964, to order PT&T to cut its charges by approximately half and to refund all excessive charges retroactively. PT&T immediately appealed the decision to the California Supreme Court, which upheld the CPUC's findings on April 28, 1965, but overturned the refund.

Prior to the turmoil, PT&T had maintained good relations with the CPUC. One of the reasons for this was that the CPUC had followed the FCC's approach for negotiation, which allowed the phone company to present its case in private and then receive a rate increase. Strenuous relations between the CPUC and PT&T led the FCC to suspect that the impropriety surrounding the accounting techniques might not be an isolated incident, since the Bell subsidiaries used bookkeeping practices similar to those of AT&T. If PT&T had overcharged Californians, AT&T might be doing the same nationwide. Pressure on the FCC to investigate was exacerbated by the fact that it had never conducted an investigation of AT&T's accounting practices. FCC Chairman Rosel H. Hyde, a longtime ally of AT&T, resisted the investigation as being unnecessary. Faced with opposition from within the commission, he finally yielded on October 28, 1965, and ordered AT&T to disclose "wide variations in earnings," a precursor to a formal inquiry into its accounting practices.

AT&T's chairman and chief executive officer, Frederick R. Kappel, announced that the investigation was "unwarranted and unnecessary" and tried to push for a return to the old tacit agreement with the FCC of surveillance and negotiation. He predicted that the public would be the ultimate loser. Kappel summoned AT&T's chief Washington lobbyist, Edward B. Crosland, to raise opposition to the FCC decision. An AT&T shareowners committee was formed to lobby for that effort and prevent AT&T stock from falling in price. The committee included several influential figures such as Benjamin Javits, a New York attorney and brother of Senator Jacob Javits.

Despite claims that the probe was a conspiracy against telephone users, the FCC was determined to proceed with the investigation. It succeeded in confronting a barrage of telephone calls from angry stockholders, lobbyists, congressmen, and senators. The FCC chairman, now firmly supportive of the commission probe, launched an investigation into all aspects of AT&T's charges and bookkeeping. The investigation found that AT&T's records showed several accounting irregularities. AT&T was inflating operating expenses by adding expenses that did not pertain to its operations, such as lobbying and advertising. The result was a reduction in reported profits that made it easier to receive approval for petitions for rate increases. AT&T's "base rate," used to petition for rate increases, included among other things approximately $550 million for plants under construction. This was analogous to charging a potential tenant rent on a dwelling under construction. AT&T billed its customers one month, in advance for telephone charges and taxes. Advance billing gave the company interest-free use of money for one month, valued at $200 million a year. The company elected not to take faster depreciation rates for its equipment allowed under a ruling by the Internal Revenue Service. Had the company adopted the alternative depreciation method, it would have passed on these savings to the general public in the form of rate rollbacks, which would have reduced current profits and potentially made it harder to petition for rate increases. The FCC estimated that the difference in the two depreciation methods amounted to $4 billion in excessive billing between 1954 and 1966.

After two and a half months of testimony by more than sixty witnesses, the FCC concluded on July 5, 1967, that AT&T's rate of return was higher than that of any comparable public utility and should therefore be reduced, from 8.5 percent to 7 or 7.5 percent. In addition, AT&T's accounting techniques should be amended. The FCC's verdict amounted to an annual cut of $120 million in AT&T's revenues.

Impact of Event

The development of microwave technology brought to the market significant transformations, by enabling carriers to connect users without wire facilities. The new technology revolutionized service and allowed expansion into otherwise inaccessible and unprofitable areas. In 1969, the FCC authorized Microwave Communications,

Inc. (MCI) to construct and lease microwave facilities under a specialized common-carrier status. Soon thereafter, several other companies applied for the specialized common-carrier status.

Faced with overwhelming competition, AT&T tried to block the entry of new companies on the grounds that they would skim off the most profitable customers, thus taking away profits that AT&T used to subsidize service to unprofitable geographical locations. AT&T was forced to provide services to those locations under the terms of the Communications Act, but the new competitors would not be. In 1971, the FCC reaffirmed its inclination to limit AT&T's dominance and rejected this "cream-skimming" contention.

One of the difficulties the FCC had to confront in regulating a natural monopoly was how to assess AT&T's fair rate of return, which ultimately would influence long-distance rates. Although the theory of monopoly regulation is extensive, the telecommunications industry had specific issues that needed to be addressed. These included the lag between the time a rate is filed and when it becomes effective, the administrative costs of monitoring AT&T's activities, and the inefficiencies resulting from a lack of incentives to compete.

A solution the FCC contemplated was to peg AT&T's profits as a specified rate of return on investment. This policy's shortcoming was that it would induce AT&T to increase its investments in an attempt to maximize its profits. The added spending might be beyond that required for efficiency.

An alternative control on profits was the FCC implementation of price caps, which limited rates rather than profits. The underlying belief was that price caps would entice AT&T to reduce its costs through efficiencies and innovation. At the same time, price caps avoided problems of wasteful overinvestment and minimized the administrative costs of regulation.

Until 1982, AT&T retained control over long-distance and local telephone service. As a regulated monopoly, AT&T exercised complete control over local telephone networks, thereby thwarting attempts by other long-distance carriers to connect one caller to another. These bottlenecks were not always explicit but appeared in several forms. Specific cases included delayed and inferior interconnections, excessive pricing, or denial of the service in an effort to preserve market share.

In early 1982, these bottlenecks were regarded as evidence of market power requiring government scrutiny of AT&T's activities. U.S. District Judge Harold Greene issued a modified final judgment effectively ending AT&T's dominance over these facilities and forcing it to divest itself from the local exchange companies by January 1, 1984. The decision severed the relationship between the local exchange companies, which continued to operate as local monopolies, and AT&T's long-distance services.

A major breakthrough in the modified final judgment was that it forced the local exchange carriers to provide all long-distance carriers with access of "equal type and quality" to the ultimate customer. This led to the implementation of "1+" equal access codes by which a caller could reach the specific long-distance carrier of his or her choice without having to dial a complicated string of codes.

It is important to note that even while the long-distance market experienced an increasing degree of competition, local telephone markets remained dominated by single carriers. The FCC feared that opening the market to other carriers could lead to market instability because of cutthroat competition. The FCC opted for a regulated monopoly whereby local rates were subject to price ceilings.

With the modified final judgment of 1984 in force, AT&T had to reevaluate its pricing and marketing strategies to confront the competitive challenge mounted by two rivals, US Sprint and MCI. AT&T's pricing strategy was significantly limited by the competitive carrier proceedings of 1971, in which the FCC had determined the illegality of nonuniform pricing by a dominant carrier. AT&T therefore had to charge a standard price to all customers. The FCC hoped that eliminating entry barriers to the long-distance market would prevent any carrier from raising prices above competitive levels, as that would prompt entry into the market by firms offering lower prices. The FCC concluded that the increased competition brought about by actual or potential market entry would replace the need for monitoring, eliminating regulatory costs as well as any potential antitrust concerns.

Bibliography

Averch, Harvey A., and Leland L. Johnson. "Behavior of the Firm Under Regulatory Constraint." *American Economic Review* 52 (December, 1962): 1052-1069. A classic article on the economics of monopoly regulation, for the more sophisticated reader. Requires some background in economic and mathematical analysis.

Evans, David S., ed. *Breaking Up Bell: Essays on Industrial Organization and Regulation.* New York: North-Holland, 1983. A classic textbook on the issues surrounding telephone regulation, price ceilings, and rate control.

Faulhaber, Gerald R. *Telecommunications in Turmoil.* Cambridge, Mass.: Ballinger, 1987. A textbook on developments and reorganizations in the telecommunications industry following the breakup of AT&T. Ties the changes to public policy issues.

Johnson, Leland L. *Competition and Cross-Subsidization in the Telephone Industry.* Santa Monica, Calif.: RAND Corporation, 1982. Written for a nontechnical audience. Summarizes the economics of regulation before the breakup of AT&T.

Larson, Alexander C., Calvin S. Monson, and Patricia J. Nobles. "Competitive Necessity and Pricing in Telecommunications Regulation." *Federal Communications Law Journal* 42 (December 1, 1989): 1. A detailed article on competition in telecommunications, written from a legal perspective. Easy to read, with many nontechnical references.

Shooshan, Harry M., III, ed. *Disconnecting Bell.* New York: Pergamon Press, 1984. Discusses the Bell breakup and the impact of the AT&T divestiture.

Stehman, Jonas Warren. *The Financial History of the American Telephone and Telegraph Company.* 1925. Reprint. New York: A. M. Kelley, 1967. A historical reference that tracks AT&T's financial activities. Simple and nontechnical.

Stone, K. Aubrey. *I'm Sorry, the Monopoly You Have Reached Is Not in Service.* New

York: Ballantine Books, 1973. Provides excellent detail on the events that culminated in the FCC decision to launch its first investigation of AT&T. A simple, easy-to-read text for someone who hates technical reading.

Sam Ramsey Hakim

Cross-References

Parliament Nationalizes the British Telephone System (1911), p. 218; The U.S. Government Loses Its Suit Against Alcoa (1924), p. 431; Alcoa Is Found in Violation of the Sherman Antitrust Act (1945), p. 869; The Supreme Court Rules Against a Procter & Gamble Merger (1967), p. 1309; AT&T and GTE Install Fiber-Optic Telephone Systems (1977), p. 1647; AT&T Agrees to Be Broken Up as Part of an Antitrust Settlement (1982), p. 1821.

ATLANTIC RICHFIELD DISCOVERS OIL AT PRUDHOE BAY, ALASKA

Category of event: New products
Time: December 26, 1967
Locale: Prudhoe Bay, Alaska

The search for new oil fields produced a major find at Prudhoe Bay, Alaska, setting off a lengthy battle with environmentalists over the development of this resource

Principal personages:

ROBERT O. ANDERSON (1917-   ), the head of Atlantic Richfield and one of the great oil wildcatters

TED STEVENS (1923-   ), the state of Alaska's primary spokesman in the Senate

MO UDALL (1922-   ), the most vocal critic of the Alaskan oil pipeline in the United States House of Representatives

Summary of Event

The Naval Petroleum Reserve was created on the North Slope of Alaska in 1923, nearly a half century before the first oil was to flow from wells in America's northernmost state to consumers in the lower forty-eight states. During the 1920's and again in the 1930's, the challenge of Alaska's uncharted resources combined with projected shortages in the United States and world petroleum markets to encourage exploratory drilling in Alaska. On both occasions, however, the exploratory wells came up dry. The exploratory ventures were seen more as a hedge against the future than the first step in massive commercial development of Alaska's oil wealth. The cost of drilling in Alaska appeared prohibitive, and the technology for transporting significant quantities of any oil discovered there did not yet exist. During the late 1940's and early 1950's, oil was discovered in Kuwait and in new, rich oil fields elsewhere in the Middle East. Oil could be produced much more cheaply in those fields than in the United States. Transportation costs had fallen as well. Interest in Alaska's unproven reserves therefore fell even lower. Given the conditions of the 1950's, when American leaders still talked in Congress about America's strategic petroleum reserves in Saudi Arabia and when the danger of market gluts and depressed prices resulting from the new fields in the Middle East had become the principal problems confronting producers, concern with the danger of shortfalls in supply faded fast. Most of the remaining interest in further exploratory drilling in Alaska disappeared as well.

The world oil market changed dramatically during the late 1950's and early 1960's. The major Western oil companies that had controlled the world petroleum market for nearly a half century began to lose their hold on the market. The existing profit-sharing system with host governments, which a decade before had replaced the concession system, no longer satisfied the governments of the states in which oil was produced, especially in an era of falling oil prices and concomitant falling governmental revenue. In 1960, Standard Oil of New Jersey's unilateral attempt to reduce the posted price of oil spurred governments of five oil-producing states, representing three-fourths of the oil then being exported, to unite in an openly declared effort to wrest control over price and production from the major oil companies. Out of their frustration was born the Organization of Petroleum Exporting Countries (OPEC). OPEC would not achieve major international status until the Arab oil embargo of 1973, but its creation served as an early warning that the United States would be better served by having its strategic petroleum reserves nearer to home, as in the Naval Petroleum Reserve in Alaska.

Also contributing to reawakening interest in Alaska were increases in the posted price of oil during the 1960's. The expanding Western economies increased their demand for oil and, at the urging of the producer state governments, the Western petroleum corporations regularly increased the posted price of oil on the international markets. The cost of producing oil in Alaska no longer seemed quite as commercially prohibitive as it once had.

During the mid-1960's, the increasing price of oil and decreased confidence in maintaining a supply of cheap oil from abroad combined to lure an expanding number of American firms into exploratory ventures abroad (for example, Occidental in Libya) and at home (chiefly along the Outer Continental Shelf). Consistent with this atmosphere, the California-based Richfield Company, together with its Humble subsidiary, launched a joint exploratory project with the Atlantic Refining Company on the North Slope of Alaska's Prudhoe Bay. Under the leadership of Robert O. Anderson, one of America's last great oil wildcatters, the Atlantic Richfield Company (later ARCO) obtained the majority of the government leases then being granted for exploratory and developmental activity in Alaska. Even after its initial well proved to be dry in 1966, Atlantic Richfield pressed on with its exploratory efforts.

The exploratory well Atlantic Richfield began drilling in 1967 might well have been the last such well tried in Alaska for some time, if not forever, had it too come up dry. On December 26, 1967, however, the well christened Prudhoe Bay State Number 1 produced oil. Approximately six months later, a second well confirmed the presence of a vast commercial-scale pool of oil beneath Prudhoe Bay's frozen banks. In time, the pool would be estimated to contain ten billion barrels, making it the largest oil field ever discovered in North America. With the potential to produce two million barrels of oil a day, the field was estimated to have a higher production capacity than all but two other fields in the world.

Impact of Event

Had the oil field been developed rapidly, the history of the petroleum industry during the next quarter century could have been written differently. The United States would have had far less need for imported oil in the early 1970's, and the Arab oil embargo in 1973 would have been far less effective. Additional years might even have been required for OPEC to obtain control over the price and production of oil in its member countries. As it was, the significance of finding oil in Alaska was initially blunted by the technological problem of transporting the oil eight hundred miles to port facilities for shipment south and by equally vexing political problems making it difficult for oil producers in Alaska to get the oil to American consumers in the lower forty-eight states.

Technologically, moving the oil from wellhead to gas tank meant overcoming the obstacles to producing the oil in volume in the subzero temperatures of Alaska's North Slope and transporting it by pipeline through the frozen tundra either to the port of Valdez for shipment by tankers to California or across Alaska and then Canada to consumers in the United States. These obstacles appeared surmountable to Atlantic Richfield, which supported the Valdez route and initially expected to ship oil from that port within three years. No sooner had the second well confirmed the presence of large reserves than the heavy equipment for constructing a pipeline began to arrive in Alaska.

The political obstacles to exploiting the oil field proved to be less negotiable. Many environmentalists doubted that the petroleum industry had the knowledge to build a safe eight-hundred-mile pipeline across Alaska's frozen landscape without doing significant ecological damage. If a pipeline did have to be built, most environmentalists advocated as less risky the longer route across Canada. They made it clear that they would do everything in their power to prevent the construction of the Valdez pipeline.

The Santa Barbara oil spill in 1969 and the National Environmental Protection Act (NEPA) passed in its wake came at approximately the same time that the oil companies were requesting a federal right of way to build the Valdez pipeline. The NEPA required the United States Department of the Interior to prepare a justifying environmental impact statement before granting permission to begin activity on any project likely to have a substantial impact on the environment. On March 20, 1970, the Department of the Interior sought to comply with the letter of the law by issuing an eight-page statement of impact that downplayed potential damage to the environment. Within a week, the Wilderness Society, the Friends of the Earth, and the Environmental Defense Fund jointly sued the Department of the Interior for violating the National Environmental Protection Act and the 1920 Mineral Leasing Act. Three weeks later, on April 13, 1970, a court injunction halted construction on the pipeline until a definitive court ruling on compliance with the NEPA could be obtained.

Work on the pipeline remained suspended for nearly four years. Two of those years were spent in judicial wrangling. On March 20, 1972, the Department of the Interior produced an expanded nine-volume environmental impact statement to justify its approval of the pipeline's construction, but the injunction remained in effect until August 15, 1972, when the case was appealed to the Supreme Court. The equipment sent to Alaska to build the pipeline was still idle in October, 1972, when the Arab-Israeli war triggered the Arab oil embargo against Western countries assisting Israel. That embargo made the Organization of Petroleum Exporting Countries a cartel effectively in control of the price and production of oil in the petroleum exporting world and produced an almost overnight quadrupling in the price of imported oil from slightly less than $3 a barrel to nearly $12 a barrel.

Also almost overnight, the atmosphere in Congress changed on the matter of constructing the trans-Alaskan pipeline. A measure to approve the Interior Department's last environmental impact statement, relieve the Department of the Interior of further obligations under the NEPA, and approve the construction of a pipeline from Prudhoe Bay to Valdez was passed on November 16, 1973, less than a month following the announcement of the Arab oil embargo. By April, 1974, the monumental $10 billion task of constructing an environmentally friendly pipeline was at last under way.

The pipeline was completed in 1977. Within a year it was carrying a million barrels of oil per day from the North Slope to port facilities in Valdez. By the early 1980's, the amount being transported had doubled, stemming America's appetite for imported oil. The development came too late to prevent a second oil crisis in 1979 from driving the price of imported oil to almost $38 per barrel but not too late to contribute to a general decline in Western demand for OPEC oil in the mid-1980's. The availability of Alaskan oil exerted such pressure on the cohesiveness of the OPEC organization that it lost substantial control over the production rates of member states and was powerless to prevent the posted price for a barrel of oil from slipping briefly below $10 before stabilizing in the late 1980's at approximately $20. Political issues played a large part in the decline of OPEC's power, but the availability of Alaskan oil surely contributed to that decline.

Bibliography

Berry, Mary Clay. *The Alaska Pipeline: The Politics of Oil and Native Land Claims.* Bloomington: Indiana University Press, 1975. An insightful account of the impact of the Alaska pipeline on the development of the "two Alaskas"—the one of natives and the one of oil.

Chasan, Daniel Jack. *Klondike '70: The Alaska Oil Boom.* New York: Praeger, 1971. A good account of the impact of oil on Alaska in the form of a very readable narrative covering the first days of the oil rush that followed Atlantic Richfield's discovery of oil.

Coates, Peter A. *The Trans-Alaska Pipeline Controversy: Technology, Conservation, and the Frontier.* Bethlehem, Pa.: Lehigh University Press, 1991. A good study of the confrontation between environmentalists and the energy developers seeking to build the trans-Alaskan pipeline, examined in the context of a century of confrontation between environmentalists and developers over Alaskan resources.

Davidson, Art. *In the Wake of the Exxon Valdez.* San Francisco, Calif.: Sierra Club Books, 1990. An in-depth, often technical analysis of the spill of approximately ten million gallons of petroleum in Prince William Sound.

Dixon, Mim. *What Happened to Fairbanks? The Effects of the Trans-Alaska Oil Pipeline on the Community of Fairbanks, Alaska.* Boulder, Colo.: Westview Press, 1979. Two years of field work produced a volume of considerable insight and a few surprises pertaining to the unintended effects of the pipeline's construction on life in Fairbanks.

Jorgensen, Joseph G. *Oil Age Eskimos*. Berkeley: University of California Press, 1990. A solid interpretation of the effect of energy development and monetary compensation for oil rights on one of the poorest groups of native Americans.

Joseph R. Rudolph, Jr.

Cross-References

Discovery of Oil at Spindletop Transforms the Oil Industry (1901), p. 24; Oil Is Discovered in Venezuela (1922), p. 385; The Teapot Dome Scandal Prompts Reforms in the Oil Industry (1924), p. 464; Oil Companies Cooperate in a Cartel Covering the Middle East (1928), p. 551; Supertankers Begin Transporting Oil (1968), p. 1336; An Offshore Oil Well Blows Out near Santa Barbara, California (1969), p. 1374; Arab Oil Producers Curtail Oil Shipments to Industrial States (1973), p. 1544; The United States Plans to Cut Dependence on Foreign Oil (1974), p. 1555; The Alaskan Oil Pipeline Opens (1977), p. 1653.

SUPERTANKERS BEGIN TRANSPORTING OIL

Category of event: Transportation
Time: 1968
Locale: Worldwide

During 1968, the world witnessed an initial proliferation of supertankers that would drastically change the economics of oil transportation and distribution and head off an oil-supply crisis

Principal personages:
GAMAL ABDEL NASSER (1918-1970), the president of Egypt, 1954-1970
LEVI ESHKOL (1895-1969), the Israeli prime minister, 1963-1969
MARCUS SAMUEL (1853-1927), the developer of the oil tanker concept
DANIEL KEITH LUDWIG (1897-1992), the owner of National Bulk Carriers

Summary of Event

On August 24, 1968, the Universe Ireland, a mammoth tanker, was christened at Ishikawajima-Harima Heavy Industries shipyard in Kure, Japan, for charter to Gulf Oil. *The Universe Ireland*, of National Bulk Carriers, owned by Daniel Keith Ludwig, was the largest ship of any kind ever built. At 312,000 deadweight tonnage (dwt), the ship dwarfed the biggest naval vessel then afloat, the U.S. nuclear carrier *Enterprise*, at 85,350 dwt. (Deadweight is a measure of everything a ship carries, including cargo, stores, and fuel.) The ship was only 115 feet shorter than the height of New York City's Empire State Building (1,135 feet in length) and drafted 74 feet of water when loaded. The *Universe Ireland*'s twin-screw propulsion system generated speeds up to 14.6 knots. Combined with a capacity of 2.5 million barrels, that speed almost halved the per-barrel cost of moving crude oil in 50,000 dwt tankers through the Suez Canal.

Events leading to the dramatic development and production schedules for supertankers went back almost seventy-six years. In 1892, Marcus Samuel developed the first ship with oil compartments separated by water-filled bulkheads. World War II created an urgent need for tanker ships to transport oil products throughout the world to support the war efforts of many nations. Tankers of this period were produced in great numbers through such efforts as the American Liberty ship program. The tankers, classified as T-2's, were built with average hauling capacities of 16,500 dwt. These ships averaged 523 feet in length and 68 feet in width, drafting 30 feet of water when loaded.

In response to increasing world demand for petroleum products, ships began to increase in size following the war. In 1950, ships averaged 28,000 dwt, 624 feet in length, and 80 feet in width, drafting 33 feet of water when loaded. By 1965, new ships averaged 120,000 dwt, were 886 feet long and 139 feet wide, and drafted 52 feet of water. Within three years, in 1968, the tankers evolved into "supertanker" configuration. The supertankers topped 200,000 dwt, averaged 1,075 feet in length, had broadened to 155 feet in width, and were drafting more than 62 feet of water when loaded.

As of December 31, 1966, there were 3,524 registered tanker vessels throughout the world. These ships totaled 102,908,800 deadweight tonnage capacity, and the average tanker was 29,200 dwt. At this same time, there were 441 vessels under construction or on order. The total deadweight tonnage for the new ships would amount to 27,385,000 dwt, or a tanker average of 62,100 dwt. During 1968 alone, shipyards worldwide launched 114 vessels, tipping the scales at 11,906,876 dwt, or a tanker average of 104,450 dwt. Thus, with one year's tanker production, the capacity for hauling crude oil products was increased approximately 12 percent over the total worldwide capacity only two years earlier.

As of August 1, 1968, nineteen tankers of 150,000 dwt or more were in service. These vessels included those owned by oil companies and those chartered from shipping companies. The larger vessels included the *Esso Mercia*, 166,800 dwt, owned by Esso Petroleum; the *N. J. Goulandris*, 188,000 dwt, chartered by British Petroleum; and the *Marisa*, 207,500 dwt, and *Murex*, 210,000 dwt, both owned by the Shell Group.

The heightened demand for supertankers during 1967 and 1968 was attributed to two significant factors. The Arab-Israeli war of mid-1967 caused disruption of the world flow of petroleum products. The fighting disrupted the operation of the Suez Canal and ultimately closed the canal to ship transport. The canal was blocked by eight sunken ships and other obstacles. Egyptian president Gamal Abdel Nasser vowed to make no effort to clear away the wreckage while Israeli troops, under the command of Prime Minister Levi Eshkol, remained on the eastern bank of the canal. The Egyptians estimated that clearing operations would take up to three months to complete after the conflict ended, but it was believed that it might be at least a year later before dredging to remove built-up silt would reopen the canal to vessels drafting or drawing 38 feet. When the canal closed, oil shippers had to bring more tankers into service to accommodate increased travel time for the trip around Africa to Europe. Some ships were brought out of retirement. The canal closure forced Persian Gulf oil producers—Europe's main suppliers—to ship their output around the Cape of Good Hope. This voyage was a twelve-thousand-mile, sixty-day round trip, versus the six-thousand-mile, thirty-six-day round trip through the Suez Canal.

The second major factor in the increasing demand for tanker capacity was a change in economic theories of oil distribution. Refineries were being located close to the consumer rather than close to the producer. This required the movement of vast quantities of crude oil rather than relatively small quantities of finished products such as gasoline. A 1968 U.S. Department of Transportation study predicted world tanker trade to jump from 935 million long tons in 1966 to 1,554 million in 1973. It was expected to more than double in the next ten years, to 3,354 million long tons in 1983. The projected figure for the year 2003 was 6,061 million long tons, and for 2043 it was 13,382 million tons. To carry on the projected oil trade, tanker capacity would need to grow from 57.1 million gross tons in 1966 to 92.5 million in 1973, 186.3 million in 1983, 292.8 million in 2003, and 488.4 million tons in 2043. According to a Litton Corporation study, tanker trade would grow by 8 percent per year to 1983, by 3 percent per year from then until 2003, and by 2 percent a year from then until 2043.

Impact of Event

Between 1966 and 1968, the amount of oil shipped through the Suez Canal dropped from a high of 3 million barrels per day to almost none in 1968. This drastic reduction resulted from the Arab-Israeli conflict and the ultimate closure of the Suez Canal to all shipping. The alternate route for the western movement of Mideast and Far East crude oil became the tanker route around the African continent, via the Cape of Good Hope. During the same period, the volume of tanker oil transport around the Cape of Good Hope jumped from 515,000 barrels per day to an estimated 4.2 million. The demand for increased capacity resulted in a tremendous surge in orders for larger tankers. This transition provided economies of scale and resulted in a sharp reduction in the unit cost of moving oil at a time when most other costs were rising.

Several factors contributed to the decreasing transportation cost. The capital cost of shipbuilding was significantly changed. Doubling all the dimensions of an 18,000 dwt tanker multiplies its carrying capacity by a factor of about eleven. It thus becomes a 200,000 dwt ship and can still be driven by one engine. Capital costs in Japanese shipyards roughly followed the succeeding pattern: $220 per ton for a 20,000 dwt vessel; $119 for a 50,000 tonner; $85 for a 100,000 tonner; $75 for a 200,000 tonner; and $68 for a 300,000 tonner. The increase in propulsion power required for the big tankers is relatively much less than the increase in carrying capacity. The larger ships also lend themselves to increased automation that helps reduce the size of the crews and promotes more efficient ship operation and loading-discharge operations.

Technology also advanced the economics of ship construction. Introduction of high-tensile steel permitted the use of thinner and lighter plates. Improved corrosion-control systems also permitted reduction in steel thickness, as less extra metal was required to allow for corrosion losses within the tanks. The new ships also implemented high-efficiency boilers for steam-driven turbines and automatic instrumentation in the engine and control rooms, both contributing to operating economies. It was estimated that a 70,000 dwt ship could deliver crude oil from the Persian Gulf to Rotterdam, The Netherlands, through the Suez Canal for $3.32 per ton. A 200,000 dwt tanker using the Cape of Good Hope route coming in and the canal in ballast going out could do the job for $2.49 per ton. A 300,000 dwt tonner using the Cape of Good Hope both ways could haul for $2.33 per ton. Another report demonstrated that on the trip from the Middle East to Japan, a 150,000 tonner could move crude oil 30 cents per ton cheaper than a 70,000 dwt vessel.

The creation of the supertanker also caused operating changes and significant environmental concerns. The sheer size of the vessels altered loading and discharge practices. The unusually deep drafts (45-74 feet) prevented the ships from docking at traditional terminals. The greater capacities required larger berthing, unloading, and storage facilities at ports. Other requirements included deepening of channels to ports where possible and more offshore terminal facilities where deeper channels would be too expensive or technically impossible. The oil industry's main problem lay in unloading the big tankers at European ports and in the United States. Solutions to this problem tended to take the form of outlying transfer terminals built by oil companies. Supertankers would come in loaded and take full advantage of their economies of scale. At the sea-based terminals, the cargo would be transferred to smaller vessels, which would move it to shallower refinery ports. Another tactic implemented was known as lightering en route. Rather than investing heavily in deep-water transfer terminals, the Royal Dutch/Shell Group embarked on a scheme to transfer part of the load from its giant tankers to smaller carriers. Two 65,000 dwt "lightering" ships met the large crude carriers at points along the route from the Persian Gulf to Europe and carried their loads into the shallower refinery ports.

The tremendous capacity of the supertankers compounded problems of pollution, especially from accidents. The breakup of the 118,000 ton *Torrey Canyon* off England in 1967 and the 800,000 barrel oil spill that resulted exacerbated the issue of insurance coverage for oil shippers. The *Torrey Canyon* disaster cost hull underwriters $16,500,000, not including the economic and aesthetic cost to the environment. The threat of insurance rates rising, perhaps by a factor of three, seriously jeopardized the economic advantages gained by the creation of supertankers. Legislation proposed by the executive branch of the U.S. government put full cleanup and damage liability on a tanker owner, regardless of fault, in an oil spill. The American Petroleum Institute sought a limit on financial liability and proposed to make the shipowner liable only if shown to be at fault, relieving the cargo owner of any liability. The U.S. government (and others) and the insurance industry were thus positioned to play an important role in determining the ultimate economies of large tankers. Issues were revisited with the 1989 oil spill in Prince William Sound caused by the *Exxon Valdez*. Larger ships presented the specter of larger disasters.

Bibliography

Bachman, W. A. "Move to Giant Tankers Fast Becoming Stampede." *The Oil and Gas Journal* 65 (October 30, 1967): 47-49. Bachman discusses the tremendous demand for new supertankers by the oil industry in its attempt to establish independence from the Suez Canal and Middle East pipelines. Japanese and European shipyards received millions of dollars in orders for new vessels ranging from 100,000 to 312,000 dwt.

"Big Ships, Big Men." *The Economist* 229 (November 2, 1968): 67-68. Describes the maiden voyage of the *Universe Ireland*, the largest ship in the world, into Bantry Bay with a cargo of crude oil from Kuwait. The owner of the ship planned to add five sister ships to the National Bulk Carriers fleet, making it the largest fleet of tanker carriers in the world.

"Ceiling on Tanker Size Still Debateable." *The Oil and Gas Journal* 66 (May 27, 1968): 64-65. Discusses the debate within the oil industry as to the economic ceiling on developing supertankers. Some oil companies placed the economic ceiling with the current state of the art at slightly above 300,000 tons. Other firms estimated the best tanker to be 250,000 tons. Included in the size issue was a range of questions on engineering, port facilities, related onshore investments, the role of the closed Suez Canal, the problem of pollution, government restrictions, and insurance rates.

"Europe's Oil Men Grab for New Supertankers." *Business Week,* April 6, 1968, 120-122. Discusses the decision of European oil companies to build or lease supertankers as the way to cut transportation costs of crude oil. The impact of closing the Suez Canal during the Arab-Israeli war is described.

Rogers, Leslie C. "Mammoth Tankers Arrive, Head Off Oil-Supply Crisis." *The Oil and Gas Journal* 66 (August 19, 1968): 29-32. Discusses the christening of the *Universe Ireland* and the role of the developing supertankers in shipping oil from the Middle East to Europe and Japan. Identifies the world's largest vessels, their owners, and their capacities.

_____ . "Suez Shutdown Hikes Cape Shipments, Bunker Sales." *The Oil and Gas Journal* 66 (May 27, 1968): 51-53. Examines the impact that closing the Suez Canal would have on oil shipping requirements for 1968. Discusses the requirements for shipping around the Cape of Good Hope in terms of demand for larger supertankers.

Wierzynski, Gregory. "Tankers Move the Oil That Moves the World." *Fortune* 76 (September 1, 1967): 80-85, 151-152. Wierzynski discusses the geography of world oil and how it is pumped and shipped from the Middle East to worldwide destinations. With the oil fields of the Middle East in turmoil and the artery of the Suez Canal ruptured, oil supply lines suddenly lengthened by thousands of miles, and the demand for tankers grew by millions of tons. Provides excellent graphics of the world oil routes and the distribution of crude from the Middle East oil fields.

John L. Farbo

Cross-References

The Panama Canal Opens (1914), p. 264; OPEC Meets for the First Time (1960), p. 1154; An Offshore Oil Well Blows Out near Santa Barbara, California (1969), p. 1374; Arab Oil Producers Curtail Oil Shipments to Industrial States (1973), p. 1544; The United States Plans to Cut Dependence on Foreign Oil (1974), p. 1555; The Alaskan Oil Pipeline Opens (1977), p. 1653; Pennzoil Sues Texaco for Interfering in Getty Oil Deal (1984), p. 1876.

JOHNSON RESTRICTS DIRECT FOREIGN INVESTMENT

Categories of event: Government and business; finance
Time: January 1, 1968
Locale: Washington, D.C.

President Johnson imposed restrictions on direct foreign investment by U.S. corporations in response to a worsening balance of payments deficit

Principal personages:

LYNDON B. JOHNSON (1908-1973), the president of the United States, 1963-1969

HENRY H. FOULER (1908-), the secretary of the U.S. treasury, 1965-1969

WILLIAM MCCHESNEY MARTIN (1906-), the chairman of the Federal Reserve Board of Governors, 1950-1970

GARDNER ACKLEY (1915-), the chairman of the President's Council of Economic Advisers, 1964-1968

Summary of Event

In a crisis atmosphere, on New Year's Day, 1968, President Lyndon B. Johnson announced the imposition of strict, mandatory curbs on capital outflows from the United States. These capital outflows were created by corporations in order to finance direct foreign investment, or purchases of machinery and factory facilities in other countries. These new restrictions were necessitated by a dramatic worsening of the nation's balance of payments in 1967. The U.S. balance of payments, an accounting system that measures flows over time and records the nation's real (exported and imported goods) and financial transactions with the rest of the world, had been recording accelerating deficits since the beginning of the decade.

In his message to the nation, Johnson indicated that the 1967 deficit in the U.S. balance of payments was estimated to be between $3.5 and $4.0 billion. He noted, moreover, that deficits of this magnitude were unsustainable and threatened not only the future prosperity of the United States but also the stability of the international financial system and the future prosperity of the free world.

The decision to restrict direct foreign investment was made secretly over the Christmas weekend. The gravity of the situation was clearly demonstrated by the unpopularity of the proposed restrictions. Nevertheless, the government saw a need to act because of nervousness in foreign exchange markets following the recent devaluation of the British pound sterling and the recurring purchase of gold reserves with currency. These developments indicated that the world's financial markets saw problems with the U.S. balance of payments.

U.S. corporations were forbidden to create capital outflows to finance direct foreign investment in Western Europe and most other developed nations. They were permitted to invest up to 35 percent of their average investment during 1965 and 1966. The funds to finance this investment could come from reinvestment of earnings from foreign countries. All earnings on direct foreign investment that were greater than 35 percent of the average investment in 1965 and 1966 had to be repatriated.

In order to maintain the economic growth and financial stability of Canada, Japan, Australia, and oil-exporting countries, these countries were exempted from restrictions. U.S. corporations were permitted to invest in developing nations up to 110 percent of their average investment there during 1965 and 1966. Funds to finance this investment could come either from the United States or from reinvested earnings. In general, U.S. corporations had to reduce bank accounts and holdings of other short-term assets to the levels during 1965 and 1966 and had to repatriate the same percentage of earnings from each of these three sectors as in 1965 and 1966.

Balance of payments problems, for which the restrictions on investment were proposed as a cure, resulted in part from the structure of the world financial system. Although the currencies of major European nations had not become convertible, as defined by the International Monetary Fund, until February of 1961, they became externally convertible de facto at the end of 1958. Under the Bretton Woods Agreement of 1944, which provided the institutions and organization for the post-World War II international financial system, general convertibility was to have been achieved in 1949.

The U.S. balance of payments had registered deficits, at first slight and then growing, from 1950 onward, following devaluations of the French franc and the British pound sterling in 1949. The U.S. balance on official reserve transactions, a summary account used at the time to measure the general overall balance of payments, averaged a deficit of $0.9 billion during the 1950-1959 period and a deficit of $1.7 billion during the 1958-1968 period.

The great concern at the time was the "dollar shortage." The so-called "dollar shortage" reflected the idea that there was a fundamental long-term imbalance in the international payments system in favor of the United States. The idea of a dollar shortage was a theoretical concept that took on a life of its own, despite underlying structural changes taking place in the international economy. An entire literature developed around the concept of a dollar shortage, and some writers forecast that the dollar shortage would be a permanent feature of the post-World War II international economy.

By the end of 1959, almost simultaneous with the de facto convertibility of major European currencies, large deficits in the U.S. balance of payments began to appear. A redistribution of world monetary gold and the accumulation by other countries of reserves in the form of dollars had already begun and soon would accelerate. The concern over the dollar shortage quickly turned to a concern over a dollar glut.

A permanent dollar shortage would have meant slower economic growth, poor allocation of world resources, and a retarding of the trend toward international integration. A dollar glut, on the other hand, would prove to be much more dangerous and would ultimately result in a collapse of the gold exchange standard that was established with the Bretton Woods Agreement. The gold exchange standard was a system of fixed exchange rates for currencies. It was also a compromise, attempting to capture the automatic adjustment mechanism of the nineteenth century gold standard, in which all major currencies could be converted into gold, while permitting a nation to devalue its currency in relation to others, so that the currency would buy less of the currencies of other nations. Devaluation allowed a country to avoid a painful drop in the prices of its products when it found that its imports exceeded its exports.

Under the Bretton Woods system, the U.S. dollar and the British pound sterling became "reserve currencies." Monetary reserves—a country's holdings of assets to support the value of its currency—could be kept in either a reserve currency or in gold. After the 1967 devaluation of the British pound sterling, the U.S. dollar became the world's premier reserve currency.

The value of the U.S. dollar was defined in terms of gold by the Bretton Woods Agreement. One ounce of monetary gold was equal to $35. All other nations defined the "par" values of their currencies in terms of the U.S. dollar. Each nation was required to keep the value of its currency within 1 percent of the currency's par value. This would be accomplished by buying or selling currency in exchange for gold or reserve currencies. Selling gold in exchange for a currency, for example, would raise the value of that currency by taking some of the currency out of world circulation.

Monetary reserves, and particularly the U.S. dollar as a reserve currency, played a key role in the Bretton Woods system. When a nation ran down its monetary reserves in attempts to keep the value of its currency above the minimum allowed, pressure would develop for the nation to devalue its currency, or reduce its par value, relative to the U.S. dollar.

The U.S. dollar had a unique role and responsibility. To the extent that other nations were willing to hold additional U.S. dollars as monetary reserves and that their citizens were willing to hold additional U.S. dollar assets as investments, the United States could continue to run a deficit in its balance of payments. That is, the United States could send its currency abroad without a devaluation since other countries used it as a reserve currency. The unique feature of the Bretton Woods system was that as long as the rest of the world was willing to accept more U.S. dollars, the United States could collect a "seigniorage," consuming and investing more than it produced. It could finance this consumption and investment with creation of additional U.S. dollars. The down side of the unique role the U.S. dollar played in the Bretton Woods system was that when the U.S. dollar was overvalued relative to other currencies, in terms of the goods and services that could be purchased with it, the United States government could not devalue the U.S. dollar or change its par value relative to other currencies.

The United States had been losing gold reserves for a number of years by the time the balance of payments crisis developed in 1968. Foreign holders of U.S. dollars had claimed gold in exchange for their dollars. In June of 1967, foreign U.S. dollar claims against the United States stood at 226 percent of the total U.S. holdings of gold reserves, meaning that the United States could redeem less than half of the dollars held in foreign countries.

Impact of Event

The restrictions on direct investment by U.S. corporations affected a number of institutions, markets, and financial practices. The impact on the U.S. balance of payments, while initially positive, proved to be transitory. By the third quarter of 1968, exports were growing faster than imports, and the balance of payments (seasonally adjusted) recorded a surplus. The return to large deficits in the balance of payments and a run on the U.S. dollar in the early 1970's, however, would ultimately cause the collapse of fixed exchange rates and the Bretton Woods system.

The restrictions on direct foreign investment by U.S. corporations did not represent a basic change in the U.S. government's policy of promoting economic development in developing nations. The restriction on investments there of 110 percent of the average in 1965 and 1966 was considered to be lenient. The policy of restricting direct foreign investment essentially was aimed at Western Europe and more specifically at the strong German mark and Germany's growing balance of payments surplus.

The major impacts of these restrictions seem to have been on the way that U.S. corporations financed their foreign activities and on the development of the Eurobond market. Eurobonds are international debt issues denominated in U.S. dollars. They are distributed in more than one country (in which the U.S. dollar is not the national currency), and the borrower is foreign. Eurobonds may be denominated in other major currencies if these bonds meet the other requirements.

The restrictions on direct foreign investment virtually forced all U.S. corporations that wanted to continue their foreign commitments and activities to participate in the expansion of the Eurobond market. The Eurobond market at the time was at a critical stage in its development. The expanded volume provided by new securities issued by U.S. corporations and the development of secondary markets made possible the participation of international institutional investors in the Eurobond market. Institutional investors, which have come to play an important role in the development of financial markets, had been largely absent from the Eurobond market prior to the mandatory restrictions on direct foreign investment by U.S. corporations. The increased demand for funds in the Eurobond market by U.S. corporations acted as an integrative force in world financial markets. Because financial markets were more integrated, interest rates became closer together and tended more to move together. In addition, one country's economic problems became more likely to be transmitted to other countries.

Participation in the Eurobond market by U.S. corporations represented a willingness to experiment with innovative financing techniques as well as enhancing their true multinational characters. Eurobond market financing also represented a willingness to separate the investment decision from the financing decision: A company could invest in a country without having to borrow money there. It could obtain the country's currency, if needed, in the international financial market.

The restrictions on direct foreign investment ended six years after they had begun, with the exception that such investment still had to be reported. The Bretton Woods system ended in 1972, eliminating some of the concerns about the dollar as a reserve currency. Currencies were allowed to "float" against one another, although in practice governments chose to intervene to maintain currency values. Seeing no need to continue the restrictions, the U.S. government ended them on January 29, 1974.

Bibliography

Foster, Susan B. "Impact of Direct Investment Abroad by United States Multinational Companies on the Balance of Payments." *Monthly Review Federal Reserve Bank of New York* 54 (July, 1972): 166-177. Foster attempts to estimate the impact of the 1968 restrictions on direct foreign investment, using existing statistical data. This article contains a detailed discussion of the concepts and the difficulties that are involved in such a measurement as well as how one might undertake such a measurement. Foster emphasizes that available data were inadequate to estimate the impact. This article is rather technical in nature though not particularly difficult to read.

Scammell, W. M. *International Monetary Policy.* 2d ed. New York: St. Martin's Press, 1965. An excellent book for someone interested in the Bretton Woods system. Well written and easy to understand, with many interesting insights. Explains the development of the Bretton Woods system and the role the International Monetary Fund played up to the early 1960's.

_____ . *International Monetary Policy: Bretton Woods and After.* New York: John Wiley & Sons, 1975. An excellent book, well written and easy to understand. Examines the development of the Bretton Woods system, changes in the international environment, and the role the International Monetary Fund played up to 1973. Contains a good discussion of the merits and shortcomings of both the Bretton Woods system and the International Monetary Fund.

Solomon, Robert. *The International Monetary System 1945-1981.* New York: Harper & Row, 1982. Excellent, well written, and easy to understand. Solomon spent many years with the U.S. Federal Reserve System and offers an insider's perspective.

Stanley, Marjorie T., and John D. Stanley. "The Impact of U.S. Regulation of Foreign Investment." *California Management Review* 15 (Winter, 1972): 56-64. The authors attempt, through use of a questionnaire, to determine whether and how the 1968 restrictions influenced the way multinational corporations financed their foreign subsidiaries. This article is not particularly difficult and contains some detailed, interesting comments on how chief corporate financial officers make decisions.

Yeager, Leland B. *International Monetary Relations: Theory, History, and Policy.* 2d ed. New York: Harper & Row, 1976. Excellent source for anyone interested in international finance. Contains a wealth of information.

Daniel C. Falkowski

Cross-References

Hoover Signs the Smoot-Hawley Tariff (1930), p. 591; The Bretton Woods Agreement Encourages Free Trade (1944), p. 851; The United States Enacts the Interest Equalization Tax (1964), p. 1235; The United States Suffers Its First Trade Deficit Since 1888 (1971), p. 1483; Nixon's Anti-Inflation Program Shocks Worldwide Markets (1971-1974), p. 1489.

BRITISH LEYLAND MOTOR CORPORATION FORMS BY MERGER

Category of event: Mergers and acquisitions
Time: January 15, 1968
Locale: London, England

British Leyland Motor Corporation, formed to slow the demise of the British automobile industry, largely failed in that effort

Principal personages:

GEORGE HARRIMAN (1908-1973), the chairman of British Motor Corporation, 1961-1968

DONALD STOKES (1914-   ), the chairman of Leyland-Triumph, 1963-1968, and chairman of British Leyland, 1968-1974

DONALD RYDER (1916-   ), an industrialist and chairman of the National Enterprise Board, 1974-1977

MICHAEL EDWARDES (1930-   ), an industrialist and chairman of British Leyland, 1977-1982

HAROLD WILSON (1916-   ), the British prime minister, 1964-1970 and 1974-1976

TONY BENN (1925-   ), the British minister of technology, 1966-1970, and minister of industry, 1974-1975

Summary of Event

Created by the merger of Leyland Motor Corporation and British Motor Holdings, British Leyland Motor Corporation (BLMC) became the only indigenously owned British producer of mass-market cars and offered a wide range of niche market models, commercial vehicles, and nonautomotive products. BLMC was among the four largest motor firms in Europe and Britain's largest exporter in value of sales. The creation of BLMC provided an opportunity to restructure the British-owned sector to reap economies of scale in manufacturing and distribution and institute the hierarchical managerial structure necessary to improve its competitive position. BLMC management, however, was unwilling or unable to implement critical measures, thereby leading to the bankruptcy and subsequent nationalization of the firm in 1974. Several attempts to revive the firm in the late 1970's and 1980's were unsuccessful, and the British-owned car industry experienced an absolute decline.

In other nations, consolidation of automobile manufacturers led to the rise of a limited number of dominant firms in domestic markets by the time of World War II. For example, General Motors, Ford, and Chrysler dominated the U.S. market. In contrast, the British automobile industry was composed of a number of small concerns well into the postwar era. This situation, reflecting the general characteristics of British atomistic capitalism, placed the firms at a cost and control disadvantage. The companies survived by exploiting a protected (until the mid-1970's) domestic market and exporting to selected markets.

The gradual consolidation of the British motor sector was motivated by a number of factors, primarily defensive in nature. The American-owned subsidiaries of Ford (which established production in 1911), General Motors (which purchased Vauxhall in 1925), and Chrysler (which acquired Rootes in 1967) were a constant threat to the British companies. Increased sales by Ford, similar product ranges, duplicated export distribution structures, and the potential for economies of scale in manufacturing convinced the two domestic sales leaders, Austin and the Nuffield Organization, to merge into the British Motor Corporation (BMC) in 1952. Over the next fifteen years, BMC kept its top sales position and expanded production, yet chairman Leonard Lord refused to integrate the production, distribution, and administrative functions of the former rivals.

Leyland, one of the country's leading bus and truck manufacturers, expanded into the car business by pursuing the strategy, used by William Morris (Lord Nuffield) to build his motor empire in the 1930's, of purchasing financially troubled companies. In 1961, Leyland acquired Standard-Triumph, traditionally the smallest of the so-called "Big Five" motor firms. Within two years, Leyland, headed by Donald Stokes, returned the automaker to profitability by moving its models from mass to niche markets and achieving greater capacity utilization rates. Leyland-Triumph's ambition and financial position was revealed in 1967 when it acquired Rover, producer of the Land Rover and upscale cars. Meanwhile, BMC bought Pressed Steel, a bodymaker, in 1965 and Jaguar one year later.

In spite of some model overlap, BMC (then called British Motor Holdings, or BMH), and Leyland-Triumph appeared to be the best match to create a British manufacturer with the scale and model range to maintain market share in the domestic and export market. As early as 1964, BMH chairman George Harriman had approached Stokes about consolidating operations. BMH was clearly in the dominant position, with twice the annual gross profit and annual car output about six times as high. When talks became serious two years later, the circumstances of the potential partners had begun to change. BMH's output had declined, and it declared a loss for fiscal year 1966. Nevertheless, an agreement that gave BMH managers and shareholders a superior position was tentatively reached. The deal, however, collapsed over assigning specific managerial responsibilities.

Chrysler's takeover of Rootes and the Labour government's emphasis on improving the competitiveness of British industry kept the merger issue alive. Stokes and Harriman rejected Minister of Technology Tony Benn's suggestion that Rootes should join BMH or Leyland but agreed to reconsider their own consolidation. In 1967, negotiations intensified as BMH's losses accelerated and Ford's market share increased. Leyland, with a better cash flow and earning an annual profit, now became a cautious aggressor, urged on by Prime Minister Harold Wilson, who believed that the merger was necessary to ensure the survival of the British industry, and the Industrial Reorganisation Corporation (IRC), which considered Stokes to be the only manager capable of reviving BMH. The IRC, established by the Labour government to facilitate such a merger, offered to mediate the negotiations and provide financial aid. Harriman, believing that he had no other choice, agreed to terms essentially dictated by Stokes on January 15, 1968. In reality, BLMC was formed by a Leyland takeover rather than an equal merger.

Impact of Event

Following the merger, Stokes and his Leyland team controlled forty-eight factories, five thousand dealers and distributors around the world, 180,000 employees, and some of the most renowned nameplates in motor history, such as Austin, Morris, MG, Jaguar, Rover, Triumph, and Land Rover. The formation of BLMC also intensified the chronic problems of the British automobile sector. The immediate task for Stokes was to create a managerial structure and corporate strategy capable of integrating and rationalizing the two organizations. In the long term, BLMC had to confront the legacy of overlapping product ranges, inflated work force, disruptive labor relations, low investment levels, outdated plant and machinery, scattered production facilities, inadequate engineering and management staff, product supply shortages, chaotic distribution structures, poor product quality, and increasing domestic and export competition.

Despite the creation of a multidivisional structure, Stokes held ultimate authority as a result of misalignment of some divisions and lack of skills in lower-level management. The chairman and managing director frequently became involved in trivial matters while the firm was guided by an ambiguous, often ad hoc, gradual rationalization program. Dedicated to arresting Ford's growing penetration of the volume car segment, BLMC methodically launched new models intended to replace existing BMH offerings. Each car was produced with highly mechanized methods, in some cases in new facilities, rather than with traditional labor-intensive techniques. Increased mechanization was an attempt to achieve economies of scale and higher productivity levels. In the absence of adequate initial investment capital, the mechanization plan was based upon the premise that the profits from one model would finance the next project, until the entire product range and manufacturing facilities of the corporation were replaced.

The strategy failed. The low quality and unattractive designs of the new models kept sales and output well below the minimum efficient scale. Costs were further increased by management's inability to supervise the new automated production methods and by frequent strikes. In an attempt to maintain market share, old models and components scheduled for discontinuation were retained, resulting in a proliferation of offerings and internecine competition. At one point, the company featured four unique sports cars. Output, exports, and profitability all declined. When the world economy moved into recession during the 1973-1974 oil shortage, BLMC experienced a cash-flow crisis. In December, 1974, Stokes turned to the government for financial assistance.

Wilson and his second Labour government were committed to preserving the

British-owned motor sector. Noting that BLMC provided exports, import substitutes, and substantial employment, the government purchased the company's equity, dispensed short-term working capital, and appointed a committee to formulate a long-term rescue strategy. The Ryder Committee, named for its chair, Donald Ryder, noted the obvious faults of BLMC and recommended a corporate blueprint similar to that used previously by Stokes. Ryder's plan centered on solving BLMC's productivity and industrial relations problems by changing executive management and committing massive public funds for capital replacement. Top managers, including Stokes, were duly dismissed. An investment schedule was drawn up with disbursements dependent upon reduced industrial action.

Controversy still surrounds much of Ryder's proposal. Vital issues such as product planning and development, staffing levels, product quality and supply, shopfloor relations, line management abilities, model range composition, and distribution structures were examined, but they were given little emphasis and not remedied. Moreover, continued unsettled labor relations issues limited the amount and effect of government investment. The ownership and management of BLMC had changed, but its operations and strategy had not. As a consequence, the results of the firm were unaltered. In 1977, Ford displaced BLMC as the domestic sales leader.

The government's intervention on behalf of BLMC established a precedent in the British motor sector. Chrysler's takeover of Rootes had not revived that firm. The parent, experiencing losses on both sides of the Atlantic, requested financial support from the Wilson government in 1975. Once again public funds were used to prevent the collapse of an automaker in Britain. Chrysler UK enacted limited measures to correct a multifaceted problem. Three years later, Chrysler sold its British operations to Peugeot, a French motor firm. Ironically, in 1979 Chrysler Corporation used loans obtained from the U.S. government to completely restructure its operations. Critics of the Wilson government's policy have claimed that action should have been taken to eliminate excess capacity and reorganize the entire British sector rather than simply supporting chronically ailing firms such as BLMC and Chrysler.

Frustrated with the lack of progress under the Ryder plan, the Labour government of James Callaghan appointed Michael Edwardes as chairman and managing director of BLMC in 1977. Edwardes was given freedom to enact the measures that he considered necessary to return the firm to profitability and private ownership. By 1979, Edwardes had embarked upon a strategy of implementing new work rules, eliminating several models, closing facilities, withdrawing from export markets, reducing the work force, and obtaining components and engineering assistance from Honda, a Japanese automaker. The state funds promised during the Ryder era were used to develop a new car range to be produced in smaller volume and to institute automated production methods. Edwardes brought capacity and employment into line with output, but by this time the British-owned sector had been radically reduced in scale and scope. The firm's results did not improve: It neared bankruptcy again in 1981 and announced annual losses throughout the rest of the 1980's. By the late 1980's, the British market was dominated by foreign manufacturing subsidiaries and imports. BLMC, rechristened Rover, held 15 percent of the domestic market in 1987, less than half the market share that BMC and BLMC had achieved in the 1960's. Rover was returned to the private sector in 1988 when British Aerospace, the country's leading aircraft manufacturer, purchased the firm. BLMC not only had failed to fulfill high expectations but also had failed to survive as a major factor in the world motor industry.

Bibliography

Bhaskar, Krish. *The Future of the UK Motor Industry*. London: Kogan Page, 1979. Primarily an analysis of British Leyland during the mid-1970's, including a review of the firm's past failures and future options. The work broadly defends the Ryder recommendations. Highly technical in some areas, but gives excellent summaries of government studies of the firm. One of the best overall assessments of British Leyland.

Edwardes, Michael. *Back from the Brink: An Apocalyptic Experience*. London: Collins, 1983. An autobiographical account of Edwardes' guidance of British Leyland. Explains the situation he inherited and criticizes the Ryder plan. The account tends to be self-serving, but it also reveals motivations for the actions taken. Valuable for its insights into how long-term decline restricts operational options.

Lewchuk, Wayne. *American Technology and the British Motor Vehicle Industry*. Cambridge, England: Cambridge University Press, 1987. Primarily an economic history. Examines the evolution of production methods in the sector and concludes that the British industry developed unique production institutions and that firms could not successfully make the transition to the mass production techniques used by rivals. A convincing interpretation that has caused some scholars to rethink their work.

Pryke, Richard. "British Leyland." In *The Nationalised Industries: Policies and Performance Since 1968*. Oxford, England: Martin Robertson, 1981. After reviewing Britain's nationalized firms, Pryke concludes that performance is not improved by government ownership. He suggests that faults at British Leyland were correctly identified and that potentially effective remedies were offered but never implemented.

Turner, Graham. *The Leyland Papers*. London: Eyre and Spottiswoode, 1971. The most comprehensive narrative of the mergers that created BMC, Leyland-Triumph, and British Leyland. A very readable account of the people and circumstances behind the British horizontal consolidation. Vital to understanding the industry up to the early 1970's. The author focuses on people in the industry and holds them responsible for its problems.

Williams, Karel. "BMC/BLMC/BL: A Misunderstood Failure." In *Why Are the British Bad at Manufacturing?* by Karel Williams, John Williams, and Dennis Thomas. London: Routledge and Kegan Paul, 1983. Clearly demonstrates that the firm suffered from the same problems under various names and compositions. This nontechnical historical analysis argues that management consistently chose inappropriate production and market strategies. The work force was often used as a scapegoat. A fine study.

Wood, Jonathan. *Wheels of Misfortune: The Rise and Fall of the British Motor Industry.* London: Sidgwick and Jackson, 1988. A narrative that traces the history of motor manufacturers from the late 1800's. Aimed at the casual reader, the work is valuable for its breadth. An excellent introduction to the sector.

Timothy R. Whisler

Cross-References

Hashimoto Forms the Roots of Nissan Motor Company (1911), p. 185; Ford Implements Assembly Line Production (1913), p. 234; A British Labour Party Victory Leads to Takeovers of Industry (1945), p. 857; Studebaker Announces Plans to Abandon U.S. Auto Production (1963), p. 1190; Japan Becomes the World's Largest Automobile Producer (1980), p. 1751; The Loan Guarantee Act Saves Chrysler (1980), p. 1763; Ford Buys Jaguar (1989), p. 2007.

FRENCH WORKERS ENGAGE IN A NATIONAL STRIKE

Category of event: Labor
Time: May, 1968
Locale: France

Police and university responses to student demonstrations in Paris provoked a general strike throughout France, eventually altering the relationships among business, labor, and government in France

Principal personages:
JACQUES CHIRAC (1932-   ), the official liaison between the French government and the striking leftist groups
CHARLES DE GAULLE (1890-1970), the president of France, 1958-1969
VALÉRY GISCARD D'ESTAING (1926-   ), the French finance minister whose austerity program set the stage for the strikes
GEORGES MARCHAIS (1920-   ), a central figure in the Communist Party during the strike
GEORGES POMPIDOU (1911-1974), the prime minister of France, 1962-1968, widely credited with persuading the Communist Party to withdraw its support for the students

Summary of Event

In May, 1958, a series of national strikes in France resulting from the government's response to Algeria's demands for independence brought down the Fourth French Republic (1946-1958) and brought to power one of Europe's most remarkable twentieth century figures, General Charles de Gaulle. Ten years later, a series of national riots rocked de Gaulle's Fifth French Republic. These riots and the labor strikes accompanying them led to major changes in labor-management-government relations in France and marked the beginning of the end of the country's rule by President de Gaulle.

When World War II ended, de Gaulle, the man who marched into Paris at the head of the liberating army, was the central player in French politics. His price for remaining in politics, however, was too high for the other political leaders in France. He demanded a new constitution built around a strong presidential figure endowed with the power to act alone when necessary to overcome the traditional fragmentary nature of French society and the paralysis of French legislative bodies. Rather than accept the titular presidency created in the Assembly-centered Fourth French Republic that emerged after the war, de Gaulle chose retirement.

Twelve years later, political storms raged over the Algerian question. The Algerians wanted independence, but the official French position was that Algeria was an integral part of France itself, not a colony but an overseas department as much a part of France as was Corsica or Normandy. The French population was violently divided over the question, and France itself drifted toward civil war as a result of the war it was conducting to hold on to Algeria. De Gaulle was summoned from retirement, this time getting his new constitution and a presidency endowed with the ability to rule France by decree in emergencies. Thus was born the Fifth French Republic.

De Gaulle opted to let Algeria go, a decision that led to more than thirty assassination attempts on his life but that gave France breathing space from the wars it had been fighting since its liberation, first against the Germans, then against the Indochinese, and finally against the Algerians. In the decade of peace that followed, France changed considerably, and so did the views of the French people regarding their leader.

President de Gaulle's rule did not so much create the conditions for a changing France as provide the pause from war necessary for the trends already at work to accelerate. By 1968, the French population, which had remained more or less frozen at forty million from 1840 to 1945, had jumped to more than fifty million. Per capita income had become the highest among the six member states of the European Economic Community. The proportion of people engaged in agriculture had fallen by half since 1945, to 12 percent of the population. The number of French people attending the universities had increased sevenfold from the number enrolled immediately following World War II. France was becoming more urban, more prosperous, and more concerned with its domestic conditions. Its government, however, continued its traditional emphasis on French influence in world affairs.

In these circumstances, the general who had quieted the storm and restored the order needed for sustained economic growth seemed increasingly out of touch with the everyday concerns of his people. He continued to emphasize French grandeur and his advocacy of a polycentrism in Eastern Europe that would enable France to lead a new Europe extending from the Atlantic Ocean to the Urals. De Gaulle seemed particularly out of touch with the 40 percent of the French people who regularly voted for the parties of the left, who had never had a share of power in the Fifth French Republic, who had experienced less of the fruits of French economic growth than had the middle class, and who particularly resented the pace and direction of policy in such areas as education and labor. To many students, the universities still seemed inaccessible; to others, both university curricula and those of the secondary schools seemed too loosely related to the demands of mass education and the realities of life in France. Meanwhile, the workers—particularly unskilled workers—were becoming restless over the distribution of the benefits of prosperity in general and the economic policies of de Gaulle's finance ministers in particular. Despite the overall growth of the French economy, the minimum wage in France remained the lowest within the European Community, and unemployment was rising. In May, 1968, the frustrations of students, workers, and even the squeezed middle-management groups fused in a month-long period of strikes, protests, and flirtation with revolution.

Impact of Event

The events began with a student rebellion at Nanterre, a new university in a depressed suburb of Paris. The students' list of complaints there matched the grievances of students throughout France. The rebellion quickly spread throughout France to other universities and even to some secondary schools as radio and television newscasts covered developments. Protests were worsened by heavyhanded tactics used to restore order by some university officials, many of whom feared a complete breakdown of order on campus if they did not act quickly. Particularly brutal and graphic were the May 3 police storming of the Sorbonne at the request of its rector and the subsequent week-long battles between police and students that culminated in police officers beating hundreds of young people on the night of May 10-11.

Spontaneously, workers and other dissident groups in France took to the streets, motivated in part by their outrage over the excessive force employed against the students and in part by the opportunity to demonstrate their own long-suppressed frustrations with the policies of the Fifth Republic. By the middle of May, a nationwide revolt against the entire system began to take shape. Street fighting and barricades could be found not only in Paris but also in Lyon, Bordeaux, and elsewhere.

Henry W. Ehrmann, one of the more prominent English-language observers of French politics, described what followed as "a psychodrama rather than a cultural, let alone political, revolution. The traditional dread of any face-to-face relationship dissolved into a feast of soul-baring." Whether the riots could have toppled the Fifth Republic remains a debatable point. Scholars agree that for them to have done so would have required a unified opposition to the government that was beyond the diverse set of groups that concurrently took to the streets under the red banners of the left to oppose the policies most grating to them. The logical rallying point for these grievances should have been the Communist Party of France and its affiliated unions; however, so general was the strike against authority, with as many as nine million people involved at its peak, that Georges Marchais and other Communist Party leaders, as well as Georges Seguy, the general secretary of the leftist General Confederation of Workers, preferred a policy of accommodation with the government, lest the events sweep them away as well. The Communist Party therefore broke with the students early on and urged the government to end the conflicts by initiating a pact between the striking unions and the business sector.

On May 25, that accommodation took the form of the Grenelle agreements (signed in a meeting of government officials, employers, and trade union leaders in the rue de Grenelle), which offered the strikers a one-third increase in the minimum wage and an across-the-board 10 percent increase in pay. The agreements also pledged to give French unions the right to organize at the workplace already enjoyed by unions in most other Western countries. By that time, however, the strikers were in no mood to compromise. Throughout France, local unions rejected the agreements and prolonged their work stoppages. Seguy was widely criticized and even booed by rank-and-file unionists for accepting the Grenelle accord. The events of May were ultimately brought to an end more by political action than by collective bargaining. In retrospect, the quelling of the uprising was de Gaulle's last contribution to the peace of French society.

When the demonstrations began at the Sorbonne, de Gaulle had been in Romania, pushing his idea of a Europe free from the interference of the superpowers and extending from the Atlantic Ocean to the Urals. As events built, he had been slow to return to France. When the events had spread to include labor protests and the participation of middle management in opposition to the government's economic policies, de Gaulle had left the country for yet another errand, this time to visit military officers in Germany. When he returned, the protests had spread nationwide. De Gaulle went into seclusion for nearly a week. Then, as France seemed to be moving toward the brink of ungovernability, he addressed the nation. Blaming the "red-flag revolutionaries" of the left for the disorder, he scheduled new elections for the Assembly, a power he possessed under the constitution he had written for France. Workers and students were offered the redress of the ballot box. The protests began to wind down, and the political right in France was able to capitalize on the longstanding fear of political chaos in the country to elect a solid majority of the right in the Assembly. Charles de Gaulle and the Gaullists still ruled France, with a little help from their friends on the right, who collectively won approximately 70 percent of the Assembly seats in the 1968 elections.

In a broader context, however, the events of May, 1968, marked the beginning of the end for de Gaulle and his policies. The radically anticapitalist nature of the strike was surprising to most commentators, who had previously assumed that the postwar expansion of the French economy had softened class antagonisms. Clearly, class conflict remained a pivotal issue in France. Governing France without exacerbating class cleavages would require a more delicate approach to economic and social policy, including educational policy, than had recently been demonstrated by the government. The events ultimately became a case study for both interest groups and the government in how to handle conflict.

Although rejected by unions at the time, the gains awarded to French workers in the Grenelle agreements were subsequently reaffirmed and expanded, both by legislative action and in collective bargaining agreements. Meanwhile, inside business firms a new attitude seemed to develop, less autocratic and more solicitous of employee concerns.

The May riots at least in part signaled a general desire for more resources to be devoted to domestic politics and fewer to foreign pursuits. The Soviet Union invaded Czechoslovakia that summer, shattering the image of the Soviet Union upon which depended de Gaulle's bid to displace American influence in Europe with French influence. These two realizations combined to foreclose de Gaulle's ability to pursue his passion, the restoration of France to a glorious and prominent place on the world stage. A year later, he would lose one of the referendums on relatively minor matters that he regularly submitted to the French people to give them an opportunity to show their support for his leadership. He resigned from the presidency and left Paris the same night.

Bibliography

Aron, Raymond. *The Elusive Revolution: Anatomy of a Student Revolt.* New York: Praeger, 1969. This analysis by one of the principal observers of French affairs is highly recommended for its insights into the motives for, strategies of, and effects of students in the events of May.

Brown, Bernard Edward. *Protest in Paris: Anatomy of a Revolt.* Morristown, N.J.: General Learning Press, 1974. One of the first and still one of the most comprehensive and best of the English-language assessments of the May protests and their impact on French politics.

Cerny, Philip G., and Martin A. Schain. *Socialism, the State, and Public Policy in France.* New York: Methuen, 1985. A good, solid overall analysis of the subject. Particularly good in analyzing the effects of the events on post-1968 economic policy in France.

Ehrmann, Henry W. *Politics in France.* 3d ed. Boston: Little, Brown, 1976. One of the best sources for putting the events of May into the broader context of French politics. The earlier editions offer more detailed information on the May strikes themselves.

Johnson, Richard. *The French Communist Party Versus the Students: Revolutionary Politics in May-June, 1968.* New Haven, Conn.: Yale University Press, 1972. An excellent analysis of the Communist Party's ambivalence toward the worker demonstrations. Leaders were fearful that the protests against all authority would cost the Communist Party itself support within the workers' movement.

Macridis, Roy C. *French Politics in Transition: The Years After DeGaulle.* Cambridge, Mass.: Winthrop, 1975. A short (161 pages), highly readable account of the Gaullist legacy and the evolution of political forces in France in the years immediately following de Gaulle's 1969 resignation from office.

Touraine, Alain. *The May Movement: Revolt and Reform, May 1968.* Translated by Leonard Mayhew. New York: Random House, 1971. Initially published in French, this authoritative work focuses on the student rebellion and workers' strikes as the midwives to a full-scale social movement in France.

Joseph R. Rudolph, Jr.

Cross-References

British Workers Fail to Achieve Objectives in a General Strike (1926), p. 510; France Nationalizes Its Banking and Industrial Sectors (1936-1946), p. 735; France Launches Its First Four-Year Plan (1946), p. 875; The European Common Market Is Established (1957), p. 1081; West Germany Bans Immigration of Workers from Outside the EEC (1973), p. 1549; French Voters Elect Mitterrand (1981), p. 1793.

CONGRESS PASSES THE CONSUMER CREDIT PROTECTION ACT

Categories of event: Consumer affairs and finance
Time: May 29, 1968
Locale: Washington, D.C.

The Consumer Credit Protection Act required creditors to provide clear and adequate information about the cost of borrowing and enacted protection regarding wage garnishment and loan sharking

Principal personages:

PAUL DOUGLAS (1892-1976), a Democratic senator from Illinois who introduced truth-in-lending legislation in the Senate

WILLIAM PROXMIRE (1915-   ), a Democratic senator from Wisconsin who supported passage of the bill in the Senate

LEONOR SULLIVAN (1903-1988), a Democratic member of the House of Representatives from Missouri who authored and gained passage of the House version of the bill

A. WILLIS ROBERTSON (1887-1971), a Democratic senator from Virginia

RICHARD H. POFF (1923-   ), a Republican member of the House of Representatives from Virginia who offered the loan-sharking amendment to the bill as part of an anticrime program

Summary of Event

The Consumer Credit Protection Act was signed into law by President Lyndon B. Johnson on May 29, 1968. The law had the longest legislative history of any consumer bill. It was introduced each year in the Senate beginning in 1960 but failed to receive committee approval for eight years. Despite the long struggle to get it passed, the final legislation was stronger than the original version.

Consumer protection began early in the history of the United States, primarily as governmental regulation of economic activities. The Interstate Commerce Act of 1887 was the first federal legislation that regulated an industry. It resulted in the creation of the first regulatory commission, which produced rules that were models for later legislation designed to ensure consumer protection. Legislation in the early twentieth century focused on the safety, purity, and advertising claims of foods, drugs, and cosmetics. The Federal Trade Commission was set up in 1914 to maintain free and fair competition and to protect consumers against unfair or misleading business practices.

After World War II, Americans were eager to buy new products. Because they had come to trust producers and believed themselves to be protected by government oversight, they had little concern about the quality or safety of products. Goods were produced as quickly as possible to satisfy demand. Advertising gained a new level of sophistication by playing to the psychological needs of individuals. In 1957, these tactics were exposed in a book called *The Hidden Persuaders* by Vance Packard, and the buying public became indignant. The consumer movement began to take shape.

The idea of truth in lending originated with Senator Paul Douglas, who believed that lenders deceived borrowers about the true annual rate of interest. The practice of charging interest on the original amount of the loan, rather than on the declining balance as an installment loan was paid off, resulted in a true annual rate that was sometimes as high as twice the stated rate. Consumers, who generally were not knowledgeable in financial matters and were unaware of the methods of interest calculation, were paying a high cost for credit. They were unable to compare the costs of borrowing from various lenders because there was no requirement of standard, accurate, and understandable disclosures of the actual cost of borrowing.

In 1960, Douglas introduced a truth-in-lending bill in the Senate. In addition to requiring disclosure of the dollar amounts of the loan, the down payment, charges not related to the financing, and the total financing charges, the bill also required finance costs to be disclosed as an annual interest rate, based on the unpaid balance of the loan. Retailers, banks, and loan companies objected to the annual percentage rate (APR) disclosure requirement. First, it was argued that consumers were accustomed to the monthly rates currently reported and would find the change confusing. Second, many sellers believed that the reporting of a much higher "true" annual rate of interest would result in reduced consumer purchases. Some argued that this would seriously hurt the economy. Other objections included the contention that the law would not do any good, since the cost of merchandise could simply be increased to hide the cost of credit, and that regulations in this area were the responsibility of the states, not of the federal government. In addition, it was feared that it would be costly and difficult to train retail personnel in the new credit procedures necessary to comply with the requirements.

Consumer protection supporters and activists were primarily liberal Democrats, and consumer protection bills were initially seen as part of a liberal agenda. Voting in committees was mostly partisan. This slowed consumer legislation in Congress. Business organizations also lobbied against most consumer legislation. Interference from the federal government was considered to be unnecessary and an infringement on their rights.

In 1960, John F. Kennedy campaigned for election as president as an advocate of consumer protection. Once elected, he proposed a "Consumer Bill of Rights," to include the right to safety (protection against dangerous products), the right to be informed (protection against fraud and misinformation), the right to choose (adequate competition), and the right to be heard (government responsiveness to consumer issues). Kennedy asked Congress to enact new food and drug regulations, strengthen antitrust laws, and pass truth-in-lending legislation.

In the version of the bill proposed in 1964, revolving credit arrangements, such as retail store credit accounts, were exempted from the annual percentage rate disclosure. The bill gained more acceptance, but it died because of strong opposition by the chair of the Committee on Banking and Currency, Senator A. Willis Robertson. In the 1966 election, senators Douglas and Robertson lost their bids for reelection so were no longer on that committee in 1967 when Senator William Proxmire reintroduced the bill. Senator Proxmire was more willing than Senator Douglas had been to bargain and compromise. The bill was debated in the Financial Institutions Subcommittee of the Committee on Banking and Currency. The bill cleared the subcommittee and the committee, then was passed by the Senate by a 92-0 vote.

Congress' attitude toward consumer bills was changing dramatically as a tide of consumer activism grew in the United States. The National Traffic and Motor Vehicle Safety Act of 1966 had proved to be a popular bill. Media coverage played an important role in the passage of that bill and helped gain attention for other pending consumer legislation.

Leonor Sullivan, an eight-term Democratic congresswoman on the Consumer Affairs Subcommittee of the House Committee on Banking and Currency, authored the House version of the truth-in-lending bill. After battling unsuccessfully to strengthen the bill in the committee, she fought vigorously on the House floor, where several amendments were added, making the bill stronger than the Senate version. The APR disclosure exemption for revolving credit was dropped. Restrictions were included on wage garnishment, whereby an individual's earnings are withheld from his or her paycheck for repayment of debt. Loan sharking was made a federal offense, with severe penalties when interest rates were charged in excess of the usury levels in each state. The bill also established a Consumer Finance Commission to study the consumer finance industry. Publicity and strong public support for the bill resulted in the stronger House version clearing the conference committee.

The main section of the bill is Title I, the Truth-in-Lending Act, which requires, before credit is extended, disclosure of the APR and all finance charges, as dollar amounts, along with other loan terms and conditions. Advertisements that included certain financing terms required further elaboration. Specifically, any advertisement that included the down payment, the amount of each payment, the number of payments, the period of repayment, the dollar amount of any finance charge, or a statement that there was no charge for credit also had to disclose the cash price or the amount of the loan; the amount of down payment or a statement that none was required; the number, amount, and frequency of payments; the annual percentage rate; and the deferred payment price or the total dollar amount of the payments. Additionally, the bill provided for the right of the consumer to cancel a consumer credit agreement within three days if a second mortgage was taken on the consumer's residence. The Federal Reserve Board was required to draft regulations that implemented the law. Regulation Z was issued on February 10, 1969. Regulations were to be enforced by nine different federal agencies, including the Federal Trade Commission, the Federal Reserve Board, the National Credit Union Administration, the Comptroller of the Currency, the Federal Deposit Insurance Corporation, the Federal Home Loan Bank Board, the Interstate Commerce Commission, the Civil Aeronautics Board, and the Agriculture Department.

Impact of Event

In 1960, when Senator Douglas first introduced truth-in-lending legislation, there was little support for consumer issues in Congress. The powerful business community and the credit industry were opposed to the bill. Politics, partisanship, and special interests stalled the bill for many years. The refusal of Senator Douglas to publicly question the ethics of members of Congress with special interests or to question banks' opposition to the bill helped enable the fight to go on for years without much publicity. Growing consumer support for protective legislation was in part the result of the consumer protection activities of Ralph Nader. Nader's investigation of shortcomings in automobile safety resulted in General Motors (GM) having him followed and investigated. The public was outraged at GM's attempts to discredit Nader. Media coverage further fueled consumer demands for protection from unscrupulous business practices. The Ninetieth Congress, which finally passed the Consumer Credit Protection Act, was described by President Johnson in his 1968 State of the Union message as "the Consumer Congress."

The Consumer Credit Protection Act was intended to protect unsophisticated consumers from the hidden costs of borrowing or buying on credit. The concern of business that customers would buy fewer goods and borrow smaller amounts when they became aware of the true annual cost of borrowing apparently was unfounded, although it is impossible to say what consumer behavior would have been in the absence of the law. Continued use of credit in the early 1980's, with its high inflation and high interest rates, seemed to indicate that consumers were willing to use credit at almost any cost. When inflation was high, consumers learned that delaying their purchases resulted in a higher cost of goods, leading them to purchase immediately even at high interest rates. They continued to use credit even when the APR rose above 20 percent. Interest rates generally dropped in the later 1980's, but credit card interest rates remained high. Consumers, however, continued to increase their credit card debt.

The original truth-in-lending bill of Senator Douglas was intended to introduce competition to the area of consumer credit. Douglas had hoped that with comparable APR information, consumers would be able to shop for the best rates. One of the results of the legislation appeared to be that some businesses ceased to advertise their credit terms and rates. Whether this was a result of the truth-in-lending act or the tight supply of money soon after the law was enacted is difficult to ascertain. The main purpose of the bill would not have been realized if creditors gave little or no information in attempts to avoid violating the law.

Businesses were concerned about the cost of implementing the regulations. Costs arose from training employees, redesigning credit agreement forms to comply with required standards, educating customers about the information being provided to them, and calculation of complex APRs. In general, businesses found that these costs were not as high as had been anticipated. The government provided rate tables to figure APRs, and training and education did not require much time for most businesses.

In 1971, the act was expanded to include a restriction on credit card issuers that they could not send unsolicited credit cards to consumers. A fifty-dollar limit was put on a credit cardholder's liability if there was unauthorized use of the card (for example, in case of a lost or stolen card). If the issuer was notified before any unauthorized use occurred, the cardholder was not liable for any charges. The Truth-in-Lending Simplification and Reform Act of 1982 was passed with a revised Regulation Z that corrected several weaknesses and ambiguities in the original law.

Further legislation covered other areas of concern. The Fair Credit Reporting Act (1971) dealt with credit reporting agencies, their practices, and consumers' rights regarding information in their credit files. The Fair Credit Billing Act (1974) dealt with billing errors and procedures to handle them. The Equal Credit Opportunity Act (1975 and 1977) prohibited discrimination in the granting of credit and provided for prompt responses to consumers regarding the acceptance or rejection of their credit applications. This act especially benefited women, who had previously had difficulties obtaining credit. The law required that credit decisions be made on the basis of qualifications regarding financial status rather than characteristics such as sex, marital status, race, age, religion, or national origin. The Fair Debt Collection Practices Act (1978) protected consumers from deceptive and abusive debt collectors and established procedures for debt collection. The Electronic Funds Transfer Act (1978) established the rights and responsibilities of users of electronic funds transfers.

Consumer outcries and the pressure put on Congress to act in the interest of its constituents, the consumers, led to this flood of legislation that followed the Consumer Credit Protection Act of 1968. It brought much more regulation to business than was previously envisioned. The cost of the regulation and the resulting benefit to consumers are difficult to measure. The impact clearly has been an increase in consumer rights and a better-informed buying public.

Bibliography

Blackburn, John D., Elliot I. Klayman, and Martin H. Malin. *The Legal Environment of Business*. 3d ed. Homewood, Ill.: Irwin, 1988. In a chapter on debtor-creditor relations, this college textbook for business students describes the laws that apply to consumer protection. It includes cases to illustrate the application of the law and the opinion of the courts on those cases.

Eiler, Andrew. *The Consumer Protection Manual*. New York: Facts on File, 1984. Describes the laws that protect consumers and gives specific advice to consumers so that they can demand the rights they have under those laws. Gives detailed information about the legal system. This is a how-to book with sample letters to help consumers put their complaints into writing to achieve results.

Faber, Doris. *Enough! The Revolt of the American Consumer*. New York: Farrar, Straus and Giroux, 1972. This well-written book gives a fascinating history of the consumer movement. Much of the book is based on interviews. Suggests additional readings that would provide the interested reader with a detailed background.

Nadel, Mark V. *The Politics of Consumer Protection*. Indianapolis: Bobbs-Merrill, 1971. Part of a policy analysis series that describes and analyzes public policies generated by national, state, and local governments. It examines consumer politics, participants in policy decisions, and the role of the press and consumer activists in influencing policy decisions.

"The Truth About Credit Is Coming." *Consumer Reports* (August, 1968): 428-431. A report from Consumers Union, a consumer protection organization that tests and reports on consumer products and consumer issues. This article informs consumers about the law and how it will affect them. The article gives opinions as well as facts.

Rajiv Kalra

Cross-References

Congress Passes the Pure Food and Drug Act (1906), p. 128; The First Morris Plan Bank Opens (1910), p. 180; The Federal Trade Commission Is Organized (1914), p. 269; The Wheeler-Lea Act Broadens FTC Control over Advertising (1938), p. 775; Congress Passes the Fair Credit Reporting Act (1970), p. 1454; Congress Prohibits Discrimination in the Granting of Credit (1975), p. 1595.

THE SUPREME COURT UPHOLDS A BAN ON HOUSING DISCRIMINATION

Category of event: Labor
Time: June 17, 1968
Locale: Washington, D.C.

In Jones v. Alfred H. Mayer Company, *the Supreme Court ruled that discrimination in the sale or rental of residential property violated the law*

Principal personages:

POTTER STEWART (1915-1985), the justice who delivered the Jones decision

LYNDON B. JOHNSON (1908-1973), the U.S. president who backed the Civil Rights Act of 1968, calling for a ban on all housing discrimination

LYMAN TRUMBULL (1813-1896), the principal author of the Civil Rights Act of 1866

EMANUEL CELLER (1888-1981), a congressional proponent of the 1968 bill

JOHN MARSHALL HARLAN (1899-1971), a dissenting justice in the Jones case

MARTIN LUTHER KING, JR. (1929-1968), a black leader whose assassination prompted House passage of the 1968 Civil Rights Act

WALTER F. MONDALE (1928-   ), a U.S. senator who helped launch the 1968 Civil Rights Act

Summary of Event

As an official response to the movement for the rights of African Americans in the 1960's as well as to an additional array of social protests, President Lyndon B. Johnson initiated, and Congress passed, the 1964 Civil Rights Act. It soon became clear that subsequent civil rights legislation was politically essential. Accordingly, the Johnson Administration directed its efforts toward passage of a fair housing bill in 1966. The heart of the bill, Title IV, sought to outlaw housing discrimination "by property owners, tract developers, real estate brokers, lending institutions and all others engaged in the sale, rental, or financing of housing." Although superficially the bill appeared to be sweeping in scope, its enforcement provisions were feeble and procedures for redress by alleged victims of these widespread forms of discrimination were prohibitively expensive and time consuming. The bill languished in Congress.

As a further step toward creation of an effective federal fair housing law, Congress in 1968 enacted another Civil Rights Act, the major provision of which, Title VIII, decreed a general ban on racial and religious discrimination in the sale and rental of housing. The ultimate effectiveness of Title VIII was dependent on judicial decisions, fresh legislation, and the outcomes of a volatile social situation across the nation.

Impetus behind fair housing legislation and the passage of a series of federal civil rights acts came in important ways from a number of black and liberal campaigns, some of long duration. For example, trade unions, churches, and civil rights organizations had formed an alliance called the National Committee Against Discrimination in Housing. It had been active since 1950 and already had by the mid-1960's played an important role in securing enactment of open housing laws, municipal ordinances, and administrative regulations pertaining to housing in seventeen states and in sixty major cities.

Fair housing laws complicated what during the 1950's and 1960's had become a "white flight" from inner cities to suburbs that was imputed largely to racial prejudice. Governmental attempts to implement or enforce open housing policies often produced a serious "white backlash." Nowhere was this more manifest than in California. There, in 1964, voters approved Proposition 14 in a state referendum. Proposition 14 declared that the state could not interfere with anyone's right to sell or rent property, or conversely the right not to sell or rent property. In effect, the proposition abrogated a number of California statutes, including the Rumford Fair Housing Act of 1963, which banned racial discrimination in housing. Proposition 14's constitutionality was soon tested before the U.S. Supreme Court, in *Reitman v. Mulkey* (1967). The proposition was judged to be a violation of the Fourteenth Amendment because it would have authorized the state of California to engage in discrimination. Nevertheless, the proposition was indicative of widespread white reactions to one major thrust of the black and liberal drive toward winning expanded civil liberties. Opposition sentiments such as those embodied in Proposition 14 had been responsible for stalling Johnson's fair housing bill in Congress for two years. Only the assassination of Martin Luther King, Jr., as the bill was being debated, led to its passage transformed into the 1968 Civil Rights Act.

Only weeks after President Johnson signed the act into law, the Supreme Court assumed its own initiative in hearing the case of *Jones v. Alfred H. Mayer Company*. Joseph Lee Jones, an African American, alleged that the Alfred H. Mayer Company had refused, on racial grounds, to sell him a home in the suburban Paddock Woods community in St. Louis County, Missouri.

In considering the case, Justice Potter Stewart, who was to deliver the majority opinion, and his affirming colleagues premised their decision not on Title VIII of the 1968 Civil Rights Act but on an obscure law, Section 1982, that had become part of the U.S. Code in 1866. Originally intended as an enforcement provision of the Thirteenth Amendment applicable to the District of Columbia, the law was nevertheless interpreted by the Court's majority to bar "*all* racial discrimination, private as well as public, in the sale or rental of property."

Justice Stewart made it clear that Section 1982 was not a comprehensive open housing law and that it did not address discrimination based on religion or national origins. It likewise did not deal with the provision of services or facilities in connection with the sale or rental of dwellings, as might be performed by a realty company. Nor did it apply to advertising, financial arrangements, and brokerage services that might be involved in sales or rentals of dwellings. Stewart's point in enumerating precisely what Section 1982 covered was to emphasize the significance of the newly enacted Civil Rights Act, stressing the need for such legislation and underscoring the responsibilities of the federal government in enforcing the rights of petitioners such as Jones.

For the majority, Justice Stewart explained the resort to Section 1982, which had been Section 1 of the Civil Rights Act of 1866. In *Hurd v. Hodge*, decided by the Court in 1948, the identical law had been invoked to respond to a situation in which an African American had been denied the chance to buy the home of his choice "solely because of (his) race and color." The source of Hurd's injury was the action of whites who agreed to bar African Americans from a particular residential area. In that case, a federal court had aided in the enforcement of the white homeowners' intentions. Thus the Hurd case did not, as the Jones case did, present the question of whether purely private discrimination, without the intervention of government, would violate Section 1982.

In Stewart's opinion, the Jones case represented the first chance for the Court squarely to confront the question of whether a wholly private conspiracy to deny the right to buy or rent property solely because of race or color was legally sustainable. The Court majority determined for Jones. It decided that historical evidence overwhelmingly supported the notion that the 1866 Civil Rights Act was intended to "secure for all men, whatever their race or color, . . . the great fundamental rights" to acquire property, to buy, sell, or rent as one chose, and to "break down *all* discrimination between black men and white men."

Impact of Event

Ten years after passage of the Civil Rights Act of 1968 and the decision in *Jones*, an exhaustive study by the federal Department of Housing and Urban Development (HUD) concluded that "a vast residue of discrimination" in the housing market remained. Black ghettos continued to exist within almost all major cities as well as in smaller communities.

Although the 1968 Civil Rights Act aimed to establish a fair housing market, in practice, as civil libertarians, black leaders, and legal scholars observed, it was more gesture than substance. The act provided no enforcement mechanisms, such as cease and desist orders aimed at violators. Charged with implementing the act, HUD, for example, lacked authority to ask for more than voluntary compliance when complaints came before it. It was incapable of imposing remedies. Similarly, as historians noted, the Justice Department, which did have authority to bring housing discrimination suits where patterns of discrimination existed, avoided tackling a number of exclusionary practices. The Justice Department, for example, made little effort to cope with "redlining," which in the arena of housing discrimination took the form of mortgage lenders marking out areas, primarily on the basis of racial composition, in which they would not lend. Although the country's financial regulatory bodies were legally required to act affirmatively to ensure fair housing, they were, many authorities concluded, derelict in issuing rules mandating nondiscrimination in mortgage lending and were slow to enforce the rules they did issue.

Notwithstanding these serious weaknesses, the act as implemented in the Jones decision did have positive effects. At the least, housing discrimination became less flagrant. A number of political scientists also found evidence of progress in the 1970 census, which indicated a light but definite trend toward residential desegregation. Moreover, spurred by largely black riots in more than one hundred American cities during 1968, President Johnson presented Congress with the most extensive federal housing program in the nation's history, an initiative calling for federal subsidization of 600,000 units annually for ten years.

The president also drew many of the same banking and construction interests that had previously abetted housing discrimination into profitable participation in his housing reform through his 1968 Housing Act's subsidization of 1.7 million units over the following three years. Johnson's successor, President Richard Nixon, continued the program with the unprecedented federal construction of 1.3 million low-income housing units during the early 1970's.

Meanwhile, the Supreme Court hewed to the course in regard to housing discrimination that it had plotted in the Jones decision. The City of Akron, Ohio, for example, had adopted a fair housing ordinance in 1964. Its dissatisfied electorate thereafter amended the city charter to provide that any ordinance regulating the sale or rental of real property had to win the approval of a majority of voters before it could become effective. The amendment, in short, nullified the city's fair housing law and reinstated customary patterns of housing discrimination.

The issue came to the Supreme Court in the case of *Hunter v. Erickson* in 1969. It afforded the liberal Court, which for fifteen years had been presided over by Chief Justice Earl Warren, an opportunity to review favorably Title VIII of the 1968 Civil Rights Act. Speaking through Justice Byron White, the Court acknowledged that it was confronted by a law that resorted to "an explicitly racial classification treating racial housing matters differently" from other legislative affairs. White declared that the charter provision was a violation of the equal protection clause of the Constitution's Fourteenth Amendment and was therefore invalid.

The Jones and the Hunter cases were only a part of the extensive civil rights adjudication engaged in by the Supreme Court during the Warren era (1954-1969). The Court had gone far toward making discrimination, racial and otherwise, illegal. The administrations of Richard Nixon and Gerald Ford, and later that of Ronald Reagan, adopted more conservative approaches—and in their time more popular ones—to racial and other forms of discrimination in all areas of American life.

Court decisions and legislative actions aside, in the early 1980's the Justice Department's Civil Rights Division declared that housing discrimination remained "rampant." Moreover, HUD estimated that there were two million instances of illegal race discrimination pertaining to housing annually and that it received only forty thousand complaints about them. In addition, the 1968 Civil Rights Act covered only 80 percent of the nation's housing units. Congress seemed willing to leave matters as they were. Legislation and Supreme Court decisions tried to establish a healthier social environment within which beneficial change could occur, but only changes in traditional attitudes over time, it seemed, could alter the facts of daily life.

Bibliography

Blasi, Vincent, ed. *The Burger Court.* New Haven, Conn.: Yale University Press, 1983. Chapter 6 deals with race discrimination and was written by a Stanford University law professor and former attorney for the National Association for the Advancement of Colored People, Paul Brest.

Cox, Archibald. *The Role of the Supreme Court in American Government.* New York: Oxford University Press, 1976. A brilliant, incisive set of lecture-essays by a distinguished legal scholar. Of particular interest here is chapter 3, but the whole of this brief book deserves reading. Superb for reflections on the Warren Court and civil rights.

Goering, John. *Housing Desegregation and Federal Policy.* Chapel Hill: University of North Carolina Press, 1986. An easily read scholarly study. Considers all major federal fair housing programs and major judicial decisions. Raises questions about limits of federal approaches to desegregation and alternatives.

Matusow, Allen J. *The Unraveling of America: A History of Liberalism in the 1960's.* New York: Harper & Row, 1984. A masterful and incisive critical survey of the subject. Chapter 7 on civil rights, including fair housing, is especially pertinent here. Worth a full reading. One of the finest general studies of the 1960's.

Metcalf, George R. *Fair Housing Comes of Age.* New York: Greenwood Press, 1988. A twenty-year retrospective evaluation of fair housing and the racial discrimination that has plagued its progress. Metcalf is a columnist who finds some bright spots but indicates that by the late 1980's discrimination was still widespread, requiring more legislation and judicial decisions.

Schwartz, Bernard, comp. *Civil Rights.* 2 vols. New York: Chelsea House, 1970. A superb combination of commentary, documents, and testimony. The Jones decision is included in full.

Clifton K. Yearley

Cross-References

The FNMA Promotes Home Ownership (1938), p. 781; Roosevelt Signs the Fair Labor Standards Act (1938), p. 792; The Civil Rights Act Prohibits Discrimination in Employment (1964), p. 1229; The Supreme Court Orders the End of Discrimination in Hiring (1971), p. 1495; Congress Prohibits Discrimination in the Granting of Credit (1975), p. 1595; The Supreme Court Rules on Affirmative Action Programs (1979), p. 1704; *Firefighters v. Stotts* Upholds Seniority Systems (1984), p. 1882.

THE WHOLESOME POULTRY PRODUCTS ACT IS PASSED

Category of event: Consumer affairs
Time: August 18, 1968
Locale: Washington, D.C.

The Wholesome Poultry Products Act required uniform standards for poultry inspection and extended requirements to establishments not previously covered

Principal personages:
JAMES L. GODDARD (1923-   ), the commissioner of the Food and Drug Administration, 1966-1968
ORVILLE L. FREEMAN (1918-   ), the United States secretary of agriculture, 1961-1969
LYNDON B. JOHNSON (1908-1973), the president of the United States, 1963-1969

Summary of Event

The Wholesome Poultry Products Act (H.R. 16363, S. 2932), passed on August 18, 1968, stipulates that poultry and poultry products must meet federal inspection standards. Prior to passage of this act, poultry processing plants were regulated by states or not at all. Poultry inspection processes varied among states, resulting in some plants having modern equipment and sanitary conditions and other plants being less well equipped. The Wholesome Poultry Products Act, also known as Public Law 90-492, requires that processors who prepare poultry and producers of foods containing poultry that are transported for sale across a state line must meet federal inspection standards and are under the jurisdiction of the United States Department of Agriculture. Establishments that prepare or produce poultry for intrastate transport fall under the jurisdiction of state inspection. This act extended coverage of federal poultry inspection standards to establishments that had not previously been covered and provided a model for establishing inspection programs at the state level.

The objective of the Wholesome Poultry Products Act was to ensure uniform inspection across all states in the United States to increase consumer protection. Most poultry and poultry products produced in the United States move across state lines or through foreign commerce, so uniform standards among states are warranted. The act stipulates that "it is essential in the public interest that the health and welfare of consumers be protected by assuring that poultry products distributed to them are wholesome, not adulterated, and properly marked, labeled, and packaged."

The Wholesome Poultry Products Act followed the Wholesome Meat Act, passed in 1967. A consumer-protection movement had increased Americans' awareness of potential health and safety risks of meat-based food products. Consumer advocates and President Lyndon B. Johnson publicly supported improvements in inspection standards for food products in the United States. Once the Wholesome Meat Act was passed, the Amalgamated Meat Cutters joined with some members of Congress in requesting the poultry act. The meat cutters acted in part because they did not want to face regulation stricter than that applied to poultry processors. Later, a seafood act was introduced to complete consumer protection from animal foods.

Attention has been given to the safety of the practices of the meat processing industry since publication of Upton Sinclair's novel *The Jungle* (1906). That book alerted consumers to concerns about the safety of meat processing. The first law governing meat inspection, the Federal Meat Inspection Act, was implemented in 1907 as a direct result of Sinclair's book. Criticism of inspection practices of the 1960's may have led consumers to believe that conditions were still similar to those in the early 1900's. A resurgence in interest in food safety by policymakers led to the 1960's revisions of the meat act and the introduction of related acts, including the Wholesome Poultry Products Act.

Widespread consumer concern about the safety of the meat and poultry products available at supermarkets, commissaries, and delicatessens had the potential to substantially affect consumption. Because of the potential negative impact from consumer uneasiness, it was important to successfully implement the new poultry inspection standards to restore consumer confidence in poultry products and to avoid substantial losses to producers of poultry and related foods.

Poultry products include, in addition to fresh and frozen poultry carcasses and pieces, canned and frozen foods containing poultry. The frozen foods industry had expanded by the 1960's to include prepared casseroles, dinners, entrées, hors d'oeuvres, pizzas, pot pies, and sauces. Also included in the 1968 Wholesome Poultry Products Act, and not previously included in standard inspections, were vending commissaries that prepare poultry products for off-premise sale. A commissary preparing such food items as casseroles, entrées, platters, and salads containing poultry was required to meet federally approved inspection guidelines throughout the facility.

The Fair Packaging and Labeling Act of 1966 was primarily targeted at nonfood items typically sold in grocery stores, but food and beverage packaging was affected by regulations for product weights or measures and manufacturer address requirements on packages. The Wholesome Poultry Products Act in some respects is an extension of the packaging and labeling act. The Wholesome Poultry Products Act requires that packaging be safe and free of contamination and that the poultry products being sold be represented accurately on the packaging. Specifically, labeling must not be false or misleading in terms of the origin of the poultry product, the quantity of the poultry product, or any additional ingredients to poultry offered in the package. Ingredients must be listed in order of quantity. Additionally, poultry packaging must disclose the name and address of the manufacturer, packer, or distributor. All required information must be placed on the package in a prominent place where the consumer is likely to read it.

The inherent nature of poultry is such that bacteria are easily bred when processing conditions are less than optimal. Under the act, inspections must be set up to detect disease or other types of contamination in poultry. When poultry products are condemned because of contamination or disease, the specific reason for condemnation must be scientifically presented. The act states that adulterated poultry, which cannot be legally sold, is defined as containing additives that are unsafe as defined by the Federal Food, Drug, and Cosmetic Act; containing any poisonous substances; consisting of decomposed, unhealthful, or unwholesome substances; or having been exposed to radiation. Further, poultry processed under unsanitary conditions that may cause contamination is considered to be adulterated.

To reduce the chance of adulteration to poultry, federal standards were mandated for buildings that house meat and poultry packers, including preparers of frozen foods containing meats and poultry. The standards include specifications for plumbing and sewers, water quality, water temperatures, detergents for washing utensils, ceiling and floor surfaces, room sizes, lighting, and worker uniforms. These specifications were created primarily to increase the cleanliness of processing plants.

The secretary of agriculture or his or her delegate is authorized to enforce the Wholesome Poultry Products Act. As a result of the act, the Consumer Marketing Service of the United States Department of Agriculture provided training programs for state inspectors so that they would become familiar with federal standards and be able to implement uniform inspections. Each state was given two years after passage of the act to establish inspection programs. An additional one-year grace period could be granted to states making progress toward implementation. Penalties for noncompliance include an exclusion of the state from interstate commerce of poultry and poultry products as well as monetary fines.

Impact of Event

In response to the inclusion of commissaries under the jurisdiction of the Wholesome Meat Act of 1967, the National Automatic Merchandising Association formed a Meat Inspection Committee. This committee worked with state agencies and the United States Department of Agriculture to establish standard guidelines that would logically apply to commissaries, which differ substantially from slaughterhouses. The Meat Inspection Committee continued to work as the Wholesome Poultry Products Act was implemented.

Because most consumers in the United States obtain their poultry and poultry products from supermarkets or other retail establishments, the Wholesome Poultry Products Act of 1968 affects the purchasing confidence of many people. Exempted from the act are people who raise and slaughter poultry exclusively for their own use or who custom slaughter for people who have delivered poultry and will retrieve it for their own use. It would be virtually impossible to routinely inspect all small slaughterhouses such as these. Because inspections are not required and standards equal to those for commercial distribution need not be met, there is a greater chance that poultry processed in these slaughterhouses will not be safe.

Labeling requirements are waived for deliveries to certain consumers. For example, wholesale distribution directly to restaurants and hotels for use in their dining rooms is exempted, with the provision that the poultry is sound and healthy. The labeling exemptions eliminate burdens from industries that would not present packaging to the ultimate consumer for examination.

The cost of the Wholesome Poultry Products Act to the federal government is substantial. According to the act, the federal government provides half of the costs for establishing inspection training programs for the states. The states are individually responsible for the other half of training expenses. Traditionally, the federal government has provided inspectors free of cost to plants, a practice that is being continued by states. Although the initial costs of implementation of the act were substantial, the tradeoff in consumer confidence has the potential to offset the costs. As a result of the act, consumers are provided with more information about sanitary plant conditions, poultry quality, and specific product contents. This increased confidence in proper information and healthy conditions often leads to increased purchases and feelings of goodwill toward retailers of poultry.

Uniformity among poultry producers, processors, and retailers was expected to be achieved as inspection standards from state to state were homogenized. Implementation, however, proved to be a monumental task. Even though it would appear to be economically beneficial to leave the inspection process to federal representatives, the autonomous nature of states and industries provided motivation for them to become involved in the training of inspectors and the implementation of the act. By the original deadline for state implementation of federally approved poultry inspectors, forty-nine states had been granted a one-year extension, as they were making good progress toward meeting designated standards. North Dakota, the only state not to be given an extension, was notified by the Department of Agriculture that its progress toward an inspection program was not well enough under way, and federal inspectors were given jurisdiction to take over the regulation process there.

In actions related to the Wholesome Poultry Products Act, engineers were hired to redesign plants, plumbing and sewage facilities were updated and improved, and water treatment and purification systems were designed. All these changes have resulted in cleaner plants, safer poultry treatment, and better working conditions in poultry houses.

One of the biggest challenges after enactment of the Wholesome Poultry Products Act was to set into practice the authority of the Department of Agriculture to regulate the conditions of the act. Largely because poultry consumers receive access to information about the origins of the products they purchase, poultry houses were eager to comply with regulations and maintain positive public images. Although inspection processes are not foolproof, there are established practices to be followed by inspectors and plant operators so that safe poultry and poultry products will be delivered to supermarkets and served in commissaries.

Bibliography

"Frozen Prepared Foods Must Meet Federal Inspection Standards." *Quick Frozen Foods* 32 (February, 1970): 125-126. Discusses standards imposed as a result of the

Wholesome Poultry Products Act, particularly those specific to prepared frozen foods.

Hartley, David E. "NAMA Meat Inspection Guidelines: Commissaries, Labeling, and the Law." *Vend* 24 (February 1, 1970): 23-26. Key effects of the Wholesome Poultry Products Act on commissaries are discussed. Also discusses questions about the purposes, jurisdiction, implementation, and costs of the act.

——————— . "Status Report: State-Federal Meat and Poultry Inspection." *Vend* 23 (December 1, 1969): 39-40. A member of the public health council for the National Automatic Merchandising Association provides an update on implementation of the Wholesome Poultry Products Act. The impact of the act on commissaries is addressed.

Semling, Harold V., Jr. "Congress Seeks Stronger Poultry Inspection Law." *Food Processing-Marketing* 29 (February, 1968): 85. This article, written prior to the passage of the Wholesome Poultry Products Act, discusses the forces behind introduction of the act.

Sinclair, Upton. *The Jungle*. 1906. Reprint. New York: Viking Press, 1946. This novel is credited with alerting the public to unsanitary practices in meat preparation and processing. As a result of information disclosed in this book, the first legislation governing meat processing was introduced and passed.

U.S. Congress. Senate. Committee on Agriculture and Forestry. Subcommittee on Agricultural Research and General Legislation. *Wholesome Poultry Products Act.* 90th Congress, 2d session, 1968. This is the complete act, listing all specifications made for the law. Amendments are noted, and definitions are explicit. Uses technical language.

Virginia Ann Paulins

Cross-References

Congress Passes the Pure Food and Drug Act (1906), p. 128; Congress Requires Premarket Clearance for Products (1938), p. 787; Congress Sets Standards for Chemical Additives in Food (1958), p. 1097; Vons Opens Its First Tianguis Marketplace (1987), p. 1943; The Environmental Protection Agency Is Created (1970), p. 1460; The United States Bans Chilean Fruit After Cyanide Scare (1989), p. 1986.

AN OFFSHORE OIL WELL BLOWS OUT NEAR SANTA BARBARA, CALIFORNIA

Category of event: Consumer affairs
Time: January 28, 1969
Locale: Santa Barbara Channel, near Santa Barbara, California

An offshore oil well blew out near Santa Barbara, California, covering the coast with oil and raising concern over the environmental dangers of developing offshore oil resources

Principal personages:
> GEORGE H. BROWN (1942-), the naval officer responsible for responding to pollution in the Santa Barbara Channel
> FRED L. HARTLEY (1917-), the Canadian-born president of the Union Oil Company, owner of the well that blew out
> STEWART L. UDALL (1920-), the U.S. secretary of the interior who approved of leasing offshore plots for development
> WALTER HICKEL (1919-), the U.S. secretary of the interior at the time of the Santa Barbara blowout

Summary of Event

Large-scale drilling for oil along the outer continental shelf (OCS) of the United States was still a developing industry when the Union Oil Company's well six miles at sea off California's coast blew out on January 28, 1969. Although pierside drilling had been done in that area as early as 1896, when drilling at the Summerfield, California, field was extended into the Pacific Ocean by drilling from a wooden pier, the yield had been small—a barrel or two a day. Underwater drilling was used mostly in lakes and other inland areas.

It was not until the early twentieth century that exploration for and development of underwater oil deposits first occurred on a large scale, and even then it was basically in America's quieter waters, initially in Louisiana lakes and then, in the 1930's, in the Gulf waters immediately off the Texas and Louisiana shorelines. The pioneering work of one of the once lesser-known American petroleum independents, Oklahoma-based Kerr-McGee, developed the technology necessary to permit the drilling for oil beyond the three-mile limit on the outer continental shelf of the United States and the safe delivery of that oil to onshore users.

It was not until the period following World War II that offshore drilling really began, inaugurated by Kerr-McGee's successful 1947 drilling operation from a mobile platform more than ten miles off the coast of Louisiana in the Gulf of Mexico. It was not until later still that offshore drilling began to develop momentum. A more rapid expansion of the industry was precluded by two factors. The cost of drilling offshore was nearly three times the expense of onshore petroleum development during the 1950's. In addition, the federal government and the states squabbled over ownership of the OCS and the royalties and taxes to be gained from the development of the resources recovered from it.

By the 1960's, however, the ownership issue had been at least temporarily resolved by a 1953 agreement dividing ownership of offshore OCS resources between the states and the federal government. Though much tinkered with in the 1970's, the basis of this agreement survived into the 1990's. Meanwhile, during the 1960's the cost of onshore drilling was becoming increasingly high. Perhaps most important, though, the economic boom of the 1960's created a major increase in America's appetite for oil. At the same time, developments abroad were beginning to raise serious concerns about the reliability of imported oil as a fuel source, and a quota system designed to protect domestic producers limited to 12 percent the percentage of America's petroleum use that could be imported from abroad. The combination of these concerns and developments propelled the expansion of the offshore drilling industry. Even environmental arguments initially worked to its advantage. Compared to coal, oil was a preferred energy source from an environmental standpoint. The dangers of offshore drilling had yet to be demonstrated, whereas the health, safety, and environmental costs of producing, transporting, and consuming coal were well known.

By 1969, offshore oil platforms could be found around the coastlines of the United States, and a dozen of these drilling platforms were functioning in a fifty-mile stretch in California's Santa Barbara Channel, four in federal waters and eight in the state's coastal waters. The operators of these platforms included such major oil firms as Gulf Oil Company and Mobil Oil, in addition to Union Oil. On January 28, 1969, Union Oil and the offshore oil industry hit a barrier. Drillers at a Union rig in federal waters approximately six miles off the coast of Santa Barbara encountered a geological anomaly. A blowout occurred, releasing thousands of barrels of oil into the Santa Barbara Channel. The release represented an environmental calamity of considerable proportions that had to be dealt with by the young naval officer responsible for pollution control in the channel, Lieutenant George H. Brown, and had to be explained to a general public and congressional audience suddenly skeptical of offshore drilling by Fred L. Hartley, the president of the Union Oil Company.

Impact of Event

Although the Santa Barbara oil spill was small compared to such subsequent environmental disasters as the *Exxon Valdez* spill in Alaska in 1989 and the oil released into the Persian Gulf during the Iraq-Iran war, it was nevertheless a very dramatic and costly one. Six thousand barrels of oil seeped into the Santa Barbara Channel. The resultant oil slick was reputed to have covered an eight-hundred-square-mile area. The part of it that washed ashore spread its contamination over nearly thirty miles of one of America's most famous beachfronts. The leakage took ten days to halt. Capping the disaster, a second eruption occurred on February 12, and it was not contained until March 3. Even then, limited seepage continued.

The political effects were nearly as dramatic and affected the offshore drilling industry not only in the Santa Barbara Channel but also nationwide. Former Secretary of the Interior Stewart L. Udall testified that he had harbored doubts about the offshore drilling industry even when he approved the leases that permitted the drilling operations in Santa Barbara Channel, but that he had eventually granted them in February of 1966 because of the pressure placed on him by the Bureau of the Budget. His successor, Interior Secretary Walter Hickel, suspended all drilling in the channel immediately after the spill, but three weeks later he reversed his order. President Richard M. Nixon appointed a study commission that eventually would recommend, to the anger of environmentalists, that drilling be resumed in order to empty the field as the surest precaution against a future oil eruption in Santa Barbara Channel. The melee continued for more than two years, with the Department of the Interior holding hearings in 1971 on granting additional leases for drilling in Santa Barbara Channel. Only with President Nixon's order of September 20, 1971, barring construction of additional platforms in the channel's federal waters, was the issue finally resolved at the federal level.

The offshore oil industry fared better at the state level, despite the flood of bad publicity it received. The city of Santa Barbara had fought hard and consistently in the past to avoid the dangers of offshore drilling. It had argued for fifteen years against drilling operations in federal waters and had fought successfully against drilling in the state waters immediately off its coast. Its injury was thus accorded special attention. Nevertheless, a bill designed to prevent future drilling off California's shoreline failed in the California legislature in July of 1969. The following month, a federal district court refused to issue a federal injunction against further drilling activity. The major drilling activity had always been in the federal waters, and from that perspective the presidential order of 1971 essentially spelled the end of meaningful drilling operations in southern California's coastal waters and a shift of the offshore industry back to the Gulf of Mexico. By 1973, 95 percent of all offshore petroleum produced in the United States was coming from the Gulf. This amounted to more than a million barrels of oil per day, compared to slightly more than fifty thousand barrels per day being recovered from California waters.

In the aftermath of the Santa Barbara spill, environmentalists were able to achieve federal legislation with an applicability well beyond the oil industry. The National Environmental Protection Act of 1969 (NEPA) was signed into law on January 1, 1970, less than a year after the Santa Barbara blowout. The NEPA established a federal office charged with protecting the environment. Under its terms, the Department of the Interior is required to file an environmental impact statement any time a contemplated federal action might have a significant effect on the environment. The act clearly was intended to apply to actions such as leasing the OCS or federal wilderness areas for mineral resource extraction.

The NEPA had an immediate and significant delaying effect on the development of the oil fields discovered on the north slope of Alaska's Prudhoe Bay in 1967. In the short run, however, other factors exerted a much greater influence than did the NEPA on the history of America's offshore oil industry outside California. Various developments affected the cost of developing domestic oil onshore, and political events abroad influenced the supply of oil. Even though after 1970 the industry had to function within the framework of new environmental legislation, offshore development of oil and gas reserves continued to expand, though at a slower rate, in the Gulf of Mexico.

By the late 1960's, the cost differential between oil produced by offshore drilling and via onshore development in the lower forty-eight states was already closing. America's older, onshore oil fields were drying up, and new wells had to go deeper and employ ever-more-expensive secondary and tertiary recovery techniques in order to develop commercially significant deposits of oil. Meanwhile, as already noted, the expansion of the American economy was creating a tremendous demand for energy in general and oil in particular, at a time when foreign sources of oil were already beginning to appear much less secure than had once been assumed. Furthermore, what was happening in the United States was occurring throughout the Western world. By increasing substantially their energy consumption following World War II, by turning increasingly to oil as a principal energy source, by depending on oil from abroad for that energy, and by increasingly depending on a handful of large oil-exporting states in the Middle East for much of that oil, the Western oil-importing world was gradually creating a vulnerability that had not existed before. That degree of vulnerability is often exploited in international politics.

It was the Arab oil embargo of 1973 that documented in clear terms the dangers of energy dependency. It did more than the Santa Barbara oil spill to set back the offshore drilling industry. In demonstrating America's need for a new, significant source of domestic petroleum development, it opened the way for the belated development of oilfields in Alaska, sources already known to contain perhaps ten times the amount of oil then projected to be recoverable from environmentally risky offshore drilling.

Bibliography

Baldwin, Pamela L., and Malcolm F. Baldwin. *Onshore Planning for Offshore Oil.* Washington, D.C.: Conservation Foundation, 1975. A good statement of the need to plan for both the environmental dangers and the urban management problems associated with an offshore oil industry in order to minimize environmental damage.

Dam, Kenneth W. *Oil Resources: Who Gets What How?* Chicago: University of Chicago Press, 1976. Primarily a study of North Sea licensing procedures versus those in other areas. Dam's work provides a clear view of the complicated nature of energy development as a political and administrative problem as much as a technological one.

Easton, Robert. *Black Tide: The Santa Barbara Oil Spill and Its Consequences.* New York: Delacorte Press, 1972. A very readable dramatized account of the Santa Barbara oil spill, from the blowout on the offshore well and the immediate action in Washington to the political aftershocks of the spill as they affected the offshore drilling industry.

Ezell, John S. *Innovations in Energy: The Story of Kerr-McGee.* Norman: University of Oklahoma Press, 1979. An excellent, highly readable account of the petroleum corporation that pioneered the development of modern offshore drilling.

Mitchell, Edward J., ed. *The Question of Offshore Oil.* Washington, D.C.: American Enterprise Institute for Public Policy Research, 1976. Composed of materials assembled at a mid-1970's conference on the promise of offshore oil, this book provides extensive information on the value and environmental impact of developing America's offshore reserves.

Joseph R. Rudolph, Jr.

Cross-References

OPEC Meets for the First Time (1960), p. 1154; Atlantic Richfield Discovers Oil at Prudhoe Bay, Alaska (1967), p. 1331; Supertankers Begin Transporting Oil (1968), p. 1336; Arab Oil Producers Curtail Oil Shipments to Industrial States (1973), p. 1544; The Alaskan Oil Pipeline Opens (1977), p. 1653; The Three Mile Island Accident Prompts Reforms in Nuclear Power (1979), p. 1693.

THE SATURDAY EVENING POST PUBLISHES ITS FINAL ISSUE

Category of event: Foundings and dissolutions
Time: February 8, 1969
Locale: Philadelphia, Pennsylvania

The Saturday Evening Post*'s cessation of publication was part of the advertising trend favoring television and specialty magazines over general mass circulation magazines*

Principal personages:
MARTIN S. ACKERMAN (1932-   ), the chief executive officer of the Curtis Publishing Company who presided over the magazine's demise
CYRUS H. K. CURTIS (1850-1933), the founder of the Curtis Publishing Company
GEORGE HORACE LORIMER (1869-1937), the editor-in-chief of *The Saturday Evening Post*, 1899-1937
WALTER D. FULLER (1882-1964), the president of the Curtis Publishing Company, 1934-1950
BEN HIBBS (1901-1975), an editor of *The Saturday Evening Post*, 1942-1962
MATTHEW J. CULLIGAN (1918-   ), the president of the Curtis Publishing Company, 1962-1964
JOHN M. CLIFFORD (1904-1979), the president of the Curtis Publishing Company, 1964-1968
WILLIAM A. EMERSON, JR. (1923-   ), the editor-in-chief of *The Saturday Evening Post*, 1963-1969

Summary of Event

As a cost-savings measure to preserve the Curtis Publishing Company, its board of directors ended publication of *The Saturday Evening Post* on February 8, 1969, even though the nostalgic and newsworthy magazine was beloved by millions of Americans. The magazine was recognized as a sentimental and articulate mirror of the American way of life.

The Curtis Publishing Company was founded by Cyrus H. K. Curtis on June 25, 1891. The company purchased *The Saturday Evening Post* in 1897, for $1,000. By 1909, circulation had reached 905,400, with an advertising rate of $3,000 per page. Four years later, circulation topped two million a week. At the same time, Curtis' *Ladies' Home Journal* was making great inroads into the women's market. Accelerating quickly, *The Saturday Evening Post* netted $16 million after taxes in 1925. In 1949, Curtis Publishing earned $3.5 million on $71.6 million in overall business. In the 1950's, annual advertising revenues from *The Saturday Evening Post* soared to almost $80 million.

Cumulative losses of $62 million during the 1960's, with a decrease in *Post* advertising as a major factor in the decline, led Curtis to sell the *Ladies' Home Journal* and *American Home* in 1968. Curtis Publishing has also owned *Country Gentleman*, which it sold in 1955. When *The Saturday Evening Post* folded, Curtis still retained *Holiday*, *Jack and Jill*, and for a brief while, *Status*.

Martin S. Ackerman, who became president of Curtis Publishing in April, 1968, denied any intent during his apprenticeship to fold *The Saturday Evening Post*, according to *The Wall Street Journal*. Ackerman, an aggressive, thirty-six-year-old entrepreneur, brought $5 million to the ailing Curtis Publishing at the onset of his brief tenure. In his book *The Curtis Affair* (1970), Ackerman cites numerous reasons for that magazine's downfall, with the loss of advertising the most important factor. Advertising revenues declined to a mere $41 million in 1967 as television viewing increased. Well-publicized rumors that Curtis Publishing might default led advertisers to lose confidence in the magazine. *Life* and *Look*, both of which folded in the early 1970's, seemed to be more dependable mass outlets than was *The Saturday Evening Post*.

Ackerman took the bold step of slashing *Post* subscriptions from six million to three million in 1968. At that time, it cost $12 to fulfill each one-year subscription. Ackerman raised the cost of a *Post* subscription from $3.95 to $8.00 and instigated an experimental "A" edition. This edition aimed at a more affluent, urban, and sophisticated audience, which advertisers preferred to the small-town, middle-class readership that had been *The Saturday Evening Post*'s milieu.

These efforts came too late, in Ackerman's opinion, and he blamed the Curtis leadership for not seeking changes in management earlier. Ackerman claimed that Curtis had failed to keep up with the times and could have developed a broader base to include newspapers, book publishing, and broadcasting.

Business acumen had been a trait of the early years at *The Saturday Evening Post*. Cyrus Curtis had his eye on advertising from the start, when he purchased the weekly in 1897 from publisher A. W. Smythe for $1,000. Curtis blended editorship with commercial promotion by signing on George Horace Lorimer as the first editor-in-chief. Curtis required Lorimer to write advertising copy as well as to edit the magazine. *The Saturday Evening Post* was one of the first magazines to capitalize on advertising revenues for profit while selling at less than production costs. It sold for a nickel a copy at newsstands until April, 1942.

Under Lorimer, who served successfully as editor-in-chief for thirty-eight years, the magazine brought notable young writers to its pages, publishing work by William Faulkner, F. Scott Fitzgerald, Edith Wharton, and Ring Lardner. This carried on the magazine's tradition from the nineteenth century, when the magazine/newssheet had printed stories by Edgar Allan Poe, James Fenimore Cooper, and Harriet Beecher Stowe. Barring William McKinley, every United States president during Lorimer's reign, from Grover Cleveland to Herbert Hoover, published in the magazine.

Walter D. Fuller expanded the holdings of the Curtis enterprises during his productive presidency from 1934 to 1950. A conscientious leader, Fuller developed the Curtis

Circulation Company for distributing all the Curtis magazines. He purchased a paper mill and constructed a printing complex in Sharon Hill, Pennsylvania. As Ackerman later pointed out, owning the paper mill and printing presses led to losses, since the loss of every advertising page meant less work for the paper mill and on the presses, translating into idle paid time for employees. Under Fuller, Curtis ignored an opportunity to buy the National Broadcasting Company's Blue Network, which later became the American Broadcasting Company (ABC). Subsequently, Curtis also passed up a chance to buy the Columbia Broadcasting System (CBS) for about $10 million.

Editorial quality of *The Saturday Evening Post* remained excellent under the leadership of Ben Hibbs, editor-in-chief from 1942 to 1962. After completely revamping the magazine's format, Hibbs proved once again that high-standard journalism still appealed to *Post* readers. During this time, Norman Rockwell illustrated *Post* covers and Ambassador Joseph E. Davies, Cecil S. Forester, Captain Harry C. Butcher, and General Holland M. Smith appeared on *Post* pages. All-time circulation highs were achieved on February 14, 1953, with the first installation of Bing Crosby's "Call Me Lucky," and on November 5, 1955, with the first installment of Arthur Godfrey's serial "This Is My Story."

Trouble brewed in the early 1960's. The magazine drew damaging libel suits for such muckraking articles as "The Story of a Football Fix" and "The Automakers and Their Mighty Works." Libel suits cost Curtis a reported $40 million. Even with annual cost savings of $16 million under company president Matthew J. Culligan, who served from 1962 to 1964, outstanding debts frequently could not be paid. A financial reprieve came when copper was discovered under Curtis-owned timberlands in Ontario. Sale of rights to the copper brought $24 million to Curtis Publishing from Texas Gulf Sulphur Company in 1965. With John M. Clifford at the presidential helm from 1965 to 1968, Curtis could achieve only small profits.

Despite the libel suits, *The Saturday Evening Post* maintained high writing standards under the editorship of William A. Emerson, Jr., who assumed the position in 1963. Emerson, a man with a sense of humor, said he would edit the *Post* as long as it amused him to do so, which was until the final issue. Authors for the Emerson version of *The Post* included Arthur Miller, James Gavin, John Kenneth Galbraith, James Michener, Russell Baker, and Daniel Patrick Moynihan. Thousands of readers wrote to Curtis Publishing after *The Saturday Evening Post* folded, asking that the magazine be given a second chance. As one editor said when the magazine was dying, "If goodwill were cash, the beloved *Post* would be rich."

Impact of Event

From a journalistic point of view, there were fewer outlets for superior writers of fiction and nonfiction after the demise of *The Saturday Evening Post*. From a business perspective, the event caught the attention of publishers as one more clear signal that general interest magazines with a mass, national circulation were no longer attracting sufficient advertising dollars. Other highly visible magazines that perished near this time were *The American* (1956), *Collier's* (1957), *Coronet* (1961), *Reporter* (1968), *Life* (1972), *Look* (1972), and *The Saturday Review*, which merged with *World Magazine* in 1973.

Although these failures give the appearance that magazine publishing was on the decline, a substantial growth occurred between 1963 and 1974 in both the number of American magazines and in their total circulation. The most significant trend was the rise in the number and sales of specialty magazines designed to take up where television left off on such topics as sports, air travel, crafts, autos, business, parenting, and metropolitan hubs, as covered by such publications as *New York* and *Philadelphia*. Even though many magazines shut down, during this period the total number of American magazines rose 47.6 percent, with a parallel 43 percent increase in overall circulation. Numerous general interest magazines entered the marketplace but achieved low sales. Thus, the total circulation figures of general magazines remained steady.

The downfall of the picture magazines *Life* and *Look* further indicated that advertisers preferred television and the new specialty publications. Increased circulation for *Life* and *Look* created soaring overhead costs at the same time that television reached dominance in pictorial news coverage. Rumors drifted throughout the media industry, spread by trade journals and gossip sheets, that *Life* and *Look* were doomed. As confidence faded, advertisers pushed further into the television market. In 1968, the *Life* page rate for four-color advertising had risen to $64,200, $20,000 more than the price of one minute of network television advertising time. As printing costs rose, postal rates increased. *Look* administrators blamed postal rate increases, in large part, for the magazine's demise in October, 1972.

Events such as the closing of *The Saturday Evening Post* and *Life* showed that editorial excellence was no longer as important to sustaining a magazine as was effective business management. By the 1980's, magazine management was relegated largely to relatives and heirs of founders, with strong editors unable to have much of an impact. At *The Saturday Evening Post*, aging conservatives still influenced the board of directors as late as the 1960's. Ackerman criticized the magazine's inability to keep up with the times, which he saw as resulting from unsuitable high-level management.

Historically, magazines have died during periods of economic instability and in the face of competition for the reader's time. For example, the bicycle fad, automobiles, radio, and motion pictures caused such magazines as *Century*, *North American Review*, and *Living Age* to fold. In the 1960's and 1970's, television acted as a much more direct and successful rival for leisure time. *The Saturday Evening Post* was revised, but as a quarterly publication, in the summer of 1971. It began monthly publication in 1974.

Bibliography

Ackerman, Martin S. *The Curtis Affair*. Los Angeles: Nash, 1970. A clear, concise rundown of Ackerman's actions and opinions during his ten months as president and chief executive officer of Curtis Publishing Company. Readable and relatively unbiased.

Culligan, Matthew J. *The Curtis-Culligan Story: From Cyrus to Horace, to Joe.* New York: Crown Publishers, 1970. Colorful but less than erudite perspective on the Culligan years. Interesting for his point of view. Brief index.

Friedrich, Otto. *Decline and Fall.* New York: Harper and Row, 1970. A very readable account of the magazine's demise, starting in September, 1962, when Friedrich went to work for *The Saturday Evening Post.* He served as number-two editor under William A. Emerson, Jr. Gives a full history of the magazine. Good index.

——————. "I Am Marty Ackerman. I Am Thirty-six Years Old. And I Am Very Rich." *Harper's Magazine* 239 (December, 1969): 92-121. Condensation of chapters about Ackerman from *Decline and Fall.* Very readable. May be all a student of *The Saturday Evening Post* needs to know about its last months and days.

Kobak, James B. "Growing, Changing, and Stable." *Folio: The Magazine for Magazine Management* 3 (October, 1974): 87-95. A plethora of facts, figures, and charts showing the foundings and discontinuances of magazines, listed by category rather than title. Useful.

Rankin, William Parkman. *Business Management of General Consumer Magazines.* New York: Praeger, 1980. Particularly relevant are chapter 4, "The Economic Development of Early Magazines," chapter 5, "*The Saturday Evening Post,*" and chapter 8, "*Life.*" Very good bibliography.

Wood, James Playsted. *The Curtis Magazines.* New York: Ronald Press Company, 1971. A clear if unevenly written history of the inexorable downfall of *The Saturday Evening Post.* Less personal than other accounts. Good index.

Anne Magnuson

Cross-References

Forbes Magazine Is Founded (1917), p. 314; *Reader's Digest* Is Founded (1922), p. 390; Henry Luce Founds *Time* Magazine (1923), p. 412; Henry Luce Founds *Fortune* Magazine (1930), p. 585; The 1939 World's Fair Introduces Regular Television Service (1939), p. 803; NBC Is Ordered to Divest Itself of a Radio Network (1941), p. 827; Community Antenna Television Is Introduced (1949), p. 953; Fred Silverman Rescues ABC Television's Ratings (1975-1978), p. 1578.

CONGRESS BEGINS HEARINGS ON COST OVERRUNS FOR THE C-5A GALAXY

Categories of event: Government and business; new products
Time: September 3, 1969
Locale: Washington, D.C.

Lockheed Aircraft Corporation suffered $2.1 billion in cost overruns in manufacturing the U.S. Air Force's C-5A Galaxy transport plane

Principal personages:
WILLIAM PROXMIRE (1915-   ), a senator from Wisconsin, 1957-1987
ROBERT MCNAMARA (1916-   ), the U.S. secretary of defense, 1960-1967
ERNEST FITZGERALD (1927-   ), the deputy for management systems, Office of the Assistant Secretary of the Air Force for Financial Management, 1965-1969
L. MENDEL RIVERS (1905-1970), a congressman from South Carolina, 1941-1970
WILLIAM MOORHEAD (1923-1987), a congressman from Pennsylvania, 1959-1981

Summary of Event

In 1965, the Lockheed Aircraft Corporation was awarded the bid to build the C-5A Galaxy super transport plane for the U.S. Air Force (USAF). The C5-A aircraft was the largest aircraft in the world. The plane was 246 feet long, with a 223-foot wing span and a tail six stories high. It had four 16-foot, 7,000-pound turbine jet engines and a load capacity of about 250,000 pounds of tanks, helicopters, cannons, trucks, or other equipment. According to original specifications, the plane could fly nearly 3,000 miles at speeds exceeding 600 miles per hour; land, unload, and take off on a 4,000-foot dirt runway; then return to its base without refueling.

The three major competitors for the enormous military contract were Douglas Aircraft Corporation, Boeing Company, and Lockheed. The award-winning proposal was for 115 aircraft and an anticipated cost to the Pentagon of $1.9 billion.

On Wednesday, September 3, 1969, the United States Senate, under the charge of Senator William Proxmire (D-Wisconsin), began hearings concerning the possibility of a $2.1 billion cost overrun in the production of the C-5A aircraft by Lockheed. These Senate hearings received national attention not only because of the significant amount of potential cost overruns but also because of the political and industrial practices hinted at and accusations made by numerous witnesses. How Lockheed could find itself in the financial situation it did requires a review of the history of the contract negotiations and manufacturing practices.

In April, 1965, the three primary contractors submitted their final bids for the

115-plane contract. Boeing was highest with a bid of $2.3 billion, Douglas was second with a bid of $2.0 billion, and Lockheed was the low bidder at $1.9 billion. In addition to the bids, the contractors provided more than 200,000 pages of supporting technical data to the Air Force. This material included cost projections, construction schedules, and aircraft performance data. A C-5A Evaluation Group from the Air Force Systems Command, consisting of four hundred analysts, spent five months reviewing the materials and evaluating the bids. The project team eliminated the Douglas bid on the grounds of required design changes and a fear that such changes would cause delays in the schedule and increases in costs. The Boeing proposal was selected based on design superiority. This recommendation was sent to the top levels of the Air Force and the Department of Defense for the final decision.

Air Force Secretary Eugene Zuckert, USAF Chief of Staff General John P. McConnell, and others overruled the selection board recommendation and awarded the contract to Lockheed-Georgia of Marietta, Georgia. Senator Richard Russell (D-Georgia), chairman of the Senate Armed Services Committee, may have provided considerable influence on President Lyndon B. Johnson concerning final contract selection criteria. Such speculation is difficult to prove.

The contract negotiated for the C5-A with Lockheed-Georgia included a new method of contracting known as Total Package Procurement (TPP). This contracting methodology was introduced under Secretary of Defense Robert McNamara by Robert Charles, newly appointed assistant secretary of the Air Force for installations and logistics. The TPP concept was to have contractors submit proposals covering research, development, and production, including performance and delivery commitments. This process differed from previous military contracts in that previously, contractors bid only for an initial research and development contract. Although research and development generally represent about 20 percent of the total cost of a weapons system, the winning contractor was normally assured of receiving the follow-on contract for actual production. Having already invested millions of dollars in the initial research and development, the Defense Department was almost forced to accept the company's bid for the production contract because the complexity of the research made it almost impossible to switch to another contractor. The TPP was intended to give the government more controls over the entire acquisition process, since the entire package could be detailed at the initial contracting stage.

One of the obvious problems of the TPP concept became evident during the congressional hearings on the Lockheed cost overruns on the C5-A. The time frame of major military contracts can sometimes range from five to ten years. In the case of the C5-A contract, for example, the Air Force and Lockheed were negotiating in 1965 on the basis of cost estimates for work that would not be completed until 1972. For Lockheed, this time frame proved disastrous in estimating costs with precision. The Lockheed contract required five experimental planes, an initial production run of 53 planes (Run A), and an optional second run of 57 additional planes (Run B), for a total of 115 aircraft. In addition, Lockheed was to provide for flight and ground test programs, crew and maintenance training for six squadrons, ground support equipment, and spare parts. The contract also contained penalty clauses. Specifically, schedule delays would bring penalties of $12,000 per day for each of the first sixteen planes delivered late, with a maximum penalty of $11 million. The contractor would also absorb the costs of correcting any structural deficiencies and would earn no profit on costs incurred as a result of design changes.

Although the terms of the contract appeared strict, there was an additional clause that later proved to be a loophole for extreme cost overruns. This clause contained a very complex and sophisticated repricing formula. Simply put, it used the cost experience on the 53 planes in production Run A as a basis for renegotiating the cost of the additional 57 planes in Run B. If costs on Run A rose above the ceiling price (30 percent over target price), the over-ceiling percentage was multiplied by a factor of 1.5. The multiplication factor rose to 2 if costs went higher than 140 percent of the target. The resulting figure was then used to multiply the original target cost of Run B, producing new, higher target and ceiling prices for Run B. It was this confusing environment that eventually led to the well-publicized congressional hearings by Senator William Proxmire in September, 1969, on substantial cost overruns on the C5-A project.

Impact of Event

There was no single contributing factor to the cost overruns on the C5-A Galaxy. The nature of the aircraft, the apparent underbid, political influences, and inefficient management caused Lockheed to ultimately suffer losses of approximately $648 million on the C5-A contract.

Soon after the contract award, engineers at the Lockheed-Georgia plant began to encounter a series of unforeseen technical problems with aircraft design. In early 1966, Lockheed was forced to redesign the wing, nose, and other parts as a result of wind tunnel tests demonstrating too much drag on short takeoffs. In changing the original design, weight became a problem, and designers had to plan for lighter but more expensive metals in the aircraft construction. These design problems caused concern to Air Force plant representatives. They issued a "cure notice" on February 1, 1967, stating that unless the technical deficiencies were soon solved, the contract might be terminated for default.

Lockheed was forced to expand the scope of its development program and in so doing incurred extraordinary labor costs for the project. Forced to live up to contract specifications, Lockheed had to spend millions of extra dollars, money not anticipated in the company's original cost estimates. The extra costs began showing up as increased overhead on Lockheed's monthly program reports to the Air Force in early 1966. To curb this trend, Lockheed claimed that initial budget estimates had been mistaken and simply increased the budget for this developmental stage. The overruns therefore disappeared.

In early 1966, Ernest Fitzgerald, deputy for management systems in the Office of the Assistant Secretary of the Air Force for Financial Management, wrote a report describing potentially disturbing overhead increases. These sharp increases continued for three years, until the Air Force was forced to publicly acknowledge the cost problems that Lockheed was incurring. Finally, on November 13, 1968, Fitzgerald testified before Senator Proxmire's hearings on military procurement that on the basis of the Air Force's records, the projected overrun for the total C5-A program would probably reach $2.1 billion, and that Lockheed would run more than 100 percent over its original target price. Fitzgerald attempted to explain the overruns by indicating an initial underestimation of costs, ineffective cost controls, and problems tied in with the repricing formula in the contract award. The news of a potential $2 billion cost overrun made front-page headlines across the United States. Senator Proxmire blasted the Air Force for concealing the cost increase from Congress and requested that the General Accounting Office (GAO) investigate the entire C-5A program.

On November 14, 1969, the Department of Defense formally announced its decision to limit the C5-A program to four squadrons, or 81 planes. Although appearing to be a cost-saving move, the contract for 81 planes still cost half a billion dollars more than the original contract for 115 planes. Lockheed, upset by the decision, protested the decision by filing an appeal notice with the Armed Services Board of Contract Appeals. Although the decision to build only 81 planes stood, an agreement was made to stretch out the production schedule for Lockheed until January, 1973.

Although the cost overruns of the C5-A by Lockheed appear to stem from unusual mismanagement or bad planning, it is not uncommon for military contracts to greatly exceed original estimates. The nature of the military-industrial-congressional system that produces these projects is subject to cost overruns, abuse, inefficiencies, and sometimes waste. Other programs have suffered extreme cost overruns. Both in terms of percentage and actual dollars, the $2.1 billion C-5A cost overrun set no records in defense contracting. In 1970, the Department of Defense informed the Senate Armed Services Committee that twenty-seven of its major weapons programs were showing an aggregate cost growth of $15 billion. Other examples of cost overruns include the F-111 fighter, contracted with General Dynamics for $3.3 billion (114 percent overrun), and the FB-111 bomber, also contracted with General Dynamics for $469 million (64 percent overrun). The Mark 48 torpedo, contracted with Westinghouse, showed an increase of cost of $2.9 billion (426 percent overrun). The Minuteman III missile, contracted with Boeing, showed an increase of $993 million, or 23 percent. Other Boeing contracts included the SRAM missile, with an increase of $717 million (193 percent), and the Minuteman II missile, with an increase of $226 million (5 percent). The Phoenix missile contract with Hughes Aircraft had a $596 million cost overrun, or a 66 percent increase. The Sparrow F missile, contracted with Raytheon, showed an increase of $370 million, a 53 percent overrun. The A-7D attack plane, contracted with Ling-Temco-Vought, showed an increase of $291 million, or 27 percent over original contract price. The Condor missile contract with North American Rockwell identified an increase of $131 million, or 60 percent. Finally the CVAN 68 carrier, contracted with Newport News Shipbuilding, showed an increase of $177 million, or 27 percent over the original contract price.

On the basis of the multiple cost overruns identified above, it appears that cost controls over military procurement programs are less than adequate. Until the military-industrial-congressional system for contracting military projects is changed, taxpayers will continue to support a flawed acquisition process.

Bibliography

"Aircraft Maker Hurts from C-5A Cutback, Lag in L-1011 Orders." *Business Week* (February 14, 1970): 46-48. Addresses the relatively poor financial position of the Lockheed Corporation, specifically the bleak financial outlook because of lack of orders for the firm's long-distance commercial airbus, the L-1011, and the estimated loss of $500 million on production of the C5-A Galaxy.

"Cost Overruns Bring on the SEC." *Business Week* (June 6, 1970): 31-32. Discusses the introduction of the Securities and Exchange Commission into inquiries regarding whether defense companies with escalating contract costs have been giving stockholders adequate notice of their financial difficulties. This applies specifically to the Lockheed Corporation and apparent cost overruns in the production of the C5-A Galaxy for the Air Force.

"Lockheed Asks DOD Fiscal Help." *Aviation Week & Space Technology* 92 (March 9, 1970): 224-225. Discusses Lockheed Corporation's appeals to the Pentagon for immediate financial relief totaling about $650 million, pending settlements of four military contracts. One of these contracts, for the C5-A Galaxy, is requiring an additional $435-500 million in payments to Lockheed to complete the planned delivery of 81 aircraft during 1971 and 1972.

"Lockheed Flies into Heavier Flak." *Business Week* (May 30, 1970): 28-29. Discusses the potential loss of $648 million for the Lockheed Corporation in its production of the C5-A Galaxy. Senator William Proxmire demanded full disclosure of Lockheed's corporate cash flow situation as well as assurances that money advanced to Lockheed on military projects will not be diverted to any commercial venture.

Miller, B. "Complex Problems Hit Lockheed." *Aviation Week & Space Technology* 92 (March 30, 1970): 56-60. Discusses the financial turmoil of the Lockheed Corporation and the primary reasons for the situation. Included in the problem is the fixed-cost nature of three military contracts, including the C5-A, AH-56A, and SRAM. Lockheed blames spiraling inflation and the unknown costs of advanced technology as the primary reasons for the cost overruns.

"Pentagon Plans Aid to Lockheed: Financiers Fear L-1011 Problems." *Aviation Week & Space Technology* 92 (March 16, 1970): 22-23. Discusses Lockheed's financial trouble with four major military contracts, including the C5-A super transport, the Air Force short-range attack missile (SRAM), and the Army AH-56A high-speed armed helicopter. Each of these contracts was awarded under the now discredited Total Procurement Package concept evolved during the administration of Defense Secretary Robert S. McNamara.

Rice, Berkeley. *The C5-A Scandal*. Boston: Houghton Mifflin, 1971. Rice provides an excellent chronology of the development and production of the C5-A Galaxy. The discussion describes the initial bid competitions among Boeing, Douglas, and

Lockheed and how the decision was made to award Lockheed the contract. He also details how key corporate and government officials were involved with the production of the C5-A and the ultimate congressional hearing regarding the substantial cost overruns on the project.

John L. Farbo

Cross-References

The U.S. Government Begins Using Cost-Plus Contracts (1914), p. 246; The DC-3 Opens a New Era of Commercial Air Travel (1936), p. 752; The Boeing 707 Begins Commercial Service (1958), p. 1112; A European Consortium Plans the Airbus (1967), p. 1303; McDonnell Aircraft and Douglas Aircraft Merge (1967), p. 1314.

THE UNITED STATES BANS CYCLAMATES FROM CONSUMER MARKETS

Category of event: Consumer affairs
Time: October 18, 1969
Locale: Washington, D.C.

Evidence that consumption of cyclamates may be harmful to humans' health led to their removal from the United States marketplace

Principal personages:
HERBERT LEY, JR. (1923-   ), the commissioner of the United States Food and Drug Administration, 1968-1969
ROBERT FINCH (1925-   ), the secretary of Health, Education, and Welfare, 1969-1970
MARVIN S. LEGATOR (1926-   ), an FDA scientist who studied the effect of cyclohexylamine injections on rats
UMBERTO SAFFIOTTI (1928-   ), a doctor affiliated with the National Cancer Institute who was instrumental in forwarding the results of cyclamate research to the Department of Health, Education, and Welfare

Summary of Event

On October 18, 1969, Secretary of Health, Education, and Welfare Robert Finch announced that food products containing cyclamates would be banned from the U.S. markets effective February 1, 1970. This decision was made after several scientific studies revealed that certain amounts of cyclamates were harmful to chicken embryos and rats.

Prior to the development of artificial sweeteners, only natural sugars, in forms such as sugarcane, corn syrup, maple sugar, and honey, were used in food products. These sugars are high in calories and are unhealthy for a small proportion of people afflicted with medical conditions such as diabetes. Artificial sweeteners have much lower caloric contents than natural sugars and can be used by consumers who cannot safely ingest sugar. Only a small percentage of the United States population must abstain from sugar, but many consumers choose to purchase foods and beverages produced with low-calorie sugar substitutes as part of weight-control programs.

A growth in consumption of artificial sweeteners would coincide with a reduction in the market for sugar. This shift threatened sugar producers, who supported testing and research on the artificial substances to determine if they might have adverse physiological effects on consumers.

Because some consumers need to restrict or discontinue consumption of sugar for medical reasons and other consumers wish to reduce caloric intake, a substantial market for artificial sweeteners had developed in the United States by the mid-1960's.

Ideally, a sugar substitute should taste identical to sugar, perform as sugar does in food preparation, and not adversely affect the health of those consuming it. Chemists have attempted to create such a product, but time and research have shown that many artificial sweeteners have limited merits.

In the two decades prior to 1969, cyclamates had been the primary substitute for sugar in diet-type food products. A cyclamate is an artificial (chemically produced) salt of sodium or calcium. Cyclamates have a sweet taste similar to that of sugar and contribute virtually no calories to foods and beverages in which they are used. By the late 1960's, the consumption of diet soft drinks, diet fruit jams and jellies, and table sugar substitutes had become widespread. Using cyclamates as sweeteners, soft drinks were made calorie free, and canned fruits and jams were produced with significantly reduced caloric contents.

Diet soft drink producers consumed more than half the cyclamates produced in the United States and, according to *Business Week*, collectively manufactured products worth $420 million at retail prices in 1969. Of all soft drinks sold in 1969, 15 percent were diet drinks. These drinks thus had substantial effects on the financial performance of manufacturers.

Producers of artificial sweeteners pursued development of their products because they believed there was a potentially large market of diet-conscious people who would willingly pay for the sweetening agents. The possibility for large profits was a motivating factor for producers, as artificial sweeteners sold for more than four times as much as granulated sugar. Furthermore, it was expected that consumers would eagerly purchase low-calorie prepared canned foods and beverages. A government advisory panel for the Food and Drug Administration (FDA) estimated in 1968 that 75 percent of the U.S. population consumed artificial sweeteners and that 70 percent of these sweeteners were used in soft drinks. At that time, about half a dozen companies were marketing brands of artificial sweeteners for table use, most of which contained cyclamates. Brand names of the sweetening products included Sugarcane 99, Crystal Sweet, Sweet 'n' Low, Sweetness & Light, Zero-Cal, and Sugarine. Diet soft drinks were sold under brand names such as Diet Pepsi, Fresca, Like, Tab, and Diet-Rite.

As new food and pharmaceutical products are developed, the FDA must approve their distribution in the United States. Once products have been approved for distribution, researchers may continue to test them to better observe the physiological effects the products have on humans. Such research is often initiated when a group or organization suggests that there may be a potential hazard as a result of consumption. In 1958, an amendment to the Food and Drug Administration Act known as the Delaney Amendment was passed. It requires that food additives that are shown to cause cancer in either animals or humans be removed from the consumer market.

Research concerning the effects of consumption of cyclamates occurred throughout the time they were marketed in the United States. Several preliminary research panels concurred that consumption of cyclamates was safe. In December, 1968, a government advisory panel, in a report to the FDA, concluded that no research warranted a reduction from the current recommended consumption limit of 5 grams (the equivalent of more than three quarts of artificially sweetened beverages) of cyclamates per day. The FDA responded with a more guarded recommendation to the public that research was ongoing and that, pending results, consumers should consume no more than 50 milligrams per day. The panel reported that according to soft drink labeling information, a 12-ounce can contained between 0.3 and 0.6 grams of cyclamates. Even one soft drink would exceed the lower recommended limit. In April, 1969, changes in labeling of products containing cyclamates were recommended by the FDA to allow consumers to more easily stay within the safe consumption levels. At that time, concern about safe intake levels was primarily in response to the knowledge that consuming more than 5 grams of cyclamates per day has a laxative effect on humans and to the results of laboratory experiments that had shown liver changes in animals that consumed cyclamates.

Early in October, 1969, researchers hired by Abbott Laboratories, which manufactured more than half of all cyclamates sold in the United States, found possibly malignant tumors in rats that were fed high doses of cyclamates. This information was passed along to the Department of Health, Education, and Welfare (HEW) through reports from the National Cancer Institute and Abbott Laboratories. As a result of the reports and as advised by the National Academy of Sciences, Robert Finch announced on October 18 that cyclamates would be removed from U.S. markets.

Impact of Event

The immediate reaction to the ban by manufacturers of cyclamates and of foods and beverages containing cyclamates was surprise. Earlier in 1969, new products containing cyclamates had been introduced to the consumer market. Other products were continuing to be developed, and HEW statements had recently ruled cyclamates to be safe for consumption.

Consumers responded with mixed reactions to the cyclamate ban. Some were concerned for their health and immediately wanted products without the controversial cyclamates. Others were concerned that they might not have low-calorie alternatives to their favorite products. As a result, many stores reported unusually heavy sales of cyclamate-containing products in the week immediately following the ban. Apparently, consumers stocked up on the items that they expected to be removed from supermarket shelves. The Royal Crown Cola company, producer of Diet-Rite, the leading diet soft drink in 1969, surveyed consumers to determine their reactions to the cyclamate issue. The results of the survey indicated that consumers were not concerned about their consumption of cyclamates even though they were aware of the controversy.

Many retail stores chose to remove cyclamate-containing products before the February 1 deadline. Other stores left cyclamate products on the shelves but discontinued orders of new products. Most stores endured a slowdown in sales of diet products following the announcement of the ban.

Producers of diet-plan beverages that were formulated and marketed as substitutes for traditional meals found an exemption from the ban by repackaging their products and distributing them through drugstores as prescription items. This move enabled them to avoid huge losses on their inventories.

Diet soft drink manufacturers dealt with the transition to cyclamate-free products remarkably well. Fortunately for the manufacturers, the ban was announced in October, a traditionally slow sales and advertising period. Soft drinks are not produced very long in advance of distribution, so manufacturers were not hampered by large inventories that might become worthless.

Fruit canners did not fare as well as soft drink producers, as they had just completed a seasonal pack when the ban was announced. Further, canners and jam producers generally had proportionately more diet products in their product mix than did soft drink producers. Manufacturers of diet-type canned fruits and vegetables successfully secured an extension in the phase-out time for cyclamates. They effectively extended the deadline to September 1, 1970. This extension enabled them to deplete most of the inventory that had been canned prior to the ban announcement.

With the impending deadline for the ban of cyclamates quickly approaching, manufacturers of foods and beverages were eager to discover a cyclamate replacement that would save the market for their products. Soft drink manufacturers overwhelmingly switched from cyclamates to saccharin. Saccharin did not replicate the taste of sugar as well as did cyclamates. Saccharin also had the unfortunate drawback of a bitter aftertaste. A small amount of sugar could be added to a drink to squelch the bitter aftertaste, but this added approximately forty calories to the product. Manufacturers were concerned about the marketability of this substitute, afraid that middle-aged consumers would not consider the reduction of a few calories to be enough of a benefit to purchase the diet drink and that consumers concerned about the effect of sugar on teeth would not be satisfied with the addition of sugar.

Following the October announcement of the cyclamates ban, advertising was heavy among diet product producers, both those that used cyclamates and those that did not. Many products that were marketed as diet or sugar-free and never did use cyclamates increased their advertising for two reasons. Firth, they now had an advantage over the cyclamate-containing products. Second, their producers wanted to be certain that consumers knew that cyclamates were not used in the products.

Although it is difficult to measure the effectiveness of advertising, it is clear that consumers responded favorably to new diet products that replaced those containing cyclamates. Saccharin had been produced since 1901. It became the sweetener of choice for diet products for more than two decades, until health risks similar to those earlier discovered for cyclamates were associated with it. Nutra Sweet emerged as the replacement of saccharin in the 1980's. Because of the potential volume of sales and profits generated from diet foods and beverages, research targeting the physiological effects of currently consumed artificial sweetener and the development of new artificial sweeteners continues.

Bibliography

Cohen, Stanley E. "Cyclamates Incident May Raise Some Questions for Government Marketers." *Advertising Age* 40 (October 27, 1969): 107. Discusses controversial issues and the impact of the cyclamate ban on producers and policymakers.

"Cyclamates: How Sweet It Isn't. . ." *Chemical Week* 105 (October 29, 1969): 30-31. Discusses the economic impact of the cyclamate ban on producers of cyclamates.

"Diet Industry Has a Hungry Look." *Business Week* (October 25, 1969): 41-42. Discusses the impact of the cyclamate ban on producers of diet soft drinks and other diet foods.

Donlon, Thomas B., and Kathryn Sederberg. "Food, Drink People React Swiftly to Cyclamate Ban: Ads May Increase." *Advertising Age* 40 (October 27, 1969): 1. Discusses the impact on advertising resulting from the cyclamate ban. Specific companies' strategies for new advertising are shared.

Semling, H. V., Jr. "FDA Establishing Cyclamate Policy, Economic Woes Being Heard." *Food Processing* 31 (April, 1970): 71-72. Highlights the new policy on cyclamates used for pharmaceutical products and the phase-out schedule for cyclamates in food products. The economic impact of the ban is discussed.

Virginia Ann Paulins

Cross-References

Congress Passes the Pure Food and Drug Act (1906), p. 128; Congress Requires Premarket Clearance for Products (1938), p. 787; Congress Sets Standards for Chemical Additives in Food (1958), p. 1097; The Wholesome Poultry Products Act Is Passed (1968), p. 1369; Health Consciousness Creates Huge New Markets (1970's), p. 1416.

THE BANNING OF DDT SIGNALS NEW ENVIRONMENTAL AWARENESS

Category of event: Consumer affairs
Time: November 20, 1969
Locale: Washington, D.C.

By banning the use of DDT, the United States took a first step in addressing environmental concerns relating to many products

Principal personages:
RACHEL CARSON (1907-1964), a marine biologist, the author of *Silent Spring*
PAUL HERMANN MÜLLER (1899-1965), the inventor of DDT
WILLIAM LONGGOOD (1917-   ), a Pulitzer Prize-winning journalist, author of *The Poisons in Your Food*

Summary of Event

In the spring of 1972, amid considerable controversy, the United States Environmental Protection Agency (EPA) banned dichloro-diphenyl-trichloroethane (DDT) for use as a pesticide in the United States. This followed a ban on use in residential areas issued by the federal government on November 20, 1969. The DDT ban had a far-reaching impact on humanity, the environment, and business. Widespread use of other toxic or dangerous pesticides, however, continued in the United States and elsewhere.

DDT, which consists of chlorinated hydrocarbons or organochlorides, was acquired by the United States from Switzerland in 1942. It was discovered by Paul Hermann Müller, who won a Nobel Prize for the discovery. Prior to the discovery of DDT, there were hundreds of different pesticides in use. Many of these pesticides were effective on only one or a few pests. Some of the more infamous pesticides included Paris green, which contained arsenic but was extremely effective on potato bugs; lead arsenate, used to eliminate gypsy moth caterpillars; and calcium arsenate, used against cotton pests in the South. One problem associated with early pesticides was that they were often as dangerous to plants as they were to insects.

DDT was an important discovery because insecticides that had been in use were scarce because of World War II. In addition, DDT was effective against a variety of insects, including lice and mosquitoes. It was discovered after the war that DDT also was effective against a number of agricultural pests that plagued American farm production and Americans in general.

By 1960, DDT was a household word. Its use was so widespread that almost every person in the United States either had used the product or had heard of its use. It was partially because DDT was so well known that it was singled out for study by scientists who noticed irregularities in the environment.

At this time, during the peak of DDT use, two books were written about pesticides and their impact on the environment. One of the books, *Silent Spring* (1962), written by marine biologist Rachel Carson, extensively outlined the effects of DDT on humans and on the environment. According to Carson, humans can become poisoned by DDT in a number of ways: by breathing the oily fumes that occur when it is sprayed, by ingesting food that has been sprayed with DDT, and by absorbing it through the skin. Because DDT is fat soluble, it is stored in organs rich in fatty substances such as the liver, the kidneys, and the adrenal and thyroid glands. DDT had been linked to cancer and blood disorders.

DDT did not disseminate in the environment. Accumulations of DDT remained in the soil and continued to contaminate plants and insects. Birds or other animals that ate insects or animals contaminated by DDT died or passed the contamination on to other animals through the food chain. There were questions as to whether DDT poisoning could be passed from a mother to her child through mother's milk and about a variety of illnesses that could result from DDT poisoning.

Another significant book written during this time was *The Poisons in Your Food* (1960) by journalist William Longgood. It was an important work because it was the first major journalistic attack against pesticides. It caused the general public to become aware of the dangers of pesticides, outlining a number of toxic pesticides that had been used to restrict insects and promote agricultural growth. The book indicated that many poisons remained in food and were therefore consumed by human beings.

Both these books stirred public interest in environmental concerns. That public concern led to the establishment in 1970 of the Environmental Protection Agency (EPA), whose purpose was to protect and improve the environment. The EPA was responsible for controlling pollution through standard setting, enforcement, and research in the areas of solid waste, toxic substances, radiation, and noise. One of the first acts of the EPA was to amend the Federal Insecticide, Fungicide, and Rodenticide Act of 1947 to restrict the use of DDT.

The federal government had banned use of DDT in residential areas on November 20, 1969, and called for a virtual halt to its use by 1971. Other countries took similar action. The EPA issued a cancellation order on the use of DDT in January, 1971. The Department of Agriculture appealed the order. In October of 1971, the EPA held hearings to determine the nature of the hazards of DDT use or misuse and the nature of benefits of the use of DDT. The EPA tried to determine if harms to humans associated with DDT occurred because it was misused or necessarily resulted even with proper use. The harms of using DDT then had to be weighed against the benefits of its use. One of the benefits of its use was increased food production, particularly important for countries that were dense in population. Land had to be very productive to feed the people of such countries. The use of DDT also had eliminated hoards of mosquitoes, which had caused epidemic outbreaks of malaria, and it had eliminated lice infestations, which were responsible for numerous typhus epidemics. The EPA determined, however, that the harmful effects of DDT outweighed the benefits. If it remained in the environment for a long enough time, it could endanger a large number of people. DDT therefore was banned for use and production in the United States. European countries later followed suit.

Impact of Event

The banning of DDT in the United States and in Europe, along with hearings on pesticides and their use, alerted the public to the importance of environmental and ecological issues. The American public became involved by joining groups such as Greenpeace, the Sierra Club, the Audubon Society, the National Wildlife Federation, and the Wilderness Society. Membership in these groups soon numbered in the millions. These groups lobbied Congress to pass additional laws to protect the environment. Lobbying efforts soon resulted in legislation concerning clean air, water pollution, noise control, drinking water, and toxic substances. These acts identified pollutants and set standards for their release into the environment. Standards were meant to identify the levels at which certain pollutants would be dangerous to people or the environment and to restrict emissions to those levels or below. The standards focused on factories and sewage plants at first. Later, standards would be expanded to include all polluters.

Compliance with the standards was expensive. The EPA forced many companies to develop new processes or products in order to conform to standards. For example, auto companies were forced to alter their auto emission systems to include a part called a catalytic converter. Auto companies also were forced to design more fuel-efficient vehicles, since gasoline had been identified as a pollutant as well as a natural resource. These changes added an estimated $800 to the cost of each American car. Other companies were required to find alternative places to dump their refuse or to do research and development on alternate uses for refuse. Even biodegradable refuse and, under some conditions, clean but warm water were deemed harmful to the environment. Areas previously used as dump sites were discovered to contain toxic substances, and companies found to have used the sites were forced to pay to have these sites cleaned.

During 1988, corporations paid an estimated $86 billion for pollution control, an amount equal to 2 percent of the Gross National Product. The Comprehensive Environmental Response, Compensation, and Liability Act was passed in 1980 in part to help firms pay the high costs of cleaning up old dump sites. Under this act, firms unable to pay to clean sites received assistance from the government, which had funds from petroleum and chemical production taxes set aside for this purpose. Business costs escalated in other ways, as firms were sued because of harm done to the environment. Hooker Chemical Company faced one such suit. When dangerous chemicals seeped from its barrels into the groundwater, people in a small community near Niagara Falls, New York, since called Love Canal, experienced increased rates of cancer, birth defects, and other illnesses. The costs of settling the resulting suit was in the billions of dollars.

Costs continued to rise as other harmful or possibly harmful practices were identified. For American business, making a profit became complicated by concerns over environmental issues and possible future liabilities. Companies producing pesticides, for example, had to be concerned about the health and welfare of the populations of areas in which the pesticides were produced and used. The Food and Drug Administration (FDA) and the Environmental Protection Agency shared the responsibility for protecting the public from harmful substances in food. Manufacturers of pesticides and chemicals had to perform tests and prove the safety of their products as well as showing that residues did not accumulate beyond allowed levels. The FDA and EPA relied largely on tests conducted by the manufacturers themselves when registering pesticides. Consequently, some harmful pesticides, including Dieldrin, Diazinon, Malathion, and Lindane, remained in use. Pesticides by nature are harmful to at least some forms of life and may cause cancer, birth defects, or nerve damage in humans. Some chemicals have not been tested for possible harmful effects. During the Ronald Reagan Administration, testing all but halted. Concern mounted about pesticides such as alar in apples, heptachlor in dairy products, and ethylene dibromide (EDB) in muffin and cake mixes. The release of toxic fumes from a chemical plant in Bhopal, India, in 1984 served as an example of the potential deadliness of pesticides. Thousands of people were killed in their sleep by toxic pesticide fumes, and hundreds of thousands more were injured.

The banning of DDT led to banning of other harmful substances in the United States and elsewhere. For countries with weaker economies or that are densely populated, the choice to restrict pesticides carried different costs and benefits. The risks of using harmful pesticides had to be balanced against the possibility of starvation or epidemic, and some countries could not afford the chemicals that could be used instead of those proved to be harmful. Pesticides will continue to be produced and used as long as insects continue to develop immunities to the chemicals being used. The challenges for business are to continue to balance pesticide use with other forms of pest control and to develop new safe and effective products. That concern with safety will also hold for wider environmental problems such as air and water pollution.

Bibliography

Beatty, Rita Gray. *The DDT Myth*. New York: John Day, 1973. Defends the use of DDT and refutes the findings of previous studies. Recounts studies of successful use. Includes tables comparing DDT to other sources of pollution and identifies some natural toxins found in the environment. Contains a selected list of references and an index.

Carson, Rachel. *Silent Spring*. Boston: Houghton Mifflin, 1962. An in-depth report on the results of early studies on the use of DDT and other dangerous chemicals. Outlines the dangers to the environment and to humans. Contains an index and an excellent list of principal sources.

Duggleby, John. *Pesticides*. New York: Macmillan, 1990. This forty-five-page hardcover book discusses what pesticides do, how to measure danger, and alternatives to pesticide use. Juvenile reading. Contains a section with addresses to write for further reading, a glossary of terms, and an index.

Greer, Douglas E. "Environmental Protection." In *Business, Government, and Society*. New York: Macmillan 1993. This chapter in a textbook reviews the topic of environmental policies by asking relevant questions. Contains an appendix on clean air and a section of notes which contains lists for additional reading. Written for undergraduate students.

Gunn, D. L., and J. G. R. Stevens. *Pesticides and Human Welfare*. Oxford, England; Oxford University Press, 1976. Presents a balanced opinion on the use of pesticides. Discusses the problems, strategies for use, and the legal environment up to 1975. Detailed appendix outlining terminology, reading lists at the end of each chapter.

Mott, Lawrie, and Karen Snyder. *Pesticide Alert: A Guide to Pesticides in Fruits and Vegetables*. San Francisco: Sierra Club Books, 1987. This softcover manual discusses pesticide residues and federal regulation of pesticides. Lists several fruits and vegetables and pesticide uses for each. Intended for the adult reader, this manual contains notes, a section on sources of additional information, and further reading. Also contains a glossary, a bibliography, and an index.

Taylor, Ron. *Facts on Pesticides and Fertilizers in Farming*. New York: Franklin Watts, 1990. Discusses pesticides and their uses in thirty-two pages. Contains four-color illustrations and color photos. An excellent and very brief introduction to ecology for the juvenile reader. Contains a glossary, an index, and a list of relevant addresses to write for additional information.

Wharton, James. *Before Silent Spring*. Princeton, N.J.: Princeton University Press, 1974. Discusses recognition of insect problems and regulations in force prior to 1962. Also includes a history of pesticides and public health. Contains bibliographic notes by chapter and an index. Meant as a source of information for the adult reader.

Elizabeth Gaydou

Cross-References

Congress Passes the Pure Food and Drug Act (1906), p. 128; Congress Passes the Motor Vehicle Air Pollution Control Act (1965), p. 1265; Health Consciousness Creates Huge New Markets (1970's), p. 1416; The Environmental Protection Agency Is Created (1970), p. 1460; The Three Mile Island Accident Prompts Reforms in Nuclear Power (1979), p. 1693; Toxic Gas Leaks from a Union Carbide Plant in Bhopal, India (1984), p. 1893; The United States Bans Chilean Fruit After Cyanide Scare (1989), p. 1986.

DENIM JEANS BECOME ACCEPTED AS FASHION

Category of event: Marketing
Time: The 1970's
Locale: The United States

By 1975, fashion designers were an established part of the huge market for blue denim jeans

Principal personages:
CALVIN KLEIN (1942-), an influential American designer who promoted jeans with provocative, often controversial advertising
GEORGES MARCIANO (1947-), a cofounder of Guess, one of the most successful blue jeans companies
LEVI STRAUSS (1829-1902), the original designer and the first manufacturer and retailer of blue denim jeans

Summary of Event

By the mid-1970's, American fashion designers had latched on to blue denim. They fashioned this fabric into jeans and a variety of apparel and accessory items that were marketed successfully around the world. *American Fabrics and Fashions*, a trade publication, stated that one of the major worldwide trends of the 1970's was the denim craze.

To understand why designers of high fashion invested time, talent, and money into denim, a fabric of the laboring class and the hippie movement, a review of the fabric and the nonverbal communication symbols associated with denim, and blue denim jeans in particular, is necessary. An understanding of the dynamics of fashion and society explains why this unusual union of high fashion designers and denim occurred.

The history of denim, a twill weave originally made of 100 percent cotton, goes back to Nimes, France, where the fabric was manufactured as early as A.D. 300. The fabric's original name was serge de Nimes, later Americanized to "denim." One of the first uses of denim in the United States was as a covering for Conestoga wagons that carried pioneers west.

The origin of jeans is attributed to Levi Strauss, a Jewish immigrant from Germany. In 1850, Strauss, loaded with a bolt of canvas to be fashioned into tents for gold miners, arrived in San Francisco. He was immediately informed by a miner of a more urgent need, for sturdy pants. Strauss measured the man on the spot, and for six dollars in gold dust, he sewed the canvas into jeans. News quickly spread of these sturdy jeans, and Strauss's supply of canvas was soon depleted. He requested a new supply from a sister living in New York. Instead of canvas, she sent denim dyed a dark indigo blue. Thus, blue denim and jeans became a pair, and the Levi Strauss Company was born.

In 1873, Strauss patented the use of metal rivets at major stress points on jeans. The rivets, first added to placate miners whose pockets kept tearing, are still a distinctive feature of jeans. By the turn of the century, durable jeans known simply as Levi's covered the legs of the working population of the West.

During the first half of the twentieth century, blue denim jeans remained a form of dress for the laboring class. The fabric proved to be durable and comfortable, and the design of the garment allowed for freedom of movement, enabling the wearer to accomplish work without hindrance.

Jeans were introduced to the higher classes of the eastern United States with the dude ranch craze of the 1930's. Pictures of cowboys clad in embroidered satin shirts, wide-brimmed hats, boots, and jeans filled travel brochures and advertisements. Even though vacationing on Western dude ranches came into vogue, jeans did not become a fashion item during this period of history.

Blue denim jeans were declared an essential commodity during World War II and were sold only to people engaged in defense work. After the war, jeans were limited to the market for work clothes until they were adopted as an almost obligatory uniform by the youth of the 1960's. Subsequently, blue denim jeans' popularity grew dramatically, as did symbolic meanings attached to them.

Social historians of fashion have attempted to explain the widespread acceptance of jeans. One explanation is the "trickle up" fashion theory. According to the theory, fashion may begin at a low level in society and proceed to higher levels as it is accepted by the masses of people. The widespread adoption of jeans by youth of the 1960's supports this theory, in that many wearers were wealthy and cast off designer clothing for jeans.

Another explanation of the widespread acceptance of jeans pertains to jeans as a symbol of the counterculture youth revolution of the 1950's and 1960's. The leaders of the movement adopted denim jeans. The message of distance between youths and parents and others in authority was clearly communicated when the young followers of the counterculture donned their often faded, mutilated jeans, to the anguish of those in positions of authority.

Other historians, of fashion have advocated that jeans, with their ties to the West, were a form of folk costume, a costume that citizens of the United States recognized as truly American. According to this theory, wearers believed that blue jeans displayed their attribute of being hard workers while showing a bit of sportiness.

Some observers believe that the mass acceptance of jeans over such a long period is a result of aging baby boomers wanting to remain youthful, or at least to revisit their youth. The trade publications *Women's Wear Daily* and *Daily News Record* substantiated this claim in the early 1990's by frequently featuring designers' lines that are reminiscent of garments from the 1960's and 1970's. The baby-boomers in their thirties and forties may have been searching for the fountain of youth via dress.

Textile scientists observed that the nature of denim fabric is a primary reason for its acceptance as fashion. The versatile fabric is capable of being produced in different weights easily adapted to seasonal garments, apparel accessories, and nonapparel items. Denim is comfortable because of the flexibility, absorbency, and pleasant feel of cotton, from which the majority of it is made. The range of color and finish possibilities of denim has allowed the fabric to stay in fashion over a long period of time and yet constantly be given new looks to satisfy consumers' desire for change.

Demographers looked at the changing population as a basis of explanation for the denim craze. As the first baby-boomers reached young adulthood, the market for apparel increased dramatically. At the same time, women entered the job market in large numbers. With this event, a change in traditional dress for women was observed. For the first time in history, women began wearing pants as frequently as skirted garments. In what can be seen as a statement of equality, many women wore pants that were similar to, or in some cases identical to, those worn by men.

Mass acceptance of blue jeans and other denim items came in the mid-1970's. The fabric had moved beyond the counterculture and youth. *Advertising Age* cited denim as the hottest fabric in the world in 1974. During a five-year period from 1969 to 1974, a pair of denim jeans increased in price from $7 to $15 in the United States. In the Soviet Union, a pair of used American jeans commanded a black market price of $75. In 1974, the six leading producers of denim fell one hundred million yards short of meeting the international demand for the fabric. The designers who elected to use denim in their lines were astute and reaped financial rewards for their fashion acumen.

Impact of Event

The versatility of denim was exploited in the market. With each finish, color, or design change, the demand for denim increased. Fashion designers with logos permanently affixed to the outside of the denim products could not meet demand, especially in the jeans market. By the mid-1970's, designer jeans had captured 10 percent of jeans sales, and at their peak in the 1980's, they had 17 percent of sales. The four top-volume brand-name manufacturers were Levi Strauss, Lee, Wrangler, and Brittania. With sueded, sanded, striped, and colored fabric used for hot pants, pantsuits, and fully lined suits as well as jeans, versatile denim was a product with a long fashion cycle.

Geographic market expansion marked the blue denim explosion. Textile manufacturers cast their eyes toward Europe, where ownership of jeans was not as widespread. Burlington opened a denim plant in Ireland to meet European needs. Cone Mills, a longtime exporter of denim, jumped significantly in exports from about 10 percent of its denim production in the early 1960's to 30 percent in the late 1970's. Denim fabric and products were exported to Japan, Australia, and South America. American apparel manufacturers were more successful at competing with foreign manufacturers in jeanswear than in other apparel items. The volume of jeans produced made it cost effective to automate jeans manufacturing; other fashion items did not have volume or product longevity to warrant automation.

The advantages of United States jeans manufacturers in the world market resulted in part from location in the largest single-country market and ready access to an efficient shipping industry that enabled them to respond to fashion changes and to distribute quickly. Blue jeans are perceived by the world as a garment that originated in America; manufacture in the United States adds status to a product.

The denim and advertising industries benefited each other. The top fifteen jeans manufacturers of 1980 spent $28.7 million on television advertising during the first half of the year. Levi Strauss's 1980 worldwide advertising budget was $85 million. Some analysts believe that the billion dollar annual market for designer jeans during the late 1970's and the 1980's was created and sustained by advertising. The success of designer jeans advertising convinced apparel manufacturers of the merits of advertising.

Calvin Klein set the pace and theme in designer jeans advertisements beginning with his 1980's ads, in which actress Brooke Shields proclaimed "You know what comes between me and my Calvins? Nothing," and "If my jeans could talk, I'd be ruined." A forty-eight-page ad titled "Sex, Bikes, and Jeans" was packaged with the October, 1991, *Vanity Fair*. Klein adopted risque themes from European advertisements but pioneered the "outsert" separate advertising package sold with a magazine. Others using "sexploitation" ads to market jeans included Georges Marciano of Guess? Gloria Vanderbilt, and Jordache. Efforts to halt the ads only seemed to increase sales.

The textile wet processing industry has benefited from and been burdened by the strong denim market. This industry has responded quickly to demands for fashion change by developing new colors and finishes. Everything from stones to chemicals to gunshots blasts have been used to give jeans new looks to meet consumer demand. The burdens placed on the wet processing industry primarily have been environmental ones. By cleaning wastewater in indigo dyeing operations, recycling chemicals in acid wash plants, and discovering why some prefaded jeans turned yellow, the wet processing segment of the textile industry led in finding solutions to problems. One promising answer to some of the environmental problems of stone-washing facilities was the use of cellulase, an enzyme that eats away the surface of denim, resulting in a soft feel and distressed look much like that of stone-washed denim. Stones often clog filters in machinery and sewer lines, whereas the enzyme is biologically friendly and safe to use. The cellulase enzyme market was expected to grow at the rate of 10 percent per year throughout the 1990's because of this new use.

A cottage industry that began in the 1960's with the purpose of individualizing denim garments with embroidery, sequins, and other surface decoration led to new ways to market some goods and services. This primarily women's industry expanded product lines to include knitted garments and an assortment of folk art items. The ingenuity shown in marketing the products evolved into annual craft fairs and flea markets.

The acceptance of casual dress, known as sportswear in the apparel industry, is one of the longest lasting effects of the denim craze. Casualness toward dress brought fabrics formerly used in work clothes to the mainstream of fashion. In addition to denim, there is chambray, a medium-weight, plain-weave fabric frequently used in dress shirts, blouses, and better dresses. Not only did changes occur in the uses of some fabrics, but in addition new styles of garments became a part of the American wardrobe. For example, shorts became accepted as standard casual dress for both men and women. This acceptance is extraordinary, considering that shorts had never before been appropriate for women's outer dress. Demand for more casual dress made sportswear one of the largest segments of the apparel market.

The major manufacturers of jeans recognized and promoted casual dress. Levi Strauss, the largest jeans manufacturer, early in the 1970's acquired Korocorp Industries. This acquisition brought to Levi's the successful Koret of California line of sportswear. The Dockers line, targeted to baby-boomers in the 1980's, also expanded the Levi's line of casual wear. Major manufacturers added fleece garment lines as well as coordinates.

The acceptance of denim almost defies explanation, but its impact and importance are without question. Denim is so much a part of the culture that Brighton Museum and Art Gallery featured it in an exposition in 1990. Warner Brothers produced a feature-length film titled *So Fine* (1981), a comedy chronicling the marketing success of jeans with see-through plastic rear pockets. The "country" look, including blue jeans, and the art form of country music became closely tied. U.S. presidents Jimmy Carter and Bill Clinton used blue jeans to identify with the American people; it is no coincidence that they both chose to be known by informal names. The economic importance of denim can be measured in part by the size of the jeans market, valued at approximately $4 billion dollars annually in the early 1990's. U. S. consumers spent about 10 percent of their clothing budget on jeans. Denim sales were strong at all price levels and in each segment of the market. Denim as fashion had become big business.

Bibliography

Gurel, Lois M., and Marianne S. Beeson. *Dimensions of Dress and Adornment*. Dubuque, Iowa: Kendall/Hunt, 1975. A book of readings offering insights into reasons for the adoption of denim.

Hamburger, Estelle. *Fashion Business: It's All Yours*. San Francisco: Canfield Press, 1976. Contains an essay about the "denimania" movement. The author presents an overview in a lighthearted manner.

Hollen, Norma, Sara Kadolph, Anna Langford, and Jane Saddler. *Textiles*. 6th ed. New York: Macmillan, 1988. Presents information about the fabrication of denim. Easy to read.

Lewis, Ethel. *The Romance of Textiles*. New York: Macmillan, 1953. A history of many fabrics, including denim, and information about well-known textiles.

Rubin, Leonard G. *The World of Fashion*. San Francisco: Canfield Press, 1976. Presents American fashion trends and ideas in an introductory manner. Uses plain language to tell how the fashion industry operates.

Sue Bailey

Cross-References

Walter Dill Scott Publishes *The Theory of Advertising* (1903), p. 80; Du Pont Announces the Discovery of Nylon 66 (1938), p. 798; Health Consciousness Creates Huge New Markets (1970's), p. 1416; The U.S. Advertising Industry Organizes Self-Regulation (1971), p. 1501.

DRIVE-THROUGH SERVICES PROLIFERATE

Category of event: Marketing
Time: The 1970's
Locale: The United States

The drive-through concept of quick service began with drive-in restaurants and spread to banks, newsstands, and various types of retail stores

Principal personages:
RAY KROC (1902-1984), the entrepreneur who brought McDonald's restaurants to prominence
RICHARD McDONALD (1909?-　　), one of the brothers, along with Maurice, who founded the McDonald's restaurants
MAURICE McDONALD (1902-1971), one of the brothers who founded the McDonald's restaurants
HARLAND SANDERS (1890-1980), the founder of Kentucky Fried Chicken

Summary of Event

Prior to the drive-through phenomenon of the 1970's, there was a gradual build-up of factors that created the phenomenon. After World War II, gasoline rationing disappeared, allowing increased use of automobiles. People began to move to the suburbs, but continued to work in the city. Highway construction gradually increased to accommodate the commuter population from the suburbs, and freeways were built. Because of longer commutes, people had to start earlier to get to work on time and spent larger parts of the day in their cars. Enterprising people with an eye for business saw a niche for drive-in service. The first drive-ins, at restaurants, accommodated customers either by having carhops come to cars to fill orders or had customers place orders at a window, without going inside. Customers would eat in their cars or take food with them.

Ray Kroc, a salesman for Mult-A-Mixer machines, which made milkshakes, discovered a small self-service restaurant that was using eight of his Mult-A-Mixers all at once, every day. He drove out to San Bernardino, California, to see the McDonald brothers, Richard and Maurice, at work in their restaurant and studied the operation for a few days. He saw the details that made their little restaurant so successful: It was clean, was well organized, and offered food at reasonable prices. Customers kept coming back. The restaurant had eliminated carhops, instead having customers step up to a counter to place orders. Kroc later instituted drive-through service. In 1954, Kroc signed an agreement with the McDonald brothers to sell franchises of McDonald's restaurants and at the same time install his Mult-A-Mixers in each new McDonald's. Twenty-two years later, in 1976, McDonald's sales hit the $1 billion mark. Compared to International Business Machines, which took forty-six years to achieve the $1 billion mark, and Xerox, which took sixty-three years, that growth was phenomenal. Other restaurant chains began to franchise, and the drive-through idea developed with these fast food franchises. Although McDonald's restaurants were not the first to offer drive-in or drive-through service, their success prompted imitation. It was much more convenient to stay in the car and order through a loudspeaker, then drive up to a window, pay for and receive the order, and drive off.

Drive-through services proliferated beyond fast food franchises. Press Box News of Lancaster, Pennsylvania, set up drive-through newsstands in such high-traffic locations as shopping center parking lots and highway intersections in New Jersey and Pennsylvania. Drivers could pull up to the window, pay for a newspaper or magazine, and drive off. The newsstands also offered coffee, cigarettes, film, and soft drinks. Other companies offered film processing through drive-up service. Attendants in tiny booths accepted rolls of film, sent them to processors, and gave them back to customers who returned several days later.

Banks became twenty-four hour institutions with the introduction of the automatic teller machine (ATM). This convenience meant that people did not have to carry so much cash, since cash would be available even when the bank was closed. Drivers could pull up to an ATM near the curb, step out of the car briefly, and perform a transaction quickly. Even in the daytime banking hours, drive-through banking made transactions much more convenient. People could do their banking from their cars simply by depositing or withdrawing money through tubes monitored by tellers inside the bank.

The drive-through service concept caught on in other product and service lines. Drive-through wedding services became available in Nevada.

In the 1990's, two California hospitals began providing drive-through flu shots for people too busy during flu season. Pharmacy 1 Express is a drive-through franchise based in Indianapolis, Indiana. It fills prescriptions while customers wait in their cars. The first outlet opened in 1989, operating from the premise that people wanted prescriptions to be filled quickly and might feel too ill to leave their cars. The company soon made plans to expand into Florida and Kentucky. A limited product list of pharmaceuticals and over-the-counter drugs kept the overhead low and helped promote the image of a specialized professional pharmacy.

Successful drive-through operations shared some characteristics. Locations had to be conveniently accessible by car. They offered a limited inventory or even a single product or service, reducing the space required and catering to people with a known single shopping need that they wanted to satisfy quickly.

The McDonald brothers had had an earlier operation with twenty-five menu items, a fry cook who produced greasy food, carhops, silverware that could be stolen and breakable dishes. They reduced their menu choices to nine, got rid of the carhops, and made cleanliness a priority. The plan worked, and that was when Ray Kroc came along. The McDonald's transformation exemplified how American business could change to accommodate drive-through service.

Impact of Event

The American idea of drive-throughs caught on in Canada and overseas between

1970 and 1979. In that time frame, McDonald's alone established outlets in Europe, Hong Kong, Japan, Singapore, Costa Rica, the Virgin Islands, and Panama. As of 1991, McDonald's had franchises in more than fifty countries. As does any successful franchise, McDonald's met the particular needs of each country. At the same time, McDonald's introduced new foods in many countries; today, french fries are common in Japan. As drive-through services spread, new ideas continued to crop up for services that would appeal to commuters and anyone else who is in a hurry. Drive-through cleaning establishments made it easy to drop cleaning off on the way to work. Drive-through photo booths operate in the same way.

Certain locations are favorable for drive-through services because of the volume of commuter traffic. Many of these locations sprouted small communities of businesses, each offering drive-through or quick service.

Environmental concerns entered the picture. A California Restaurant Association study on possible pollution by cars waiting in restaurant drive-through lanes resulted in proof that cars parked and later restarted cause more pollution than those in idle. The South Coast Air Quality Management District had proposed a ban on drive-throughs but withdrew it in August, 1990. The California Restaurant Association and nine fast food chains spent $125,000 on their study because they believed that the ban might again be proposed.

Good news for investors in the Sonic Corporation, a later arrival in the drive-through arena, came in the form of a surge in net income, with a 232 percent increase, for fiscal year 1990. The company exceeded $3 million in revenue, and its share price jumped from 19 cents to 49 cents. The growth in company earnings was attributed to better management and employee-incentive programs.

Drive-through services began to face heavy competition, especially in the fast food category. The good idea of drive-through had caught on, and businesses now had to implement it better to survive. The result of competition has been an increase in purchases of equipment as well as more efficient planning of traffic surrounding the businesses.

The American life-style has speeded up since the early drive-throughs of the 1950's attempted to meet the accelerated pace of commuters. The drive-ins and drive-throughs of the 1950's inspired the tremendous increase of drive-throughs in the 1970's. Highway construction, continued upgrading of existing drive-through service generated growth in the drive-through sector.

The increase in drive-through service can be traced forward to effects on suppliers and their products. When many women began working outside the home in the 1960's, there was an increased demand for quick-service food. The hamburger became king. Ground beef consumption in the United States increased by 50 percent from 1965 to 1975, according to the Institute of Policy Planning at Pennsylvania State University. Certainly much of the meat was consumed at home, but fast food restaurants accounted for much of it.

The desire for convenience grew. Trends in the food industry provide good examples. Major sources for prepared food are fast food restaurants, table service restaurants, and supermarkets. In 1989, fast food restaurants had a 41 percent share of the prepared food market, table service restaurants had 33 percent, and supermarkets had 12 percent. By 1991, fast food restaurants claimed a 51 percent share of the prepared food market, table service restaurants had 23 percent, and supermarkets had 14 percent. Fast food appeared to be taking business from traditional restaurants.

Drive-through service tended to be accompanied by franchising or by branching into many locations. Establishments tended to be small, with limited services and products, and therefore were easy and inexpensive to duplicate. Chains of identical outlets thus spread across the United States and, in some cases, around the world. No mater what community a hungry customer enters, for example, he or she can almost count on finding familiar food. That fact has added to the success of drive-through restaurants and other drive-through establishments. Customers like to make some choices quickly, and familiar products aid in that process.

Bibliography

Alpert, Mark. *"Extra! Extra!" Fortune* 121 (January 1, 1990): 14. Describes how a high-traffic location and commuters in a hurry led to success for Press Box News, a chain of newsstands offering newspapers and magazines as well as coffee, film, and other products.

Kroc, Ray, with Robert Anderson. *Grinding It Out: The Making of McDonald's* Chicago. Henry Regnery, 1977. Begins with Kroc's visit to the McDonald brothers in 1954, when he discovered their efficient operation, and traces the development of the McDonald's chain.

Love, John F. *McDonald's: Behind the Arches*. New York: Bantam Books, 1986. Includes much information on the origins of McDonald's. Relatively unbiased but written in cooperation with the company.

"No Waiting." *U.S. News & World Report* 109 (November 26, 1990): 20. Describes innovations in quick delivery of products and services, including the drive-through flu shots offered by two California hospitals.

Whittemore, Meg. "Advice for the Entrepreneur Who Sees Franchising as the Best Route to 'Being My Own Boss.'" *Nation's Business* 78 (February, 1990): 70. Describes features that make franchises successful, using several enterprises as examples, including Pharmacy 1 Express. Details what they have in common, including good locations, simplicity of products and services, and efficiency.

Corinne Elliott

Cross-References

Clarence Saunders Introduces the Self-Service Grocery (1916), p. 302; Invention of the Slug Rejector Spreads Use of Vending Machines (1930's), p. 579; Kroc Agrees to Franchise McDonald's (1954), p. 1025; The Environmental Protection Agency Is Created (1970), p. 1460; A Home Shopping Service Is Offered on Cable Television (1985), p. 1909.

THE FEDERAL TRADE COMMISSION ENDORSES COMPARATIVE ADVERTISING

Category of event: Advertising
Time: The 1970's
Locale: The United States

By encouraging marketers to name competitors in comparative advertisements, Federal Trade Commission officials hoped to provide consumers with product-related information

Principal personages:
ROBERT PITOFSKY (1929-   ), the director of the FTC Bureau of Consumer Protection, 1970-1973
ANDREW KERSHAW (1921-1978), the chairman of the Ogilvy & Mather advertising agency
STANLEY TANNENBAUM (1928-   ), the chairman of the Kenyon & Eckhardt advertising agency
WILLIAM WILKIE (1944-   ), a leader in comparative advertising effectiveness research
PAUL FARRIS (1946-   ), a leader in comparative advertising effectiveness research

Summary of Event

During the 1970's, several important Federal Trade Commission (FTC) officials suggested that marketers should directly name their competitors in media advertising instead of referring to them as "Brand X." Although the series of letters and speeches delivered by FTC personnel in the early 1970's did not convey the regulatory agency's official position, endorsing comparative advertising was consistent with the FTC goal of enhancing the consumer decision-making process through more complete information. The logic supporting such a stance by members of the FTC essentially held that comparative advertising allowed consumers to weigh the benefits of identified products. This stance received widespread support from consumer advocates, but many advertising executives worried that the negative aspects of the technique would damage the credibility of all advertising.

Salespersons have incorporated product comparisons in their presentations for years. Prior to the 1970's, however, the use of comparative advertising by marketers was relatively rare, for a number of reasons. Governmental regulatory agencies, advertising industry associations, and the media—particularly network television—strongly discouraged its use. In addition, many advertisers thought that naming a competing brand would provide it with "free" publicity or that consumers would perceive the named brand as a victim of sorts and purchase it instead of the sponsor out of sympathy. To circumvent this reluctance to use comparative advertising, marketers who valued the format were forced to rely on "Brand X" comparisons or "beep" sounds to replace brand names in spoken ads.

Comparative advertising is by no means a recent phenomenon. The famous British writer and poet Joseph Addison published an article in the September 14, 1710, *Tatler* that claimed that half of the advertisements at that time were comparative in nature. In the United States, Plymouth advertisements of the early 1930's asked consumers to "Look at All Three" before buying an automobile. Many such advertisements existed prior to the 1970's.

One of the most memorable indirect comparison campaigns (in which the competitor was not actually named but instead was implied) was run in the car rental industry during the 1960's by "Number 2" Avis against "Number 1" Hertz. Some innovative market entrants, such as *Penthouse* magazine, also managed to use implied comparisons during this period. *Penthouse* left no doubt who was being challenged, using the headline "We're going rabbit hunting" and a picture of a rabbit seen through a rifle sight in a full-page newspaper advertisement placed in *The New York Times*.

Perhaps encouraged by some of the preceding examples, Robert Pitofsky, the FTC's director of consumer protection, issued a series of letters in 1971 in support of the proposition that the nebulous "Brand X" comparisons required by the American Broadcasting Company (ABC) and Columbia Broadcasting System (CBS) television networks actually helped advertisers mislead and deceive consumers. For example, Shell Oil Company claimed that Shell with "Platformate" outperformed "Brand X" without platformate in terms of gas mileage. The problem was that "Brand X" turned out to be Shell without platformate, and most other gasoline brands included a similar additive. Advertisers were able to make exaggerated claims about their products, claims they could substantiate if challenged by claiming that "Brand X" was some unknown product that was obviously inferior.

Such loopholes, combined with mounting pressure by consumer advocates, prompted Pitofsky to ask ABC and CBS to follow the lead of the National Broadcasting Company (NBC) and allow sponsors to directly name competing brands in product-related comparisons. Both networks agreed to allow the direct naming of competitors in commercials for a one-year trial period, which was eventually extended. All three networks had agreed that direct comparisons were acceptable by the end of 1973. NBC published its comparative advertising guidelines early in 1974.

The American Association of Advertising Agencies' (AAAA) *Policy Statement and Guidelines for Comparative Advertising* was released in April, 1974, and appeared to be based on NBC's guidelines. The AAAA consistently had discouraged use of direct comparison statements in advertising over the years but bowed to pressures of the time and recognized the format by establishing a set of rules.

Joan Bernstein, deputy director of the FTC's Bureau of Consumer Protection, elaborated at an AAAA meeting in November, 1973, on the commission's reasoning behind backing overt comparisons between competing brands in advertisements. According to Bernstein, advertisers and their agencies were more skilled in delivering information to target audiences than was the government. Allowing marketers to use direct comparisons in persuasive messages would result in consumers obtaining information not previously available to them. In addition, advertising that directly named competing brands was more likely to result in advertisers policing one another. Finally, although Bernstein is not on record as mentioning it at this particular meeting, FTC officials were known to believe that direct comparisons in advertisements would result in lower prices as well as quality improvements.

Various FTC officials continued to encourage the use of comparative advertising throughout the decade. In November of 1977, for example, Tracy Weston, a deputy director of the FTC's Bureau of Consumer Protection, staunchly defended the strategy during a speech at the annual meeting of the National Advertising Review Board (NARB). With William Tankersley (the president of the Council of Better Business Bureaus who had blasted comparative advertising for eroding advertising's credibility one month before) seated before him, Weston said that the strategy was no more of a problem than was traditional advertising. Weston said that comparative advertisements were providing consumers with information more effectively than did their noncomparative counterparts, were heightening competition, and were prompting consumers to ask marketers tough questions about their brands. Comparative claims tended to warn consumers that they should be careful about accepting the results of product tests because the tests may have been manipulated, according to Weston. He concluded that the ads probably resulted in less FTC action because shoppers had a more balanced understanding of the market.

The FTC formally endorsed comparative advertising in 1979 and stated that even advertisements that disparaged competitors were legal as long as the comparisons were not false or deceptive. In addition, the commission established a standard for substantiating comparative claims that was no more strict than standards used to validate noncomparative claims. The definition for comparative advertising formally set forth stated that the strategy should compare competing brands on the basis of features that can be measured objectively and that brands involved in the advertisement must be distinctly identified by verbal or visual means or by both.

Impact of Event

The major impact of the FTC's backing of comparative advertising during the 1970's was the increased frequency of its use. Firms across a widening array of industries employed brand comparisons as a major marketing tactic. For some mature product categories, such as automobiles and soft drinks, comparative advertising has become a mainstay. The increasing use of the comparison format remained controversial, however, and resulted in litigation and research to analyze its effectiveness.

Opposition to comparative advertising has come from a variety of sources in the advertising industry. The print media have had little to say concerning the topic, but two out of the three major television networks were initially against its use. Industry associations, regulatory entities, advertisers, and their agencies have all expressed concern about using the format at one time or another. Doubts concerning comparative advertising lingered, and it is unlikely that disdain for the tactic will ever completely disappear.

One advertising agency, Ogilvy & Mather, was particularly outspoken against the use of comparative advertisements during the 1970's. Andrew Kershaw, the agency's chairman, became the most vocal opponent of comparative advertising, warning managers in 1976 that its use would intensify the distrust of corporations by consumers. Kershaw also strongly believed that the use of comparative advertisements would erode the effectiveness of advertising by damaging sponsors' credibility. Although the agency had amassed data to support its position against comparative advertising, Executive Vice President Graham Phillips cautiously admitted at a 1980 AAAA conference that the strategy could work when employed under certain conditions.

Other industry executives took exception to Ogilvy & Mather's attack on comparative advertising. In a widely publicized debate before the annual meeting of the AAAA in 1976, Stanley Tannenbaum, then chairman of the Kenyon & Eckhardt advertising agency, took a stance in favor of comparative advertising, against Andrew Kershaw. Tannenbaum hailed comparative advertising as the industry's own brand of consumerism when executed properly, because it stimulated consumers to compare before making a purchase decision. It also served as an incentive for marketers to produce better products.

Analysts have found general agreement across the advertising industry that comparative advertising results in significantly more legal problems than does noncomparative advertising. Comparative advertising campaigns that are challenged can be resolved through a number of channels, including the National Advertising Division of the Council of Better Business Bureaus (NAD), the National Advertising Review Board (NARB) on appeal from the NAD, the television network officials, the Federal Trade Commission, and federal court, under section 43(a) of the Lanham Trademark Act. The likelihood of litigation arising from comparative advertising claims increased when President Ronald Reagan signed into law the Trademark Law Revision Act of 1988, which closed a loophole in the Lanham Trademark Act of 1946. The original Lanham Act prohibited only false claims about a marketer's own brands, whereas the Trademark Revision Act specifically prohibited false claims concerning competing brands as well.

An early example of problematic comparative advertising (from a legal standpoint) that has been widely cited was Schick's controversial Fleximatic electric razor campaign. Schick's print and television advertisements claimed that the Fleximatic shaved closer than Norelco, Remington, and Sunbeam brands. Lawsuits and countersuits were initiated, and complaints were filed with the NARB. Ronson, one competitor not named in Schick's campaign, quickly attacked Schick in national magazine advertisements, claiming that it was not named in the Schick campaign because the Ronson shaver was superior.

Based on issues relating to the shaving test's validity, the NAD—which is the NARB's investigative unit—challenged Schick's comparisons with the competitors named in the campaign. On appeal, the NARB disagreed with eleven of the thirteen

NAD findings concerning the test procedures but agreed that overall, Schick's comparative advertisements were false and deceptive because they implied more than the limited testing procedures could determine. The Schick campaign was halted.

In *U-Haul International v. Jartran, Inc.*, a false comparative advertising case filed under Section 43(a) of the Lanham Trademark Act, the Ninth Circuit Court of Appeals found Jartran's campaign to be deliberately false and deceptive and awarded more than $40 million in damages and legal fees to U-Haul. Jartran had claimed a price advantage compared to U-Haul but based the claims on a comparison of its own special introductory prices versus U-Haul's regular prices for the same service. In addition, Jartran deliberately distorted pictures showing its truck next to the U-Haul version to make the U-Haul truck appear smaller and less attractive.

The results of research studies focused on the effectiveness of comparison advertising are inconclusive. This is perhaps a fitting finale for any discussion of such a controversial topic. Even the scientific issues concerning its usefulness to those who pay for it do not agree. The only closing statement that can be made with any degree of certainty is that the practice of comparative advertising will continue because many marketers have achieved increased sales by using it, but they will do so at the risk of being counterattacked from a number of different directions.

Bibliography

Buchanan, Bruce, and Doron Goldman. "Us Versus Them: The Minefield of Comparative Ads." *Harvard Business Review* 67 (May/June, 1989): 38-50. A "how-to" discussion for marketers who want to avoid lawsuits charging false and deceptive claims. Good examples from legal case history.

Howard, Niles. "Battle Over Comparative Ads." *Dun's Review* 110 (November, 1977): 60-62. Discusses several legal conflicts between marketers using comparative advertising campaigns. Includes opinions of various industry officials.

Meyerowitz, Steven A. "Brand X Strikes Back! The Developing Law of Comparative Advertising." *Business Marketing* 70 (August, 1985): 81-86. Good discussion of the legal and regulatory aspects of comparative advertising. Includes cases.

Muehling, Darrel D., and Norman Kangun. "The Multi-Dimensionality of Comparative Advertising: Implications for the Federal Trade Commission." *Journal of Public Policy and Marketing* 4 (1985): 112-128. Thorough description of comparative advertising. Includes a complete description of the many varieties of comparative advertisements actually in use.

Muehling, Darrel D., Donald E. Stem, Jr., and Peter Raven. "Comparative Advertising: Views from Advertisers, Agencies, Media, and Policy Makers." *Journal of Advertising Research* 29 (October/November, 1989): 38-48. Explores perceptions of comparative advertising held by advertisers, agencies, the media and regulators.

Rogers, John C., and Terrell G. Williams. "Comparative Advertising Effectiveness: Practitioners' Perceptions Versus Academic Research Findings." *Journal of Advertising Research* 29 (October/November, 1989): 22-37. A balanced, thorough discussion of the effectiveness of comparative advertising.

Tannenbaum, Stanley I., and Andrew G. Kershaw. "For and Against Comparative Advertising." *Advertising Age* 47 (July 5, 1976): 25-26, 28. Interesting "pro-con" discussion of the controversial use of comparative advertising, delivered by two top advertising executives.

Ulanoff, Stanley M. *Comparison Advertising: An Historical Retrospective.* Cambridge, Mass.: Marketing Science Institute, 1975. Discusses historical aspects of comparative advertising. Provides a good background on the topic. Includes visual examples of comparative advertisements as well as information concerning regulation.

Wilkie, William L., and Paul W. Farris. "Comparison Advertising: Problems and Potential." *Journal of Marketing* 39 (October, 1975): 7-15. Good background discussion of comparative advertising. The primary reference point for almost all comparative advertising research since.

William T. Neese

Cross-References

Walter Dill Scott Publishes *The Theory of Advertising* (1903), p. 80; Advertisers Adopt a Truth in Advertising Code (1913), p. 229; The Federal Trade Commission Is Organized (1914), p. 269; The Wheeler-Lea Act Broadens FTC Control over Advertising (1938), p. 775; The U.S. Advertising Industry Organizes Self-Regulation (1971), p. 1501.

HEALTH CONSCIOUSNESS CREATES
HUGE NEW MARKETS

Category of event: Marketing
Time: The 1970's
Locale: The United States

Growing awareness of the importance of a healthy diet and exercise opened new markets among American consumers

Principal personages:
ADELLE DAVIS (1904-1974), a biochemist and author of four books on nutrition
BENJAMIN GAYELORD HAUSER (1895-1984), a nutritionist and chiropractor
CARLTON FREDERICKS (1910-1987), a psychiatrist and biochemist
LINUS PAULING (1901-1994), a biochemist and proponent of Vitamin C as a preventive medicine
RACHEL CARSON (1907-1964), a marine biologist
RALPH NADER (1934-   ), a consumer advocate who wrote about the dangers of chemicals in food

Summary of Event

In the 1970's, several health issues generated concern about nutrition and exercise. The pesticide DDT and cyclamates, an artificial sweetener, were banned in the United States in 1969. Other pesticides and food additives soon came under scrutiny. Doctors and researchers made news by linking cholesterol and heart attacks; findings showed that exercise could reduce cholesterol while strengthening the heart. People began to take up jogging; joggers then began buying clothing and shoes for their exercise. Manufacturers of athletic shoes touted specialized shoes for that form of exercise.

The World Food Congress, sponsored by the United Nations Food and Agriculture Organization (FAO) at the Hague in June, 1970, brought together nations concerned with a host of problems including agricultural productivity and the purity of the environment. Addeke H. Boerma, director-general of the FAO, stated that it would be futile to discuss hunger and malnutrition in isolation from other related problems such as overpopulation. He believed that radical steps had to be taken to cure the entire problem as a whole; if such steps were not taken, the problems could result in outbreaks of violence. At this same conference, delegates expressed concern regarding new plant varieties that were the backbone of the green revolution and the large amounts of fertilizer, pesticides, herbicides, and irrigation required to grow these new plants. Chemical use would prove to be problematic in a monsoon country such as India, where such herbicides, fertilizers, and pesticides would be washed into the River Ganges and the Bay of Bengal, causing pollution of unpredictable magnitude. There was also fear for the oceans of the world, not only from pollutants that were meant to increase yields of food plants but also from future oil spills that could reduce another valuable food source, marine life.

Meanwhile, these same concerns were being addressed by scientists in the United States and elsewhere. Numerous books were published on the subject of pesticides and herbicides as well as on the effect of food additives on the human body. Health-conscious biochemists such as Adelle Davis and Benjamin Gayelord Hauser wrote books about the benefits of pure food. James Trager stated in an article that three groups of people buy what had become known as health foods: people who have a desire for good food, people concerned about environmental decay brought on by persistent use of pesticides and herbicides, and people who believe that what they eat affects their health and well-being. Trager stated that in 1971 there were fifteen hundred to two thousand health food stores in the United States, adding a billion dollars a year to the economy. Davis stated that health food stores appealed to both the "establishment" and the "young, hip" generation. With a master's degree in biochemistry from the University of Southern California, she had sold nearly two million copies of her books on the subject of pure food by 1970.

With the rise in popularity of health food stores and growing awareness of the environment, farmers and ranchers took up organic farming, producing food without artificial fertilizers, pesticides, or herbicides. California growers in particular reflected the increase in interest in organic food. That state appeared to lead the U.S. movement toward health consciousness. Farmers there were among the first in the country to adopt organic methods on a large scale, and consumers swarmed to health food stores and embraced healthy food products. Furthermore, the California climate was conducive to year-round outdoor exercise.

In 1970, organic food was found mostly in health food stores, small country stores, and through co-ops, groups of people that got together to order large amounts to take advantage of quantity discounts. The leaders of this movement were found mostly on the two coasts and in the Midwest in 1970. As of 1992, the amount of revenue generated by the sale of organic foods in the marketplace had grown to an estimated $1.4 billion dollars.

In 1976, psychiatrist and biochemist Carlton Fredericks published a book, *Psycho-Nutrition*, in which he showed how diets planned on an individual basis could heal people with a wide variety of ailments ranging from simple allergies to chemical imbalances and schizophrenia. His appearances on television talk shows provided publicity for that book and his later publications. The buying public appeared to be willing to accept broad claims of the benefits of a proper diet.

While the World Food Congress addressed problems raised by the new plant strains that began the green revolution, researchers continued to test new plant strains. They also rediscovered plant varieties that had fallen out of use. Examples include amaranth, and ancient Aztec grain with a buckwheat flavor; spelt, an ancient grain that first had its resurgence in Europe and then gained popularity in the United States; quinoa, a complete protein grain known as the Chilean mother grain, grown high in the Andes; and kamut, a grain brought to the United States from Egypt. Health food producers soon marketed these rediscovered grains in pasta form and in cereals.

Health consciousness affected markets in addition to that for food. People became increasingly aware of the importance of exercise. Markets for athletic shoes, equipment, and clothing grew tremendously. As exercise gained in social status, equipment became a status symbol. Sweatsuits came out in glamorous lines and were worn by people who rarely exercised but wanted to give the appearance that they did. General-purpose gym shoes were replaced by shoes designed for specific forms of exercise. Jogging shoes proved to be particularly popular, even for people who never went jogging. Exercise equipment that found new markets ranged from rowing machines and stationary bicycles to large, multiuse home gyms. Sales of bicycles boomed. Later, mountain bikes would become popular, in part as a result of the increasing desire to escape urban life and get in touch with nature, at least temporarily.

Athletic equipment and footwear took sophisticated turns in regard to comfort and utility. Wooden tennis rackets were replaced by ones made of metal and other materials, for example. Sophistication naturally came at a price, and innovators with new ideas reaped substantial profits.

Consumers in many cases needed to be educated about healthy practices. Cookbooks and exercise books proliferated, as did periodicals. *Vegetarian Times*, for example, promoted the benefits of doing without meat. Magazines also developed around the many newly popular participant sports.

Impact of Event

From health food stores to organic gardening and farming to the growth of interest in exercise, the entire health movement has proliferated since the 1970's. Many of the new products and trends introduced in that decade became entrenched parts of the marketplace.

Doctors recommend exercise to keep circulatory systems in good shape, and people discovered that they felt better as a result of exercise. The result was often an overall increase in fitness consciousness, with greater attention also paid to diet. Many people attracted to health consciousness in the 1970's remained steady consumers of health-related products. By 1990, many of those early converts had passed their health consciousness on to their children, a new generation of consumers.

Health consciousness extended into the field of health care itself. Consumers of medical care gradually became aware of alternatives to traditional Western medicine as it became more expensive and as the alternatives proved to be effective. *The New England Journal of Medicine* reported that by 1990, one-third of all Americans were using some form of alternative health treatment. These alternatives included relaxation techniques, spiritual healing, biofeedback, acupuncture, and herbal medicine. These alternative treatments accounted for $10.3 billion in expenditures in 1990, with insurance covering $2.4 billion of that total. Traditional physicians began to take notice of this trend and studied these alternatives. In 1992, the National Institutes of Health in Bethesda, Maryland, established an office for the study of unconventional medicine.

Surveys on the sales of sporting goods show steady increases in sales. From 1980 to 1991, for example, the market for sporting goods as a whole grew from $16.7 billion to $45.1 billion. Sales of athletic clothing grew from $3.1 billion to $11.9 billion over the same period of time. Footwear sales, including shoes for jogging and running, tennis, aerobics, basketball, golf, and other sports, grew from $1.7 billion to $6.8 billion. Equipment sales nearly doubled, from $6.5 billion to $12.5 billion. Sales of bicycles and related supplies more than doubled, from $1.2 billion to $2.5 billion.

Part of the increase in sales came from the increased sophistication of products. The large number of buyers made it feasible to develop new products, such as basketball shoes with air pumps. Buyers proved eager to try out each innovation, and prices of products skyrocketed. Sophisticated products became so popular that simpler products were crowded out of the market. Single-speed bicycles, for example, are almost impossible to find for adult riders.

Athletes became conscious of the link between exercise and diet, partly as a result of the many books and articles published on the subject. Endurance athletes load up on carbohydrates before they begin strenuous activity and consume drinks containing electrolytes while they exercise. Backpackers carry food, often in the form of dried fruits and nuts, while on the trails.

Organic foods increased in sales, but their market share remained small. In 1992, organic foods accounted for $1.4 billion in sales out of the approximately $200 billion for all farm products.

Health consciousness created huge new markets in the United States and elsewhere in the industrialized world. Other parts of the world, however, still struggled with basic problems of food distribution, overpopulation, and the difficulties created by herbicides, pesticides, and fertilizers. These were the very problems that had, in part, spurred the movement toward health consciousness.

Bibliography

Detje, F. W. "Reform, Revolution, and Food." *Science News* 98 (July 25, 1970): 86. Discusses concerns voiced by representatives attending the World Food Congress in 1970. These concerns included use of pesticides and herbicides and how Third World nations can avoid contamination when monsoon rains wash toxins into rivers.

Eisenberg, David M., et al. "Alternative Medicine in the United States: Prevalence, Costs, and Patterns of Use." *The New England Journal of Medicine*, January 28, 1993, 246. Gives statistics on use of alternative medicine. By 1990, one-third of all Americans were using some form of health treatment alternative such as relaxation techniques, spiritual healing, biofeedback, acupuncture, and herbal medicine. Americans spent $10.3 billion on these treatments; insurance covered $2.4 billion.

Goldman, M. C. "Sharp Rise in Organic Food Demand." *Organic Gardening and Farming* 17 (April, 1970): 66-70. Reports the rising interest in food produced without herbicides, pesticides, or fertilizers. Tells how farmers and ranchers successfully provided organic food.

Jacobson, Michael F. *The Complete Eater's Digest and Nutrition Scoreboard.* 1st ed., rev. and updated. Garden City, N.Y.: Anchor Press/Doubleday, 1985. A consumer's fact book of food additives and healthful eating. A good source for understanding what is listed on food labels and how it may affect the consumer.

Lansing, Elizabeth. "Image to Shed, More Food to Grow." *Life* 69 (December 11, 1970): 52. Discusses how the organic gardening movement is growing and why. Also tells how families and other groups are succeeding with this enterprise.

Trager, James. "Health Food: Why and Why Not." *Vogue* 157 (January 1, 1971): 122-123+. Casts a somewhat skeptical eye at much of the health food movement. Covers extremes in the health food movement.

Corinne Elliott

Cross-References

Congress Passes the Pure Food and Drug Act (1906), p. 128; Congress Sets Standards for Chemical Additives in Food (1958), p. 1097; New Rice and Wheat Strains Launch the Green Revolution (1960's), p. 1133; The Wholesome Poultry Products Act Is Passed (1968), p. 1369; The United States Bans Cyclamates from Consumer Markets (1969), p. 1390; The Banning of DDT Signals New Environmental Awareness (1969), p. 1395; Toxic Gas Leaks from a Union Carbide Plant in Bhopal, India (1984), p. 1893; The United States Bans Chilean Fruit After Cyanide Scare (1989), p. 1986; Bush Signs the Clean Air Act of 1990 (1990), p. 2034.

RETAILERS BEGIN USING HIGH TECHNOLOGY TO CONTROL SHRINKAGE

Categories of event: Retailing and business practices
Time: The 1970's
Locale: The United States

By using computers and other technical innovations, retailers better secured merchandise, identified types of shrinkage, and located departments with the greatest shrinkage

> *Principal personages:*
> RONALD ASSAF (1935-   ), the cofounder and president of Sensormatic Electronic Corporation
> CARTER W. CLARKE (1926-   ), the president of Security Tag Systems
> ARTHUR MINASY (1925-   ), the chair and chief executive officer of Knogo Corporation
> THOMAS A. NICOLETTE (1950-   ), the president of Knogo Corporation

Summary of Event

Sophisticated accounting and control methods merged with technology during the 1970's to alert retailers to the depth and breadth of inventory shrinkage. The major causes of shrinkage were identified as employee theft, customer theft, and employee errors. Shrinkage is the difference between the retail value of all merchandise purchased by a retail store minus sales, markdowns, and the retail value of the merchandise in stock.

In 1972, the Federal Bureau of Investigation conservatively estimated the annual value of retail shrinkage at $2.5 billion, more than twice the shrinkage in 1962. Retailers themselves estimated the value of shoplifting alone at $3.2 billion in 1972. In the early 1970's, shrinkage was believed to average about 1 percent of sales, but by the mid-1970's, shrinkage had leaped to nearly 2.5 percent. Many retailers experienced shrinkage as high as 3 and 4 percent of sales. One study conducted in the mid-1970's reported that shoplifting alone siphoned off 4 percent of total retail sales. Retailers recognized that this meant a significant loss of profits in a business that averaged profits of only 2 to 3 percent of sales.

The primary focus of retail security until the mid-1970's was on shoplifting, defined as a nonemployee entering a retail store without using force and stealing merchandise. The deterrents that had been used to stop shoplifting through the 1960's included wide-angled mirrors, employees trained to reduce the opportunities for theft, catwalk and other viewing areas that were disguised from the selling floor, store design and display of merchandise to discourage theft, and security guards. The introduction of electronic surveillance occurred in the 1950's with the advent of the closed-circuit television camera (CCTV); however, CCTV was in limited use to protect stock as late as the 1960's.

An act of shoplifting in the mid-1960's in a Kroger grocery store resulted in the idea for a more reliable device for preventing nonemployee theft. Manager Ronald Assaf returned to the store after unsuccessfully chasing a shoplifter for several blocks. His tinkering cousin, John Welsh, was in the store. Assaf made the statement that Welsh could make a million dollars if he would invent something to prevent shoplifting. Welsh proceeded to do just that. In 1968, the first electronic article surveillance (EAS) system was marketed by Sensormatic Electronic Corporation of Hollywood, Florida, a company founded by Ronald Assaf, John Welsh, and James Rogers. Sensormatic had difficulty marketing its product and even had to pay the first store to use the system. It was five years before the corporation realized a profit.

The first Sensormatic EAS system used inconspicuous tags placed on the inside of apparel items and sensing devices at exits that would detect a tag carried out. After a few embarrassing incidents, such as when a commanding officer's wife was caught shoplifting in a military PX, Sensormatic realized that store management wanted only to deter shoplifters, not to "catch" them. Retailers wanted to avoid embarrassing situations as well as the cost of prosecution. To achieve the retailers' goal of discouraging shoplifters, Sensormatic developed large and somewhat heavy white tags that were placed on garments where they could be seen clearly.

Other companies that began marketing electronic surveillance systems during the 1960's included Knogo Corporation of Westbury, New York; Checkmate Systems of Lionville, Pennsylvania; D-Tektamatic Corporation of Atlanta, Georgia; Stop-Lifter International of Dallas, Texas; and I.D. Engineering of Peabody, Massachusetts. Combined sales in the industry in 1972 were less than $5 million. The technology existed, but its marketing and distribution were minimal.

Retailers were also slow to adopt computers. Retailing experts identified fear, mistrust, cost, and misuse as reasons for the slow acceptance of computers. Consumers of the early 1970's opposed the use of computer-based scanning checkout systems in supermarkets. The Universal Product Code (UPC symbol) placed on food products enabled supermarkets to use computerized checkout systems but was especially disliked by national consumer organizations. As of mid-1975, only about twenty-five supermarkets in North America had fully computerized checkout systems. Some bold experiments did take place. Woodward and Lothrop in Washington, D.C., with the help of International Business Machines (IBM), installed a model computer system for a department store in 1966. Montgomery Ward opened a computer-operated store in Rockford, Illinois, in 1970. Ward claimed that half of the goods sold in the store would be merchandised by computer.

Retailers that did computerize gained a new and closer look at shrinkage. Theft by employees typically accounted for about 50 to 60 percent of shrinkage. Errors by employees accounted for about 10 percent, and theft by nonemployees accounted for the rest. Computerization minimized shrinkage resulting from accounting and bookkeeping errors. The extent and methods of internal theft, known as pilferage, were recognized for the first time.

Retailers of the 1970's continued to fight traditional shoplifting and pilferage while a new type or shrinkage, electronic theft, was evolving. As point of sale (POS) computers were linked with electronic credit systems, an environment was created that gave birth to electronic theft through its many methods of acquiring money illegally. Electronic theft often involved collusion of employees and nonemployees. Computers and other technical innovations gave retailers a new look at who was stealing and how. Old attitudes toward store theft held by retail managers, law enforcement officers, and judicial systems were being eroded. Retailers demanded new and creative ways to curtail rising shrinkage.

Impact of Event

An immediate reaction to the rise in retail shrinkage during the 1970's was the creation and implementation of awareness programs. In Philadelphia, Bernard Kant, then president of Gimbels, initiated a broad antishoplifting campaign known as STEM (Shoplifters Take Everybody's Money). He rallied the Philadelphia Retail Merchants Association to set up an advisory board of civic-minded people and businesses to fight the problem, which was likened to a spreading disease in the city. STEM worked to prevent retail theft by increasing public awareness and by alerting both police officers and judges to the retail problem. The advisory board sought to speed up the legal process and to win tougher sentences. STEM is believed to have cut Philadelphia's retail shrinkage by 20 percent. Civic groups similar to STEM were started in San Diego, California, and Tampa, Florida. Retailers in Corry, Pennsylvania, organized a different type of awareness program called Call Alert System. When a merchant was hit by a shoplifter, he or she called the police and the chamber of commerce. The chamber of commerce called two different merchants, and they each placed two calls. The process continued until all eighty participating retailers were alerted. The chain of calls took fifteen minutes. The awareness generated by the calls resulted in smaller losses from shoplifting. The National Retail Merchants Association (NRMA) and the International Newspaper Advertising Executives (INAE) joined forces in an antishoplifting effort designed to make the public aware that shoplifting was a crime. More than two hundred newspapers ran ads developed by the NRMA. Despite the awareness programs, it was announced at the first national Shoplifting Prevention Conference in 1980 that shoplifting cost retailers $16 billion a year. Americans were paying five cents of every shopping dollar to cover shoplifting thefts.

As theft continued to rise during the 1980's, retailers became more receptive to technical innovations, including improved EAS tag and label systems, point-of-sale (POS) surveillance cameras, and subliminal behavior modification packages. Companies specializing in equipment to prevent and detect theft were encouraged by increased profits to improve their systems and broaden their market. By 1990, there were about thirty companies manufacturing EAS systems, components, or specialized software.

Knogo, the first company to sell hard tags that must be removed by a cashier, announced in 1981 a line of adhesive-backed sensor strips that could be attached to items as varied as hammers and caviar. Supermarkets and hardware stores were

Knogo's new target market. Knogo placed KnoGlo (the first tag filled with ink and electronics) and WaferLITE (a small, lightweight tag for women's specialty stores) on the market. Knogo developed a system that emitted sounds and activated lights if someone removed a tag or label in the fitting room. During the 1980's, Checkpoint Systems and Avery's Soabar Products Group collaborated to improve imprinting capabilities in order to expand their lines of tags and labels. Security Tag Systems developed a label that could be used directly on merchandise with metal and foil content, such as cans and cigarette packs. In 1986, Sensormatic announced a new EAS system of labels called Ultra Max for use in discount stores, drugstores, and home improvement centers. Two other markets targeted in the late 1980's by various manufacturers of EAS labels were libraries and bookstores.

During the 1980's, Sensormatic also marketed a deterrent to internal theft known as POS/EM. POS/EM was the first cash register/video interface system that offered stores the opportunity for simultaneous, real-time cash register transaction evaluation. Others marketing closed circuit video systems during the 1980's included Viacom Industry, Jensen Video Sonics, and Security Tag Systems.

Eastbourne, a company founded in 1987, marketed the Eastbourne Protection System, an exception report software package. This system automatically produced standard reports on such information as employees ringing no-receipt returns and returns rung by credit card. Marshall Field's, Saks, and Bergdorf Goodman had installed this system by 1990.

Sound Threshold Systems and Viaticus Group, two companies founded during the 1980's, designed subliminal behavior modification packages for retailers. Both companies claimed to use only socially accepted messages that reminded people to be honest. Sound Threshold Systems claimed to reduce shrinkage in stores by up to 1 percent. David Riccio, the president of Viaticus, stated that research showed shoplifting reductions between 20 and 40 percent in some settings using this approach. Although retailers were not quick to advertise their use of subliminal behavior modification messages, the *Stores* trade journal reported in 1990 that seven of the top ten specialty stores and four of the top ten department stores had the equipment. They also reported that six hundred installations had occurred in drugstores, consumer electronics outlets, and home supply centers. Supermarkets also purchased the packages.

Even with a variety of technical systems in place to control shrinkage, retailers and others recognized that more was required to prevent theft. Programs, seminars, courses, articles, and entire publications emphasizing protection of retail assets from shrinkage proliferated. Best Products of Richmond, Virginia, gave each new employee a pamphlet detailing security rules and outlining the employee's role in reducing shrinkage. Best Products and many other retailers offered cash rewards for tips resulting in apprehension of a dishonest employee or shoplifter. Bank of America published a twenty-page report, "Crime Prevention for Small Business," listing numerous suggestions for prevention of shrinkage. College-level retailing textbooks published in the 1990's almost universally dedicated a chapter or more to shrinkage, with greater emphasis than in the past placed on the detection and prevention of employee theft. The National Retail Federation (formerly the National Retail Merchants Association and the American Retail Federation), through seminars, publications, and other means, has provided retailers with excellent information concerning such issues as emerging technology, legal advice, and social problems including the use of illegal narcotics and its impact on retail shrinkage.

Because retailers accepted and implemented the technology available during the 1980's to assist in the prevention and detection of theft, companies developing these products continued to upgrade and expand their lines. Security systems were used not only in retail sales but also by libraries, museums, and other businesses that needed to secure products and information. In retail, technology continued to expand. As of the early 1990's, advances were expected in customer service areas, interactive video terminals, holographic and laser video disk systems that would allow customers to simulate the use of products, automated mannequins, automated (robotic) sales assistants, mobile point-of-sale systems, and artificial intelligence in the back office.

Bibliography

Beisel, John. *Contemporary Retailing*. New York: Macmillan, 1987. Provides security information as related to store layout and merchandise placement. Makes numerous suggestions on how to prevent shoplifting and employee theft.

Bolen, William. *Contemporary Retailing*. 3d ed. Englewood Cliffs, N.J.: Prentice-Hall, 1988. Methods of theft are covered in depth. Presents ten areas of concern that must be addressed by a store's retail security program.

Hodgetts, Richard. *Effective Supervision: A Practical Approach*. New York: McGraw-Hill, 1987. Topics covered include selection of employees; motivating, appraising, and rewarding employees; and dealing with discipline. Presents many suggestions for selecting employees.

Mason, J. Barry, et al. *Retailing*. 3d ed. Boston: Irwin, 1988. Good coverage of EAS systems. Discusses use of civil recovery procedures.

Morgenstein, Melvin, and Harriet Strongin. *Modern Retailing: Management Principles and Practices*. 3d ed. New York: John Wiley & Sons, 1992. Outlines features of store security that minimize retail crime. Covers procedures for handling merchandise.

Sue Bailey

Cross-References

Invention of the Slug Rejector Spreads Use of Vending Machines (1930's), p. 579; Congress Passes the Consumer Credit Protection Act (1968), p. 1358; Drive-Through Services Proliferate (1970's), p. 1406; Congress Passes the Fair Credit Reporting Act (1970), p. 1454; Sony Introduces the Betamax (1975), p. 1573; Electronic Technology Creates the Possibility of Telecommuting (1980's), p. 1733.

THE U.S. GOVERNMENT REFORMS CHILD PRODUCT SAFETY LAWS

Category of event: Consumer affairs
Time: The 1970's
Locale: Washington, D.C.

Federal legislation prevented the marketing of potentially harmful children's products

Principal personages:

EDWARD M. SWARTZ (1934-), an attorney, and child toy safety advocate

RALPH NADER (1934-), an attorney and consumer advocate

TERRENCE SCANLON (1939-), the chair of the Consumer Product Safety Commission

JAMES FLORIO (1937-), the chairman of the House Reauthorization Subcommittee on Commerce, Consumer Protection, and Competitiveness

PEGGY CHARREN (1928-), the founder of Action for Children's Television

Summary of Event

During the 1970's, the federal government of the United States undertook a concerted effort to improve the safety of toys and other products used by children. This effort was presaged by passage of the Child Protection Act of 1966, which prohibited sale of any hazardous substance that might cause harm to children, if it failed to display a warning label on either the product or its package. The Food and Drug Administration (FDA) was responsible for enforcing this act, which amended the Hazardous Substances Labeling Act of 1960. Prior to this act, signed into law on November 3, 1966, toy manufacturers were not held accountable for product safety or for reducing the risk of injuries sustained to children using their products.

On November 6, 1969, the Child Protection and Toy Safety Act was passed, extending the requirements of manufacturers by prohibiting any toxic, corrosive, or flammable toy or article that could cause personal injury or illness to children. In addition, if a product could cause an electrical, fire, or mechanical hazard to children, a label was to be displayed on the product or its package warning of its potential danger. The law gave the secretary of health, education, and welfare the authority to ban what the FDA classified as a hazardous substance.

The FDA was also responsible for carrying out the 1953 Flammable Fabrics Act, passed to ban highly inflammable nightgowns and children's clothing that would burst into flame when exposed to open flames. Unfortunately, the standards were not stringent. For example, if a six-inch sample of a material was held at a 45 degree angle from a flame for one second and did not catch fire, it passed the test. If the material burned at a rate of five inches or less in three and one-half seconds, it passed the test.

On October 27, 1972, the Consumer Protect Safety Act established the Consumer Product Safety Commission (CPSC), which was empowered to develop safety standards for most consumer products other than food, drugs, and automobiles. The CPSC was charged with protecting the public against unreasonable risks of injury from consumer products, assisting consumers in evaluating the relative safety of competing product brands, reducing the conflicts between state and local regulations, and promoting research and investigation into the causes and prevention of product-related death, illness, and injury.

Prior to the establishment of the CPSC, the toy industry regulated itself. In 1968, the National Commission on Product Safety (NCPS) found in its final report to the United States Congress that self-regulation by trade associations such as the Toy Manufacturers of America (TMA) and organizations that give seals of approval, such as Good Housekeeping, were ineffective. The TMA did not force its members to comply with its standards, and organizations such as Good Housekeeping were more concerned that advertising claims were truthful than with testing and certifying products' safety to children.

One toy safety advocate who testified before the NCPS was Edward M. Swartz, an attorney who represented several clients in court to obtain compensation for injuries suffered by their children as a result of playing with hazardous toys. At the 1968 NCPS hearings, Swartz demonstrated how dangerous toys could be to their child users. Swartz became an advocate on toy safety issues and wrote several books, including *Toys That Don't Care* (1971) and *Toys That Kill* (1986).

Swartz's research uncovered several unsafe products that were marketed in the 1970's having not been found to be dangerous by the CPSC. One product was the Wham-O Manufacturing Company's boomerang. Another unsafe product, marketed by PBI Incorporated, was a projectile toy that was advertised to the wholesale trade as a safe, flexible plastic toy, even though it had sharp edges and was potentially blinding. F. A. O. Schwartz marketed a fiberglass bow and wooden arrow set. The wooden arrows had rubber tips, but they were removable. The toy was advertised as being harmless.

During the 1970's, the Ideal Toy Corporation made a "Kookie Kamera" that was marketed as nontoxic and not intended for internal consumption. The product caused several cases of nausea, which may have led to vomiting and even asphyxiation as a result of blockage of the trachea in small children. Another product, the Newman Company's "Loonie Straw," was designed to be reusable. The problem was that instructions called for the straw not to be washed in hot water. It was intended to be used to drink milk, making it probable that bacterial germs would be bred in the unsanitary straw.

From 1973 to 1977, the CPSC received more than one hundred death certificates related to the ingestion of small objects. Forty-five of these deaths were related to toys and nursery products. In 1976, it was estimated by a CPSC study that 46,500 children under the age of ten were treated in hospital emergency rooms for injuries related to small parts. Twenty-five of forty-five deaths involving children's products were of children less than three years old.

During 1978, the CPSC received more than 180 oral and written comments from businesses, trade associations, and consumer groups regarding the safety of consumer products. In response, on August 7, 1978, the Consumer Product Safety Act tightened up safety regulations and required every manufacturer, distributor, or retailer who obtained information that a product either was unsafe or did not comply with the CPSC regulations to immediately inform the CPSC.

Impact of Event

The effects of regulation on how toys were manufactured and marketed were mixed. In 1980, the CPSC banned the sale of toys with small parts intended for children under the age of three if the parts could accidentally be swallowed or become dangerously lodged in their throats. By 1989, however, the CPSC still had not clearly defined what constituted a small part and if small-part toys should be banned in general. Toymakers still claimed that accidents being researched were isolated incidents; the CPSC concurred in most cases.

On the other hand, many products were banned because of the CPSC's enforcement of the Child Protection Act and Child Protection and Toy Safety Act. In the 1970's, products called crackerballs were categorized as hazardous substances. Crackerballs consisted of small quantities of gunpowder and particles of sand or flint in papier-mâché coatings. When thrown against any hard surface, they would explode with a loud noise. Lawn dart sets were required to carry warning labels, and they could not be sold at toy stores. In 1977, the CPSC required bicycles to have capped brake wires, treads on the pedals to prevent foot slippage, and reflectors for night riding.

One area of concern for product safety advocates was that under product safety laws, toy manufacturers were permitted to market products with labels recommending the age group for which the toy would be most suitable. The labels did not indicate that the toy would be hazardous to any child younger than the recommended age. As a result, many adults believed that the recommended age group was based on intellectual capacity or dexterity, not on safety standards.

In 1977, Parker Brothers marketed a product called Rivitron, a plastic construction toy for children aged six to twelve. After an eight-year-old boy died from ingesting a small part of the toy, the CPSC found the death to be an isolated case. Parker Brothers added chemicals to the toy rivets, giving them a bad taste so that children would be deterred from putting the parts in their mouths.

In 1987, the CPSC under Commissioner Terrence Scanlon seized goods valued at almost $4 million during spot checks. Seizures represented 1.5 million units of toys. James Florio, chairman of the House Reauthorization Subcommittee on Commerce, Consumer Protection, and Competitiveness, criticized the CPSC for being relatively weak during the 1980's. Florio and his committee believed that confiscating $4 million worth of products from a $12 billion industry showed ineffectiveness as a safety commission.

Many critics of toy manufacturers believed that the public was unaware of the dangers that children faced when playing with toys that were not being stringently monitored by the CPSC. On the other hand, toy manufacturers believed that regulations were too stringent and the public too demanding. They argued that many injuries to children were not caused by the children and their toys but by the lack of parental supervision.

In 1968, Peggy Charren had founded Action for Children's Television (ACT). Charren was a critic of toy-based programs, which she believed were exploiting children and should have been scrutinized by the television industry and the Federal Communications Commission. In 1987, when Mattel announced a line of gun toys to be used in interaction with a television show, she unsuccessfully tried to stop the marketing of these products, claiming that simulating the shooting of a television figure would give children the wrong impression of real shooting. Charren's movement gave a new interpretation to product safety, expanding beyond physical features and taking into consideration the potential danger of marketing products that could lead to an unsafe situation or foster dangerous behavior.

Toy manufacturers were faced with other criticisms that may have led to decreased sales. In 1987, consumer advocate and attorney Ralph Nader found that television advertising manipulated child viewers to buy toy products that were not safe. For example, Nader found that plastic toy parts were more hazardous than were wood products, but that television advertising focused on plastic toys. Toy manufacturers responded that critics were more concerned with an antibusiness philosophy than with objections to the actual safety of toys.

Although the CPSC generally supported consumer advocates, in 1991 Toys "R" Us was permitted to sell wind-up dolls, even though children under three years of age could be injured by choking on some of the parts. Sale of the dolls was allowed because they were not intended for children of that age. Throughout the 1980's and 1990's, attorney Edward Swartz compiled lists of dangerous toys. Although many legal battles were won by the toy manufacturing industry, advocates such as Swartz, Nader, and Charren influenced the CPSC and the toy manufacturers to ensure that toys were safe. Toy manufacturers became more cognizant of their market and of the pressure that consumer advocates placed by lobbying legislators to strengthen product safety rules for children. Efforts that began in earnest in the 1970's thus continued to bear fruit into the 1990's, with effects sure to continue.

Bibliography

Dadd, Debra Lynn. *Non-Toxic and Natural: How to Avoid Dangerous Everyday Products and Buy or Make Safe Ones.* Los Angeles: Jeremy P. Tarcher, 1984. Designed to enable the selection of products that are nontoxic. Describes how to make safe products, choose brands that are safe, and pick products that will help protect the environment. A special section on toys describes the safest toys to purchase for young children.

Oppenheim, Joanne. *Buy Me! Buy Me!* New York: Pantheon Books, 1987. The first section describes the toy business as an industry and how it changed what children play with in the 1980's. The second section lists toys that are appropriate and safe for children of various age groups. The third section is a directory listing the names and addresses of organizations and toy suppliers, enabling the reader to obtain further information on purchasing toys for children.

Stern, Sydney Ladensohn, and Ted Schoenhaus. *Toyland: The High Stakes Game of the Toy Industry*. Chicago: Contemporary Books, 1990. A brief history of the toy industry, with a focus on the 1980's. Gives an objective and reasonably unbiased account of the toy industry's response to its customers from a safety perspective.

Swartz, Edward M. *Toys That Don't Care*. Boston: Gambit, 1971. Discusses the unsafe toys manufactured and purchased for children and what can be done to increase safety. Written by an attorney who is an advocate for safe toys. An excellent source, but written from a subjective viewpoint, that of a product liability and negligence trial attorney.

_____ . *Toys That Kill*. New York: Vintage Books, 1986. A sequel to *Toys That Don't Care*. A history and list of unsafe toys manufactured in the 1970's and 1980's. An excellent source, but subjective.

Martin J. Lecker

Cross-References

Hasbro Advertises Toys on Television (1952), p. 986; Congress Sets Standards for Chemical Additives in Food (1958), p. 1097; The United States Bans Cyclamates from Consumer Markets (1969), p. 1390; Nixon Signs the Consumer Product Safety Act (1972), p. 1522; The FTC Conducts Hearings on Ads Aimed at Children (1978), p. 1658.

AMTRAK TAKES OVER MOST U.S. INTERCITY TRAIN TRAFFIC

Categories of event: Transportation; government and business
Time: 1970
Locale: Washington, D.C.

New modes of transportation threatened railroads with extinction and forced the federal government to take radical measures to save them, including passing the Rail Passenger Service Act

> *Principal personages:*
> RICHARD M. NIXON (1913-1994), the president of the United States, 1969-1974
> JOHN A. VOLPE (1908-   ), the U.S. secretary of transportation under Nixon
> ROGER LEWIS (1912-1987), the first president of the Amtrak corporation
> RONALD REAGAN (1911-   ), the president of the United States, 1981-1989

Summary of Event

When the U.S. Congress created Amtrak in 1970, it took one in a series of steps increasing government involvement in railroad transportation. Railroads had an important role in the development of the United States. Trains carried passengers and supplies to the frontier and brought back food, lumber, and minerals to the population centers of the East. The federal government encouraged the growth of railroads by giving their builders enormous land grants, including not only rights of way but millions of acres on both sides of the tracks. This land increased tremendously in value because of the presence of the railroad tracks.

In the Midwest, railroads were responsible for the change from subsistence farming to the raising of single crops such as wheat and corn. In the West, ranchers were able to thrive because they had a means of shipping their cattle and sheep to major markets. California became a rich state in part because growers were able to ship fruits and vegetables to the eastern markets on rapid trains that had freight cars specially designed to prevent spoilage in transit. Cities such as New York and Chicago were able to grow to enormous proportions because trains brought in abundant food.

The so-called "railroad barons" received their land grants and exclusive operating territories on the condition that they provide efficient and equitable transportation for both passengers and freight. When rapid growth of railroads took place in the nineteenth century, no one could foresee the changes in transportation that would be wrought by the Industrial Revolution and later technological and social developments.

One of the earliest developments that threatened railroads was Henry Ford's adoption in 1913 of assembly lines for mass production of his famous Model T automobiles. This innovation allowed the price of cars to fall dramatically, changing automobiles from toys of the rich to a practical means of transportation for the entire population and marking the beginning of the end of the golden era of passenger travel on railroads.

Automobiles became an American passion. More women began driving as manufacturers competed by making their products more stylish and easier to handle. U.S. auto manufacturers began making annual style changes to encourage sales. Trade-ins of good used cars on new models made it possible for nearly every American to own some kind of car. Two-car families with two-car garages became a common part of the American scene.

The demand for automobiles brought a demand for paved highways. State governments responded by creating more highways, and the attractive highways increased the demand for automobiles. In the 1960's, under President Lyndon Johnson's administration, the government spent billions of dollars on a nationwide system of superhighways.

Along with automobiles came trucks and buses. Large long-haul diesel trucks encroached on the railroads' freight business, while buses encroached on the railroads' passenger business. Buses of the Greyhound line in particular became a common sight across the nation. Cars, trucks, and buses, not being confined to steel rails, could take people anywhere they wanted to go. As a result, the entire American landscape changed. New towns and cities sprang up that were not dependent on any linkage to railroad tracks.

At the end of World War II came the worst blow of all to the railroads' passenger business. The federal government was eager to encourage the growth of airlines for many reasons. For one thing, the business of manufacturing airplanes had long been an important asset to the American economy. The federal government helped to encourage air transportation by setting strict safety standards through the Civil Aeronautics Board.

There were plenty of pilots to fly these planes, because the government had trained thousands of men to be aviators during World War II. These experienced pilots provided safe, reliable service that helped to build the public image of air travel. Flying a passenger plane was easy for men who had flown bombing raids over Germany and Japan.

In spite of dramatic air crashes that sometimes killed hundreds of passengers, the public came to realize that, statistically speaking, air travel was the safest form available. The incredible savings in time made air travel hard to ignore. It took the fastest trains three full days to carry a load of passengers from Los Angeles to New York, while an airliner could make the same trip in a few hours. A business traveler could zoom from San Francisco to Los Angeles in one hour, while the same trip could easily take ten hours by car, covering four hundred miles of highways.

Trains were subject to long delays because of weather conditions, but airliners could avoid most adverse weather by flying above the clouds. Younger people, especially business travelers, abandoned train travel, and it became apparent that train clientele increasingly consisted of elderly people who were afraid of flying and had plenty of time on their hands.

Eventually, only one-third of 1 percent of Americans traveling between cities used trains. By the mid-1950's, 85 to 90 percent of the total passenger traffic in the United States went by automobile. The volume of traffic on interstate highways connecting America's cities illustrated that trains could no longer handle the endless stream of humanity hurtling along in private automobiles.

The basic problem was that railroads had become outmoded as a means of human transportation. Railroad companies, however, had obtained their rights of way from the government on the basis of a commitment to provide public transportation. Passenger traffic now not only caused the railroads to lose money but also interfered with the profitable transportation of freight. Freight trains had to be shunted off to sidings to stand idle while passenger trains that were half empty sped by. One possible solution was to build separate lines for passenger trains, but this was so obviously unprofitable that no railroad company considered such an investment.

President Richard M. Nixon supported the idea of government subsidization of passenger trains and was influential in the creation of Amtrak, the official nickname for the National Railroad Passenger Corporation, created by the Rail Passenger Service Act of 1970. Amtrak soon took over virtually all intercity passenger train service, although the semi-independent corporation was not involved in rail commuter service. Amtrak management eliminated many famous old passenger trains and cut down service to approximately 240 trains each day serving about 500 stations over 23,000 miles of tracks. Even with radical cost cutting, Amtrak continued to lose money, and there were periodic outcries to stop wasting taxpayers' money on an obsolete form of transportation and to let passenger trains pass into history, along with stagecoaches and riverboats.

Impact of Event

Many American railroad corporations were in desperate financial straits by 1970. The federal government was forced to subsidize them to prevent a complete collapse of rail transportation. Amtrak brought immediate relief. Freed from the duty of running passenger trains full of empty seats, the railroads were able to concentrate on hauling freight, the business that brought them profits.

The railroads were able to cash in on mushrooming international trade by providing "land bridges" across America. Japan, the largest exporting nation in the world, found that it was relatively inexpensive and fast to send cargo ships to ports in Seattle, San Francisco, and Los Angeles, where cargoes could be off-loaded onto flatcars and whizzed across the continent to ports such as New York, Baltimore, and Atlanta. The cargoes would then proceed to Europe, Africa, and the Middle East. The alternative was to send ships thousands of miles on circuitous routes around the Cape of Magellan or through the Panama Canal to reach their final destinations.

New methods of transporting freight were developed to adapt to changing conditions of international trade. The most innovative idea was containerization. Instead of being packaged in whatever form manufacturers chose, manufactured goods came to be customarily packed in huge, standard-size, all-metal containers that are weatherproof and tamper-proof. Freight no longer had to be slowly loaded into the holds of freighters in small parcels that had to be carefully placed but instead could be piled quickly. The containers were easy to tie down and easy to load and unload with winches. When they reached American ports, the containers could be quickly unloaded onto ordinary railroad flatcars. Huge "doublestack" freight trains requiring minimal crews became a familiar sight. Containerization was bitterly fought by labor organizations representing stevedores and other cargo ship employees. Unions obtained some concessions for their senior members but had to accept the loss of many jobs.

Amtrak did not provide much help for train travelers. Service continued to deteriorate under the new federally subsidized corporation. Many business leaders, government officials, economists, and journalists agreed that long-distance passenger trains were nothing but a form of amusement, like the trains at Disneyland. The only passenger trains that were needed were those providing commuter service over relatively short distances, and these did not need government support. The dominant modes of transportation between cities continued to be planes and automobiles.

With the coaches and Pullman cars getting older and shabbier, the wonderful dining cars of the past being replaced by canteen cars serving packaged food, and the rails themselves deteriorating so that passengers were sometimes badly shaken, the incentive to travel by train decreased. Older people who could remember the glory days of train travel were dying or traveling less frequently.

In the light of these developments, President Ronald Reagan, faced with huge budget problems, called for the breakup of Amtrak and the destruction of the remaining intercity passenger trains. Long-distance train travel managed to continue because of political pressure; some of the most famous surviving trains passed through states represented by influential United States senators. The future of Amtrak remained uncertain. It continued to operate passenger trains between major cities and acquired badly needed new equipment to provide greater speed and comfort.

It became obvious that trains were not an efficient means of transporting people in a vast country such as the United States. American travelers valued their time too greatly and became accustomed to the convenience and speed of travel by automobile and airline. Passenger trains continued to exist primarily because some people were afraid to fly, because some nostalgia buffs favored them for aesthetic reasons, and because some politicians continued to fight for them for their own political advantage.

Intercity passenger trains likely will remain part of the American scene, especially in areas of exceptional scenic beauty and areas of high population density, such as the Northeast Corridor between Boston and Washington, D.C. The passenger train, however, can never hope to recapture more than a fraction of its former glory.

Bibliography
Frailey, Fred W. *Zephyrs, Chiefs, and Other Orphans: The First Five Years of Amtrak.*

Godfrey, Ill.: RPC Publications, 1977. A detailed study of the first five years of Amtrak's operations, attempting to determine which trains were attracting passenger business and which were operating at a loss, and why. Frailey, who is nostalgic about the golden years of train travel, is critical of management and government. Contains many facts and figures. Illustrated with photos of Amtrak trains.

Hilton, George W. *Amtrak: The National Railroad Passenger Corporation*. Washington, D.C.: American Enterprise Institute for Public Policy Research, 1980. Hilton, a professor of economics at the University of California, Los Angeles, describes the decline of passenger traffic and blames railroad management for deliberately discouraging passenger travel by downgrading the quality of service. Concludes that Amtrak serves no useful function but subsidizes people who enjoy traveling by train. Predicts that Amtrak will eventually pass out of existence.

Itzkoff, Donald M. *Off the Track: The Decline of the Intercity Passenger Train in the United States*. Westport, Conn.: Greenwood Press, 1985. Itzkoff concludes that the glamour of railroad travel has vanished forever. He is pessimistic about the future of Amtrak. Extensively footnoted and supplemented with an excellent bibliography. Contains photographs of interiors and exteriors of great passenger trains of the past.

Kidder, Tracy. "Trains in Trouble." *The Atlantic* 238 (August, 1976): 29-39. A survey of the American passenger trains operating under Amtrak. Explains the factors leading to the gradual deterioration of passenger service and discusses possible hope for rail travel revival because of increasing congestion on highways and freeways.

Lyon, Peter. *To Hell in a Day Coach: An Exasperated Look at American Railroads*. Philadelphia: J. B. Lippincott, 1968. An amusing and informative history of American railroads from their beginnings up until the time when it became obvious that the federal government was going to have to take drastic action to preserve passenger service. Lyon blames the railroads for sabotaging their passenger service in favor of the more lucrative freight business.

Orenstein, Jeffrey. *United States Railroad Policy: Uncle Sam at the Throttle*. Chicago: Nelson-Hall, 1990. An explanation and evaluation of U.S. public policy toward American railroads by a political scientist. Presents an overview of the history of American railroading. Discusses Amtrak in considerable detail and offers recommendations for improving government's subsidization and supervision of the nation's railroads.

Pindell, Terry. *Making Tracks: An American Rail Odyssey*. New York: Grove Weidenfeld, 1990. Pindell is a passenger train enthusiast and recounts the history of America's great passenger lines. He spent most of 1988 riding all twenty-one Amtrak routes, covering thirty thousand miles and visiting all but three states. He is a staunch advocate of preserving and improving passenger train service through Amtrak.

Bill Delaney

Cross-References

Ford Implements Assembly Line Production (1913), p. 234; Congress Authorizes Private Carriers for Airmail (1925), p. 493; The Air Commerce Act Creates a Federal Airways System (1926), p. 499; Congress Centralizes Regulation of U.S. Commercial Air Traffic (1940), p. 815; Truman Orders the Seizure of Railways (1946), p. 880; The Boeing 707 Begins Commercial Service (1958), p. 1112.

CURT FLOOD TESTS BASEBALL'S RESERVE CLAUSE

Categories of event: Labor; monopolies and cartels
Time: January 16, 1970
Locale: Washington, D.C.

Curt Flood challenged major league baseball's reserve clause in a lawsuit alleging that the clause violated federal antitrust laws but lost his case in a 5-3 decision of the U.S. Supreme Court

Principal personages:

CURT FLOOD (1938-), an outfielder for the St. Louis Cardinals baseball team from 1958 to 1969

HARRY A. BLACKMUN (1908-), an associate justice of the U.S. Supreme Court

ARTHUR J. GOLDBERG (1908-1990), a prominent trial lawyer and member of the U.S. Supreme Court

BOWIE KUHN (1926-), the commissioner of major league baseball from 1969 to 1984

WILLIAM O. DOUGLAS (1898-1980), an associate justice of the U.S. Supreme Court from 1939 to 1975

IRVING BEN COOPER (1902-), a judge for the U.S. District Court, Southern District New York

MARVIN MILLER (1917-), the executive director of the Major League Baseball Players Association from 1966 to 1983

Summary of Event

On January 16, 1970, Curt Flood initiated a lawsuit arguing that baseball's reserve clause was unlawful. The reserve clause had been judged lawful by the U.S. Supreme Court in 1922 and was a cornerstone of the standard baseball player contract. On June 19, 1972, the U.S. Supreme Court ruled, in a 5-3 decision, that the reserve clause was "an established aberration" and that it was a matter for legislative, not judicial, resolution.

Curt Flood was born in 1938 and began his major league baseball career at the age of eighteen by playing briefly (four at bats) for the Cincinnati Reds of the National League in 1956 and 1957. Prior to the 1958 season, the Reds traded him, exchanged his playing contract for the contracts of other baseball players, to the St. Louis Cardinals of the National League. Flood's twelve-year career as an outfielder with the Cardinals was remarkable. Over the course of his fifteen-year career (which also included thirty-five at bats with the Washington Senators of the American League), Flood made 6,357 appearances at bat and achieved a career batting average of .293 and a career slugging average of .389. He received the Gold Glove Award (for fielding excellence) seven times. He appeared in the 1964, 1967, and 1968 World Series and had his best batting year in 1967 with a .335 average. Flood was one of the top major league baseball players of the 1960's.

On October 7, 1969, the Cardinals traded Flood, then thirty-one years old, to the Philadelphia Phillies of the National League. In December, 1969, Flood registered a complaint about the transaction with Commissioner of Baseball Bowie Kuhn. He requested that he be allowed to become a "free agent," free to negotiate the best deal with any major league club. Kuhn rejected his request, citing the reserve clause in each baseball player's contract.

At the time of Flood's request, all teams and players in major league baseball were bound by the reserve clause found in all players' contracts. The reserve clause specified that once a player had signed a Uniform Player's Contract with a baseball team, the player and team were to negotiate each year if necessary. If there was no agreement by March 1 of a year, the club had the right to renew the contract for one year. The clause had been interpreted to mean that these renewals could go on indefinitely, giving the team the rights to the player's baseball services until the player retired. Unless the team released the player from his contract, he could not negotiate with other teams. The team had the right to assign the player's contract to another team without obtaining the player's permission. The player was then tied to his new team by his contract's reserve clause.

The reserve clause had its legal underpinnings in two decisions of the U.S. Supreme Court. In 1922, the Court ruled in *Federal Baseball Club of Baltimore v. National League of Professional Baseball Clubs* (259 U.S. 200) that the baseball business was not interstate commerce and therefore was not subject to federal antitrust laws. This curious decision gave to baseball's owners and commissioners the privilege of colluding to raise product prices or to reduce the price of labor. In 1953, the Court accepted the case of *Toolson v. New York Yankees* (346 U.S. 356), in which several baseball players directly challenged baseball's reserve clause. The Court issued a one-page opinion affirming its 1922 decision without considering the underlying issues of the reserve clause.

The next challenge to the reserve clause came after Commissioner Kuhn rejected Flood's request to be made a free agent. Flood instituted a lawsuit on January 16, 1970, in federal court in New York. The lawsuit alleged that the reserve clause violated federal and state antitrust laws, was unconstitutional under the Thirteenth Amendment of the U.S. Constitution, and violated other labor and civil rights statutes. Judge Irving Ben Cooper heard his case during May and June of 1970. Flood was represented in his lawsuit by Arthur J. Goldberg, a former member of the U.S. Supreme Court. Judge Cooper rejected all of Flood's arguments, deciding the case (*Flood v. Kuhn*, 316 F.Supp. 271) in favor of major league baseball.

Judge Cooper's decision considered both the constitutional and the antitrust law arguments. First, he observed that a "showing of compulsion" was necessary to find that a contract constituted involuntary servitude, prohibited by the Thirteenth Amendment to the U.S. Constitution. Since a baseball player had a right to retire from baseball and undertake a new career, Judge Cooper concluded that compulsion was not present in the reserve clause. Second, Judge Cooper cited the U.S. Supreme Court's exemption of baseball from the federal antitrust laws and argued that baseball's reserve clause was at the heart of this exemption. Moreover, since baseball was exempt from federal antitrust laws, baseball was also exempt from state antitrust laws.

Although Judge Cooper ruled against Flood, his decision also concluded that the conflicts between team owners and players over the reserve clause were reconcilable. He believed that collective bargaining between the players' union (the Major League Baseball Players Association) and the team owners was capable of producing a reform acceptable to both sides.

Flood appealed Judge Cooper's decision to the U.S. Court of Appeals for the Second Circuit. In a 3-0 ruling (*Flood v. Kuhn*, 443 F.2d 264) in 1971, the court of appeals upheld Judge Cooper's decision. In a concurring opinion, Judge Moore noted that it was up to Congress, not the courts, to repeal baseball's exemption from the antitrust laws.

The Supreme Court accepted an appeal of the case and heard arguments on March 20, 1972. In a 5-3 vote, the Court ruled (*Flood v. Kuhn*, 407 U.S. 258) against Flood on June 19, 1972, affirming its previous exemption of baseball from the antitrust laws. Justice Harry A. Blackmun, writing for the majority, declared that baseball was a business and that the antitrust exemption was an aberration. Nevertheless, the exemption had been in place for five decades, and Blackmun affirmed the importance of adhering to precedent. Blackmun, as well as Chief Justice Warren Burger in a separate concurring opinion, followed the appeals court in arguing that the matter should be resolved by the U.S. Congress, not the federal courts.

In a dissenting opinion, Justice William O. Douglas argued that the Court was responsible for correcting the errors of its earlier decisions. He reasoned that baseball had become like other big businesses and should be subject to antitrust laws. In a separate dissenting opinion, Justice Thurgood Marshall argued that Congress had done nothing to right the inequities stemming from the reserve clause and that it was time that they were corrected by the courts. All three dissenters wanted to send the case back to District Court, which would then determine if the reserve clause violated federal and state antitrust laws.

Impact of Event

The federal court rulings in the Flood case were not particularly surprising, as Flood's case was relatively weak. Although he ran a photography store in St. Louis, he did not claim that his business suffered losses as a result of the trade. In addition, Flood could not establish the extent of his damages in baseball stemming from the reserve clause. Robert Nathan, an economist, testified at Flood's trial that Flood and all other major league baseball players suffered reduced salaries because of the reserve clause. Unfortunately for Flood, Nathan did not provide any evidence on the magnitude of the damages.

Baseball scholar Gerald Scully argued that Flood's lawyers mistakenly based much of their case on the Thirteenth Amendment's prohibition of involuntary servitude.

Scully stressed that a stronger case could have been made by focusing on labor law and emphasizing the excessive control management exercised over players. Others have argued that the case against the reserve clause should not have been brought by a star player but instead by a journeyman player whose damages were more transparent.

The immediate impact of the Flood case was to send a signal to both players and managers that the courts were not going to strike down baseball's reserve clause. If the reserve clause was to be eliminated or modified, it would be through negotiations between the team owners and the players' union. In fact, changes that would lead to partial elimination of the reserve clause were already under way prior to the Flood case. The 1970-1972 Basic Agreement between the players association and the owners had specified that the reserve clause was a required subject for collective bargaining. In addition, the 1969 Basic Agreement had specified that all disputes concerning the Basic Agreement would be submitted to a three-arbitrator panel to resolve. One arbitrator was appointed by the owners, the second by the players, and the third by the first two arbitrators.

The owners' victory in the Flood case was short-lived. The 1973-1975 Basic Agreement restricted the reserve clause by allowing players with ten years of experience (and the last five years with a single club) to veto a trade to another club. After the Flood decision was announced, the owners proposed in early 1973 to allow arbitration to be used to settle salary disputes between players and owners. The players agreed to the use of salary arbitration beginning with the 1974 season.

The critical event in changing the reserve clause came with pitcher Andy Messersmith's dispute with the Los Angeles Dodgers. Messersmith had played the 1975 season without a contract and at season's end proclaimed himself to be a free agent. The players association sent his case to arbitration, arguing that the reserve clause did not tie a player perpetually to a given team but merely granted the baseball team a one-year option to renew the player's contract. To the shock of all parties involved, arbitrator Peter Seitz decided in favor of Messersmith on December 23, 1975. The ruling essentially freed all players to negotiate with other clubs after playing one season without a signed contract.

The players association eventually compromised with the owners by agreeing on a six-year reserve clause in the 1976 Basic Agreement. After six years in the majors, players could become free agents, subject to a reentry draft by major league teams. In 1984, a "Memorandum of Settlement" ended the reentry draft and granted players with six years of experience the right to negotiate with any team.

Since the 1975 Messersmith decision, player salaries have escalated dramatically. This is consistent with economic theory. When a player was constrained to deal with only one club by the reserve clause, the alternative to accepting the club's offer was to work outside baseball, usually at a much lower salary. When a player is free to negotiate with other clubs, the alternative to accepting the club's offer is to accept another club's offer. Since the player's productivity is much higher inside baseball than outside, an offer from another team will be much higher than an offer from a business other than baseball. This pushes up the salary that the player's original team is willing to offer the player.

It is noticeable that the Flood decision reaffirming baseball's exemption from the antitrust laws did not stop the reserve clause from being heavily modified. It should, therefore, be no surprise that other major sports that did not have the benefit of an exemption from antitrust laws also modified their reserve clauses during the 1970's and 1980's. For example, the National Basketball Association allowed players in some circumstances to solicit offers from other basketball teams. The player's current team could, however, match the offer and retain the player. Compared to salaries under a reserve clause system, players' salaries are substantially higher. Perhaps the most surprising development was the ability of the National Football League to avoid modifying its reserve clause system for seventeen years after the Messersmith decision. Finally, in 1993, football players under some circumstances were allowed to negotiate with other teams. The effect on football players' salaries from modifying football's reserve clause was likely to be dramatic.

Bibliography

Dworkin, James B. *Owners Versus Players: Baseball and Collective Bargaining.* Boston: Auburn House, 1981. Reviews the history and impact of collective bargaining on major league baseball. Provides a short overview of the major antitrust cases, including Flood's, questioning baseball's reserve clause.

Kuhn, Bowie. *Hardball: The Education of a Baseball Commissioner.* New York: Times Books, 1987. The former commissioner of baseball provides his version of the important events in baseball from 1969 to 1984. Chapter 6 recounts the events surrounding Curt Flood's lawsuit.

Noll, Roger G., ed. *Government and the Sports Business.* Washington, D.C.: Brookings Institution, 1974. An influential collection of writings by academic economists on the economics of professional sports. Topics covered include racial discrimination, competition between teams, the relationship between productivity and pay, and the profitability of sports teams.

Scully, Gerald W. *The Business of Major League Baseball.* Chicago: University of Chicago Press, 1989. Scully explains how economic incentives critically affect the baseball business. He analyzes racial discrimination, free agency, owner collusion, financial incentives of teams to win pennants, team profits, baseball's high salaries, and television contracts.

Seymour, Harold. *Baseball: The Golden Age.* New York: Oxford University Press, 1971. An excellent history of major league baseball in its formative years. Seymour retells famous stories and recounts the major changes in the organization and management of the game.

Sommers, Paul M., ed. *Diamonds Are Forever: The Business of Baseball.* Washington, D.C.: Brookings Institution, 1992. A collection of articles by academic economists. Topics covered include the baseball players' labor market, player pay, competitive team balance, and racial discrimination.

Will, George. *Men at Work: The Craft of Baseball*. New York: Macmillan, 1990. An excellent book providing a unique perspective on the game of baseball by one of the best-known commentators on modern American politics and society.

Sumner J. La Croix

Cross-References

The Yankees Acquire Babe Ruth (1920), p. 341; The Wagner Act Promotes Union Organization (1935), p. 706; The Brooklyn Dodgers Move to Los Angeles (1957-1958), p. 1076; The NFL-AFL Merger Creates a Sports-Industry Giant (1966), p. 1298; Professional Baseball Players Go on Strike (1972), p. 1512; The Boston Celtics Sell Shares in the Team (1986), p. 1939.

THE U.S. GOVERNMENT BANS CIGARETTE ADS ON BROADCAST MEDIA

Category of event: Advertising
Time: April 1, 1970
Locale: Washington, D.C.

As of January 1, 1971, cigarette advertising was banned from the American broadcast media

Principal personages:

LUTHER TERRY (1911-1985), the United States surgeon general in 1962; formed the Advisory Committee on Smoking and Health

FRANK E. MOSS (1911-   ), the chair of the Senate Commerce Committee hearings on the effects of smoking

JOSEPH CULLMAN III (1912-   ), the chair of Philip Morris and spokesperson for tobacco manufacturers at the Senate Consumer Subcommittee hearings

WALLACE BENNETT (1898-   ), the U.S. senator who introduced the bill that required health warning labels on cigarette packages beginning in 1965

JOHN F. BANZHAF III (1940-   ), the executive director of Action on Smoking and Health, an antismoking public interest group

Summary of Event

The Public Health Cigarette Smoking Act of 1969 banned cigarette advertising from American radio and television beginning January 1, 1971. It also allowed the Federal Trade Commission (FTC) to consider warnings in printed advertising after July 1, 1971. Warnings on cigarette packages were changed, and under the act, the FTC was required to give Congress six months notice of any pending changes in rules concerning cigarettes. The legislation was signed by President Richard Nixon on April 1, 1970. After passage of the act, two voluntary agreements were reached between the FTC and cigarette manufacturers. The companies agreed to list tar and nicotine content in their advertising and also agreed to feature the health warning label in print advertising.

Pressure to curb cigarette advertising originated with a 1939 study that for the first time scientifically linked smoking with lung cancer. Between 1950 and 1954, fourteen major studies linked cigarette smoking with specific serious diseases. In response to these studies, cigarette manufacturers created the Tobacco Industry Research Committee, a lobby group to fund research on the use and health effects of tobacco. The group later changed its name to the Council for Tobacco Research—USA. In 1957, the Legal and Monetary Affairs Subcommittee of the House Government Operations Committee held six days of congressional hearings, with John A. Blatnik as the chair. As a result of these hearings, Senator Wallace Bennett introduced a bill that would require cigarette packs to carry warning labels, and Senator Richard Neuberger proposed removing tobacco from the list of crops that qualify for agricultural price supports. Five years later, in 1962, Surgeon General Luther Terry formed the Advisory Committee on Smoking and Health.

Two years later, on January 11, 1964, the surgeon general announced the results of that committee's findings. The press conference to announce the results was held on a Saturday in anticipation of the adverse effect the study might have on the stock prices of tobacco companies. The study established a link between cigarette smoking and diseases ranging from lung cancer to cardiovascular diseases and cirrhosis of the liver. Two weeks later, the Public Health Service announced its acceptance, in full, of the Advisory Committee's report. In subsequent weeks, several congressmen introduced legislation related to the controversy and called for hearings.

On March 16, 1964, three days of Federal Trade Commission hearings on cigarette labeling and advertising rules began. A proposed rule had been circulated in advance. One section required that a health warning appear in all advertising and on cigarette packages. Drafts of two warning statements were presented, each indicating that cigarette smoking can lead to death. Another section of the rule attempted to ban "words, pictures, symbols, sounds, devices or demonstrations. . . that would lead the public to believe cigarette smoking promotes good health or physical well-being."

The FTC was overruled by Congress on part of its proposal. Warnings were to be required only on packages, not in advertising, according to the Cigarette Labeling Act of 1965. The ban on radio and television advertising came later, by an act of Congress, not through the FTC or the Federal Communications Commission (FCC). The required inclusion of the health warning on all print advertisements also came later. This was the result of a voluntary agreement between the commission and cigarette manufacturers in 1972, when a congressional ban on commission action forcing this requirement was expiring.

The ruling requiring warning labels was to take effect on January 1, 1965. In the nine-month period between the commission's hearings and the first of January, the cigarette industry mobilized. Within one month of the hearings, the industry announced the creation of a voluntary code, intended to signify to Congress and the public that the industry was interested in regulating itself and that the FTC was an obstacle to self-regulation. Robert B. Meyner, a former governor of New Jersey, was hired to administer the code and given the authority to issue fines of up to $100,000 to violators. Essentially, the code prohibited advertising aimed at persons under twenty-one years of age and prohibited cigarette advertising from making positive health claims. The code limitations were difficult to interpret and enforce. These difficulties eventually led to an agreement that eventually banned cigarette advertising from the broadcast media.

The agreement was prompted by the pending expiration on July 1, 1969, of the Cigarette Labeling Act of 1965. The Federal Communications Commission unexpectedly announced in February, 1969, that if Congress allowed the 1965 act to expire, the FCC would propose a rule that would ban cigarette advertising from the airwaves.

At this point, several options were available. If Congress did not act and allowed the 1965 legislation to expire, this would permit the FCC to enact its proposed restrictions. Alternatively, Congress could have extended the 1965 ban or could have taken action on the health warning label, making it more or less stringent.

Antismoking forces hoped that Congress would not act, thereby allowing for the more encompassing regulations proposed by the FCC. Instead, the House Interstate and Foreign Commerce Committee held thirteen days of hearings two months before the ban was to expire. The arguments and many of the witnesses were the same as those heard in the 1965 hearings.

In testimony before the House Commerce Committee, Warren Braren, former manager of the New York office of the Code Authority, made it clear that the National Association of Broadcasters (NAB) deliberately misled Congress and the public into believing that voluntary industry self-regulation in reducing youth appeal was meaningful. He revealed that television networks and advertising agencies regularly overruled Code Authority staff members in interpretation of standards. The Code Authority operated entirely on voluntary submissions by advertising agencies. Some tobacco sponsors simply had not subscribed to the code, and those that did made their own judgments on whether their commercials needed to be reviewed.

The bill that passed the House of Representatives on June 18, 1969, however, appeared to represent a victory for the cigarette industry. It prohibited the states permanently, and the federal agencies for six more years, from enacting regulations on cigarette advertising, in exchange for a strengthened package warning label.

The bill as passed by the House, however, sparked a severe backlash in the Senate and at the state level as well as in the private sector. *The New York Times*, for example, announced that it would require a health warning in any cigarette advertisement appearing in that newspaper.

The Senate Commerce Committee, chaired by Frank E. Moss, held a one-day hearing, with only five witnesses appearing. Speaking for the tobacco manufacturers in July, 1969, Joseph Cullman III, chairman of Philip Morris, told the Senate Consumer Subcommittee that the industry was ready to end all advertising on television and radio on December 31, 1969, if the broadcasters would cooperate, and in any event would agree to cease advertising by September, 1970, when existing agreements expired. The announcement by Cullman caught many broadcasters by surprise. They had proposed to phase out cigarette ads over a three-year period beginning in January, 1970. Cigarette advertising accounted for $225 million a year in revenue to broadcasters, and they had hoped that a gradual reduction would help in the development of contingency plans to recover a portion of the lost revenue.

Meanwhile, the National Association of Broadcasters (NAB) Television and Radio Code Review Boards announced a plan on July 8, 1969, to stop advertising on radio and television beginning January 1, 1970. In addition, cigarette manufacturers were required to continue carrying warning labels on their packages. The agreement stipulated that member stations of the NAB would phase out cigarette commercials on the air beginning January 1, 1970. The Review Boards also said that they would prohibit cigarette commercials during or adjacent to any program that was primarily directed at youth and would further study ways to reduce the appeal of cigarettes to minors. The announcement amounted to a victory for critics of tobacco, most notably the FCC, which had threatened to ban all cigarette commercials from the airwaves.

The tobacco industry, in presenting its proposal, showed concern that broadcasters might sue for antitrust violations, on the grounds that the cigarette companies had acted in collusion. The industry included a request for antitrust protection in presenting its proposal.

The bill that emerged from Congress on March 19, 1970, called the Public Health Cigarette Smoking Act of 1969, banned cigarette advertising from radio and television beginning January 1, 1971. It also agreed to allow the FTC to consider warnings in printed advertising after July 1, 1971. Cigarette package warning labels were changed to: "Warning: The Surgeon General Has Determined that Cigarette Smoking Is Dangerous to Your Health."

Impact of Event

Attitudes within the tobacco industry regarding the ban were mixed. It is commonly assumed in the industry that advertising does not increase the size of the overall cigarette market. Instead, it affects the competitive position of the various brands. The primary effect of the advertising ban, therefore, would be to freeze the market shares currently held by each of the brands. Print ads could still affect market share but were not believed to be as powerful. The money saved by not producing and placing advertising in the broadcast media would be substantial. As an added bonus, the industry hoped that a cessation of cigarette advertising would yield a respite in the growing volume of antismoking advertising.

It was expected that the industry's decision to discontinue expensive television campaigns would be accompanied by stepped-up spending on print advertising, coupons, and contests. The chairman of American Brands predicted that "the battleground for cigarette sales advertising will probably switch to other media." Newspaper and magazine publishers, unlike broadcasters, are not federally licensed and are protected by the First Amendment's freedom-of-speech provision. There was no indication that publishers would voluntarily ban cigarette advertising, since it amounted to approximately $50 million in annual revenue. Furthermore, there was less pressure to ban print advertising of cigarettes, since these ads primarily reached an adult audience and were less intrusive than television ads.

Opinions varied on how cigarette sales would be affected by a ban on broadcast advertising. In Great Britain, where cigarette ads were banned from television in 1965, sales initially fell but then recovered to reach record levels. In the United States, per capita cigarette sales had begun declining in 1968. This decline had been attributed in part to a drop in the number of new, young smokers. This market segment had become increasingly concerned about the health threats of smoking. That concern resulted in part from antismoking advertisements that the television networks were required to run, free of charge, after passage of the 1967 Fairness Doctrine.

The tobacco industry's initial response to the broadcast advertising ban was to find alternative means to get its message to the public. Liggett & Myers, Philip Morris, and R. J. Reynolds all signed contracts with automobile racing organizations as a way to keep their brands on television, announcing that the races would be named after popular brands, for example the "L&M Continental Championship," the "Marlboro Championship," and the "Winston 500." Some industry observers saw this as an attempt at a "rear door" reentry by cigarette makers into the television market. Advertisers also positioned displays strategically at racetracks so that they would be captured by television cameras covering the events.

Within one month of the imposed ban on broadcast media advertising, the number of pages of cigarette advertising in consumer magazines more than doubled as compared to the same period of the previous year. Although some increase was anticipated, its magnitude caught the magazine industry by surprise and created a controversy. This stemmed from the impression that the increase in cigarette advertising might convey in the light of the magazine industry's somewhat delicate position regarding health warnings. Congress had barred the Federal Trade Commission from requiring health hazard warnings in cigarette print ads before July 1, 1971, but not after.

Twenty months after the broadcast advertising ban went into effect, the FTC urged the government to buy broadcast time for antismoking advertising. Smoking had hit record high levels since the ads left the airwaves. In 1972, a total of 554 billion cigarettes were smoked, 3 percent more than in the preceding year. The tobacco industry apparently had survived the controversy that began with the 1964 surgeon general's report. Analysts correctly predicted that the industry would witness at least a decade of strong, steady growth. Some attributed this growth to the increase in the 25-to-44 age bracket, a group that accounted for a large proportion of cigarette consumption. Others argued that the ban had not yet had its full effect, since most young consumers had seen cigarette ads for most of their lives. John F. Banzhaf III, executive director of Action on Smoking and Health, an antismoking public interest group, stated that to date the greatest impact of the ruling was that antismoking messages were appearing far less frequently, since broadcasters no longer had to air them for free to balance cigarette ads. The effects of cigarette advertising were seen to be long-term, while the antismoking ads seemed to have an effect for a shorter period.

In the 1970's, public and medical research interest turned to the effects of smoking on nonsmokers. In 1972, the surgeon general issued the first report suggesting that secondhand smoke was dangerous to nonsmokers. In 1975, Minnesota passed the first state law requiring businesses, restaurants, and other institutions to establish nonsmoking areas. The concern regarding secondhand smoke continued, with an increasing number of local governments and businesses restricting smoking in public areas.

The cigarette industry continued to target new generations of smokers. Through print and billboard advertising, sales promotions, public relations, and giveaways, the industry continued to aggressively promote its brands. In 1988, tobacco companies spent more than one billion dollars on advertising and more than two billion dollars on promotion. The restriction on broadcast advertising and the required warning labels on packages and advertisements appear to have had a limited impact in the face of advertising that promises smokers increased status, social acceptance, and glamour. The cigarette industry has defended itself against charges of irresponsibility by claiming that individuals are free to decide whether to smoke and that it simply is meeting an existing consumer demand. The industry is particularly defensive regarding charges that ads are targeted toward children. It argues that ads do not encourage people to start smoking, but rather to switch brands.

Bibliography

Doron, Gideon. *The Smoking Paradox: Public Regulation in the Cigarette Industry.* Cambridge, Mass.: Abt Books, 1979. Provides a succinct overview of the conflicting interests at the center of the debate regarding cigarette smoking.

Fritschler, A. Lee. *Smoking and Politics: Policymaking and the Federal Bureaucracy.* 3d ed. Englewood Cliffs, N.J.: Prentice-Hall, 1983, A comprehensive review of the debate and negotiations that surrounded the decision to ban cigarette advertising from television and radio. Provides an insightful summary of the political maneuvering that accompanied the decision.

Sobel, Robert. *They Satisfy: The Cigarette in American Life.* New York: Anchor Press, 1978. An extensive history of the tobacco industry and its changing economics, with a dispassionate account of the political struggle regarding cigarette advertising.

Tollison, Robert D., ed. *Smoking and Society: Toward a More Balanced Assessment.* Lexington, Mass.: Lexington Books, 1986. Presents an assessment of the debate regarding cigarettes from the standpoint of its impact on society. Does not directly review legal aspects, but provides a collection of articles that provide essential background information.

White, Larry C. *Merchants of Death: The American Tobacco Industry.* New York: Beech Tree Books, 1988. A somewhat biased presentation (as evidenced by its title) that provides a readable account of the techniques that tobacco companies have used to market their brands.

Elaine Sherman
Andrew M. Forman

Cross-References

Congress Passes the Pure Food and Drug Act (1906), p. 128; The Wheeler-Lea Act Broadens FTC Control over Advertising (1938), p. 775; The U.S. Advertising Industry Organizes Self-Regulation (1971), p. 1501; R. J. Reynolds Introduces Premier, a Smokeless Cigarette (1988), p. 1976.

CONGRESS PASSES THE RICO ACT

Category of event: Business practices
Time: October 15, 1970
Locale: Washington, D.C.

Congress passed the Racketeer Influenced and Corrupt Organizations Act to fight organized crime, but it was used most prominently to prosecute white-collar criminals

Principal personages:
G. ROBERT BLAKEY (1936-   ), an attorney who drafted the RICO Act
RUDOLPH GIULIANI (1944-   ), the prosecutor most famous for using RICO
CARL ICAHN (1936-   ), a prominent takeover artist who was one of the first to be threatened with RICO indictments
MICHAEL MILKEN (1946-   ), a powerful investment banker who was Giuliani's chief target
WILLIAM REHNQUIST (1924-   ), the Chief Justice of the United States who criticized prosecutors for using RICO in ways not intended by Congress

Summary of Event

In 1970, Congress wound up debates on what appeared to be a simple piece of legislation but actually, as the financial community would learn, was quite complex. Signed into law on October 15, it became known as the Racketeer Influenced and Corrupt Organizations (RICO) Act. The origin of the name was evocative, since its intended target was organized crime.

The measure's history stretched as far back as the Senate investigations of organized crime in 1950. These investigations demonstrated strikingly, through testimony by underworld figures, that legitimate businesses had been infiltrated by criminal elements. Congress considered legislation to prevent this infiltration and a few weak statutes actually were passed, but the problem remained. In 1967, a presidential commission recommended a stiff new law to deal with the issue. Discussions that followed culminated in the 1970 debates.

G. Robert Blakey, who as a Senate committee counsel in 1969 drafted the bill that became the RICO Act, later claimed that the resulting law would make fair the fight between legitimate businesses and the twin Goliaths of organized crime and white-collar crime. Almost all the legislators debating the issue, however, indicated that the primary objective was to provide penalties for gangster elements. Senator Robert Dole (R-Kansas) said that it was impossible to put too much stress on the importance of the legislative attack on organized crime. White-collar crime received little attention.

Even so, the term "organized crime" did not appear in the final version of the law, partly in deference to the sensibilities of the Italian American community. Representative Mario Biaggi (D-New York) was vocal on this score, as were others. Some members of Congress doubted that a precise definition of organized crime was possible. Instead, the term employed was "racketeering activities," defined to include a pattern of racketeering activity or the collection of an unlawful debt as well as the establishment or operation of any illegal enterprise engaged in, or the activities of which affect, interstate or foreign commerce. Also included were "acts or threats of murder, kidnapping, gambling, arson, robbery, bribery, extortion, or dealing in narcotics or other dangerous drugs." In addition, counterfeiting, embezzlement from pension and welfare funds, extortionate credit transactions, obstruction of criminal investigations, and certain dealings with labor unions fell under the racketeering label. All of this was expected, since all of these activities were within the purview of criminal elements.

The acronym for the law, RICO, came into question. One account is that the name was inspired by the character played by Edward G. Robinson in the 1930 film *Little Caesar*, Rico Bendello. Apparently no connection was meant to be made to the Italian American community.

Mail fraud also came under the strictures of the new act, as did fraud in the sale of securities and the felonious manufacture, importation, receiving, concealment, buying, selling, or otherwise dealing in narcotic or other dangerous drugs, punishable under any law of the United States. The context makes it clear that the target of the law was individuals and groups collectively known as organized crime.

Activities falling under the rubric of white-collar crime were not intended to come under the RICO statute. One of the few moments of levity during the debates on the bill came from a congressman who voiced objection to the measure on the basis that whatever the original motives of lawmakers, the courts would be flooded with cases involving all kinds of things not intended to be covered. The law already was recognized to have the potential for overreaching by zealous prosecutors. For example, the congressman suggested, suppose several members of Congress played poker for money on a regular basis. Would this mean that they had been running an organized gambling business and could get twenty-year prison sentences? Could the federal government also confiscate the pot?

Subsection a of section 1962, which deals with prohibited activities, contains a laundry list of illegal activities. Securities activities are mentioned in this section. The act regulates the disposition of income that comes, directly or indirectly, from a pattern of racketeering activity or through collection of an unlawful debt in which a person has participated as a principal. That income, or the proceeds of such income, cannot be sued to invest, directly or indirectly, in the acquisition of any interest in, or the operation of, any enterprise engaged in interstate or foreign commerce or any enterprise that affects interstate or foreign commerce. The purchase of securities with such income is not necessarily illegal. Securities purchases made in the open market for purposes of investment and without the intention of controlling or participating in the control of the issuer of the securities are not unlawful. Securities purchases would be lawful if the holdings (after the purchase) of the purchaser, the members of his or her immediate family, and any accomplices in any pattern of racketeering activity or the collection of an unlawful debt come to less than 1 percent of the outstanding securities of any single class; further, these holdings cannot confer, either in law or in fact, the power to elect one or more directors of the issuer of the securities.

The penalties for RICO violations were severe. Even if a business were run legitimately, it could be confiscated if it had been purchased with illegally obtained money, and in civil cases treble damages could be levied. Funds and assets could be seized even prior to any trial; suspected criminals thus could be punished before their guilt was assessed. The penalties were so severe that even as the law was passed, some attorneys doubted its constitutionality. RICO's defenders replied that such measures were needed to ferret out money obtained from "mob" activities.

The RICO Act provided for both civil and criminal prosecution when an enterprise engaged in two or more predicate acts within a ten-year period that involved interstate commerce. Under terms of the legislation, even two acts within this time period would constitute a pattern of racketeering activity.

There is debate as to whether legislators considered targets for the law other than "mob" activity and organized crime. Definitions included in the measure describe racketeering activity as including "any offense involving . . . fraud in the sale of securities, or the felonious manufacture, importation, receiving, concealment, buying, selling, or otherwise dealing in narcotic or other dangerous drugs, punishable under any law of the United States."

The context indicates that the legislators meant to address organized crime specifically, not the more common white-collar variety. The wording of the law, however, provided opportunities for energetic and imaginative prosecutors to bring cases outside the scope of organized crime. The initial cases under RICO did involve criminal activities undertaken by career criminals. That was the public's understanding of the purpose of the law. As late as 1980, a reporter wrote, "RICO stands for the Racketeer Influenced and Corrupt Organizations statute, a federal law enacted in 1970 that gave the government a powerful new weapon in its fight against organized crime's takeover of legitimate businesses. . . . The idea, as the Justice Department put it in a training memo to its lawyers and agents, is 'to hit organized crime in the pocketbook.' "

Impact of Event

Contained in the law were provisions for civil cases, which were used mostly against financial operators. It took time for this use of RICO to become widespread and gain acceptance. There was only one decision involving "civil RICO" in 1972, and only one other case before 1975. Only nine decisions were reported before the 1980's. It was then that matters changed. As New York federal judge Gerard Goettel noted, virtually any fraud case or even a commercial case with overtones of fraud might qualify as racketeering, since use of the mail and telephones brought illegal activity under the definition of racketeering.

One of the first uses of civil RICO in the securities industry came in 1982, when financier and takeover artist Carl Icahn was attempting to raid the Marshall Field organization, in his biggest attempted takeover up to that time. Attorneys for the large department store alleged violations of securities law in Icahn's strategy and also invoked RICO provisions, charging that Icahn had obtained some of the funds for the raid from a "pattern of racketeering." This pattern was evidenced by a consent order from the New Jersey Bureau of Securities, a New York Stock Exchange censure, four fines from the Chicago Board Options Exchange, and other minor charges. Nothing came of this, as Marshall Field entered into a merger with Batus, and the matter was dropped.

Of the approximately 270 trial court decisions before 1985, 3 percent were decided before 1980, 2 percent in 1980, 7 percent in 1981, 13 percent in 1982, 33 percent in 1983, and 43 percent in 1984. Of this number, 57 involved securities transactions. These fell into three categories: brokers providing false information to clients to encourage trading, the "churning" of client accounts (engaging in excessive trading as a means of generating commissions), and issuing prospectuses with misrepresentations. For example, a client sued Harris, Upham after a broker with that firm told him of a pending takeover of a furniture warehouse chain; the takeover rumor was false. The client's total losses from acting on it came to $2.6 million. In 1985, activity related to RICO prosecutions picked up, as prosecutors and litigators fixed upon the law as a superb instrument to terrify businesspeople.

This new activity did not sit well with many disparate organizations. The American Civil Liberties Union, the National Association of Manufacturers, and the American Federation of Labor-Congress of Industrial Organizations (AFL-CIO), among others, objected to the uses to which the law was put. The law and its use also had critics in the legal profession. Chief Justice of the United States William Rehnquist told a Brookings Institution seminar in April, 1989, that civil RICO was being used in ways that Congress never intended, implying that its constitutionality might be tested and found wanting. In two of the most important cases to be heard by the Supreme Court, however, the Court did not strike down civil RICO prosecutions. A majority in both cases instead threw the matter back to the legislature. RICO may have been a poorly drafted statute, it concluded, but rewriting was a job for Congress, not the courts. Four justices pronounced the wording of the law unconstitutionally ambiguous.

Casting about for means to thwart corporate raiders, target companies started turning to civil RICO. There was talk of using RICO against T. Boone Pickens during the contest for control of Unocal, but nothing materialized. In 1986, officials at the Staley corporation spoke of "extortion" and "bribery," and two parts of its complaint dealt with racketeering activity.

The most important use of RICO, however, was made by Rudolph Giuliani, the U.S. attorney for the Southern District of New York who in the late 1980's led the campaign against Wall Street malefactors. In 1988, he invoked RICO against the investment bank of Princeton/Newport. The prosecution destroyed that company, though it later was found innocent of wrongdoing. Government seizure of assets played a large part in destroying Princeton/Newport. Giuliani's biggest attack was against the investment bank of Drexel Burnham Lambert and its star banker, Michael Milken. Threatened with RICO action, Drexel agreed to pay $650 million in fines and restitution and to place Milken on a leave of absence. To some, this penalty seemed to be overkill, since the slightest doubt of Drexel's ability to remain in business would, in effect, force it out of business. Ultimately, Drexel did file for bankruptcy in 1990. It was the biggest casualty of RICO, though probably one of the last, because the law was used only sparingly thereafter.

Bibliography

Bailey, Fenton. *Fall from Grace: The Untold Story of Michael Milken*. Secaucus, N.J.: Carol Publishing Group, 1992. Contains a harsh criticism of RICO and an analysis of its use. Bailey is a British journalist who had access to Drexel files.

Bruck, Connie. *The Predators' Ball*. New York: Simon & Schuster, 1988. An early exposé of Drexel and Milken, generally supportive of the use of RICO. Bruck gained entry to Drexel, and this book is the result of investigative journalism.

Kornbluth, Jesse. *Highly Confident: The Crime and Punishment of Michael Milken*. New York: Morrow, 1992. Written with Milken's cooperation, this is a highly personal pro-Milken and anti-Giuliani account of the demise of Drexel Burnham Lambert and the incarceration of Milken. Kornbluth concentrates on the human side of the story and demonstrates only a slight knowledge of RICO.

Sobel, Robert. *Dangerous Dreamers: The Financial Innovators from Charles Merrill to Michael Milken*. New York: J. Wiley & Sons, 1993. Contains an account of the passage of the RICO statute and analysis of how it was used. Valuable for insights into the early and later views of how RICO should be employed.

Stewart, James. *Den of Thieves*. New York: Simon & Schuster, 1991. Stewart is generally sympathetic to RICO and believes its use was justified in certain criminal and civil cases. Stewart was an editor of *The Wall Street Journal* with ties to Giuliani.

Robert Sobel

Cross-References

The Canada Cement Affair Prompts Legislative Reform (1909), p. 174; Merrill Lynch Concentrates on Small Investors (1940's), p. 809; Kohlberg Kravis Roberts Pioneers the Leveraged Buyout (1977), p. 1641; Pennzoil Sues Texaco for Interfering in Getty Oil Deal (1984), p. 1876; Insider Trading Scandals Mar the Emerging Junk Bond Market (1986), p. 1921; Drexel and Michael Milken Are Charged with Insider Trading (1988), p. 1958; The Recruit Scandal Surfaces in Japan (1988), p. 1964.

CONGRESS PASSES THE FAIR CREDIT REPORTING ACT

Categories of event: Finance and consumer affairs
Time: October 26, 1970
Locale: Washington, D.C.

The Fair Credit Reporting Act caused policies to be implemented to ensure the proper maintenance and disclosure of credit information

Principal personages:
WILLIAM PROXMIRE (1915-   ), a senator from Wisconsin
RICHARD H. LEHMAN (1948-   ), a congressman from California
ALAN J. DIXON (1927-   ), a senator from Illinois
ALAN CRANSTON (1914-   ), a senator from California
ESTEBAN EDWARD TORRES (1930-   ), a congressman from California

Summary of Event

The Fair Credit Reporting Act (an amendment to the Consumer Credit Protection Act of 1968), was passed by Congress on October 26, 1970, and became law in April of 1971. Senator William Proxmire of Wisconsin was instrumental in the passage of this legislation.

Section 602 of the Fair Credit Reporting Act (FCRA) outlined the need for this law. First, the banking system is dependent upon fair and accurate credit reporting. Inaccurate credit reports directly impair the efficiency of the banking system, and unfair credit reporting methods undermine the public confidence essential to the continued functioning of the banking system. Second, elaborate mechanisms exist to investigate and evaluate creditworthiness, credit standing, credit capacity, character, and general reputation of consumers. Consumer reporting agencies have assumed a vital role in assembling and evaluating consumer credit and other information on consumers. There is a need to ensure that consumer reporting agencies exercise their responsibilities with fairness, impartiality, and a respect for consumers' right to privacy.

The FCRA had four primary objectives. They were to establish acceptable purposes for which a consumer credit report may be obtained; to define the consumer's rights regarding credit reports, with particular emphasis on giving consumers access to their reports and procedures for correcting inaccurate information; to establish requirements for handling an adverse credit decision that resulted in whole or in part from information contained in a credit report; and to define the responsibilities of credit reporting agencies.

In general, it was the realization by Congress that consumer credit has had major impacts on economic activity as a whole that spurred the legislation. Consumers' inability to obtain credit for expensive items such as automobiles and large appliances negatively affected economic factors such as employment, production, and income, ultimately magnifying the business cycle, particularly in downturns. Financial institutions, as the grantors of consumer credit and the users of information supplied by credit reporting agencies, weighted their credit decisions heavily on the information supplied. Timely, accurate, and intelligible information was necessary for proper credit decisions. Consumers also needed to be protected from ramifications resulting from inaccurate, untimely, or improper credit information.

Consumers by far were the most heavily affected by the passage of this legislation. Consumers rely heavily upon consumer credit as a means of purchasing expensive items and raising their standards of living by purchasing goods for current use with future income. Reporting agencies faced higher costs as a result of the legislation but gained a greater reputation for accuracy and usefulness.

The following information is usually contained within a consumer credit file: name; address; previous address; Social Security number; date of birth; employer; length of employment; previous employment; credit history including creditors, balances, and payment patterns; and public filings such as mortgages, chattels, marriages, divorces, collections suits, and bankruptcies. The FCRA made all information within a consumer's credit report accessible to the consumer.

Consumers can get access to their credit files in several ways. If a consumer is denied credit on a credit application, the lending institution is required to mail a detailed letter outlining the reasons for denial and including the name, address, and telephone number of any reporting agency consulted. The consumer may take this letter to the reporting agency within thirty days of the date of the letter to discuss and obtain a free copy of the report. A consumer who has not been denied credit may obtain a copy of his or her file from the local reporting service for a nominal fee. A consumer must provide proper identification in order to obtain a copy of his or her credit file. The FCRA identifies the type of material available to the consumer. The consumer has the right to know all the information in the file, with the exception of medical records. This includes names of people or companies that have obtained the report within the past six months and the names of those who received the report for employment purposes within the past two years.

The FCRA greatly benefits consumers by allowing them to dispute information contained within their files. Erroneous or inaccurate information can be contested and asked to be verified by the reporting agency. The consumer has the right to place within the credit file a consumer statement outlining his or her interpretation of negative information. This statement is then part of the file and is presented to future users. The consumer statement is usually limited to one hundred words. The FCRA limits the amount of time that unfavorable information can be reported on a consumer. Seven years is the maximum, with the exception of bankruptcies, which are reported for ten years.

In some instances, an investigative credit report may be compiled on an individual. It includes all the information mentioned above. In addition, it includes information on the character, reputation, and living style of the consumer. This information is obtained from interviews with friends, associates, and neighbors. The consumer has the same rights of access to this report as to an ordinary credit file.

The final major area that the FCRA addresses is consumers' right to privacy. Credit information is basically for use by the consumer, the reporting agency, authorized credit grantors, employers, and insurance companies. To restrict dissemination to proper users, those who request credit information must prove their identity and their reason for wanting access to a consumer's credit file. For users who obtain information under false pretenses, the law provides for fines of up to $5,000, prison sentences up to one year, or both. The same penalties apply to officers and employees of reporting agencies who misuse information. Consumers are allowed to pursue civil litigation against reporting agencies and are entitled to compensation for any financial injury, extra penalties imposed by the court, court costs, and attorney fees. Consumers can discuss complaints with credit reporting agencies by contacting the Federal Trade Commission.

Impact of Event

Consumers were not the only parties affected by the FCRA. Reporting agencies assumed a more clearly defined fiduciary responsibility to act in good faith and trust. Their goals are to maintain timely and accurate files on consumers, handle disputes in a timely manner, and investigate complaints and inaccurate information on consumers. They must also ensure the confidentiality of their information while still making it available to the proper users. Failure to follow proper procedures and guidelines can result not only in consumer complaints but also in lawsuits, fines, or even imprisonment for employees of reporting agencies.

Consumer credit grantors also were affected by the FCRA. Lenders need to be careful when disclosing credit information. It must be both timely and accurate. Letters denying credit must be sent out on time, and procedures need to be in place to handle direct requests made to the organization. Lenders need to be careful with outside requests so as to not be viewed as credit reporting agencies. The final area lenders must address is the use of information for decision-making purposes. Many lenders place great weight in consumer credit decisions on the information obtained from credit files. It is essential that lenders have reliable information in order to make proper credit decisions. Lenders also use credit reporting agencies to screen borrowers. This works in two ways for lenders. It improves their credit quality by eliminating marginal borrowers and also gives them access to potential new customers. Lenders are bound by privacy laws and are forbidden to give copies of reports to consumers or other lenders.

The FCRA had major ramifications for consumers applying for credit, credit reporting agencies, and lenders who relied upon information for decision-making purposes. The emphasis of this act was that information contained within a credit file must be timely and accurate, accessible to all concerned parties, and inaccessible to unconcerned parties. The FCRA and subsequent amendments dealt with these issues.

On September 13, 1989, the United States House of Representatives Subcommittee on Consumer Affairs and Coinage of the Committee on Banking, Finances, and Urban Affairs met to discuss multiple concerns regarding the FCRA. Chairman Richard H. Lehman summarized the concerns. He stated that the act had existed essentially without amendment for nearly twenty years and that the credit reporting industry apparently had been successful in convincing Congress that it worked well in its present form. He noted, however, that people had concerns about privacy and other aspects of their rights under the act. There had been complaints about the difficulty of getting inaccurate information removed from credit files, the length of time to get disputed information reinvestigated, name mix-ups, and denials of credit being based upon the number of inquiries in a credit report. He also noted that Vice President Dan Quayle had had his credit report made available with what appeared to be insufficient checks by the credit reporter of the purpose intended. Finally, Lehman noted that $104 billion in consumer installment credit was outstanding when the act was passed. By 1989, that figure had reached approximately $700 billion.

On October 22, 1991, the United States Senate Subcommittee on Consumer and Regulatory Affairs conducted hearings on the FCRA. In his opening statement, chairman Alan J. Dixon expressed reasons for the hearing. Consumer credit had increased sixfold since the act was first introduced, and the number of reports had increased fivefold. A revolution in computer technology had changed not only the shape of the credit reporting industry but also methods of record keeping and dissemination of consumer data. Witnesses at the hearing were asked to comment on credit report inaccuracies, complaints about errors and obsolete information, consumer access to reports and knowledge of rights, privacy issues and prescreening, enforcement of the FCRA, and credit repair organizations.

At this hearing, Senator Alan Cranston of California noted that he had introduced to the Senate a companion bill to legislation in the House of Representatives proposed by Richard H. Lehman. Cranston's bill proposed education of consumers about the credit reporting process, greater protection of privacy rights, and response to the massive changes in information technology and business credit needs. The meeting was concluded with the members of the subcommittee assuring Dixon that they were looking forward to passing the necessary amendments to the FCRA.

On October 24, 1991, the United States House of Representatives Subcommittee on Consumer Affairs and Coinage met to discuss the FCRA. Chairman Esteban Edward Torres conducted the hearings. The primary purpose of the meeting was to overview legislation (H.R. 3596) introduced earlier in the week by the chairman to reform the FCRA. His legislation addressed problems primarily pertaining to lack of privacy induced by the use of computer technology, the rampant inaccuracy of information contained within credit reports, and the imbalance of power between business credit grantors and consumers. After much debate and testimony, Torres concluded the meeting by stating that it appeared that reform was essential. He ended by stressing the impacts these injustices had upon many Americans, particularly consumers.

The FCRA was passed, and later amended, to enhance the proper maintenance and use of consumer information for credit, employment, and other related purposes. It outlines the responsibilities for all parties involved in the granting of consumer credit. In its inception in the early 1970's, it dealt with relatively small volumes of information and limited technology. In the late 1980's, the amount of information and technology had increased to the point where the original intentions of the law were compromised. This led Congress to hold many hearings and pass amendments to the original law to bring it back into compliance with its original intentions.

Bibliography

Beares, Paul. "Regulation of Consumer Credit." In *Consumer Lending*. Washington, D.C.: American Bankers Association, 1987. An excellent book dealing with all phases of consumer credit. Written from a banker's perspective, but easy reading for the layperson. Discusses in detail the process of granting consumer credit. This chapter in particular focuses on legislation and regulation.

Cole, Robert H. "Regulation of Consumer Credit." In *Consumer and Commercial Credit Management*. 8th ed. Homewood, Ill.: Irwin, 1988. This chapter discusses consumer credit regulation in detail. Chapter 9 in the same volume details the operations of credit reporting agencies.

U.S. Congress. House. Committee on Banking, Finance, and Urban Affairs. Subcommittee on Consumer Affairs and Coinage. *Fair Credit Reporting Act: Hearing*. 101st Congress, 1st session, 1989. Hearings discussing problems, loopholes, and noncompliance by credit reporting agencies.

U.S. Congress. House. Committee on Banking, Finance, and Urban Affairs. Subcommittee on Consumer Affairs and Coinage. *Fair Credit Reporting Act: Hearing*. 102d Congress, 1st session, 1991. Hearings discussing pending legislation designed to modernize and amend the FCRA. Discussions include abuses and reclarifications of the intended purpose of the original act.

U.S. Congress. House. Committee on Banking, Finance, and Urban Affairs. Subcommittee on Consumer Affairs and Coinage. Give Yourself Credit (Guide to Consumer Credit Laws). 102d Congress, 2d session, 1992. A detailed guide covering consumer credit regulations. Uses a question-and-answer approach. Written in everyday language. Actual consumer situations are included. Chapter 5, "Your Credit File," is directly applicable to this article.

U.S. Congress. Senate. Committee on Banking, Housing, and Urban Affairs. Subcommittee on Consumer and Regulatory Affairs. Fair Credit Reporting Act: Hearing. 102d Congress, 1st session, 1991. Senate hearings and testimonials relating to proposed amendments prompted primarily by the explosive growth of consumer credit, in conjunction with implementation of computer technology as a means of managing credit information.

William C. Ward III

Cross-References

The Federal Reserve Act Creates a U.S. Central Bank (1913), p. 240; Congress Passes the Consumer Credit Protection Act (1968), p. 1358; Congress Prohibits Discrimination in the Granting of Credit (1975), p. 1595; Congress Deregulates Banks and Savings and Loans (1980-1982), p. 1757; Bush Responds to the Savings and Loan Crisis (1989), p. 1991.

THE ENVIRONMENTAL PROTECTION AGENCY IS CREATED

Categories of event: Government and business; consumer affairs
Time: December 2, 1970
Locale: Washington, D.C.

A large consensus on the need to consolidate the many programs designed to protect the environment led Congress to approve President Nixon's proposal to create the Environmental Protection Agency

Principal personages:
RICHARD M. NIXON (1913-1994), the president of the United States, 1969-1974
JOHN D. DINGELL (1926-   ), a congressman
RUSSELL E. TRAIN (1920-   ), the chair of the Council on Environmental Quality
Roy L. Ash (1918-   ), the chairman of the President's Advisory Council on Executive Organization
PARKE C. BRINKLEY, the president of the National Agricultural Chemicals Association

Summary of Event

The nature and extent of governmental involvement in setting environmental policy was dramatically changed by two nearly concurrent developments. First, the passage of the National Environmental Policy Act of 1969 established the President's Council on Environmental Quality (CEQ). The second development was initiated on July 9, 1970, when President Richard M. Nixon forwarded a plan to Congress to create an independent Environmental Protection Agency (EPA). The plan required consolidation of several programs from the Interior Department (for example, water quality administration and pesticide research programs), the Department of Health, Education, and Welfare (for example, air pollution control and solid waste management), the Department of Agriculture (for example, pesticide registration, licensing, and monitoring functions), the Federal Radiation Council (for example, setting of radiation standards), and the CEQ (for example, ecological research).

Subsequent congressional hearings and floor debates led to the formal endorsement of President Nixon's plan. Hearings were conducted under the auspices of the House Government Operations Subcommittee on Executive and Legislative Reorganization and the Senate Government Operations Subcommittee on Executive Reorganization and Government Research. Individuals providing supportive testimonies included Russell E. Train, the chairman of the CEQ, Roy L. Ash, the chairman of the President's Advisory Council on Executive Organization, and Parke C. Brinkley, the president of the National Agricultural Chemicals Association.

Train stressed that the EPA would contribute to the effectiveness of efforts to reduce pollution. He indicated that its authority would stem from previously enacted legislation such as the Clean Air Act; the Federal Water Pollution Control Act; the Solid Waste Disposal Act of 1965; the Federal Insecticides, Fungicide, and Rodenticide Act, and the Atomic Energy Act. Additional authority would come from selected administrative units such as the Council on Environmental Quality, the National Air Pollution Control Administration, the Federal Water Quality Administration, and the Bureau of Sports Fisheries and Wildlife. Ash testified that the programs for combating pollution were spread across several agencies at that time and that this fragmentation did not serve the public interest. He envisaged that the EPA would have a 1971 budget of $1.4 billion and approximately six thousand people on staff. He also indicated the following EPA objectives with regard to pollution control: to conduct research and to set standards, to formulate coordinated policy, to recognize new environmental problems as they arise and develop new programs to address them, to integrate pollution control and enforcement, to simplify tasks of state and local governments, and to clarify the responsibility of private industry. Other testimony focused on the advantages to industry and to Congress of dealing with only one agency on pollution control matters.

The House Government Operations Committee endorsed Nixon's reorganization plan on September 23, 1970. Although most House members favored the plan, John D. Dingell (D-Michigan) contended that the new EPA could be a source of new delays and wastes rather than enhancing the effectiveness of pollution control efforts. He criticized the plan because it excluded water and sewer programs in the domain of the Department of Agriculture and the Department of Housing and Urban Development as well as the environmental programs of the Defense and Transportation departments. He sought establishment of a cabinet-level Department of Environmental Quality instead of the proposed EPA. The House eventually endorsed the plan by defeating a veto resolution opposing the creation of the EPA. In the Senate, the Government Operations Committee presented a report expressing its endorsement for the establishment of the EPA. The reorganization plan became effective on December 2, 1970.

Impact of Event

The EPA has been forced to cope with enormous performance expectations. The agency was created at a time of popular dissatisfaction with earlier attempts at pollution control. Responding to demands from the electorate for effective efforts to protect the environment, Congress passed several legislative measures that were ambitious in scope and that served to heighten expectations of what the EPA should deliver. In addition, the EPA's considerable authority stemmed from a legislative mandate to establish and administer standards for industry aimed at protecting the environment in the United States. In a report titled *Research and Development in the Environmental Protection Agency*, the Environmental Research Assessment Committee of the National Research Council elegantly summarized the far-reaching scope and importance of effective environmental policy for industry. The report noted that once agents have been released into the environment as by-products of production, natural processes acting on them can cause changes in the quality of the ambient environment. These changes have potentially adverse consequences for human health and welfare, weather and climate, managed and natural ecosystems, and the use of resources for alternative purposes.

Because environmental protection is a multifaceted and complex topic, it is difficult to assess the risks and costs associated with any decision or policy. Such assessments often are confounded by value judgments (for example, the tradeoff between "necessary" economic progress and "acceptable" environmental damage), conflicting viewpoints (for example, the differing agendas of industry and environmental groups), and a genuine lack of knowledge (for example, uncertainty over the thresholds of exposure to substances likely to harm human beings, and a clear understanding of the causal links between the intensity and duration of environmental pollution and societal costs such as birth defects, poor health, and premature deaths). Decisions and actions of the EPA thus were fated to become the subject of debate.

An objective appraisal of the EPA's decision-making impact should consider the benefits directly attributable to the agency and the costs at which they were achieved. The EPA claimed that emissions of lead, carbon monoxide, and sulfur oxides respectively fell by 97 percent, 41 percent, and 25 percent between 1970 and 1990. Although these benefits appear impressive, they can be attributed in part to factors largely unrelated to environmental regulation.

Cost implications further undermine the benefits associated with EPA regulations. The EPA grew into a massive bureaucracy several times larger than its size at inception. In 1992, it accounted for an operating budget of $4.5 billion and a staff of eighteen thousand. The EPA itself estimated that compliance with its regulations cost Americans $115 billion in 1990, or an annual pollution control cost of $450 per person per year. That figure was a remarkable 2.1 percent of the country's gross national product. That figure was higher than corresponding percentages for most Western European countries and was more than twice the 0.9 percent of GNP spent by the United States in 1972. Furthermore, the EPA's 1992 budget represented one-third of the entire annual spending on federal regulatory bodies.

The burgeoning cost estimates focus attention on value judgments associated with lives saved as a direct consequence of EPA regulations. Some studies show that the cost of saving one life through EPA regulations ranges from $100 million to as much as $5.7 trillion. More generous estimates of the number of lives saved lower this cost. EPA critics such as John Goodman of the National Center for Policy Analysis have questioned the wisdom of incurring such astounding costs, noting that regulating for health is a policy at war with itself, since the reduction of living standards associated with increased regulatory costs will cause additional deaths. Even if the EPA's claims regarding lives saved were accurate, the price paid to save one life through environmental regulation could cover the cost of many other lives at risk from other causes, such as malnutrition.

Businesses have often exploited environmental politics and policies to hurt competitors or to discourage new competition. Ethanol manufacturers, for example, formed a strategic alliance with environmentalists to hurt the oil industry. This alliance influenced the 1990 amendments to the Clean Air Act in a manner designed to enhance demand for their alternative fuel. Many businesses share the view that the EPA possesses sweeping and potent authority that can unreasonably restrict their operations. This view has some merit. Federal agencies usually have either broad authority covering virtually all industries or focused power that deeply affects operations of specific industries. In contrast, the powers of the EPA are unparalleled in both breadth and depth. Nevertheless, some aspects of environmental pollution are less amenable to direct EPA control than others.

Although the EPA derives its authority from several congressional statutes focused either on protecting the environment or on protecting the public against health hazards, the agency does not carry unlimited powers to achieve statutory goals. On the contrary, the EPA is constrained by procedures and limitations that may not be consistent across statutes. As one illustration, the Clean Air Act states that the EPA's decisions concerning ambient air quality should not focus on economic or technical considerations but on protection of public health. In contrast, under the Federal Environmental Pesticide Control Act, the EPA cannot cancel the registration of a pesticide because it poses an unreasonable risk to the public unless the impact of cancellation on economic factors such as prices of agricultural commodities and retail food prices have been considered.

The political ramifications of environmental policy decisions are formidable. Political realities may inhibit EPA regulatory actions even if they are essential from a public interest standpoint, and even if they are mandated by law. Often, EPA policy is influenced heavily by extraneous considerations such as the likelihood of legal challenges. Because almost four out of five EPA decisions are litigated, it appears that environmental policy is shaped more by court orders and settlement negotiations than by EPA directives. For example, one area that has witnessed controversy and litigation involves the Comprehensive Environmental Response, Compensation, and Liability Act (CERCLA) of 1980, more widely known as Superfund. Essentially, Superfund is a large trust fund, financed through tax dollars and levies on petroleum and certain chemical products, that the EPA utilizes to clean up toxic spills and hazardous waste sites. The law also empowers the EPA to pursue parties responsible for these environmental hazards and to get them to reimburse the fund for cleanup costs. This has led to much resentment, because in some cases the parties held responsible were only tenuously linked to the object of the cleanups for which they were forced to pay.

Additional constraints on the EPA are imposed by Congress, through the large number of committees that supervise EPA activities, and the White House, through control over key appointments and budgetary oversight through the Office of Management and Budget. Taken together, the preceding political factors may have significantly undermined the effectiveness of U.S. environmental policy. Some policy regulations overtly subordinate environmental protection goals to political feasibility. For example, EPA regulations discourage the replacement of old plants by holding them to lower pollution standards than new plants. This may be irrational both economically and environmentally, but it is politically essential.

Key functions of the EPA include establishing standards to control and safeguard the environment and conducting research that contributes meaningfully to environmental decision-making. These tasks pose special challenges. First, establishing standards is a difficult undertaking given the enormous imbalance between the current level of knowledge and the amount of work that remains to be done. Of the approximately seventy thousand chemicals in the EPA Toxic Substances Control Inventory in the early 1990's, information concerning health implications were available for only ninety-six hundred. Second, although the EPA's research should aim to provide scientific bases for environmental decision-making, such research is not likely to be perceived as objective by the regulated parties. Given the high frequency of litigation in environmental matters, the EPA is likely to draw on findings from EPA-initiated research programs to bolster its arguments in an adversarial legal setting. Unfortunately, the validity of sound EPA-initiated research may appear suspect because the EPA is a participant in a litigated, adversarial regulation process.

Other evidence suggests that the bulk of available environmental research and knowledge may not be effectively used by the EPA for decision-making purposes. The Environmental Research Assessment Committee reported in 1977 that environmental research and development is actively pursued by many agencies other than the EPA, including the departments of Agriculture; Commerce; Health, Education and Welfare; and Interior. The National Science Foundation and the Energy Research and Development Administration are among the other agencies that contribute. Although most of these research efforts could help decision-making at the EPA, the report found detailed information on the efforts lacking.

In summary, environmental regulation is an extremely vital and complex area. Enforcing environmental policies often constrains industrial operations; therefore, businesses usually resist or oppose EPA directives via judicial means. Environmental regulation is also an enormously costly enterprise. Because of pervasive value judgments in this area, it is not surprising that some people advocate the abolition of the EPA, calling for a replacement with another system based on common law and torts. Others see the effect of the EPA as beneficial in net.

Bibliography

Brimelow, Peter, and Leslie Spencer. "Should We Abolish the EPA?" *Forbes* (September 14, 1992): 432-443. Evaluates common law and torts as an alternative to the bureaucratic approach for tackling environmental problems.
_____ . "You Can't Get There from Here." *Forbes* (July 6, 1992): 59-64. An informative performance assessment of the EPA. Analyzes the complexity of environmental legislation, focuses on cost/benefit factors, and critically appraises the EPA's bureaucratic approach to solving pollution problems.
Committee on Environmental Decision Making. *Decision Making in the Environmental Protection Agency*. Washington, D.C.: National Academy of Sciences,

1977. A useful assessment of the EPA's decision-making framework.

Environmental Research Assessment Committee. *Research and Development in the Environmental Protection Agency.* Washington, D.C.: National Academy of Sciences, 1977. A detailed and insightful account of the EPA's research policies and practices.

Washington Environmental Research Center. *Managing the Environment.* Washington, D.C.: U.S. Government Printing Office, 1973. Although dated, this source contains informative articles on a variety of environmental management topics.

Siva Balasubramanian

Cross-References

Congress Passes the Motor Vehicle Air Pollution Control Act (1965), p. 1265; An Offshore Oil Well Blows Out near Santa Barbara, California (1969), p. 1374; The Three Mile Island Accident Prompts Reforms in Nuclear Power (1979), p. 1693; Bush Signs the Clean Air Act of 1990 (1990), p. 2034; World Leaders Confer on the Environment and Development (1992), p. 2061.

NIXON SIGNS THE OCCUPATIONAL SAFETY AND HEALTH ACT

Category of event: Labor
Time: December 29, 1970
Locale: Washington, D.C.

The Occupational Safety and Health Act of 1970 gave the federal government the responsibility of establishing and enforcing safety standards in the workplace

Principal personages:
>RICHARD M. NIXON (1913-1994), a conservative Republican president who strongly supported the passage of legislation to improve safety in the workplace
>HARRISON A. WILLIAMS, JR. (1919-   ), the principal author of the Occupational Safety and Health Act
>GEORGE P. SHULTZ (1920-   ), the secretary of labor during the hearings on the bill, a strong supporter of the legislation
>JIMMY CARTER (1924-   ), the Democratic president who in the late 1970's undertook a substantial revision of OSHA procedures

Summary of Event

On December 29, 1970, President Richard M. Nixon signed the Occupational Safety and Health Act, mandating that the U.S. Department of Labor establish health and safety standards in the workplace with the goal of achieving the "highest degree of health and safety protection for the employee." This was one of a series of statutes, sometimes referred to as "public interest labor laws," that began with the Landrum-Griffin Labor-Management Reporting and Disclosure Act of 1959. The purview of OSHA is expansive, involving both health and safety standards. In the 1970's, the Occupational Safety and Health Administration (OSHA), created by the act, stressed direct government regulation of safety in the workplace. In the 1980's, OSHA extended its efforts to the communication of information, primarily through the labeling of hazardous chemicals.

OSHA enforcement involves inspections, financial penalties, and recourse to criminal prosecutions. The act grew out of growing concern for issues related to the environment and awareness of dangers in the workplace, particularly asbestosis (a lung disease caused by breathing asbestos particles), respiratory diseases among cotton workers, and various forms of cancer. Between 1964 and 1969, the injury rate in manufacturing increased by almost 25 percent. Efforts to address black lung disease had been addressed in the Federal Coal Mine Health and Safety Act of 1969. Other acts had been passed to protect certain workers, such as longshoremen and construction workers, but the OSHA regulations superseded these laws and extended to many previously uncovered sectors. Causing considerable controversy were situations in which employers knew of dangers but workers did not.

The high cost of safety made it unlikely that standards would be met unless mandated by government statute. It was also hoped that OSHA would alleviate some of the problems associated with state-administered workers' compensation programs. Some injuries were not compensated or were not adequately compensated, yet the costs of workers' compensation programs were very high. Advocates of new regulations proposed injury prevention as a way of reducing compensation payments. In addition, it was argued that workers' compensation programs might cause people to feign injuries, be less cautious, or stay out of work longer than necessary. By increasing time at work and reducing expenditures on workers' compensation, increased safety would be better for the individuals directly involved and for society as a whole. It was also pointed out that since employers paid into the workers' compensation program and since benefits to workers differed among states, the cost of injuries was not uniform among the states. As a result, incentives for employers to provide safe workplaces were not the same. In addition, a given safety standard might have different costs in different states, depending on such factors as wage rates and prevailing technology in use. Secretary of Labor George Shultz pointed to the increasing incidence of workplace injuries and the costs of medical care and workers' compensation claims as evidence of the need for passage of the OSHA law. In congressional hearings it was pointed out that in some European countries national standards had been imposed, but they had met with mixed results. In sectors such as steel and chemicals, the U.S. safety record was far better than that of the United Kingdom, even though the latter country had a national safety program.

The Senate bill (S. 2193, P.L. 91-596) was proposed by Harrison A. Williams, Jr., of New Jersey, its principal author. The act created three new federal agencies: the Occupational Safety and Health Administration (OSHA) in the Department of Labor; the National Institute of Occupational Safety and Health (NIOSH) in the Department of Health, Education, and Welfare; and an independent Occupational Safety and Health Review Commission. The first two agencies were to conduct inspections and investigations, and the third was intended to hear appeals by employers relating to the decisions of the first two agencies. A 1978 Supreme Court decision prevented OSHA from conducting inspections without cause, limiting the ability to catch violators in the act. The decision, however, allowed for warrants permitting inspections. States maintained the right to establish their own safety programs provided that they receive prior approval from OSHA. State standards therefore had to match those at the federal level or provide greater protection. OSHA provided workers with a form of redress beyond that provided through collective bargaining agreements. Equally important, the Supreme Court ruled in *Alexander v. Gardner-Denver* (1974) that workers could seek statutory redress even after making use of the grievance procedures established in a collective bargaining agreement.

The mandate of the OSHA law represented a shift from issues of cost efficiency in production to equity. The goal was to eliminate injuries in the workplace without explicit consideration of costs and benefits. The legislation represented a movement away from a system for determining reparations after an accident to an approach intended to set standards that would prevent accidents. OSHA brought to the forefront a number of issues central to the future of industrial relations in the United States. Previous legislation such as the Fair Labor Standards Act of 1938 and its amendments set limits on wages, hours, and other conditions of employment, but the way production was conducted was left to be decided by employers and workers. The theory of "compensating wage differentials" argued that unsafe, high-risk jobs would require higher wages to attract workers. Workers who chose those occupations would be compensated for the risk by higher wages. In cases in which the allocation of workers among jobs was unacceptable, unions, through collective bargaining, would negotiate a package of wages and safety standards mutually agreeable to both the employer and the employee. The justification for direct government intrusion into the way production was conducted rested on two premises. To the extent that the way goods are produced affects people other than the employer and the employee, the interest of those others may justify a role for the government. As an example, exposure of pregnant women to certain chemicals may be a health hazard not only to them but also to their future children. Society may feel compelled to limit such exposure in the interests of the unborn even if the women are willing to risk exposure. OSHA policies sought to control the social costs of unsafe workplaces. A second justification arises in cases in which the risk of disease or injury is not known or is underestimated by the worker. In this context, workers are unable to make informed decisions. From a purely monetary perspective, there may even exist incentives for employers to conceal true risks from employees. In this case, the role of the government may take the form of setting standards or providing information.

Impact of Event

From its very passage, the OSHA law was plagued with problems. The act provided no penalties to employees who were careless or deliberately unsafe, only an encouragement to act safely. The act provided for sanctions against employers including citations and fines. When corrective measures prescribed by OSHA were not adhered to, the agency had recourse to the courts. In 1972, twenty-four hundred citations were issued under the act. The number increased to forty-three thousand in 1973. Companies found it especially difficult to understand what OSHA expected and how the OSHA standards were to be implemented. The Subcommittee on Labor of the Committee on Labor and Public Welfare of the United States Senate held numerous oversight hearings at which employers vociferously addressed the uneven enforcement of the act, the trivial nature of many standards, and the excessive costs of adherence to standards. Enforcement efforts have been criticized for unevenness and for responding to the preferences of the political party in office.

Since the mandate of OSHA can be carried out either by state programs or at the federal level, any assessment must look at the two distinct modes of implementation. Although states were allowed to establish their own mechanisms for enforcement, standards were to at least equal those at the federal level. In part, the federal statute was a response to the failure of state programs to adequately address the problems of workplace injuries, yet the statute allowed for state implementation of the program for two principal reasons. First, some legislators were concerned with states' rights, particularly in the light of problems with implementing federal programs. Second, there were more than two thousand state inspectors, with millions of dollars spent on safety by states. The federal government was not interested in dismantling the state programs or assuming this additional cost.

In September, 1991, a fire at an Imperial Food Products poultry plant in Hamlet, North Carolina, killed twenty-five workers who were trapped in the factory after the employer had locked the exit doors from the outside. OSHA found serious deficiencies in the enforcement of standards at the state level, precipitating an examination of the state programs. Particular attention was paid to the failure of states to adjust their standards to changes in federal rules. States with separate programs included Alaska, Arizona, California, Hawaii, Indiana, Iowa, Kentucky, Maryland, Michigan, Minnesota, Nevada, New Mexico, Oregon, South Carolina, Tennessee, Utah, Vermont, Virginia, Washington, and Wyoming, in addition to Puerto Rico and the Virgin Islands.

At the federal level, critics of OSHA have come from many camps. Employers have argued that OSHA rules and regulations are trivial and have led to large increases in the cost of doing business. Organized labor has at times argued that the standards are not stringent enough, while in other cases, in which the standards have led to job losses, unions have argued that the standards are too strict. In 1990, maximum fines for each violation were raised from $10,000 to $30,000, and willful violations that led to death were changed from misdemeanors to felonies.

Despite annual expenditures in the early 1990's of approximately $400 million, there is little evidence that OSHA has had the effect of reducing injuries in the workplace. Two explanations are given for the ineffectiveness of OSHA. Some argue that the penalties for violating safety standards are so low that it is more profitable for firms to violate the standards and pay fines if caught rather than make changes to meet standards. In addition, the likelihood of a firm being inspected is very small, so the chances of being caught are very low. The second explanation is that OSHA has concentrated on standards for machinery and equipment while ignoring the human aspect in many accidents. Safe machines do not ensure a safe workplace in the absence of safe operation and supervision. The question is why Congress has continued to support OSHA.

Two factors seem to explain continued support. One is that OSHA has been able to increase compliance. In other words, it is able to impose penalties that reduce the likelihood of firms repeatedly violating standards. It can force compliance even if that does not translate immediately into fewer injuries. A second factor is the significant indirect influence of OSHA on the structure of American industry. Large firms and unionized firms tend to be safer in part because of the ability to bear the costs of increased safety and also because of economies of scale associated with safety. An expenditure to make a machine safer will be more cost effective if the machine is used by ten people rather than by one person. OSHA, by concentrating on sectors with the greatest incidence of injuries, intrudes most on small, nonunion operations. As a consequence, costs are driven up in these firms, giving large firms and unionized firms cost advantages. These are the same firms that are able to influence political decisions the most. It comes as no surprise that these firms support continuation of OSHA. Support may come in the guise of promotion of safety, but large firms also gain a cost advantage as a result of safety and health regulation.

A number of lessons have been learned from experience with OSHA. One is the need to consider cost effectiveness in establishing safety standards. In this context, the move toward performance-based regulatory policies was inevitable. In October, 1978, Eula Bingham, director of OSHA during the Jimmy Carter Administration, modified or eliminated almost a thousand OSHA regulations. President Ronald Reagan's efforts to deregulate led to further reductions in OSHA efforts. The total budget for OSHA went from $97 million in 1975 to $248 million in 1989. By 1989, despite the increase in budget, the staff was still smaller than in 1980, with most of the reduction coming from enforcement personnel.

During the Reagan Administration, the Office of Management and Budget (OMB) was given oversight power. OSHA had to submit proposed reforms to the OMB, which could then hold up implementation. A 1986 court decision required that OMB not restrict OSHA when it faced a statutory deadline. Unions used this rule on behalf of OSHA to get regulations on formaldehyde and lead, among other job hazards. The Office of Management and Budget has estimated that the regulatory costs of OSHA were $2.7 billion in 1987 and $12.7 billion in 1989. The growth in OSHA is evidenced by the following statistics. In 1972, there were 28,900 inspections, 89,600 discovered violations, and $2.1 million in penalties. In contrast, in 1989, there were 58,400 inspections, 154,900 discovered violations, and $45 million in penalties.

Bibliography

Bartel, Ann P., and Lacy Glenn Thomas. "Direct and Indirect Effects of Regulations: A New Look at OSHA's Impact." *Journal of Law and Economics* 28 (1985): 1-26. Data for the 1974-1978 period show no significant effect of OSHA on injury rates.

Gray, Wayne B., and Carol Adaire Jones. "Longitudinal Patterns of Compliance with OSHA in the Manufacturing Sector." *The Journal of Human Resources* 26 (Fall, 1991): 623-653. This empirical study looks at the pattern of response to the regulatory efforts of OSHA.

U.S. Congress. Senate. Committee on Labor and Public Welfare. Subcommittee on Labor. *Legislative History of the Occupational Safety and Health Act of 1970*. 92d Congress, 1st session. Senate document 2193. Documents the various amendments to the bill and the positions of interested groups.

Viscusi, W. Kip. *Fatal Tradeoffs*. New York: Oxford University Press, 1992. A detailed economic discussion of how risk is evaluated. Empirical evidence is used to examine the effectiveness of OSHA in the 1970's and 1980's. The author is the leading economic authority on risk in the workplace.

Warren, A. C., Jr., ed. "Occupational Safety and Health." *Law and Contemporary*

Problems 38 (Summer/Autumn, 1974): 583-757. A collection of eight articles looking at the legal and economic aspects associated with the implementation of OSHA.

John F. O'Connell

Cross-References

The U.S. Government Creates the Department of Commerce and Labor (1903), p. 86; Congress Passes the Pure Food and Drug Act (1906), p. 128; Roosevelt Signs the Fair Labor Standards Act (1938), p. 792; The Landrum-Griffin Act Targets Union Corruption (1959), p. 1122; The Three Mile Island Accident Prompts Reforms in Nuclear Power (1979), p. 1693; Bush Signs the Clean Air Act of 1990 (1990), p. 2034.

NEW YORK STATE ALLOWS OFF-TRACK BETTING

Category of event: Government and business
Time: 1971
Locale: New York State

New York State established off-track betting in 1971, arguing that it would raise funds for education

Principal personages:
PAUL FINO (1913-   ), a New York congressman instrumental in creating an atmosphere favorable to passage of off-track betting legislation
PAUL SCREVANE (1914-   ), the first administrator in charge of off-track betting
STEVEN G. CRIST (1956-   ), a noted racing journalist, one of the earliest and most persistent critics of off-track betting

Summary of Event

During the immediate post-World War II period, horse racing in the United States was a vehicle for gambling and little more. State officials posed few objections, as wagering on thoroughbred racing was a bonanza for those states in which it flourished. Governments came to view racing as a cash cow, to be milked to provide funding for a variety of purposes.

Along with casino gambling in Nevada, betting on horses at tracks was one of the few forms of gambling that were legal in the United States during the early 1960's. It would be difficult to estimate the total amount of illegal gambling that occurred in the country in forms ranging from numbers rackets to social card games to illegal bets on football, basketball, and baseball games and other sporting events. Most probably, illegal wagering could be measured in the tens of billions of dollars annually.

Fear of taints from gambling, which had caused scandals in baseball, football, and basketball, led leaders of those sports to oppose legalized gambling of any kind, although newspapers regularly reported odds and point spreads on games. In 1975, for example, the state of Delaware introduced a lottery based on scores of National Football League (NFL) games. The NFL sued the state on the ground that the lottery would harm the sport's reputation. The lottery was unpopular anyway, because gamblers soon learned that they could get larger payouts on the Las Vegas betting line than through the lottery.

Horse racing was different, having a tradition of wagering. Where wagering existed, controls were tight and had been tested over time. Legal wagering on horse races, however, required attendance at the tracks. This distinction helped make the sport appealing. Wealthy gamblers might travel to Las Vegas casinos; the middle class drove to the local track. Those unwilling or uninterested in going to the track to bet could do so with illegal bookies, who were not difficult to find.

One exception offered a suggestion of what might have been and what was to come.

The Irish Sweepstakes, initiated in 1930, combined horse racing with a lottery. The sweepstakes was popular in some circles, and although it was illegal, the results were duly reported by the press. The country seemed to approve of that type of lottery and, by extension, gambling on horse racing. If that was true, proponents of wagering suggested, legalized gambling tied to races would not face strong opposition and could provide a basis for taxation. The craving for additional revenues that could come painlessly through legalization of wagering pressured legislatures to act.

Legalization of any form of gambling was a touchy matter, since throughout the country there were powerful forces in opposition. Equally strong forces favored gambling taxes, however, since the alternatives of raising other taxes or cutting spending were unpalatable.

There were several ways of gathering gambling taxes. One possibility was off-track betting (OTB), tying a new form of gambling to one accepted in almost all states. Another method would be casino gambling. The somewhat unsavory reputation of casinos and fears that they would attract an unwholesome element mitigated against them.

Because wagering on horses was already lawful, taxing it seemed to be the best means of raising tax revenues from gambling. The arguments were vaguely reminiscent of those employed in 1932, when Democratic presidential candidate Franklin D. Roosevelt urged the repeal of Prohibition. Such an action, accompanied by imposition of taxes on alcohol, would raise revenues, provide enjoyment for a portion of the population, and create jobs. A 1963 poll of New Yorkers indicated the same types of sentiments. Every segment of the population—all races, religions, and income and age groups—favored OTB. Even churchgoers, who were thought to be in opposition, came out in favor, by a margin of 69 percent in favor to 29 percent opposed.

Some trepidation remained. One-fourth of the respondents thought that OTB would have an unfavorable impact on the lower classes, and a third of them offered this as their major reason for opposition. Some saw opportunities for graft in OTB, while others feared an influx of organized crime. Moreover, there appeared to be significant differences in the public's perceptions regarding wagering at tracks, which seemed like a sport, compared to betting at OTB installations, with the latter somehow suspect. Fully 64 percent of respondents said that they would never bet at an OTB installation; 21 percent thought they might do so less than once a week; another 13 percent expected to be there once a week; and only 2 percent said they would be daily attendees.

OTB thus had strong support. The only real questions were when, how, and under whose management it would take place. A subsidiary question was whether it, like the Irish Sweepstakes, would be connected in some way with a lottery.

This was an appealing notion. Lotteries had a long history. During the early national period, many jurisdictions had employed them in response to ongoing resentment against direct taxation. Beginning in 1934, several state legislatures debated lotteries, most of them modeled on the Irish Sweepstakes. Proponents hoped to overcome opposition by earmarking the proceeds for worthwhile causes. A proposal in New

York, for example, would have used funds generated by lotteries for unemployment relief. At the time, Congressman Edward Kennedy called for a national lottery, but his version would not have been based on racing. Nothing came of these proposals.

Congressman Paul Fino (D-New York) introduced bills for a national lottery every year from 1953 into the early 1960's. Fino developed the strongest case made to that time for lotteries, noting that not only would funds be raised through them for worthwhile public causes, but there could be tax cuts as well. In addition, organized crime, which controlled illegal betting, would be dealt a crushing blow.

In 1953, the New Hampshire legislature began debating the worthiness of a lottery. Some of the suggested lottery plans involved a tie-in with thoroughbred racing, but most did not. In 1964, a lottery based upon numbers drawn at random was introduced. When the federal government declared its intention to tax the proceeds from that lottery, New Hampshire started to base lottery drawings on the results of horse races, which were exempt from the wagering tax. The initial success of this lottery encouraged other states, especially in the Northeast, to accelerate their plans for such gambling.

New York legislators considered such a lottery bill, with the funds generated to be used for hospitals. In 1964, a private concern, the American Sweepstakes Corporation, succeeded in placing on the California ballot a proposal whereby it would have an exclusive ten-year franchise to operate a statewide lottery combined with horse racing. The company intended to remit 65 percent of the take to the state, the funds to be used to help operate schools. American Sweepstakes would get 13 percent, and the remaining 22 percent would go for prizes and operating costs. Opposition to gambling, a poor presentation of the plan, and the relatively low payout contributed to the plan being defeated overwhelmingly at the polls.

In the absence of intervention by racing interests, in 1971 New York State instituted OTB. At the time, proponents claimed that OTB would raise revenues, help the tracks, and lessen organized crime's grip on sports betting. Racing industry leaders, including the influential Jockey Club, were adamantly opposed to OTB and would have nothing to do with it. This opposition perhaps erased racing's best hope for prosperity and set the stage for the decline of thoroughbred racing in the United States.

Impact of Event

Handled intelligently, OTB might have evolved into the kind of introduction to racing that Little League provides for baseball. At attractive locales, providing restaurants, bars, and chairs and tables at which patrons could socialize and watch the races on multiple television sets, OTB parlors might have become akin to social clubs to which couples might repair for an afternoon's or evening's entertainment. Familiarized with racing in this way, the next step then might be a visit to the track itself and the transformation of bystanders into fans. Several industry leaders, most notably journalist Steven G. Crist, recommended the establishment of a string of such OTB installations. Crist and others who supported him were ignored.

As it turned out, the New York OTB parlors primarily were storefronts and abandoned restaurants. Rarely cleaned, without chairs or furniture of any kind, and with poor facilities for following races, they attracted a generally seedy clientele concerned with gambling and not at all interested in the sport. Moreover, those who wagered at the track got better odds, as did those who used the services of illegal bookies. Finally, middle-class Americans, seeing the kinds of people who frequented the OTB parlors, got the impression that the same types would be found in great numbers at the tracks. This discouraged attendance at the tracks. Rather than introducing people to horse racing and encouraging them to visit the track, OTB actually kept people away.

Nevertheless, OTB was a financial success. The state took the bulk of the earnings and distributed a small amount to the tracks that made wagering possible. In 1978, OTB betting totaled $1.2 billion, against $1.6 billion at the tracks themselves. By 1993, approximately 100,000 people a day were betting on races in the state's OTB parlors. Most of them rarely visited the tracks.

How much OTB harmed track attendance is a matter of contention, but that it had an impact is beyond doubt. The fact that track attendance in New York declined by almost half from 1970 through 1977 can be ascribed largely to OTB. Paul Screvane, the state official in charge of OTB, claimed the tracks actually benefited, noting that in its first five years OTB contributed $140 million to racing. Screvane ignored the many millions of dollars invested in the tracks, the horses, and other parts of the sport. In fact, the investment in racing and ancillary activities in the state was more than the total for professional baseball, basketball, and football combined, and these other sports made many times what racing did, by selling television rights.

In 1977, New York Racing Association (NYRA) Secretary and Vice President James P. Heffernan told reporter Gene Stevens that he believed that the primary function of the NYRA was to raise money for the state of New York. A decade and a half later, this attitude still prevailed. Of the wagering dollar, approximately 84 cents was returned to the parimutuel bettor. The states offering horse racing did their best to get as much of the rest as possible. Even so, horse racing offered a more attractive return to bettors than did most lotteries, which typically returned about half of the amount spent on tickets as prizes.

The decline in track attendance barely troubled owners of and investors in the leading stables. Owners primarily enjoyed the status and the amenities that came from being at the center of the sport. Large crowds in attendance were unnecessary.

Not until the early 1990's did those few industry leaders who had favored OTB recognize the dangers the Jockey Club had foreseen. D. Wayne Lucas, whose interests were in breeding and training, not racing, opined that without fans at the track there are no tracks, and without the tracks, little remained for people in his position. Even the NYRA, which had fumbled opportunities for a quarter of a century, finally awoke to its errors. Some of its leaders talked of participation in a revamped OTB industry, based on the kinds of plans presented earlier by Crist and others.

They might have been thinking about an already existing facility outside of Pittsburgh, in New Castle, Pennsylvania. There, in a shopping mall, the English wagering firm of Ladbroke Group PLC constructed an establishment that was clean and attractive and had places to eat and drink. Satellite dishes on the roof brought in televised races from several tracks, on which the customers wagered. It opened in 1990 and accommodated an average of eleven hundred patrons daily, more than attended events at many tracks. Other similar operations opened in other states. Some people within the racing industry, noting that Ladbroke had purchased four tracks, suspected that the firm anticipated a time when tracks would exist merely to provide races for offtrack bettors. Manager Ted McKenna thought the racetrack had become a necessary evil for OTB. In other words, the tail of OTB was wagging the dog of the tracks. Had places such as New Castle been opened when OTB became a reality in New York, they might have provided a more positive introduction to the track.

In 1989, Suffolk Downs closed down, and Hialeah was forced to suspend operations. These events were to thoroughbred racing what the shuttering of Yankee Stadium would have been for baseball. Although Hialeah reopened in November, 1991, the one-year recess was shocking. The closing of one of the nation's premier tracks was barely noted outside the sport, however, as few Americans were concerned about the state of horse racing. In 1993, New York Governor Mario Cuomo announced that the entire OTB situation would be reviewed.

Bibliography

Clotfelter, Charles, and Philip J. Cook. *Selling Hope: State Lotteries in America.* Cambridge, Mass.: Harvard University Press, 1989. The best study of the lottery in America, with a discussion of off-track betting.

Crist, Steven. *The Horse Traders: Inside the Billion Dollar Breeding Industry That Rules Racing Today.* New York: Norton, 1986. Crist is a premier track journalist who in this book analyzes the economics of the industry.

Reed, William F. "Fading Fast." *Sports Illustrated* 74 (April 22, 1991): 90-96. Reed documents the decline of thoroughbred racing, placing much of the blame on the rise of organized gambling.

Seligman, Daniel. "Privatize the Bookie." *Fortune* 123 (June 3, 1991): 248-249. A column suggesting that New York State would raise more revenues through OTB if it were privatized. Identifies inefficient management by the state as reducing profits from OTB.

Wolfson, Louis. *The Future Looks Bleak for the Thoroughbred Racing and Breeding Industry.* Miami, Fla.: Wolfson, 1986. One of the leading critics of the way off-track betting developed in New York offers his suggestions for alternatives.

Robert Sobel

Cross-References

Charles Ponzi Cheats Thousands in an Investment Scheme (1919-1920), p. 324; The Yankees Acquire Babe Ruth (1920), p. 341; The Brooklyn Dodgers Move to Los Angeles (1957-1958), p. 1076; Atlantic City Legalizes Casino Gambling (1976), p. 1600; The Boston Celtics Sell Shares in the Team (1986), p. 1939.

NIXON REMOVES AN EMBARGO ON TRADE WITH CHINA

Category of event: International business and commerce
Time: 1971
Locale: The United States and the People's Republic of China

President Richard M. Nixon took a step toward world peace by announcing a change regarding U.S. trade policy concerning the People's Republic of China

Principal personages:
RICHARD M. NIXON (1913-1994), the president of the United States, 1969-1974
HENRY KISSINGER (1923-   ), Nixon's national security adviser
ZHOU ENLAI (1898-1976), the premier of the People's Republic of China

Summary of Event

"I will undertake what I deeply hope will become a journey for peace, peace not just for our generation but for future generations on this earth we share together." So said President Richard M. Nixon in a televised speech on July 15, 1971. The speech announced a major shift in U.S. trade policy with the People's Republic of China. On February 21, 1972, at the invitation of Premier Zhou Enlai of the People's Republic of China, Nixon began a historic week-long visit to Beijing that created new and lasting commercial relations between the two countries. On February 27, the two leaders signed the Shanghai Communiqué, establishing some basic guidelines for U.S. and Chinese economic policy reforms, setting the stage to re-establish mutually beneficial trade relations.

Trade relations between the two countries had changed dramatically following the outbreak of the Korean War. Twenty-two years earlier, on June 28, 1950, President Harry S Truman had declared a national emergency and placed an embargo on all U.S. exports to China. He was granted authority to do this primarily under the Export Control Act of 1949 and the Trading with the Enemy Act of 1917. When Communist China had entered the Korean War early in 1949, the United States began imposing selective trade controls on that country. By July 20, 1950, the United States had successfully blockaded all strategic export items, including ammunition, atomic energy materials, and petroleum. In October, 1950, Chinese Communist forces joined the North Korean army.

The trade embargo and the trade controls imposed by allies of the United States were basically acts of economic warfare designed to weaken China's capacity to wage war in Korea. Partners in the North Atlantic Treaty Organization (NATO) had placed greater restrictions on their trade with China than with other Communist countries such as the Soviet Union. As a result, the list of products banned for export to China was more comprehensive than those for other Communist countries. The effectiveness of the embargo, however, was strongly undermined. If China could not buy goods from Western Europe or Japan, it could get them from the Soviet Union or Eastern Europe, if perhaps at a higher cost.

After the Korean War ended, commercial pressures for decontrol began to build in a number of Western European countries and in Japan. Removal of many of the restrictions occurred in a piecemeal fashion as allies began to disregard them. As early as 1957, the United States officially reduced the list of banned exports to China, putting China on the same basis as other Communist countries. As a result, allied controls did not prevent China from getting most goods but merely imposed higher resource costs on the Chinese economy.

Between 1949 and 1970, economic growth in Communist China fluctuated. In 1950 and 1951, the country experienced strong growth, but it leveled off in 1952. From 1953 to 1956, the growth continued under a program of expansion known as the First Five-Year Plan. Another leveling occurred in 1957, followed by the Great Leap Forward of 1958 to 1960, which produced dramatic growth followed by a depression. From 1960 to 1962, the deep depression affected most areas of the Chinese economy, including agriculture, industry, and foreign trade. Gradual economic recovery began after the 1962 harvest and continued until 1966, when China's economic growth rate exceeded that of the Great Leap Forward. The Cultural Revolution beginning in 1966 once again set China's economy back.

On March 28, 1969, U.S. National Security Adviser Henry Kissinger gave a directive to review the U.S. trade embargo with China. As a result, the United States modified trade controls against China in two ways. First, the ban on travel to the People's Republic of China was removed. Second, the United States allowed U.S. tourists to purchase up to $100 worth of Chinese goods and bring them back to the United States. These steps, perhaps in combination with growing Soviet aggressiveness around the world at the time, caused China to begin a reassessment of its policies concerning the United States.

When President Nixon took his historic trip to China in February of 1972, he was well received. In addition to promoting the progressive development of trade between the two countries, the Shanghai Communiqué of February 27 also stated that both sides viewed bilateral trade as mutually beneficial and agreed that economic relations based on equality were in the interest of citizens of both countries.

Nixon's televised speech had announced a policy shift that was formalized in the Shanghai Communiqué, but it was not until 1980 that trade relations with China normalized. In February, 1977, President Jimmy Carter's administration announced that it would continue to follow the guidelines of the Shanghai Communiqué and sought normalization of trade with China. In 1979, Vice President Walter Mondale gave a speech in Beijing stating that U.S. trade interests were served by China's expanding exports of natural resources and industrial products. On January 24, 1980, Congress passed the U.S.-China Trade Agreement, granting most-favored-nation status for Chinese exports to the United States. As President Carter noted, this agreement was the most important step that the United States could take to provide greater economic benefits to both countries. The two nations had come a long way since the early 1970's in reconciling trade relations.

Impact of Event

Although learning to trade with China was a complex undertaking, many companies succeeded. For example, after the signing of the Shanghai Communiqué, ten American companies were invited to attend the Canton Trade Fair held in the spring of 1972. One of these companies stands out as an example of establishing successful long-term trade with China. Seabrook International Foods, Inc., was a manufacturer of finished fabrics and home furnishing products, also distributing frozen foods. By 1979, its annual consolidated sales were $827.9 million. Seabrook's success prompted questions concerning trade with China. What factors helped Seabrook succeed? Did the success depend on the particular line of products, or did other more general factors contribute? What other companies would succeed in establishing trade with China? Would many other companies move jobs to the Far East, as Seabrook had?

The National Council for U.S.-China Trade conducted a survey and found several common factors in companies trading in China. The survey found that such factors as the managerial attitude of the U.S. firm, its product characteristics, and familiarity with the Chinese culture could all affect a company's success. A company was more successful when its employees were sincere, patient, and able to establish personal relationships with their Chinese partners. Successful products filled empty product niches rather than competing with established products. An understanding of Chinese business practices, social customs, politics, and language also improved chances of success. If a company lacked understanding of differences in business practices, negotiation styles, and social customs, it was more likely to fail. Differences in ideology and culture, insincerity, and communication breakdown also ranked high on the list of reasons why American companies failed in their ventures into China.

The survey drew five important primary conclusions. First, it found that companies experienced in trading and negotiating with the Chinese were more likely to enter future negotiations. Second, most firms agreed that the Chinese were concerned with establishing long-term relationships. As a result, a firm had to be prepared to invest time, money, and resources to build up a good working relationship. Third, the survey showed that the type of industry did not seem to matter. The Chinese were willing to trade many different products, as long as they fit with national priorities. Therefore, companies had to be familiar with national policies. Fourth, knowledge of Chinese business practices and understanding of Chinese culture was not in itself a key to success. A company also needed a genuine interest in working toward common goals. Fifth, in doing business with China, the American firm had to face the problems of conducting trade with a socialist economy. A firm had to learn how to deal with cultural differences and complexities involved in a trading atmosphere in which political and economic relations merge.

An American company could do business with one or more Chinese foreign trade corporations, which included the China National Machinery Import and Export

Corporation, the China National Technical Import and Export Corporation, the China National Chemicals Import and Export Corporation, the China National Metals and Minerals Import and Export Corporation, the China National Light Industrial Products Import and Export Corporation, the China National Native Produce and Animals By-Products Import and Export Corporation, the China National Arts and Crafts Import and Export Corporation, the China National Textiles Import and Export Corporation, and the China National Cereals, Oils, and Foodstuffs Import and Export Corporation. Five industries took the greatest advantage of the open trade with China: textiles, tourism, petroleum products, computers and high-tech equipment, and insurance.

By 1980, textiles had grown to about 20 percent of the total volume of annual exports from China, making up 3 percent of the world's textile trade. Chinese economic planners saw the potential for increased exports of Chinese textiles through targeting the United States as one of China's major markets.

Although tourism was not listed as a national priority, by 1980 it had become a potentially large source of foreign exchange earnings for China. Because of a shortage of hotels and other facilities, the Chinese had to turn away almost 75 percent of all tourist applications. Nearly one million tourists visited China in 1979 alone. The potential for increased tourism induced the Chinese to build more hotels. A number of major hotel chains discussed prospects of constructing hotels in China.

Until 1956, geologists considered China as a nation poor in petroleum resources. In that year, oil was discovered in T'a-ch'eng. China soon had enough oil to meet its needs, with surplus oil available for export. This presented several major oil companies with the opportunity to expand through offshore drilling. By 1979, China exported 10 percent of its production of crude oil, maintaining that level throughout the 1980's.

Development of trade in computers and other equipment involving high technology depended on the world's political climate. The Soviet invasion of Afghanistan in 1979 led to a softening of the military stance the United States took with China, clearing the way for sales of military support and dual-use equipment. Companies began to sell computer systems with general-purpose simulation capabilities for training and advanced research. For example, companies such as Electronics Associates, Inc., were able to make deals that previously were impossible. In 1979, that company sold a $4.47 million computer to Harbin University. In 1980, it sold a $10.5 million computer to the China Precision Machinery Corporation in Beijing. Although companies still faced the frustration of having to obtain export licenses to complete sales, the open door to China created huge opportunities for those willing to take the risk.

Because U.S. investors faced various risks with their ventures in China, insurance was vital to establishing and maintaining business relationships. These risks included those involved with currency fluctuations and with the relationships between capitalist and socialist firms, along with all the usual risks of business dealings. Major U.S. corporations formed joint ventures with the Chinese. The American International Group, Inc., merged in 1980 with the People's Insurance Company of China to become known as the China-American Insurance Company. Other companies soon followed.

Although the Chinese market was important for some American industries, products, and firms, the Chinese market was limited for American goods in general. Establishing trade with China was almost certainly of greater political than economic importance. Implementing the guidelines of the Shanghai Communiqué created a policy that led to normalization of relations between China and the United States through the trade channel. Becoming trading partners and working for mutual economic benefit moved the countries, and the world, closer to peace.

Bibliography

Buss, Claude A. *China: The People's Republic of China and Richard Nixon.* San Francisco, Calif.: W. H. Freeman, 1972. A thin volume giving an outline of Chinese history as well as a discussion of relationships with the United States.

Choudhury, G. W. *China in World Affairs: The Foreign Policy of the PRC Since 1970.* Boulder, Colo.: Westview Press, 1982. A good general source on China's foreign policy. Chapter 4 discusses Nixon's visits to China. Other chapters discuss relationships with other countries.

Cohen, Jerome Alan. "The Origins of the Embargo: A Short History." In *China Trade Prospects and U.S. Policy,* by Jerome Alan Cohen, Robert F. Dernberger, and John R. Garson. New York: Praeger, 1971. Written before the signing of the Shanghai Communiqué, this book nevertheless gives important highlights of the event, makes predictions as to who would benefit, and lists reasons why the embargo should be removed. Some predictions proved to be correct; others were wildly wrong.

Congressional Quarterly, Inc. *China and U.S. Foreign Policy.* Edited by William B. Dickinson, Jr. Washington, D.C.: Author, 1973. Includes a brief summary of U.S. policy toward China along with a diplomatic history. Discusses House and Senate hearings on China and includes the text of statements by Nixon concerning China, including his televised speech from July 15, 1971.

De Pauw, John W. "Introduction." In *U.S.-Chinese Trade Negotiations.* New York: Praeger, 1981. An excellent summary of the events. Also provides interesting tables showing increases in U.S. trade with China between 1970 and 1980. Good on specific details of negotiating business contracts, examples of difficulties encountered with Chinese trade, and methods for overcoming the impediments inherent in the U.S.-Chinese trade system.

Tung, Rosalie L. *U.S.-China Trade Negotiations.* New York: Pergamon Press, 1982. Contains the findings of the questionnaire from the National Council for U.S.-China Trade. Each chapter details case studies of separate success stories. Includes interviews with presidents of major corporations. Interesting, informative, and easy to read.

Patrick Bridgemon

Cross-References

The General Agreement on Tariffs and Trade Is Signed (1947), p. 914; China Begins Its First Five-Year Plan (1953), p. 1003; The Asian Development Bank Is Chartered (1965), p. 1276; China Begins the Cultural Revolution (1966), p. 1281; Great Britain and China Agree on Control of Hong Kong (1984), p. 1887; Avon Begins Operations in China (1990's), p. 2012.

THE UNITED STATES SUFFERS ITS FIRST TRADE DEFICIT SINCE 1888

Category of event: International business and commerce
Time: 1971
Locale: The United States

In 1971, the United States suffered its first trade deficit since 1888, importing more than it exported, on its way to becoming a net debtor nation by the end of 1987

Principal personages:
RICHARD M. NIXON (1913-1994), the president of the United States, 1969-1974
RONALD REAGAN (1911-   ), the president of the United States, 1981-1989
ARTHUR BURNS (1904-1987), the chairman of the Board of Governors of the Federal Reserve System, 1970-1978

Summary of Event

In 1971, the United States suffered its first balance of trade deficit since 1888, importing $2.26 billion more in goods and services than it exported. The United States recorded a surplus on its trade account in only two of the following fourteen years. In 1973 and 1975, the United States exported $911 million and $8.9 billion more, respectively, than it imported. Between 1980 and 1987, the U.S. trade deficit virtually exploded, growing at a compound annual rate of 29.7 percent, from $25.5 billion in 1980 to $159.5 billion in 1987, the year in which the United States became a net debtor nation, owing more to the rest of the world as a whole than it was owed.

To understand the causes and significance of these developments and events, it is necessary to understand the rudimentary elements of balance of payments accounting and theory. The balance of trade is a part of the overall balance of payments. The balance of payments is a bookkeeping system that records all transactions between nations, including the flows of physical goods and services as well as the financial flows between nations. As a flow concept, the balance of payments must have a time dimension. In general, balance of payments statements are reported on an annual or quarterly basis. They can be reported in terms of the country in question versus the rest of the world or versus a particular region or a particular country. For example, the United States Department of Commerce reports the balance of payments for the United States in its *Survey of Current Business* on a quarterly and annual basis. The U.S. balance of payments is reported relative to the rest of the world and relative to various regions and countries.

A nation cannot simply import more than it exports. It must pay for any excess of imports over exports in one of several ways. It can use up foreign assets that were the result of past investments, spend foreign currency reserve balances or gold reserves it had accumulated in the past, or borrow. A relatively small percentage of imported goods takes the form of gifts or aid from one country to another; these imports do not have to be paid for.

Concern about trade deficits centers on the fact that they cannot continue indefinitely. Eventually, reserves of foreign currency and assets will be used up, and other countries eventually will become resistant to lending to trading partners that, because of persistent trade deficits, show little evidence of being able to earn the foreign currency to pay back loans through selling goods and services on the international market. Persistent trade deficits may indicate the need for a reduction in living standards in the deficit country. In simple terms, a trade deficit indicates that a country is consuming and investing more than it produces. Reducing the trade deficit may require reducing consumption of goods and services, thus lowering the standard of living.

The foregoing information about the balance of payments should aid in understanding the history of the United States' balance of trade. In 1960, the United States had a surplus on its balance of trade of $4.9 billion. The value of the United States' exports in that year was one-third higher than the value of its imports. By 1964, the surplus on the U.S. balance of trade had peaked at $6.8 billion. Exports in that year were 37 percent greater than imports.

In 1960, imports and exports were only 2.9 percent and 4.0 percent of the gross national product of the United States, or total value of all goods and services produced in the country that year. U.S. imports and exports were 11 percent and 16 percent, respectively, of world trade, making the United States an important part of the international marketplace.

This asymmetric position—the United States was important to the world economy, but the converse was not true—allowed the United States, the largest trading nation in the world, to operate as though it were a "closed economy" for purposes of domestic macroeconomic policy. A closed economy is one that is closed off from international markets. Because foreign trade was so small relative to the level of U.S. production, policymakers could ignore the effects of international transactions on the U.S. economy when analyzing proposed policies.

In 1964, there was little evidence to indicate that in just seven years the United States would suffer its first deficit in eighty-three years in its balance of trade. The balance of payments problem of the moment was a capital outflow from the United States. The subsidiaries of U.S. multinational corporations, foreign corporations, international agencies, and foreign governments were using the U.S. capital markets to raise funds to finance foreign projects. Dollars were flowing out of the United States, and the rest of the world was becoming more indebted to the United States.

From 1964 to 1971, the United States' imports grew at a compound annual rate of 13.3 percent, while its exports grew at only a rate of 8.3 percent. In 1971, the United States suffered a $2.6 billion deficit in its balance of trade, the first such deficit since 1888.

The reversal in trading position of the United States can be traced to at least one cause. In the late 1960's, the United States' international competitive position deteriorated as the country's domestic inflation rate, the rate of increase of prices, accelerated. Americans were willing and able to pay higher prices for American goods. Because foreign prices as a whole did not rise as rapidly as did American prices, goods produced in the United States became relatively more expensive. This caused potential foreign buyers to shun American goods, reducing U.S. exports. At the same time, foreign goods appeared increasingly attractive to American buyers because of their relatively lower prices. Imports therefore increased. A combination of falling exports and rising imports led naturally to a balance of trade deficit. The trade deficit thus can be traced to the relatively high inflation rate in the United States.

Impact of Event

The worsening balance of trade position of the United States led to worldwide concern. In May of 1971, a wave of speculation began that the deutsche mark was going to be allowed to increase in value relative to the dollar. Confidence in the dollar waned, and by early summer the fundamental weakness in the U.S. balance of payments became apparent. A widespread belief developed that even though the United States suffered from a high rate of unemployment and sluggish growth, inflation was not being brought under control. Normally, policymakers perceive inflation as a cure for unemployment and vice versa; the problems are not supposed to coexist. Confidence in the dollar ebbed further.

Various suggestions came from monetary policymakers including Arthur Burns, chairman of the Board of Governors of the U.S. Federal Reserve System. As chairman of the Board of Governors, Burns directed policy related to the functioning of the U.S. banking system and markets for U.S. treasury bonds. On August 15, 1971, President Richard M. Nixon announced his selection from among the various policy suggestions offered. The United States would suspend the privilege of converting U.S. dollars into gold as well as imposing a 10 percent tax on imports. Major world currencies at the time were all convertible into gold at fixed prices; suspension of convertibility meant that the United States recognized that the dollar had fallen in value relative to gold and relative to other currencies. Suspension of convertibility lowered the desirability of the dollar. Foreign countries would not be as willing to take dollars in exchange for goods knowing that dollars could no longer be traded for gold on demand. This effect, combined with the tax on imports, was intended in part to lower the trade deficit.

The dollar was the world's principal reserve currency at the time, meaning that it was the primary currency used in international exchanges and in settling debts. The exchange rates, or values, of most of the world's currencies were defined in terms of the U.S. dollar as part of the Bretton Woods System, under which countries had agreed to maintain the values of their currencies within narrow bands. It was clear that the dollar had become overvalued relative to most major currencies, with the agreed-upon fixed rates of exchange making the dollar appear more valuable than it in fact was. The questions were how much the dollar's value had to fall and how the fall could be achieved. Two alternatives were to allow the dollar to find its own value in the world market, thus eliminating fixed exchange rates, or to negotiate a new set of fixed exchange rates.

The latter alternative was chosen. The Smithsonian Conference was convened in Washington, D.C., in December of 1971 in an attempt to save the Bretton Woods System of fixed exchange rates. Representatives of the ten largest industrial nations in the Western world reached an agreement, known as the Smithsonian Agreement, to devalue the U.S. dollar by 8.57 percent, which was accomplished by raising the official price of gold from $35 to $38 per ounce. The Smithsonian Agreement, moreover, allowed currency values to fluctuate 2.25 percent above and below the fixed rates, allowing some flexibility before the rates would need adjustment.

In June of 1972, the new regime of exchange rates established only six months earlier began to collapse. By the second quarter of 1973, the world's major currencies were "floating." Rather than being fixed in terms of relative values, the world's major currencies traded for each other at rates determined by daily market transactions in the international market for foreign exchange. The Bretton Woods System, which had been dying a slow, agonizing death, finally collapsed.

The early 1980's witnessed the United States moving very rapidly from being the world's largest net creditor nation to being the world's largest net debtor nation. At the end of 1980, the United States was a net creditor to the rest of the world in the amount of $393 billion. By 1987, the United States had become a net debtor; by the end of 1991, it had accumulated $362 billion in debt. Essentially, this debt was incurred to pay for excesses of imports over exports.

The twin deficit theory argues that the tax cuts of the early 1980's, promoted by President Ronald Reagan, were not followed by spending cuts of equal magnitude. The U.S. government therefore ran huge fiscal deficits and had to borrow to finance its spending. The increased demand for funds by the U.S. government put upward pressure on interest rates, attracting foreign investors in search of higher interest rates. The inflow of capital into the United States and the increased demand for U.S. dollars resulted in an increased value of the dollar as measured against the major currencies of the world. The high value of the U.S. dollar made U.S. exports expensive to the world and made imports cheaper to Americans. A product with a given dollar price becomes more expensive to a foreign buyer as the value of the dollar increases relative to other currencies. This change in the prices of American goods relative to prices in the rest of the world led to a tendency for the U.S. trade deficit to increase.

The U.S. dollar rose in value throughout the early 1980's, and imports grew at astounding rates. The United States ran ever-larger trade deficits, and the value of the dollar kept rising, contrary to accepted theory, which predicts that a country running a trade deficit will find the value of its currency declining. As other countries accumulate a currency, the theory predicts, they will find it less attractive to accumulate even more and will be less willing to take it in trade for goods. That currency therefore should fall in value, rather than rise in value as the U.S. dollar did. Government borrowing apparently offset the effects on the dollar that resulted from trade deficits.

The trade deficit of 1971 thus signaled the beginning of a variety of problems in the U.S. economy. Policymakers faced increasingly unpleasant choices in overcoming trade deficits, debt to foreign countries, government budget deficits, inflation, unemployment, and slow economic growth. The multitude of goals and problems meant that some would have to be ignored.

Bibliography

Federal Reserve Bank of Atlanta. "Atlanta Fed Research Points to Validity of Twin Deficits Notion." *Economics Update* 4 (July-September, 1991): 6-7, 10. This brief article presents arguments for the twin deficit theory, reviews previous research, and presents a review of the Atlanta Fed's current research on this topic.

Howard, David H. "Implications of the U.S. Current Account Deficit." *Journal of Economic Perspectives* 3 (Fall, 1989): 153-165. Reviews some of the current empirical literature, concluding that the trade deficit is caused by an insufficiency of domestic savings. Concludes that the United States has gone from the position of a large net creditor to one of a large net debtor. The Feldstein Horioka Puzzle, the high correlation of saving and investment across countries, is discussed. Concludes that evidence indicates that capital is not very mobile internationally.

Pigott, Charles. "Economic Consequences of Continued U.S. External Deficits." *Federal Reserve Bank of New York Quarterly Review* 13 (Winter/Spring, 1989): 4-15. Concludes that the U.S. trade deficit is fundamentally a result of the imbalance between savings and investment. Policymakers cannot ignore it simply because some of the dire consequences predicted have not come to pass. Actual consequences include job loss and overcapacity in U.S. manufacturing during the early 1980's and slow U.S. domestic growth in more recent years. The most dire consequences could include a significant increase in the real U.S. long-term interest rate, which in turn could reduce both the future level of investment and productivity growth.

Scholl, Russell B., Raymond J. Mataloni, Jr., and Steve D. Bezirgaian. "The International Investment Position of the United States in 1991." *Survey of Current Business* 72 (June, 1992): 46-59. Discusses the difficulties in determining the net international investment position of the United States, concluding that the country became a net debtor in 1987, rather than in 1985 as reported earlier.

Solomon, Robert. *The International Monetary System 1945-1981*. New York: Harper & Row, 1982. This book is excellent, well written, and easy to understand. Solomon spent many years at the Federal Reserve System. His perspective, as both a participant in and an objective observer of developments in the international monetary system, is unique.

Yeager, Leland B. *International Monetary Relations: Theory, History, and Policy*. 2d ed. New York: Harper & Row, 1976. An excellent source for anyone interested in international finance. Contains a wealth of information.

Daniel C. Falkowski

Cross-References

The Bretton Woods Agreement Encourages Free Trade (1944), p. 851; The General Agreement on Tariffs and Trade Is Signed (1947), p. 914; The United States Enacts the Interest Equalization Tax (1964), p. 1235; Johnson Restricts Direct Foreign Investment (1968), p. 1341; Nixon's Anti-Inflation Program Shocks Worldwide Markets (1971-1974), p. 1489; The North American Free Trade Agreement Goes into Effect (1994), p. 2072.

NIXON'S ANTI-INFLATION PROGRAM SHOCKS WORLDWIDE MARKETS

Categories of event: Government and business; finance
Time: 1971-1974
Locale: Washington, D.C.

Richard M. Nixon's Economic Stabilization Program slowed inflation temporarily in the United States and established a new standard for currency exchange rates internationally

Principal personages:

RICHARD M. NIXON (1913-1994), the president of the United States, 1969-1974

JOHN CONNALLY (1917-   ), the secretary of the treasury, 1971-1972

GEORGE P. SHULTZ (1920-   ), the director of the Office of Management and Budget, 1970-1972

HERBERT STEIN (1916-   ), the chairman of the Council of Economic Advisers, 1969-1974

Summary of Event

On August 15, 1971, President Richard M. Nixon appeared before a nationwide television audience to announce that the United States would immediately embark on an unprecedented economic stabilization program. Domestically, the cornerstone of the program was to be the most extensive use, during a period of peacetime, of wage and price controls. In addition, President Nixon announced that the United States would immediately suspend all conversions of the dollar into gold. In essence, the United States had left the gold standard established by the Bretton Woods Agreements of 1944. Nixon also informed the world that a 10 percent surcharge would be placed on about half of the products imported into the country.

Nixon took over the presidency in 1969 during a period of broad economic expansion. The economy was described by many as "overheated": inflation was rising while the growth rate of real output was falling. In 1970, Congress passed legislation giving the president authority to implement price controls. Nixon initially opposed this course of action. His position softened as inflation continued to rise along with unemployment. Businesspeople were unaccustomed to seeing high inflation and high unemployment at the same time. The mood among managers shifted toward support of government action to change economic conditions.

When a balance-of-payments crisis arose in 1971, with the balance shifting toward relatively more imports and fewer exports, the Nixon Administration began to plan a program of action. For the first time since 1888, the United States found itself with a trade deficit, having imported more than it exported. The persistent outflow of funds that resulted from the trade deficit overwhelmed foreign markets. The U.S. dollar became overvalued—its exchange rates with other currencies overstating its true value—in many foreign markets, particularly that of Japan. Overvaluation of the dollar made imported goods cheaper than domestic products, contributing to the trade deficit.

The above factors led Nixon to present his multifaceted Economic Stabilization Program. He disclosed that for a ninety-day period a freeze would be placed on the prices of most products and on increases in wages in most industries. The major objective was to prove that the government was committed to taking direct action to stop inflation. Another important consideration was that time was needed to develop a plan of controls and to create an infrastructure to meet the goals for economic stability. This initial ninety-day period became known as Phase I, or simply as the freeze.

Nixon announced that a new organization would be created to act as a focal point for the wage and price control program. This commission was named the Cost-of-Living Council (CLC). Secretary of the Treasury John Connally was appointed chairman, and Arnold R. Weber, a Nixon economic adviser, was named executive director.

At the same time that Nixon announced Phase I domestic controls, he also suspended the convertibility of the U.S. dollar into gold. Under International Monetary Fund (IMF) rules, the value of the U.S. dollar was pegged to gold; that is, the United States was obligated to redeem its currency in gold at the rate of $35 per ounce. Connally had attempted to influence foreign banks to invest excess U.S. dollars in American securities rather than redeeming them in gold. A few countries had begun to do so, but Nixon's announcement made the issue moot.

Phase I ended on November 13, 1971, just as Nixon promised that it would. A month before Phase I ended, Nixon outlined the basics of how Phase II would operate. Wage and price controls would continue under the scrutiny of several newly created administrative boards. A Price Commission was created, consisting of seven public figures from outside government. A Pay Board was created, consisting of fifteen members with five representatives each from labor, business, and government. Additionally, a Committee on Interest and Dividends was created, headed by Arthur Burns, chairman of the Federal Reserve Board. All these commissions operated under the supervision of the CLC. The Pay Board and Price Commission were to formulate standards of permissible compensation, prices, and rents. The Pay Board set as its goal reduction of average annual wage increases to 5.5 percent. The Price Commission set as its goal reduction of inflation, or the annual rate of increase of prices, to a range of 2 to 3 percent. The Committee on Interest and Dividends announced a guideline limiting increases in corporate dividends to 4 percent. Interest rates were left to be determined by the marketplace.

The Phase II program was designed largely by George Shultz, director of the Office of Management and Budget; Herbert Stein, chairman of the council of Economic Advisers; and Connally. This same group advised Nixon on the stabilization program as a whole. The irony was that this group generally was opposed to the concept of direct control of the economy by the government. Perhaps for this reason, the keystone of the Phase II program was that it would be transitory in nature. Phase II ended on January 10, 1973, with abolition of the Pay Board and Price Commission.

Phase III officially began the next day. The CLC took over direct control of wage and price administration. Phase III was characterized by the progressive trimming back of controls, relaxing of reporting requirements, and switching to voluntary compliance. Phase III ended on June 12, 1973. Nixon announced that a selective freeze would immediately be placed on the prices of specified goods for a period of no more than sixty days. Wages were not subject to the freeze. The purposes of this second freeze were to impose an additional shock on any existing inflationary psychology, to stop speculative pricing activity, and to provide time for the planning of the fourth and final phase of the program. Phase IV began in August, 1973. It was to be a transitory period replacing the second freeze with an environment of marginal controls that would be reduced gradually to no controls at all. Phase IV and Nixon's program as a whole ended on April 30, 1974. The CLC was disbanded on June 30, 1974.

While the domestic program was running through its various phases, the international component of the program was generating reactions of its own. Shortly after Nixon's initial announcement of the program, the governors of the World Bank Group, along with leaders of the IMF, convened in Washington, D.C. The meeting centered on the need for restructuring of the worldwide monetary system and a reversal of the growing tendency toward restrictive trade agreements. Finance ministers and central bank governors met again at the Smithsonian Institution in Washington, D.C., on December 17 and 18, 1971. There they jointly agreed on a realignment of currency exchange rates that included an 8.57 percent devaluation of the U.S. dollar against gold. The official price of gold rose from $35 to $38 per ounce. In return for this concession by the United States, several international trade partners such as Canada, Japan, and the European Economic Community agreed to grant short-term trade concessions. Nixon made a surprise visit to this meeting and personally signed the Smithsonian Agreement, which resulted from the meeting. At the same time, he announced removal of the 10 percent surcharge on imports.

Impact of Event

Nixon's anti-inflation program spurred different reactions from various sectors in the United States and abroad. Labor initially denounced the wage freeze. Labor leader George Meany expressed fears that the wage freeze would be discriminatory against organized labor. Despite this type of vocal criticism, labor followed a general course of acceptance.

The business community reacted favorably. For example, the steel and the aluminum industries fell in line even though it meant postponing price increases they had scheduled to offset wage increases. American business executives whose firms traded globally supported the 10 percent surcharge on imports because it offered them the opportunity to regain a competitive advantage in international markets.

The public and investors generally approved. A Gallup poll conducted on August 19, 1971, reported that 70 percent of the public approved of the economic program. A Harris poll on September 7, 1971, reported that the freeze was supported by 73 percent of those interviewed. Reaction on Wall Street was highly favorable as well. On the day after the announcement, the New York Stock Exchange recorded the largest single-day gain in history and the largest single-day trading volume ever.

Nixon's announcement came as a surprise to overseas commercial, financial, and diplomatic sectors. Anger and bewilderment were expressed, especially with regard to the United States severing its ties with the gold standard and to imposition of the 10 percent surcharge on imported goods. Foreign stock markets slumped. The U.S. dollar immediately plunged in value internationally. Most European governments acted quickly to close their foreign exchange markets immediately following Nixon's announcement. When they reopened a few days later, it was on the basis of floating currencies, or currency exchange rates determined by market forces rather than by government decree.

Phase I was a simple, if harsh, device to alter inflationary expectations. Short-term results were soon identifiable. The Consumer Price Index (CPI) rose by only .3 percent over the period of the freeze. Wholesale prices eased slightly. Compliance with the freeze was high.

Outcomes in subsequent phases were not as consistently positive. During Phase II, the rate of increase for both prices and wages subsided. On the average, the Pay Board met its goal of no more than a 5.5 percent increase in wages. After the first year of the program, the CPI dropped from about a 4 percent annual increase to a 2.5 percent increase. This was within the range of the Price Commission's goals. Employment increased by about 2.4 million jobs during Phase II. Unemployment decreased from 5.9 percent to 5.5 percent. Productivity rose. Economic recovery on the whole was exemplified by an 8.9 percent rise in the Gross National Product (GNP).

On the negative side, not all sectors of the economy shared equally in these results. Such depressed industries as textiles, shoes, machine parts, and steel saw less favorable results in terms of productivity, unemployment, and containment of inflation. Business leaders in these industries were pessimistic. Many industries did not share in the ability to maintain wage increases under 5.5 percent. For the food and agricultural sectors, the second freeze resulted in serious shortages that brought an early end to the program. Early successes were followed by setbacks, as inflation increased in 1973-1974, led by food and energy prices. In general, the later phases of the program did not bring about long-term gains for the economy.

Internationally, the floating currency exchange rates that resulted from Nixon's proclamation bogged down trade markets for a number of months. Despite the preliminary international support of the Smithsonian Agreement to devalue the dollar, exchange markets found great difficulty in achieving stability. Devaluation had been expected to help reverse the U.S. balance-of-payments deficit. It did not consistently do so. The U.S. dollar was still in trouble as the program reached its end, and the trade deficit was higher than ever. The impact of leaving the gold standard could not be evaluated for a number of years. Most of the impact on American business was felt by those firms trading in international markets. The world currency outlook became more stable as the focus shifted from both gold and the U.S. dollar as standards of value to other currencies.

Several facets of Nixon's program deserve attention. Wage and price controls appear to hold the possibility of success over a short period of time even within a peacetime environment. Nixon's program resulted in short-term amelioration of inflationary pressure. After a period of time, however, the administration of the program became intricate. Eventually equity considerations became more difficult to control. Pressures grew to "catch up" on wage or price increases. Price controls in some sectors resulted in supply shortages. Controls were effective in the short run as a device to deal with special transitory pressure on the economy. They did not prove to be dependable in generating a long-run solution to the problems of unemployment and inflation.

Bibliography

Miller, Roger LeRoy, and Raburn M. Williams. *The New Economics of Richard Nixon: Freezes, Floats, and Fiscal Policy*. San Francisco: Canfield Press, 1972. This eighty-eight-page booklet presents a critical analysis of Nixon's program. Presents in appendices the full text of Nixon's original announcement and executive orders. Recommended for review of opinions of a dissenting author.

Nikolaieff, George A., ed. *Stabilizing America's Economy*. New York: H. W. Wilson, 1972. Contains reprints of articles, excerpts from books, and addresses associated with Nixon's program. Presents viewpoints contemporaneous to the events. Gives reactions to events as they unfolded.

Sobel, Lester A., ed. *Inflation and the Nixon Administration*. 2 vols. New York: Facts on File, 1974-1975. Presents major economic events in chronological order. Presents detailed facts in objective style. Allows the reader to review the details of Nixon's program with minimal interpretation by editors.

United States Gold Commission. *Report to the Congress of the Commission on the Role of Gold in the Domestic and International Monetary Systems*. 2 vols. Washington, D.C.: The United States Gold Commission, 1982. Volume 1 presents the major findings of the report; volume 2 provides detailed annexes. Furnishes an exhaustive study to assess and make recommendations regarding gold in domestic and international monetary systems.

Weber, Arnold Robert. *In Pursuit of Price Stability: The Wage-Price Freeze of 1971*. Washington, D.C.: Brookings Institution, 1973. Part of a series on wage-price policy compiled by the Brookings Institution. Gives an insider's view of why and how the freeze was implemented; the point of view is that of an administrator of the program.

Weber, Arnold Robert, and Daniel J. B. Mitchell. *The Pay Board's Progress: Wage Controls in Phase II*. Washington, D.C.: Brookings Institution, 1978. Another in the Brookings Institution series on wage-price controls. Presents the details of planning and implementation of Phase II. Also presents one view on the results of the program. Emphasis is on wage controls and the Pay Board, as presented by a participant.

Victor J. LaPorte, Jr.

Cross-References

Keynes Publishes *The General Theory* (1936), p. 740; Roosevelt Signs the Emergency Price Control Act (1942), p. 833; The Bretton Woods Agreement Encourages Free Trade (1944), p. 851; The European Common Market Is Established (1957), p. 1081; The United States Suffers Its First Trade Deficit Since 1888 (1971), p. 1483.

THE SUPREME COURT ORDERS THE END OF DISCRIMINATION IN HIRING

Category of event: Labor
Time: March 8, 1971
Locale: Washington, D.C.

In Griggs et al. v. Duke Power Company, *the Supreme Court ruled that employers could not require qualifications for jobs that were discriminatory in effect unless those qualifications were proved necessary for the job*

Principal personages:
WILLIE S. GRIGGS, a black worker who led the class action suit
WARREN BURGER (1907-   ), the Supreme Court justice who delivered the Griggs decision
HUBERT H. HUMPHREY (1911-1978), a U.S. senator who supported the Civil Rights Act of 1964
JOHN TOWER (1925-1991), a senator who sought amendments allowing job tests
HERMAN TALMADGE (1913-   ), a senator who was concerned about Title VII of the Civil Rights Act
ASA PHILIP RANDOLPH (1889-1979), a black union leader and lifelong enemy of employment discrimination
LYNDON B. JOHNSON (1908-1973), the president of the United States, 1963-1969
MARTIN LUTHER KING, JR. (1929-1968), a black leader and organizer of Operation Breadbasket
JESSE JACKSON (1941-   ), a King aide who led the boycott of biased employers

Summary of Event

Legal challenges to the constitutionality of Title VII of the federal Civil Rights Act of 1964 brought the case of *Griggs et al. v. Duke Power Company* before the U.S. Supreme Court for argument in December, 1970. The Court's decision, read by Chief Justice Warren Burger, was rendered on March 8, 1971.

Beginning in 1866, the American Congress enacted a series of civil rights laws that ostensibly safeguarded citizens' nonpolitical rights, notably those personal liberties guaranteed to U.S. citizens by the Thirteenth and Fourteenth Amendments to the Constitution. The Civil Rights Act of 1964 became law amid the turbulence of the 1960's associated with the "Black Revolution," campaigns for the rights of women, battles for alternative life-styles, environmentalism, and bitter debate over the Vietnam War. The Civil Rights Act of 1964 represented the most sweeping legislation of its kind.

President John F. Kennedy, contrary to his political instincts, launched the civil rights bill in June, 1963, five months before his assassination. Anxious to build the Great Society, President Lyndon B. Johnson, Kennedy's successor, was deeply committed both personally and politically to the principles embodied in the bill. So, too, were liberal members of the Congress, some of whom, including Hubert H. Humphrey, Michael Joseph Mansfield, and Carey Estes Kefauver, were veteran civil libertarians, while others including Samuel James Erwin had become dedicated converts.

The real initiatives for fresh civil rights legislation lay outside the White House and Congress, most notably among black leaders. By 1963, Martin Luther King, Jr., and young aides such as Jesse Jackson had begun their dramatic peaceful assaults on segregation in various Southern cities. Almost simultaneously, they had launched Operation Breadbasket, a grass-roots effort to bring an end to discriminatory practices that kept substantial numbers of African Americans out of the work force and gravely handicapped their economic opportunities. It was this type of discrimination in particular that was dealt with in Title VII of the 1964 Civil Rights Act.

Although hiring discrimination affected many groups, the plight of African Americans, the nation's largest minority, was singularly bad in the early 1960's, and in some regards it was worsening. Long a leader against discrimination in trade unions and a proponent of equal employment opportunities, the president of the Brotherhood of Sleeping Car Porters, Asa Philip Randolph, outlined the effects of hiring and job discrimination to a U.S. Senate subcommittee in 1962. Randolph pointed to the relatively small number of skilled black workers in the nation, to segregation and racial barriers in trade unions and in apprenticeship programs, to a disproportionate concentration of black workers in unskilled occupations, and to new technologies that were diminishing industry's need for unskilled labor. He noted that the percentage of black carpenters, painters, bricklayers, and plasterers, for example, had declined precipitously since 1950. In addition, the unemployment rate for black workers was nearly three times the rate for whites.

Such was the background against which Willie S. Griggs and thirteen fellow black coworkers at the Duke Power Company's Dan River Steam Station in Draper, North Carolina, brought a class action suit against their employer. All the black workers at the Dan River Plant worked in the Labor Department, in which the highest paying jobs paid less than the lowest paying jobs that whites held in the plant's four other departments. Promotions within departments were normally made on the basis of seniority, and transferees into a department usually began in the lowest positions.

In 1955, the Duke Power Company began requiring a high school diploma for assignment to any department except Labor. When the company eliminated its previous policies of segregation and stopped restricting black workers to the Labor Department, a high school diploma remained a prerequisite for transfer to other departments. In 1965, the company announced that for new employees, placement in any department except Labor was dependent on the achievement of adequate scores on two professionally designed high school equivalency tests. It was in this regard that the Griggs case invoked Title VII of the 1964 Civil Rights Act. The workers argued that black workers were less likely than whites to pass the tests but that performance on the tests was unrelated to ability to perform jobs.

The longest debate in American legislative history had preceded passage of the Civil Rights Act. Congress had laboriously made clear its intent in regard to Title VII: It was to achieve equality of employment opportunities and to remove previous barriers that had favored identifiable groups of white workers. No part of the act barred employers from utilizing "neutral" tests, practices, or procedures in selecting or promoting employees.

Delivering the opinion of the Supreme Court in the case, Chief Justice Warren Burger reiterated these congressional objectives. Speaking for a unanimous Court, Burger declared that even when an employer's tests, procedures, or practices were "neutral" in their intent, they could not be maintained if their effect was to freeze the status quo of prior discriminatory employment practices. What the Civil Rights Act and Title VII proscribed were any "artificial, arbitrary, and unnecessary barriers to employment" when such barriers served to discriminate on the basis of race, color, religion, sex, or any other impermissible classification. Burger acknowledged that the test requirements instituted by the Duke Power Company were intended to improve the overall quality of its work force. The Chief Justice noted, however, that employment practices that could not be shown to be related to job performance and that disproportionately excluded black workers from employment opportunities were clearly prohibited. An employer's good intent or absence of discriminatory intent, Burger continued, did not redeem employment procedures or testing mechanisms that operated as "built-in headwinds" for minority groups and were unrelated to measurements of job performance. Burger emphasized that the purpose of Title VII was to protect the employer's right to insist that any job applicant, black or white, must meet the applicable job qualifications. Title VII in fact was designed to facilitate hiring on the basis of job qualifications rather than on the basis of race or color.

Impact of Event

Title VII of the Civil Rights Act of 1964, however strongly President Johnson and liberal members of Congress felt about its objectives, did not miraculously abolish ingrained discriminatory hiring and employment practices. Despite the vast powers that Johnson derived from being the head of the country's largest employer, the federal government itself, and from having some control over billions of dollars in federal contracts, his power was circumscribed. The federal bureaucracy, many observers noted, was lethargic, and the country's great corporations and unions could not lightly be antagonized, particularly because the president required their support to attain other goals of his Great Society. After appointing Vice President Hubert H. Humphrey, one of the country's leading civil libertarians, to lead the President's Committee on Equal Employment Opportunity in February, 1965, Johnson abruptly removed him the following September. Taking this as a signal of presidential will, the agencies charged with implementing fair employment policies tended to drift.

There were gains, most notably in the changed public attitudes about race. Whereas in 1944 only 45 percent of whites polled believed that African Americans should have as good a chance as whites to secure jobs, in 1963, 80 percent espoused that belief. The U.S. Civil Service Commission increased the percentage of black workers in government jobs, principally in the Post Office. The Civil Rights Commission, however, found that the enforcement of nondiscrimination provisos in government contracts was almost nonexistent, and the Equal Employment Opportunity Commission (EEOC) that had been created to oversee applications of Title VII struggled without enforcement powers. Operation Breadbasket, initiated by Martin Luther King, Jr., and conducted largely by his aide, Jesse Jackson, had boycotted businesses until they opened jobs to black workers, but its efforts and success gradually diminished. Black unemployment ran four to five times as high as unemployment among whites. The problem was especially severe in inner cities.

By the early 1970's, there were signs of improvement. Enforced or not, the Civil Rights Act of 1964 encouraged employers to hire more black workers. This cause was aided by labor shortages of the 1960's as well as improvements in the education of black labor force entrants. Moreover, by 1972, Congress had granted the EEOC power to initiate legal action against businesses showing evidence of employment discrimination, and major offenders were soon forced to comply with Title VII's mandates. For these reasons, among others, black men nearly tripled their employment in white collar jobs. Black women also gained in employment generally, with strong gains in white collar jobs. Accordingly, the gap between white and black incomes narrowed significantly. The median income of black employees, for example, had been 59 percent of that of whites in 1959. By 1969, the proportion had risen to 69 percent. Employed black women, during the same period, raised their median income to 93 percent of that of white female employees, although women generally were paid less than were men.

By March, 1971, when Chief Justice Burger delivered the Court's decision in the Griggs case, some observers believed that despite the Civil Rights Act of 1964, the gap in opportunities between blacks and other Americans was widening. Increases in the numbers of black high school dropouts, black welfare recipients, and black women giving birth out of wedlock, as well as in venereal disease, drug abuse, and crime among African Americans, seemed to substantiate such assertions. According to some observers, the African American population had taken on the configurations of a distinct underclass.

As indicated above, however, there was heartening evidence that black workers were closing economic gaps between them and mainstream white society. Challenges to hiring and promotional barriers through Title VII and an empowered EEOC were important contributing factors to the hastening of this process. The liberal position taken by the Burger Supreme Court in giving specific weight to Title VII's objectives in the Griggs case also undoubtedly strengthened federal and state attacks on employment discrimination. To many black leaders, such decisions proved the worth of the 1964 Civil Rights Act. As Roy Wilkins told the Fifty-fifth Annual Convention of the

National Association for the Advancement of Colored People (NAACP), the principal value of the act was the recognition by Congress that African Americans are constitutional citizens, recognition necessary to begin the pursuit of happiness through political, social, and economic progress. Wilkins might have gone further. As legal scholars observed, the *Griggs* decision went beyond the Constitution. The Constitution prohibited only intentional discrimination, and the illegality of such discrimination had for decades been beyond legal question. After the Griggs opinion, legislation such as the 1964 Civil Rights Act's Title VII was interpreted to prohibit *de facto* discriminatory effects of employment practices as well.

Bibliography

Auerbach, Jerold S., ed. *American Labor: The Twentieth Century*. Indianapolis: Bobbs-Merrill, 1969. Commentary and documents presented clearly by a labor historian and other specialists. Part 4 is particularly relevant, dealing with civil and economic rights, race, segregation, employer and union job discrimination, and the impacts of automation. Part 3 also deals with major labor legislation.

Berger, Morroe. *Equality by Statute: The Revolution in Civil Rights*. New York: Octagon Books, 1978. A clearly written, intelligent survey of subject. Chapter 4 examines efforts to reduce employment discrimination in New York State as a mirror of national problems. Chapter 1 details creation of the EEOC and increments to its powers. Chapter 5 is an acute analysis of the effects of law in controlling prejudice and discrimination.

Blasi, Vincent, ed. *The Burger Court: The Counter-Revolution That Wasn't*. New Haven, Conn.: Yale University Press, 1983. The main thesis linking these expert analyses of the Burger Court is that it continued its work much in the same liberal spirit in regard to civil rights as its predecessor, led by Chief Justice Earl Warren. The Griggs case is treated in chapters 6 and 7, in context with analogous cases. Contains photos and biographies of Burger Court justices.

Matusow, Allen J. *The Unraveling of America: A History of Liberalism in the 1960s*. New York: Harper & Row, 1984. An outstanding survey. Richly detailed and critical but well balanced. Places the Griggs case in context with a gamut of racial and employment problems. A fine historical survey, clearly written and engaging.

Schwartz, Bernard, comp. *Civil Rights*. 2 vols. New York: Chelsea House, 1970. Consists of federal legislation, extracts from congressional debates, and Supreme Court decisions, with commentary by the compiler. An outstanding work for the background and context of Title VII.

Whalen, Charles, and Barbara Whalen. *The Longest Debate: A Legislative History of the 1964 Civil Rights Act*. Washington, D.C.: Seven Locks Press, 1985. Written by an outstanding congressman and civil libertarian with his columnist wife. This is an informative, engaging commentary and excerpting of testimony on an extraordinarily complex and politically difficult bill. Ample discussion of the EEOC and Title VII.

Clifton K. Yearley

Cross-References

The Wagner Act Promotes Union Organization (1935), p. 706; Roosevelt Signs the Fair Labor Standards Act (1938), p. 792; The Taft-Hartley Act Passes over Truman's Veto (1947), p. 908; The Civil Rights Act Prohibits Discrimination in Employment (1964), p. 1229; The Pregnancy Discrimination Act Extends Employment Rights (1978), p. 1682; The Supreme Court Rules on Affirmative Action Programs (1979), p. 1704; *Firefighters v. Stotts* Upholds Seniority Systems (1984), p. 1882; The Supreme Court Upholds Quotas as a Remedy for Discrimination (1986), p. 1915.

THE U.S. ADVERTISING INDUSTRY ORGANIZES SELF-REGULATION

Category of event: Advertising
Time: May 18, 1971
Locale: Washington, D.C.

The National Advertising Review Board (NARB) was established by various advertising industry organizations to institutionalize self-regulation in order to stem the prospect of increased governmental regulation of advertising

Principal personages:
WILLIAM EWEN (1913-   ), the executive director of the National Advertising Review Board
CHARLES YOST, the first chairman of the National Advertising Review Board
FRED BAKER, a past chairman of the American Advertising Federation
HOWARD BELL (1926-   ), the president of the American Advertising Federation
VICTOR ELTING, JR. (1905-1980), the chairman of the American Advertising Federation

Summary of Event

In response to a growing threat of tighter governmental regulation, the advertising industry in the United States created an elaborate self-regulatory apparatus in 1971 to curtail deceptive practices in advertising. This apparatus included the National Advertising Division (NAD) of the Council of Better Business Bureaus (CBBB) and the National Advertising Review Board (NARB). The initial phase of any investigation on any deceptive advertising case would be conducted by the former body; if the judgment rendered by the NAD was satisfactory, the case stood resolved. If the case remained unresolved or unsatisfactorily resolved at the NAD level, the NARB represented a higher (and final) court of appeals within the self-regulatory apparatus.

The late 1960's and early 1970's witnessed an unprecedented amount of congressional and federal attention to consumer protection issues. Criticism and publicity focused on alleged inaction by the Federal Trade Commission (FTC) during the early 1960's. This attention led to new leadership and a revitalization of this agency. In the early 1970's, the FTC processed an unusually large number of cases, with typical sanctions harsher than before.

The advertising industry perceived a need for an active response to these developments. Three people made seminal contributions to building the advertising self-regulatory apparatus: Howard Bell, president of the American Advertising Federation (AAF); Victor Elting, Jr., chairman of the AAF; and Fred Baker, a past chairman of the AAF. At the annual meeting of the AAF in June, 1970, both Bell and Elting stressed the importance of advertising self-regulation. Elting later proposed a structure for a regulatory apparatus, patterned closely after the system used successfully in Great Britain.

The British model contained two principal tiers: the Code of Advertising Practice Committee (CAP) and the Advertising Standards Authority (ASA). Elting also envisioned a two-tier system. To render the self-regulatory system powerful, Elting's proposal initially included a sanction mechanism that had worked effectively in Great Britain. The British system was equipped to punish offending (that is, deceptive) advertisers through sanctions ranging from confidential blacklisting to public disclosure of offending advertisers. Elting's proposed sanction mechanism was abandoned eventually because incorporating it into the proposed self-regulation system would violate U.S. antitrust laws (the British system did not face similar antitrust laws); for example, sanctions directed at a firm by an industry body would constitute an unfair restraint of trade under the Sherman Antitrust Act.

In 1970 and 1971, the proposal to institutionalize advertising self-regulation won the support of four influential industry groups: the AAF, the American Association of Advertising Agencies, the Association of National Advertisers, and the Council for Better Business Bureaus. Representatives were drawn from these four organizations to form a National Advertising Review Council (NARC), which served as a supervisory and policy-making body for both the NAD and the NARB but was not directly involved in routine disposition of complaints and cases.

The administrative structure envisaged was as follows. When first submitted, any complaint would be processed by the NAD to determine whether the case involved misleading or deceptive advertising and was national in scope. If the complaint failed to meet these requirements, it would be dismissed. For complaints that satisfied these requirements, the NAD would ask the advertisers involved to discuss and substantiate claims in their advertisements. The NAD would then judge whether the substantiation was satisfactory and indicate appropriate remedies if necessary.

If the case remained unresolved at the NAD level, either because the advertiser did not agree with the NAD or because the NAD found the advertiser unwilling to cooperate, the case would be referred to the NARB, which would consist of thirty advertisers, ten representatives of advertising agencies, and ten public members noted for their contributions to the public interest. A special panel of five NARB members would hear each case referred to the NARB. If the panel decided that the advertisement involved was not misleading, the case would be dismissed; however, if the NARB found the advertisement to be deceptive, the advertiser would be directed to make suitable changes. If the advertiser failed to comply with this directive, a public announcement outlining the case details, the NARB decision, and the advertiser's position would be made. In addition, the matter would be submitted to an appropriate federal agency.

Because the NARB structure dealt with only national advertisements, a similar structure was proposed to consider misleading commercials at local levels. Local Advertising Review Boards (LARBs) would be patterned after the NARB, with board membership made up of the same mix of advertisers, advertising agency representatives, and members of the general public. It was proposed that local Better Business Bureaus would work with the LARBs to resolve local cases in a manner analogous to the interaction of the NAD with the NARB at the national level. In 1971, William Ewen of the Borden Company was chosen as the first executive director of the NARB. He chose Charles Yost, then U.S. ambassador to the United Nations, to be the chairman of the NARB.

Impact of Event

By November, 1971, several complaints alleging deception in advertisements had been referred to the NARB. Most complaints had originated from consumer activists and were designed to test the fairness and expedience of the newly established self-regulatory system. During this period, the NARB was reluctant to make its proceedings public. The ostensible intent of this secrecy was to safeguard the interests of the advertisers involved, who preferred that the self-regulatory apparatus be a forum for settling disputes without the embarrassing publicity that often accompanied skirmishes with regulatory agencies such as the FTC. This nondisclosure policy was criticized even within the advertising industry. Although the industry had a body of useful precedents and information in the NARB cases, the advertisers could not benefit from it because they were denied access to it.

Two important steps were taken in 1972. First, it was decided to make the NARB decisions public. Second, Yost announced new procedures to facilitate the generation of more cases through monitoring activities as opposed to complaints and referrals. As a consequence, NARB activities benefited from public scrutiny and became more focused on cases that truly involved deceptive or misleading advertising.

To assess the impact of the NARB, it is useful to review decisions of various NARB panels. Some panels led to case dismissals that reinforced prior NAD action. For example, one panel was formed following an appeal by Mark Silbergald, a consumer activist, to overturn a previous NAD dismissal of his complaint concerning a commercial for Luden's Fifth Avenue candy bar. In this advertisement, an actor in a football uniform claimed to have consumed an entire case of candy bars before a game in order to become tough, mean, and smart. The NARB concurred with the NAD's decision that the advertisement was a satire that was not meant to deceive.

Several other NARB panels judged advertisements in their respective cases to be misleading or deceptive. In all such cases, the advertisers were forced to modify or discontinue the offending advertisements. One case centered on a commercial from the American Dairy Association (ADA) that claimed that milk provides instant energy. Reversing a previous NAD decision, the NARB panel ruled that the advertisement contained false claims. The ADA indicated that it was not currently using the offending advertisement and promised not to use it in the future.

In at least one instance, the NARB panel did not deliberate on a case because of an assurance that the offending advertisement would not be used again. The case concerned an advertising claim by Zenith Radio Corporation that its product was made in the United States. The company disagreed with an earlier NAD ruling that this claim was misleading because 14.5 percent of the product's components were of foreign origin. When the case was referred to the NARB, Zenith agreed to discontinue use of the advertisement.

A few of the NARB cases concerned comparative advertisements that allegedly disparaged competitors without adequate substantiation. One panel deliberated over a commercial by Drackett Company that compared its Behold furniture polish with Lemon Pledge. The manufacturers of Lemon Pledge lodged a complaint with the NAD, which judged the advertisement in question to be misleading. When Drackett appealed this decision, the NARB concurred with the NAD's verdict. The NARB's reasoning was that although Behold was proven to be superior on one attribute (removing oil-based stains), Drackett's advertisement misleadingly implied overall superiority. The panel indicated that advertisements that claimed total superiority faced the burden of substantiation with regard to all product attributes.

Some cases were resolved outside the self-regulatory system, with minimal NARB contribution. As one example, an advertisement claimed that No Nonsense Pantyhose (manufactured by Kayser-Roth Corporation) were superior to L'eggs Pantyhose (manufactured by Hanes Corporation). Hanes filed a complaint with the NARB and initiated a damage suit against Kayser-Roth for $20 million. Kayser-Roth responded with a countersuit for $30 million. Before the NARB could offer a conclusive verdict, the two contending parties reached an out-of-court settlement that stopped further use of the No Nonsense advertisement.

A common denominator in the cases in which the NARB reversed NAD decisions is that the advertisements in question were required to be either modified or discontinued. Such NARB judgments were less harsh on the offending advertiser than those in similar cases in which the FTC had rendered judgment. The NARB found the advertisement to be misleading or deceptive in all such cases, and the FTC was known to impose more severe penalties, such as corrective advertising, when an advertisement was judged to be deceptive.

A complaint frequently directed at the NARB is that it takes more time than necessary or desirable to dispose of cases. Various industry leaders suggested that advertising self-regulation serves no useful purpose if the process is notoriously lengthy. For example, if an advertisement's intended life is only six months and the self-regulatory process takes that long to render a decision, the outcome may be moot. Even if advertisers with offending commercials are required to terminate their campaigns, such directives may be painless because those commercials already were scheduled to be dropped.

Some of the NARB's judgments involved cases initiated through monitoring activities. For example, a Sperry Rand Corporation commercial claimed that its Remington electric shaver was superior to Schick's Flexamatic electric razor. Sperry Rand refused to provide supporting material to help the NARB reach a decision because the firm was engaged in litigation with Schick at that time. This case was terminated following an assurance that the advertisement in question would not be used again. This case demonstrates an aspect central to any successful industry self-regulation effort: the interests of individual firms in the industry were protected even though they did not initiate action through formal complaint channels.

The NARB made important contributions in two other areas: advertising to children and advertising to women. A children's review unit was constituted as part of the NAD in 1974 and was mandated to work within the children's television advertising guidelines formulated by the Association of National Advertisers. In a 1975 report, a NARB panel concluded that advertisers sometimes relied on outdated standards in messages directed at women. The panel outlined issues and questions to be considered by advertisers and advertising agencies when developing messages that either include or target women.

The NARB had a considerable impact on how important constituencies such as Congress, consumer groups, and government agencies evaluate the advertising industry and whether they perceive any need to regulate it. Self-regulation served the advertising trade as a means of eradicating deception and as a means of dealing with public criticism, with its attendant threat of government regulation. The NARB has attracted praise from federal officials and consumer activists over the years. The bulk of evidence suggests that the NARB has succeeded in achieving its goals.

Bibliography

Colford, Steven W. "Speed Up the NAD, Industry Unit Told." *Advertising Age* 60 (May 1, 1989): 3. Summarizes recommendations made to revitalize the NARB, mostly by minimizing the time for processing cases.

Kintner, Earl W. *A Primer on the Law of Deceptive Practices: A Guide for the Businessman.* New York: Macmillan, 1971. Discusses the foundations of laws concerning unfair and deceptive business practices, including advertising.

Ulanoff, Stanley M. *Advertising in America.* New York: Hastings House, 1977. Offers a relatively strong historical orientation. Several sections pertain to legal and regulatory issues.

Zanot, Eric J. *The National Advertising Review Board, 1971-1975.* Lexington, KY.: Association for Education in Journalism, 1979. Offers an insider's perspective on the NARB during its formative years.

——————. "The National Advertising Review Board, 1971-1976." *Journalism Monographs* 59 (February, 1979): 1-46. Exhaustive review and critique of the formative years of the NARB.

Siva Balasubramanian

Cross-References

Advertisers Adopt a Truth in Advertising Code (1913), p. 229; The Federal Trade Commission Is Organized (1914), p. 269; WEAF Airs the First Paid Radio Commercial (1922), p. 396; Congress Establishes the Federal Communications Commission (1934), p. 685; The Wheeler-Lea Act Broadens FTC Control over Advertising (1938), p. 775; Hasbro Advertises Toys on Television (1952), p. 986; The FTC Conducts Hearings on Ads Aimed at Children (1978), p. 1658.

AN INDEPENDENT AGENCY TAKES OVER
U.S. POSTAL SERVICE

Category of event: Government and business
Time: July 1, 1971
Locale: Washington, D.C.

*The Postal Reorganization Act of 1970 replaced the U.S. Post Office Department
with the semi-independent U.S. Postal Service, established to modernize mail delivery, make operations more efficient, and be self-supporting*

Principal personages:
RICHARD M. NIXON (1913-1994), the president of the United States,
1969-1974
FREDERICK R. KAPPEL (1902-   ), the head of the President's Commission on Postal Organization under President Lyndon B. Johnson
LAWRENCE O'BRIEN (1917-1990), the postmaster general under President Johnson
WINTON M. BLOUNT (1921-   ), the postmaster general under President Nixon

Summary of Event

President Richard M. Nixon signed the Postal Reorganization Act on August 12,
1970. The reorganization was the culmination of an effort begun during the administration of Lyndon B. Johnson, when the President's Commission on Postal Organization, popularly known as the Kappel Commission, recommended that the Post
Office Department be made independent and self-supporting.

The U.S. Postal Service, as an independent, government-owned agency, replaced
the Post Office Department. An eleven-member commission managed the service.
The commission was composed of nine governors who were appointed by the
president and confirmed by the Senate. Their terms were staggered, and no more than
five governors could come from one political party. Also serving on the commission
were the postmaster general and a deputy postmaster general, both of whom were
appointed by the governors. The postmaster general was no longer a member of the
president's cabinet. The new agency was phased in during 1971.

The Postal Service was freed from the financial control of Congress and was
authorized to issue bonds for capital improvement. A limit of $10 billion was placed
on outstanding debt, with a $2 billion annual limit on new issues. Proceeds of bond
issues were initially used to modernize buildings and automate processes. The service
was expected to move toward self-sufficiency but would continue to be subsidized
until able to break even. The subsidy took the place of large rate increases.

Significant improvements were made to operations. Political appointments of local
postmasters were replaced by a merit system. Specific criteria were established for

hiring and promotion. Postal workers were given the right to negotiate for wages and benefits. Binding arbitration would be used to settle labor disputes. As part of the Reorganization Act, postal workers received an 8 percent pay raise.

The cost of stamps was raised to eight cents for first-class mail. A similar increase was instituted for bulk mail. Increases for second-class mail would be phased in gradually. A five-member Postal Rate Commission would have the authority to set future rate increases, with Congress retaining the right of veto.

New services were provided to customers, including the Priority Mail next-day delivery system and Mailgrams, letters sent by telegraphs. To handle customer complaints, an Office of Consumer Advocate was established. The entire operation was decentralized. Regional directors were given greater autonomy, and the number of regions was reduced to five.

In 1970, the Post Office Department handled more than eighty-seven billion pieces of mail, making it the largest postal operation in the world. It was also the largest civilian government agency, employing more than 750,000 workers, a payroll comparable to those of General Motors Corporation and American Telephone and Telegraph (AT&T). The Post Office Department was plagued by problems in all phases of its operation. A deficit of $2.6 billion was expected in 1970. The operation relied heavily on manual work, with clerks able to hand-sort only eighteen letters a minute. The Post Office relied on the airlines and Amtrak to deliver intercity mail. Route cutbacks slowed down the mail. Coast-to-coast delivery took ten days, and intracity delivery often took two days. Second-class mail delivery of newspapers and magazines was frequently delayed by as much as ten days.

The problems of the Post Office Department were widely believed to be caused by political influence. Postmaster jobs were filled by political appointees, and within-the-ranks promotion was considered unlikely for someone without political connections. The inefficiency and the lack of capital improvements were blamed on Congress, which often failed to appropriate funds for automation or building improvements. Within the Nixon Administration, there was a strong desire to implement modern management techniques throughout government operations, including the Post Office.

Working conditions for postal workers were below the standard of industry of the time. The Post Office experienced a turnover rate of 23 percent, lower than the industry average of the time. It took thirteen weeks to hire a new worker. Post Offices in some large cities experienced difficulty filling vacant positions; in 1970, more than nine hundred position were unfilled in New York City. Post Office jobs started at a salary of $6,176, and the top pay grade was $8,440, reached after twenty-one years of service. Most buildings were not air conditioned. Many had no parking lots or cafeterias, and toilet facilities were often inadequate. Few Post Offices had doctors or first aid available for workers, and accident rates were high.

Prior to the Depression, Post Office Department jobs were desirable. After World War II, there was increased labor competition from industry, and the Post Office had difficulty attracting workers. The department, under the Civil Service System, was not able to pay differential rates in high-cost areas such as New York City. In 1970, 10 percent of that city's postal workers qualified for welfare. After three years of service, garbage collectors in New York City were paid more than postal workers with twenty years of service.

The idea of reorganizing the Post Office Department originated with Lawrence O'Brien, who was postmaster general in the Johnson Administration and who believed that the Post Office should be made independent and self-sufficient. President Johnson established the President's Commission on Postal Organization and appointed Frederick R. Kappel, former chairman of AT&T, as chairman of the commission. In June, 1968, the commission recommended that the Post Office Department be reorganized and placed on a self-sufficient basis. President Nixon's postal reform message on May 27, 1969, endorsed the proposal. Opposition reached a peak in March, 1970, when the New York postal workers staged an illegal strike. Congress added a binding arbitration clause to the legislation. In April, 1970, the American Federation of Labor-Congress of Industrial Organizations (AFL-CIO), with George Meany as bargainer, reached an agreement with the government to end the strike. On August 12, 1970, President Nixon signed the Postal Reorganization Act, which authorized the creation of the U.S. Postal Service. On June 26, 1971, an eight cent first-class stamp was issued with the U.S. Postal Service emblem, and on July 1, 1971, the service was born.

Impact of Event

The Postal Reorganization Act shifted control of the postal system from Congress and the president to the managers of the new U.S. Postal Service. This provided immediate political advantage to the White House and Congress, which no longer could be directly blamed for the failings of the system.

Until 1979, the Postal Service ran annual operating deficits. In 1979, the service reported an operating surplus of $470,000. Deficits occurred even though postal rates rose significantly after reorganization. The cost of mailing first-class letters rose 150 percent from 1970 to 1977, with similar increases for second-class and bulk mail.

Firms were able to compete with the Postal Service to deliver bulk mail, but not first-class mail. After 1971, this competition accelerated. The business community showed concern about the increased cost of bulk-mail advertising and other kinds of business mail. The bulk-mail industry was the most affected by the change. After 1971, costs of bulk mail continued to rise, and service did not measurably improve.

Firms that entered the bulk-mail business at the time of reorganization were able to offer lower rates because they delivered advertising mail door to door. No mailing labels or sorting was necessary, thus reducing costs. Leading firms included Independent Postal Systems of America of Oklahoma City, Oklahoma; Consumer Communications Services Corporation of Columbus, Ohio; American Postal Corporation of Los Angeles, California; Pacific Postal System of San Francisco, California; and Continental Postal Service of Charlotte, North Carolina.

Some firms began delivering their own bills to customers. Virginia Electric and

Power Company was able to deliver its own monthly bills for as little as five cents apiece in urban areas at a time when the Postal Service charged eight cents. Under the Reorganization Act, it was legal for firms to deliver their own first-class mail.

The greatest concern within the Postal Service was the increased competition from the United Parcel Service, which soon had half of the small-parcel delivery market. The competitive advantage United Parcel Service enjoyed resulted from its reputation for reliable, consistent, and rapid delivery and from its ability to charge lower rates than those of the Postal Service.

Management improvements in the new Postal Service focused on improving airmail service, with a goal of next-day delivery for airmail. Airlines depended on airmail for revenue. After reorganization, the Postal Service was able to negotiate terms with carriers. There was fear within the airline industry of the resulting increase in competition. Airmail standards set by the Postal Service were next-day delivery for destinations within six hundred miles with all other deliveries to be made within two days. The Mail Express program was inaugurated, with door-to-door delivery by courier.

The Postal Service experienced a 35 percent increase in productivity from 1970 to 1980. According to the Postal Service's own reports, by 1980 the system succeeded in delivering 95 percent of first-class mail within one day. Intercity mail traveling less than six hundred miles was delivered within two days 86 percent of the time, and cross-country mail was delivered within three days 87 percent of the time.

The first U.S. Postal Service bonds were issued in October, 1971, in the amount of $250 million. The bonds were issued for capital improvement, with two areas of initial focus. A bulk mail system was designed to include twenty-one processing centers using modern technology, computers, and conveyor systems. The second project was a letter mail code sort system. A pilot plant was built in Cincinnati, Ohio, and used optical scanning equipment and other technologies to sort mail.

After the reorganization, there were significant cuts in headquarters and regional staffs. The new agency started with $3 billion in assets and $1 billion in cash, which could be invested in U.S. government securities. In 1972, the service ordered a hiring freeze in an attempt to reduce costs. Labor contracts did not allow a reduction in force, so inducements for early retirement were offered. Experienced postal managers responded to the offer, significantly reducing the Postal Service deficit for 1973. The loss of experienced managers, however, resulted in deterioration of service and public criticism. The backlash resulted in additional hiring and subsequent growth of the deficit.

Postal unions were able to negotiate no-layoff clauses in their contracts; nonunion postal employees did not have such protection and significant reductions in work-force levels occurred. From 1970 to 1980, the number of full-time-equivalent postal employees declined by forty-six thousand. After 1971, wages increased at a higher rate than that of other government workers, primarily because of cost-of-living adjustments included in union contracts. During the inflation-plagued 1970's, postal wages more than doubled.

Federal Express was founded in 1971 as a competitor to the government's mail operation. The reorganization of the Postal Service and the emergence of Federal Express and other overnight delivery services revolutionized the way business mail was sent and received. In 1980, Mail Boxes Etc. of San Diego, California, extended innovations in service to the individual consumer. For hundreds of years, it had been believed that mail delivery must be provided by a protected government monopoly. The 1971 reorganization of the Postal Service challenged that basic belief and made possible advances in mail delivery and processing.

Bibliography

Blount, Winton Malcolm. "Overhauling the Mails: Interview with Postmaster General Blount." *U.S. News and World Report* 68 (May 4, 1970): 46-51. An interview with the postmaster general at the time reorganization was under consideration by Congress. Shows the extent of operational considerations and the optimism of Post Office Department management for reform.

Fleishman, Joel L., ed. *The Future of the Postal Service.* New York: Praeger, 1983. Good critical analysis of the effects of reorganization on government, labor, business, and the communications industry. Includes international comparisons as well as detailed economic information. Recommends further restructuring and management improvements.

Fowler, Dorothy Ganfield. *Unmailable: Congress and the Post Office.* Athens: University of Georgia Press, 1977. A highly readable history of the Postal Service from the appointment of Benjamin Franklin as postmaster general in 1753 to the formation of the U.S. Postal Service in 1971. Covers the important role the Postal Service has played in American history and the relationship between Congress and the postal service. Good focus on the dynamics that led to reorganization.

Fuller, Wayne E. "The Politics and the Post Office" and "Epilogue." In *The American Mail: Enlarger of the Common Life.* Chicago: University of Chicago Press, 1972. A history of political control of the Post Office, from establishment to reorganization in 1971. A balanced report that illuminates both positive and negative aspects of this control. The epilogue recounts the congressional debate leading to passage of the Reorganization Act.

Nixon, Richard M. *Nixon: The Second Year of His Presidency.* Washington, D.C.: Congressional Quarterly, 1971. Contains Nixon's statements on the postal reorganization, the postal strike, and the settlement of the strike.

_____ . "Toward a Better Postal Service." In *Setting the Course, the First Year: Major Policy Statement by President Richard Nixon.* New York: Funk & Wagnalls, 1970. Contains Nixon's policy statements on the need for reorganization. The chapter outlines the structural and political problems inherent in the Post Office Department as well as the basic objectives of reform.

Sandford, David. "Post Office Blues, the Mail That Costs More and Comes Sometimes." *The New Republic* 162 (March 21, 1970): 19-22. Focuses on customer frustration with Post Office Department performance prior to reorganization. Particular emphasis is placed on problems experienced by weekly news magazines regarding delays in second-class mail delivery. Inequities in the rate structure are covered.

Tierney, John T. *Postal Reorganization: Managing the Public's Business.* Boston: Auburn House, 1981. An in-depth study of the reorganization of the Postal Service, from a broad perspective essentially favorable toward the system. Focuses on managerial initiatives within the postal system and the changing dynamics of labor relations. Also shows the effects of competition on the operation of the postal service.

_____ . "Untangling the Mess in the Post Office." *Business Week*, March 28, 1970, 78-80. A survey of the problems plaguing the reorganization of the Post Office Department. Covers all aspects, including labor, systems performance, management, and political influence. Comparison with other nations is included. Good coverage of the political concerns that led to reorganization.

Alene Staley

Cross-References

The Post Office Begins Transcontinental Airmail Delivery (1920), p. 357; Congress Authorizes Private Carriers for Airmail (1925), p. 493; The U.S. Government Creates the Tennessee Valley Authority (1933), p. 650; Amtrak Takes Over Most U.S. Intercity Train Traffic (1970), p. 1431; Federal Express Begins Operations (1973), p. 1538; AT&T Agrees to be Broken Up as Part of an Antitrust Settlement (1982), p. 1821; Great Britain Announces Plans to Privatize British Telecom (1982), p. 1831.

PROFESSIONAL BASEBALL PLAYERS GO ON STRIKE

Category of event: Labor
Time: April 1-13, 1972
Locale: The United States and Canada

Major league baseball players engaged in a brief strike that set the tone for future labor relations in professional sports

Principal personages:
  MARVIN MILLER (1917-   ), the executive director of the Major
    League Baseball Players Association
  JOHN GAHERIN, the chief negotiator for the major league team owners
  BOWIE KUHN (1926-   ), the commissioner of baseball from 1969 to
    1984

Summary of Event

Sports fans throughout America look forward to the opening of the major league baseball season, an annual ritual that through the decades has acquired almost mythic overtones in the public consciousness. The first games of each new year, played during the traditional season of renewal, are a leisurely prelude to the sterner competitions of the summer and fall. Opening day is a celebration that seems to draw out baseball's pastoral qualities, emphasizing the game's allure as a haven from more troubling concerns.

The spring of 1972, however, was different. On April 1, only a few days before the season's scheduled opening, the Major League Baseball Players Association (MLBPA) announced that its members were on strike pending resolution of a dispute with baseball's twenty-four team owners over contributions to the players' pension fund. The strike was a relatively short one, lasting less than two weeks before a compromise on the pension fund issue was reached, but the dispute went on long enough to disrupt the season's first week and force the cancellation of eighty-six regular-season games. The national pastime itself had come to reflect the same mundane troubles that many fans sought to escape.

The 1972 strike was precipitated by a relatively minor dispute. In 1969, the owners and players had agreed to a revision of the general contract (known as the "Basic Agreement") that called for the owners to contribute $5,450,000 each year to the pension fund for retired players. By 1972, however, inflation had reduced the value of the owners' contribution, and player representatives asked for a $1,072,000 addition to the annual payment to reflect cost-of-living increases. The owner-sponsored Player Relations Committee, headed by John Gaherin, offered to raise the total by $490,000, but as spring training ended and the April 5 opening of the season approached, neither side was willing to compromise. The thirteen-day strike, which was settled when owners agreed to allow $500,000 in income earned by the fund to be used to increase payments, cost the owners an estimated $5 million in revenue and the players roughly $1 million in pay, sums far in excess of the amount in dispute.

Although the issue at hand was minor, larger issues in baseball's labor-management relationship were not. In fact, both sides were spoiling for a fight. Team owners were eager to test and, if possible, break the MLBPA; the young union, on the other hand, was looking for a chance to flex its muscles and show the owners that their century-long domination of baseball's power structure was nearing an end. "The owners are intent on making the players eat dirt," said Marvin Miller, the MLBPA's executive director and driving force. "They want the players to bend down and kiss their shoes." Owners were equally combative in public. "All you hear from the players nowadays is gimme, gimme, gimme and threat, threat, threat. I'm getting sick of it," said Oakland Athletics owner Charlie Finley. St. Louis Cardinals owner Gussie Busch told reporters, "We're not going to give them another damn cent. And if they want to strike, let them strike."

Such public comments by owners reflected a confidence that bordered on arrogance. Indeed, the owners seemed to have good reason to feel secure in their power; baseball's history of labor-management conflicts was an almost uninterrupted litany of owner victories and player losses. For decades, major league owners had squelched every real challenge to their power, crushing rival leagues and winning important legal decisions with regularity. The owners' hand was bolstered in particular by two trump cards: a 1922 U.S. Supreme Court decision that exempted organized baseball from antitrust legislation, and the notorious "reserve clause," a portion of the Basic Agreement that was used to bind players to their teams in perpetuity.

The antitrust exemption, which stemmed from the Supreme Court's much-criticized ruling that baseball was not a "trade or commerce in the commonly accepted use of these words," allowed the owners to run the major leagues as a legal monopoly; the reserve clause, which deprived players of the right to negotiate with rival teams, made the owners' bargaining strength overwhelming in most cases. Although St. Louis Cardinals outfielder Curt Flood's 1970 challenge to the legality of the reserve clause was under Supreme Court review at the time of the strike, the clause was still in full effect. (In fact, the Court's June, 1972, ruling in the Flood case extended the owner's string of successes in labor disputes; the reserve clause would retain its potency until 1975, when it was vitiated by an arbitrator.)

If a player was dissatisfied with a contract offer from his team, therefore, his only real recourse was to refuse to play. Salary holdouts were common but were seldom very effective. Stars from every era of the game had waged salary wars with their bosses, but with little leverage apart from the uncertain help of public opinion, even such legends as Babe Ruth and Joe DiMaggio were generally forced to accept management's terms.

In the spring of 1966, for example, Los Angeles Dodgers stars Sandy Koufax and Don Drysdale engaged in a celebrated joint holdout asking for salaries of $175,000 apiece. Koufax settled for $125,000 and Drysdale for $110,000; though their holdout ranked as one of the most successful on record, each received far less than he thought he was worth. (In 1962, Drysdale, one of baseball's top pitchers, had made a reported $35,000; in unrelated court proceedings, the Dodgers reported a profit of $4,347,177 for the 1962 season.) When the 1972 strike began, Finley was already engaged in another highly publicized salary battle with Oakland's young pitching sensation Vida Blue, who was seeking a raise from $14,500 after a spectacular 1971 season. Blue settled for $50,000 plus $13,000 in bonus money, little more than half of what he had sought, and the acrimony generated by the bitter holdout cast a shadow over what had promised to be a brilliant career.

Stars such as Koufax, Drysdale, and Blue, however, were rare exceptions. Most of the six hundred or so major league players earned salaries closer to the $13,500 minimum than to the figures commanded by the top players; in 1970, for example, the average player earned roughly $22,000. Rank-and-file players did not, for the most part, have the leverage needed to win concessions in individual holdouts. For such players, united action offered the only real prospect of bargaining power.

Baseball player unions, though, had a century-long history of ineffectiveness. Owners had traditionally dealt with attempts to organize their workers by adopting divide-and-conquer tactics and by blacklisting activist players. The MLBPA had been organized in the late 1950's, but the diplomatic approach of its first chief negotiator, Judge Robert Cannon, inspired neither fear in owners nor confidence in players.

The man who changed the players' fortunes was Marvin Miller, a career labor negotiator who took the helm of the MLBPA in 1966 after spending sixteen years working for the United Steelworkers of America. The owners were incensed by the hard-nosed Miller's appointment and forbade the use of pension funds to pay his $50,000-plus salary, forcing the MLBPA to raise its yearly dues to more than $300 per player. Miller, though, proved well worth the money. In short order, he more than doubled the minimum player salary and brokered the 1969 pension deal. When his negotiations over the 1972 pension increase reached an impasse, player representatives voted 47-0 (with one abstention) to call a strike. United behind Miller, the MLBPA in 1972 represented the most formidable labor foe the owners had faced in decades. The short strike offered proof of the union's new power: Baseball players had at last stood together to win concessions from their bosses.

Impact of Event

The spring interruption did not seem to affect the quality of play in the 1972 season, which featured several exciting pennant races and a memorable World Series won by Finley's Oakland team. The most significant on-field consequence of the strike was felt by the Boston Red Sox, who lost the American League Eastern Division title—and a chance to compete in postseason play—by one half-game to the Detroit Tigers. The strike settlement stipulated that none of the canceled games would be made up; the Red Sox, however, lost one more game to the strike than the Tigers did, and the unplayed game provided Detroit's margin of victory.

During the 1972 strike, both labor and management expressed concern over the possible effect of a prolonged strike on fan interest. By the early 1970's, the explosive growth of the popularity of professional football was threatening to deprive baseball of its traditional status as the national pastime, and other spectator sports were vying with the major leagues for fan loyalty. Owners and players alike were denounced in the media as greedy businessmen, and both sides worried that the public wrangling over money might disenchant fans and lead to a long-term loss of interest in the sport. "We don't want to give the fan an opportunity to see if he can live without baseball," one Baltimore Orioles executive remarked. "God knows there are plenty of other things to do in the summer." Despite such fears, baseball's popularity showed no lasting effects; in fact, major league attendance for the 1970's as a whole rose by 18 percent from the previous decade.

The millions lost by the owners in revenue and by the players in salaries represented perhaps the least important consequence of the strike. Both sides were clearly more concerned with the symbolic effect of their actions; the players had made their declaration of independence, and the owners had expressed a continued unwillingness to share power. Hard feelings between labor and management persisted, portending future struggles.

The most significant part of the strike settlement, ironically, proved not to involve the central issue, the pension fund, at all. The new Basic Agreement contained a provision calling for binding arbitration of future salary disputes by outside parties, a concession the owners would soon come to regret. It was arbitrator Peter Seitz who pulled the teeth of the reserve clause in 1975, not by judging the provision illegal but by ruling simply that its language did not bind players to their clubs for longer than one year. The decision ushered in the free-agent era, and competitive bidding among owners for top players soon pushed salaries to undreamed-of levels.

In 1976, in the wake of Seitz's decision, the owners locked players out of training camps briefly as a negotiating ploy, but the season was not affected. In 1981, however, full-scale warfare erupted between the factions, and more than a third of the season was lost to a midsummer strike. The owners, having learned the lessons of 1972, took out a $2 million strike-insurance policy before the 1981 season and collected more than $40 million as compensation for lost revenue. Players were generally much less well prepared, but the MLBPA again held its ground. Thereafter, the owners changed their tactics; rather than trying to break the union through direct confrontation, they tried to hold down salaries by refusing to bid for free-agent players. A series of arbitration decisions found the owners guilty of illegal collusion, however, and the affected players were awarded millions of dollars in damages.

The success of the MLBPA can perhaps best be measured with respect to its counterpart in professional football, America's other most lucrative spectator sport. The National Football League Players Association (NFLPA), hamstrung by leadership disputes and poor decision-making, failed to achieve anything like the gains made by Miller and his colleagues in the 1970's and 1980's. Even though pro football did not enjoy baseball's treasured antitrust exemption, football salaries consistently lagged far behind baseball salaries. In 1987, a midseason strike by the NFLPA ended in disaster for the players, as strikebreakers and substitute players quickly eroded the union's strength. The result was the virtual destruction of the NFLPA, which subsequently decertified itself as the players' negotiating arm in order to allow its members to pursue independent legal challenges to their employers' policies.

The 1972 baseball strike was the opening shot in a new phase of an ongoing war over sports revenues. Although fans and media analysts would continue to lament the intrusion of such prosaic concerns on their favorite diversions, the enormous and seemingly ever-growing sums involved made such battles appear to be a permanent adjunct of modern sports.

Bibliography

Dworkin, James B. *Owners Versus Players: Baseball and Collective Bargaining*. Boston: Auburn House, 1981. A useful overview of baseball's labor relations up to the time of the sport's biggest strike.

James, Bill. *The Bill James Historical Baseball Abstract*. Rev. ed. New York: Villard Books, 1988. A fascinating compendium of history, anecdote, and penetrating statistical analysis. Contains much useful and hard-to-find information on attendance figures, player salaries, and labor disputes from throughout the game's history. Unique and indispensable.

Kuhn, Bowie. *Hardball: The Education of a Baseball Commissioner*. New York: Times Books, 1987. Commentary on the game's crises by its commissioner from 1969 to 1984, who was often taken to task for his inaction during the momentous events of the time.

Miller, Marvin. *A Whole Different Ball Game: The Sport and Business of Baseball*. Secaucus, N.J.: Carol Publishing Group, 1991. Reflections on the owner-player disputes of the 1970's and 1980's by the players' champion of the era. Provides an interesting contrast of perspectives with Kuhn's book.

Scully, Gerald W. *The Business of Major League Baseball*. Chicago: University of Chicago Press, 1989. A useful discussion of how economics affects big-league baseball on a variety of levels.

Robert McClenaghan

Cross-References

The Yankees Acquire Babe Ruth (1920), p. 341; The Brooklyn Dodgers Move to Los Angeles (1957-1958), p. 1076; The NFL-AFL Merger Creates a Sports-Industry Giant (1966), p. 1298; Curt Flood Tests Baseball's Reserve Clause (1970), p. 1437; The Boston Celtics Sell Shares in the Team (1986), p. 1939.

THE POCKET CALCULATOR IS MARKETED

Category of event: New products
Time: September, 1972
Locale: The United States

With the introduction of a pocket calculator to the market, Texas Instruments provoked turmoil in the computing machine industry

Principal personages:

MARK SHEPHERD, JR. (1923-   ), the president and chief executive officer of Texas Instruments during the 1970's

JERRY D. MERRYMAN (1932-   ), the project manager of the Texas Instruments team that developed the first portable calculator

EDWARD A. WHITE (1928-   ), the president and chairman of Bowmar during the 1970's

Summary of Event

The marketing of the pocket calculator was one of the major events in the marketplace in 1972. In September, three new models of calculator were introduced by Texas Instruments, which also announced that more new products would be offered over the next year or so. The products from Texas Instruments were made entirely from American components, in contrast to the Japanese-made calculators that dominated the market at the time. Japan's manufacturers benefited from relatively low wage rates. The new calculators were made from one or more chip components made by Texas Instruments, which also manufactured the keyboard and the plastic case. The labor required for assembly was much less than for the earlier machines, allowing the American firm to be competitive. Entrance of Texas Instruments into the market set the stage for dramatic price competition. Japanese products would soon become less competitive because of freight charges.

Texas Instruments had not been in any consumer goods market up until then, although it had produced components for calculating machines. The company thought that personal calculators were a good opportunity because no strong brand loyalty had yet developed. The products also had an obvious tie-in with the company's existing electronics expertise.

Of the three new calculator models, one was a portable priced at $119.95. The other two, for the desk, were priced at $84.95 and $99.95. A huge increase in sales was anticipated as prices fell as a result of technical improvements. At first, business offices were expected to be the main buyers, as they replaced old adding machines, but personal use by individuals, including students, offered substantial sales.

The portable model was known as a pocket calculator or a hand-held calculator. It weighed less than a pound and could fit into a shirt pocket or handbag. The simplest models on the market could do addition, subtraction, multiplication, and division, as well as chain calculations involving a stored constant. Most had eight- or ten-digit illuminated display boards. Some had a fixed, and some a floating, decimal point. More expensive versions had a memory function that stored a number for later recall and could perform other operations such as square roots, logarithms, and statistical analysis. When the Texas Instruments pocket model, the TI-2500, was brought out, its main competitors were the Rapidman 800 ($75-$80), the Abatron 800 ($79), the Craig 451 ($104-$110), the Bowmar 901B ($120), and the Witco ($100). None of these models had a memory function. Calculators with the memory function included the Sharp ELSI-8M ($200-$212) and the Canon Pocketronic ($168-$179).

The technological breakthrough in hand-held calculators was the chip, or integrated circuit. The quarter-inch square contained the entire operational logic of the machine, doing the equivalent work of six thousand transistors. The single integrated circuit was the last step in the evolution of calculators from mechanical, to electromechanical with tubes and transistors, then to machines with seven or eight integrated circuits. The technology of the integrated circuit had been developed by Texas Instruments itself, using the metal-oxide semiconductor process in work for defense and aerospace. Texas Instruments had come to dominate the market for semiconductor chips, supplying to most of the other makers of small calculators, before making its own venture into the consumer market.

One of the companies deploying Texas Instruments components was Bowmar. The president and chairman of Bowmar, Edward A. White, was perhaps the chief visionary in the hand-held calculator business. Sensing that the one-chip development was the wave of the future, he decided to build his own calculators around Texas Instruments components, ordering in advance the first chips produced in 1971. These went into the Bowmar model, which achieved initial success. About half of the first half million pocket calculators sold in the United States were Bowmars. White chose a marketing strategy that went far beyond the office supply stores that were the main outlet for earlier computation machines. He included department and specialty stores as well as luxury goods stores. Many of the first pocket calculators sold were gifts for educated middle- and upper-class people.

At the time Texas Instruments entered the market for pocket calculators, the purpose of the product was not understood by everyone. As with the introduction of the personal computer, many people asked whether it was a tool or simply a toy. Some people who purchased a pocket calculator as a gift may have thought is was a nice gadget to serve inessential purposes, a good present for a man or woman who has everything. Businesses were quick to see the uses of portable calculators, not only for employees inside the office but also for anyone who moves around and uses numbers, such as buyers. Higher sales at tax return time indicated that people used them for tax work. The use of pocket calculators in academic work also was established early on. Before the end of 1972, the Harvard Graduate School of Business Administration was renting pocket calculators to students for classroom use.

Impact of Event

The introduction of American-made electronic pocket calculators, and in particular the entry of component-maker Texas Instruments into the consumer market with its own machines, prompted dramatic changes in the market for calculators. The Japanese were caught unawares by the new technology. Although Japan produced semiconductors, they evidently were inferior to those made by Texas Instruments. Japanese chip producers could not believe that chips could be sold so cheaply and complained about American companies dumping chips in Japan when, in fact, the chips were selling for more in Japan than in the United States. In addition, Japanese companies focused on desktop devices and were slow to switch from vacuum-tube to solid-state displays.

Within weeks of the introduction of Texas Instruments' portable calculator, such products were the hottest selling consumer electronics product since the transistor radio, and American made goods were dominating the rapidly expanding business. The first pocket device, coming out in 1970, had a price of $400, but Christmas shoppers in 1972 could buy one for as little as $75. Total sales were expected to be 1.2 million for the year, more than double the number in 1971. The principal purchasers were businesses and professional people, accounting for 75 percent of sales.

A typical department store would sell seven or eight different brands of calculators. Several companies had entered the business in 1972. Competition led to price cuts every few weeks in the latter half of the year. The competing companies included Commodore, Craig, Bowmar, Rapid Data, and Ragen Precision Industries. All these companies, except Commodore, suffered a drop in stock price over the course of the year because of reduced prices and profit margins. Japanese companies retained a presence in the market. At a time when there was already a prospect of a shakeout resulting from intense competition, some firms were thinking of entering the market. These included Hewlett-Packard and Sperry Rand.

The intensity of price competition prompted by Texas Instruments' pocket model had begun even before the product was launched. The suggested retail price was first set at $149. Bowmar brought the price of its product down from $179 to $139. Texas Instruments responded by introducing its pocket calculator at a price of $119.95. Further price reductions were made possible by production efficiencies, with the price falling to $69.95, then $59.95, then $44.95, all within three months in 1974. Bowmar was able to match the first two price cuts.

Although most consumer goods markets were in recession in 1974, the still-immature market for hand-held calculators was growing spectacularly, with sales in the United States up 80 percent from the previous year. Prices had fallen by about 40 percent, and one simple calculator was selling for $17. Estimates of the worldwide market saw growth continuing until 1977, with a plateau of forty million units sold annually.

The shakeout of companies was apparent at the end of 1974, by which time about twenty companies had dropped out. At one time, about ninety companies had been in the market. In the long term, there would be about ten.

The most successful companies in the industry have been integrated ones making most of their own components. These companies include Texas Instruments, National Semiconductor, and Rockwell International. Bowmar set up its own chip-manufacturing plant in 1974, hoping thereby to overcome its disadvantage against Texas Instruments. Some foreign companies that perform only assembly have also done well. These include Canada's Commodore Business Machines and Japan's Casio Computer Company and Sharp Electronics.

Intense competition in the industry was the main impact of the introduction of the pocket calculator. Many companies entered the market, but most dropped out. Competition for sales forced drastic reductions in prices.

Price cutting caused problems for retailers. Rapid unannounced price reductions took value from any of the product held in inventory. Texas Instruments also annoyed some retailers by cutting prices and then not delivering calculators, at the same time selling them by direct mail. These tensions were seen as an opportunity by Rockwell International, which had its marketing staff focus on department stores. Texas Instruments president, Mark Shepherd, Jr., had long-term expansion plans that included setting up his own retail outlets selling calculators and other products.

The success of the pocket calculator spurred the development of models to do more complicated operations. Scientific calculators carry out calculations in advanced mathematics and science, proving useful to architects, statisticians, and engineers. Business calculators could handle time value and interest-rate problems easily and therefore were valuable for bankers, stockbrokers, accountants, and security analysts. Calculators came to be seen as necessities and were built into wristwatches and telephones. Talking calculators were developed for people with visual impairments. The impact of pocket calculators in everyday life has been very wide. In some occupations, a calculator is all but indispensable. Schools have come to accept them as tools for students rather than solely as crutches to aid those with poor arithmetic skills.

Bibliography

Ahlers, D. M. "Management Information Systems: From Spyglass to Pocket Calculator." *Financial Executive* 44 (July, 1976): 44-52. Situates the pocket calculator as the latest device to improved efficiency in commerce. Nicely written and interesting.

Lederer, Victor. "Calculators: The Applications Are Unlimited. *Administrative Management* 38 (July, 1977): 53-58. Describes many possibilities for use of calculators. Written with enthusiasm.

Murray, Thomas J. "The Mess in Consumer Electronics." *Dun's Review* 109 (June, 1977) 72-73. Comments on the competitive turmoil in the consumer electronics market.

Oliva, Ralph A., M. Dean Lamont, and Linda R. Fowler. *The Great International Math on Keys Book.* Dallas, Tex.: Texas Instruments Learning Center, 1976. Explains the functions of the calculator and its use in mathematical and scientific problems. Also includes puzzles and games. A simple introduction to the calculator.

"Pocket Calculators: Number Power." *Management Accounting* 57 (December, 1975): 54-56. Reviews the uses of pocket calculators in managerial accounting.

"The Semiconductor Becomes a New Marketing Force." *Business Week*, August 24, 1974, 34-39. Explains that the shakeout in the calculator market shows that integrated companies, which make their own components, are at an advantage. Large-scale manufacturing promised cost savings. Foreign markets are mentioned as the future battleground.

"Texas Instruments: Pushing Hard into the Consumer Markets." *Business Week*, August 24, 1974, 39-41. Describes Texas Instruments' strategy to develop an expanding business in consumer goods, with retail outlets planned. Bad relations with retailers are also reported.

Richard Barrett

Cross-References

Morita Licenses Transistor Technology (1953), p. 1009; Jobs and Wozniak Found Apple Computer (1976), p. 1611; VisiCalc Spreadsheet Software Is Marketed (1979), p. 1687; Electronic Technology Creates the Possibility of Telecommuting (1980's), p. 1733; IBM Introduces Its Personal Computer (1981), p. 1809.

NIXON SIGNS THE CONSUMER PRODUCT SAFETY ACT

Category of event: Consumer affairs
Time: October 28, 1972
Locale: Washington, D.C.

The Consumer Product Safety Act established an independent agency of the federal government to investigate the causes of product-related injuries and to develop regulations to control their occurrence

Principal personages:

WARREN GRANT MAGNUSON (1905-1989), a U.S. senator from California and a member of the Senate Committee on Commerce

JOHN E. MOSS (1915-   ), a U.S. senator from California and a member of the Senate Committee on Commerce

RICHARD M. NIXON (1913-1994), the thirty-seventh president of the United States

CHARLES PERCY (1919-   ), a U.S. senator from Illinois, the sponsor of the bill

Summary of Event

The Consumer Product Safety Act of 1972 (CPSA) established the Consumer Product Safety Commission (CPSC) as an independent agency of the federal government. The CPSC was given authority to identify unsafe products, establish standards for labeling and product safety, recall defective products, and ban products that posed unreasonable risks to consumers. In order to ensure compliance with its directives, the CPSC was given authority to impose civil and criminal penalties, including fines and jail sentences.

Prior to the enactment of the CPSA, attempts to reduce hazards associated with consumer products were fragmented and produced uneven results. Federal, state, and local laws addressed safety issues in a limited, piecemeal manner. Industry self-regulation was occasionally attempted by trade associations, testing laboratories, or other standards-making groups. Competitive economic forces often delayed or weakened the establishment of standards, and the inability of the industry legally to enforce standards once they were set often made these attempts little more than window dressing. In 1967, members of Congress decided that there had to be a consistent approach to the problems of injuries resulting from the use of consumer products.

The House of Representatives and the Senate enacted PL 90-146 in June, 1967, creating the National Commission on Public Safety. The commission was given the responsibility of identifying products presenting unreasonable hazards to consumers, examining existing means of protecting consumers from these hazards, and recommending appropriate legislative action.

In June, 1970, the commission reported the magnitude of the problem: 20 million people were injured each year because of incidents related to consumer products; 110,000 people were permanently disabled from such accidents; and 30,000 deaths resulted each year. The cost to the country was estimated to be more than $5.5 billion a year. The commission suggested that consumers were in more dangerous environments in their own homes than when driving on the highway. The commission outlined sixteen categories of products as providing unreasonably hazardous risks to the consumer. Architectural glass used for sliding doors in homes caused approximately 150,000 injuries a year; the commission recommended that safety-glazed materials be required for this use. Hot-water vaporizers that were capable of heating water to 180 degrees repeatedly caused second- and third-degree burns to young children. High-rise bicycles with "banana" seats, high handlebars, and small front wheels encouraged stunt riding and frequently resulted in injuries. Furniture polish with 95 percent petroleum distillates were packaged in screw-cap bottles, colored to resemble soft drinks, and attractively scented; many children who drank these suffered fatal chemical pneumonia. Power rotary lawn mowers sliced through fingers and toes and sent objects hurtling toward bystanders. Other products that the commission identified as posing unreasonable potential hazards to consumers included color television sets, fireworks, floor furnaces, glass bottles, household chemicals, infant furniture, ladders, power tools, protective headgear (especially football helmets), unvented gas heaters, and wringer washing machines.

The commission maintained that it was not entirely the responsibility of consumers to protect themselves, because they could reasonably be expected neither to understand all the existing hazards nor to know how to deal effectively with the hazards. Although consumers were becoming increasingly successful at receiving compensation for injuries through common law, manufacturers in general had not responded by taking preventive measures.

The commission suggested that a national program was needed to prevent further accidents and injuries. At hearings before the U.S. Senate Committee on Commerce on June 24, 1970, the National Commission on Public Safety recommended that an independent agency, the Consumer Product Safety Commission, be formed. Hearings were held between May of 1971 and February of 1972. These hearings allowed individuals representing both businesses and organizations concerned with health and safety issues to testify. Competing legislation included proposals to give the responsibility for oversight to the existing secretary of health, education, and welfare rather than to an independent agency. One proposal would have permitted the adoption of an existing private standard as a federal safety standard; this proposal, however, was criticized on the grounds that it might result in the acceptance of private standards that were inadequate or anticompetitive. Witnesses at the hearings testified on the problems of hazardous household products, the function and effectiveness of state and local laws, and the role of advertising and the need for public education and debated whether the American economy would reward or punish producers of safe consumer products, which were likely to carry higher prices. Manufacturers, legislators, college professors, attorneys, publishers, representatives of trade and professional associations, engineers, and physicians provided information and opinions on the proposed legislation.

The process brought about intense lobbying and heated debates. Companies saw the CPSC as a potential source of harassment, with government decisions affecting their industries. Sponsors of the legislation complained that regular government agencies listened too closely to the very industries that they were directed to regulate and ignored the voice of the consumer. Long filibustering sessions and angry accusations nearly killed the legislation. Observers claimed that key sponsors could have brought the issue to a vote sooner but were not present when votes on stopping the filibustering were taken. The Richard M. Nixon Administration publicly supported the legislation, but key aides supported the filibustering. The Grocery Manufacturers of America, a business lobby, distributed information kits on how to fight the bill in Congress, calling the legislation a threat to free enterprise. Opponents warned of the authority the agency could have, claiming that it had the potential to turn against the consumer, side with big business, and increase the costs of products to consumers.

Impact of Event

As it was passed in 1972, the Consumer Product Safety Act charged the CPSC with four main tasks: to protect the public from unreasonable risks of injury associated with the use of consumer products; to be of assistance to consumers in evaluating and comparing the safety of consumer products; to develop uniform safety standards for consumer products; and to encourage research and investigation into the causes and prevention of product-related deaths, illnesses, and injuries. "Consumer products" were defined both as things sold to customers as well as things distributed for the use of customers (such as component parts). Specifically excluded were tobacco and tobacco products, motor vehicles and equipment, pesticides, firearms and ammunition, aircraft, boats and equipment, drugs, cosmetics, and foods, as these fell under the jurisdiction of other existing agencies. Responsibility for a product was extended to include producers, importers, and, basically, anyone who handled the product in the stream of commerce.

The CPSC established a National Electronic Injury Surveillance System (NEISS) in order to collect and investigate information on injuries and deaths related to consumer products. NEISS is a computer-based system tied into more than one hundred hospital emergency rooms. The information in this system allows the commission to compute a product "hazard index." Products with the highest hazard indices—such as cleaning agents, swings and slides, liquid fuels, snowmobiles, and all-terrain vehicles—are targeted for further studies and possible regulation. The CPSC is authorized to perform in-depth studies on accidents and to investigate the effects and costs of these injuries to individuals and the country as a whole. If the CPSC believes there is significant cause, it can investigate the industry and product in question with the goal of encouraging voluntary industry safety standards or initiate mandatory safety standards of its own. If CPSC investigators believe that safety standards are required, they will research the product, develop test methods if necessary, and propose an appropriate safety standard. Proposals for appropriate standards are also solicited from the affected industry. Interested organizations, individuals, and industry representatives testify during open hearings on the proposed standards. After the hearings, the standards may be modified or enacted as proposed. Products that fail to meet the standards within a set period of time (from one to six months) may be pulled from store shelves, and manufacturers may face fines as well as jail sentences. If adequate safety standards cannot be designed, court action may be taken to have the products banned. So that unreasonable demands are not placed on a small company, fines for violations may be limited, or establishments of particular sizes may be given extensions of time in which to comply with regulations.

The establishment of specific standards is a process that is frequently viewed with concern by the manufacturers involved. When changes in manufacturing, product design, or labeling are suggested, manufacturers' associations respond with proposals, which include estimates of the additional costs necessary to implement the changes. Cost/benefit criteria are considered to determine if the benefits of a proposed action can be justified by the attendant costs. This not an easy issue to revolve. For example, the changes that were contemplated in the design of power lawn mowers included locating pull cords away from chokes and throttles, installing footguards, redesigning exhaust systems, and installing automatic cutoffs. The enacted changes increased the price of the power lawn mower to the consumer by an average of twenty-two dollars.

Manufacturers, legislators, and administrative figures all were aware of the potential power of CPSC. The establishment and enforcement of standards had the potential to raise the costs of manufacturing and, consequently, increase prices to consumers. Regulations had the potential to limit the types and quality of consumer products on the market. Passing the Consumer Product Safety Act did not bring an end to the debate. The CPSC's first action was to establish flammability standards for mattresses. As soon as the new regulations were established, the CPSC was promptly taken to court both by manufacturers' associations and by consumer groups unhappy with the standards. Manufacturers claimed that they were being unfairly asked to absorb the costs of switching materials and conducting new testing procedures; the problem, the manufacturers alleged, was really caused by careless cigarette smokers. Consumer groups claimed that the standards were not strict enough, since small manufacturers were given additional time during which they could sell mattresses that did not meet the flammability standards if such mattresses were prominently so labeled. Consumer groups wanted only safe mattresses on the market, without a time delay. In spite of the potential for unlimited power claimed by opponents, the CPSC—a watchdog agency—soon became the watched.

Critics of regulatory agencies argue that solutions to safety problems cost money and that these costs will be passed along to consumers. Direct costs, such as those involved in retooling, testing, labeling, and changes in personnel and material, are relatively easy to determine. Trade associations and manufacturers argue that government standards actually limit consumers' freedom of choice, increase costs, put people out of work, and lead to excessive governmental control. Many associations advocate self-regulation in order to preempt government involvement. Consumer-protection advocates contend that if self-regulation could solve the problem, there would not be any problem. They also argue that costs are inevitable when safety is concerned. Indirect costs, including hospital and doctors' fees, time lost from work, and pain and suffering from injuries, must be paid, whether by injured consumers, insurance companies, or manufacturers. Regardless of who pays directly, the ultimate cost is passed on, whether to the consumer or to the public as a whole.

Bibliography

Commerce Clearing House. *Consumer Product Safety Act: Law and Explanation.* Chicago: Author, 1972. Contains the text of the law and an overview of its meaning and intent.

Evans, Joel R., ed. *Consumerism in the United States: An Inter-Industry Analysis.* New York: Praeger, 1980. The history of consumerism is examined in ten industries. The roles of consumer groups, industries, individual companies, and the government are explored. Describes the effects of consumerism and legislation and the reactions by the businesses studied.

Katz, Robert N., ed. *Protecting the Consumer Interests.* Cambridge, Mass.: Ballinger, 1976. An edited version of papers presented by the National Affiliation of Concerned Business Students. Chapter 10, "The Consumer Product Safety Commission: Its Clout, Its Candor, and Its Challenge," by R. David Pittle, is an especially valuable essay.

Mayer, Robert N. *The Consumer Movement: Guardians of the Marketplace.* Boston: Twayne, 1989. A history of consumerism as a social movement, with an examination of the factors that affect the success of regulatory action. Attempts to quantify the economic impact of consumer-protection policies.

U.S. Consumer Product Safety Commission. *Regulatory Responsibilities of the U.S. Consumer Product Safety Commission: Study Guide.* Washington, D.C.: Government Printing Office, 1976. Developed as a training manual for entry-level inspectors. Easy to read. Excellent definitions, with detailed lists and explanations of products that are specifically not covered by legislation. Has quizzes and answers.

Sharon C. Wagner

Cross-References

Congress Passes the Pure Food and Drug Act (1906), p. 128; Nader's *Unsafe at Any Speed* Launches a Consumer Movement (1965), p. 1270; The United States Bans Cyclamates from Consumer Markets (1969), p. 1390; The Banning of DDT Signals New Environmental Awareness (1969), p. 1395; The U.S. Government Reforms Child Product Safety Laws (1970's), p. 1426; Congress Passes the Magnuson-Moss Warranty Act (1975), p. 1584.

ITT ACTIONS CAUSE SUSPICION OF INVOLVEMENT IN A CHILEAN COUP

Categories of event: Business practices; international business and commerce
Time: 1973
Locale: Santiago, Chile; New York, New York; and Washington, D.C.

After the Chilean electoral victory of Salvador Allende, International Telephone and Telegraph (ITT) representatives became involved in attempts to destabilize the government

Principal personages:
HAROLD GENEEN (1910-   ), the chief executive officer of ITT
SALVADOR ALLENDE (1908-1973), the president of Chile, 1970-1973
HENRY KISSINGER (1923-   ), the national security adviser to President Richard M. Nixon

Summary of Event

On September 4, 1970, Salvador Allende, the Marxist candidate for president of Chile, received the most votes of all candidates in the country's presidential election. Since he did not have a majority, the election was to be decided in the legislature. The United States government, acting through the State Department and the Central Intelligence Agency (CIA), had opposed Allende and had contributed at least $300,000 to defeat him. Almost immediately after the election, Henry Kissinger, then national security adviser to President Richard M. Nixon, developed a program at the CIA to prevent Allende from coming to power.

At the September 9, 1970, board of directors meeting of International Telephone and Telegraph (ITT), Harold Geneen, the chief executive officer, informed the board that Chiltelco, a telephone company in Chile in which ITT had a substantial stake, was in danger of being nationalized if Allende were elected. ITT's presence in Chile went back to 1927, when Chiltelco was granted a fifty-year concession that subsequently had been extended. Telephone operations are a capital-intensive business, and ITT made substantial investments in the company. During the 1960's, it provided Chiltelco with $40 million in new financing and reinvested all earnings above $19 million. As a result, Chiltelco's assets increased substantially. According to an audit in the late 1960's accepted both by the government and by ITT, it had a net worth of $200 million. By 1970, however, ITT had sold off a minority position in Chiltelco, bringing its investment down to $153 million.

Ever since the nationalization of ITT's Cuban telephone company by Fidel Castro—without strong protests or action by President Dwight D. Eisenhower—Geneen had been concerned about other properties that might meet with a similar fate. He feared that President Nixon would be tempted to follow the Eisenhower example and meant to do what he could to prevent confiscation. Geneen knew of the CIA plan to prevent Allende's election. Without asking approval from the ITT board of directors, he approached former CIA Director John McCone, who had become a member of the ITT board, and told McCone that he was prepared to spend as much as $1 million in support of any plan that was adopted by the government for the purpose of bringing about a coalition of the opposition to Allende so that when the Chilean legislature met to select the next president, Allende would be rejected. Geneen added that the offer had been transmitted to Kissinger. McCone indicated that he supported the plan.

Two days later, Jack Neal, a former State Department official who was in charge of international relations for ITT, telephoned Viron Peter Vaky, Kissinger's assistant for Latin American affairs, to tell him that Geneen was willing to come to Washington to discuss ITT's interests in Chile and that ITT was prepared to assist financially in a government operation there. Neal also proposed trying to interest other companies with investments in Chile in cooperating with the CIA but added that he had not had much success in this attempt. Vaky told Neal that he would pass on the information but apparently did not do so.

Meanwhile, Geneen asked McCone to go to Washington to sound out his contacts there regarding ideas on blocking Allende's election. McCone agreed to do so. He met with CIA Director Richard Helms and informed him of Geneen's offer. McCone also contacted Kissinger and told him of Geneen's offer. Kissinger thanked McCone and said that he would hear from him again. Kissinger did not indicate support for the plan, however, so McCone assumed that nothing would be done.

Kissinger had only one reference to ITT in his 1,496-page memoir, *White House Years* (1979), and that in the form of a footnote. "My own attitude was that any covert action in Chile should be carried out exclusively by our government; this was not a field for private enterprise. Accordingly, I turned down ITT's offer of $1 million to help influence the election. I may have agreed with the objective, but certainly not the vehicle."

Later on, in a congressional investigation of the matter, ITT board member Felix Rohatyn testified that Geneen had always taken the position that the company did not "participate" in the plot in Chile. In a carefully worded statement, Geneen said "ITT did not encourage or participate in any way in any alleged plot for a military coup in Chile to block the election of Dr. Allende." Moreover, the corporation "didn't contribute money to any person or to any agency of government to block the election of Dr. Allende." Finally, he claimed "ITT did not take any action to cause economic chaos in Chile in an attempt to block the election of Dr. Allende, nor did it advocate that any others take such steps."

Even so, ITT field representatives were in continual contact with CIA operatives and Allende's opponents. The key figures in this contact were Robert Berrellez, a former newspaper reporter who had specialized in Latin American affairs, and Harold Hendrix, a Pulitzer Prize-winning reporter. Both went to Santiago that summer to represent ITT and were under the direct control of Ned Gerrity, ITT's chief public relations officer.

Berrellez and Hendrix sent detailed memos to the home office that later were submitted to Congress and released to the public. From them one can obtain the picture of a corporation concerned with the nationalization of its remaining property in that part of the world. The memos also reveal that, as anticommunist Americans as well as ITT officials, board members were troubled by the growth of communism in Latin America.

In early October, it appeared that General Roberto Viaux, who had worked with the CIA, was planning a coup, which was opposed by General Rene Schneider, who had strong connections with the American State Department. The United States therefore was on both sides of the matter. To further complicate matters, Colonel Camilo Valenzuela also hoped to overthrow the government and was encouraged by the CIA.

On October 15, the CIA opted to defuse the situation, and Viaux was told that he would not be supported by the United States. CIA officials soon had second thoughts and backed Viaux. On October 17, several Chilean officers were provided with arms by the American military attaché, and Valenzuela informed Viaux that all preparations had been made. On October 19 and 20, there were two bungled attempts to kidnap Schneider. On October 22, Schneider was killed during yet another kidnapping effort. Riots erupted, and outgoing President Eduardo Frei declared a state of national emergency. This prompted Jorge Allesandri, who was Allende's chief opponent, to withdraw from the presidential race, asking his supporters to vote for Allende.

Allende won the October 24 balloting in the legislature by a margin of 153-35 with seven abstentions and so became president of Chile. He took office on November 3. Most of the key cabinet posts went to communists. On November 20, the government seized subsidiaries of Ralston Purina and Indiana Brass. Six days later, Allende spoke of his intention to nationalize American-owned copper mines, utilities, and banks.

This prompted a CIA response. On November 13, the agency approved an initial $25,000 for support of Christian Democrat candidates in the forthcoming local elections, and on November 19 it authorized the expenditure of $725,000 for a new covert operations program. In January, 1971, it authorized the use of an additional $1,240,000 for the purchase of radio stations and newspapers to support anti-Allende candidates. None of these efforts was supported by financial contributions by American firms, although some, including ITT, were kept informed.

ITT formed the Ad Hoc Committee on Chile, which brought together large corporations with Chilean interests as a lobbying team. At the same time, ITT representatives approached Allende Administration officials to initiate talks on possible compensation for seized properties. To provide compensation would be in his interests, Gerrity said. In a February 11 memo to Geneen, he wrote that Allende might be told that if a mutually acceptable solution could be found, he would improve relations with the United States and at the same time have a model to use in other nationalizations. Any funds that companies received in compensation might be invested in Chile, perhaps in ITT's chain of Sheraton hotels. ITT's president, Tim Dunleavy, presented the idea to Allende and told him that if a compensation plan worked, Chile's credit rating would go up around the world. ITT would go to the banks and tell them how fairly the company had been treated.

This approach failed. On April 28, the Chilean government proclaimed that it would nationalize Chiltelco and pay ITT a price of slightly more than $13 million. The company replied that Chiltelco was worth at least $153 million and that its insurance with the Overseas Private Investment Corporation (OPIC) covered only $92 million of that. ITT also lodged a protest with the State Department.

All the while, Allende made speeches denouncing Western imperialists. He suggested arbitration by the International Telecommunications Union coupled with an immediate takeover, a plan that ITT rejected. Talks were broken off on August 31. The Allende government froze Chiltelco's bank accounts, and on September 16 it established a three-member team to run the company. As anticipated, ITT filed additional protests while Neal designed a program designed to disrupt the Chilean economy. Nothing came of this, but the Export-Import Bank denied a Chilean loan request and the CIA added another $815,000 to its fund to assist opposition parties. This did not deter the Chilean government, which on September 29 seized control of Chiltelco.

Confiscations and nationalization ultimately worked against Allende. Pressure from the United States resulted in a stoppage of World Bank loans. Middle-class and wealthy Chileans fled the country, which experienced huge capital outflows. It was against this background that a coup developed on September 11, 1973, during which Allende was overthrown and was either killed or committed suicide. A right-wing military junta, to be headed by General Augusto Pinochet, took over in Santiago and soon thereafter opened negotiations with ITT regarding compensation for Chiltelco. This stirred rumors that ITT had supported Allende's opponents, was responsible for his death, and now was about to receive its payoff.

Impact of Event

The Chilean coup occurred at a time when the United States was torn by the aftermath of the Nixon impeachment crisis and the controversy surrounding President Gerald Ford's pardon of Nixon. The Vietnam War continued, and national morale was low, as was confidence in the federal government. The possibility that the United States—aided and abetted by ITT—had taken a role in the coup resulted in added criticisms. ITT offices in Rome, Zurich, and Madrid were bombed, and special precautions against similar violence were taken in New York City and elsewhere. As a result of its activities in Chile, ITT received a reputation as a rogue elephant of a company. Geneen's standing, once quite high, was besmirched.

Most of the story soon came out, when the Subcommittee on Multinational Corporations of the Senate Committee on Foreign Relations investigated the matter. Throughout the public hearings, ITT representatives insisted that they did nothing wrong and defended the company's attempts to influence government policy against Allende. Geneen appeared before the committee. He portrayed ITT as attempting to work with the American government in Chile but denied any involvement in the coup.

Rumors of ITT's involvement appeared and persisted, and stories were leaked to the press. This was compounded by the publication of an article by British journalist Anthony Sampson, titled "The Geneen Machine," in *New York* magazine. Sampson's book *The Sovereign State of ITT* (1973) appeared soon thereafter. It documented the affair in a lively and plausible manner. The book was a best-seller and was credited with sparking new riots against ITT installations around the world.

This was not the end of the story. In November, 1978, Stanley Sporkin, head of the Security and Exchange Commission's division of enforcement, charged that from 1970 to 1975 ITT had expended $8.7 million to fund illegal activities in Chile, Indonesia, Italy, Turkey, and several other countries. ITT replied that all payments were "consistent with the laws of their jurisdiction but may have been applied in a manner contrary to current corporate policies." It added that all such activities had ended in 1976.

The incident provoked a new round of debate about the role of business in politics and government affairs. Multinational corporations had a long history of involvement in the politics of the less developed countries in which they operated, sometimes treating the governments of those countries as contractors or agents whose purpose was to fulfill corporate objectives. Corporate officials claimed that bribery and other forms of corruption that they undertook were all part of the game of politics in these countries. Nevertheless, because of such cases as ITT's involvement in Chile, greater attention was paid to corporate dealings overseas.

Bibliography

MacEoin, Gary. *No Peaceful Way: Chile's Struggle for Dignity.* New York: Sheed and Ward, 1974. A work generally sympathetic to Allende and critical of ITT.

Petras, James, and Morris Morley. *The United States and Chile.* New York: Monthly Review Press, 1975. Important primarily because of its collection of documents relating to ITT's involvement in Chile.

Rojas, Robinson. *The Murder of Allende and the End of the Chilean Way to Socialism.* New York: Harper and Row, 1976. Strongly pro-Allende, considering him to be an independent reformer who was murdered for attempting to free his country from foreign domination.

Sampson, Anthony. *The Sovereign State of ITT.* New York: Stein and Day, 1973. A strongly anti-ITT book that was a best-seller. Marred by omissions and not reflective of later scholarship.

Sigmund, Paul. *The Overthrow of Allende and the Politics of Chile, 1964-1976.* Pittsburgh, Pa.: University of Pittsburgh Press, 1977. The most complete and scholarly work on the subject.

Sobel, Robert. *I.T.T.: The Management of Opportunity.* New York: Times Books, 1982. Written independently but with the company's cooperation, this book contains a chapter dealing with ITT's involvement in Chile.

Zanartu, Mario, and John Kennedy. *The Overall Development of Chile.* Notre Dame, Ind.: University of Notre Dame Press, 1969. A good source for background material on the Chilean economy.

Robert Sobel

Cross-References

Oil Companies Cooperate in a Cartel Covering the Middle East (1928), p. 551; The United Fruit Company Instigates a Coup in Guatemala (1954), p. 1040; Frei "Chileanizes" Chile's Copper Industry (1964-1970), p. 1207; Johnson Restricts Direct Foreign Investment (1968), p. 1341; The World Health Organization Condemns Use of Infant Formula (1981), p. 1798; Toxic Gas Leaks from a Union Carbide Plant in Bhopal, India (1984), p. 1893; The United States Bans Chilean Fruit After Cyanide Scare (1989), p. 1986; Elimination of Secret Swiss Bank Accounts Ends a Myth (1991), p. 2045.

IRAN ANNOUNCES NATIONALIZATION OF FOREIGN OIL INTERESTS

Category of event: Government and business
Time: March 20, 1973
Locale: Iran

By nullifying a contract with oil companies that was not due to expire until 1979, Iran set the stage for crucial events in the history of world economic relations

Principal personages:
MOHAMMAD REZA SHAH PAHLAVI (1919-1980), the shah of Iran, 1941-1979
AHMAD ZAKI YAMANI (1930-   ), the oil minister of Saudi Arabia, 1962-1986
FAISAL (c. 1905-1975), the king of Saudi Arabia, 1964-1975
MOHAMMAD MOSSADEGH (1880-1967), the prime minister of Iran, 1951-1953

Summary of Event

On March 16, 1973, the shah of Iran, Mohammad Reza Shah Pahlavi, announced that oil companies had handed over operation of the Iranian oil industry. Foreign-owned oil companies were to become customers for rather than producers of oil from Iran. On March 20, the shah announced that the takeover would take effect on that day, and that production and refining facilities would be controlled by the National Iranian Oil Company (NIOC).

Thus the St. Moritz Agreement initially discussed by the shah and senior oil company officials on February 26, 1973, was concluded, replacing the 1954 agreement between Iran and consortium companies. The agreement embodying the new conditions was signed in the middle of July and ratified by the Majlis (Iranian parliament) on July 31. The new deal provided for increased production capacity, assured Iran of a price per barrel no lower than that of the other Persian Gulf producers, and made crude oil available to NIOC for direct exports. NIOC still needed the oil companies' expertise in exploration and exploitation. Under the new agreement, Iran was committed to long-term oil sales to the consortium companies and received only 4 percent of oil production for independent export and domestic use. The agreement reflected Iran's lack of expertise to run its own oil industry and a commitment to continued links with the West.

Taking advantage of its increased control, NIOC offered some of its surplus oil to international bidding. This proved to be of far-reaching importance. Given the prevailing concern about a prospective energy shortage and the heavy dependence of Japan on Iranian oil, Japanese companies offered the highest bid at $17.80 a barrel. This relatively high price provided Iran and other Persian Gulf producers with a solid base for negotiations with the oil companies. Negotiations opened, but when the fourth Arab-Israeli war broke out on October 6 and Iraq nationalized U.S. interests in the Basrah Petroleum Company, talks collapsed on October 12. Thus the stage was set for the second oil crisis since World War II, involving tremendous escalation of oil prices.

The primary actors in the oil trade following World War II were the international oil companies, the consuming-country governments, and the oil-exporting countries. The industry during this period was dominated by seven interlocked firms—Exxon, Mobil, Standard Oil of California, Texaco, Gulf, British Petroleum, and Royal Dutch/Shell—collectively known as the majors or the Seven Sisters. These were later joined and challenged by newcomers, both independent private companies and state-backed companies. The United States was by far the most important consuming country. Its political and military power, the fact that five of the majors and as many of the independents were based there, and its status as the largest single oil market gave the United States particular importance. Western Europe, however, provided the largest market for the oil-exporting countries. Of the thirteen members of the Organization of Petroleum Exporting Countries (OPEC), Saudi Arabia was the most important, followed by Iran, Iraq, Kuwait, Venezuela, and Libya.

The history of world oil following World War II was shaped by three major crises: a shortage of supplies at the close of World War II, the 1973-1974 oil price shocks, and the 1979 price increases. The first postwar energy crisis was resolved by the international system that the United States organized around Middle East oil. Because the system had been organized by the United States in accordance with its own interests, other countries viewed it as not in their best interests. Conflicts led to the second oil crisis, that of 1973-1974. A drive for greater control by OPEC governments over oil-production operations, in the form of participation or nationalization, along with Arab frustration at the lack of progress in securing Israeli withdrawals from the occupied territories, was instrumental in initiating the oil price revolution of the early 1970's.

The demand for nationalization had a long history. In 1951, Prime Minister Mohammad Mossadegh nationalized the Iranian oil fields, but they were given back three years later. In 1961, Iraq nationalized the unexploited acreage in the Iraq Petroleum Company concession. In 1967, Algeria nationalized British Petroleum's Algerian retail network as the first step in a process that led to national control of the country's oil industry. Algeria's nationalizations and its success in selling its oil put the other oil-exporting countries under pressure to seize control of their oil industries. Subsequently, in 1971 OPEC announced a demand for effective participation in ownership of the companies' producing assets. Persian Gulf exporting countries initially sought 20 percent participation.

In October, 1971, representatives of twenty-three international oil companies met in London, armed with an antitrust waiver from the U.S. Department of Justice, to prepare to confront OPEC on participation. Meanwhile, political developments encouraged Libya to nationalize British Petroleum facilities on December 7, 1971. Negotiations between OPEC and the oil companies got under way early in 1972.

Ahmad Zaki Yamani pursued the talks on behalf of the Persian Gulf producers. A series of meetings followed. On February 16, King Faisal of Saudi Arabia intervened by issuing a blunt warning to the oil companies, which soon accepted the principle of 20 percent government participation. The two sides were still far apart regarding other items of the deal. Talks between Yamani and the companies continued from April to June with little progress, accompanied by warnings of impending unilateral action by OPEC.

At this juncture, a number of significant events altered the complexion of the participation talks. On June 1, 1972, negotiations between Iraq and the Iraq Petroleum Company (IPC), which had started in January along with the Persian Gulf participation talks, broke down, and Iraq announced its nationalization of the IPC's fields in northern Iraq. The Iraqi nationalization put additional pressure on other Persian Gulf countries and the companies. The next shock came less than a month later. On June 28, the shah announced a new program for Iran's oil industry. He demanded an immediate increase in production and a greater direct role for NIOC in all branches of the industry. The oil companies' refusal to meet the shah's demand culminated in the nationalization of March 20, 1973.

Impact of Event

Rivalry between various oil-exporting countries tended to spur OPEC on, leading to a leapfrog process in which one group secured gains only to be outdone by another group. Unprecedented economic growth in the oil-consuming countries encouraged a sharp rise in market process for petroleum products, as did the fourth Arab-Israeli war and the associated oil embargo and Arab oil-production cutbacks. After 1974, the price of oil stabilized to some extent, but in 1979, as a result of the shutdown of Iranian oil production during the Iranian revolution, the price skyrocketed once again.

These unprecedented price increases represented a fundamental reordering of power relationships as well as the largest nonviolent transfer of wealth in human history. The oil-exporting countries triumphed in asserting the power of nation-states over international companies, in addition to forcing the consuming countries to transfer significant streams of income to the exporting countries.

The rises in oil prices challenged the world economy. Higher prices meant slower rates of growth, since production was more expensive; increased inflation; and serious balance-of-payments problems, as countries had to send more of their currencies to oil exporters. Higher prices also meant, paradoxically, increased availability of adequate energy supplies, as they encouraged conservation and development of new sources. Because of such conflicting effects, response to the crisis was especially difficult, as measures that alleviated one part of the problem aggravated other parts. The United States assumed leadership, urging a collective multilateral reaction to OPEC and discouraging other consuming countries from concluding bilateral agreements with the exporting countries. Western Europe and Japan did not want to antagonize OPEC or to be associated with U.S. support for Israel and thus were reluctant to follow the U.S. lead.

Though highly significant, the economic consequences of the oil price explosion proved to be manageable. By 1978, the Middle East appeared to be stabilized. Disunity among oil consumers, heavy dependence upon Middle East oil, rivalry among oil companies, and the national aspirations and militancy of the Middle Eastern suppliers remained strongly evident. A complex of such factors combined to produce yet another oil crisis in 1979. Consuming countries failed to develop effective energy policies because of their lack of cooperation and the international oil companies' reluctance to develop new sources of oil and alternative sources of energy.

The dependence of the exporting countries upon the international oil companies persisted. The less wealthy exporters looked to the international companies for the capital and the expertise to maintain and expand their oil-producing operations. In addition, the majors were still the only ones capable of performing most secondary and tertiary recovery work and also the only source of the technology for the liquefaction of petroleum gases. Exporting countries looked to their former concessionaires for aid in moving into downstream operations, such as refineries, and sought their assistance in economic development programs as well as the companies' political support within the consuming countries. As the exporting countries assumed formal control over their oil-producing assets, as Iran had done, the companies came under widespread attack in the consuming countries.

The most significant impact of the price rise on the oil companies was the greatly increased value of their assets. Prior to 1973, oil company profits lagged behind those in other U.S. industries, but the tightening of the market and the price explosion led to an enormous increase in profits earned outside the United States. Oil production continued to be the most profitable sector, both in the United States and in the OPEC countries. Because of long-term uncertainty and the volatility of their earnings, however, the oil companies intensified their efforts to diversify into other fields.

The oil companies became very active in the coal industry, controlling large portions of U.S. coal resources and production. They also performed a large proportion of the work in synthetic fuels. Oil companies also made major nonenergy acquisitions. In 1974, Mobil began its takeover of Marcor, best known for its Montgomery Ward outlets. Exxon developed a chain of small computer-related companies, and Gulf spent several hundred million dollars to secure control of Kewanee, a company that derived most of its income from sales of chemicals. Aside from Texaco, each of the majors acquired significant holdings outside the traditional oil, gas, and petrochemical fields. In their diversification strategies, the oil companies looked for new growth areas and recognized that they had to dominate new energy sources and technologies. In addition to diversifying, oil companies also began to acquire each other; for example, British Petroleum took over Standard Oil of Ohio.

The diversification schemes accounted for only a small portion of the companies' total sales. Profits went up greatly in 1973-1974, but costs also rose—particularly for crude oil—and profits soon fell below the average rate of return in other industries. For all the turbulence, the companies survived. The governments of oil-exporting countries were not always able to manage without them even after taking control, as demonstrated by Iran, which succumbed to revolution and the dramatic fall of the shah. Although those events had other causes, economic difficulties and problems in relationships with international companies certainly played a role.

Bibliography

Amirsadeghi, Hossein, ed. *Twentieth Century Iran.* New York: Holmes & Meier, 1977. A number of American, British, and Iranian specialists provide a useful introduction to the history of Iran in the twentieth century. About thirty pages are devoted to a concise and interesting account of the development of the Iranian oil industry.

Lenczowski, George, ed. *Iran Under the Pahlavis.* Stanford, Calif.: Hoover Institution Press, 1978. An excellent detailed summary of achievements of Iran to 1975, written by several authorities in the field. A relatively long chapter describes Iranian oil policy from 1925 to 1975. Other chapters cover social, economic, educational, cultural, and foreign policy.

Sampson, Anthony. *The Seven Sisters: The Great Oil Companies and the World They Shaped.* New York: Viking Press, 1975. Describes how one of the world's biggest and most critical industries came to be dominated by seven giant companies. Essentially a book about political consequences of oil rather than its economic basis. A highly readable and absorbing account.

Schneider, Steven A. *The Oil Price Revolution.* Baltimore: The Johns Hopkins University Press, 1983. An excellent, detailed, and comprehensive account that seeks to explain the oil crises by examining the interrelationships between governments and companies.

Seymour, Ian. *OPEC: Instrument of Change.* New York: St. Martin's Press, 1981. Recalls OPEC's record of achievements and its rise from relative obscurity to world eminence. Detailed and accurate on a technical level. Highlights the broad sweep of events that enabled OPEC members to regain control of their destinies after so many years of subservience.

Shwadran, Benjamin. *Middle East Oil Crises Since 1973.* Boulder, Colo.: Westview Press, 1986. A well-organized, lucid account. Delineates changes in the power equation, the political atmosphere, and the resources of the participants since 1973. Provides persuasive evidence that the absence of strategic planning, narrow vision, and economic forces were major factors in the crises.

Kambiz Tabibzadeh

Cross-References

The Supreme Court Decides to Break Up Standard Oil (1911), p. 206; Oil Is Discovered in Venezuela (1922), p. 385; Oil Companies Cooperate in a Cartel Covering the Middle East (1928), p. 551; Supertankers Begin Transporting Oil (1968), p. 1336; Arab Oil Producers Curtail Oil Shipments to Industrial States (1973), p. 1544; The United States Plans to Cut Dependence on Foreign Oil (1974), p. 1555; Carter Orders Deregulation of Oil Prices (1979), p. 1699.

FEDERAL EXPRESS BEGINS OPERATIONS

Category of event: Foundings and dissolutions
Time: April 17, 1973
Locale: Little Rock, Arkansas

Fred Smith developed Federal Express into an alternative to the United States Postal Service

Principal personages:
FRED SMITH (1944-   ), the founder of Federal Express
ARTHUR BASS (1940-   ), one of Smith's closest aides, a key figure in Federal Express' early history
HENRY CROWN (1896-1990), a Chicago financier who helped Smith find necessary financing

Summary of Event

Until the mid-1970's, Americans who desired rapid delivery of small packages and documents had to settle for airmail transmission by the United States Postal Service. There was no certainty of when packages would arrive. Several private companies provided express delivery, the most prominent being Emery Air Freight and Flying Tiger, but these were relatively small operations, each of which did less than $100 million a year in total business. They each had few offices, some in out-of-the-way commercial areas and none outside major population centers. Moreover, they concentrated on commercial customers wanting to send bulk items. Emery and Flying Tiger competed not with the post office but rather with furniture moving companies that used trucks and railroad cars to transport large items. Neither company thought it possible or desirable to expand out of this base. To do so would require large amounts of capital and a different kind of work force from that currently employed. Besides, to deliver mail in competition with the U.S. Postal Service was illegal at the time.

While a student at Yale University, Fred Smith arrived at the conclusion that he could provide better service than provided by the post office. Smith came from a family with deep roots in transportation. One of his grandfathers had been a riverboat captain, and his father had founded the Dixie Greyhound Bus Lines. Later, Smith's father founded a chain of restaurants that, when sold, fetched $22 million. Part of this legacy would be used by Smith in his own business ventures.

In 1965, Smith sketched in a term paper the outlines of a new kind of transportation company to challenge the postal service. His professor was unimpressed. Perhaps it could be done, he conceded, but as noted, federal regulations precluded competition with the post office. Even if these regulations were overcome, large airlines would have the edge in creating such a service. A start-up company would not have a chance. Smith's paper received a grade of C.

In 1969, after serving in the Marine Corps, Smith purchased a controlling interest in Arkansas Aviation Sales, a firm based in Little Rock, Arkansas, that provided maintenance services for corporate airplanes and had annual revenues of $1 million. Smith expanded the company into the purchase and sales of used airplanes. From the beginning, he intended this company to provide the base for an express mail carrier.

Smith commissioned two firms to study the matter. They reported widespread dissatisfaction with existing services. One found that although more than 60 percent of all traffic flowed between cities in the largest twenty-five markets, 80 percent of small, urgent shipments originated or terminated outside them. Shippers or receivers at these places had to wait for available scheduled carriers to pick up or deliver packages at distant locations. At a time when manufacturing and research facilities increasingly were choosing locations outside central cities and had an urgent need for rapid deliveries, such a service as Smith had in mind seemed to meet the demands of a growing potential clientele.

The other report noted that nine out of ten domestic commercial airlines were inoperational between 10 P.M. and 8 A.M. This meant that airlanes were uncluttered in those hours, so that takeoffs and landings would be unproblematic and relatively unlikely to be delayed. The task of creating a company that would concentrate on overnight deliveries would be eased.

Armed with these findings, Smith set about raising funds to start operations. He soon learned just how high the capital requirements would be, and he met with investor skepticism similar to that shown by his professor. Smith committed all of his own capital, more than $8 million. This impressed some private investors, who added another $40 million. Several banks contributed a similar amount, bringing the total to $90 million. This made Smith's company the largest single venture capital start-up in American history to that time.

Smith called the company Federal Express and incorporated it on June 1, 1971. He purchased thirty-three twin-engine Dassault Falcons, largely because they were small enough to slip under the Civil Aeronautics Board's certification requirements for nationwide freight services. He then put his business plan into action.

Drawing upon the standards of the United Parcel Service, Smith limited the size of packages to seventy-five pounds. These parcels would be picked up or deposited at central receiving stations and then sent to a central hub location, from which they would be rerouted to their final destinations. After some consideration, Smith decided upon Memphis, Tennessee, as his first hub. Initially, Federal Express offered three services: guaranteed overnight delivery, a reduced rate for second-day delivery, and a "courier pack," an envelope in which the sender would deposit documents to be delivered the next day for a flat fee of $5.

Smith went to great lengths to publicize his company. Trucks and planes were brightly painted in orange, purple, and white, and full-page advertisements stressing reliability were placed in leading publications and emphasized the company's promise of "Absolutely, Positively, Overnight." This was necessary not only to obtain business but also to provide the image required to obtain additional financing. "We purchased the credibility we needed to entice capital sources," Smith explained.

Operations began on April 17, 1973, with service to twenty-two cities. Revenues that year came to $6.1 million, on which the company reported a loss of $4.7 million. More money was needed, a situation that became chronic in the company's early years. Smith obtained assistance from Chicago-based financier Henry Crown, who helped him obtain a $23.7 million loan from Chase Manhattan Bank.

A year later, Federal Express lost $13.4 million on revenues of $17.3 million. The company fell into technical default, and Smith liquidated all of his holdings to help pay bills. On one occasion, he used $27,000 won at a Las Vegas blackjack table to meet a payroll. Couriers would leave their wristwatches for security against fuel purchases and would hide the Falcons when sheriffs came to repossess them.

During this period, Federal Express benefited from unforeseen developments. The company came into being at a time when airline traffic was expanding rapidly. Total industry revenues, which came to $7.2 billion in 1970, rose to $11.2 billion in 1972, then to $19.9 billion in 1977. Finding themselves in the unusual position of being short of carriers because of expanding demand, the major delivery services concentrated on their prime markets and dropped services to many smaller cities. Federal Express filled the gap. In addition, there was a long United Parcel Service strike in 1974, followed by the collapse the following year of rival REA Air Express. These events provided Federal Express with new opportunities.

Furthermore, Federal Express began operations at a time when more Americans than ever before were demanding the kinds of services available previously to relatively few people. Arthur Bass, one of Smith's early executives who became the company president, stated that modern communications had given people in out-of-the-way areas the same expectations for service as those who lived in large cities. Urban businesspeople expected rapid deliveries, but so did shopkeepers in villages and towns. Bass's ambition was to serve both constituencies, but that would take time. Other technologies, such as xerography and telephonics, also had taken time to diffuse from large businesses to smaller businesses and individuals.

Smith saw the United States business community as being in the midst of an evolution into a new form. He intended Federal Express to be nothing short of the logistics arm of a whole new society that was in the process of being created, a society built not around automobile and steel production but instead around service industries and high-technology endeavors in electronics, optics, and medical science.

Impact of Event

Federal Express posted an $11.5 million loss in 1975, but as the year wore on it became evident that a turnaround was taking place. In 1976, the company had revenues of $75 million and a net profit of $3.6 million.

As a result of legislation passed in 1977, Federal Express was permitted to operate larger aircraft, and Smith promptly purchased used Boeing 727-100's from several airlines, greatly expanding capacity. That year, Federal Express reported revenues of $160 million and earnings of $20 million, sufficiently impressive for Smith to plan the first public stock offering. This came in April, 1978, with 1,075,000 shares offered at $3 a share. By 1980, when Federal Express had earnings slightly under $60 million on revenues of $590 million, the stock's price was up to $24. Smith was a celebrity, and the development of Federal Express became the subject of many articles and business school case studies. Smith continued to talk about innovation and his developing business philosophy. To one interviewer, he noted that to some degree the term "entrepreneur" had taken on the connotation of "gambler." He did not see it that way. Many times action was not the most risky path. Rather, risk came with standing still in a rapidly changing environment.

Federal Express became a glamour company on the stock market. In 1983, it posted revenues of more than $1 billion, on which it earned $89 million.

Smith's successes revolutionized postal services not only in the United States but also in most developed countries. As the pace of business and government quickened, express services became more important. By the 1980's, the U.S. Postal Service recognized this fact and began offering many of the same services as Federal Express.

Federal Express invigorated other express companies and encouraged newcomers, but its successes also led to the departure of some rivals, such as the aforementioned REA Air Express. The leading competitor of Federal Express in the early 1980's was Emery Air Freight, which still concentrated on large parcels. Federal Express' rapid growth encouraged Emery to enter the small-package and letter markets in 1978. Emery tried to break into the market by offering low prices, leading to a price war. Emery foundered, unable to translate its expertise in cargo into this new area. Smith noted that price cutting will not help a company that cannot deliver its product. Airborne Freight, another competitor, made the same mistake.

In 1982, United Parcel Service (UPS), an enterprise with $5 billion in annual revenues, began offering express service. Even that company, with some of the best management in America, had difficulties, which Smith immediately spotted. UPS was the best in the business at what it did, Smith told reporters, adding that its business was moving low-priority, consumer-oriented parcels for which time is not a factor. Federal Express specialized in emergency deliveries. As did Emery and other competitors, UPS had difficulties matching the efficiency and service of Federal Express. The same was true for Purolator Courier and others that entered the market later with hopes of replicating Smith's successes.

In 1989, Smith opened negotiations for an acquisition of Flying Tiger. The companies both were involved with express services, but while Federal Express concentrated on shipments of less than 150 pounds, Flying Tiger, like other older companies, catered to customers having much heavier loads to transport. In addition, Federal Express used smaller planes than Flying Tiger's Boeing 747's. Smith's offer of $895 million was approved by Flying Tiger, and the U.S. Justice Department approved the deal as not being a combination in restraint of trade. With Flying Tiger in his camp, Smith was well-positioned to expand freight services, especially in Europe.

This was a major acquisition. Flying Tiger had revenues of $1.4 billion in its most recent fiscal year, on which it had earned $89 million. There was a downside to the deal: The merged companies had a debt of $2.1 billion, which some analysts thought would be difficult to service.

Smith continued to sharpen his techniques and improve service, in the process giving Federal Express the reputation of being one of the best-managed companies in the world. By the late 1980's, he had devised five strategic goals for the firm: to improve service while differentiating the company from rivals such as UPS; to lower rates, both to expand the client base and to contest markets with rivals; to get close to the customer, maintaining dialogues with customers to make certain that services offered changed as customer needs evolved; to maximize electronic and technological capacities, keeping abreast of developing technologies and applying them to the business before rivals could react; and to improve cash flow and financial performance, not only to provide funds for expansion but also to increase dividends, keep the price of the common stock high, service shareholders, and ensure a strong market for future stock offerings.

Smith continued to take risks, some of which turned out badly. In the mid-1980's, he offered a service he called Zapmail. Federal Express offered to deliver documents anywhere in the United States within hours of deposit at one of its facilities. Zapmail would be made possible through the use of fax machines, relatively rare at the time but soon ubiquitous. This time Smith acted too soon. The market was not yet ready for faxing, and the service barely got off the ground. Federal Express finally abandoned Zapmail, but not until it lost more than $1 billion on the project.

Meanwhile, the express service expanded rapidly. Federal Express surpassed $2 billion in revenues in 1984, $3 billion in 1986, and $5 billion in 1988. By then, it had 53 percent of the U.S. market, followed by UPS with 19 percent.

Bibliography

"All Strung Up: Federal Express." *The Economist* 327 (April 17, 1993): 70. Discusses financial problems experienced by Federal Express as a result of European operations.

Curry, Gloria. "Package Delivery Services: The Options Are Plentiful." *The Office* 110 (August, 1989): 60. Contains a good analysis of the company, along with comparisons to its rivals.

Nash, Kim S. "Unix Net Helps Fedex Say 'No Problem.' " *Computerworld* 26 (November 23, 1992): 1. Describes a computer networking project begun by Federal Express with the intent of improving the tracking of packages.

Sigafoos, Robert A. *Absolutely, Positively Overnight: The Story of Federal Express.* New York: New American Library, 1984. The first history of the company. Chatty and informal, with little analysis.

Trimble, Vance. *Overnight Success: Federal Express and Frederick Smith, Its Renegade Creator.* New York: Crown, 1993. Written without cooperation from the company or Smith. Trimble describes the company's successes and failures as well as offering some unflattering details of the founder's life.

Robert Sobel

Cross-References

The Post Office Begins Transcontinental Airmail Delivery (1920), p. 357; Congress Authorizes Private Carriers for Airmail (1925), p. 493; The Air Commerce Act Creates a Federal Airways System (1926), p. 499; An Independent Agency Takes Over U.S. Postal Service (1971), p. 1506; Electronic Technology Creates the Possibility of Telecommuting (1980's), p. 1733.

ARAB OIL PRODUCERS CURTAIL OIL SHIPMENTS TO INDUSTRIAL STATES

Category of event: International business and commerce
Time: October 17, 1973
Locale: Kuwait City, Kuwait

In response to the United States' decision to supply Israel during the October, 1973, Yom Kippur War, Arab oil ministers agreed to reduce oil shipments to nonfriendly oil importers

Principal personages:

FAISAL (c. 1905-1975), the king of Saudi Arabia, prime force in initiating the embargo

HENRY A. KISSINGER (1923-   ), the White House national security adviser and chief foreign policy negotiator in the Nixon Administration

ANWAR EL-SADAT (1918-1981), the president of Egypt, 1970-1981

Summary of Event

The decision by Arab oil-exporting states to withhold oil from states supporting Israel during the October, 1973, Yom Kippur War was a watershed in the history of modern Western civilization. It revealed the fragile roots of the Western life-style, which had come to rest on an energy source Western countries did not control and for which there was no ready substitute. It also drove a wedge between members of the Western alliance based on their differing degrees of vulnerability to the disruption of their energy supplies. Western countries bid against one another for oil on the spot market, driving up the price of oil and providing the Organization of Petroleum Exporting Countries (OPEC) with the moment it needed to wrest control over the price and production of petroleum from the cartel of private oil companies that had controlled the international oil market for much of the twentieth century.

The developments leading to this event are easily summarized. The degree to which the moment could have been avoided and the seriousness of the embargo itself, however, became subjects of hot debate for years following the embargo.

By 1973, the major oil corporations that had collectively managed the world petroleum industry for nearly half a century were beginning to lose their grip on the market. New oil companies had gone multinational and had invested heavily in states that had only recently begun producing oil on a large scale. Because a state was often the only foreign source of supply for a company, the governments of new oil-producing states such as Libya were able to extract greater revenue from the development of their oil fields than the larger corporations (Standard Oil of New Jersey, British Petroleum, Shell Oil, Mobil, Gulf, Texaco, and Standard Oil of California), with multiple sources, were conceding to their host governments. To satisfy the latter, the larger firms were forced to increase the posted price of oil. Under the 50/50 profit-sharing system then being employed, higher prices allowed the companies to give their hosts revenues per barrel that matched the revenues that governments such as that of Libya were receiving from the smaller, more vulnerable oil companies such as Occidental. These concessions, in turn, became the basis for new rounds of negotiations between Libya and Occidental. Libya would press its advantage, and the new concessions wrung out of Occidental would then generate another round of negotiations between the major oil companies and OPEC's more established members. Further price increases and tensions in the oil market followed.

Only thinly masked by this process was the fact that the major oil companies had already lost their former power to dictate the market price to producing states. Furthermore, many of the older oil-producing states were no longer satisfied with the 50/50 agreement and demanded the right to buy into the majors' operations within their borders. Matters reached a head at the September, 1973, OPEC meeting in Vienna, Austria, when several delegates noted the windfall profits the oil companies were reaping, under the 50/50 agreement, from increases in the market price of oil. They called for a new system for determining the revenue of the oil-producing states. Discussion was scheduled to continue at a follow-up meeting in October.

Meanwhile, within the Middle East tensions had again been rising between Israel and its neighboring Arab states. The Saudis regularly sent—often through the multinational oil firms—warnings to Henry A. Kissinger, President Richard M. Nixon's national security adviser, and others in Washington that in the event of another Arab-Israeli war, assistance by the United States to Israel would almost certainly trigger retaliation in the global petroleum market. That market was already short of supply because of the demand for oil resulting from exceptionally high growth rates in Western economies during the 1968-1973 period.

Far from adjusting to this new reality, the Nixon Administration had contributed to an even greater tightening of the market in the early 1970's. It had dropped a quota system that had limited America's oil imports to 12 percent of the oil consumed in the United States. In slightly more than a year, American demand for imported oil shot above six million barrels per day, nearly twice the level of 1971. The federal government, nurtured on decades of abundant, cheap oil and preoccupied with the then-breaking Watergate scandal, ignored the warnings of Arab states even as tensions continued to build between Israel and Egypt, Jordan, and Syria, all of which had lost land to Israel in the June, 1967, war. King Faisal of Saudi Arabia had a special stake in the resolution of these territorial disputes. The June war had left Israel in control of Jerusalem. As the official protector of Islam's holy places (Mecca, Medina, and Jerusalem), Saudi Arabia was expected to do everything in its power to reopen Arab access to Jerusalem.

It was against this economic and political backdrop that the Egyptians and Syrians launched a surprise attack as Israel celebrated Yom Kippur on October 6, 1973. In the initial days of the war, their armies enjoyed considerable success in entering lands Israel had occupied since 1967. Israel had to deplete its supply of war materials to halt the Arab advance. For the first time during an Arab-Israeli war, Israel had to request military assistance from the United States. On October 14, as the scheduled OPEC session drew near, highly visible American Air Force transports carrying military equipment touched down in Israel.

On October 16, the delegates of the five Arab states along the Persian Gulf, along with a delegate from Iran, met in Kuwait City, Kuwait, to discuss the evolving situation. As OPEC moved to increase the posted price of oil without further consultation with the oil industry, the Arab delegates opted on October 17 to impose a 5 percent cut in oil deliveries on states friendly to Israel. An additional 5 percent cut per month would occur until the oil-importing states officially endorsed United Nations Resolution 242, which called on Israel to relinquish the land it had seized in the 1967 war. The announcement of these cuts spurred a round of fear-laden buying and resultant price increases on the spot market. On October 20, 1973, fear turned to panic as Saudi Arabia responded to President Nixon's announcement of a $22 billion military assistance package for Israel by cutting off all oil shipments to the United States, Holland, and other pro-Israel states. The following day, Aramco (Arabian-American Oil Company) executives were summoned to King Faisal's royal palace to help plan the details of implementing the embargo.

Impact of Event

The Arab oil embargo had profound political and economic ramifications. Both the developed, oil-importing world and the developing world felt its direct and indirect consequences, as did the multinational oil companies. A major disruption in the flow of oil was not among these consequences.

The Western oil companies had little choice but to accept the Arab prohibition against shipping Arab oil to blacklisted states. At the same time, however, they controlled a global petroleum distribution network that was not limited to moving only Arab oil. The embargo involved only the Arab oil-exporting countries, not the full membership of the Organization of Petroleum Exporting Countries. Following a rule of "equal misery," the major oil companies rerouted Arab oil initially destined for embargoed states to nonembargoed areas and filled the needs of the embargoed countries by rerouting shipments of oil from non-Arab OPEC suppliers to the blacklisted countries and those targeted for substantial reductions in their oil deliveries. Accomplishing the task required an enormous effort, in part because the type of oil needed (heavy, light, crude, refined) varied from oil-importing state to oil-importing state. Nevertheless, as a result of industry action all consumers received approximately the same percentage of their scheduled deliveries and no consumer experienced more than a 20 percent shortfall in its contracted delivery amount during the embargo period. The Arab states did not control enough of the production or distribution networks to make more of an impact.

The perceived danger of an oil supply disruption nevertheless remained high throughout the oil-importing world. Western countries regularly competed against one another for oil supplies on the spot (noncontracted) oil market, on occasion purchasing more oil than they had the capacity to use immediately or store. By the time the embargo ended in March, 1974, and the crisis had passed, OPEC had been able to use this demand for oil to establish a market price of OPEC oil at nearly $12 a barrel, four times the precrisis price. It took the oil-importing countries nearly three years of general inflation, corrective interest rates, and resultant increases in unemployment rolls to adjust their economies to these costs.

The political fallout from the embargo was also substantial. The political demands made on importing states by the Arab world forced Japan and several of America's North Atlantic Treaty Organization allies to break with the United States in their response to Arab demands in order to avoid being placed on the embargo list or having their oil shipments curtailed. In the oil-importing countries, energy became a major political issue. Oil companies were often scapegoated for permitting the energy crisis to occur. In the oil-producing states, the events of October, 1973, accelerated an ongoing redefinition of the multinational oil companies' role in the oil-producing world. The principal oil companies not only lost control to the emergent OPEC cartel of the pricing and production of oil but also were generally downgraded to being the contracted producer of oil for the oil-exporting states. In many instances, these states used their new wealth and power to buy out the oil companies' operations inside their borders.

The big losers in the post-embargo world, however, were the states in the developing world that did not produce oil. Economic development is an energy-intensive process, whether pursued through mechanization of agriculture or through industrial diversification. Even before 1973, with oil priced at $2.50 a barrel, energy costs posed an obstacle to development in many countries. After October, 1973, much of the Third World was essentially priced out of development and for nearly a generation locked into a situation of continued poverty. The price of oil nearly reached $40 a barrel before it plunged below $10 and finally stabilized at about $20 a barrel during the late 1980's and early 1990's. Ironically, few Third World countries condemned the OPEC states for exploiting their leverage against the richer Northern Hemisphere countries and escalating the price of oil. Most of those countries dreamed of some day finding themselves in a cartel of coffee, tin, or phosphate producers that could make similar changes to the world markets. This dreamed-of opportunity appears to have been wasted. None of the larger, suddenly richer OPEC states noticeably distinguished itself by using its newfound wealth to significantly improve its own underdeveloped status during the decade of high oil prices that followed the Arab oil embargo of 1973.

Bibliography

Bromley, Simon. *American Hegemony and World Oil*. University Park: Pennsylvania State University Press, 1991. A good study of the effect of the energy crisis on U.S. influence in international relations since 1973, cast in a broad discussion of the significance of energy in global economic and political affairs since 1945.

Daedalus (Fall, 1975). This special issue, devoted to the oil crisis, is the single best source of information on the multiple dimensions of the first oil crisis and its effects on the states, multinational oil companies, and international organizations caught up in it.

Gelb, Alan, et al. *Oil Windfalls*. New York: Oxford University Press, 1988. An excellent analysis of the impact on six OPEC producers of the windfall revenue resulting from sharp oil price increases.

Kapstein, Ethan B. *The Insecure Alliance*. New York: Oxford University Press, 1990. An outstanding study of Western efforts to respond to seven energy crises in the twentieth century.

Licklider, Roy. *Political Power and the Arab Oil Weapon*. Berkeley: University of California Press, 1988. A well-developed examination of the Arab oil embargo of 1973 and its success in advancing the interests of Arab oil-exporting states.

Lieber, Robert. *Oil and the Middle East War: Europe in the Energy Crisis*. Cambridge, Mass.: Center for International Affairs, Harvard University, 1976. A short, outstanding analysis of the failure of the European Community to respond to the oil crisis as a community and of the counterproductive effects of its members' individual responses to the crisis.

Sowayegh, Abdulaziz al-. *Arab Petropolitics*. New York: St. Martin's Press, 1984. An excellent work on the politicization of Arab oil, the use of oil as a weapon to influence negotiations concerning Palestine, and the general success of the policy to 1973. The author concludes that the embargo marked the culmination, not the beginning, of the Arab world's efforts to use oil for political gains.

Tetreault, Mary Ann. *The Organization of Arab Petroleum Exporting Countries: History, Policies, and Prospects*. Westport, Conn.: Greenwood Press, 1981. Probably the best readily accessible, comprehensive study of the Organization of Arab Petroleum Exporting Countries (OAPEC). Covers its structure, its policies, and its relationship with OPEC.

Venn, Fiona. *Oil Diplomacy in the Twentieth Century*. New York: St. Martin's Press, 1986. A compact, readable, scholarly work on the influence of oil on international relations. As Venn notes, no other resource has come close to having an equivalent influence on international politics or finance.

Yergin, Daniel. *The Prize: The Epic Quest for Oil, Money, and Power*. New York: Simon & Schuster, 1991. A massive study of the development of the international oil industry, with as much attention devoted to the personalities and politics involved as to the historical events that marked the evolution of the petroleum industry.

Joseph R. Rudolph, Jr.

Cross-References

Oil Is Discovered in Venezuela (1922), p. 385; Oil Companies Cooperate in a Cartel Covering the Middle East (1928), p. 551; OPEC Meets for the First Time (1960), p. 1154; Iran Announces Nationalization of Foreign Oil Interests (1973), p. 1533; The United States Plans to Cut Dependence on Foreign Oil (1974), p. 1555; Carter Orders Deregulation of Oil Prices (1979), p. 1699.

WEST GERMANY BANS IMMIGRATION OF WORKERS FROM OUTSIDE THE EEC

Category of event: Labor
Time: November 23, 1973
Locale: West Germany

The Federal Republic of Germany announced that it would cease all recruiting of workers from countries outside the Common Market, thus reversing a policy in place for more than a decade

Principal personages:
WALTER ARENDT (1925-   ), the West German minister of labor and social welfare, 1969-1976
WILLY BRANDT (1913-1992), the West German chancellor, 1969-1974
JOSEF STINGL (1919-   ), the director of the German Labor Exchange, 1968-1984

Summary of Event

On November 23, 1973, the West German government announced that it would no longer admit foreigners seeking work in Germany who came from countries outside the European Common Market. It thus brought to an end a policy that had characterized the German employment scene for more than a decade.

In the early years following World War II, the inhabitants of the western occupation zones, which were later to become the Federal Republic of Germany, were flooded with people from elsewhere. Some twelve million Germans, formerly residents of territories claimed by the victorious Allies, poured into the three western occupation zones from the Baltic states, East Prussia, Danzig, Silesia, the Sudetenland, Poland, Hungary, Romania, and Yugoslavia. There were at least 100,000 refugees from the Soviet forces who could not be repatriated. Thus in the first years after the end of World War II, Germany had no lack of individuals willing to work, facing instead a lack of jobs.

As the West German economy began to recover under the stimulus provided by the Marshall Plan, industry required more workers. At the same time, as the economy in the Soviet zone faltered under the heavy load of reparations, many Germans who had lived for years in that part of Germany fled to the west. Before erection of the Berlin Wall in 1961, three million East Germans managed to make it across the zonal border and added to the numbers already living in western Germany. West Germany also offered a sanctuary to some 800,000 people of German extraction who had settled in Poland and the Soviet Union years earlier. Together, the native inhabitants of West Germany and all these new immigrants added up to 62 million people. The population was one of the most dense in Europe, with 250 people per square kilometer.

Thanks to currency reform, Marshall Plan aid, and a strong work ethic, German industry created jobs for all the West German inhabitants able and willing to work. From the early 1950's to the late 1960's, West Germany enjoyed full employment. In the late 1950's and throughout most of the 1960's, there were more jobs than could be filled from the native population. These unfilled jobs provided a magnet for people from other parts of Europe, where job opportunities were less plentiful.

The first to take advantage of the many job opportunities were Italians, especially Italians from central and southern Italy. Italians poured north of the Alps, principally to Germany but also to France, Belgium, The Netherlands, and even tiny Luxembourg. By the mid-1960's, however, the pent-up pressure from underdeveloped southern Italy had been relieved. Thereafter, as the need for labor continued in Germany, it had to be met from elsewhere. Workers came from Spain, Portugal, Greece, Turkey, and Yugoslavia. By 1974, 2.2 million foreign workers held jobs in West Germany; they amounted to about 10 percent of the work force.

The root cause of this large migration was population pressure in the underdeveloped parts of Europe and the Mediterranean basin. Both Greece and Turkey, for example, had population growth rates that vastly exceeded the number of jobs being created in their underdeveloped economies. One expert estimated in the late 1960's that if current trends continued, by 1980 Greece would have between 270,000 and 670,000 excess workers and Turkey would have between 4.3 and 5.4 million. These pressures propelled large numbers of Greeks and Turks, and later Yugoslavs as well, northward and westward into Germany, many to take jobs that German workers scorned, including unskilled or semiskilled work in factories and "dirty" service sector jobs such as garbage collection. By the early 1970's, West Germany was admitting a thousand times more immigrants per citizen than was the United States.

The concept of the free movement of labor from areas of surplus to areas of deficit was an essential part of the economic unification of Europe that began with the formation of the Common Market, or European Economic Community (EEC) in 1957. Although the underlying treaty provided for free movement of labor among the members, regulations governing that movement were first put in place in 1961, when workers from any member country could accept an officially listed position in another country provided that no native workers were available to take the listed position. In 1964, the native preference was dropped, and the distinction between "permanent" and "seasonal" workers also disappeared. Furthermore, if a position could not be filled by an applicant from anywhere in the European Economic Community, the position could be filled by an applicant from outside the EEC. Workers who remained for four years in one job were eligible for an unrestricted work permit; that is, they could transfer to other employment if they desired. They could also bring their families to join them if housing (generally in short supply in West Germany) was available. By 1968, when the restriction of work applicants to those positions formally listed with the official employment service was dropped, the EEC essentially had established complete freedom of movement for EEC nationals.

The agreements by which Greece and Turkey became associate members of the EEC (signed in 1961 and 1963, respectively) provided for the gradual introduction of freedom of movement within the EEC for Greeks and Turks. The timetable for Greece was suspended when a coup d'état overthrew the democratic government. The timetable for Turkey envisaged the introduction of limited freedom of movement in 1976, with complete freedom of movement in 1985. These arrangements were upset by the termination of foreign hiring in the action taken on November 23, 1973.

Most foreign laborers who came to Germany were officially recruited. Special recruitment agreements were signed with Italy (1955), Greece (1960), Spain (1960), Turkey (1961), Morocco (1963), Portugal (1964), Tunisia (1965), and Yugoslavia (1968). These treaties were implemented through the Federal Employment Office, located in Nuremberg. To facilitate the recruitment process, German officials attached to the Employment Office were stationed in Athens, Greece; Verona, Italy; Madrid, Spain; Istanbul, Turkey; Belgrade, Yugoslavia; Lisbon, Portugal; Casablanca, Morocco; and Tunis, Tunisia. Offices issued work permits to more than two million foreign workers. Work permits initially were valid for one year, but for employees still at the same jobs, they were subject to renewal. The offices in recruiting areas were closed following the termination of foreign recruitment on November 23, 1973.

Although the vast majority of foreign workers in Germany entered following official recruitment, some "illegals" also seeped in. German authorities estimated that they amounted to about 10 percent of all foreign workers in Germany. Many such workers were brought in by middlemen who peddled them to employers who wanted to evade the official recruiting process. Following the termination of official recruitment, the West German government stepped up its efforts to prevent illegal immigration. Tougher laws governing "illegals" were passed in 1975.

Notwithstanding the termination of official recruitment in 1973, the number of foreign workers in Germany declined only moderately after that date. Those foreigners who had already been there for five years were entitled to indefinite extensions of their work permits. Legislation passed in 1978 and 1979 entitled them to extend their residence permits as well.

Impact of Event

The termination of official recruitment of foreign labor on November 23, 1973, marked the end of the great postwar economic boom in Germany. From that point onward, unemployment began to rise in Germany, as well as elsewhere in the EEC. By the early 1990's, it had reached 10 percent of the labor force in Germany. The shortage of labor that had characterized the developed nations of the EEC—not only Germany but also France, The Netherlands, Belgium, and Luxembourg—had turned into a surplus. Experts are divided on the causes of this unemployment.

A major cause of unemployment was the two oil shocks, the first in 1973 and the second in 1978. Chancellor Willy Brandt justified the decision announced on November 23, 1973, as a response to the anticipated economic effects of the first oil shock, caused by the announcement by Arab countries that they would curtail oil shipments to certain nations. These two shocks brought about a significant rise in production costs, hampering further expansion of industry. The result was a significant decrease in the number of manufacturing jobs in the years after 1973, and it was particularly these semiskilled factory jobs for which foreigners were recruited. As Germany expanded educational opportunities for its citizens, fewer of them were willing to take monotonous factory jobs; many submitted to unemployment rather than accept such positions.

In addition, during the period of labor shortages many employers substituted capital equipment for labor. This process continued well into the 1970's and 1980's, as electronic machine controls and new types of machines made such substitutions possible. Many jobs for which foreign workers had been hired were eliminated, yet those workers who had been in Germany for more than five years were entitled to remain. Thus foreigners added to the numbers of unemployed even though few new foreign workers were admitted. Labor Minister Walter Arendt declared that those foreign workers who already had jobs were not likely to be affected by the government's decision, but as the number of manufacturing jobs declined, some did become unemployed.

Some economists argue that the substitution of capital for labor was accelerated by government and trade union policy. The socialist government that ruled Germany during the early 1970's, under the chancellorship of Willy Brandt, was committed to a policy of income redistribution. The government taxed more heavily the incomes of the upper and upper-middle classes as well as encouraging wage settlements in which wages increased more rapidly than the growth of productivity. The result was that the availability of capital declined at the same time that real wages, and real wage costs, rose. Expansion of factories that might have taken place and provided new manufacturing jobs did not occur.

Europe's less buoyant economy operated against a backdrop of declining world expansion. The two oil shocks transferred vast sums of money from the advanced industrialized countries to the Middle East. This money was therefore not available, or available only in more limited amounts, to fuel additional economic expansion in the industrialized world.

Conservative economists argue that another factor adding to unemployment in Europe was the ever-increasing social costs associated with it. Health benefits, unemployment benefits, substantial vacation benefits, and other social costs, many enshrined in collective bargaining agreements, left less money for production. Moreover, it became increasingly difficult to fire excess employees. This in turn led employers to use overtime rather than take on additional employees when the business cycle turned up, so that recoveries did not cause the job growth that had previously occurred. As a result, most of the job growth after 1973 was in the public sector.

Other factors also played a part. Although by the 1970's the exodus from agricultural work was largely complete, the postwar baby boom added larger numbers of Germans to the work force, even though the German birth rate had dropped below the replacement level by the late 1960's. In addition, many women entered the work force, taking many white-collar jobs that might otherwise have been occupied by men.

Although the announcement of Germany's decision to cease recruiting foreign labor was the most striking sign of a fundamental change of direction in the European economy, it was not an isolated event. Most of the other advanced industrial economies of Europe took similar steps at about the same time. In 1976, the Dutch Parliament passed a law on foreign laborers that limited the number of foreign employees to twenty per employer. Moreover, employers that wanted to hire a foreigner for a job had to demonstrate that the position could not be filled locally and that it was essential to their operation.

Most highly developed European nations took the position that their population densities were already such that they could not, and should not, in principle become immigration countries. They continued to welcome their own nationals who sought repatriation for any reason, but they took an increasingly negative view of people who wanted to immigrate but who had no prior connection with the land in which they wished to settle. In many European countries, housing was in short supply, and it was argued that this restricted supply should go first to citizens in need. In cases such as that of The Netherlands, which had one of the highest population densities in the world—more than three hundred persons per square kilometer—the rejection of further immigration is easier to understand.

Nevertheless, the end of foreign recruitment posed major problems for the areas from which the bulk of the foreign workers had been recruited. Turkey in particular was heavily affected. It was still in the process of urbanization, and employment opportunities in Turkey's cities were inadequate to accommodate the large number of Turks pouring out of agricultural areas. Another area heavily affected by the end of recruitment was Yugoslavia, where the inability to export surplus labor may have contributed to the breakup of the country in the early 1990's.

The pressures from the native unemployed also made more difficult the position of foreign workers long resident in the industrialized countries. The growth of xenophobia was expressed in acts of violence against foreign workers in almost all the highly industrialized countries of Europe. As unemployment persisted or increased, the number of acts of violence tended also to increase.

The decision of the German government to terminate the practice of recruiting foreign labor for German factories in 1973 marked a turning point in Europe's economic progress since World War II. It signaled the end of the rapid economic expansion that had characterized the 1950's and 1960's.

Bibliography

Böhning, W. R. *The Migration of Workers in the United Kingdom and the European Community.* London: Oxford University Press, 1972. Although this study antedates the termination of German recruitment of foreign workers and focuses on the likely impact of British accession to the EEC on international labor migration, it gives substantial information on the effects of the "free migration" policies of the EEC on various member countries.

Entorf, Horst, Wolfgang Franz, Heinz Koenig, and Werner Smolny. "The Development of German Employment and Unemployment: Estimation and Simulation of a

Small Macro Model." In *Europe's Unemployment Problem*, edited by Jacques H. Drèze and Charles R. Bean. Cambridge, Mass.: MIT Press, 1990. Although this study focuses on development of the appropriate algorithm to describe the evolution of the labor market in West Germany, particularly in more recent years, it gives many details that are helpful in understanding the relationship of the immigration ban to the unemployment problem generally.

Franz, Wolfgang, and Heinz Koenig. "The Nature and Causes of Unemployment in the Federal Republic of Germany Since the 1970's: An Empirical Investigation." In *The Rise in Unemployment*, edited by Charles Bean, P. R. G. Layard, and S. J. Nickell. Oxford, England: Basil Blackwell, 1986. This account of the German unemployment problem gives numerous statistical details and applies some standard econometric models. It takes note of the fact that although the concept of labor mobility implied the further migration of migrant laborers or return to their land of origin when labor demand diminished, this did not occur to any degree in Germany, perhaps because the migrants were aware that they had become accustomed to a higher standard of living than they could hope to achieve at home.

Organisation for Economic Co-operation and Development. Manpower Policy in Germany. OECD Reviews of Manpower and Social Policies 13. Paris: Author, 1974. Oriented toward public policy measures. Gives many details as to the way in which manpower policy operated in Germany in the years prior to the cessation of foreign recruitment. Its underlying assumption is that full employment can be achieved and maintained through governmental economic policy, a goal that has proved far less easy to achieve in the years since this booklet was published.

Reimann, Horst, and Helga Reimann. "Federal Republic of Germany." In *International Labor Migration in Europe*, edited by Ronald E. Krane. New York: Praeger, 1979. The Reimanns provide the best short description of the entire process of recruiting foreign labor for German manufacturers. They also discuss some of the social problems that developed in relations between Germans and "guest workers."

Nancy M. Gordon

Cross-References

The United States Begins the Bracero Program (1942), p. 840; The Truman Administration Launches the Marshall Plan (1947), p. 902; The European Common Market Is Established (1957), p. 1081; Firms Begin Replacing Skilled Laborers with Automatic Tools (1960's), p. 1128; Sara Lee Opens an Automated Factory (1964), p. 1202; Arab Oil Producers Curtail Oil Shipments to Industrial States (1973), p. 1544; CAD/CAM Revolutionizes Engineering and Manufacturing (1980's), p. 1721; The European Market Unifies (1992), p. 2051.

THE UNITED STATES PLANS TO CUT DEPENDENCE ON FOREIGN OIL

Category of event: International business and commerce
Time: 1974
Locale: Washington, D.C.

In 1974, responding to disruptions in world oil supplies, the Federal Energy Administration formulated plans to reduce U.S. dependence on foreign oil, plans that later became national legislation

Principal personages:

RICHARD M. NIXON (1913-1994), the president of the United States, 1969-1974

GERALD R. FORD (1913-   ), the president of the United States, 1974-1977

JIMMY CARTER (1924-   ), the president of the United States, 1977-1981

RONALD REAGAN (1911-   ), the president of the United States, 1981-1989

JAMES R. SCHLESINGER (1929-   ), the secretary of the Department of Energy, 1977-1979

Summary of Event

In the late 1960's and early 1970's, the economy of the United States became dependent upon oil imports, especially from the Middle East. The growth of American dependence on imported oil was made dramatically clear by the disruption in world oil supply caused by the Arab oil embargo of 1973-1974. The embargo prompted Congress to pass the Emergency Petroleum Allocation Act of 1973, implementing a number of policies designed to reduce U.S. dependence on foreign oil. The act also created the Federal Energy Administration (FEA) to implement and enforce the legislation and to formulate policies to reduce dependence on oil imports. A number of the FEA's recommendations, developed in 1974, were passed into legislation in the Energy Policy and Conservation Act of 1975. These statutes and regulatory policies laid the foundation for a continuing federal role in the domestic oil and natural gas industries.

American oil companies had been developing oil and gas reserves in the Middle East since the mid-1930's. By the mid-1950's, American domestic demand began to outpace domestic oil production. At the end of 1955, imported oil accounted for less than 15 percent of America's domestic energy consumption, but the figure was growing rapidly. As the American economy began to demand increasing amounts of petroleum, the relationship between the United States and the Middle East continued to grow.

In 1972 and 1973, oil production in the United States (excluding Alaska) declined by about 360,000 barrels each year. This came at a time when American demand for oil was increasing dramatically. The American population had increased 30 percent since 1950, but energy consumption had doubled. Almost all the increases in U.S. energy consumption were filled by oil imports. In 1970, foreign oil accounted for 22 percent of domestic consumption; by 1973, 36 percent. In 1970, the United States imported 3.2 million barrels of oil per day; by 1972, that figure had risen to 4.5 million barrels. In the summer of 1973, months before the Arab oil embargo, the United States was importing 6.2 million barrels of oil each day, largely from the Middle East.

In 1971, federal control of oil and gas prices was instituted as part of the federally mandated general freeze on wages and prices. This action was a response to an inflation rate of nearly 5 percent per year. Although most of the price controls ended by 1974, continuing public disenchantment with oil and gas shortages and price increases meant that price controls on the domestic petroleum industry would continue in various forms until 1981.

The members of the Organization of Petroleum Exporting Countries (OPEC) met in Kuwait City on October 16, 1973. The OPEC ministers decided to raise the price of a barrel of OPEC oil, which had become a measure of world oil prices, from $2.90 to $5.11. In January, 1974, OPEC raised the price again, to $11.65 per barrel. Many of the Arab oil-producing nations also had embargoed shipments of oil to the United States in October of 1973 in retaliation for U.S. support of Israel.

The prospect of the exhaustion of domestic oil stocks, together with the Arab oil embargo, portended disaster for the American economy. On November 7, 1973, President Richard M. Nixon announced that if preventive measures were not taken, the American economy would soon fall 10 percent short of its energy needs. Nixon called for Project Independence, a series of policies designed to eliminate U.S. dependence on imports by 1980. Many oil industry executives and policy experts believed the goal to be unrealistic.

Nixon called for voluntary conservation of energy and lower thermostat settings, lower standards for air quality to aid factories and the auto industry, reduced highway speeds, acceleration of the building and licensing of nuclear power plants, incentives to increase the production of coal and lignite, a halt on changing utilities from coal to oil, increased oil production on the outer continental shelf, and increased production from the federal naval petroleum reserves. Although the coal, lignite, and nuclear power options were slowed by environmental concerns, in the next two years Congress passed legislation calling for a national 55 mile per hour speed limit and tax breaks for home insulation. Congress also passed legislation to speed up the Alaskan pipeline project.

More comprehensive legislation was needed, however, to address the immediate problem of the shortage in petroleum supplies. As domestic oil supplies became scarce in late November, 1973, political action groups representing the independent and smaller refiners, transporters, and marketers called for the federal government to allocate limited crude oil stocks for the immediate future, a plan that would be designed to ensure fairness in crude oil stocks while also preserving competition.

On November 27, 1973, Congress passed the Emergency Petroleum Allocation Act (EPAA). A primary goal of the EPAA was to aid vulnerable end-users of oil. This meant federally mandated allocations of crude and refined oil to small and independent domestic refiners, transporters, and marketers. This policy often meant that integrated companies with large crude oil stocks had to sell oil at controlled prices to their less-well-supplied competitors. The EPAA also continued the complex series of price controls on domestic oil and provided for gasoline rationing. To implement, administer, and enforce these policies, the EPAA authorized the president to create a federal energy agency.

Accordingly, President Nixon created the Federal Energy Administration (FEA) to implement and enforce the provisions of the EPAA. The FEA also endeavored to develop a workable set of policies from the energy initiatives proposed in Project Independence. The FEA devised a number of proposals to reduce U.S. dependence on foreign oil and completed its report in November, 1974. Some of these proposals that would soon become federal legislation included higher fuel efficiency standards for automobiles, higher efficiency standards for electrical appliances, and standards for home and office insulation and heating and cooling equipment.

Impact of Event

Gerald Ford became president of the United States in August, 1974. He proposed federal decontrol of oil and natural gas prices in the hope that rising prices would spur domestic oil production. To maintain some control on oil prices, Ford proposed a Windfall Profits Tax. Ford also proposed large-scale development of coal mines, coal-fired power plants, and synthetic-fuel plants. Ultimately, these plans were canceled or scaled down.

Congress included some of Ford's proposals in the Energy Policy and Conservation Act (EPCA) of 1975. Instead of decontrol of petroleum prices as Ford advocated, however, the EPCA continued the complex and controversial price controls on oil and gas. Federal allocation of domestic oil and natural gas continued as well. The FEA was given authority to implement and enforce the new regulations. The attempt to control prices and allocate oil and gas proved to be just as complex, controversial, and difficult as under the EPAA.

The EPCA gave increased powers to the president to intervene in the domestic petroleum industry. The president could require power plants to use coal, if available, rather than oil; order the development of new coal mines; and further allocate and appropriate domestic stocks of oil and gas. The president could also order mandatory conservation measures and rationing of oil and natural gas.

The EPCA required higher fuel efficiency standards for a host of products, including automobiles and electrical appliances. The EPCA required manufacturers of electrical appliances to label their products with information on their energy efficiency. The EPCA also mandated fuel-efficiency standards for automobiles that later became the Corporate Average Fuel Economy (CAFE) standards. The new standards established by the EPCA mandated that the average fuel efficiency of a new car would have to double over a ten-year period, from 13 miles per gallon to 27.5 miles per gallon.

Another significant aspect of the EPCA was the establishment of the Strategic Petroleum Reserve (SPR), in which the federal government, together with the American oil companies, would establish reserve oil stocks for emergencies in the case of a future disruption in world oil supplies. The EPCA also called for U.S. participation in the International Energy Program, whereby Great Britain, Japan, West Germany, and the United States would all develop reserve systems that they could coordinate and share in the event of another oil supply disruption. The EPCA ratified American participation.

President Jimmy Carter came into office in 1977 also committed to reducing American dependence on foreign oil. In April, Carter announced several goals, including a reduction of oil imports to one-eighth of total energy consumption by 1985. In an effort to reduce demand for energy, Carter proposed the Crude Oil Equalization Tax, which would have taxed oil at the wellhead, and instituted a new pricing system. The Carter Administration hoped that this new pricing system would let oil prices rise gradually to discourage consumption and reduce dependence on foreign crude oil. Carter also submitted to Congress the Department of Energy Organization Act; Congress approved the bill in August, 1977. The bill created the Department of Energy (DOE) and placed most of the previous energy agencies under the DOE umbrella, including the Federal Energy Administration, the Energy Resources and Development Administration, and the Federal Power Commission. Carter appointed James R. Schlesinger, the secretary of defense in the Nixon Administration, to be the first secretary of energy.

The Iranian revolution of January, 1979, removed large amounts of petroleum from world markets, pushing prices up to $30 per barrel and bringing on a second oil price shock and supply disruption. OPEC used the opportunity to raise its prices. By December, 1979, the price was above $30 per barrel; in some spot markets, it was $45 per barrel.

The whirlwind of congressional activity and executive actions taken during the Nixon and Ford administrations had done little to reduce American dependence on foreign oil. The complex set of energy regulations was of little help to President Carter in the crisis of 1978-1979. The American economy was still dependent on imported oil for nearly half of its energy consumption in the last years of the 1970's.

In the midst of the severe worldwide inflation of oil prices, pressure increased for the Carter Administration to decontrol U.S. prices. The ensuing price increases would, the government hoped, make domestic exploration economical. In April, 1979, Carter announced a phased process of decontrol of oil prices over thirty months. To satisfy consumers, Carter proposed a new tax on American oil companies that became the Windfall Profits Tax Act of 1980.

Ronald Reagan assumed the presidency in 1981 strongly committed to reducing federal regulations. In his first month in office, Reagan formally ended the federal pricing system, lifting all the controls on oil and gas. The Reagan Administration also pledged to reevaluate the Department of Energy, which had become a political symbol of overregulation. President Reagan considered abolishing the DOE but finally decided to reduce its budget.

It was not long after federal decontrol of prices occurred, however, that world oil prices began to fall. Beginning in 1981, world oil prices began a five-year deflationary trend. By 1983, oil prices had fallen to below $30 per barrel. Price deflation also reduced the political and economic threat of high prices and gasoline lines. As the American economy recovered from the oil shocks of 1973 and 1979, controversy over imported oil also abated. The Reagan Administration, previously concerned with removing federal hindrances to economic growth, took the opportunity to push through Congress a measure that increased the federal tax on gasoline by five cents. It was hoped that this act would check potential increases in consumption caused by falling prices while also raising revenue to meet mounting federal expenditures.

Ironically, falling oil prices on the world markets in the early 1980's resulted in large part from OPEC's success in raising prices in the 1970's. Higher prices made oil production in non-OPEC areas, such as the North Sea, Alaska, Mexico, and the southwestern United States, more economically feasible. The U.S. national economy still depended on foreign oil for approximately 25 percent of its petroleum requirements. Greater non-OPEC production, however, was creating a glut of oil on the world market, leading to price deflation.

With the price of oil falling and supply on the rise, public and private alternative fuel programs became uneconomical. In 1981, the Reagan Administration slashed federal funding for solar energy programs as well as the Synthetic Fuels Corporation, established by Carter. American oil companies cut back their shale oil and coal gasification projects.

In 1990 and 1991, the United States, under United Nations auspices, militarily intervened in a conflict involving Iraq, Kuwait, and Saudi Arabia. The action was motivated in part by a desire to keep Middle Easter oil flowing to the United States, which still had not eliminated its dependence on foreign oil.

Bibliography

Krueger, Robert B. *The United States and International Oil: A Report for the Federal Energy Administration on U.S. Firms and Government Policy*. New York: Praeger, 1975. Presents policy options considered in the 1970's. Also contains brief but informative histories of federal and state regulation of the petroleum industry and of U.S. diplomacy with the oil producing nations of the world.

Melosi, Martin V. "Energy Intensive Society, 1945-1970" and "Scarcity Decade—1970's." In *Coping with Abundance: Energy and Environment in Industrial America*. Philadelphia: Temple University Press, 1985. These chapters give an excellent overview of the formation of energy policy, detailing the forces behind the growing federal regulation of the energy industries in the United States after World War II.

Nash, Gerald D. *United States Oil Policy, 1890-1964* Pittsburgh, Pa.: University of

Pittsburgh Press, 1968. Although Nash's work does not cover the 1970's, it is a good source for readers seeking an introduction to the subject of public policy regarding the oil, coal, and natural gas industries.

Sherrill, Robert. *The Oil Follies of 1970-1980: How the Petroleum Industries Stole the Show (and Much More Besides)*. Garden City, N.Y.: Anchor Press/Doubleday, 1983. The best source for a detailed treatment of the politics of petroleum regulation in the 1970's. Shows the ways in which the divergent segments of the American political economy shape energy policy.

Vietor, Richard H. K. *Energy Policy in America Since 1945: A Study of Business-Government Relations*. New York: Cambridge University Press, 1984. This work covers the oil, coal, and natural gas industries and their regulatory relationships with federal and state governments. Contains useful and detailed analysis of the issues of imports, price control, and allocation.

Yergin, Daniel. *The Prize: The Epic Quest for Oil, Money, and Power*. New York: Simon and Schuster, 1991. Covers many aspects of petroleum issues, including actions and policies of oil producing and consuming nations, international relations, and the business strategies of oil firms. Best in its treatment of the international aspects of the petroleum industry, this work also has concise coverage of domestic regulatory policy.

Bruce Andre Beaubouef

Cross-References

Oil Companies Cooperate in a Cartel Covering the Middle East (1928), p. 551; OPEC Meets for the First Time (1960), p. 1154; Atlantic Richfield Discovers Oil at Prudhoe Bay, Alaska (1967), p. 1331; An Offshore Oil Well Blows Out near Santa Barbara, California (1969), p. 1374; Nixon's Anti-Inflation Program Shocks Worldwide Markets (1971-1974), p. 1489; Iran Announces Nationalization of Foreign Oil Interests (1973), p. 1533; Arab Oil Producers Curtail Oil Shipments to Industrial States (1973), p. 1544; The Alaskan Oil Pipeline Opens (1977), p. 1653; Carter Orders Deregulation of Oil Prices (1979), p. 1699.

THE EMPLOYEE RETIREMENT INCOME SECURITY ACT OF 1974 IS PASSED

Category of event: Labor
Time: September 2, 1974
Locale: Washington, D.C.

By establishing fiduciary, funding, vesting, and disclosure rules and plan termination insurance, ERISA attempted to protect employees' rights to retirement and other benefits

Principal personages:
JACOB JAVITS (1904-1986), a Republican senator from New York, cosponsor of pension reform legislation
RUSSELL B. LONG (1918-), a Democratic senator from Louisiana, chairman of the Senate Finance Committee
HARRISON WILLIAMS (1919-), a Democratic senator from New Jersey, cosponsor of pension reform legislation
RICHARD M. NIXON (1913-1994), the president of the United States, 1969-1974
JOHN H. DENT (1908-1988), a Democratic congressman from Pennsylvania, chairman of the General Subcommittee on Labor
GERALD FORD (1913-), the president of the United States, 1974-1977
RALPH NADER (1934-), a consumer advocate

Summary of Event

On September 2 (Labor Day), 1974, President Gerald Ford signed the Employee Retirement Income Security Act of 1974 (ERISA) into law. ERISA established complex rules concerning employee benefit plan disclosure, fiduciary responsibility, funding, and vesting. Vesting refers to an employee's nonforfeitable right to a pension, a right earned, for example, after a fixed number of years of service. The law also established pension plan termination insurance and the Pension Benefit Guaranty Corporation.

ERISA was the culmination of eight years of investigations, hearings, and legislative proposals that responded to reports of abuse in the private pension and group insurance system, particularly with respect to the absence of vesting and funding standards in some plans. ERISA mandated practices that had become increasingly common among large corporate plans. The law's supporters thus included a wide range of interests, such as the American Bankers' Association and the United Auto Workers union. ERISA was moderate in scope and did not include certain reforms, such as the mandating of private employee benefit coverage for everyone in the work force, that were advocated at the time by Ralph Nader and other public interest advocates.

The American Express Company adopted the first pension plan in the United States in 1875. By 1940, more than four million American employees were covered by private pensions. The Revenue Act of 1942 allowed a company to receive a guarantee that pension contributions would be tax deductible, and this provision encouraged growth in coverage. The War Labor Board also encouraged growth during World War II by exempting employee benefit plans from wage freezes. A similar provision was made during the Korean War. Furthermore, in 1948 the Seventh Circuit Court of Appeals upheld a ruling in a case involving the Inland Steel Company that pensions are mandatory subjects of collective bargaining. This decision opened the door to collective bargaining by unions for employee benefits. Pension assets rose from $2.4 billion in 1940 to $52 billion in 1960. By 1970, more than twenty-six million American employees were covered by private pensions.

In 1958, the Welfare and Pension Plan Disclosure Act (WPPDA) established disclosure requirements for employee benefit plans. The WPPDA was amended in 1962 to establish criminal sanctions. The WPPDA's disclosure requirements, however, were limited in scope.

In 1963 and 1964, pension plans gained public attention when Studebaker's factory in South Bend, Indiana, closed. About forty-five hundred Studebaker employees under the age of sixty received only 15 percent of the retirement benefits they had earned, and many received no benefits at all. President John F. Kennedy had appointed a Committee on Corporate Pension Funds in 1962, and in 1965 the committee recommended stricter standards for plan funding and vesting of employees' pension benefits. This recommendation led to a 1968 House bill that would have established fiduciary standards for administrators of employee benefit plans, but the bill died.

In a message to Congress on December 8, 1971, President Richard M. Nixon proposed legislation to establish vesting and fiduciary standards and to permit individual retirement accounts (IRAs). A House Banking and Currency Committee task force investigated pension reform that year as well. In 1972, the National Broadcasting Company encouraged popular support for pension reform legislation by airing a television news documentary, *Pensions: The Broken Promise*, that depicted abuses in the pension system.

The House Ways and Means Committee, chaired by Wilbur Mills, held hearings in 1972 on H.R. 12272, the Nixon Administration's bill. H.R. 12272 included provisions on disclosure, fiduciary responsibility, and vesting, but not on funding and plan termination insurance. The most controversial part of the bill was its proposal for increasing the limits on the tax deductibility of pension benefits for self-employed individuals and their employees (Keogh or HR 10 plans) and IRAs. More than twenty national and local bar associations and the American Medical Association testified in favor of the Keogh plans and IRAs. The American Federation of Labor-Congress of Industrial Organizations (AFL-CIO) strongly opposed the Nixon bill because of these provisions. The bill died in the House.

In September, 1972, the Senate Labor and Public Welfare Committee, chaired by Harrison Williams, reported a bill that would have regulated pension plans, but the bill died when Senator Russell Long argued that it was primarily tax legislation and so was the province of his Senate Finance Committee. The Senate Finance Committee reported the bill out only after removing its provisions concerning vesting, funding, and termination insurance.

By early 1973, public support for pension reform was widespread, and jurisdictional disputes were to be swept aside. Congressman Carl Perkins, chairman of the Education and Labor Committee, testified that he had received several thousand letters in support of pension reform. Later that year, Ralph Nader and Kate Blackwell published *You and Your Pension*, a book that further encouraged popular support for pension reform by providing examples of insufficiently funded plans, the absence of vesting rules, and excessively complex plan provisions.

In September, 1973, the Senate Labor and Public Welfare Committee reported a bill cosponsored by Jacob Javits and chairman Harrison Williams. At the same time, the Senate Finance Committee sponsored a complementary bill. The two bills were merged into S. 4, which passed the Senate. The bill set minimum fiduciary, funding, portability, and vesting standards, established plan termination insurance, established IRAs, and extended limits on Keogh plans. (Portability refers to allowing employees to transfer pension assets to a new employer or to a centralized trust fund when they change jobs). Weeks later, in October, 1973, the House Education and Labor Committee reported H.R. 2, which omitted S. 4's provisions on portability, Keogh plans, and IRAs but was similar to it in other respects.

During 1972 and 1973, the House Ways and Means Committee held hearings concerning H.R. 12272; the Senate Labor and Public Welfare Committee held hearings concerning S. 4; and the General Subcommittee on Labor, chaired by John H. Dent, held hearings concerning H.R. 2. In the course of these hearings, organized labor gave only mixed support to pension reform legislation. For example, a representative of the Amalgamated Clothing Workers Union testified that jointly sponsored labor-management trusts should be exempt from retirement legislation. In fact, industry groups such as the national Chamber of Commerce and the American Bankers' Association, along with Towers, Perrin, Foster, and Crosby, a consulting firm, gave stronger support to the proposed vesting, disclosure, and fiduciary rules than did the AFL-CIO. The AFL-CIO did not testify during the S. 4 and H.R. 2 hearings. The United Steelworkers, the United Auto Workers, and other industrial unions, along with some craft unions, did not support the proposed legislation, especially its termination insurance provisions, probably because pension funds in the steel and auto industries were underfunded. In testimony concerning H.R. 2, Ralph Nader excoriated the labor movement for its weak support of pension legislation.

In February, 1974, the House Ways and Means Committee passed a revised H.R. 2 bill that included improvements to Keogh plans and established IRAs. The House-Senate conference committee reported a final compromise version of H.R. 2 and S. 4 in August, 1974. The conference committee's bill passed the Senate unanimously, 85-0. In the House, only two representatives voted against ERISA. President Ford signed the bill on September 2, 1974.

Impact of Event

ERISA established new rules on disclosure, vesting, eligibility, funding, and fiduciary responsibility. It established individual retirement accounts and increased the amount that self-employed individuals could contribute to their own pension plans. It established limits on contributions and benefits to highly paid individuals and restated the Internal Revenue Code's rules on integration of pensions with Social Security benefits. It also established the Pension Benefit Guaranty Corporation and a $1 per participant tax on single-employer plans to cover the newly created plan termination insurance.

With respect to disclosure, ERISA required that plan sponsors (both single employers and multiemployer trusts that sponsor benefit plans) provide participants with a summary of the formal, relatively technical, plan document that governs their pension plan. The summary, called a summary plan description, was required to be written in a manner calculated to be understood by the average plan participant. ERISA required that each plan administrator produce a detailed annual report that, in the case of pension and profit sharing plans, was required to be audited by a certified public accountant. It also required plan administrators to provide each plan participant with a summary of this annual report. Furthermore, the law required that the plan administrator provide an estimate of a participant's benefit upon request.

With respect to eligibility, ERISA required that plans could not require more stringent eligibility requirements than participants being twenty-five years of age or older, with at least one year of service, although with full immediate vesting, plans could require three years of service. Plans could no longer exclude employees because they were too old unless those employees began work within five years of the normal retirement age for the plan.

With respect to vesting, ERISA allowed plan participants to vest according to one of three rules: full vesting at ten years, the five to fifteen rule (25 percent vesting at five years of service increasing by 5 percent in the following five years and by 10 percent for five more years) and the rule of forty-five (50 percent vesting when the sum of age and years of service equals forty-five, increasing 10 percent per year thereafter). It also required that pension plans' normal form of benefit be a 50 percent joint and survivor benefit, that is, a pension amount at normal retirement age that has been actuarially reduced to provide a 50 percent benefit to the participant's spouse in the event of the participant's death.

With respect to funding, ERISA required that plans fully fund the cost accruing each year and that unfunded past service liabilities be funded over thirty years, with the exception of pre-existing past service liabilities, which could be funded over forty years. With respect to fiduciary standards, ERISA required that plans name a fiduciary and that the named fiduciary and any cofiduciaries must act exclusively for the benefit of plan participants. The law required that fiduciaries act as would a prudent person in like capacity. The law also required that fiduciaries diversify assets and prohibited the exchange of property or lending of money between a plan and a party-in-interest, defined as a fiduciary or the relative of a fiduciary, a person providing services to a plan, an employer, or a related union.

With respect to Keogh plans and IRAs, ERISA raised the tax-deductible amounts that a self-employed person could contribute to $7,500, or 15 percent of earnings if less. It also allowed individuals not otherwise covered by a pension plan to establish an IRA.

With respect to limitations on contributions and benefits, it limited contributions to profit sharing plans to $25,000 or 25 percent of compensation, whichever was less, and limited benefits under pension plans to $75,000 or 100 percent of final average earnings, whichever was less. Both limits were indexed for inflation and were intended to prevent highly paid individuals from taking undue advantage of tax deductions for qualified pension plans.

Several writers, including Nader and Blackwell, raised important concerns about ERISA's efficacy. One characteristic of America's private system of pension and other benefits is that coverage is skewed toward higher-paid employees and employees of large firms. For example, in 1978, those whose preretirement income was more than 43 percent in excess of the median worker's had pensions worth 93 percent more than the median amount, as pointed out by Teresa Ghilarducci. Similarly, according to another study, in 1988, 65 percent of workers in firms with more than five hundred employees were covered by pension plans, while only about 12 percent of workers in firms with fewer than twenty-five employees were covered. By failing to mandate benefits and doing little to tighten restrictions on offsetting Social Security benefits from pension benefits (called integration), ERISA did little to alleviate the skew in coverage toward higher-paid workers.

The additional disclosures and plan termination insurance that ERISA required were costly, and administrative costs associated with compliance with ERISA may have had a depressing effect on plan adoption rates, especially among small firms. Although coverage rates of private pension plans grew from 15 percent of the work force in 1940 to 45 percent in 1970, the coverage rate remained constant at about 45 percent from 1970 to 1987. In particular, coverage among firms with fewer than twenty-five employees declined by about 15 percent from 1979 to 1988.

ERISA opened a floodgate for regulation of employee benefit plans. From 1974 through 1992, fifteen laws regulating employee benefit programs were passed. For example, the Tax Equity and Fiscal Responsibility Act of 1982 reduced the limitations on contributions and benefits, the Retirement Equity Act mandated further spousal benefits, and the Tax Reform Act of 1986 reduced the minimum years of service for vesting to five. The premium required for plan termination insurance increased dramatically, twentyfold for some plans. As of 1993, approximately half of the American work force lacked private pension coverage, and much of the remainder expected only modest benefits from the private pension system.

Bibliography

Ghilarducci, Teresa. *Labor's Capital: The Economics and Politics of Private Pensions*. Cambridge, Mass.: MIT Press, 1992. The best available analysis of the

American pension system and its institutional context. The book is critical of the American employee benefit system and recommends several directions for reform.

Ippolito, Richard. *Pensions, Economics, and Public Policy*. Homewood, Ill.: Dow Jones-Irwin, 1986. A quantitative study of public policy on pensions by an official of the Pension Benefit Guaranty Corporation. Excessive emphasis on some unions' interest in plan termination insurance as a factor in ERISA's evolution.

Mamorsky, Jeffrey D. *Employee Benefit Law: ERISA and Beyond*. New York: Law Journal Seminars-Press, 1980-   . The 1992 version is by a prominent pension attorney. The best available legal analysis of ERISA and subsequent employee benefit plan regulation. Includes discussion of pension and profit sharing plans.

Nader, Ralph, and Kate Blackwell. *You and Your Pension*. New York: Grossman, 1973. Written by the country's leading consumer advocate and published one year before ERISA was passed. Includes illuminating anecdotes and recommendations for pension reform, many of which were adopted by Congress. The book was surprisingly well received by the pension community.

Rosenbloom, Jerry S. ed. *The Handbook of Employee Benefits*. Homewood, Ill.: Dow Jones-Irwin, 1984. Good introduction to practical administrative tasks associated with implementing ERISA and subsequent employee benefit regulation.

Turner, J. A., and D. J. Beller, eds. *Trends in Pensions 1992*. Washington, D.C.: U.S. Government Printing Office, 1992. Includes useful, up-to-date statistical data about pensions.

Mitchell Langbert

Cross-References

The Wagner Act Promotes Union Organization (1935), p. 706; The Social Security Act Provides Benefits for Workers (1935), p. 711; The Taft-Hartley Act Passes over Truman's Veto (1947), p. 908; The Landrum-Griffin Act Targets Union Corruption (1959), p. 1122; Studebaker Announces Plans to Abandon U.S. Auto Production (1963), p. 1190.

CONGRESS CREATES THE COMMODITY FUTURES TRADING COMMISSION

Category of event: Finance
Time: October 23, 1974
Locale: Washington, D.C.

Through creation of the CFTC as an independent agency with the mandate to regulate U.S. commodity futures markets, Congress sought to ensure the economic usefulness of futures markets

Principal personages:
> WILLIAM R. POAGE (1899-1987), the chair of the House Agriculture Committee and a strong proponent of the Commodity Futures Trading Commission Act
> HERMAN E. TALMADGE (1913-), the chair of the Senate Agriculture and Forestry Committee and a strong supporter of the act
> WILLIAM T. BAGLEY (1928-), the first chairman of the CFTC
> GEORGE E. BROWN, JR. (1920-), a member of the House Agriculture Committee and a strong supporter of the act
> CARL T. CURTIS (1905-), a member of the Senate Agriculture and Forestry Committee

Summary of Event

The Commodity Futures Trading Commission Act of 1974 made comprehensive changes in the Commodity Exchange Act of 1936. It created an independent Commodity Futures Trading Commission (CFTC) charged with regulating how farm and other commodities were traded on exchanges. The CFTC was entrusted with strengthening regulation of the United States' commodity futures trading industry to ensure fair practices and honest dealings in futures exchanges. It was empowered to regulate and control all activities on the exchanges.

Formal commodity markets developed in the United States in the late 1700's. After keeping enough of a crop for his or her own needs, a farmer brought grain and livestock to the local market. Because of the rhythms of nature, most farmers brought their products to market at about the same time. Supplies of meat and grains generally exceeded the current demand of meatpackers and millers, causing the prices of commodities to slump. The price problem was further worsened by inadequate storage facilities and lack of standards for quality.

Several months after the harvest, the supply of commodities would shrink. With no stored commodities to draw from, prices would skyrocket, and people would often go hungry. Millers and meatpackers also faced problems when they lacked the raw materials necessary to run their operations. Closures and bankruptcies would result. The minimal proceeds that farmers received for their produce at harvest time were inadequate for the construction and development of storage and farming assets.

Transportation and storage facilities improved in response to the inadequacy of local markets in meeting the needs of suppliers and buyers of commodities. Forward contracting between farmers and merchants developed to offset, at least partially, the fundamental problem of demand and availability of the commodities. Forward contracting involved an agreement for the delivery of a commodity at a predetermined future date. All the terms and conditions of the contract regarding the price, quality, quantity, and packaging of the commodity and the place and mode of delivery were predetermined. Forward markets did little to control the risk arising out of crop failures, losses in transit, and bankruptcies in a volatile price environment. Moreover, lack of regulation resulted in lack of a reliable mechanism to ensure performance by the parties to a contract.

There were two major shortcomings of forward trading: a lack of secondary markets for forward contracts to enable the participants to "bail out" of a contract if they so desired, and a lack of a performance guarantee. These problems were eliminated as a system of futures trading developed in the United States. The development of futures markets accelerated with increasing needs for large-scale risk transfer and centralized pricing in the agriculture forward markets.

In 1848, the Chicago Board of Trade (CBOT) was formed by eighty-two merchants. While Chicago became the primary location for the distribution and export of grains, New York developed into a similar center for cotton. These centers promoted competition and attracted traders from all over the world. Participants soon developed uniform systems for trading in these centers.

Futures trading on the CBOT began in 1865. Trading in futures, or contracts to deliver a commodity at a future date, required market participants to make and rely on forecasts of supply and demand. Prices that emerged for futures contracts reflected a consensus of those forecasts. High futures prices, for example, indicated a consensus that demand would be relatively high or supply would be relatively low.

Futures trading allowed hedging of price risks. A seller or buyer could lock in a price through a futures contract rather than take the risk of the price changing unfavorably before the delivery date. This reduction of risk allowed commodity handlers to operate at lower costs.

Rules and procedures for trading, clearing, and settling contracts were adopted in the late 1800's. Standardization of contracts and delivery dates also took place. Increased efficiency of commodity trading, however, rarely resulted in increased prices for farmers. Abuses in the commodity markets were frequent. These abuses arose from the very structure of the commodity markets. A speculator could enter into a large futures contract with a relatively small commitment of funds, since payment was promised in the future. The markets were dominated by large traders and speculators who exercised their economic power and manipulated markets to their advantage. Farmers had little faith in these markets but little choice about where to sell their produce. This lack of faith of farmers led to a revolt against the futures markets, and in 1893 the United States Congress came close to imposing prohibitive taxes on futures trading. During the first years of the twentieth century, the revolt against futures trading softened as a result of price increases for farm products and development of cooperative farm marketing. Pressure still was building for federal regulation to ensure more stable and reliable futures prices and markets.

With passage of the Cotton Futures Trading Act of 1914, Congress attempted to regulate a farm product market for the first time. The end of World War I saw declining farm prices and increased demands for the regulation of futures trading. By passing the Grain Futures Act of 1922, Congress extended its regulation of futures trading.

The Grain Futures Act empowered the secretary of agriculture to regulate the activities of a futures exchange but not those of the futures traders. Under the act, it was the responsibility of an exchange to prevent price manipulation on the exchange. Although the act provided for legal action against price manipulators, it proved inadequate in dealing with market abuses.

The ineffectiveness of the Grain Futures Act resulted in the passage of the Commodity Exchange Act of 1936, which extended the regulatory net to other commodities and made price manipulation a criminal offense. Broader powers were granted to deal with abuses and to prosecute any offending trader. The act was also designed to curb excessive speculation and to bring commodity brokerage under regulation.

Several minor changes were made to the Commodity Exchange Act between 1936 and 1967. In 1968, Congress set minimum financial standards for commission traders and increased the penalties for certain violations such as price manipulation. Until the early 1970's, the government's stockpiles of commodities played an important role in stabilizing prices. The government would buy farm products in times of declining prices and high output, then serve as a supplier in periods of low farm output. As the shift to a market-oriented economy free of government interference gained strength, government reduced its role in the commodities markets, and merchants increased their reliance on futures markets to protect themselves against substantial price changes.

Although many futures markets had been regulated to varying degrees since 1914, several important markets including metals, coffee, cocoa, and sugar were still completely unregulated by the federal government. The volume of trading on the futures markets was rapidly increasing, by 1973 reaching $500 billion annually, much greater than the volume of financial securities trading on exchanges. It was apparent that futures markets had far-reaching effects on consumers, affecting them from their grocery bills to their housing costs. It also became apparent that commodities markets were just as important as securities markets for the country's economic development, resulting in demands for a single regulatory authority that would oversee and regulate the activities of all commodities markets. On October 23, 1974, Congress passed the Commodity Futures Trading Commission Act, thereby creating the CFTC. On April 21, 1975, the CFTC assumed all regulatory powers and functions pertaining to futures trading.

Impact of Event
The CFTC's task of overseeing and regulating a rapidly expanding and growing

futures market was enormous. The commission was charged with regulating "any item of goods or services traded on a futures basis." Within a week of assuming regulatory responsibility, the CFTC proposed rules to prevent fraud in commodities options and gold and silver futures contracts. By July 18, 1975, the CFTC had expanded its scope of regulation from thirty-eight futures markets for farm products to eighty-two markets for all types of futures trading. Later in the same year, the CFTC approved trading on the first two financial futures, one for Government National Mortgage Association (GNMA) mortgage certificates and the other for ninety-day U.S. Treasury bills.

During the first nine months of its operations, the CFTC rejected a request by Jack W. Savage, who previously had been convicted of mail fraud, for registration as a commodity trading adviser. The commission also filed its first injunction proceedings against City Commodities, Inc. of Minnesota for fraud and other violations of futures laws.

During its first year, the CFTC put in place procedures for reparations, handling confidential data, and receiving reports required of foreign traders. It also enlarged its reporting requirements to new commodities. In 1976, the CFTC's enforcement division launched two hundred fraud investigations. In 1977, the CFTC proposed regulating options markets and suggested rules for consumer protection. During this early period, the CFTC handled several major crises including a rise of coffee futures from $0.55 per pound to $1.50 in response to floods in Colombia and frost damage to the coffee crop in Brazil. The CFTC also charged the Hunt family of Dallas, Texas, with taking futures positions in soybeans that far exceeded the speculative limits. The U.S. district court in Chicago found the Hunt family in violation of rules and imposed a civil penalty of $500,000. It also prohibited family members from trading soybean futures for two years.

In 1977, the CFTC declared that it was legal for floor traders to engage in dual trade—for themselves and for customers—as long as the customers' orders were executed first. Trading firms were responsible for appropriate supervision of their employees.

On November 2, 1978, William T. Bagley retired as the first chairman of the CFTC. In his letter of resignation to President Jimmy Carter, he noted that the CFTC, after some initial start-up problems, had emerged as an efficient operating agency with a uniform set of trading rules and procedures.

The CFTC later designated several new contracts and contract markets including the Amex Commodities Exchange, Inc., for futures on GNMA certificates, the New York Futures Exchange for financial instruments and foreign currencies, and the Chicago Board of Trade for options on Treasury bond futures. Introduction of stock index futures contracts provided an effective means of hedging the overall direction of the stock market. By the end of 1982, stock index futures were trading on several exchanges.

During the last week of December, 1979, the Soviet Union invaded Afghanistan. On January 4, 1980, President Carter imposed an embargo on previously contracted wheat exports to the Soviet Union. In view of this embargo and the prospects of an abundant crop, commodity prices were expected to plummet. Traders and experts were concerned that this sudden shock, coupled with uncertainty about the price support program of the United States Department of Agriculture, would result in chaos in the marketplace. Large price declines were expected to result in margin calls in excess of $400 million. The CFTC, after wide-ranging consultations, called for a two-day suspension of the trading of wheat, corn, oats, soybeans, soybean meal, and soybean oil. The two-day suspension gave the markets time to consider market conditions more carefully, and an almost certain market crisis was averted. The CFTC has since effectively intervened several times to avoid or reduce crisis in several commodities, including silver and crude oil futures.

Standardized futures contracts in which quantity, quality, and location are established help meet specific requirements of buyers and sellers. Price is the only variable, and it is discovered through auction trading on the floor of an exchange. Farmers, merchants, and investors use futures contracts to protect themselves against fluctuating cash prices. Availability of nontraditional contracts such as futures on stock indexes, government bonds, foreign currencies, and other financial instruments provide means of hedging for all investors. Speculators, who generally have no trade interest in the underlying instrument or commodity, assume the risk the hedgers are attempting to avoid. Futures exchanges play the crucial role of clearing and settling contracts in these risk-transfer activities.

Bibliography

Commodity Futures Trading Commission. *Commodity Futures Trading Commission: The First Ten Years.* Washington, D.C.: Author, 1984. This sixty-four-page book describes events in the first ten years of the CFTC. It details the challenges faced by the CFTC and how they were managed.

Kolb, Robert W. *Understanding Futures Markets.* Miami, Fla.: Kolb Publishing Company, 1991. This well-written book provides easy access to details about specific futures markets.

Schwarz, Edward W., Joanne M. Hill, and Thomas Schneeweis. *Financial Futures: Fundamentals, Strategies, and Application.* Homewood, Ill.: Irwin, 1986. A good source of information on the theories, applications, and strategic use of financial futures.

Stebbins, Christine D. *Commodity Trading Manual.* Chicago: Board of Trade of the City of Chicago, 1989. A well-written reference manual dealing with a variety of topics ranging from historical development to day-to-day operations of a futures exchange.

Teweles, Richard J., and Frank J. Jones. *The Futures Game.* 2d ed. New York: McGraw-Hill, 1987. The first three chapters provide insights into the nature and mechanics of futures markets. Much of the remainder of the book deals with individual futures markets.

Rajiv Kalra

Cross-References

The Federal Trade Commission Is Organized (1914), p. 269; Congress Passes the Agricultural Marketing Act (1929), p. 569; Roosevelt Creates the Commodity Credit Corporation (1933), p. 668; The Securities Exchange Act Establishes the SEC (1934), p. 679; Eisenhower Begins the Food for Peace Program (1954), p. 1052; Insider Trading Scandals Mar the Emerging Junk Bond Market (1986), p. 1921.

SONY INTRODUCES THE BETAMAX

Category of event: New products
Time: 1975
Locale: Japan and the United States

Although the first to offer videocassette technology, Sony and its Beta format was quickly defeated by VHS technology

Principal personages:
    AKIO MORITA (1921-   ), the chairman of Sony
    JACK VALENTI (1921-   ), the president of the Motion Picture Association who led the battle against the introduction of Sony Betamax machines in the 1980's
    KONOSUKE MATSUSHITA (1894-1989), the chairman of Matsushita

Summary of Event

In September, 1974, Sony proposed to Matsushita and JVC that they jointly adopt the new Sony videocassette recorder (VCR) under development. The Sony VCR was nearly completed, and Sony already had started manufacturing dies and had made other preparations for production. Sony also showed the Betamax prototype to RCA in the hope of persuading the American manufacturer to adopt the Sony design. The eventual demise of Sony's Beta format and the corollary domination of the VHS technology proved to be a dramatic story of management and innovation in the electronics industry.

Magnetic video recording technology, invented in the United States by Ampex Corporation, a small California business that developed the video recorder in 1956, languished as a consumer technology because of its high cost. A single unit cost $50,000 and used magnetic tape as opposed to earlier audio tape. In the 1950's, the American manufacturer found that the Japanese firms Sony, JVC, and Matsushita had studied its design and had started to reduce the machine's price through use of solid-state electronic circuits. In addition to foreign competitors, Ampex met fierce competition from American rivals with experience in sound recording, such as RCA. RCA chose another ill-fated technology to support, the videodisc system. Throughout the 1960's RCA and the Japanese companies experimented with a variety of film reproduction techniques, including bulky reel-to-reel formats. Prices remained high until, in 1971, Sony designed a cassette model with a three-quarter-inch tape. Known as the U-Matic, the machine contained the basic concepts of the Beta and rival VHS formats and was inexpensive enough to be purchased by schools or large institutions. The price remained too high for the consumer market. With the U-Matic as a conceptual basis for technology, the Japanese dominated the market, leaving American competitors and the poorly conceived RCA videodisc behind.

Progress on the basic technology continued, split between two competing concepts, the Beta format and others based on a half-inch tape. Manufacturers, some of whom had signed cross-licensing agreements for video recording patents, wanted a single standard format. Such standardization would benefit both producers and consumers. Meanwhile, both Sony and JVC proceeded to develop the Beta machine. In 1974, JVC announced that it had a competing design under development, which it called the VHS. Both formats had borrowed heavily from the U-Matic and thus did not differ enough to ensure technological advantage for one or the other.

The VCR market expanded rapidly. In 1976, Japan exported 139,000 units; a scant two years later, the number of units exported had ballooned to 973,000, with a value of $126 billion. As prices fell further, the market grew by leaps and bounds. In 1982, Japan exported fifteen million VCRs, 80 percent of the total produced.

Without a clear advantage in the machinery, none of the manufacturers had a clear-cut advantage, despite Sony's lead. Instead, the market dictated the technology. By 1976, other major Japanese manufacturers had moved to the VHS technology. Hitachi, Mitsubishi, and Matsushita all introduced their own models or adopted the VHS format. Sharp soon adopted VHS as well, and Beta began its slide to oblivion. In 1978, the Beta format accounted for 594,000 units, while VHS accounted for 878,000 units. Within five years, Beta format production had grown to more than 4.5 million units, but VHS production had risen to three times that amount, at 13.6 million.

What accounted for the massive shift in consumer tastes? Most of the pioneers had missed the most useful feature of VCRs and touted a less useful, although increasingly popular, feature. Originally, companies expected that the primary use of VCRs would be for playing movies purchased at stores, and they downplayed the machines' ability to record. Americans in particular came to use the recording feature to "time shift," taping a program shown at one time for viewing at another, more convenient time.

In 1976, VHS technology took another step forward when JVC attempted to gain a foothold in the U.S. market through an agreement with RCA. Although JVC failed to reach that agreement, the company turned its attention to similar agreements with European companies. Those agreements, concluded with most of the major European electronics companies by 1978, all but eliminated Beta. JVC also offered options such as stereo sound recording, slow motion and still functions, and portability, all of which marked it as a superior product to the Sony machine. As scholars of the technology concluded, only by offering better special features could Sony have gained a niche once its tape format was surpassed by VHS.

Faced with the prospects of losing further ground to JVC and the VHS format, Akio Morita of Sony approached the Japanese government. He asked that the government intervene in the industry by establishing a single standard, one that favored the Beta format. Morita argued that the diversity of formats was splitting the market and threatened Japan's entire electronics export industry. As quickly as Sony could lobby for its format, the VHS companies responded by pointing out that more companies had adopted VHS and that the consumers should decide. The Ministry of International Trade and Industry (MITI) attempted to get the principals to meet and adopt a single standard, but both JVC and Sony announced that they would accept no format other than their own.

Meanwhile, the major VHS competitors gained sales, distribution, or side agreements with U.S. companies, particularly RCA, which offered to sell VCRs under the name Selectavision for $1,000, undercutting the price of the Betamax units. Zenith, which had signed a similar agreement with Sony to sell the Betamax, had to lower prices dramatically. Zenith and Sony still could not address the longer playing time for a tape offered by the VHS technology.

At the same time, a new opponent to the entire technology arose in the form of the motion picture industry, which suddenly realized that with two machines hooked together, anyone could copy film cassettes sold by the manufacturers. VCR manufacturers originally thought that cassettes of films would create the major source of demand for the machines. The potential to copy motion pictures represented a source of lost revenue for the industry that held the copyrights on them. The Motion Picture Association started to investigate legal actions against the recording industry, and Universal Studios ultimately brought a suit against Sony that went to the Supreme Court. Eventually, the Court ruled that videocassette technology itself did not constitute copyright infringement and thus could be sold without interference. Motion picture makers quickly realized that, unable to keep VCRs off the market, they had to find a way to take advantage of them. They did that by marketing their films through video sales at first, then—but only reluctantly—through rentals. An enormous industry bloomed as a result.

By 1977, JVC, Sharp, and Matsushita were the primary VHS manufacturers, while Pioneer, Aiwa, Sanyo, Toshiba, and Zenith all produced Beta machines. The technology impetus continued to reside with the VHS manufacturers, who introduced a four-hour version of VHS for export. As early as 1980, JVC had introduced multispeed six hour machines, four-head machines, and portable two-head machines, and within four more years JVC had added one-touch timers, compact camcorders, stereo sound functions, and random search functions. By the late 1980's, the Beta technology had all but disappeared.

Impact of Event

The Betamax-VHS struggle constituted a battle for a new technology to win over a marketplace while emerging victorious over a competing technology. It resembled the difficulties that IBM had in cornering the personal computer market, despite the fact that it had introduced many of the new features and had a virtual lock on the original technology. The Sony Betamax's troubles stemmed from the fact that it could not compete with the longer-format tapes. At the same time, the competitors' machines, derived from the same U-Matic design, remained close enough in other features that Sony could not gain a technological edge.

Unable to dictate a single industry standard because of the strength of the VHS format, Sony found itself seeking government support, a sure sign of a technology behind the times. Sony's inability to reach side agreements early with either its competitors or its overseas distributors, who themselves eventually would manufacture the technology with Japanese internal parts, left it without a strong base upon which to force a single standard. Sony never found a way to improve the cassette technology for longer programming.

At the same time, videocassette technology had to establish itself as a consumer product and survive the Hollywood-directed campaigns to block its sale. Motion picture studios feared copyright infringements that would derive from bootleg copies of films. At first, the motion picture companies envisioned the tape technology almost strictly in terms of playing prerecorded Hollywood films. Studios such as Disney released separate groups of its films, one group intended for rental and another group for sale. Few people in the film industry predicted that rentals, subject to copyright fees, would constitute the primary use of VCRs. Again, consumers set the pace, eschewing purchases and opting instead for rentals. Pornographic films in particular proved popular because of the privacy offered by the VCR technology. Within a short time, consumers themselves had pushed the boundaries of the market to emphasize rentals in all areas. Larger video rental stores found that they had to drop adult titles from their inventory to attract families and general viewers. Later, a legion of specialized videos appeared, featuring rock music, lectures, "how-tos," and celebrities hawking fitness and workout programs. Video rental businesses became the libraries of the 1990's.

Although virtually all types of businesses, from drug stores to grocery stores to one-stop gas and food stations, offered rentals, several chains developed into national leaders, including Blockbuster and Videotowne. Those chains not only rented the latest releases but also sold them. When home computer games became available on a broad scale, the video rental houses also rented video games. A fusion of those products came in the early 1990's, when the video game "Street Fighter II Turbo" was touted for a month in video stores with offers of free rentals of videocassettes produced by the manufacturer of "Street Fighter II Turbo."

As of 1993, the ultimate fusion still lurked on the horizon, namely that of the personal computer and the television. Attempts to mate television technology with personal computers already had yielded an interactive system that allowed people to receive education or training, browse through real estate offerings, or take nationwide polls. Such technology promised ultimately to expand to videorecorders, which in the future would be modified into digital technology. At that point, interactive tapes would allow "personalized" motion picture tapes, allowing viewers to choose among different endings to motion pictures.

Sony's inability to establish itself as the frontrunner in the VCR market resulted from a failure to understand consumer demands for the new machines. Although it made the initial technological breakthrough, Sony locked itself into technology that was neither compatible with other systems nor flexible enough to beat them at their own game.

Bibliography

Cusumano, Michael, Yiorgos Mylonadis, and Richard Rosenbloom. "Strategic Maneuvering and Mass-Market Dynamics: The Triumph of VHS Over Beta." *Business History Review* 66 (Spring, 1992): 51-94. By examining the marketing strategies and corporate approaches to VCRs, the authors provide a thorough analysis of the business strategies employed by the major competitors. They ignore political influences for the most part and do not dwell on consumer tastes or demands.

Gilder, George. *Life After Television.* New York: W. W. Norton, 1992. One of the most insightful analyses of the interrelationship between computer technology and television. Gilder maintains that telephone signals should be sent over the airwaves and that television should be carried to personal computers through fiber optical technology, creating an interactive computing, videocassette, and television technology.

Lardner, James. *Fast Forward: Hollywood, the Japanese, and the Onslaught of the VCR.* New York: Norton, 1987. The first book to survey the VCR wars. Provides a detailed history of the development of VCRs. Lardner examines political as well as technological factors that led to the dominance of VHS technology.

Luther, Arch C. *Digital Video in the PC Environment.* New York: McGraw-Hill, 1989. Examines the combinations of technologies that will characterize television and videocassette recording in the near future. Written more for specialists in computers and/or electronics. The author develops the important distinctions between passive and interactive use of technology.

Morita, Akio. *Made in Japan.* New York: Dutton, 1986. Morita's own story of Sony, including his perceptions of the advantages of Japanese manufacturing.

Rosenbloom, Richard S., and Michael A. Cusumano. "Technological Pioneering and Competitive Advantage: The Birth of the VCR Industry." *California Management Review* 29 (Summer, 1987): 51-76. Focuses on technological developments at Ampex, Sony, and other companies.

Larry Schweikart

Cross-References

The National Broadcasting Company Is Founded (1926), p. 522; The 1976 Copyright Act Reflects Technological Change (1976), p. 1626; Electronic Technology Creates the Possibility of Telecommuting (1980's), p. 1733; Video Rental Outlets Gain Popularity (1980's), p. 1745; IBM Introduces Its Personal Computer (1981), p. 1809; U.S. Courts Restrict Rights to Photocopy Anthologies (1991), p. 2040.

FRED SILVERMAN RESCUES ABC
TELEVISION'S RATINGS

Categories of event: Marketing and management
Time: 1975-1978
Locale: New York, New York

Fred Silverman took ABC from third to first in network television ratings, and the network's fortunes declined after his departure

Principal personages:

FRED SILVERMAN (1937-   ), the president of ABC Entertainment, 1975-1978

WILLIAM S. PALEY (1901-1990), the chair of CBS, 1929-1990

LEONARD GOLDBERG (1934-   ), the programming chief at ABC, 1966-1969

LEONARD GOLDENSON (1905-   ), the chief executive officer of ABC beginning in 1953

Summary of Event

Fred Silverman, the first person to hold top programming positions at each of the three major television networks, left the Columbia Broadcasting System (CBS) in 1975 to work for the American Broadcasting Company (ABC). In one year, ABC went from third to first in the ratings, an unparalleled feat in the history of broadcasting. Silverman left ABC for a position at the National Broadcasting Company (NBC) in 1978.

Silverman worked with Fred Pierce (the president of ABC Television) to retool the already established 1975-1976 schedule. They used the "family viewing hour," the first hour of evening network transmission, to experiment with new programs and new talent, saving their strongest programs, such as *NFL Football, Baretta,* and *Starsky and Hutch,* for the 9 P.M. (8 P.M. in the Midwest) slot. The strategy worked so well that ABC held a slim lead in ratings at midyear.

ABC was able to increase its lead with a string of midseason additions to the programming schedule. *Laverne and Shirley* became a successful *Happy Days* spinoff, and shows such as *The Bionic Woman* and *Charlie's Angels* cemented ABC's top position.

ABC's rapid success was the result of several factors. First, the network responded to the wishes of the viewing public, which were discovered through audience research. Second, the viewing public's taste shifted in favor of action-oriented, sexually provocative shows. ABC provided this type of programming more quickly than its competition. Third, Silverman showed great ability to promote programs. Fourth, the managements at both CBS and NBC proved to be unwilling to change, offering opportunities for ABC to succeed with innovation.

Silverman's remarkable success fostered a number of changes in network television operations. Particularly telling would be the other networks' efforts to copy programming innovations. Histories of network television generally refer to the 1970's as "the Silverman years," indicating his power and influence.

Silverman had been at CBS since 1963 and had been the head of daytime programming before becoming programming chief in 1970. He carried many of his ideas and programming philosophies with him when he left for ABC. CBS had long been the top network in terms of ratings, but many of its programs, such as *The Beverly Hillbillies* and *The Andy Griffith Show*, were aimed at rural audiences. Silverman advocated a new strategy: He would target programs for a more urban, younger audience. The "baby boom" after World War II made the group between eighteen and thirty-four years of age a significant portion of the population. The strategy to target this group was not without risk, but the potential rewards were high. Advertisers liked the ability to appeal to the younger segment, and the audiences of the early 1970's continued to watch Silverman's CBS programs.

One of Silverman's strengths was his ability to masterfully schedule programs. Historically, network television scheduling theory had been based on the principle that the average viewer prefers to make as few choices as possible. Emphasis was on keeping a consistent flow of programs throughout an evening and giving viewers no reason to change channels. Silverman could build a schedule better than any of his counterparts. Although he never strayed far from the formula of adventure series and sitcoms with liberal doses of sexual innuendo, his shows were filled with likable characters and recognizable stars.

Silverman recognized the need to minimize risk. He understood the value of protecting a weaker show by having strong shows surround it and was not above "counterprogramming," offering a show that would appeal to a small audience that was not interested in the "popular" program on another network at the time. Silverman also had the talent necessary to fix a script and to obtain the maximum amount of benefit from his shows through series spinoffs and cross-pollination of stars. Perhaps Silverman's greatest skill was being able to realize what the public wanted and then offering it. Silverman was one of the first to use and respond to audience research on a large scale.

When Silverman left CBS in 1975, his new employer, ABC, was the perennial also-ran in network television. ABC had fewer affiliates, a smaller operating budget, and less production capability than its competitors. ABC did, however, have a basically sound programming plan in place, and Silverman was able to make great strides by doing what he knew best: rescheduling, fine tuning, and promoting. Some executives at CBS were never entirely comfortable with Silverman's down-to-earth attitude; those at ABC welcomed him with open arms because they were less concerned with image and more concerned with how many people were watching.

Silverman's ratings triumph at ABC was fashioned in part by competitors shortcomings. Both NBC and CBS were complacent, conservative network operations, somewhat out of touch with the average audience member. The management structure at NBC was complex and cumbersome. CBS was still very much under the control of its founder, William S. Paley, a man who typically did not give his executives much freedom. ABC was able to move quickly and to change course dramatically in large part because it had not been terribly successful. Long accustomed to being in third place, ABC could only improve its position; thus Silverman had more freedom and more flexibility than he had at CBS.

Silverman had developed a shrewder sense of programming than most, but he also was able to maintain a genuine enjoyment for his work. He was perceived as more down to earth than his seemingly more elitist colleagues. Some of his critics suggested that he was so successful in programming for the masses because he was a "common man" himself. For most of his career, Silverman responded to these jibes as though they were compliments, exhibiting pride at his skill in responding to the desires of the average American.

Silverman was courted by NBC in late 1977 and left ABC when his contract expired in June, 1978. As with many executive changes, this one seemed to have more to it than an increase in salary and benefits. Silverman would become the president of NBC, and he would be fully responsible for network television operations. Some have said that the move was fueled by Silverman's desire for more authority and flexibility. Others have noted Silverman's desire to be seen as a person of vision rather than as a refiner of others' ideas. For whatever reasons, Silverman left ABC and became the first individual to have held the position of head of programming at all three major television networks.

Network television programming is a complex undertaking. Certainly some of Silverman's success resulted from luck, but he knew his target audience better than most and he recognized what network advertisers wanted: large numbers of likely customers for their products. When Silverman went to NBC, most observers expected him to continue the kind of programming he had shepherded so well at ABC, shows that featured young, good-looking actors who often did not wear much clothing. As Silverman talked of programming quality and the need to downplay the importance of ratings points, most people were shocked or at least pleasantly surprised. Whether Silverman would be able to take the programming high road given NBC's previous history and current problems remained to be seen. What was clear was that ABC began to slide in the ratings race, as had CBS, after Silverman departed. Silverman's plans of action at CBS and ABC were similar, but his success apparently could not be carried on by others.

Impact of Event

Fred Silverman's success had a major impact on network television programming. All three networks rushed to implement his strategy of appealing to the tastes of young urban audiences. Programming became more cyclic than creative, and a successful new program would soon spawn many imitators, resulting in overexposure.

Historically, network programming philosophy had been to appeal to the broadest possible constituency. Television became a mass medium, with programs aimed at the lowest common denominator. For a number of reasons, this type of programming made good economic sense. Advertisers wanted a stable, consistent audience base, and they generally were not interested in supporting controversial programs. Costs of production were escalating rapidly, so failure was very expensive. Safe programs similar to those already on the air therefore had greater appeal than shows that differed and could offer either greater success or potential failure. The need to draw large audiences meant that shows could not appeal only to narrow interests.

Demographic experiments undertaken by Silverman at CBS and ABC changed television programming philosophy. Previously, the emphasis was on how many people were watching. The emphasis changed to whether a program could deliver a large share of a particular target market. Popular shows that appealed to the wrong demographics were cancelled, to be replaced by programs that could better deliver the desired demographics.

The ability to target specific demographic segments pleased advertisers, but it also led to a drop in total network audience. As the networks became less interested in certain segments, including the very old and the very young, independent and cable stations began to gain strength and ratings by offering programs to these groups. Ironically, as the independent and cable stations began to offer programs for groups such as young children and senior citizens, additional "target markets" were created, and advertisers began to support independent and cable endeavors as well, often to the financial detriment of network programs and revenues.

A programming change that would prove to be a mixed blessing was the signing of talent, including performers, writers, and producers to exclusive long-term contracts. These contracts could lock in talent but played a large part in doubling the average production cost of a half-hour sitcom in just five years.

The ratings services began to generate "instant numbers" in the early 1970's. As programming executives began to rely on them, shows were often given shorter periods in which to prove themselves. Networks became likely to buy a smaller number of initial episodes of each series, and try larger numbers of series. By the end of the 1970's, even Fred Silverman would have trouble finding enough "good" programs to satisfy the networks' voracious appetites.

Silverman had the ability to create formulaic programs that appealed to audiences. The other networks tried to copy his programs but were not as successful. Silverman's unique talents as a programmer and promoter always seemed to keep him a step ahead. Silverman had a more "hands-on" approach than his network counterparts and seemed to be more attuned to the desires of the audience. Silverman also maintained an edge through his creative use of promotion. Silverman would give his brief—often ten seconds—promotional commercials careful attention and would usually succeed in capturing a provocative or suggestive moment from a show to act as an effective enticement. Soon after Silverman left ABC, the network lost its first-place standing in the ratings. Many of Silverman's programs were still on the air, but no one else at ABC was able to fine tune and promote like he did. The shift was subtle but noticeable. ABC became more of an imitator than an innovator.

By the early 1980's, all three major television networks were having difficulties. The programming changes initiated during the 1970's continued to define the medium, but not always with positive results. Questions were raised concerning the networks' motives for profits at the expense of long-term development and whether advertisers had too much power over program scheduling and development. Questions were also raised about a relatively new trend, organized boycotts and letter-writing campaigns aimed at cleaning up the airwaves by eliminating some of the sex and violence from shows.

Even as television struggles to remain a mass medium, it increasingly targets programs at narrower segments. As long as broadcasting remains primarily a privately owned, commercially financed operation, network programming will likely continue on the course set by Fred Silverman.

Bibliography

Bedell, Sally. *Up the Tube: Prime-Time TV and the Silverman Years.* New York: Viking Press, 1981. A detailed look at the life and career of Fred Silverman. Pays particular attention to his tenures at each of the three major networks. Interesting reading, accessible to the general reader.

Blum, Richard A., and Richard D. Lindheim. *Primetime: Network Television Programming.* Boston: Focal Press, 1987. A model of network programming activities. Less a history than a description of the programming process, including job descriptions and relationships. Fairly technically oriented. Useful in helping the reader understand how programs are developed.

Head, Sydney W., and Christopher H. Sterling. *Broadcasting in America: A Survey of Electronic Media.* Boston: Houghton-Mifflin, 1987. A detailed and analytic look at the electronic media. An excellent resource and one of the most popular textbooks in the field.

Quinlan, Sterling. *Inside ABC: American Broadcasting Company's Rise to Power.* New York: Hastings House, 1979. Quinlan, a former ABC employee, looks at the history and development of the network, concentrating on personalities. Opinionated, but still offers a reasonably balanced perspective.

Slater, Robert. *This . . . Is CBS: A Chronicle of Sixty Years.* Englewood Cliffs, N.J.: Prentice-Hall, 1988. A historical narrative of CBS, more a chronicle of events than an analysis. Chapter 11 looks at Silverman's tenure at CBS.

Sterling, Christopher H., and John M. Kittross. *Stay Tuned: A Concise History of American Broadcasting.* Belmont, Calif.: Wadsworth, 1978. A good overview of radio and television, organized both chronologically and by topic. A popular textbook.

William J. Wallace

Cross-References

Howard Hughes Builds a Business Empire (1924-1976), p. 442; Radio's Payola

Scandal Leads to Congressional Action (1960), p. 1148; Sony Introduces the Betamax (1975), p. 1573; Video Rental Outlets Gain Popularity (1980's), p. 1745; The Cable News Network Debuts (1980), p. 1768; The Fox Television Network Goes on the Air (1986), p. 1928.

CONGRESS PASSES THE MAGNUSON-MOSS WARRANTY ACT

Category of event: Consumer affairs
Time: January 4, 1975
Locale: Washington, D.C.

The Magnuson-Moss Warranty Act imposed important requirements on manufacturers and sellers that offer written warranties to consumers

Principal personages:

WARREN GRANT MAGNUSON (1905-1989), a U.S. senator who coauthored the Magnuson-Moss Warranty Act
JOHN E. MOSS (1915-   ), a U.S. congressman who coauthored the Magnuson-Moss Warranty Act
GERALD R. FORD (1913-   ), the president of the United States, 1974-1977

Summary of Event

The Magnuson-Moss Warranty Act of 1975 imposed important disclosure requirements upon sellers that provide written product warranties to consumers, addressed and sought to simplify the procedures for enforcing such warranties, and limited or proscribed certain common practices of product warrantors. This act, the first major federal effort to reform warranty law, represented the culmination of several years of federally-prescribed studies of consumer-directed written warranties.

Prior to 1975, state law, in the form of the Uniform Commercial Code (UCC), governed the creation, interpretation, and enforcement of product warranties. The UCC was the law in virtually all states and, in Article 2, included several provisions governing warranties. For example, the UCC governed express warranties or oral or written statements by sellers that they will stand behind the goods they sell. It also governed implied warranties, warranties arising because of the sales contract and existing regardless of the presence of an express warranty.

The two most important implied warranties are the implied warranty of merchantability and the implied warranty of fitness for a particular purpose. The implied warranty of merchantability arises in sales by merchants or dealers in a particular type of good. It requires that the goods be fit for their ordinary use or purpose. For example, under the UCC, merchant sellers by implication warrant that automobiles are generally safe to drive and that washing machines are capable of washing clothes. In both cases, the sellers are warranting that their product meets general industry standards. The implied warranty of fitness for a particular purpose requires that sellers select appropriate goods in those cases in which buyers rely on the sellers' expertise to do so. For example, a contractor needing a certain type of exterior paint to complete a project might inform the seller that he or she is relying on the seller's expertise in identifying suitable paint. The implied warranty of fitness for a particular purpose would arise in that sale. If the paint is unfit for the stated purpose, then the seller has breached the implied warranty.

Although the UCC's regime of express and implied warranties represented the most comprehensive product warranty rules ever adopted, a number of federal studies in the 1960's and 1970's revealed the UCC's shortcomings, particularly in its rules related to written warranties. These studies suggested that some written warranties were so general that they communicated nothing about product quality, were often misleading, and were usually imposed by the product seller or manufacturer rather than being the result of bargaining between the seller and buyer.

The studies' more specific observations identified some of the key problems with written warranties. For example, it became evident that in many sales of durable goods such as automobiles and large appliances, sellers were not communicating their warranties to buyers. Instead, buyers would often learn of a warranty after having received the product. The warranty in those cases was largely unimportant in the sale because the buyer knew nothing of it until after agreeing to purchase the product. In those cases in which the buyer knew of a written warranty, the seller often would include a disclaimer of implied warranties and/or a limitation of consequential damages (damages other than the reduced worth of a defective product; for example, the damages from a basement flood caused by a defective valve on a hot water heater). The net result of such a warranty was that the buyer would lack the benefits of the implied warranties and consequential damages. Buyers often were confronted with conditions of qualification for warranty protection. These conditions might include a requirement to send a warranty card to a manufacturer to ensure coverage, a provision that the defective product be sent to a distant manufacturer for service, or a requirement that the buyer take the product to a local retailer for service despite the manufacturer's unwillingness to compensate the retailer adequately for the services provided. Another conclusion of the federal studies was that many purchasers who enjoyed rights under the UCC's warranty provisions were unwilling to litigate because the amount of the claim, often only the difference between the actual and warranted value of the product, would not justify pursuing an action against the manufacturer or seller of the product.

On January 4, 1975, Congress' effort to correct these problems, the Magnuson-Moss Warranty Act, became law. In general, the act requires manufacturers and sellers who use written product warranties to disclose to purchasers the scope, effect, and limitations, if any, of a warranty; requires warrantors to establish informal dispute resolution programs for consumers who have claims based on written warranties; and prohibits warrantors from using a written warranty to disclaim the UCC's implied warranties. It is important to note that the act does not require that product sellers make written warranties; it applies only to those sellers that elect to use such warranties.

Impact of Event

The disclosure provisions of the Magnuson-Moss Warranty Act were likely its most significant provisions. These provisions were intended to respond to the less-than-clear language often used by sellers in their written warranties and to provide consumers with more information, with which they could make better choices. The most important disclosure requirement is that warrantors clearly label written warranties as either "full" or "limited." A full warranty requires the warrantor or its designated representative to repair the defective product at no cost to the consumer, and, if repair is not possible, to replace the product at no cost. If the warrantor or its representative is unable to repair or replace the product, then the warrantor must refund the purchase price. The warrantor may specify the duration of the full warranty. The act classifies all warranties that fall short of the coverage of full warranties as limited warranties and requires that the warrantors label them as such.

The Magnuson-Moss Warranty Act requires that all consumer-directed written warranties be stated in clear and unambiguous language. Consumers should know the following information after reading the written warranty: which parts and repairs are covered by the warranty, whether any expenses are excluded from coverage, how long the warranty lasts, the necessary steps in obtaining repairs, what the company will do if the product fails, whether the warranty covers consequential damages, and any conditions or limitations on the warranty. The act also includes some important requirements and prohibitions. It requires that consumers be apprised of their written warranty options before the sale, compels warrantors that want to limit or avoid consequential damages to include conspicuous language to that effect in the written warranty, and proscribes the use of warranty cards and other devices that may pose obstacles to purchasers unless the written warranty itself includes such requirements. The act also prohibits a warrantor that makes a written full or limited warranty from disclaiming any implied warranties.

To encourage the resolution of consumer warranty claims, the Magnuson-Moss Warranty Act requires all product warrantors to establish internal means of informal dispute resolution for these claims. Although the act does not require resort to informal resolution, it encourages consumers to use this method. If a consumer makes reasonable efforts to comply with the warrantor's wishes and if the warrantor is unable to remedy the consumer's claim adequately, then the consumer has the right, if he or she prevails in a later lawsuit against the warrantor, to recover from the warrantor the reasonable value of attorney fees and court costs arising from the litigation.

The Magnuson-Moss Warranty Act has had a varied but overall positive effect on consumer-directed warranty transactions. For example, the act's disclosure provisions appear to have had their intended effect of providing consumers with information so that they can make better purchasing decisions. After passage of the act, the federal government commissioned several studies to examine its effect. In general, the findings suggested that consumers were pleased with the warranty information required by Magnuson-Moss and used this information to make informed choices among comparable products.

Additional studies sought to determine whether and to what extent the act influenced potential warrantors. The findings suggested that product manufacturers and sellers were not more reluctant to make written warranties after the act. In fact, it appeared that many product marketers sought to use the act's requirements to their advantage by offering full warranties to consumers. The studies also suggested that warranties appearing after passage of the act were more readable and included more product information than did their predecessors. Finally, the studies revealed that virtually all warrantors were complying with the act's prohibition against implied warranty disclaimers but warrantors were more inclined to include conspicuous limitations of consequential damages in their written warranties.

The act's provision prohibiting warrantors from using their written warranties to disclaim implied warranties has had a significant influence on both warrantors and consumers. Perhaps the single most deceptive practice before the adoption of Magnuson-Moss was a warrantor's assertion of product quality through a written warranty coupled with an almost contradictory provision disclaiming the UCC's implied warranties of merchantability and fitness for a particular purpose. The written warranty would suggest to most reasonable consumers that the product was of good quality, would include language that often restricted the consumer's options in case the product was less than advertised, and then would eliminate resort to implied warranties, which provided the only other recourse should the written warranty fail for some reason.

Despite the act's attempt to simplify the dispute process, dispute resolution remained the biggest problem for consumers wishing to pursue warranty actions against product warrantors. Whether the product deviates from a written warranty or is of poor quality continued to be a key issue in warranty disputes. Although the Magnuson-Moss Warranty Act improved the dispute process and encouraged warrantors to cure the problem, the act did not, and likely could not, eliminate frivolous consumer claims, unreasonable warrantor reactions to legitimate claims, and high litigation costs for those cases in which both sides strongly support their positions and are therefore unwilling to resolve their dispute in an informal manner.

A final and largely unanswered question raised by the act concerns the effects of federal intervention in an area such as warranty law that historically had been governed by states' laws. This question becomes more important when examined within the context of congressional efforts to reform another area reserved to states' laws, product liability. Magnuson-Moss received wide support in Congress, but proposed product liability reform legislation, introduced in every Congress from 1979 through the 1980's, never became law. It is unclear why this is so.

Bibliography

Arthur Young & Company. *Warranties Rules Consumer Baseline Study.* Washington, D.C.: Government Printing Office, 1979. A comprehensive, lengthy (250 pages), and technical study of the effects of Magnuson-Moss. An excellent and methodologically sound work intended for serious researchers.

Reitz, Curtis R. *Consumer Protection Under the Magnuson-Moss Warranty Act.* Philadelphia, Pa.: American Law Institute-American Bar Association Committee on Continuing Professional Education, 1978. A comprehensive, readable (150 pages) treatment of the legal environment that provoked the adoption of Magnuson-Moss, the act itself, and the potential legal and business issues that might arise because of the act.

Schmitt, Jacqueline, Lawrence Kanter, and Rachel Miller. *Impact Report on the Magnuson-Moss Warranty Act*. Washington, D.C.: Government Printing Office, 1980. An excellent and brief (thirty-three pages) early source on the impact of Magnuson-Moss. Focuses on industry reaction to the act and whether the act has influenced sellers. Discusses such issues as continued use of written warranties whether new warranties are limited or full, and intelligibility of warranties.

U.S. Code Congressional and Administrative News. 93d Congress, 2d session. St. Paul, Minn.: West, 1975. Highly recommended reading for those interested in the legislative history of the act. Includes excellent summaries of industry practices prior to adoption of the act and strong detail on the legislative intent of Congress in adopting it. Good reference, combined with the Arthur Young study, for determining whether Congress' intent squares with the act's effects.

U.S. Federal Trade Commission. *A Businessperson's Guide to Federal Warranty Law*. Washington, D.C.: Government Printing Office, 1987. A brief (twenty-three pages) primer on the provisions of the Magnuson-Moss Warranty Act. A particularly good source for those who receive written warranties and want to know their rights.

Nim Razook

Cross-References

Nader's *Unsafe at Any Speed* Launches a Consumer Movement (1965), p. 1270; Congress Passes the Consumer Credit Protection Act (1968), p. 1358; Congress Passes the Fair Credit Reporting Act (1970), p. 1454; Nixon Signs the Consumer Product Safety Act (1972), p. 1522; Sears Agrees to an FTC Order Baning Bait-and-Switch Tactics (1976), p. 1631.

THE ECONOMIC COMMUNITY OF WEST AFRICAN STATES FORMS

Category of event: International business and commerce
Time: May 28, 1975
Locale: Lagos, Nigeria

The ECOWAS facilitated cooperative mobilization of national resources for subregional development and self-reliance

Principal personages:
LUIZ CABREL (1931-), the president of Guinea Bissau
FÉLIX HOUPHOUËT-BOIGNY (1905-), the president of Ivory Coast
YAKUBU GOWON (1934-), the head of the federal military government of Nigeria, 1966-1975
OLUSEGUN OBASANJO (1937-), the Nigerian head of state in 1976 who signed the Lome Protocols for Nigeria
WILLIAM RICHARD TOLBERT, JR. (1913-1980), the president of Liberia, 1971-1980
LÉOPOLD SENGHOR (1906-), the president of Senegal
GNASSINGBE EYADÉMA (1937-), the president of Togo

Summary of Event

The Treaty of the Economic Community of West African States (ECOWAS), also known as the Treaty of Lagos, was signed on May 28, 1975, by representatives of fifteen sovereign states. The instrument set up a transnational framework for economic cooperation and sociocultural exchanges, with a view to the eventual unity of the nations of West Africa. The treaty was the culmination of a decade of effort by subregional leaders to establish a viable intergovernmental forum for optimal mobilization of national resources to achieve subregional development and continental progress. The ECOWAS was the first of such unions in Africa to cross ethnographic, linguistic, and colonial partitions in favor of a multipurpose, polglot community.

Before the formation of the ECOWAS, subregional groupings in Africa tended to be fragmented. The fractional tendency, often associated with past colonial orientation, was evident, for example, in such formations as the francophonic West African Customs Union (1962), the Union Africaine et Malgache de Co-operation Economique (1964), and the Afro-Malagasy Common Organization (1966). The same tendency existed in the former British dependencies. The East African Community and Common Market, comprising Kenya, Tanzania, and Uganda, was organized in 1967 to replace the defunct East African Common Services Organization, created by a British Order-in-Council.

Regional fragmentation led to a multiplicity of intergovernmental groupings and loyalties. The many groupings included the Central African Customs and Economic Union, Economic Community of the Great Lakes Countries, Mano River Union,

Permanent Inter-State Committee on Drought Control in the Sahel, Niger Basin Authority, Organization for the Management and Development of the Kangera River Basin, Organization for the Development of the River Gambia, Organization for the Development of the Senegal River, and South African Economic Development Coordination Conference. Despite the fractional tendencies, economic integration was found to be helpful in promoting development efforts in postcolonial Africa.

In 1965, the Untied Nations Economic Commission for Africa (ECA) adopted resolution 142 (VII), which urged its West African members to plan for the erection of a framework for the harmonization of economic and social development in the subregion. The resolution called on member states to consider the existing models and experiences of economic integration both in Africa and overseas as possible structures for a West African community. An ongoing power struggle between the Organization of African Unity (OAU) and the ECA hampered progress until the early 1970's. The OAU, faced with formal constraints and realities, finally conceded to the ECA in matters of economic planning.

Disagreements with the OAU notwithstanding, the ECA pursued its objectives. In October, 1966, the ECA sponsored a conference in Niamey, Niger, on West African economic cooperation, at which eleven state participants agreed to economic integration on an incremental basis, starting with the creation of permanent committees for energy and transportation. The articles of association were consequently formalized and presented to a later conference of the leaders at Accra, Ghana, from April 27 to May 5, 1967. The conference concluded with the adoption of the articles of association for an Economic Community of West Africa. The twelve signatories were Benin, Ghana, Ivory Coast, Liberia, Mali, Mauritania, Niger, Nigeria, Senegal, Sierra Leone, Togo, and Upper Volta (later Burkina Faso).

The instrument became a basis for cooperation and integration. It provided for the harmonization of development efforts on a range of matters. Integration, however, came slowly. At a subsequent summit at Monrovia, Liberia, in April, 1968, the leaders of nine states in the subregion adopted a resolution to establish a West African Common Market. The conference also approved a protocol for a West African regional group and the drafting of a treaty that would be discussed at the next summit scheduled at Ouagadougou, Upper Volta, later that year.

Meanwhile, however, the francophonic Customs Union of West African States had revised its statue in January, 1966, and in March adopted a new convention. On the basis of Accra Protocol of 1967, the union reconstituted itself on May 21, 1970, as the West African Economic Community. The organization, headquartered in Ouagadougou, had goals including economic cooperation for balanced development.

At another level, the Nigerian administration of Yakubu Gowon, along with the leaders of Togo, Ivory Coast, Senegal, and Benin, pursued plans for the formation of a broad-based Economic Community of West African States (ECOWAS). After protracted negotiations, the ECOWAS treaty was signed at Lagos, Nigeria, on May 28, 1975, by state functionaries representing Benin, Gambia, Ghana, Guinea, Guinea Bissau, Ivory Coast, Liberia, Mali, Mauritania, Niger, Nigeria, Senegal, Sierra

Leone, Togo, and Upper Volta. Cape Verde acceded to the treaty in 1977. The West African Economic Community associated with the ECOWAS despite occasional differences in perspective.

The Treaty of Lagos provides for subregional cooperation in all fields of economic activity and promotional exchanges in social and cultural matters. The pact prescribes the phased elimination of intracommunity barriers and the harmonization of industrial, fiscal, and economic policies. The institutional structure of the ECOWAS comprises the Authority of Heads of State and Government, a council of ministers, an executive secretariat, the tribunal, and technical and specialized commissions. Article 50 of the treaty established the Fund for Co-operation, Compensation, and Development, which is the core of ECOWAS efforts. Despite funding constraints, ECOWAS has made significant achievements.

Impact of Event

The ECOWAS structure cut across ethnographic partitions and residual imperial cleavages, bringing former colonial entities together to achieve subregional governance in social, cultural, and economic affairs. The community framework has enhanced relational equity among member states as well as between the ECOWAS and third parties. Economic integration has offered member states a defensive formation in their dealings with other regional and transnational groupings. The ECOWAS secures resources for national development from other nations and promotes transnational cooperation without threatening sovereign individuality. The ECOWAS soon appeared to be the likely model for a proposed African common market.

The ECOWAS in 1984 approved a broad-based program of action to promote industrial enterprise and support direct investments. The Lome Declaration on Economic Recovery of 1984 became the basis of the ECOWAS Economic Recovery Programme launched on July 8, 1987. The Recovery Programme comprised relief, rehabilitation, and reform measures involving ninety-six national projects and forty regional schemes, together budgeted at $926 million.

The ECOWAS interacts with intergovernmental and nongovernmental organizations in furtherance goals for industrialization. These organizations include the African Development Bank Group, European Development Fund, Federation of West African Chambers of Commerce, Organization of African Trade Union Unity, and agencies of the United Nations. The ECA had failed in 1971 to secure the general agreement of African governments for a transcontinental network of roads partly because of concern about the prospect of large-scale smuggling. The ECOWAS in 1981 reconsidered the proposal and assumed responsibility for a subregional network of roads and air traffic facilities at an estimated cost of $2 billion. Even at the risk of overreaching its resources, the ECOWAS authorized surveys for a subregional network of railroads, with an initial outlay for the Togo-Upper Volta-Niger-Mali section.

The ECOWAS Fund, created in 1977, formed a primary pivot of ECOWAS programs. The fund supports cooperative ventures, finances development projects, and awards compensatory sums to member states adversely affected by its trade liberalization measures. The fund has supported major ECOWAS projects, including a $12.5 million loan in 1982 for telecommunication works across seven states and the INTELCOM I projects for domestic and external communication. The ECOWAS recognizes that telecommunication is a necessity for effective integration, but funding constraints forced delays in projected development.

The ECOWAS plan for the free movement of goods, services, and personnel suffered from infrastructural as well as policy barriers. Member states have had to deal with conflicting immigration policies, particularly in relation to the implementation of the *Protocol Relating to Free Movement of Persons, Right of Residence and Establishment* of May 29, 1979. Implementation began on a controversial note, exemplified by Nigeria's massive expulsion of "illegal immigrants" in the early 1980's. The reluctance of states to accept mass migration showed the fragile texture of the protocol. The ECOWAS initiated a plan in 1990 for the inception of legal residence cards within the community.

The community acknowledged the scope of its energy resources and requirements. In 1982, the ECOWAS launched its Integrated and Comprehensive Energy Policy, under which it set up an Energy Resources Development Fund and the Dakar-based Regional Information Centre and Database to aid the assessment, conservation, and systematic exploitation of energy resources through targeted research and development. The Regional Information Centre and Database provides policy and project information on renewable energy.

Agriculture presents a special challenge to the efforts of the community because of its bearing on self-reliance, industrialization, and rural development. The challenge is underscored by the fact that in some ECOWAS nations agriculture accounts for as much as half of the gross national product and is the basis of industrial stability among rural populations. Export trade in raw materials has placed stress on land, labor, and infrastructure in the farming districts. The capacity of farmers to meet the food and nutrition needs of the subregion remained in question.

Protocols for the elimination of trade and customs barriers have faced major barriers. The barriers include bureaucratic handcuffs, constitutional uncertainties, political inaction, and irregular contributions to the Fund. The Third Summit of the Authority agreed, in May, 1980, to a phased procedure for the elimination of restrictions on industrial goods and priority items. By May 30, 1981, only four states had ratified the protocol of Rules of Origin, defining the source and compositional value of products moved in and out of the subregion. The ECOWAS nevertheless anticipated a functional common market and a viable monetary cooperation. An agreement of May 28, 1979, on a customs union was supportive of existing arrangements and a common customs tariff, including a free trade zone for raw agricultural goods and indigenous handicrafts.

The ECOWAS adopted a protocol on nonaggression in 1979 and a protocol on mutual defense assistance in 1981. The latter established a defense council and a defense commission as well as committing member states to contributory participation in the Allied Armed Forces of the Community (AAFC). The AAFC, founded on the principles of nonaggression and mutual defense, ensures the territorial integrity of member states and checks disintegrative forces within the community. The overriding policy of the ECOWAS, however, has been the peaceful settlement of disputes, for which the community's Standing Mediation Committee was established. The committee in 1990 intervened in the Liberian crisis and later dispatched a peacekeeping force. The tribunal's jurisdiction is limited to disputes arising from application or interpretation of the ECOWAS treaty.

The frequent incursion of the military in African politics and the reluctance of dictatorships to accommodate democratic political organization in the subregion have affected the pace of progress in ECOWAS programs. Political instability has therefore contributed to economic instability in the subregion.

Bibliography

Andemicael, Berhanykun. *The OAU and UN: Relations Between the Organization of African Unity and the United Nations*. New York: Africana, 1976. Discusses the conflicting principles and dispositions of the two institutions, particularly in the sphere of economic development in Africa.

Brownlie, Ian, comp. *Basic Documents of African Affairs*. Oxford, England: Clarendon Press, 1971. Thematically arranges and annotates the documents in historical order. Part 1 in particular is relevant to the development of corporatist organizations in the postcolonial period between 1963 and 1967.

Mazrui, Ali A. *Africa's International Relations: The Diplomacy of Dependency and Change*. Boulder, Colo.: Westview Press, 1977. Examines African politics, government, and foreign relations. An interesting analysis of the interplay of power and politics in the management of underdeveloped and dependent economies.

Meier, Gerald M. ed. *Leading Issues in Economic Development: Studies in International Poverty*. New York: Oxford University Press, 1984. Among other pertinent facts of economic development, discusses in chapter 7 the constraints of capital deficiency on economic planning and industrial growth in developing nations.

Munu, Alhaji M. *The Future of ECOWAS*. Lagos: Nigerian Institute of International Affairs, 1989. A summary and succinct overview of the challenges and prospects for economic integration in West Africa.

Renniger, John P. *Multinational Cooperation for Development in West Africa*. New York: Pergamon Press, 1979. The focus is on West African economic integration. Examines the character and scope of transnational cooperation in the subregion, with focus on the relationship between gross national product and primary industrial production in the subregion.

Robson, Peter. *Economic Integration in Africa*. Evanston, Ill.: Northwestern University Press, 1968. The theoretical positions taken in this book are well argued and factually supported. The author restates the advantages usually associated with economies of scale and scope. The facts suggest that economic integration and customs unions, for example, are able to secure such advantages in proper circumstances.

Wionczek, Miguel S., ed. *Latin American Economic Integration*. New York: Praeger, 1966. A volume of studies on Latin America, useful for a comparative understanding of the approaches and problems of economic integration in developing areas, including the limitations of foreign exchange and the remedial strategy of import substitution.

Satch Ejike

Cross-References

Canada Seeks Preferential Trade Status from Great Britain (1932), p. 624; The European Common Market Is Established (1957), p. 1081; The Organization for Economic Cooperation and Development Forms (1961), p. 1169; The EEC Adopts a Common Agricultural Policy (1967), p. 1320; The European Market Unifies (1992), p. 2051; The North American Free Trade Agreement Goes into Effect (1994), p. 2072.

CONGRESS PROHIBITS DISCRIMINATION IN THE GRANTING OF CREDIT

Categories of event: Finance and consumer affairs
Time: October 28, 1975
Locale: Washington, D.C.

The Equal Credit Opportunity Act passed in 1975 included policies to eliminate credit discrimination and eased the ability of women and minority group members to get loans

Principal personages:
WILLIAM BROCK (1930-   ), a senator from Tennessee
JOE BIDEN (1942-   ), a senator from Delaware
WILLIAM PROXMIRE (1915-   ), a senator from Wisconsin
JAKE GARN (1932-   ), a senator from Utah
PARREN J. MITCHELL (1922-   ), a congressman from Maryland
LINDY BOGGS (1916-   ), a congresswoman from Louisiana
PATRICIA SCHROEDER (1940-   ), a congresswoman from Colorado
FRANK ANNUNZIO (1915-   ), a congressman from Illinois
FERNAND J. ST. GERMAIN (1928-   ), a congressman from Rhode Island

Summary of Event

Portions of the Equal Credit Opportunity Act were enacted in 1974. The intent of this act was to protect individuals applying for credit from facing discrimination based upon gender and marital status. In 1975, the act was amended several times to prohibit credit discrimination based on race, color, national origin, religion, and age. The prohibition on age discrimination has one exception, in that an individual applying for credit must have reached the age of majority in his or her home state and must be deemed competent to sign a legally binding contract.

On January 29, 1975, Senator William Brock proposed a bill in Congress to amend the Equal Credit Opportunity Act to ban age discrimination. Further amendments were proposed on June 9, 1975, when Senator Jake Garn suggested that the act encompass not only consumer loans but also all consumer lease agreements, since they were also forms of consumer credit. Later in the month, Senators William Proxmire and Joe Biden proposed further legislation related to consumer leasing requiring lenders to disclose all terms of leases to borrowers. On June 12, 1975, senators Biden and Proxmire proposed a bill encompassing criteria to prohibit consumer credit discrimination based upon the following personal characteristics: race, color, religion, national origin, political affiliation, sex, marital status, receipt of public assistance, or exercise of rights under this act. Both the original act and its amendments applied only to individuals applying for consumer credit, not business credit.

Credit is the process of obtaining funds from a lending institution in order to purchase goods and services. The ability of a consumer to obtain credit substantially raises his or her standard of living, as items can be obtained in the present and can be paid for with future income. The creditor (lender) has the ultimate authority as to whom will be granted credit and thus who will have this opportunity.

Traditionally in American society, those deemed by lenders as worthy credit applicants were white and male. There was some logic to this in the fact that prior to the 1960's a majority of the better-paid work force with greater likelihood of repaying loans, fell into these two categories. The composition of America's work force began to change drastically in the 1960's as women and minority group members began to enter the work force in large numbers and take jobs with better pay, more responsibility, and greater longevity. This change increased the ability of women and minorities to derive incomes and to be able to repay their debts. Old paradigms die hard, however, and lenders were conditioned to believe that these groups were poor credit risks. Congress recognized the social changes taking place and the civil unrest erupting during this time period and enacted various legislation to guarantee equal opportunity. Equality in the process of receiving credit was a relatively low priority, so legislation regarding it was proposed relatively late.

The Federal Reserve Board was the primary regulator involved in monitoring banks' compliance with this act. Federal Reserve Regulation B was incorporated into the guidelines of banks and was monitored through bank examinations. This regulation codified the intent of the act.

Creditors are in the business of assessing and managing risk, or the chance of loss. Creditors need to assess five different things when evaluating a consumer credit request: character (will the borrower pay), capacity (can he or she pay), conditions (anything particular or unique to the loan request), capital (the borrower's accumulated wealth), and collateral (the security for the loan). A prudent lender would apply these "five C's" of credit to make a credit decision. These are the criteria that theoretically determine the creditworthiness of a borrower; factors such as age, sex, race, national origin, and religion are not accurate predictors of a borrower's willingness and ability to repay a debt and therefore should not be part of the lending decision. Passage of the amended Equal Credit Opportunity Act on October 28, 1975, thus reflected Congress' desire to exclude irrelevant factors from lending decisions.

Impact of Event

The passage of the Equal Credit Opportunity Act affected all parties involved in the granting and monitoring of consumer credit. This act was directly related to consumers and their attempts to obtain credit. It stipulated that creditors could not ask the sex, race, color, religion, or national origin of an applicant for credit. Loans using real estate as collateral or for home purchases were exempt because of dower rights of married applicants and government monitoring of other categories for fair housing. The law also established that no individual can be discouraged from applying for credit, each individual is entitled to have credit files maintained in his or her own name, a spouse is not required to sign a loan agreement unless he or she would be responsible for the credit (with the exceptions related to real estate mentioned above), and poor credit obtained with a former spouse could not be used against a borrower who had established good credit in his or her own name. Creditors may ask about obligations to pay child support or alimony and if applicants are receiving alimony, child support, or public assistance. This information did not have to be revealed and creditors were not allowed to use receipt of public assistance as a reason for denial of credit. In the case of female applicants, questions regarding types of birth control methods used and plans to have children were deemed illegal. Creditors had the right to determine whether applicants had reached the age of majority but could not deny a consumer credit because of his or her inability to obtain life insurance. Any other discrimination based on age was prohibited.

In the event that a consumer was denied credit, the Equal Credit Opportunity Act spelled out the procedures that must be followed. The lender had thirty days from the date of the application to inform the borrower of the decision on the loan. The creditor had to provide the borrower with the following information in writing: the action that had been taken (acceptance of the agreement, denial or change in the terms), a statement of the consumer's rights, the name and address of the federal agency responsible for credit regulation, and whether information was obtained through a credit reporting agency.

Consumers were not the only parties affected by the passage of this legislation. Everyone in the business of granting credit to consumers was forced to comply with this legislation. The process of conforming began when a lender started to discuss the process of credit with an applicant. Lenders could not use sexist, racist, or other types of discriminatory language that might discourage or offend applicants applying for credit. Credit applications reflected the impact of this law. They included statements that the lender did not discriminate based on the disallowed factors. Individuals involved in the credit application process needed to have proper training to ensure that they were meeting the requirements of the law. Lenders needed not only proper training but also clerical staff to support the paperwork generated by the law, for example, written denial notices that had to be sent out on time. The act added direct costs to lenders through the paperwork, training, and compliance measures required. The paybacks for these added costs have been better customer relations, a more positive image of business, and the possibility of entering new and profitable markets as new groups were able to obtain credit.

The passage of any regulation requires monitoring by appropriate regulators. The Equal Credit Opportunity Act (ECOA) covers a vast spectrum of businesses, with different regulators each responsible for their own area. Commercial banks were regulated either by the Comptroller of the Currency or the Federal Reserve Board. Savings and loans were regulated by the Federal Home Loan Bank Board, and credit unions were regulated by the National Credit Union Association. Individual states also had responsibilities in ensuring compliance with the law.

Each regulator had various mechanisms to enforce the law. For example, a major portion of a commercial bank's examination dealt with consumer credit compliance. Bank examiners were often more concerned with loans that were denied then with loans that were made. Regulators have used compliance with ECOA and other consumer regulations in deciding whether to allow banks to merge with or acquire other banks.

Prior to 1986, small business owners were not protected under the Equal Credit Opportunity Act. Small businesses are viewed as high credit risks. Statistics show that more than half of new small businesses will fail within their first few years, with the most frequent cause of small business failure being inadequate financing brought about by inadequate cash flow. Applicants for small business loans commonly were as bad to provide the following information to the lender: cash flow forecast, a clearly stated purpose for the loan, the amount of the loan, and the time frame and source of repayment. Lenders often required a loan proposal including the above information and a detailed business plan. Most small businesses and their owners are one and the same. Even though loan requests are for business purposes, loans are made to individuals. Congress decided to extend equal credit opportunity to business owners as well as consumers.

On March 19, 1985, Parren J. Mitchell and Lindy Boggs proposed a bill to the House of Representatives to amend the Equal Credit Opportunity Act to include owners of small businesses. The bill particularly focused on small business loans to women and minority group members. Congresswoman Patricia Schroeder, Cochair of the Congressional Caucus on Women's Issues, presented details regarding the discrimination women experienced in obtaining credit to finance small businesses. Her arguments included the fact that women were rapidly entering the work force as the owners of their own companies and that women were playing a critical role in the creation of jobs. Congressmen Frank Annunzio and Fernand J. St. Germain also played critical roles in the passage of this amendment through their work as members of the Subcommittee on Consumer Affairs and Coinage of the Committee on Banking, Finance, and Urban Affairs. St. Germain remarked that this bill was special to him because he had floor managed the original act in 1974. The amendment exempted large businesses from protection. All banks, savings and loans, credit unions, department stores, credit card issuers, and car and appliance dealers had to comply with this regulation and act without discrimination in their credit decisions regarding loans to small businesses.

The Equal Credit Opportunity Act had major effects on those involved in granting, receiving, and regulating consumer credit. The 1986 amendments extended those effects to those involved with loans to small businesses and to the businesses themselves. The economic environment of the late 1980's and early 1990's favored small businesses and women and minority group members were the fastest-growing segments of small-business owners. This was brought about in large part by the Equal Credit Opportunity Act amendments prohibiting credit discrimination and increasing opportunities for all borrowers.

Bibliography

Beares, Paul. "Regulation of Consumer Credit." In *Consumer Lending*. Washington, D.C.: American Bankers Association, 1987. An excellent book dealing with all phases of consumer credit. Written from a banker's perspective, but easy reading for the layperson. Discusses in detail the process of consumer credit, the five C's of credit, and consumer credit management. A must for all consumer lenders.

Board of Governors of the Federal Reserve. *A Guide to Business Credit and the Equal Credit Opportunity Act*. Washington, D.C.: Author, 1986. A twelve-page brochure explaining the requirements to obtain a small business loan. Lists federal enforcement agencies and alternative sources of capital.

Cole, Richard H. "Regulation of Consumer Credit." *In Consumer and Commercial Credit Management*. 8th ed. Homewood, Ill.: Irwin, 1988. Chapter 6, "Regulation of Consumer Credit," goes into consumer lending regulation in detail. The book is an excellent reference on both consumer and business credit.

Federal Reserve Bank of Philadelphia. *How the Equal Credit Opportunity Act Affects You*. Philadelphia: Author, 1986. Puts the ECOA into perspective for the average individual. Describes who ECOA applies to, lenders' responsibilities, what to do in the case of errors, and consumer remedies. A straightforward publication that is easy to understand.

Sirota, David. "Other Government Activities in Real Estate Finance." In *Essentials of Real Estate Finance*. Chicago: Real Estate Education Company, 1992. This chapter lists all federal government regulations pertaining to residential real estate financing. The book in general covers all aspects of consumer real estate finance. An excellent reference for all mortgage lenders.

U.S. Congress. House. Committee on Banking, Finance and Urban Affairs, Subcommittee on Consumer Affairs and Coinage. *To Amend the Equal Credit Opportunity Act*. 99th Congress, 2d session, 1986. House Document 1575. Government hearings and testimonies amending the ECOA to include small businesses. Includes arguments pertaining to the amendment from both opponents and proponents.

U.S. Congress. Senate. Committee on Banking, Housing, and Urban Affairs, Subcommittee on Consumer Affairs. *Equal Credit Opportunity Act Amendments and Consumer Leasing Act—1975*. 94th Congress, 1st session, 1975. Summary of the legislation and discussions prior to enacting the ECOA. Includes the bills proposed in Congress and testimony regarding them.

William C. Ward III

Cross-References

The Federal Reserve Act Creates a U.S. Central Bank (1913), p. 240; Congress Passes the Equal Pay Act (1963), p. 1185; The Civil Rights Act Prohibits Discrimination in Employment (1964), p. 1229; Congress Passes the Consumer Credit Protection Act (1968), p. 1358; Congress Passes the Fair Credit Reporting Act (1970), p. 1454; Congress Deregulates Banks and Savings and Loans (1980-1982), p. 1757; Bush Responds to the Savings and Loan Crisis (1989), p. 1991.

ATLANTIC CITY LEGALIZES CASINO GAMBLING

Categories of event: Government and business; new products
Time: 1976
Locale: Atlantic City, New Jersey

By permitting legalized casino gambling, Atlantic City became a competitor to Las Vegas in the organized gambling industry

Principal personages:
    DONALD TRUMP (1946-   ), a New York developer who created Trump Castle
    STEVE WYNN (1941-   ), a casino promoter in Las Vegas who successfully opened new operations in Atlantic City
    BILL HARRAH (1911-1978), an early Las Vegas casino builder who created Harrah's in Nevada and New Jersey
    MERV GRIFFIN (1925-   ), an entertainment figure who bid against Trump for Atlantic City casinos

Summary of Event

Since the 1930's, legal casino gambling within the United States had been confined to Nevada and (with minor exceptions) Indian reservations. Casino gambling took a giant step toward penetrating more deeply into American society in 1976, when New Jersey voters legalized the practice. Atlantic City residents hoped that taxes on gambling revenues as well as tourist dollars would restore the luster to what once was the jewel of East Coast resorts. Opened in 1854 to beach visitors, Atlantic City started to attract vacationers as early as 1870, when the boardwalk was finished. After World War II, however, it fell in popularity as a vacation destination. It had no superhighway to connect it to New York or other urban areas, and, except for the boardwalk, it had no attraction to compete with California or Florida beaches.

A vote in 1974 had failed to legalize casinos statewide. Supporters of gambling in New Jersey sculpted a different measure in 1976 that restricted gambling to Atlantic City. Various states already had permitted lotteries for more than a decade (New Jersey itself had a lottery), and casinos had gone up along the California-Nevada border in Lake Tahoe. Casino gambling offered dice and card games, roulette wheels, on-the-spot sports betting, and slot machines, all with the odds stacked clearly in favor of the casino, or "the house." The advantage to the house varied, depending on the game. A rule of thumb was that the smaller the bet (as in nickel slot machines), the higher the chance of a payoff but the lower the percentage of money bet that was returned to the bettor, since the highest payoffs were relatively low amounts.

Gambling in America represented essentially a "frontier" activity, one that embodied such western traits as individuality, risk, and opportunism. The "gambling bug" had tended to move westward, until it alighted in Nevada, close enough to incubate in the warmth of California's economy but far enough removed that it did not directly influence the Golden State. According to this interpretation, the spread of gambling back to the East represented a natural phenomenon of eastern areas trying to regain their frontier spirit. Ultimately, however, the dynamics of voter mentality demanded that gambling show material rewards rather than merely an individualistic, opportunistic spirit, before it would be approved at the polls.

Las Vegas and Nevada gaming in general had long been associated with organized crime figures such as Benjamin "Bugsy" Siegel, who claimed credit for creating Las Vegas, and frequent mobster visitors. Gaming came under intense investigation by federal and state officials. New Jersey's voters wanted to make sure that any Atlantic City gambling remained free of organized crime's influence.

The traditional philosophy of casino management was epitomized by Bill Harrah, whose Harrah's catered to professional gamblers. Harrah and others had directed the older generation of casinos in Nevada, giving complimentary rooms, meals, and show tickets to, or "comping," the gamblers that they identified as potential "high rollers." With returns to the casinos vastly exceeding the cost to the casinos of the complimentary free rooms and meals handed out to the high rollers, casinos in the relatively noncompetitive environment that existed prior to 1976 made hefty profits. Although organized crime originally had a foothold in many of the casinos, by the 1970's Nevada's gaming commission had weeded out most of that influence.

Even before the competition from Atlantic City, a new generation of casino owners in Las Vegas sought to keep gamblers in the hotels for longer periods of time by offering attractions and shows aimed at family members. That trend accelerated once the threat from Atlantic City was realized. Las Vegas tried to be seen as a center for entertainment, while Atlantic City focused on gambling as its primary attraction.

Impact of Event

The opening of Atlantic City as a "second Las Vegas" let the gambling genie out of its bottle. Although far superior in attractions and casino management, Las Vegas lost its mystique of being the only gambling resort in America. Estimating exactly how much Atlantic City cost Las Vegas in lost revenue is difficult, but some statistics are illustrative. In 1982, Atlantic City attracted twenty-three million visitors, twice the number that visited Las Vegas. Its gross revenues from gaming were $1.5 billion, or roughly equal to those of Las Vegas. The gaming revenues-to-visitors ratio suggested that Atlantic City was far less effective in getting visitors to gamble. Atlantic City's visitors left quickly, while Las Vegas visitors increasingly lengthened their stays.

Part of the reason for Las Vegas' effectiveness in convincing visitors to stay longer and to part with their dollars came from a fundamental reassessment made by Las Vegas hotels and casinos when Atlantic City opened to gambling. Realizing that they could no longer rely only on gamblers, since that market would suffer from inroads made by Atlantic City, they entered into a frenzy of new casino building aimed at family entertainment. Many of the new hotels copied the successful family-oriented Mirage Hotel created by Steve Wynn and, to a lesser extent, the theme-oriented

Caesar's Palace. The Mirage featured dolphin pools, white tiger enclaves, game arcades for children, a volcano that erupted every hour, the hugely popular Siegfried and Roy magic and illusion show, and many other nongambling attractions. Caesar's, renovated in 1992 and 1993, had Disney-type robot attractions, costumed employees who wore Roman togas and battle gear, an enclosed shopping mall, and an IMAX theater.

No casino better captured the new philosophy than the Excalibur, opened in 1990 by the owners of Circus Circus, who had considerable experience in family entertainment. The Excalibur was built to resemble King Arthur's magical castle and featured a jousting tournament, a "virtual reality" ride, and an extensive game area for children. Other hotels quickly imitated the Excalibur, with the Luxor and the MGM Hotel/ Casinos opening in 1993. Those hotels contained such nongambling entertainment as IMAX theaters, virtual reality rides, and even self-contained amusement parks, patterned after the amusement park at the Mall of America.

By the late 1980's, most of the organized crime influence had been driven out by large, publicly held corporations such as Holiday Inn, Harrah's, and Ramada Inns. The new owners of the casinos were less interested in using the legal gambling operations as a cover for illegal income than in maximizing their profits in the gaming establishments themselves. New computer technology produced video poker machines as well as traditional slot machines that featured randomly spinning objects, such as fruit, numbers, or characters. Regardless of the format, a typical slot machine or video poker machine could take in a profit of $100,000 in a year. Many casinos even introduced "frequent gambler" cards, which carried computer-coded information that allowed selected customers to receive complimentary drinks, meals, or even hotel rooms. The cards and associated discounts were intended to lure patrons into gambling more than they otherwise would have. In 1991, Atlantic City casinos gave out nearly $500 million in complimentary goods and services.

The new corporate owners of Atlantic City and Nevada casinos advertised heavily. To entice New Yorkers and visitors to the East Coast to make the trip, Atlantic City casinos gave away more than $247 million in coins and bus coupons in 1991 alone. Room prices rarely covered the cost to the hotel; the hope was that guests would gamble in the hotel's casino rather than venturing out. "Comps" and advertising were easily paid for out of gambling revenues, but financing the construction of expensive hotel-casinos required considerable capital investment.

Among the early sources for Atlantic City casino financing was Michael Milken, famous for his convictions on violations of securities laws in the 1980's. Veteran corporate hotel and casino operators such as Holiday Inn, Hyatt, and Ramada Inns had no difficulty raising cash. New entrants and those inexperienced in American casino gaming, such as the Playboy organization and Donald Trump, found the going more difficult. As a result, several paid far more for their facilities than was proved to be justified. Trump paid more than $1 billion for the Taj Mahal, and Merv Griffin's takeover of Trump's Resorts International exceeded $1 billion in borrowed capital. Some of the ventures represented a misunderstanding of the market. Playboy, for example, tried to create a fancy, European-style casino, not realizing that most Atlantic City bettors were more of the nickel slot machine variety, unwilling to spend a lot of money on luxurious accommodations and elaborate shows. Trump ran so low on funds that he could not afford a swimming pool for the Taj Mahal. Trump even competed against himself for a short time. In 1985, he bought the Trump Castle from Barron Hilton, and in 1986, he bought Holiday Inn's Boardwalk property, which he called the Trump Plaza Hotel and Casino.

Inexperience was exhibited in operating the casinos as well as in capitalizing them. Trump, for example, allowed his wife Ivana, who had no casino managerial experience, to run Trump Castle. Whereas veteran casino managers such as Steve Wynn made certain that the "high rollers" got the most prestigious suites, Ivana took the Castle's fanciest suite for herself. Trump's ego and inexperience also led him to acquire controlling interest in Resorts International and its Taj Mahal, the world's largest casino, which was unfinished at the time and was estimated to need more than $500 million to complete. Meanwhile, Resorts International had attracted the interest of show business producer Merv Griffin, who put out a bid to acquire the stock in Resorts International from Trump in a deal that allowed Trump to keep the Taj Mahal. Griffin used junk bond financing provided by Michael Milken (in his last major deal) to purchase Resorts International from Trump in November, 1988. More than $1 billion in borrowed funds went into the deal. Within a short time, both Griffin and Trump were in bankruptcy court.

Legalized gambling spread to other states that were enticed by the promise of huge revenues. In April of 1989, Iowa passed a casino bill allowing gambling on casino boats traveling on the Mississipi and Missouri rivers. Davenport set its sights on becoming the center of the river gambling activity, which proponents claimed would attract nearly 800,000 gamblers each year, generating more than $90 million. Boom towns of the Old West sought to return to their former glory by legalizing casino gambling.

Analysts of commercial gambling predicted that by the end of the twentieth century, many other cities and states would join the trend. Chicago had plans as of 1993 for a $2 billion gambling zone, with Caesar's World, Hilton, and Circus Circus all planning development. In 1992, the Mashantucket Pequot Indians opened a casino in Foxwoods, Connecticut. Legalization of casino games in Indiana, Missouri, New York, Pennsylvania, and Washington was pending. By 1992, every state except Utah and Hawaii had laws that permitted at least one form of commercial gambling, including lotteries, casinos, dog and horse racing, jai alai, bingo, sports betting, or charity "Las Vegas nights."

In 1987, the U.S. Supreme Court allowed Indian tribes to offer on their reservations any types of gambling that were allowed in the state where the reservation was located. Indian tribes in other states immediately started to lobby for gambling of other types on their reservations. In several states, reservation gambling touched off sharp debate among those who contended that the Indians had unfair advantages, such as freedom from federal taxation, or that gambling was not permitted in other forms in the state. Indian groups maintained that such charges represented revived forms of racism and oppression of Native Americans, but several states rejected Indian attempts to expand gambling activities into other areas.

The quiet proliferation of legalized gambling included legalization of video slot machines in Maryland, Montana, Oregon, South Dakota, and West Virginia. Minnesota, by 1993, had more casinos than did New Jersey. The advent of casinos owned and operated by individual states appeared likely. Many states already had targeted lottery money for specific state expenditures. In the case of Ohio, for example, all lottery profits went for education; in other states, lottery money funded highway construction. The visible returns were offset by unseen and subtle harms from creation of a public mentality that wealth came from chance or luck rather than from skill and effort, and the notion that public goods could be obtained and financed without sacrifice. With this tradeoff, it was hardly surprising that both the public and corporate America supported the spread of organized gambling.

One final aspect of legalized gambling involved the increasing sophistication of video and computer technology. "Virtual reality" games had reached the market by the early 1990's, offering consumers the chance to "live" in imaginary situations. It was only a matter of time before gambling and virtual reality joined forces. One could imagine bets on virtual reality games in which people would "walk" over computerized virtual reality suspension bridges, with odds set on survival after a bridge collapse, or, for the true risk-takers, virtual reality games of Russian roulette. Bettors had long displayed their willingness to gamble on anything. New technologies were sure to be employed to offer fresh approaches and new attractions.

Bibliography

Abt, Vicki. *The Business of Risk: Commercial Gambling in Mainstream America*. Lawrence: University of Kansas Press, 1985. A scholarly approach to the sociological impact of legalized gambling on American values.

Findlay, John. *People of Chance: Gambling in America from Jamestown to Las Vegas*. New York: Oxford University Press, 1986. A broad investigation of gambling. Findlay argues that gambling had distinctly "frontier" or western roots and that it reflected American values of opportunism, risk taking, and individualism. Well documented and stronger in analysis than many other books on American gambling.

Johnston, David. *Temples of Chance: How America Inc. Bought Out Murder Inc. to Win Control of the Casino Business*. New York: Doubleday, 1992. A journalist's entertaining and timely discussion of the new generation of corporate-owned casinos. A pioneering history of the rise of Atlantic City and subsequent legalization of gambling in other states.

Sasuly, Richard. *Bookies and Bettors: Two Hundred Years of Gambling*. New York: Holt, Rinehart & Winston, 1982. Examines in depth the history of gambling in the United States. Particularly helpful in understanding the laws involved in gambling.

Stuart, Winston. *Nation of Gamblers: America's Billion-Dollar-a-Day Habit*. Englewood Cliffs, N.J.: Prentice-Hall, 1984. An international approach that emphasizes British horse racing as much as Las Vegas craps tables. Makes only weak attempts to discuss the impact of casino gambling in the United States.

Larry Schweikart

Cross-References

Charles Ponzi Cheats Thousands in an Investment Scheme (1919-1920), p. 324; The Yankees Acquire Babe Ruth (1920), p. 341; Congress Passes the RICO Act (1970), p. 1449; New York State Allows Off-Track Betting (1971), p. 1472; Drexel and Michael Milken Are Charged with Insider Trading (1988), p. 1958.

THE CONCORDE FLIES PASSENGERS AT SUPERSONIC SPEEDS

Category of event: Transportation
Time: January 21, 1976
Locale: London, England, and Paris, France

The Concorde made inaugural flights on January 21, 1976, between London, England, and the Persian Gulf emirate of Bahrain and between Paris, France, and Rio de Janeiro, Brazil

Principal personages:

SIR ARCHIBALD RUSSELL (1904-   ), a designer with the British Aircraft Corporation

PIERRE SATRE (1909-   ), the technical director at Sud-Aviation

JULIAN AMERY (1919-   ), the British minister of aviation, 1962-1964

GEOFFROY DE COURCE (1912-   ), the French minister of aviation, 1962

WILLIAM T. COLEMAN, JR. (1920-   ), the U.S. secretary of transportation, 1975-1977

Summary of Event

On January 21, 1976, the Anglo-French Concorde became the world's first supersonic airliner to carry passengers on scheduled commercial flights. British Airways flew a Concorde from London's Heathrow Airport to the Persian Gulf emirate of Bahrain in three hours and thirty-eight minutes. At about the same time, Air France flew a Concorde from Paris' Charles de Gaulle Airport to Rio de Janeiro, Brazil, in seven hours and twenty-five minutes. The Concordes' cruising speeds were about twice the speed of sound, or 1,350 miles per hour. On May 24, 1976, the United States and Europe became linked for the first time with commercial supersonic air transportation. British Airways inaugurated flights between Dulles International Airport in Washington, D.C., and Heathrow Airport. Likewise, Air France inaugurated flights between Dulles International Airport and Charles de Gaulle Airport. The London-Washington, D.C., flight was flown in an unprecedented time of three hours and forty minutes. The Paris-Washington, D.C., flight was flown in a time of three hours and fifty-five minutes.

Events leading to the development and production of the Anglo-French Concorde went back almost twenty years and included approximately $3 billion in investment costs. Issues surrounding the development and final production of the supersonic transport (SST) were extremely complex and at times highly emotional. The concept of developing an SST brought with it environmental concerns and questions, safety issues both in the air and on the ground, political intrigue of international proportions, and enormous economic problems from costs of operations, research, and development.

In England, the decision to begin the SST project was made in October, 1956. Under the promotion of Morien Morgan with the Royal Aircraft Establishment in Farnborough, England, it was decided at the Aviation Ministry headquarters in London to begin development of a supersonic aircraft. This decision was based on the intense competition from the American Boeing 707 and Douglas DC-8 subsonic jets going into commercial service. There was little point in developing another subsonic plane; the alternative was to go above the speed of sound. In November, 1956, at Farnborough, the first meeting of the Supersonic Transport Aircraft Committee, known as STAC, was held. Members of the STAC proposed that development costs would be in the range of $165 million to $260 million, depending on the range, speed, and payload of the chosen SST. The committee also projected that by 1970, there would be world market for at least 150 to 500 supersonic planes. Estimates were that the supersonic plane would recover its entire research and development cost through thirty sales. The British, in order to continue development of an SST, needed a European partner as a way of sharing the costs and preempting objections to proposed funding by England's Treasury.

In 1960, the British government gave the newly organized British Aircraft Corporation (BAC) $1 million for an SST feasibility study. Sir Archibald Russell, BAC's chief supersonic designer, visited Pierre Satre, the technical director at the French firm of Sud-Aviation. Satre's suggestion was to evolve an SST from Sud-Aviation's highly successful subsonic Caravelle transport. By September, 1962, an agreement was reached by Sud and BAC design teams on a new SST, the Super Caravelle.

There was a bitter battle over the choice of engines with two British engine firms, Bristol-Siddeley and Rolls-Royce, as contenders. Sir Arnold Hall, the managing director of Bristol-Siddeley, in collaboration with the French aero-engine company SNECMA, was eventually awarded the contract for the engines. The engine chosen was a "civilianized" version of the Olympus, which Bristol had been developing for the multirole TRS-2 combat plane.

On November 29, 1962, the Concorde Consortium was created by an agreement between England and the French Republic, signed by Ministers of Aviation Julian Amery and Geoffroy De Cource. The first Concorde, Model 001, rolled out from Sud-Aviation's St. Martin-du-Touch assembly plant on December 11, 1968. The second, Model 002, was completed at the British Aircraft Corporation a few months later. Eight years later, on January 21, 1976, the Concorde became the world's first supersonic airliner to carry passengers on scheduled commercial flights.

Development of the SST did not come easy for the Anglo-French consortium. The nature of supersonic flight created numerous problems and uncertainties not present for subsonic flight. The SST traveled faster than the speed of sound. Sound travels at 760 miles per hour at sea level at a temperature of 59 degrees Fahrenheit. This speed drops to about 660 miles per hour at sixty-five thousand feet, cruising altitude for the SST, where the air temperature drops to 70 degrees below zero. The Concorde was designed to fly at a maximum of 1,450 miles per hour. The European designers could use an aluminum alloy construction and stay below the critical skin-friction temperatures that required other airframe alloys, such as titanium. The Concorde was designed with a slender curved wing surface. The design incorporated widely separated engine nacelles, each housing two Olympus 593 jet engines. The Concorde was also designed with a "droop snoot," providing three positions: the supersonic configuration, a heat-visor retracted position for subsonic flight, and a nose-lowered position for landing patterns.

Impact of Event

Early SST designers were faced with questions such as the intensity and ionization effect of cosmic rays at flight altitudes of sixty to seventy thousand feet. The "cascade effect" concerned the intensification of cosmic radiation when particles from outer space struck a metallic cover. Scientists looked for ways to shield passengers from this hazard inside the aluminum or titanium shell of an SST flying high above the protective blanket of the troposphere. Experts questioned whether the risk of being struck by meteorites was any greater for the SST than for subsonic jets and looked for evidence on wind shear of jet streams in the stratosphere. Other questions concerned the strength and frequency of clear air turbulence above forty-five thousand feet, whether the higher ozone content of the air at SST cruise altitude would affect the materials of the aircraft, whether SST flights would upset or destroy the protective nature of the earth's ozone layer, the effect of aerodynamic heating on material strength, and the tolerable strength of sonic booms over populated areas. These and other questions consumed the designers and researchers involved in developing the Concorde.

Through design research and flight tests, many of the questions were resolved or realized to be less significant than anticipated. Several issues did develop into environmental, economic, and international issues. In late 1975, the British and French governments requested permission to use the Concorde at New York's John F. Kennedy International Airport and at Dulles International Airport for scheduled flights between the United States and Europe. In December, 1975, as a result of strong opposition from anti-Concorde environmental groups, the U.S. House of Representatives approved a six-month ban on SSTs coming into the United States so that the impact of flights could be studied. Secretary of Transportation William T. Coleman, Jr., held hearings to prepare for a decision by February 5, 1976, as to whether to allow the Concorde into U.S. airspace. The British and French, if denied landing rights, threatened to take the United States to an international court, claiming that treaties had been violated. The treaties in question were the Chicago Convention and Bermuda agreements of February 11, 1946, and March 27, 1946. These treaties prohibited the United States from banning aircraft that both France and Great Britain had certified to be safe. The Environmental Defense Fund contended that the United States had the right to ban SST aircraft on environmental grounds.

Under pressure from both sides, Coleman decided to allow limited Concorde service at Dulles and John F. Kennedy airports for a sixteen-month trial period. Service into John F. Kennedy Airport, however, was delayed by a ban by the Port Authority of New York and New Jersey until a pending suit was pursued by the airlines. During the test period, detailed records were to be kept on the Concorde's noise levels, vibration, and engine emission levels. Other provisions included that the plane would not fly at supersonic speeds over the continental United States; that all flights could be cancelled by the United States with four months notice, or immediately if they proved harmful to the health and safety of Americans; and that at the end of a year, four months of study would begin to determine if the trial period should be extended.

The Concorde's noise was one of the primary issues in determining whether the plane should be allowed into U.S. airports. The Federal Aviation Administration measured the effective perceived noise in decibels. After three months of monitoring the Concorde's departure noise at 3.5 nautical miles was found to vary from 105 to 130 decibels. The Concorde's approach noise at one nautical mile from threshold varied from 115 to 130 decibels. These readings were approximately equal to noise levels of other four-engine jets, such as the Boeing 747, on landing but were twice as loud on takeoff.

Another issue of significance was the economics of Concorde's operation and its tremendous investment costs. In 1956, early predictions of Great Britain's STAC were for a world market of 150 to 500 supersonic planes. In November, 1976, Great Britain's Gerald Kaufman and France's Marcel Cavaille said that production of the Concorde would not continue beyond the sixteen vehicles then contracted for with BAC and Sud-Aviation. There was no demand by U.S. airline corporations for the plane. Given that the planes could not fly at supersonic speeds over populated areas because of the sonic boom phenomenon, markets for the SST had to be separated by at least three thousand miles, with flight paths over mostly water or desert. Studies indicated that there were only twelve to fifteen routes in the world for which the Concorde was suitable. The planes were expensive, at a price of approximately $74 million each and had a limited seating capacity of one hundred passengers. The plane's range was about four thousand miles. These statistics compared to a Boeing 747 with a cost of $35 million, seating capacity of 360, and a range of six thousand miles. In addition, the International Air Transport Association negotiated that the fares for the Concorde flights should be equivalent to current first-class fares plus 20 percent. The marketing promotion for the Anglo-French Concorde was thus limited to the elite business traveler who considered speed over cost of transportation. Given these factors, the recovery of research and development costs for Great Britain and France would never occur.

Bibliography

Alpern, David, Evert Clark, and James Bishop. "The Concorde Furor." *Newsweek* 87 (February 16, 1976): 16-21. Reporters discuss the decision by Transportation Secretary William T. Coleman, Jr., to allow the controversial Anglo-French supersonic jet to land in Washington and in New York for a sixteen-month trial period. They also address several of the issues related to supersonic flight such as international relations, the ozone layer, air pollution, noise pollution, and economics.

"Concordes Arrive to Enthusiasm." *Aviation Week and Space Technology* 104 (May 31, 1976): 7, 22-24. Describes the inaugural dual landings on May 24, 1976, of the Concorde flights by Air France and British Airways into Dulles International Airport. Discusses the general reaction of spectators and how the airlines intended to schedule their transatlantic flights.

Dwiggins, Don. *The SST: Here It Comes, Ready or Not*. Garden City, N.Y.: Doubleday, 1968. A history of the development stages of the SST in Europe and the Soviet Union. Also includes the initial research efforts of U.S. aerospace firms in regarding production of a commercial SST, later dropped because of lack of funding from the U.S. Congress.

Ellingsworth, Rosalind K. "Concorde Stresses Time, Service." *Aviation Week and Space Technology* 105 (August 16, 1976): 25-28. Discusses the efforts that Air France and British Airways made to accommodate passengers on transatlantic Concorde flights, including ensuring reliable departure times.

Gillman, Peter. "Supersonic Bust." *The Atlantic* 239 (January, 1977): 72-81. Gillman discusses the economic disaster of the Concorde, which cost at least fifteen times the original estimates. He discusses the history of its development and the numerous problems encountered in both development and commercial utilization on a worldwide basis.

Kozicharow, Eugene. "Concorde Legal Questions Raised." *Aviation Week and Space Technology* 104 (January 12, 1976): 12-14. Examines the issues raised by both sides of the debate on allowing the Concorde into U.S. airports on a regularly scheduled basis.

―――――― . "Concorde Wins Sixteen-Month Trial in U.S." *Aviation Week and Space Technology* 104 (February 9, 1976): 27-29. Discusses the environmental quality task force, headed by the Federal Aviation Administration, organized to monitor Concorde transport operations at John F. Kennedy and Dulles International Airports.

Ropelewski, Robert. "Air France Poised for Concorde Service." *Aviation Week and Space Technology* 104 (January 19, 1976): 31-33. Describes how Air France intended to streamline handling of passengers on the ground, provide a faster pace for flight and cabin crews, and train maintenance technicians in the complexities of the Concorde.

John L. Farbo

Cross-References

The Boeing 707 Begins Commercial Service (1958), p. 1112; A European Consortium Plans the Airbus (1967), p. 1303; McDonnell Aircraft and Douglas Aircraft Merge (1967), p. 1314; Congress Begins Hearings on Cost Overruns for the C-5A Galaxy (1969), p. 1384; Carter Signs the Airline Deregulation Act (1978), p. 1676; Braniff International Suspends Flight Operations (1982), p. 1826.

JOBS AND WOZNIAK FOUND APPLE COMPUTER

Category of event: Foundings and dissolutions
Time: April 1, 1976
Locale: Santa Clara Valley, California

In 1976, Steven Jobs and Stephen Wozniak founded Apple Computer, Inc., which became the world's second-largest manufacturer of personal computers

Principal personages:
STEVEN JOBS (1955-), a cofounder of Apple Computer
STEPHEN WOZNIAK (1950-), a cofounder of Apple Computer
MIKE MARKKULA (1942-), a former Intel marketing manager appointed as Apple's first chairman in May, 1977
MICHAEL SCOTT (1943-), the first president of Apple Computer
JOHN SCULLEY (1939-), a business executive who joined Apple Computer in 1983 and later became chief executive officer

Summary of Event

Apple Computer was officially founded on April 1, 1976, by twenty-one-year-old Steven Jobs and twenty-six-year-old Stephen Wozniak. Their initial idea was to assemble computers for their friends. They did not realize the potential that their ideas had to revolutionize the personal computer industry. Ultimately, their goal became making computer technology widely accessible to the mass population. These entrepreneurs recognized that most consumers at that time saw computers as too expensive and too complex to use. Jobs envisioned the firm offering products that contributed to human efficiency as much as had the electric typewriter, the calculator, and the photocopy machine.

Jobs and Wozniak were graduates of Santa Clara's Homestead High School and began collaborating in 1976 at the Home Brew Computer Club, a group of young computer enthusiasts located in Palo Alto, California. Wozniak was a superior product engineer and designer, while Jobs had a grasp of the demands of the marketplace. They designed their first machine in Jobs's bedroom and used $1,300 from the sale of Jobs's Volkswagen and Wozniak's scientific calculator to assemble their first working model in Jobs's parents' garage. They chose Apple as the name for their venture as conveying a nonthreatening yet high-technology image. The name also recalled Jobs's fond memories of time he spent on an Oregon farm. Jobs and Wozniak's original plan was to limit production to circuit boards. After Jobs's first sales call yielded an order for fifty units, they rethought their strategy and decided to offer fully assembled microcomputers.

The first model, the Apple I, was introduced and sold without a monitor, keyboard, or casing, at a price of $666. It was the first single-board computer with on-board read-only memory (ROM), which told the machine how to load other programs from an external source, and with a built-in video interface. Orders for their "personal computer," mainly from hobbyists, soon reached six hundred units. Jobs and Wozniak now faced the problem of improving the original model without sacrificing its key selling features, its simplicity and compactness. Their efforts resulted in the introduction of the Apple II, the first fully assembled, programmable microcomputer that did not require that users know how to solder, wire, or program. The Apple II featured considerable versatility and inspired numerous independent firms to develop third-party add-on devices and software programs. The resulting software library soon included more than ten thousand programs ranging from games to sophisticated business applications.

Demand soon outstripped the founders' ability to produce the machine. They turned to Mike Markkula, who had been a marketing manager at Intel, a fast-growing manufacturer of integrated circuits. Markkula contributed at least $91,000 to the company (by some estimates, as much as $250,000), secured a line of credit with the Bank of America, raised over one-half million dollars from venture capitalists, and was named chairman of the company in May, 1977. One month later, Michael Scott was brought in as president of the firm.

Markkula wrote Apple's first business plan. Its objectives included capturing a market share at least twice that of the nearest competitor, realizing at least 20 percent pretax profits, and growing to $500 million in annual sales within ten years by continuing to make significant contributions to the home computer industry. In addition, the plan called for the establishment and maintenance of a corporate culture that was conducive to personal growth and development for the firm's employees. The plan also called for an "easy exit" for its founders within five years, should they wish to disassociate themselves from the enterprise.

The firm's strategy called for continual marketing of peripheral products for the basic computer so as to generate sales equal to or greater than the initial computer purchase, the allocation of funds for research and development to guarantee technological leadership, and the ability to attract and retain outstanding personnel. The plan called for initially targeting the hobbyist market, as a stepping-stone to wider distribution. The company also sought to refine manufacturing processes to reduce costs. Apple computers were to be designed and marketed as more economical than a dedicated system in specific applications, even though a particular user might not use all the features of the computer.

By the end of 1977, Wozniak had improved substantially upon the original model by adding a keyboard, a color monitor, and expansion capabilities for peripheral devices. These features gave the new model, the Apple II, considerable flexibility and enticed a number of companies to develop software programs for the company, as well as a plethora of add-on devices.

By 1980, with the help of Regis McKenna, a well-respected public relations expert in Silicon Valley, the California center for computer technology, Apple had sold more than 130,000 units. Revenues grew from less than $8 million in 1978 to $117 million. The company went public in 1980 with one of the largest stock offerings in history, underwritten in cooperation with Morgan Stanley, Inc. The first day of trading took Apple stock from the underwriters' price of $22 per share to $29, bringing the market value of Apple to $1.2 billion.

The Apple II Plus model did not fare as well as its predecessors. The Apple III, aimed at the professional market, was hampered by production problems that resulted in a recall of some units. These problems and the attention required to solve them offered International Business Machines (IBM) an opportunity to introduce its long-awaited entry in the personal computer market.

The problems with the Apple II Plus and Apple III models were at least partially responsible for the firm's first major managerial shake-up. Apple president Michael Scott fired forty employees. Scott was then dismissed by Markkula, who became president. Jobs assumed Markkula's former position as chairman. Meanwhile, Wozniak was injured in 1981 and took a leave of absence from the firm. After his recovery, Wozniak founded an organization dedicated to fostering a spirit of cooperation among people. He expressed an interest in returning to Apple in a trouble-shooting capacity, with a mission to restore the spirit that led Apple to its early successes.

In January, 1983, Jobs announced the introduction of the Apple IIe, a successor to the Apple II Plus. He simultaneously announced the introduction of Lisa, the first of a generation of computers aimed at the business market. Lisa incorporated many of the technological advances to date and added several unique features, including the first hand-held "mouse" input device. This mechanism allowed the user to execute commands by invoking a series of user-friendly "menus" by moving the mouse and clicking buttons rather than by typing commands. This innovation also allowed the user to more easily produce high-quality graphics that previously would have required a complex series of keystrokes. Computer novices could now master use of the computer in a matter of minutes, rather than the weeks mastery had taken in the past.

As the company evolved, its approach to management changed dramatically. Realizing that selling computers had become a more complex marketing problem, Jobs sought help. Computers no longer would sell themselves on the basis of their technological innovations. In April, 1983, perceiving that marketing expertise was lacking within the firm, Jobs recruited John Sculley from PepsiCo. The move was controversial given that Sculley had developed his reputation selling soft drinks in a mature market, an environment very unlike the growth industry of personal computers. Some foresaw a conflict of corporate cultures between the freewheeling style of Silicon Valley and the more traditional style that Sculley embodied. Although an outsider, Sculley brought marketing skills to Apple that had been missing.

Impact of Event

In 1984, Apple introduced the Macintosh. This model, dubbed the computer "for the rest of us," incorporated a graphical user interface inspired by Xerox's Alto Computer. Macintosh was developed for the business (focusing on productivity and desktop publishing) and education markets. Its compact design and ease of use caught the attention of the market, though the original models were criticized for lacking the computing power required for some business applications. After a series of modifications and upgrades, the computer gained widespread acceptance.

In 1985, after a series of tumultuous conflicts with Sculley and Apple's board of directors, Jobs resigned his position, closing the chapter on Apple's origin and founders. Jobs later formed his own firm, Next, Inc., dedicated to providing sophisticated workstations for the education markets.

By 1986, with the introduction of the Mac Plus and the Laserwriter printer, Apple had begun to make significant inroads into the business market. The company also embarked on a cost- and price-reduction program, allowing it to sell aggressively to large businesses, a historically weak market for Apple. Combining traditional computer applications such as word processing and spreadsheets with pioneering concepts such as desktop publishing, three-dimensional computer-assisted design, and interactive multimedia tools (with text, animation, and sound) carried the Apple tradition for innovation forward.

Apple's unique approach to personal computing altered the manner in which computer manufacturers compete. Apple pioneered the concept of integrating hardware and software to offer new possibilities. For example, integration of high-resolution displays with scalable fonts (alphanumeric characters that could be printed in a variety of sizes) and graphics capabilities allows people to create sophisticated documents on their personal computers. Through the integration of a microphone and a CD-ROM drive with specialized software, people could now work with sound, video, and animation. Most other computer manufacturers could not integrate hardware and software as expediently because they did not manage the software development for their systems. Most, instead, licensed the same system software (MS-DOS) from the same company (Microsoft). As a result, many of their products were indistinguishable and companies often competed solely on the basis of price. Manufacturers of "clones" of IBM computers set off price wars in the hardware arena. Although Apple lowered prices to remain competitive, much of its sales growth has come through product innovation.

In a surprising change in direction, given the maverick style of the firm's beginnings, strategic partnerships became increasingly important for Apple. The company collaborated with Sony in introducing the Macintosh Powerbook notebook computer, and in 1990 Apple announced that it was working with Sharp on a pen-based group of products to include electronic books and communication devices. In 1991, in a move that shocked the computer industry, Apple and rival IBM announced a joint venture to develop new software, operating systems, and hardware that would allow easier integration of the products of the two firms.

Apple Computer rose from origins in a garage to become the second-largest manufacturer of personal computers, behind IBM. The company's Macintosh line became known for its user friendliness and superior graphics capabilities. Although some significant product features have been mimicked by competing firms, Apple has successfully redefined how general users view personal computing. As a result of planning and the vision of Jobs and Wozniak in Apple's early years, personal computing has become accessible to the general population. Through a continual series of product innovations, the firm has continued to redefine how people process and transmit information.

Bibliography

Levering, Robert, Michael Katz, and Milton Moskowitz. *The Computer Entrepreneurs: Who's Making It Big and How in America's Upstart Industry*. New York: New American Library, 1984. A series of brief biographical sketches of the pioneers of the computer industry, including Apple's founders and their contemporaries.

Moritz, Michael. *The Little Kingdom: The Private Story of Apple Computer*. New York: William Morrow, 1984. Covers the early history of the firm and provides behind-the-scenes insight into the founders and the unique corporate culture they fostered.

Price, Rob, Jill Savini, and Thom Marchionna. *So Far: The First Ten Years of a Vision*. Cupertino, Calif.: Apple Computer, 1987. Although published as a public relations vehicle for the firm, this richly-illustrated volume provides an interesting and entertaining historical overview of the firm's early years.

Rose, Frank. *West of Eden: The End of Innocence at Apple Computer*. New York: Viking Press, 1989. A behind-the-scenes account of the managerial upheaval at Apple Computer that led Steve Jobs to leave the company as it sought to penetrate the business market.

Sculley, John. *Odyssey, Pepsi to Apple: A Journey of Adventure, Ideas, and the Future*. New York: Harper & Row, 1987. A readable personal account of the firm from the standpoint of Apple's chief executive officer and successor to Steve Jobs. Focuses on the struggle between Sculley and Jobs and its implications for the direction of the firm.

Andrew M. Forman
Elaine Sherman

Cross-References

IBM Changes Its Name and Product Line (1924), p. 447; VisiCalc Spreadsheet Software Is Marketed (1979), p. 1687; CAD/CAM Revolutionizes Engineering and Manufacturing (1980's), p. 1721; Electronic Technology Creates the Possibility of Telecommuting (1980's), p. 1733; IBM Introduces Its Personal Computer (1981), p. 1809.

GENENTECH IS FOUNDED

Category of event: Foundings and dissolutions
Time: April 7, 1976
Locale: San Francisco, California

Genentech played a pioneering role in commercializing biotechnology

Principal personages:

ROBERT SWANSON (1947-   ), a venture capitalist and cofounder of
     Genentech
HERBERT BOYER (1936-   ), a biochemist/microbiologist and cofoun-
     der of Genentech
KIRK RAAB (1935-   ), the chief executive officer of Genentech who
     took office in 1990

Summary of Event

Genentech was the largest and best-known of the early efforts to commercialize biotechnology research. The company has been viewed by some as laying the foundation for the biotechnology industry. In addition to having a pioneering role in commercializing biotechnology, Genentech achieved a major feat by using public financing to fund clinical trials of drugs.

In the early 1990's, the biotechnology industry remained in its infancy, and not many products had come out of it. The products that have come out indicate the industry's potential. Biotechnology may produce drugs to cure diseases such as cancer and acquired immune deficiency syndrome (AIDS), increase the yields of agricultural products, and even make computers faster using "biochips." Continued growth of the biotechnology industry is likely to revolutionize the operations of drug and pharmaceutical producers, chemical companies, and farms.

Biotechnology has been defined as the application of biological organisms, systems, or processes to manufacturing or service industries. Of the collection of technologies that are called biotechnology, the one most discussed is genetic engineering. The true potential of biotechnology was unleashed when James Watson and Francis Crick worked out the double helix structure of deoxyribonucleic acid (DNA), the chemical blueprint for all living creatures. The fact that DNA reproduces itself opened the possibility of making DNA do what people wanted it to do. If genetic instructions for the manufacture of a desirable protein could be identified and inserted into the DNA of a living cell, then that cell would be able not only to manufacture the protein but also to pass on that ability to future generations of cells. In the early 1970's, techniques for transferring genes from organisms into bacteria were first developed. At this time, much of the biotechnology research conducted was in university laboratories.

Robert Swanson, a venture capitalist working for Kleiner and Perkins, had a bachelor's degree in chemistry and a master's degree in management. Swanson was intrigued by the commercial potential of recombinant DNA and was following research efforts in this area. In 1976, Swanson read a paper on recombinant DNA by Herbert Boyer, who was working at the University of California. Swanson arranged a meeting to discuss the commercial potential of techniques developed by Boyer. Between January and April of 1976, Boyer and Swanson made more detailed investigations of specific technological and market opportunities. On April 7, 1976, Swanson and Boyer incorporated Genentech, each taking twenty-five thousand shares of common stock in return for the cash and assets of their partnership. Kleiner and Perkins provided $200,000 of seed capital in exchange for twenty thousand shares.

Genentech's goals were to select products that were in great demand and to specifically engineer microorganisms to produce those products. The founders believed that any product produced by a living organism would eventually be within the company's reach.

In the next two years, Genentech played a pioneering role in product development. In August, 1977, a little more than a year after the company was founded, Genentech scientists cloned DNA in a bacteria culture to produce somatostatin. This was the first human protein ever produced in a microorganism. In August, 1978, Genentech and City of Hope Medical Center in Duarte, California, jointly announced that they had produced insulin using biotechnology. This product was licensed to Eli Lilly and was the first product using recombinant DNA technology to reach the market.

To continue its research efforts and commercialize technology, Genentech needed more funds than could be raised internally. Swanson hired a sales and marketing force to sell the company itself. On October 14, 1980, Genentech offered its shares publicly, even though it had no product ready for sale. Shares issued for $35 apiece at 10 A.M. hit $86 by the afternoon. Genentech used proceeds from the stock sale to fund clinical trials of a drug, becoming the first company to do so. Previously, research and development partnerships had been associated with real estate or oil and gas development.

Impact of Event

Efforts by Genentech have had significant impacts on the performance of Genentech itself, the founding of other biotechnology firms, and the operations of giant drug and pharmaceutical firms. In addition, biotechnology has spawned related new technologies such as rational drug design.

By 1992, Genentech's research had aided in developing seven of the thirteen biotechnology-based pharmaceuticals on the market. It was the first biotechnology company to take three of its own products from the laboratory to the marketplace. Genentech has shown considerable commitment to research, investing approximately half of its revenues in research. This was three times the average of pharmaceutical companies and the highest among firms in the biotechnology industry.

Genentech's performance was steady but not spectacular. Contrary to expectations, none of its first three products was a runaway success. Each of the three products, the

Protropin human growth hormone (hGH), the Activase tissue plasminogen activator (t-PA) blood clot dissolving agent, and Actimmune interferon gamma, faced different problems.

In 1985, Genentech received approval from the Food and Drug Administration (FDA) to market its first product, Protropin. Genentech applied for "orphan drug" status and obtained it, since there were only ten thousand children in the United States who lacked the natural hormone and would not reach full height without it. The orphan drug status gave Genentech tax incentives and exclusive marketing rights for seven years. The intent of the Orphan Drug Act of 1983 was to provide incentives to drug companies to research cures for rare illnesses.

Eli Lilly developed a different version of the growth hormone, and the FDA granted orphan drug status to that drug as well. Genentech sued to block the approval for Lilly's product. The courts refused, stating that Lilly's drug was sufficiently different from Genentech's. Several fundamental questions were raised. Analysts questioned whether a highly profitable drug, or one with potential applications outside the small group of primary patients, should be eligible for special status. The growth hormone could have much wider applications as a wound-healing drug or could be used to treat people of short stature unrelated to a hormone deficiency. By 1991, Protropin had annual sales of $185.1 million and showed steady growth.

In early 1987, Genentech applied to the FDA for approval of Activase t-PA (tissue plasminogen activator), which is used to dissolve blood clots during a heart attack. Streptokinase (sold by SmithKline) was already used for the same purpose. Initial tests comparing Activase with Streptokinase suggested that Activase was twice as effective. This improved performance was reflected in its price: Streptokinase was $200 to $300 a dose, and Activase had a projected price of $2,200 a dose. Genentech's application to market Activase was rejected by the FDA. Part of the reason for refusal was that tests had been conducted on a pool of fewer than two hundred patients. Genentech's excellent public relations mobilized public opinion, and the FDA approved when Genentech reapplied six months later, in November, 1987.

The company's sales forecast of $400 million per year was not reached. The initial euphoria about Activase started to fade as reports about excessive bleeding in patients using Activase came in. In view of the increased risk, many doctors did not believe that the performance difference between Activase and Streptokinase justified the higher price. Activase appeared to be an improvement, not a breakthrough. Sales of Activase in 1988 were approximately $180 million. By 1991, sales of Activase were only $196.5 million, and in 1992 sales fell to $182.1 million. Genentech's problems were compounded by the introduction of competing products.

Genentech received approval for its third product, Actimmune interferon gamma, in 1990. This drug is used to treat an inherited immune system impairment called chronic granulomatous disease. Few people have this disease, so sales of the product were only $1.7 million in 1991 and $2.9 million in 1992.

In the pipeline were increased applications of the three existing products as well as new products to treat patients with cystic fibrosis and breast and ovarian cancer, an

AIDS vaccine, and a drug to reduce pain during childbirth. On February 3, 1990, Genentech announced sale of a controlling stake to Roche Holding Ltd., the Swiss parent of giant drugmaker F. Hoffman-La Roche and Company. This move resulted in an infusion of $492 million in cash that would be used to support research. Kirk Raab took Swanson's place as chief executive officer, and Swanson became chairman of the board of directors. The change signaled a shift from entrepreneurial and visionary management to a more traditional corporate control.

About six hundred biotechnology companies had been founded by 1993, nearly all of them in the United States. Among them were Applied Biosystems, Chiron, Life Technologies, Centocor, Cetus, and Amgen, all of which met considerable success. Only about a dozen biotechnology products had reached the market, leaving many biotechnology firms at the stage of product development and testing.

The growth of biotechnology products has been steady rather than spectacular. A decade after Genentech's launch, industry sales reached approximately $700 million. About $300 million was accounted for by diagnostic tests, with the remainder sales of drugs and vaccines.

The commercial performance of biodrugs was disappointing partly because expectations were so high. Many drugs that seemed promising ended up having side effects, such as interleukin-2, or treated only rare diseases. Biotechnology-based pharmaceuticals have also been limited by the delivery system. Most of these drugs had to be injected, since they would be absorbed by the stomach wall if swallowed. If it becomes possible to take these drugs orally, the market for them may expand.

Despite these problems, as of the early 1990's most analysts saw tremendous potential in the biotechnology industry. More than one hundred biotechnology-based drugs were in clinical tests. The diagnostic test market was also expected to grow as mapping of the human genome became more precise. This may allow early identification of birth defects and susceptibility to certain diseases.

Biotechnology-based drugs have numerous advantages over synthetically produced drugs that currently dominate the market. Most biodrugs have fewer side effects. In addition, finding a suitable synthetic drug is a major challenge. Hundreds or thousands of chemicals are exposed to cells to see if there is any effect. The success rate is very low in this type of haphazard research. Biotechnology has a higher success rate because it starts its search for a cure based on what biologists know about a disease and how the body fights it.

The success of biotechnology has also acted as a catalyst in bringing new techniques in the design of pharmaceuticals. One line of research is developing chemicals similar to short strands of DNA that would short-circuit harmful genetic messages. These drugs would focus narrowly on a target disease and not interfere with anything else, thus avoiding side effects.

Biotechnology has also influenced the way traditional drug and pharmaceutical firms treat synthetic drugs. Some drug designers in these companies are experimenting with what is called rational drug design. Instead of the hit-and-miss screening traditionally used, scientists use recombinant DNA and other genetic engineering tools to make large quantities of natural proteins, then use them as research tools for designing better synthetic products.

Bibliography

Elkington, John. *The Gene Factory: Inside the Genetic and Biotechnology Business.* New York: Carroll & Graf, 1985. Very useful source for information on the potential benefits from the biotechnology industry.

Gannes, Stuart, and Gene Bylinsky. "The Big Boys Are Joining the Biotech Party." *Fortune* 116 (July 6, 1987): 58-64. Has a discussion of corporate giants interested in biotechnology firms.

Hamilton, Joan. "Genentech's Custody Case Over an Orphan Drug." *Business Week*, March 23, 1987, 39. Discusses Genentech's problems with marketing Protropin.

_____ . "The Search for Superdrugs." *Business Week*, May 13, 1991, 92-96. Provides information on extensions of biotechnology.

Hamilton, Joan, Laura Jereski, and Joseph Weber. "Why Genentech Ditched the Dream of Independence." *Business Week*, February 19, 1990, 36-37. Discussion of the deal struck with Hoffman-La Roche.

Mahar, Maggie. "The Genentech Mystique: How Much Science, How Much Hype?" *Barron's* 68 (January 11, 1988): 8-9, 20-31. Has a discussion of Genentech's founding and its launch of Activase.

Quinn, James Brian. "Genentech, Inc. (A)." In *The Strategy Process: Concepts, Contexts, and Cases*, edited by Henry Mintzberg and James Brian Quinn. 2d ed. Englewood Cliffs, N.J.: Prentice-Hall, 1991. A good summary of the founding and initial years of Genentech.

Wyke, Alexandra. "The Genetic Alternative: A Survey of Biotechnology." *The Economist* 307 (April 30, 1988): s1-s18. An informative survey covering the development and future of the biotechnology industry.

Kamala Arogyaswamy

Cross-References

Federal Express Begins Operations (1973). p. 1538; Jobs and Wozniak Found Apple Computer (1976), p. 1611; Kohlbert Kravis Roberts Pioneers the Leveraged Buyout (1977), p. 1641; The Supreme Court Rules That Life Forms Can Be Patented (1980), p. 1778.

PRICE CLUB INTRODUCES THE WAREHOUSE CLUB CONCEPT

Categories of event: Marketing, foundings and dissolutions
Time: July 12, 1976
Locale: San Diego, California

Price Club revolutionized traditional approaches to product distribution by open-ing a cash-and-carry warehouse stocking brand-name merchandise to be sold at low prices primarily to small businesses

Principal personages:
SOL PRICE (1916-   ), a cofounder of Price Club
ROBERT E. PRICE (1942-   ), a cofounder of Price Club
MITCHELL G. LYNN (1948-   ), the president of the Price Company, 1991-1993
JAMES D. SINEGAL (1936-   ), a Price Club executive and cofounder of Costco
JEFFREY H. BROTMAN (1942-   ), a cofounder of Costco
SAMUEL M. WALTON (1918-1992), a cofounder of Wal-Mart, instrumen-tal in formation of Sam's Wholesale Club

Summary of Event

In 1976, Sol Price and his son Robert created the membership warehouse store when they opened the first Price Club outlet, in San Diego, on July 12. Their goal was to attract the buying power of small businesses by offering merchandise at volume discounts. The first Price Club restricted membership to "wholesale" members. For the right to shop at Price Club, businesspersons were required to pay a $25 annual membership fee. Price Club initially targeted the small business owner with no efficient way of buying wholesale. The Prices learned in their first year, however, that focusing exclusively on this business sector was not as lucrative as anticipated. Therefore, in its second year Price Club broadened its base. Membership was extended to select consumer groups, such as credit union members and public sector employees, who were exempted from paying membership fees but were charged 5 percent more than business customers for merchandise.

Eventually, Price Club abandoned the 5 percent surcharge for the nonbusiness members and established two types of membership: Business membership (for busi-ness owners, nonprofit organizations, and government agencies) and Gold Star mem-bership (for members of select credit unions and employee groups, state-licensed professionals, and public service employees). Both groups' annual membership fees became $25. Business members had the advantage of shopping at the warehouse during the week an hour or two before the store was open to Gold Star members.

Price Club soon was followed by warehouse imitators that were patterned closely after Price Club's philosophy and operations. Costco Wholesale Club and Sam's Wholesale Club (a division of Wal-Mart) both began operation in 1983. Pace Membership Warehouse (a division of Kmart) and B. J.'s Wholesalers opened shortly thereafter.

Although warehouse clubs were recognized as an interesting phenomenon on the fringe of retailing during their early years, it was not until around 1985 that they were seen as a major force in the industry. One important factor favoring the growth of warehouse clubs was the repeal of fair trade laws, formally referred to as resale price maintenance laws. From the early 1930's to 1976, a series of state laws and federal enabling acts allowed manufacturers to determine their products' minimum retail prices to consumers. This form of restriction of competition was permitted on the grounds that it would encourage retailers to compete on the basis of customer service rather than price. On March 11, 1976, the demise of fair trade laws occurred when the Consumer Goods Pricing Act of 1975 went into effect. This act in essence repealed the Miller-Tydings Act of 1937 and the McGuire Act of 1952. The 1975 act abolished the use of fair trade pricing for interstate commerce.

As economic conditions became less favorable, warehouse clubs underwent an explosive expansion. Consumers became increasingly concerned with getting the best value for their shrinking dollar. They were willing to seek out retailers who could offer them, at lower prices, nationally recognized brands and the quality and status they implied.

Manufacturers were also eager to reduce their inventories and find alternatives to selling to retailers, which often ordered late and paid late. Warehouse clubs, unlike some other retailers, rarely asked for special deals such as promotional allowances, extended payment terms, and return privileges. Many manufacturers therefore began to look on warehouse clubs as a market force to be courted.

Owners of small businesses needed to find an efficient means to purchase products in relatively small quantities at wholesale prices. When warehouse clubs started, a primary focus was to offer this viable retailing alternative to small businesses.

Consumers who had become disenchanted with traditional retailers also contributed to the success of warehouse clubs. Poor service, frequent sales that distorted prices and required consumer monitoring, and a lack of distinctive merchandise antagonized consumers and eroded loyalty to department stores and other traditional retailers. As consumers became more concerned with finding a place were they could regularly buy nationally recognized brands at rock-bottom prices, warehouse clubs seemed to provide a refreshing and economical option.

Impact of Event

Although warehouse clubs started small, with a single Price Club store in San Diego, they became a major force in the selling of products to small businesses and selected groups of consumers. In the early 1990's, there were more than a dozen different warehouse clubs. In 1992, however, the top five (Sam's Wholesale Club, Price Club, Costco, Pace, and B. J.'s Wholesale Club) controlled more than 90 percent of the approximately six hundred warehouse club outlets and more than 95 percent of all warehouse clubs' estimated sales.

The largest players in the warehouse club arena achieved their success by making similar assumptions about their target audience and by following similar strategies related to their facilities and operations. Warehouse clubs purchase most of their goods directly from manufacturers in large quantities at rock-bottom prices and ship these goods directly to individual outlets, avoiding the cost of maintaining a central warehouse. These savings are passed on to customers, who are able to buy merchandise near wholesale prices.

In keeping with their low-price philosophy, warehouse clubs began with a basic platform. Shopping was limited to card-carrying members, purchases were on a cash basis, there were no home deliveries, and customers either brought their own shopping bags or had their purchases put in discarded boxes near the cash registers.

A club usually operates out of a large warehouse, typically 100,000 square feet or larger, in a low-rent area. Clubs usually carry between 3,500 and 5,000 items, compared with about ten times that number carried by a typical discount store of the same size. Although the warehouse store carries a vast array of product categories, the selection of brands, sizes, and models in each category is narrow. For example, a store may carry only two types of refrigerators and one brand of garbage bags. Generally the products are sold either in outsized packaging (for example, rice in ten-pound bags, soy sauce in gallon containers, and peanut butter in two-pound jars) or in shrink-wrapped "multi-packs" containing several individual items. Few prices are below three dollars. The rationale behind this limited selection is that it creates efficiencies in buying, stocking, and selling merchandise.

The merchandise is displayed on concrete floors or simple pipe racks and steel shelves. Broad aisles allow forklifts to restock shelves with pallets of fresh goods. Advertising, personal selling, and post-sales service are minimized. Because of the bare-bones, no-frills decor and the no-advertising, no-delivery policies (Price Club introduced delivery in 1989), coupled with annual membership fees, warehouse clubs are able to survive on low markups above cost.

Warehouses typically turn over merchandise between fifteen and twenty-two times each year. This is more than triple a big discount store's turnover. A 100,000-square-foot warehouse of the early 1990's generates about $900 in sales per square foot of space, about ten times the volume of discount retailers. A typical warehouse club priced its products at 8 to 10 percent above cost, about one-third of the typical discount store markup. Because of the tremendous volume that a warehouse club can produce, its pretax profits may be higher than those of discount retailers.

In the early 1990's, it was estimated that roughly one in five households shopped at a warehouse club. The clubs seemed to attract middle- and upper-class consumers and small businesses. Half to two-thirds of the shoppers at wholesale clubs are consumers rather than businesses, and their numbers are predicted to grow as clubs broaden their services. Although in terms of size, the business members are a slight minority, this group generated about 60 percent of all sales.

Warehouse clubs have added some new features and innovations in their stores. Price Club developed a variety of subsidiary businesses under the umbrella of Price Club Industries (PCI). For example, it operated a meatpacking plant, candy packaging operation, optical lab, photo processing lab, and pharmacy. Its private label products include Gibson's Gourmet Ranch ground beef, Hattie Brooks Candy, and Club Classic Clothing. In each case, PCI believed that the quality of its own products matched national brands and sold at a lower price. Some Price Club stores featured a "Tech Center" offering sales assistance with business machines and computer products. Price Club also introduced fresh bakery products, deli departments, and fresh meats in most warehouses. "Touch & Shop," an interactive shopping system, allowed customers to select upscale products by touching a video display screen. Many warehouse clubs also departed from their strict cash-and-carry policies of the past and began to accept credit cards. Some introduced business delivery services.

Although some analysts believe that the warehouse club phenomenon will continue to grow, others see that after years of rapid expansion, warehouse club leaders are involved in head-on competition in some markets. Competition also comes from spinoff operations including home-improvement clubs such as Home Depot and office clubs such as Staples and Office Depot. At the same time, some non-club retailers are fighting to regain lost sales. Supermarkets, for example, are now offering "warehouse" sections and club-size packaging as part of their product mix.

Consolidation of warehouse clubs and some alteration of marketing and operational strategies are likely to occur in the future. In 1993, only six of the major twenty players that started out in the warehouse business were still around. Moreover, in the fall of 1993, Price Club and Costco merged to form Price/Costco Inc., and Sam's Wholesale Club made efforts to augment its base by adding Pace warehouse clubs to its operations.

Expansion for the warehouse clubs may involve entering new markets, particularly in the Midwest and Northeast, as well as overseas. Couponing, private-label merchandising, and advertising, all perceived as unnecessary expenses in warehouse clubs' early days, may soon be viewed as necessary expenses in the future, as warehouse operations and retailers implement one another's best ideas to stay competitive.

Bibliography

Degen, James M. "Warehouse Clubs Move from Revolution to Evolution." *Marketing News* 26 (August 3, 1992): 8. Discusses how market forces such as baby boomers, small businesses, and in-home offices are important factors in the growth of warehouse clubs. A helpful pie chart shows the market shares of the major warehouse clubs.

Dunkin, Amy, Todd Mason, Lois Therrien, and Teresa Carson. "Boom Times in a Bargain-Hunter's Paradise." *Business Week*, March 11, 1985, 116, 120. Discusses how warehouse clubs have become a booming phenomenon that blurs the distinction between retailing and wholesaling. Easy to read.

Gelbtuch, Howard C. "The Warehouse Club Industry." *The Appraisal Journal* 58

(April, 1990): 153-159. Analysis of the way warehouse clubs emerged as a significant form of mass merchandising during the 1980's. Excellent overview of warehouse club operations, history, and relative growth and sales.

Jakobson, Cathryn. "They Can Get It for You Wholesale." *The New York Times Magazine* 138 (December 4, 1988): 24-25, 54, 56. Provides an excellent look at how Sol Price and his warehouse clubs sparked a revolution in the retail trade. Gives historical background surrounding the opening of the first Price Club in San Diego and delineates key philosophical and operational assumptions about warehouse clubs. Well researched and clearly written.

Kaikati, Jack G. "The Boom in Warehouse Clubs." *Business Horizons* 30 (March/April, 1987): 68-73. One of the best and most comprehensive discussions of warehouse clubs, covering their evolution and factors that contributed to the growth of warehouse clubs. Written for an undergraduate audience or for those with some basic marketing background.

Morgenstein, Melvin, and Harriet Strongin. *Modern Retailing: Management Principles and Practices*. 3d ed. Englewood Cliffs, N.J.: Prentice Hall, 1992. Discusses how warehouse clubs are one of the retail innovators, along with off-price retailers, factory outlets, warehouse-style home centers, and warehouse stores. A helpful graph shows how the five major warehouse club competitors' sales grew from 1983 to 1991.

Teutsch, Austin. *The Sam Walton Story: The Retailing of Middle America*. Austin, Tex.: Diamond Books, 1990. A former employee of Sam Walton tells the story of the inception and growth of Wal-Mart and Sam's Wholesale Club. Easy to read.

John E. Richardson

Cross-References

The First Major U.S. Shopping Center Opens (1922), p. 380; The Miller-Tydings Act Legalizes Retail Price Maintenance (1937), p. 764; The First Two-Story, Fully Enclosed Shopping Mall Opens (1956), p. 1070; The U.S. Service Economy Emerges (1960's), p. 1138; Drive-Through Services Proliferate (1970's), p. 1406; A Home Shopping Service Is Offered on Cable Television (1985), p. 1909.

THE 1976 COPYRIGHT ACT REFLECTS
TECHNOLOGICAL CHANGE

Category of event: Government and business
Time: October 19, 1976
Locale: Washington, D. C.

The Copyright Act of 1976 attempted to correct the imbalance between the competing rights of copyright owners and users that had developed as a result of technological change

> *Principal personages:*
> STANLEY H. FULD (1903-   ), the chair of the National Commission on New Technological Uses of Copyrighted Works
> ROBERT W. KASTENMEIER (1924-   ), the chair of the House Judiciary Subcommittee on Courts, Civil Liberties, and the Administration of Justice
> JOHN L. McCLELLAN (1896-1977), the chair of the Senate Judiciary Subcommittee on Patents, Trademarks, and Copyrights
> BARBARA RINGER (1925-   ), the register of copyrights

Summary of Event

Prior to enactment of the 1976 Copyright Act, which became effective on January 1, 1978, the last wholesale revision of United States copyright law took place in 1909. In the intervening decades, technological advances in communications rendered many provisions of the 1909 act ineffective. A number of efforts to amend the copyright law in piecemeal fashion were introduced, but it was not until the Legislative Appropriations Act of 1955 provided funds for research by the Copyright Office of the Library of Congress that a more general effort to revise the copyright law was undertaken.

Congressional hearings on proposed revisions began on May 26, 1965, before the House Judiciary Subcommittee on Courts, Civil Liberties, and the Administration of Justice, which ultimately voted favorably on the proposed legislation. Prior to approving the bill, however, the subcommittee jettisoned an entire section devoted to copyright issues raised by cable television's secondary transmission of broadcast signals. This would prove to be the issue upon which the legislation would founder for some time. Senator John L. McClellan, chair of the Senate Judiciary Subcommittee on Patents, Trademarks, and Copyrights, which had begun its hearings on August 18, 1965, insisted that any copyright legislation that passed must address the status of the cable industry. His concern grew out of the Federal Communications Commission's failure to adopt a new cable regulatory scheme that would relax restrictions on the carriage of signals. It was only after the FCC approved such regulations in 1972 that McClellan resumed his efforts to push through a new copyright bill.

Active debate on the copyright bill resumed in 1974 with the Ninety-third Congress. The bill finally passed in the Senate on February 19, 1976, and in the House of Representatives on September 22, 1976. President Gerald R. Ford signed the bill into law on October 19, 1976.

The new copyright statute was divided into eight chapters. The first chapter defined the subject matter of copyright, stated what rights copyright affords, and outlined the limitations on those rights. Chapter 2 was concerned with the ownership and transfer of copyrights. The third chapter dealt with the duration of copyrights. Chapter 4 dealt with formalities such as the form and placement of copyright notice and the details of depositing and registering a copyrighted work. Chapter 5 addressed copyright infringement and its remedies. Chapter 6 concerned the manufacture, importation, and public distribution of copies. Chapter 7 dealt with the organization and responsibilities of the Copyright Office. Finally, chapter 8 established the Copyright Royalty Tribunal.

Perhaps the most conspicuous change in U.S. copyright law had to do with the utilization, in the 1976 act, of compulsory licenses—such as the annual fees levied on jukeboxes—to balance the competing interests of copyright owners and users. Analogously, several sections of the new act established statutory royalty rates, such as those connected with secondary transmission by cable television, the collection of which was to be overseen by the Copyright Royalty Tribunal, itself created by the 1976 act.

Less conspicuously, but more profoundly, the statute amended U.S. copyright law by making four major changes: abolishing common law copyright; changing the concept of copyright by clarifying what it protects; creating an electronic copyright to supplement the print copyright; and codifying the doctrine of fair use. In addition, the statute marked, as noted by Barbara Ringer, then the register of copyrights, a shift in the philosophical underpinnings of copyright, resolving a centuries-old debate whether copyright was a natural law property right or only a statutory grant of limited monopoly, in favor of the latter. Chapter 1 of the act opens with a proclamation of the exclusive rights of copyright owners, which are five: the right to reproduce a work; the right to prepare derivative works, such as abridgments; the right to distribute copies of a work to the public; the right to perform a work in public; and the right to display a work in public. The bulk of this chapter is devoted to limitations on these rights.

Impact of Event

Prior to the 1976 act, copyright had been governed by two systems of law: federal statutory copyright and common law copyright, which was largely the province of individual states. By decreeing that a work was copyrighted the moment it was fixed in a tangible medium of expression, the new statute did away with the concept of common law copyright, which previously had governed works prior to publication, when statutory law took over.

The elimination of common law copyright clarified the concept of copyright protection by making it clear that what was being protected was an original work of authorship, which must fall into one of three categories: an imaginative work, such as a novel; a derivative work, such as a film based on the novel; or a compilation of previously existing materials, such as an anthology. In the latter two cases, copyright now protected only the original aspects of the work: that is, in the case of a derivative work, only the new elements added to the underlying work, and in the case of a compilation, only the collection as a whole (although copying an individual short story in a collection, for example, might violate the copyright of that story). Thus, the impact of this reconceptualization of copyright protection was to do away with earlier confusion of the original work of authorship with the material object embodying it, such as a compilation or film. Under the 1976 act, the two must be merged in order for copyright protection to attach.

Common law copyright lived on, however, in a new copyright created by the 1976 statute: the electronic copyright. The electronic copyright was meant to cover television and also apply to computers and software. It differed fundamentally from print copyright in that the subject matter consisted of works that are performed rather than published. These performances—for example, a live telecast of a National Football League game—may or may not be based on writing of some kind and may have no author per se. The statute gets around these requirements by making performance equivalent to publication if any fixation (even simultaneous transmission and recording) takes place and making the employer of those creating the work its "author." The electronic copyright is thus equivalent to common law copyright protection of an improvised stage performance.

The fourth, and potentially the most far-reaching, major change introduced by the 1976 act was the codification of what had always been a judicially determined doctrine limiting the powers of copyright holders, the doctrine of fair use. United States copyright law originated with the Constitution, which, in article I, section 8, clause 8, empowers Congress "to promote the progress of science and the useful arts, by securing for limited times to authors and inventors the exclusive right to their respective writings and discoveries." The original idea was to provide creators with the incentive of a limited monopoly while at the same time allowing those who followed to build on ideas that already had been formulated and disseminated. This is clearly a delicate balance to maintain, requiring constant adjustment. American law traditionally responded by allowing fair use to remain a rule of reason developed and applied by the judiciary. Even when codified, the fair use doctrine consisted of a number of significantly nonexclusive factors that are reconfigured with each new infringement case that arises.

Section 107, the fair use section of the 1976 act, was not intended to change previous judicial interpretations of the doctrine. Section 107 was loosely formulated, refraining from formally defining "fair use" and including a list of exemptions from the restrictions of copyright, such as criticism and research. The section also included a list of four factors to be considered by judges when weighing fair use defenses raised against claims of copyright infringement. First was the purpose and character of the use, including whether such use is of a commercial nature or is for nonprofit educational purposes. Second was the nature of the copyrighted work. Third was the amount and substantially of the portion used in relation to the copyrighted work as a whole. The fourth consideration was the effect of the use on the potential market for or value of the copyrighted work. The fact that a work is unpublished was not to bar a finding of fair use.

The final proviso, indicating that even unpublished work is subject to fair use, was an addition to the act, adopted by Congress in 1992 largely in response to constriction of the fair use doctrine resulting from several Supreme Court decisions. *Harper & Row Publishers v. Nation Enterprises* (1985) revolved around the unauthorized publication by the magazine *The Nation* of excerpts, concerning the pardon of President Richard M. Nixon, from President Ford's forthcoming memoir. The most notorious of similar cases is *Salinger v. Random House* (1987).

In both the Nation and Salinger cases, the courts refused to acknowledge as fair use what might in an earlier time have been seen as minimal borrowing. One of the pivotal issues in both cases was the unpublished nature of the infringed works. As the Supreme Court reasoned in the Nation case, perhaps because the fair use doctrine was based on the author's implied consent to reasonable use of his or her work upon publication, fair use was not traditionally recognized as a defense to charges of copying works not yet released for public consumption.

Arguably, the fair use doctrine was intended to protect copyright owners from competitors, not consumers. In the Salinger case, however, fair use was pressed into service as a rationale for censorship. In this case, the writer J. D. Salinger brought suit seeking an injunction against publication of an unauthorized biography that included quotations and paraphrases from his correspondence with various persons who had deposited these letters with archives, seeking to protect personal interests. In view of the purpose of federal copyright laws, that type of deposit is a misuse of what is fundamentally a property right.

When the fair use proviso regarding unpublished works was proposed, largely in reaction to demands made by reporters, historians, biographers, and book publishers, it was vigorously opposed by the computer software industry, which feared that such a change in the copyright law would legitimize already rampant piracy of programs. These copyright owners argued that fair use of their products, unlike books, would of necessity involve extensive copying. The battle between these interest groups was reflected in congressional debate over the proviso, which raged for two years. Finally, a compromise was reached late in 1992, with the Senate adopting the seemingly restrictive language of the House bill but adding, in the legislative history attached to the bill, that its intent was "to clearly and indisputably reject the view that the unpublished nature of the work triggers a virtual per se ruling against a finding of fair use."

Equally significant revisions of the 1976 Copyright Act doubtless will follow as a result of the continuing technological revolution. Anticipating such changes, many electronic publishing contracts were written with clauses granting publishers rights in media yet to be invented.

Bibliography

Miller, Jerome K. *U.S. Copyright Documents: An Annotated Collection for Use by Educators and Librarians.* Littleton, Colo.: Libraries Unlimited, 1981. In addition to highlighting and annotating key parts of the Copyright Act affecting its target audience, this 292-page volume includes the full text of the act, together with relevant excerpts from its legislative history.

New York Law School Law Review. *The Complete Guide to the New Copyright Law.* Dayton, Ohio: Lorenz Press, 1977. Originally published in the *New York Law School Law Review* in 1976 and 1977, this two-part symposium was intended to provide timely advice to attorneys. This collection of essays by copyright experts provides valuable insights for laypersons, particularly in the second section, which contains analyses of the differences between the 1909 and 1976 acts.

Patterson, L. Ray, and Stanley W. Lindberg. *The Nature of Copyright: A Law of Users' Rights.* Athens: University of Georgia Press, 1991. As its title indicates, this is a work with a point of view. The book is divided into three substantive sections, the first of which examines the history of U.S. copyright law, the second copyright and the Constitution, and the third the balance between authors' and users' rights.

Strong, William S. *The Copyright Book: A Practical Guide.* 4th ed. Cambridge, Mass.: MIT Press, 1993. A straightforward presentation of the rights and responsibilities connected with copyright law, addressed to the average citizen. In addition to being revised every few years, it is supplemented more frequently by unbound updates.

White, Herbert S., ed. *The Copyright Dilemma.* Chicago: American Library Association, 1978. Containing the proceedings of a 1977 conference, this volume includes essays aimed at specific copyright users as well as more generalized essays about various aspects of the 1976 act.

Lisa Paddock

Cross-References

Congress Updates Copyright Law in 1909 (1909), p. 163; ASCAP Forms to Protect Writers and Publishers of Music (1914), p. 252; Community Antenna Television Is Introduced (1949), p. 953; Sony Introduces the Betamax (1975), p. 1573; U.S. Courts Restrict Rights to Photocopy Anthologies (1991), p. 2040.

SEARS AGREES TO AN FTC ORDER BANNING BAIT-AND-SWITCH TACTICS

Categories of event: Advertising and retailing
Time: October 21, 1976
Locale: Chicago, Illinois

In response to a 1974 complaint issued by the Federal Trade Commission alleging that Sears had indulged in deceptive bait-and-switch tactics, Sears agreed to a consent order to cease and desist from such practices

Principal personages:
> LEWIS ENGMAN (1936-   ), the chairman of the Federal Trade Commission
> MORRIS THOMPSON (1939-   ), a member of the Federal Trade Commission
> ARTHUR M. WOOD (1913-   ), the chairman and chief executive officer of Sears, Roebuck and Company

Summary of Event

Bait-and-switch tactics refer to deceptive practices whereby shoppers are baited into visiting a retailer's store with bargains that are heavily advertised. Once inside the store, however, shoppers find the retailer attempting to switch their focus to products other than the advertised bargains. The basis of this switch to other (higher-priced) products frequently rests on negative arguments about the advertised product (for example, that it is out of stock or would take a long time to be delivered) or positive arguments for nonadvertised products (for example, an item could be described as possessing superior features when compared to the advertised bargain or as being readily available for delivery). This retailing practice is a clear deception because retailers not only fail to deliver on beguiling offers advertised to consumers but also compound the problem with aggressive attempts to sell products that usually cost more than the advertised products. Shoppers motivated to visit a store to purchase advertised bargains may be vulnerable to retailer manipulation to make them spend more than they had intended because they are likely to be committed to making a purchase during that visit.

The Federal Trade Commission (FTC) had forewarned retailers as early as 1959 about its vigilance with regard to bait-and-switch practices. Sears, which was the largest retailer in the United States at that time, issued the following directive in response: "Sears does not tolerate under any circumstances bait advertising or any other unfair or deceptive selling practice. Sears has developed a substantial reputation with the American public for fair dealings, and cannot afford to have that good will jeopardized." Despite this clearly articulated Sears policy, problems surfaced. The FTC announced a complaint against Sears in July, 1974, and formally lodged it in

September. The well-documented complaint alleged that Sears had violated the Federal Trade Commission Act by using bait-and-switch tactics and cited details extracted from Sears advertisements for sewing machines. Although the advertisements implied bona fide offers to sell sewing machines, the FTC charged that the experience of prospective purchasers visiting Sears retail stores was to the contrary. The complaint noted that when customers attempted to buy the advertised sewing machine, Sears salespeople would discourage the purchase, stating that the advertised item was out of stock or would take a long time to deliver. Typically, they also attempted to sell other products by disparaging the advertised product. Some salespeople made statements that contradicted the product performance characteristics mentioned in the Sears advertisements. Others highlighted negative attributes, such as the advertised product being noisy. Salespeople also drew attention to features that the advertised product lacked, such as a guarantee.

The FTC complaint alleged that the system used by Sears to compensate its salespeople encouraged bait-and-switch behavior. Compensation policy apparently rewarded salespeople for selling higher-priced sewing machines and discouraged them from selling the advertised sewing machines. In addition, compensation was linked to product sales quotas. The FTC claimed that this framework of incentives and disincentives encouraged salespeople to use bait-and-switch tactics.

The FTC complaint charged that Sears had used false, misleading, and deceptive statements and actions to induce a substantial number of customers into buying products at higher prices than they had intended to pay. The FTC considered the bait-and-switch practices to be in violation of section 5 of the Federal Trade Commission Act and to be injurious to both the public and the competitors of Sears.

FTC Commissioner Morris Thompson expressed dissent with regard to the complaint, on the grounds that it did not examine whether the goods to which prospective buyers were switched were good buys or bad buys when compared to what outlets competing with Sears were offering. In the absence of evidence establishing that the higher-priced products to which Sears allegedly steered customers were indeed bad buys relative to competitive product offerings, Thompson thought that it was improper to surmise that the public interest had suffered. His dissent characterized the Sears case as a "victimless crime" and suggested that the limited resources of the FTC might be spent better on cases that, unlike the Sears case, involved real injury to the public interest.

FTC Chairman Lewis Engman disagreed with Thompson's dissent. He opined that a bait-and-switch scheme does not constitute a victimless crime, even if the goods to which customers are switched are comparable in price and quality to those offered by competing sellers. Engman believed that customers were indeed victimized because they were likely to enter an advertiser's store, rather than competing stores, on the presumption that the product bargains advertised were offered in good faith. Bait-and-switch tactics deceptively entice customers into a retail store, thereby giving that store an unfair advantage over its competitors. Engman concluded that previous FTC orders and published guidelines clearly indicated a violation of section 5 of the Federal Trade

Commission Act when a retailer indulged in bait-and-switch tactics. According to Engman, these tactics involved a preconceived selling plan to disparage a low-priced advertised item as a ruse to sell a higher-priced product. He suggested that such selling approaches are often accompanied by low inventories of advertised products, high-pressure sales tactics directed at customers, misrepresentations about the value of advertised products, and compensation methods for salespeople that discourage the sale of low-priced advertised products.

Sears management was shocked by the allegations in the FTC complaint, which directly contradicted stated corporate policy of fairness toward customers. Some Sears executives believed that the complaint was inspired by a disgruntled former employee who had approached the FTC. The initial reaction at Sears was a vow to fight the FTC allegations. After the FTC complaint was filed, Sears consistently maintained that the cited bait-and-switch examples were isolated incidents incompatible with corporate policy.

During the subsequent proceedings before an FTC administrative law judge in early 1976, several Sears salespeople and customers testified. One witness testified, as an example of deceptive behavior, that the bolts on an inexpensive Sears sewing machine were loosened to make it unappealingly noisy when demonstrated to customers. After considering the collective evidence offered at these FTC hearings, Sears changed its stand and opted to seek a settlement rather than to aggressively oppose the FTC complaint. The proceedings ended when Sears accepted an FTC consent order announced on October 21, 1976. Arthur M. Wood, the chairman and chief executive officer of Sears, maintained that the violations of FTC standards that surfaced during the FTC hearings were also violations of Sears policy, and he expressed regret that even one such incident had occurred.

Impact of Event

The Sears claim that its policies were not responsible for bait-and-switch incidents was later vindicated to some extent. Although the original FTC complaint sought to prevent Sears from using sales quotas or employee discipline and retention methods that discouraged sales of advertised merchandise, the consent order did not address these issues. Furthermore, Sears agreed to the consent order for settlement purposes only; in other words, the consent order did not imply an admission by Sears that the law had been violated as detailed in the original FTC complaint.

The FTC consent order required Sears to cease and desist from several practices. First, Sears was precluded from making any oral or written representations concerning the sale of major home appliances when the representations were not bona fide offers to sell such appliances. Second, the company was directed to prevent the disparagement of any major home appliance that was advertised or offered for sale. Third, the demonstration or display of any advertised major home appliance was prohibited if such demonstration was designed to make the appliance appear defective. Fourth, Sears could not allow any false, misleading, or deceptive comparisons between the advertised products and other goods in the same product line. Fifth, Sears was required to ensure that sufficient quantities of advertised products were available to each store to which the advertisement applied, so that reasonably anticipated demands could be met. Sixth, Sears was mandated to maintain records of any local advertisement of its products for a period of three years following the date of publication of the advertisement. These records were required to document inventories, prices, and sales volumes on advertised products that had two or more models in their product lines and had a retail cost of $100 or more.

Sears also was required to display the following notice clearly in each of its advertisements that offered a product at a stated price: "Each of these advertised items is readily available for sale as advertised." The company was further required to post a copy of its printed advertisements and the preceding notice at a conspicuous place in each store, for the entire period to which the advertisements applied. If radio or television advertisements were used, the firm was required to post a copy of the text of the advertisement and the availability notice.

The bait-and-switch incidents generated unwelcome publicity for Sears. It is fruitful to probe the reasons for their occurrence despite company policy that disavowed such practices. Clearly, the problem was symptomatic of something fundamentally wrong at Sears in the 1970's. The traditional Sears policy of keeping inventories as low as possible may have contributed to the problem, as did incentives built into the compensation of salespeople, who could be swayed toward bait-and-switch behavior by the prospect of higher sales commissions that accompanied the sale of higher-priced merchandise. One analyst noted that many salespeople were angry with Sears management over their compensation. Their pay had kept pace neither with that of other Sears employees (only noncommission store personnel were given an across-the-board pay increase in 1974) nor with the cost of living. Although salespeople were paid a 6 percent commission, appliance sales during the 1970's had fallen to modest levels after impressive growth in postwar decades. When sales were slow, Sears allowed salespeople to take advances against future sales commissions, but they were sometimes fired if their later performance failed to neutralize such debt. This practice may have exerted pressure on salespeople and encouraged bait-and-switch tactics.

A final explanation for the bait-and-switch problem centers on the administrative structure at Sears. Because the company was very decentralized in the 1970's, Sears headquarters had limited ability to effectively control and enforce its policies on stores in remote locations. Despite government threats of sanctions, senior management may have been unable to stop the practices. Power had been ceded downward from level to level, from territory to group to store. Corporate officers in Chicago and heads of territories were unable to make local store managers do much of anything. The embarrassing and unfortunate bait-and-switch incidents conveyed a simple, uncomfortable, and dramatic irony: Although Sears grew into a behemoth in the U.S. retailing industry through a long tradition of customer orientation, its customer credibility in the mid-1970's was somewhat blemished by its very size and the attendant problem of ineffective managerial control.

As one of the most prominent cases taken on by the FTC in the early 1970's, the Sears case drew attention to one particular type of deceptive sales tactic. The publicity surrounding the case drew consumer attention, increasing awareness and therefore forcing retailers of all types to conform to the intent of the law. The case itself was one part of the increasing trend toward consumer protection and consumer activism.

Bibliography

"Federal Trade Commission Complaints and Orders 1973-1976." In *Trade Regulation Reporter*. Chicago: Commerce Clearing House, 1976. Summarizes the FTC complaint against Sears.

"Federal Trade Commission Complaints and Orders 1976-1979". In *Trade Regulation Reporter*. Chicago: Commerce Clearing House, 1979. Summarizes the FTC consent order in connection with the earlier complaint against Sears.

Katz, Donald R. *The Big Store: Inside the Crisis and Revolution at Sears*. New York: Viking, 1987. This book is unique in that it offers an inside look at the way Sears faced challenges and changes in its operational environment.

Weil, Gordon L. *Sears Roebuck, U.S.A.* New York: Stein and Day, 1977. An informative account of the growth of Sears, Roebuck. Contains a summary description of the bait-and-switch incidents.

Worthy, James C. *Shaping an American Institution: Robert E. Wood and Sears, Roebuck*. Urbana: University of Illinois Press, 1984. Analyzes the culture, values, and history that shaped Sears during the thirty years of Wood's stewardship. Offers insights into the managerial and leadership style of Wood, who was one of the chief architects of Sears' growth and dominance in the U.S. retail industry. The author's narration often reflects a positive bias toward Sears.

Siva Balasubramanian

Cross-References

Catalog Shopping by Mail Proliferates (1900's), p. 6; Advertisers Adopt a Truth in Advertising Code (1913), p. 229; The Federal Trade Commission Is Organized (1914), p. 269; Sears, Roebuck Opens Its First Retail Outlet (1925), p. 487; The Wheeler-Lea Act Broadens FTC Control over Advertising (1938), p. 775.

MURDOCH EXTENDS HIS MEDIA EMPIRE
TO THE UNITED STATES

Category of event: Foundings and dissolutions
Time: December, 1976
Locale: New York, New York

By purchasing The New York Post, *Rupert Murdoch extended his successful tabloid style of newspaper publishing from London and Australia to the United States*

Principal personages:
RUPERT MURDOCH (1931-   ), a newspaper magnate
DOROTHY SCHIFF (1903-1989), the owner and publisher of The New York Post who sold it to Murdoch
OTIS CHANDLER (1927-   ), the longtime head of newspaper operations for the Times Mirror Company
GEORGE E. McDONALD, the president of the Allied Printing Trades Council
WILLIAM KENNEDY, the president of the Pressmen's Union

Summary of Event

In December, 1976, newspaper magnate Rupert Murdoch purchased *The New York Post* for $30 million from Dorothy Schiff. Murdoch's premise in purchasing an American newspaper was founded on his previous success in publishing mass circulation newspapers. If his tabloid approach to journalism was successful in London and Australia, he believed, it should also be successful in the United States. Murdoch's purchase created an international and transatlantic newspaper connection, one that rankled the established newspaper world of New York City and created contention in other parts of the United States. The U.S. publishing community generally opposed Murdoch's incursion, partly because of his aggressive dealings in purchasing newspapers and expanding his paper kingdom and partly because of his tabloid format, which sensationalized the news and relied heavily on pictures. His formats were far removed from those of such major newspapers as *The New York Times* and *The Christian Science Monitor*, along with most other New York newspapers.

British journalist Anthony Smith, writing in *The Nation*, described Murdoch's approach as an unceasing flow of titillation, sensationalism, and voyeuristic excitement, devoid of information. Edwin Diamond later suggested in the same publication that Murdoch seemed unconcerned with the conventional standards of taste imposed by advertisers aiming at an educated middle-class audience. A journalistic variant of Gresham's Law appeared to be at work, in which newspaper publishers believed that bad journalism drives out good journalism. Murdoch believed that newspapers do not create taste, they merely reflect it.

Murdoch's American Advertising Agency comprised a team that often repeated, "You've got to hit 'em hard, mates, hard," referring to the readers. Soon, Murdoch realized why his formula was not working in New York City as well as it did in London: The United States did not have the same sharply divided class structure. In 1977, Murdoch was asked in an interview whether his "cheeky working-class formula" was applicable to New York. Murdoch replied that New York City was middle-class and did not have a working class.

Lines of battle between Murdoch and the rest of the New York newspaper establishment were drawn even more sharply when the pressmen struck in 1978. George E. McDonald was president of the Allied Printing Trades Council, the coordinating group to which nine of the ten newspaper unions belonged. He was also the president of the Mailers' Union. William Kennedy was the president of the Pressmen's Union.

Murdoch was serving as the president of the Publishers Association of New York City. Following a breakdown in negotiations, McDonald suggested bringing in Theodore Kheel as a mediator. Most of the principals in the strike opposed bringing in Kheel. Kennedy, the president of the Pressmen's Union, feared that Kheel would be the middleman in a cabal of publishers and unions other than his. The publishers were wary because the peace Kheel had brought in past strikes had come at a high price. Joseph Barletta of the *Daily News* had vetoed Kheel as a mediator in a Newspaper Guild strike at his paper the previous June. Distrust among the principals caused an early deterioration.

Meanwhile, McDonald planned a strike by his mailers' union against the already struck newspapers as a means of giving himself sufficient direct involvement to call for Kheel's designation as mediator. Once Kheel was called in as mediator for the mailers' union, McDonald thought it would be natural for him to mediate the pressmen's strike. Instead, Kheel suggested that he enter negotiations as an adviser rather than as a mediator. Kenneth Moffett, deputy director of the Federal Mediation Conciliation Service in Washington, D.C., thought that Kheel could be a positive influence. A controversy occurred when Murdoch learned of a private meeting between Kheel and Walter E. Mattson, executive vice president and general manager of *The New York Times*. Murdoch was enraged because this meeting was contrary to the understanding he had when he became president of the Publisher's Association. The original understanding was that none of the principals would discuss the terms of a settlement with anyone outside the group except by mutual agreement, and that Murdoch would be the central figure in all such moves. After a series of meetings and misunderstandings, Murdoch made a separate pact with the union and abandoned the bargaining table. He launched a Sunday edition of *The New York Post*, complete with a television supplement similar to one that the *Daily News* had been quietly planning. Murdoch thus expanded his subscriber base while other papers suffered from strikes. After the strike was settled, the *Daily News* went on a campaign to bury Murdoch by going after his subscribers and advertisers in an effort to win them away from Murdoch and thus bring down his expanding newspaper kingdom. Joseph Barletta stated in a 1979 interview that newspaper publishing in New York is not an "old boys' club," but that if Murdoch was going to be a street fighter, the establishment could play his game.

By 1979, Murdoch still had only a small share of total U.S. newspaper revenues as well as a small portion of U.S. newspaper holdings. His sprawling international media empire annually grossed close to $600 million, netted more than $45 million after taxes, and sold two and a half billion copies of ninety-two publications, mainly in Australia and Great Britain. His American properties included *The New York Post*, the weekly *Star*, two papers in San Antonio, Texas, and *The Village Voice*. The Gannett Company during the same period published seventy-seven newspapers in thirty states, dwarfing Murdoch's American holdings. The Times Mirror Company, publisher of the *Los Angeles Times*, made three times as much money as Murdoch's entire empire. Otis Chandler, head of newspaper operations for that company, stated that he was waiting to see how long it would take for Murdoch to fail in the United States.

Rather than fail, Murdoch continually analyzed his losses and adjusted the formats of his papers. Although tabloids such as *The National Enquirer* existed prior to Murdoch's arrival on the scene, those papers had gradually changed to adjust to the market. Murdoch also adjusted. After his use of lurid headlines pertaining to the Son of Sam murders in *The New York Post*, the Murdoch formula declined in the United States. Murdoch knew he had to adapt. By 1979, *The New York Post* began to display upgraded quality, even though it still featured crime, scandals, gossip, and occasional bouts of hysteria. The paper now carried a solid financial section and reported more international and metropolitan news. American newspaper publishers also learned from Murdoch. He was becoming part of the American newspaper establishment.

Impact of Event

When Murdoch bought *The New York Post* from Schiff in 1976, the initial reaction from the newspaper establishment was fear that the Murdoch format of sensationalism would squeeze out the more conservative papers that appealed to the middle and upper classes. Publishers also objected to his agressive style of acquisitions. His style and format precipitated a "bury Murdoch" campaign. The Gannett Company, a complex of publications, organized an effort to identify and reclaim every subscriber who had switched to the *Post*.

Murdoch drew criticism and animosity while generating fear among the established newspaper publishers. His aggressive manner in acquiring newspapers was abhorred, and his tabloid format caused fear among more established publishers that the quality of the newspaper world was going downhill. Some observers believed, however, that American newspapers were becoming more elitist. Murdoch offered choices by offering another style of journalism. His presence in the American market worked in two ways. Murdoch continued to adapt his style in order to make his newspapers sell, and the established media had to scramble to maintain their subscription lists. At the same time that Murdoch was becoming Americanized, he prompted action in response to his style. Other publishers had to react, going after potential subscribers in a shifting demographic environment and making other changes in their publishing operations. Many of the changes should have been made twenty years earlier. Murdoch's entry into U.S. publishing made his new competitors move faster.

Murdoch's News International Company encompassed holdings in England, Australia, and the United States, resulting in an international press network different from any in the past. Murdoch kept a tight rein on every phase of his publishing empire, compared to the American style of departmental authority. Murdoch passed judgment on his publications in every department rather than assigning authority in the various phases of publishing. He even brought in American editors to replace some of his overseas editors.

Murdoch's ownership of *The New York Post* from 1976 to 1988 was marked by flamboyance. Abe Hirschfeld acquired the *Post* in 1988. By 1993, *The Wall Street Journal* and *The New York Times* were carrying news of its bankruptcy and a subsequent bid by Murdoch to take over the newspaper once again.

A 1990 article in *The Economist* featured Murdoch's News Corporation, describing how nobody had exploited the booming media industry of the late 1980's better than Murdoch. In addition, few had borrowed more money to do it. Murdoch's willingness and ability to borrow money gave him opportunities unavailable to most others. Newspaper articles on his bids and holdings show years of being deeply in debt, but he always managed eventually to show a profit. Murdoch continued, into the 1990's, to make bids to purchase media holdings including newspapers, magazines, and radio and television stations throughout the world.

Bibliography

Diamond, Edward. "Low Road to Oblivion: Murdoch and the *Post*." *The Nation* 230 (May 24, 1980): 615-617. Explains what was often cited as Murdoch's "S" formula: scare headlines, sex, scandal, and sensation, with a fifth "S" for New York—Studio 54 people. Explains the ups and downs in readership of the *Post*. Also explains how the newspaper shutdown of 1978 helped create a *Post* monopoly until the strike was over.

Gottlieb, Martin. "Cuomo Backs Murdoch's Bid for Post." *The New York Times*, March 25, 1993, p. B1. New York Governor Mario Cuomo says Rupert Murdoch is *The New York Post*'s only hope for survival.

Kennedy, Carol. "Tough Guy in the Gentlemen's Club." *Maclean's* 94 (March 2, 1981): 10. Contains theories about why Rupert Murdoch became so aggressive, suggesting that he tried to live up to his father's reputation as a respected newspaperman. Also contains viewpoints of Murdoch's executives.

Raskin, A. H. "A Reporter at Large, II: Intrigue at the Summit." *The New Yorker* 54 (January 29, 1979): 56-85. An in-depth report about the personalities involved in the pressmen's strike of 1978.

Reilly, Patrick M. "Murdoch to Offer Interim Proposal to Acquire Post." *The Wall Street Journal*, March 26, 1993, p. B7. Describes Murdoch's submission of a plan to a federal bankruptcy judge for the purchase of *The New York Post*.

Tuccille, Jerome. *Rupert Murdoch*. New York: D. I. Fine, 1990. Describes Murdoch as standing at the center of a communications revolution that is reshaping ways of receiving information. Describes his media empire and the deals that created it.

Welles, Chris. "The Americanization of Rupert Murdoch." *Esquire* 91 (May 22, 1979): 51-59. Explains how Murdoch created such intense animosity in such a short time. He brought his own "game rules" with him, but his rules and those of the newspaper establishment changed and to some extent meshed.

Corinne Elliott

Cross-References

Reader's Digest Is Founded (1922), p. 390; Henry Luce Founds *Time* Magazine (1923), p. 585; *The Saturday Evening Post* Publishes Its Final Issue (1969), p. 1379; The Cable News Network Debuts (1980), p. 1768; *USA Today* Is Launched (1982), p. 1842; The Fox Television Network Goes on the Air (1986), p. 1928.

KOHLBERG KRAVIS ROBERTS PIONEERS THE LEVERAGED BUYOUT

Category of event: Mergers and acquisitions
Time: 1977
Locale: New York, New York

By executing its first leveraged buyouts, Kohlberg Kravis Roberts ushered in an era of debt-financed acquisitions that enabled many businesses to remain viable but led to the use of risky securities

Principal personages:

JEROME KOHLBERG, JR. (1925-   ), the original principal of Kohlberg Kravis Roberts

HENRY R. KRAVIS (1944-   ), a partner in Kohlberg Kravis Roberts

GEORGE R. ROBERTS (1944-   ), the third partner in Kohlberg Kravis Roberts

MICHAEL MILKEN (1946-   ), a bond trader at Drexel Burnham Lambert who was convicted of violations of security law

Summary of Event

In early 1977, Kohlberg Kravis Roberts (KKR), a newly formed investment banking firm, acquired three small firms, A. J. Industries, U.S. Natural Resources, and L. B. Foster. Although these transactions were comparatively small in size, they were important as the first leveraged buyouts (LBOs) executed by a specialized investment banking firm.

KKR was designed as a different type of investment banking firm, a "boutique" whose only service was LBOs. The principals—Jerome Kohlberg, Jr., Henry R. Kravis, and George R. Roberts—had worked together at Bear Stearns, a leading full-service Wall Street investment banker. While at Bear Stearns, Kohlberg had learned to execute financing packages known at the time as "bootstraps." In essence, a bootstrap raised cash based on a firm's assets and its ability to service the debt taken on as part of the transaction. Through this process—some called it "financial engineering"—the management of the company was able to maintain control, take partial ownership, and eventually cash in.

In 1965, Kohlberg arranged his first bootstrap at Bear Stearns, a $13.8 million transaction involving a producer of precious metals, I. Stern. This arrangement was eminently successful, ultimately providing management and investors with a return nearly eight times the original investment. Kohlberg followed up on this first success by arranging three more bootstraps in 1966. In 1969, he did another, this time assisted by two young investment bankers, Kravis and Roberts, who would become his partners.

In 1972, the trio pulled off another such transaction, which because of its extensive use of debt had by this time become commonly known as a leveraged buyout. This

LBO of a major Singer Corporation subsidiary represented a milestone in that it transformed a subsidiary of a publicly traded corporation into a private company.

As Kohlberg and his young associates continued to execute more transactions into the mid-1970's, they recognized that they had uncovered a major market opportunity. The conglomerate craze of the 1960's had resulted in numerous smaller companies being acquired by major corporations without much concern as to markets or other synergisms. During the 1970's, many of these conglomerates took the advice of consultants who recommended that they divest these "underperforming" divisions about whose businesses they knew little. The trio also recognized that through their innovative LBOs, they were producing far more income than were other Bear Stearns partners. This fact began to grate on them, especially since they were considered mavericks by many within the staid firm. Kohlberg developed a plan for setting up a separate business, which Kravis and Roberts elected to join.

On May 1, 1976, Kohlberg Kravis Roberts officially opened for business in New York City. Other than an interest in LBOs and tennis, the new partners had little in common. Although all three were of Jewish heritage, only Kohlberg had any significant religious background. His personal and ethical values came largely from his college experience at Swarthmore College, an institution associated with the Quakers. Kohlberg came to value the principles of tolerance and selflessness espoused by Quakerism that he had not found through his own religion. In contrast, Kravis and Roberts had attended more secular colleges that did not provide this type of experience.

At first, this disparity of values did not hamper the young organization. All three recognized that they were now on their own and needed to execute a few modest deals to become a viable firm. They agreed to start at salaries of $50,000 each, modest by New York financial standards in the 1970's.

Although the young firm had little difficulty identifying solid companies worthy of purchase, obtaining financing was a significant challenge. The concept of a leveraged buyout was still new, and the investment returns the partners claimed to have earned while at Bear Stearns seemed too good to be true. Insurance firms and banks were especially difficult to convince, but after several months of trying, Kohlberg's quiet demeanor and years of experience began to convince the skeptics.

It was with this background that KKR executed its first transactions in early 1977. The immediate effect was of only moderate significance, but the longer term impact and the implications were much more dramatic, setting the stage for an entirely new financial era in the 1980's.

Impact of Event

Although the KKR partners recognized the value of what they had initiated, the financial world was not yet ready to follow. During its second year, KKR executed no buyouts. Skeptics continued to dispute the concept that a buyout improved management's motivation to perform.

In mid-1978, Kohlberg's low-key approach began to bear larger fruit. Goldman

Sachs, a major investment banker, put KKR in touch with Jerry Saltarelli, the chief executive officer (CEO) of Houdaille, Inc., a large conglomerate. Considering alternative avenues to his retirement, the CEO refused to consider merger with another conglomerate, since he would be left with stock but little control.

By this time, KKR had established a set of principles it believed were conditions for a successful buyout. The company needed a long-established, predictable cash flow, clearly sufficient to service the debt produced by the LBO. Better candidates had usable, fully depreciated fixed assets that would cost significantly more to replace than they had cost to purchase. The best candidates operated in mature markets, in which technological upheavals were unlikely, and were relatively free of debt prior to buyout. Finally, the company needed a strong management team, all or most of whom would stay on to maintain continuity. Houdaille appeared to fit all these conditions.

In October, 1978, Houdaille and KKR went public with their plans to form an investor group to purchase all of Houdaille's shares at more than double the current market price. This was clearly a "make or break" deal for KKR, since a publicly traded firm had never gone private through a leveraged deal. Much of Wall Street was skeptical, with the result that Houdaille stock traded well below the offer price into early 1979. Only when Houdaille announced consummation of the $335 million deal did the market fully respond.

KKR's success amazed veteran Wall Street observers. The final deal incorporated a staggering array of legal instruments and participants, which included three banks, a major insurance company, and Oregon's state pension fund.

Following the coup in buying out Houdaille, KKR became an accepted "niche" investment banking firm. In 1983 alone, it purchased three more companies and initiated efforts to raise a $1 billion equity fund. As KKR successes continued, however, both internal and external problems arose. Externally, many Wall Street firms had come to accept the leveraged buyout concept, and, by 1985, many of them had established their own LBO departments. This move placed these new departments in direct competition with KKR.

Internally, the philosophical and ethical differences between Kohlberg and his younger partners began to emerge. KKR's original concept was that the partners should reap profits only when the other investors and management of bought-out companies did. In early 1984, Kohlberg had serious surgery and was absent from the firm for nearly a year. During this hiatus, Kravis and Roberts began to change the original philosophy so that KKR would make money regardless of how management and investors fared.

The combination of a more aggressive business philosophy and increased competition dramatically changed the LBO business. KKR found that it could now close transactions only by outbidding two or three rivals. This forced KKR to establish alliances with other investment banking firms to raise needed capital. A key alliance struck by KKR was with Drexel Burnham Lambert, a medium-sized investment banker.

In 1985, KKR offered to buy Storer Communications for $2 billion in the largest leveraged deal proposed at that time. When Comcast Corporation also made an offer for Storer, Michael Milken, a bond trader with Drexel, induced Ivan Boesky to invest some $9 million into Storer. According to a government indictment, this arrangement was accompanied by a secret agreement that any losses would be sustained by Drexel, not Boesky. Such an agreement violated security laws, and Milken was later sent to prison.

Clearly, KKR had gotten far away from its original values to execute deals. This change enraged Kohlberg, who by the time he returned full-time in early 1985 found himself powerless to reverse the new philosophy his younger partners had driven into KKR. In an emotional 1987 speech at KKR's annual investment conference, Kohlberg announced his resignation from the firm he had created. He formed a new firm, Kohlberg and Company.

Kohlberg's resignation had little impact on Kravis and Roberts. Although furious with Milken over the secretive Storer chicanery, KKR continued to use Drexel as additional opportunities arose. The most significant was the largest LBO ever transacted, the RJR Nabisco buyout in 1988. That transaction was valued at $29.6 billion.

By the end of the 1980's, KKR had acquired thirty-six companies at a cost of $85 billion. Although the volume of LBOs decreased in the early 1990's, the technique remained a viable option for many firms, especially for deals that could be executed without resort to high-interest "junk" bonds.

KKR itself continued as an extremely powerful enterprise. Its impact on U.S. financial history has been immense. As this fledgling firm convinced the rest of the Wall Street community of the viability of the LBO concept, it ushered in a new era. The original concept of LBOs was excellent. The idea that managements perform better when they are part-owners seems obvious in retrospect. When KKR and other LBO specialists deviated from their basic principles, however, they produced side effects, such as the Milken improprieties and indictment, that even the most ardent KKR executive would not defend.

From an overall societal standpoint, the LBO boom of the 1980's produced the most extensive indebtedness in corporate history. Some analysts believe that LBOs were to a significant extent responsible for the severe stock market selloff in October, 1987. Most conservative CEOs argue vociferously against the impact of LBOs, but not all observers agree that LBOs had negative effects on balance. Some writers contend that since indebtedness was limited to stable firms, the more cyclical firms that stayed away from LBOs actually became stronger. They argue that every postwar expansion has resulted in huge amounts of debt, so the 1980's were not an exception to be explained by LBOs. Others point out that LBOs enabled a number of large firms, Safeway being a major example, to survive, thus saving jobs.

The early portion of the 1990's provided a mixed business environment. Some sectors, such as the automobile industry, made major strides, while others stagnated. The debt binge of the 1980's had clearly abated, and "reverse LBOs" surfaced in several industries. At the same time, the LBO continued to be an important financing vehicle.

Bibliography

Bartlett, Sarah. *The Money Machine: How KKR Manufactured Power and Profits.* New York: Warner Books, 1991. This comprehensive volume represents the most thorough evaluation of KKR's legacy. Chapters most relevant to key issues include "Jerry" and "Early Days." The book is generally favorable to Jerome Kohlberg and his ethical values but generally unfavorable to Henry Kravis. The discussion of Kohlberg's early exposure to the values of Quakerism are particularly illustrative.

Faltermayer, Edmund. "The Deal Decade: Verdict on the '80s." *Fortune* 124 (August 26, 1991): 58-70. This article comments negatively on the LBO boom. It cites the decline in corporate cash flow following most transactions and argues that takeover threats siphoned valuable time away from corporate management. Excellent graphics and statistical analysis.

Fisher, Anne B. "Don't Be Afraid of the Big Bad Debt." *Fortune* 123 (April 22, 1991): 121-128. This article's thesis is that the LBO boom of the 1980's did not permanently damage the nation's competitive stature. Fisher points out that every prolonged postwar expansion has produced huge debt on corporate balance sheets. Critics claim that LBO managers tend to cut back on research and development; Fisher believes this is a naïve position.

_____ . "Employees Left Holding the Bag." *Fortune* 123 (May 20, 1991): 83-92. Describes the human impact of leveraged buyouts, with particular regard to buyouts in which workers became owners. Cites a number of examples of failure that resulted in numerous employee-owners losing their jobs. Deals mostly with Employee Stock Ownership Plans (ESOPs). Provides detailed descriptions of the human toll that sometimes results from the establishment of ESOPs.

Holland, Max. "Buyout (1979-1980)." In *When the Machine Stopped: A Cautionary Tale from Industrial America.* Boston: Harvard Business School Press, 1989. This chapter from a book focusing on the history of Burg Tool describes in detail the buyout of Burg's corporate parent, Houdaille, through the efforts of KKR. The annotated chapter also discusses much of the background to KKR's establishment as an LBO specialist.

Morgenson, Gretchen. "The Buyout That Saved Safeway." *Forbes* 146 (November 12, 1990): 88-92. Describes some of the positive impacts of leveraged buyouts. Focuses on the 1986 LBO engineered by Kohlberg Kravis Roberts that literally saved thousands of jobs. Comments favorably on KKR.

Pouschine, Tatiana, Phyllis Berman, and Mary Beth Grover. "The Takeover Game Isn't Dead, It's Just Gone Private." *Forbes* 146 (October 1, 1990): 63-74. Describes the "new" LBO model of the early 1990's, in which investment bankers executed transactions without the assistance of junk bonds. Discusses the trends in LBO volume, which—despite negative publicity in the national press—was down only slightly in the first half of 1990 compared to the same period of 1989.

Van Horne, James C. "Corporate Restructuring." In *Financial Management and Policy.* 9th ed. Englewood Cliffs, N.J.: Prentice Hall, 1992. Discusses, in syntax designed for sophomore or junior college students, the concept of the leveraged buyout and its positive and negative impacts. Also of value to readers, including businesspeople, who wish to see how academia treats the LBO issue.

Ralph W. Lindeman

Cross-References
Textron Initiates the Trend Toward Conglomeration (1948), p. 948; Pennzoil Sues Texaco for Interfering in Getty Oil Deal (1984), p. 1876; Insider Trading Scandals Mar the Emerging Junk Bond Market (1986), p. 1921; The U.S. Stock Market Crashes on 1987's "Black Monday" (1987), p. 1953; Drexel and Michael Milken Are Charged with Insider Trading (1988), p. 1958.

AT&T AND GTE INSTALL FIBER-OPTIC TELEPHONE SYSTEMS

Category of event: New products
Time: April, 1977
Locale: Chicago, Illinois, and Long Beach, California

With the installation of the AT&T and GTE fiber-optic telephone systems, the potential for high-quality, expanded telephone service was in place, as was the impetus to find other uses for the new technology

Principal personages:

JOSEPH H. MULLINS, the man responsible for the transmission equipment of the AT&T installation

MORTON I. SCHWARTZ (1934-), the man responsible for the optical cable splicing techniques used in the AT&T installation

BERT E. BASCH (1942-), the project leader responsible for GTE system design and installation

ROBERT B. LAUER (1942-), the project leader of the GTE optoelectronics group

WILL A. REENSTRA (1923-), the man responsible for installation of the AT&T equipment

HOWARD CARNES (1943-), a designer of the GTE system

RICHARD A. BEAUDETTE, a designer of the GTE system

WILLIAM POWAZINIK, the man responsible for the fabrication of the GTE light-emitting diodes

JOSEPH ZUCKER (1928-), the man responsible for the GTE optoelectronics devices

STEWART D. PERSONICK (1947-), the man in charge of measuring the quality of transmission and splice losses in the AT&T installation

Summary of Event

In April of 1977, General Telephone and Electronics (GTE) installed fiber-optic telephone service over a 5.6-mile path between a Long Beach, California, switching office and a local exchange in Artesia, California. Shortly thereafter, American Telephone and Telegraph (AT&T) switched on its own fiber-optic communications system under the streets of Chicago. The first fiber-optic public telephone systems were in place and operating, and their success or failure in providing reliable and economical expanded services would determine the fate of the infant technology of fiber optics and the divergent uses that might develop for it.

Developments in optical communication were minimal until the introduction of the laser. Charles Townes and Arthur Schawlow of Bell Laboratories proposed the concept of the laser as an intense light source in 1958, and by 1960 Theodore Maiman of Hughes Research Laboratory had succeeded in creating a functional laser. The most significant event leading to the establishment of optical fiber as a viable transmission medium was the publication of a paper in 1966 by K. C. Kao and G. A. Hockham of Standard Telecommunication Laboratory in England, in which they proposed that optical fiber could be used as a transmission medium provided that the loss in the fiber could be reduced to 20 decibels per kilometer. At the time, signal losses in optical fiber were typically about 1,000 decibels per kilometer, making the fiber almost useless as a transmission medium.

In 1970, scientists at Corning Glass Works achieved the manufacture of optical fibers with losses measuring less than 20 decibels per kilometer. With the advent of the laser as an intense light source and the development of high-quality optical fibers, the stage was set for researching the possibility of establishing a fiber-optic communications network.

Fiber optics refers to a technique for transmitting information that has been modulated with a light source from a laser or light-emitting diode (LED) along optical fibers. Light has a higher frequency on the electromagnetic spectrum than other forms of electromagnetic radiation commonly used to transmit information, such as radio waves and microwaves. Because of the higher frequency of light, a fiber-optic channel can carry much more information than can other means of data transmission. Optoelectronics is a discipline of electronics having to do with electronic devices that generate, detect, transmit, and modulate electromagnetic radiation in the infrared, visible, and ultraviolet parts of the electromagnetic spectrum. One of the basic functions of optoelectronics is to transform electrical pulses to light, then back again.

For the telephone companies, the pursuit of fiber-optic communication, over the short term, had a logistical basis. The appeal of fiber optics, in the light of increasing demand for telephone service, was that fiber-optic cable could go anywhere copper-wire pairs could go, so service could be expanded over established paths and over the same real estate. Some of the foreseeable economic and technical advantages of fiber-optic systems included longer distances between repeaters or terminals resulting from decreased signal loss, higher rates of data transmission because of greater available bandwidth, and freedom from the electromagnetic interference typical of a copper-wire environment.

GTE's Long Beach, California, fiber-optics system was designed and developed by GTE Laboratories Inc. of Waltham, Massachusetts. The pulse code modulation (PCM) equipment that provided the 1.544 megabits per second digital signals to the optical communications link was manufactured by GTE Lenkurt Incorporated of San Carlos, California. General Cable Corporation of Greenwich, Connecticut, developed the optical-fiber cable using fibers manufactured by Corning Glass Works.

The GTE system carried twenty-four simultaneous telephone conversations on two of six optical fibers. Although the total distance between switching offices was 5.6 miles, the fiber-optic cable was looped back on itself so that the total distance for the system spanned 21.6 miles, connected through eight repeaters. According to Lee L. Davenport, then president of GTE Laboratories, the success of the Long Beach,

California, installation proved that fiber-optic circuits are significantly quieter than copper-wire circuits and that it is feasible to use optical transmission systems on a permanent basis.

The installation of the Chicago fiber-optic system was a cooperative effort among American Telephone & Telegraph Company, Bell Laboratories, Western Electric Company, and Illinois Bell Telephone Company. The optical-fiber cable in the Chicago experiment contained two ribbons of twelve optical fibers each. The optical fibers were made by the Modified Chemical Vapor Deposition Process (MCVD), which was invented at AT&T Laboratories. Video encoders and other terminal equipment had been installed to enable the system to provide customer voice and data transmission, Picturephone Meeting Service (PMS), and interoffice trunk service. Most of the system's traffic was digitized and transmitted at the 44.7 megabits per second rate necessary to convey Picturephone video signals.

The half-inch-diameter Chicago cable contained two twelve-fiber ribbons. According to Joe Mullins, then head of the Bell Laboratories Fiberguide Trunk Development Department, a single pair of fibers could carry 576 conversations. One of the fiber-optic ribbons was used for commercial traffic, such as the transmission of voice, data, and video information. The rest of the fiber-optic lines were used for tests and measurements. The total distance of the Chicago optical link was about 1.6 miles.

The successful installation and operation of the Chicago system gave AT&T the necessary field experience that it would soon need for other fiber-optic installations. The success in Chicago convinced management that such systems were economically effective and led to lightwave trunk development that began in 1978 and resulted in the first standard commercial service in September, 1980. The Chicago project was also a precursor to a later AT&T commitment to lay the first transatlantic and transpacific fiber-optic cable systems, completed in 1988 and 1989, respectively.

The installation of the early fiber-optic telephone systems was the first step taken by two telecommunications giants toward the deployment of a new technology that had heretofore only been tested in the laboratory. This step signaled the beginning of a new era that would see changes in the way the world perceived the technology of telecommunications. Voice, data, and video transmissions were now riding a beam of light to their destination, instead of a copper wire. The success of the fiber-optic telephone systems was a major technological and historical event that opened the floodgate from which would be unleashed a torrent of entrepreneurial efforts taking advantage of the new technology.

Impact of Event

From its beginning with the experimental telecommunications systems in Chicago and Long Beach that demonstrated that it was technologically and economically feasible to combine electronic, laser, and fiber-optic technologies to create high-quality telecommunication systems, the science of fiber optics has grown and flourished. New telephone systems almost exclusively use optical fiber instead of copper cable, and old systems were upgraded. As of the early 1990's, only the final link

between the American home and the telephone branch exchange remained predomi-
nately copper-wire pairs. That also began to change, not because the telephone
companies wanted to provide subscribers with better-quality voice service, for
twisted-wire pairs offer excellent voice transmission to the home, but because other
services such as high-definition TV (HDTV) and data require high-bandwidth optical
technology or coaxial cable to carry the broadband signals. Therein lies a conflict
between the telephone companies and the cable television industry.

Most U.S. households have telephones and television sets. About one-fourth have
personal computers, and about half subscribe to cable television. Telephone companies have access to these homes by means of the twisted-wire pairs that connect to the
family telephone. Cable television companies gain entry by coaxial cable.

The Cable Act of 1984 prevents telephone companies from owning or operating
cable television businesses within their designated service areas. Free of any real
competition, the cable television industry experienced tremendous growth, and its
companies, for the most part, operated as unregulated monopolies. Seeing that the
cable television industry was no longer a small, struggling business in need of
protection from competition, the Federal Communications Commission (FCC) began
investigating the possibility of recommending the repeal of the Cable Act of 1984,
thereby allowing telephone companies to transmit television signals and enter into
competition with the cable television industry.

If the repeal of the Cable Act takes place, a race to provide optical fiber to the home
will begin. Huge profits can result from using high-bandwidth optical technology to
provide telephone service as well as high-definition television, data, and other services. Because coaxial cable is not an efficient conductor of electronic pulses over
long distances, signals traveling over it need to be amplified about every quarter mile.
Coaxial cable is efficient over stretches of less that three hundred feet when carrying
conventional video, but an HDTV signal would start to distort after only about one
hundred feet. Signals traveling over fiber-optic cable need reamplification only about
every thirty miles.

Telephone companies have the advantage of already having a fiber-optic backbone
installed for their communications networks but would have to bear the expense of
supplying fiber optics to the home if they are to reap the profits resulting from
customer demand for expanded services. Manufacturers of optical fiber and optoelectronics devices see tremendous potential profits in supplying the material necessary
to provide fiber optics for the local telephone loop.

The monumental quantities of information already traveling over fiber-optic telecommunications networks on beams of flashing light are blurring the distinction
between telephone voice information, entertainment systems, and computer data. It is
all simply digital data, ones and zeros. Those who would control this surging sea of
information are playing for high stakes. Losses could be staggering, but the rewards
could be in the hundreds of billions of dollars. To this end, alliances began forming in
the early 1990's among telephone, cable television, electronics, computer, entertainment, video game, and publishing companies that were destined to change the face of

television from a simple cyclopic box allowing the viewing only of programs that happen to be on the air to an interactive control center from which can be ordered selections from a huge library of movies, arcade-type video games, retail-store merchandise from video catalogs, and any program from five hundred television channels. Music, text, and instructional programs will also be available on demand. Many more innovative services were in various stages of development. Their implementation depended in large part on public demand and legislation.

Bibliography

Carey, John, and Neil Gross. "The Light Fantastic: Optoelectronics May Revolutionize Computers—and a Lot More." *Business Week*, May 10, 1993, 44-49. Looks at the fiber-optics revolution that essentially began with the deployment of fiber-optic telephone systems in 1977. Modern uses for fiber optics from medicine to aircraft wings are discussed.

Free, John. "Fiber Optics Head for Home." *Popular Science* 238 (March, 1991): 64-95. Discusses the many services that will be available in the home via fiber-optic lines.

Kuecken, John A. *Fiberoptics*. Blue Ridge Summit, Pa.: Tab, 1980. A well-written book that covers the history, basics, applications, and theory of fiber optics.

Leon, Jose C. de, ed. *Selected Articles from the GTE Lenkurt Demodulator*. San Carlos, Calif.: GTE Lenkurt, 1976. Several chapters cover events leading to the development of the concept of fiber optics. Light sources such as light-emitting diodes and lasers are discussed, as is the future role of optical communication in the telephone industry.

Noll, A. M. "The Broadbandwagon!: A Personal View of Optical Fibre to the Home." In *Telephone Company and Cable Television Competition*, edited by Stuart N. Brotman. Boston: Artech House, 1990. Noll discusses the impending conflict between telephone companies and the cable television industry over service to the home. Technical and economic issues concerning fiber-optic cable installation are viewed, and historical parallels of services are drawn.

Schwartz, Morton I. "Optical Fiber Transmission—From Conception to Prominence in Twenty Years: Emerging from Infancy into the Limelight." *IEEE Communications Magazine* 22 (May, 1984): 38-48. Includes a brief historical description of the evolution of optical fiber communications, a technical discussion of fiber-optic cable, and an overview of AT&T Bell Laboratories' fiber-optic field trials. Although some parts of this paper are slightly technical, the language is clear and very readable.

Schwartz, M. I., W. A. Reenstra, J. H. Mullins, and J. S. Cook. "The Chicago Lightwave Communications Project." *The Bell System Technical Journal* (July/ August, 1978): 1881-1888. A clear, readable description of the Bell System Chicago fiber-optic telephone system installation in 1977.

Waller, Larry. "Fiber's New Battleground: Closing the Local Loop." *Electronics* 61 (February, 1989): 94-96. An excellent article describing the conflicts between cable television and the telephone companies. Suggests solutions to some of the problems and discusses the costs and profits of providing fiber optics to the home.

Weinstein, Stephen B., and Paul W. Shumate. "Beyond the Telephone." *The Futurist* 23 (November/December, 1989): 8-12. Looks at innovative communications concepts that may drastically change the way people live.

Jose C. de Leon

Cross-References

Bell Labs Is Formed (1925), p. 470; Congress Establishes the Federal Communications Commission (1934), p. 685; Community Antenna Television Is Introduced (1949), p. 953; Electronic Technology Creates the Possibility of Telecommuting (1980's), p. 1733; AT&T Agrees to Be Broken Up as Part of an Antitrust Settlement (1982), p. 1821; The Fox Television Network Goes on the Air (1986), p. 1928.

THE ALASKAN OIL PIPELINE OPENS

Category of event: Transportation
Time: July 28, 1977
Locale: Prudhoe Bay to Valdez, Alaska

The trans-Alaskan pipeline between Prudhoe Bay and the port of Valdez, long delayed by environmental considerations, opened nearly ten years after discovery of a major oil field at Prudhoe Bay

Principal personages:
ROBERT O. ANDERSON (1917-   ), the head of Atlantic Richfield Company, the principal actor in both the discovery of oil in Alaska and the construction of the pipeline
THEODORE "TED" STEVENS (1923-   ), the primary spokesman for Alaska in the Senate
MORRIS UDALL (1922-   ), a congressman who was the most vocal critic of the pipeline in the House of Representatives

Summary of Event

The opening of the trans-Alaskan pipeline on July 28, 1977, represented a victory of energy considerations over environmental concerns and of technology over a bewildering array of problems. Tremendous problems had to be overcome in order to produce oil in the frozen wilderness of Alaska's North Slope and then transport it across nearly a thousand miles to an open port without disturbing, to any significant extent, the area's fragile physical and biological landscape.

The story of Alaska's oil begins with the creation of the Naval Petroleum Reserve on the territory's North Slope in 1923. The history unfolds essentially in three stages from that moment to the opening of the pipeline more than a half century later. During the first of these stages, which lasted until the 1960's, exploratory drilling in Alaska occurred intermittently, usually at times of projected oil shortages in the continental United States and usually more as a hedge against future shortages than as the first step in a massive commercial development of Alaska's oil wealth. Even if the technological difficulties in producing and transporting Alaskan oil could be solved, the costs involved would have made the product prohibitively expensive. The discovery of cheap oil in Kuwait and exploration of other rich oil fields in the Middle East during the late 1940's and early 1950's further dampened interest in Alaska. Exploratory drilling there slowed.

Changes in the world oil market during the late 1950's and early 1960's inaugurated the second period, one of growing interest in Alaskan oil that lasted until the "eleventh hour" discovery of oil in Prudhoe Bay in 1967. As the oil companies of the Western world began to lose the control they had exercised over the world petroleum market for half a century, particularly after the birth of the Organization of Petroleum

Exporting Countries (OPEC) in 1960, interest was rekindled in finding closer-to-home sources of oil. Meanwhile, steady increases in the posted price of oil during the 1960's closed the gap between the cost of producing Alaska's oil and the price that it could fetch on the world market.

During the mid-1960's, world oil prices increased. At the same time, world politics and the economic power of OPEC made the supply of cheap oil from abroad less secure. These conditions combined to lure an expanding number of American firms into exploratory ventures abroad and at home, chiefly along the Outer Continental Shelf. Among these adventurers was the Atlantic Richfield Company, later known as ARCO. Under the direction of Robert O. Anderson, one of America's last great oil wildcatters, Atlantic Richfield obtained the majority of the governmental leases then being granted for exploratory and developmental activity in Alaska. The company then began its search. Even after its initial well on Alaska's North Slope proved to be dry in 1966, Anderson pressed on with exploratory efforts. On December 26, 1967, in temperatures thirty degrees below zero, Atlantic Richfield struck a pool of oil that would eventually be estimated to contain ten billion barrels. This was the largest oil field ever discovered in North America.

Then came the third period, the most frenzied of all, in which Atlantic Richfield struggled for permission to build the pipeline necessary to ship oil from the often-frozen tundra of the North Slope to southern markets. While Atlantic Richfield was confirming the size of its find and evaluating its potential, environmental groups began to mobilize in opposition to the construction of any pipeline running south across Alaska's frozen landscape. Their hand was strengthened enormously by the Santa Barbara oil spill in 1969 and the National Environmental Protection Act (NEPA) passed in its wake, at approximately the same time that oil companies were requesting a federal right-of-way to build a trans-Alaskan pipeline. The NEPA required the United States Department of the Interior to prepare a justifying environmental impact statement before granting permission to begin any project likely to have substantial effects on the environment.

On March 20, 1970, the Department of the Interior sought to comply with the letter of the law by issuing an eight-page impact assessment that substantially downplayed the risk of environmental damage being caused by a Prudhoe Bay-to-Valdez pipeline. Within a week, a group of respected environmental organizations jointly sued the Department of the Interior for violating the National Environmental Protection Act. Three weeks later, a court injunction halted construction on the pipeline until such time as a definitive court ruling on compliance with the NEPA could be obtained.

The trucks and the half million tons of pipeline previously rushed to Alaska so that work could begin on the pipeline ultimately remained in storage for nearly four years. Two of those years were spent in judicial wrangling. On March 20, 1972, the Department of the Interior produced a nine-volume environmental impact statement to justify its approval of the pipeline's construction, but the injunction remained in effect until August 15 of that year, when the case was appealed to the Supreme Court. Then came the October, 1973, Arab-Israeli war and resultant Arab oil embargo on

Western countries that assisted Israel in that war. OPEC emerged as a cartel that was effective in controlling the price and production of oil. Almost overnight, the price of oil from OPEC countries quadrupled to nearly $12 per barrel. Opposition in Congress to the construction of the trans-Alaskan pipeline collapsed. A measure to approve the Interior Department's last environmental impact statement, relieve the Department of the Interior from further obligations under the NEPA, and approve the construction of the trans-Alaskan pipeline from Prudhoe Bay to Valdez was passed on November 16, 1973, less than a month following the announcement of the Arab oil embargo on shipment of petroleum to the United States. By April, 1974, the monumental task of constructing an environmentally friendly pipeline was at last under way.

Impact of Event

Almost every aspect of the production and transportation of oil in Alaska represented a technological and environmental challenge to the petroleum industry. Environmentalist groups that sought to block the development of Alaska's oil reserves were not entirely wrong when they claimed that the industry, when oil was first discovered at Prudhoe Bay, had lacked the technology to exploit the field without significant damage to the environment.

The environment of icebound Prudhoe Bay was unique in the oil industry's experience. Temperatures could drop to and remain at sixty-five degrees below zero for long periods in winter. The tundra would freeze solid. The layer of permafrost below the tundra could be as thick as a thousand feet. Steel pilings then in use for rig construction were useless.

Laying an eight-hundred-mile pipeline across the terrain posed equally taxing problems. Once thawed, the tundra took on a spongelike property and was thus unable to provide the stability needed for a pipeline. Except in winter, the ground could be extremely delicate, so delicate that even light trucks could easily disfigure it. On the other hand, laying the pipeline below the tundra posed serious threats to the permafrost itself. Unless precautions were taken, oil being pumped from wells would enter the pipeline at temperatures above 150 degrees. Oil rushing through the pipeline at that temperature could melt the permafrost.

Meanwhile, all along the stretch from Prudhoe Bay to Valdez, construction of the pipeline and the pipeline itself posed threats to the landscape as well as to the migratory paths of caribou and other animals. Environmentalists feared the damage that would be caused by construction crews as they worked and also questioned how animals would respond to the pipeline once it was in place. Subsequent shipment of Alaskan oil to California by means of tankers traveling from Valdez through Prince William Sound carried yet another set of environmental risks, as the 1989 wreck of the *Exxon Valdez* would underscore.

So formidable were the technological and environmental challenges confronting ARCO that its executives considered another pipeline route—one running across Alaska and then Canada to consumers in the American Midwest—as well as other options including shipment of oil from Prudhoe Bay by icebreaker-tankers. The

Valdez route was the shorter and generally less expensive option. In addition, because it did not cross national borders, it was also the option most in keeping with security-of-oil-supply concerns. Furthermore, it did not require negotiating tricky right-of-passage agreements with a foreign country that the trans-Canada route would have required. Nor was the Canadian route without environmental risks of its own.

At a cost of $7.7 billion, the pipeline was completed in 1977. Within a year, it was carrying a million barrels of oil per day from the North Slope to the port facilities in Valdez. Within another year, as a result of another international oil crisis and another doubling of the price of OPEC oil to more than $36 per barrel, investors in the pipeline were earning handsome profits. The principal remaining problems associated with the trans-Alaskan pipeline revolved around the problems of abundance.

By the early 1980's, the amount of oil being transported had doubled, stemming America's appetite for imported oil but also overwhelming California's ability to absorb the oil available for shipment from Alaska. Finding other outlets for Alaskan oil thus became an unforeseen inconvenience of the pipeline's success, but it was only an inconvenience. The brake placed on the growing flow of imported oil into the United States more than offset such unforeseen consequences of the shipment of Alaskan oil. Moreover, although the flow of oil from Alaska came too late to prevent a second oil crisis from occurring in 1979, it played an important part in contributing to the general decline in Western demand for OPEC oil. That decline in demand exerted such pressure on the cohesiveness of the OPEC organization that OPEC substantially lost control over the production rates of its member states and was powerless to prevent the virtual collapse in the posted price for a barrel of OPEC oil in the mid-1980's.

Bibliography

Anderson, Robert O. *Fundamentals of the Petroleum Industry*. Norman: University of Oklahoma Press, 1984. Slick, illustrated, readable, and informative, this work offers just what the title suggests: a guide to and history of U.S. and foreign oil industries, their on- and offshore operations, and the relationship between the worlds of oil and government. For beginners and general audiences.

Berry, Mary Clay. *The Alaska Pipeline: The Politics of Oil and Native Land Claims*. Bloomington: Indiana University Press, 1975. An insightful account of the impact of the Alaska pipeline on the development of the "two Alaskas," one of natives and one of oil.

Chasan, Daniel Jack. *Klondike '70: The Alaska Oil Boom*. New York: Praeger, 1971. Another good account of the impact of oil on Alaska, this time in the form of a very readable narrative covering the first days of the oil rush that followed Atlantic Richfield's discovery of oil.

Coates, Peter A. *The Trans-Alaska Pipeline Controversy: Technology, Conservation, and the Frontier*. Bethlehem, Pa.: Lehigh University Press, 1991. A good study of the confrontation between environmentalists and energy developers seeking to build the trans-Alaskan pipeline, examined in the context of a century of confrontations between environmentalists and developers over Alaskan resources.

Davidson, Art. *In the Wake of the Exxon Valdez*. San Francisco, Calif.: Sierra Club Books, 1990. An in-depth, often technical analysis of the spill of approximately ten million gallons of petroleum in Prince William Sound in 1989.

Dixon, Mim. *What Happened to Fairbanks?: The Effects of the Trans-Alaska Oil Pipeline on the Community of Fairbanks, Alaska*. Boulder, Colo.: Westview Press, 1978. Two years of field work produced a volume of considerable insight and a few surprises pertaining to the unintended effects of the pipeline's construction on life in Fairbanks.

Jorgensen, Joseph G. *Oil Age Eskimos*. Berkeley: University of California Press, 1990. A solid interpretation of the effect of energy development on one of the poorest groups of native Americans. Compensation for the oil on their Alaskan homelands later relieved poverty.

Yergin, Daniel. *The Prize: The Epic Quest for Oil, Money, and Power*. New York: Simon and Schuster, 1991. A massive study of the development of the international oil industry, with as much attention to the personalities and politics involved as to the historical events that marked the evolution of the petroleum industry in the modern world.

Joseph R. Rudolph, Jr.

Cross-References

OPEC Meets for the First Time (1960), p. 1154; Atlantic Richfield Discovers Oil at Prudhoe Bay, Alaska (1967), p. 1331; An Offshore Oil Well Blows Out near Santa Barbara, California (1969), p. 1374; Arab Oil Producers Curtail Oil Shipments to Industrial States (1973), p. 1544; The United States Plans to Cut Dependence on Foreign Oil (1974), p. 1555.

THE FTC CONDUCTS HEARINGS ON ADS
AIMED AT CHILDREN

Category of event: Advertising
Time: 1978
Locale: Washington, D.C.

The Federal Trade Commission's examination of children's advertising concluded that advertising to children was inherently unfair, but the commission did not mandate formal restrictions

Principal personages:
MICHAEL PERTSCHUK (1933-   ), a chairperson of the Federal Trade
    Commission
PEGGY CHARREN (1928-   ), a founder and leader of Action for Chil-
    dren's Television (ACT), a consumer group
DEAN BURCH (1927-1991), a former chairperson of the Federal Commu-
    nications Commission

Summary of Event

Prior to the early 1970's, most complaints concerning television advertising focused on adult-oriented messages. During the 1960's, advertisers acknowledged children as a special target market and began developing campaigns specifically geared to them. Parents, recognizing the potential impact that advertisers could have in the shaping of their children's values, began to organize and protest. The most visible and vocal protest group, Action for Children's Television (ACT), was formed in Boston, Massachusetts, in January, 1968, with Peggy Charren as its chairperson. Initially ACT focused on the content of television programming, but its attention soon shifted to the role of advertising. After attempting to influence the networks directly, by 1970 ACT turned to the federal government for assistance. In February of that year, ACT spokespersons met with representatives of the Federal Communications Commission (FCC) and presented a petition requesting that there be no sponsorship and no commercials on children's programs; that no performer be permitted to use or mention products, services, or stores by brand name during children's programs; and, as part of its public service requirement, that each station provide programming to children for at least fourteen hours per week.

The FCC, under the leadership of chairperson Dean Burch, was sympathetic to the group's concerns and asked for comments on ACT's proposed guidelines. The responses from sponsors and broadcasters were vehemently negative. The hearings did, however, prompt attention in the media. Simultaneously, a second group, the Council on Children, Media, and Merchandising (CCMM) focused specifically on food products aimed at the children's market. A founder of the group, a former member of the White House Conference on Food, Nutrition, and Health, testified that children's breakfast cereals provide little more than "empty calories."

Concern regarding the impact of television advertising to children continued to rise. By July, 1971, more than eighty thousand letters had been received by the FCC in support of the ACT proposals. Later that year, Commissioner Burch announced a permanent children's unit within the FCC. ACT, not content with relying on the FCC for action, turned to the Federal Trade Commission (FTC). The group petitioned the FTC to impose a ban on all television advertising to children for toys, food products, and vitamins. By the summer of 1972, the group began to meet with some measure of success. Three major vitamin manufacturers agreed to withdraw their ads aimed at children. In January, 1973, the national Association of Broadcasters announced changes in the Television Code that would prohibit hosts of shows from advertising to children and began to limit the number of minutes per hour of airtime that could contain children's advertising. In March, 1974, the Council of Better Business Bureaus established the Children's Advertising Review Unit.

By the mid-1970's, however, proponents of reform had discovered that although they achieved some isolated victories, major changes were difficult to attain. A series of proposals were submitted to the FTC and rejected by the broadcasting industry, and attempts to arrive at mutually agreeable guidelines were abandoned in 1974. In November of that year, the FCC issued a report at the conclusion of a three-year study. It noted that "broadcasters have a special responsibility to children" and that "special safeguards may be required" to protect children from the actions of advertisers. The commission did not, however, adopt any of ACT's proposals and actually decided against requiring specific changes in children's programming and advertising practices, expressing a preference for industry self-regulation. A lack of unequivocal research evidence on the impact of television advertising on child development was a major reason given for the decision.

Over the next few years, a stream of research studies focused on the impact of television advertising on the cognitive and emotional development of children. A 1977 National Science Foundation report reviewed policy-related statements from federal, industry, and consumer-group sources and developed a summary list of ten policy issues. This review, along with the results of scientific studies, was summarized and presented to the FTC. In 1978, the FTC published the *Staff Report on Television Advertising to Children*. This report called for a complete ban on commercials aimed at children too young to understand the true selling intent of the advertisements.

Under a series of Federal Trade Commission chairpersons (Miles Kirkpatrick, Lewis Engman, Calvin L. Collier, and Michael Pertschuk), the issue of advertising to children had received significant attention. In the early 1970's, the commission began taking action against advertisers, charging them with deceptive practices. In 1977, the commission proposed what would have been the most far-reaching and damaging set of regulations to date. The trade regulation rules, dubbed the "kidvid rule," would have banned all advertising to children on television at times when children in a particular age group composed a certain percentage of the audience (approximately 20 percent); banned advertising of products that contain more than a certain amount of sugar by weight; and required advertisers to sponsor health or nutritional disclosure messages in proportion to the amount of food advertising directed to children.

Concern over the effects of television advertising aimed at children can be traced to the early 1960's, when the National Association of Broadcasters (NAB) adopted a set of guidelines regarding the advertising of toys. Over the succeeding years, children's television advertising emerged as an issue of national concern.

Broadcasters and advertisers attempted to regulate their own business to avoid formal regulations on the part of government agencies. At the time of the FTC hearings in the late 1970's, there were at least two major voluntary codes that imparted recommended guidelines to advertisers.

The National Association of Broadcasters, in its advertising guidelines, recognized that children, especially those of preschool age, are highly dependent on the guidance and direction of the adult world around them. Since children, especially when unsupervised by adults, may not be able to judge the credibility of what they watch on television, the NAB thought that it was the ethical responsibility of the industry to protect them from their own susceptibilities. The NAB further recognized, however, that advertising to children can be an important source of information for children regarding not only specific goods and services but also many aspects of society and the world in which they live. This NAB code, presented in 1976, indicated that everyone involved in the creation, production, and presentation of advertising to children has a responsibility to ensure that such material avoids being exploitative of or inappropriate to a child's still-developing cognitive abilities and sense of value. The code then went on to state specific requirements regarding truthfulness, proper disclosure, the use of exhortative language, and the reflection of appropriate social values. The code made specific recommendations regarding certain product categories (such as toys, food, and clothing) and certain practices, such as special offers and the use of premiums and prizes.

The second code was proposed by the Children's Review Unit of the National Advertising Division (NAD) of the Council of Better Business Bureaus. The NAD was part of the self-regulatory mechanism created by advertisers, advertising agencies, better business representatives, and consumer groups. Its guidelines were predicated on five basic principles. First, advertisers should always take into account the level of knowledge, sophistication, and maturity of the audience to which their message is primarily directed. Children's limited capability for evaluating the credibility of what they watch should be considered. Second, children are imaginative, and advertisers should not exploit the imaginative quality of children. Third, advertising can play an important part in the education of children, and therefore information should be truthful and accurate. Fourth, advertisers were urged to capitalize on the potential of advertising to influence social values. Fifth, the prime responsibility to provide guidance to children remains with parents, and advertisers should play a role in fostering constructive parent-child relationships.

By 1977, it had become apparent that the issue of children's television advertising had become important both among a large segment of the populace and within government agencies. The nomination of Michael Pertschuk as head of the Federal Trade Commission by President Jimmy Carter heralded the administration's commitment to the issue. Pertschuk, through his involvement with the Senate Commerce Committee's hearings on the children's breakfast cereal market, had defined himself as a champion of the cause of child protection in the marketplace. He and his fellow commissioners launched an inquiry into advertising and children. The commission released its staff report in April, 1978. At the time, there was widespread disagreement among consumer groups regarding the scope of the problem and an outcry on the part of affected business constituencies, which charged Pertschuk with an antibusiness and proconsumer bias. Legal action initiated by a business lobby disqualified Pertschuk from voting on the issue.

In November, 1978, the FTC began hearings on children's television advertising. The commission called more than two hundred witnesses, in the most exhaustive hearing on the subject. Advertisers sensed that the "reasonably prudent" rule, which says that a commercial is not deceptive as long as a "reasonably prudent" individual could correctly evaluate the truthfulness of the claim, could be used against them, since a child could generally be classified as imprudent. In order to forestall formal restrictions, the television industry and advertisers stepped up their self-regulatory actions. Cereal companies reduced the sugar content of their products and began to emphasize nutritional qualities. The American Broadcasting Company announced a reduction in the number of its Saturday morning commercials. By early 1980, it became apparent that industry lobbyists had prevailed. FTC rule making was made subject to congressional veto without presidential intervention and "unfairness" as a criterion for judging children's advertising was dropped from the FTC's auspices. Arguing that marketplace forces can determine appropriate commercial levels better than could regulators, the FCC in 1984 rescinded all limitations on the amount of commercial content, whether directed to children or to adults.

Impact of Event

Research into the effects of television on children and the debate surrounding the issue continued. Senator Albert Gore commented in 1989 that if one were designing a hypothetical world, few people would support the idea of putting a little black box in every home, sitting every child in front of it, and then showing children twenty thousand messages a year to get them to buy something. That is, however, the situation facing children in the United States. Despite the intense attention paid to issues relevant to children's advertising, the government failed to ban or control the practice on any large scale.

Evidence indicates that the amount of advertising during breaks in children's programming increased during the 1980's. In addition, entire programs were built around products for children, including the "My Little Pony" and "Masters of the Universe" toys. Critics charged that these programs amounted to little more than thirty- or sixty-minute commercials for these lines of toys.

Children as consumers constitute three markets: a primary market, an influence market, and a future market. As a primary market, children spent more than $14 billion of their own money in 1991. As an influence market, children have demonstrated the power to influence parental decision making concerning more than $50 billion in purchases per year. Children also represent a future market for products. A common strategy for marketers is to reach consumers when they are young and to make them loyal for life.

Advertisers continued, and in many cases stepped up, their efforts to target children in the years following the 1978 FTC hearings. Television networks such as Music Television (MTV), Nickelodeon, and Whittle Communication's "Channel One" (on which children watched commercial programming in their classrooms) were developed with young consumers as their primary target market. Critics contended that some forms of children's advertising continued to be abusive. Particularly controversial was the role that commercial advertising plays in children's cognitive, attitudinal, and behavioral tendencies.

Some consumer advocates and lawmakers continued to press for stricter limits on what can be advertised to children and when. In many ways, the issues did not change. The major areas of controversy focused on the amount of advertising time aimed at children and on advertising in certain product categories such as food, toys, and alcohol.

In late 1987, the FCC launched a new investigation to determine if it should reconsider limits on commercial time in children's programming. It also reconsidered whether children's programs based on toys are actually "program-length commercials" and, if so, how they should be regulated. ACT and new pressure groups continued to lobby for action. The result of this pressure and the outcome of the investigation was the passage of the Children's Television Act in 1990. This act gave the FCC the power to enact new guidelines regarding the amount of advertising on children's programming. The act defined children as twelve years of age or younger. The act stated that broadcasters are legally required to demonstrate that they have complied with the statutory obligation to present educational and informational programming. The FCC was legally required to limit all commercial matter in order to protect the unique child audience and further required to hold broadcast licensees to the highest standard of responsible advertising practices. Congress stated that the Children's Television Act was passed in order to protect the nation's children from the excesses of commercialism and to nurture their minds through programming that not only entertains but also educates and informs. This legislation was enacted when it became apparent that self-regulation among advertisers and broadcasters would not effectively limit the amount or control the content of advertising aimed at children.

On January 2, 1992, the FCC enacted additional guidelines that limited per-hour commercial matter on cable and broadcast television to 10.5 minutes on weekends and 12 minutes on weekdays. Despite these restrictions, sales of commercial advertising on children's television programs remained strong. For the 1992-1993 season, $475 million to $500 million was expected to be spent on television advertising aimed at young consumers, an increase of almost 6 percent over the previous season. This continued increase in children's advertising is one of the factors used by advocacy groups that call for more stringent regulations.

Bibliography

Barry, Thomas E. *Children's Television Advertising*. Chicago: American Marketing Association, 1977. This eighty-page monograph addresses the key issues in the debate regarding children's television advertising. It contains the full text of several codes recommended by industry and consumer groups.

Kunkel, Dale, and Donald Roberts. "Young Minds and Marketplace Values." *Journal of Social Issues* 47, no. 1 (1991): 57-72. The authors provide a comprehensive review of the empirical research that has been done over the years on the impact of advertising on children's cognitive and emotional development. Tends to use technical jargon.

McNeal, James U. *Children as Consumers: Insights and Implications*. Lexington, Mass.: Lexington Books, 1987. The author examines the psychological development of children as they learn to be consumers. Attention is paid to the means by which advertisers target children and how children respond to their influence.

_____. *Kids as Customers*. New York: Macmillan International, 1992. In some ways an update of the 1987 book. This version is somewhat less focused on research and more oriented to management. Provides interesting insights on how marketers attempt to reach the children's market.

Palmer, Edward L., and Aimée Dorr, eds. *Children and the Faces of Television: Teaching, Violence, Selling*. New York: Academic Press, 1980. This collection of twenty-one articles addresses the issue of television's impact on children. Seven of these articles specifically address the impact of advertising and attempts to regulate the industry.

Ward, Scott. "Compromise in Commercials for Children." *Harvard Business Review* 56 (November/December, 1978): 128-136. Succinctly addresses the debate regarding children's advertising. The author summarizes the positions taken by both sides of the debate and presents an alternative to regulation based on research-based educational methods.

Andrew M. Forman
Elaine Sherman

Cross-References

The Federal Trade Commission Is Organized (1914), p. 269; Congress Establishes the Federal Communications Commission (1934), p. 685; Hasbro Advertises Toys on Television (1952), p. 986; The U.S. Government Reforms Child Product Safety Laws (1970's), p. 1426; The U.S. Advertising Industry Organizes Self-Regulation (1971), p. 1501.

VOLKSWAGEN OPENS THE FIRST FOREIGN-OWNED U.S. AUTO PLANT

Category of event: International business and commerce
Time: 1978
Locale: Westmoreland County, Pennsylvania

Volkswagen opened America's first foreign-owned auto plant in 1978 in order to preserve its U.S. market share as Japanese competition increased and production costs in Germany rose

Principal personages:

JAMES McLERNON (1927-   ), the president of Volkswagen of America, 1976-1982

HEINZ NORDHOFF (1889-1968), the Volkswagenwerk chairman who built a major automobile company from the ruins of World War II

RUDOLPH LEIDING (1914-   ), the chief executive officer of Volkswagenwerk, 1971-1974

TONI SCHMÜECKER (1921-   ), the chief executive officer of Volkswagenwerk, 1975-1981

Carl Hahn (1926-   ), the chief executive officer of Volkswagenwerk, succeeding Toni Schmüecker in 1981

MILTON J. SHAPP (1912-   ), the Pennsylvania governor who negotiated establishment of Volkswagen's U.S. auto plant

Summary of Event

In 1978, the West German automobile manufacturer Volkswagenwerk AG opened the first foreign-owned auto plant in the United States. The decision came as a response to rising manufacturing costs, resulting from unfavorable currency fluctuations, and the increasing threat of Japanese competition in the auto industry. Other countries, also eager to obtain larger shares of the U.S. car market and simultaneously avoid American import quotas, watched Volkswagen's experience with interest.

Volkswagen, West Germany's largest corporation, began its profitable history during World War II. Its single product, a small, inexpensive car called a Beetle, was introduced to the United States in 1949. Gradually redefining the American automotive scene, Volkswagen contributed about one-fourth of the 614,000 vehicles imported by the United States in the 1950's. The cars were also popular in The Netherlands, Australia, and Canada, as well as throughout Europe.

Export sales accounted for so much of Volkswagen's business that early on the company established foreign manufacturing plants to take advantage of low-wage labor, a move not followed by other automakers until years later. In 1950, South Africa began making Volkswagens out of components imported from Germany. Similar assembly began in Brazil in 1953, in Australia in 1954, and in Mexico in 1964. In

1955, Volkswagen bought a New Jersey manufacturing plant from Studebaker, hoping to assemble cars with a combination of U.S. and German parts. When the costs of the American components turned out to be higher than estimated, Volkswagen abandoned this effort before production could start.

Demand for the Beetle continued to rise. In the 1960's, the car held nearly 7 percent of the U.S. market. At the height of its success in 1970, Volkswagen sold roughly 580,000 vehicles in America, earning $112 million on $4.1 billion in sales. As the leader in automobile exports to the United States, the company unloaded a freighter full of Beetles—affectionately nicknamed Bugs—almost every day of the year from the corporation's main plant in Wolfsburg, Germany, and its other manufacturing sites.

There were several reasons for Volkswagen's popularity in the United States. The Beetle had a reputation for reliability, having been thoroughly tested during World War II and constantly refined and upgraded in subsequent years. The car's basic design never changed, because Volkswagen's legendary postwar chairman, Heinz Nordhoff, insisted that stylistic modifications be kept to a minimum. Nordhoff believed that this was an honest way to do business. It also reduced internal costs and kept the sticker price low. Clever advertising reinforced this approach. The car filled a need for a low-priced compact that U.S. auto manufacturers had long ignored.

In the early 1970's, however, the corporation suffered severe financial losses. The widespread economic growth that flourished in Germany in the 1960's decelerated. The work force at Volkswagenwerk had become excessively large, and German wages were among the world's highest. In addition, imported cars began to threaten Volkswagen's dominance in its homeland. The exchange rate between the German mark and the U.S. dollar rose 40 percent from 1969 to 1973, making Volkswagen unable to produce its cars for the same low cost, as a given price in marks now meant a higher price in dollars. The Beetle's retail price in the United States jumped 61 percent during this time period, from $1,799 to $2,895. The company lost a crucial competitive edge. In 1974, U.S. sales were 53 percent lower than the peak in 1970. Americans, seeing the variety of models offered by Japanese car manufacturers, grew tired of the steadfast Bug. Its quality had also declined, partially because of new emission control standards that forced redesign of the engine. U.S. automakers capitalized on these factors, introducing their own compact cars at prices below Volkswagen's.

To renew interest among potential customers, Volkswagen chairman Rudolf Leiding pushed the company to quickly develop a replacement for the Beetle in the early 1970's. Unveiled in 1974, the Golf left behind 1930's engineering and boasted a front-mounted, water-cooled engine and front-wheel drive. Leiding also attempted to establish a U.S. manufacturing base in order to preserve the diminishing American market. Volkswagen's supervisory board and labor representatives vehemently resisted this idea because of the company's $310 million loss the same year and the threat of displaced jobs.

Leiding ultimately resigned over this issue and was succeeded by Toni Schmüecker as chief executive officer in 1975. Formerly an executive for Ford of Germany,

Schmüecker, a diplomatic leader, convinced the board to approve a U.S. manufacturing plant to offset declining American sales. He estimated that an American-built Golf, called a Rabbit, would be 5 to 15 percent less expensive to build. In addition, the move would increase Volkswagen's competitiveness with Japanese automakers, who by then were the leaders in exports to the United States. In 1976, Volkswagen began examining prospective U.S. sites for the "breeding" of Rabbits.

The Wall Street Journal called the bidding war that ensued "the greatest industrial courtship of all time." Representatives from nearly every state east of the Mississippi attempted to lure the large German corporation, believing that its presence would bring jobs and an influx of cash into local economies. Volkswagen narrowed the choice to two sites, one near Cleveland, Ohio, and the other just southeast of Pittsburgh, Pennsylvania.

The Pennsylvania offer included a purchase option on an unfinished Chrysler plant and a generous incentive package developed by Governor Milton J. Shapp worth approximately $63 million. In May, 1976, Volkswagen officially announced the selection of this site, located in Westmoreland County near New Stanton. The company spent more than $250 million on the plant's conversion.

Former General Motors executive James L. McLernon was chosen as president of the newly created Volkswagen Manufacturing Corporation of America. Other American automotive executives were hired to complete the management team. Fifty thousand residents from surrounding counties applied for six thousand hourly jobs at the plant. In April, 1978, the first Volkswagen Rabbit rolled off the assembly line in front of a thousand delighted spectators.

Both the state of Pennsylvania and Volkswagen executives thought that this was the beginning of a mutually rewarding relationship. Problems that developed almost immediately, however, doomed America's first foreign-owned auto plant to disappointment.

Impact of Event

Volkswagen's American assembly plant, established to meet anticipated strong demand for the sporty Rabbit, produced its desired quota of 200,000 cars in 1980. For the most part, sales declined over the next decade. The company never achieved its targeted 5 percent market share. During the 1980's, the plant frequently was forced to shut down the line for extended periods in order to avoid surpluses. Problems with labor, quality control, marketing strategy, and competition from other U.S. manufacturers and growing Japanese firms kept Volkswagen from the success it had envisioned.

An adversarial relationship between workers and management resulted in several work stoppages during the first six months of operation. A wage disparity of $1.00 to $1.50 per hour between Volkswagen and the American Big Three (Ford, General Motors, and Chrysler) led to a wildcat strike by the plant's employees. Hoping to attract foreign manufacturers to the United States and demonstrate that stable labor relationships were possible under unions, United Auto Workers representatives negotiated a wage concession. This show of stability was less than convincing, however, as employees rejected the contract. Volkswagen management in Germany threatened to pull out. Finally, a fifty-cent raise was approved, but other downward adjustments were made.

Quality control problems with the early Rabbits tarnished Volkswagen's longstanding reputation for reliability, already shaken by the performance of the later Beetles. The first Rabbits tended to have mechanical defects, further hurting the brand's image of endurance established by the unstoppable Bug. Over time, Volkswagen was able to eliminate these kinks, but the initial reliability problems left the corporation vulnerable to competition from Japan. Lean production practices employed by Japanese companies led to quicker decision-making and problem-solving than occurred within the confines of traditional American or German industrial management. As a result, Japanese cars were rapidly gaining the reputation for high quality and appealing design that, at the same time, Volkswagen was losing.

The irreversible decline of the Rabbit had begun by 1980, when the American unit suffered a loss of more than $30 million. Attempting to boost sales, McLernon tried to tailor the car to the tastes of American consumers and changed its interior, headlights, and suspension. German executives criticized this decision for destroying the European mystique and contributing to the car's decline. In fact, however, much of the Japanese success can be attributed to a more calculated concern for determining consumer wishes. For example, Toyota and Honda updated models of their cars every two or three years. Volkswagen, on the other hand, imposed German styles on the United States market and saw little need for stylistic variations. The Rabbit's successor, basically the same car but renamed the Golf, was not introduced until 1983. Carl Hahn, who in 1981 replaced Schmüecker as chief executive officer upon his retirement, subscribed to Nordhoff's evolutionary approach to management. The seven-year-old Rabbit lost its appeal.

In the meantime, Japanese car makers looked to American plants like Volkswagen's as a way to avoid federal import quotas and to increase market share. In the early 1980's, Nissan Motor Corporation built a $500 million truck plant in Tennessee and Honda built a $300 million car factory in Ohio. By 1986, Toyota (through a joint venture) and Hyundai also operated North American assembly plants.

Volkswagen's initial hope of holding down prices through production in the United States was never fully realized. Although the domestic-built cars were roughly 5 percent cheaper than if they had been imported, their retail price was still about $500 higher than those of American rivals such as the Chrysler Omni and Ford Escort. By the time the retooled Golf replaced the Rabbit, its sticker price was about $9,000, $2,000 more than a Honda Civic. High manufacturing costs forced Volkswagen to relinquish the role it formerly played as a leader in the economy car class. Instead, its marketing division began emphasizing quality German engineering and technological sophistication, with limited success.

Sales of the Golf never soared in the United States. The introduction of a pickup truck and larger Jetta sedan later manufactured at New Stanton did not help Volkswagen regain its 1970 levels of popularity. In 1984, the hourly work force was reduced to fifteen hundred, producing only seventy thousand cars. Plans for a second American assembly plant were abandoned. By 1985, the Westmoreland facility had accumulated a $1 billion deficit, approximately $120 million in losses accruing each year. Confronted with declining sales and the increasing Japanese presence in the United States, Volkswagen officials announced in 1987 that the American plant would close.

If things ended poorly for Volkswagen in the United States, the outlook was different in other parts of the world. In 1986, the company acquired SEAT, a Spanish automaker. It began supplying parts for a luxury automobile built by Nissan in Asia and also signed an agreement to manufacture cars in mainland China. In addition, Volkswagen's dominance in both Mexico and Brazil continued despite high levels of inflation. Both of these countries exported Volkswagens to the United States, at a large cost savings to the corporation.

The plant's 1988 closing suggested that Volkswagen had failed to adapt its global strategy to the American market. Time-honored German managerial traditions made the firm incapable of responding to increased and intense competition in the auto industry and changing consumer preferences. The Japanese plants on American soil enjoyed greater success, despite some similar problems with labor and Big Three competition. Ironically, the Westmoreland facility was eventually taken over by Sony to produce television picture tubes. Although Volkswagen did not remain a major manufacturing force in the United States, its establishment of an American plant provided an example from which other foreign manufacturers could learn.

Bibliography

Ball, Robert. "Volkswagen Hops a Rabbit Back to Prosperity." *Fortune* 100 (August 13, 1979): 120-128. Provides a helpful rationale for the corporation's decision to manufacture Rabbits in the United States. Also gives biographical information about Toni Schmüecker and details about the company's product line, technology, and design plans.

Beaver, William. "Volkswagen's American Assembly Plant: Fahrvergnugen Was Not Enough." *Business Horizons* 35 (November/December, 1992): 19-26. An excellent article. Provides a detailed and informative account of the history of Volkswagen in America, including objective analysis of the company's successes and its problems. Includes a helpful reference list.

Dyer, Davis, Malcolm S. Salter, and Alan M. Webber. "Auto Competition in Europe: A Tale of Two Companies." In *Changing Alliances*. Boston: Harvard Business School Press, 1987. The chapter's section titled "The Trials of Volkswagen" provides a thorough account of the company's origins, rise to prominence, success, and decline. Clearly identifies the major players in the Volkswagen story.

Laux, James M. *The European Automobile Industry*. New York: Twayne, 1992. Traces the history of the automobile in Europe from around 1890 to the present. A good chronological account of the origins of businesses that have shaped this industry, including sections on the background and growth of Volkswagen.

Serafin, Raymond. "From Beetle to Bedraggled: Behind VW's Stunning U.S. Decline." *Advertising Age* 64 (September 13, 1993): 16-23. A good overview of the problems that plagued Volkswagen in the United States after its 1970 peak in popularity. Suggests that marketing and image remain the most significant obstacles to the brand's renewed success and recounts various advertising campaign strategies employed by the corporation.

"Why VW Must Build Autos in the U.S." *Business Week*, February 16, 1976, 46-51. Offers reasons for the company's venture onto American soil. Includes synopses of Volkswagen's competition, financial indebtedness, and employment practices. Also describes the position of other foreign car manufacturers as they observed Volkswagen's activities.

Alecia C. Townsend

Cross-References

Studebaker Announces Plans to Abandon U.S. Auto Production (1963), p. 1190; Ford Introduces the Mustang (1964), p. 1224; American Firms Adopt Japanese Manufacturing Techniques (1980's), p. 1716; Japan Becomes the World's Largest Automobile Producer (1980), p. 1751; The Loan Guarantee Act Saves Chrysler (1980), p. 1763; Yugo Begins Selling Cars in the United States (1985), p. 1898.

TRIGGER PRICES PROTECT THE U.S. STEEL INDUSTRY

Categories of event: International business and commerce; government and business
Time: February, 1978
Locale: Washington, D.C.

The trigger price mechanism provided temporary assistance to the U.S. steel industry as steelmakers attempted to withstand challenges from foreign steel suppliers

Principal personages:

ANTHONY M. SOLOMON (1919-   ), the head of an interagency task force that recommended establishment of a trigger price mechanism

EDGAR B. SPEER (1916-   ), the head of U.S. Steel and chairman of the American Iron and Steel Institute

JIMMY CARTER (1924-   ), the president of the United States, 1977-1981

Summary of Event

After nearly eighty years of global preeminence, the American steel industry began to lose its competitive strength in the 1950's as serious structural problems and heightened international competition threatened both profits and market share. Over the next two decades, internal problems further weakened the U.S. steel manufacturers. As important penetration into the U.S. steel market deepened, calls for increased protection of the once-mighty industry naturally increased. Thus, in February, 1978, following a report by an interagency task force, the administration of President Jimmy Carter introduced the trigger price mechanism (TPM) as a systematic protection device for the U.S. steel industry.

Termed an antidumping measure, the TPM pegged a reference price to 5 percent of the cost of production of the most efficient international steel supplier (Japan), plus 8 percent as a nominal profit plus transportation costs. Imported steel sold below the reference price was presumed to be "dumped" (sold at a price less than fair value) and would automatically trigger antidumping investigations that could lead to fines or increased tariffs. The increased risk faced by shippers and importers deterred low-priced steel imports in general and caused prices of steel that was imported into the United States to rise by as much as 10 percent, thereby allowing domestic steel firms to temporarily raise their own prices without risking further loss of market share.

The U.S. steel industry, once highly profitable and competitive, had deteriorated to a point at which its survival was threatened by imports. The industry's global dominance had been based on the existence of a large domestic and export market, international technological leadership, low-cost raw materials, plentiful skilled labor, capital adequacy, and significant economies of scale. During the 1950's and 1960's, such advantages began to slip away as a result of both the growing post-World War II global economy and actions by the U.S. government, U.S. steel manufacturers, and steelworkers.

One of the key factors in the decline of the U.S. steel manufacturers was the manner in which labor relations changed beginning in the 1960's. Prior to 1960, U.S. steelworkers were generally regarded as the most productive in the world. Because steel companies were able to easily institute price increases in order to raise wages, there was little cause for discontent on either part. As the steel industry began to encounter an increasingly competitive global environment, steelmakers became more reluctant (and, in fact, unable) to further raise steelworker compensation. In reaction, the United Steelworkers of America initiated the largest industrial strike in U.S. history in July of 1959. As a direct consequence of the strike, annual steel imports into the United States were greater than U.S. exports for the first time. The situation never reversed itself.

Eventually, the union and the steel industry reached a labor contract, but the damage had already been inflicted. The industry and its workers had entered into an adversarial relationship, leaving steel manufacturers to face compensation costs that were rising dramatically while the threat from foreign suppliers grew. In the 1950's, for example, average hourly earnings in the industry were only slightly above the average for all U.S. manufacturing employment, but by 1967 they stood at 128 percent of the manufacturing average. By 1978, they had reached 157 percent of average wages in manufacturing. Moreover, while wages rose steadily, value added per production worker failed to keep pace. Labor productivity in the U.S. steel industry rose 27 percent between 1970 and 1980, compared with about 85 percent in Japan.

Traditionally, the U.S. steel industry was able to survive such conditions simply by boosting prices. As modern steelmaking technology became available internationally, raising prices became increasingly untenable, since more and more steelmakers across the globe were acquiring the technology to manufacture quality steel cheaply. In addition, mismanagement and unwieldy corporate structures made it increasingly difficult for U.S. steel companies to attract debt and equity capital. Money to invest in research and development and in updated manufacturing facilities therefore was in short supply.

A final problem for the U.S. steel industry was the fact that the U.S. government, unlike most other national governments, had been only indirectly involved in individual business decisions affecting the steel sector. It did, however, play a significant role in setting prices and wages in the industry as a whole, beginning with the administration's threats to nationalize all steel firms under President Harry S Truman and continuing with pressure on prices in the early 1960's. Furthermore, strict governmental enforcement of environmental and worker health and safety standards dramatically increased costs for the steelmakers, while U.S. foreign aid helped Japan and Europe build modern, efficient steel industries. Essentially, the U.S. steelmakers suffered the hardships of government interference in economic decisions without having the benefit of access to public funds, as did many foreign competitors.

Thus, with a weakened U.S. industry needing to raise prices in order to survive, and with steel demand extremely price sensitive because of a weak global economy, foreign competitors in the 1960's and 1970's were able to grab a growing share of the

U.S. market. Steel imports had remained under 5 percent of the U.S. market in the 1950's. Prices of U.S. suppliers rose significantly above those of Japanese and European suppliers during the 1960's and 1970's, allowing steel imports to rise to 16.7 percent of the U.S. market in 1968 and reach a high of 18.1 percent in 1978.

Under such conditions, protection-seeking behavior in the United States intensified. In 1967, the major firms in the industry and the United Steelworkers of America forged an alliance to work on trade matters. Shortly thereafter, in 1968, Congress began considering legislation that would establish import quotas on steel. Considering the likely passage of such protectionist legislation, President Lyndon B. Johnson negotiated "voluntary export restraint" agreements, or VERs, with Japanese and European suppliers, effective through 1974. The agreements, which represented the first significant U.S. trade policy measure regarding steel, provided for import limits of 5.75 million tons in 1969 and increases of 5 percent in 1970 and 1971. The agreements eventually were seen as unnecessary and were allowed to lapse in 1974, during a world steel shortage.

In 1976, a substantial increase in foreign penetration of a depressed U.S. market prompted the U.S. industry to once again seek forms of protection. The Carter Administration, which was confronted with a substantial amount of pressure to deal with the situation, could not come up with a clear vision of how to aid the domestic suppliers without resorting to quantitative import restraints. In response, the American Iron and Steel Institute, led by U.S. Steel Corporation head Edgar B. Speer, first sought protection through a petition filed with the Office of the Special Trade Representative. Soon, however, steelmakers began to file individual antidumping lawsuits with the Treasury Department. In September, 1977, U.S. Steel brought an antidumping action against six Japanese suppliers in the largest antidumping action yet brought. As it became apparent that European mills also were dumping on a widespread scale, more than a dozen additional actions were filed by the end of the year.

The numerous actions effectively swamped the Treasury Department's ability to deal with the time-consuming and complex antidumping investigations. With five import-restriction bills pending in Congress, President Carter established a task force, headed by Under Secretary of the Treasury Anthony Solomon, to develop a solution. In December, 1977, the task force released the Solomon Report, which concluded that antidumping laws were too arcane to provide effective protection to the domestic industry. It proposed to rectify the problem with the trigger price mechanism, ostensibly an antidumping measure rather than a protectionist trade restriction.

Impact of Event

Pressured by President Carter, the U.S. steel industry accepted the TPM in February, 1978, and agreed to withdraw antidumping cases. Because U.S. producers thought they could compete successfully with Japanese mills if Japanese steel prices reflected true costs, the reference price was pegged to Japanese production cost. It was generally acknowledged that this would enable the less efficient European producers to sell in the United States at prices below their own production costs, but it was believed that such a development would not harm the U.S. producers.

By the spring of 1978, the TPM was in place. It was initially successful both in deterring imports and in forcing price increases on imported steel. Imports of steel, which had reached a high of 21.2 million tons (18.1 percent of the U.S. market) in 1978, immediately declined to 17.5 million tons in 1979. With U.S. producers operating at 91 percent of capacity, the domestic industry saw operating profits reach the highest levels in years.

Nevertheless, the TPM did not succeed in providing relief for long. Since imported and domestically produced steel could not be used interchangeably, the TPM caused average domestic steel prices to rise by only about 1 percent in 1979, not enough of an increase to provide the U.S. industry with a complete recovery. Moreover, the Japan-based reference price gave European firms more of an advantage than anticipated and eroded both the Japanese and the domestic share of the U.S. market.

These developments, together with an increase in the foreign exchange value of the dollar, prompted U.S. Steel to file a massive antidumping suit against European Community (EC) suppliers in March of 1980. In retaliation, the U.S. government immediately suspended the TPM, which had been designed to serve as an alternative to such blanket suits. Stimulated by threats of retaliation by the EC, the U.S. government and steel manufacturers reached an accord in October, 1980, that reinstated the TPM with significantly higher trigger prices as well as special provisions for quantitative import restrictions in the event of future import surges.

Despite the revitalized TPM, after an initial decline imports once again began to rise, influenced in part by a strong U.S. dollar on the foreign exchange markets. The strong dollar made it easier for foreign steel suppliers to sell steel at prices below the reference level. Some European suppliers began to sell steel in the United States at prices below the trigger level on the presumption that they could withstand TPM scrutiny. The domestic industry soon was operating at about 60 percent of capacity. At least ten major plants closed, and industry employment fell to 285,000 in 1981 from 403,000 in 1970. The steel industry's cries for protection once again arose, and threats of suits aimed at alleged subsidization of the industry in Western Europe and certain other countries reemerged.

Fearing yet another collapse of the TPM, the U.S. government itself initiated seven antidumping and countervailing duty investigations against European mills in November, 1981. At the same time, the government desperately tried to convince foreign suppliers to cut back their shipments and increase prices to the U.S. markets. In February, 1982, the seven largest U.S. steel firms filed 110 charges of unfair trading practices (with three million pages of documentation) against forty-one competitive steel suppliers in eleven countries. Those cases deemed to warrant investigations covered about $2 billion in trade, or about 20 percent of U.S. carbon steel imports in 1981. Once again, the TPM was suspended in retaliation as the investigations were initiated.

The EC reacted angrily, complaining of discrimination and harassment, and Japanese suppliers, no longer restrained by the TPM, immediately increased their shipments to the United States. By this time, it had become clear that the TPM was unable to provide any long-term protection for the domestic industry. Consequently, discussions were initiated in an attempt to reach a compromise with European suppliers. The U.S.-EC Steel Arrangement of 1982 was reached, setting limits for steel imports from the EC and voiding the antidumping investigations.

The collapse of the TPM convinced the U.S. steel industry that government intervention alone would not be enough to ensure survival and profitability. In response, capital spending and plant maintenance budgets were cut, nonsteel assets sold, white-collar staff reduced, nonunion salaries and benefits slashed, and major steelmaking facilities closed. Such moves signaled a substantial structural adjustment and slimming down by the U.S. steel industry, driven in part by the failure of the TPM to provide protection from imports in newly price-sensitive global and domestic markets.

Bibliography

Hogan, William Thomas. *Economic History of the Iron and Steel Industry in the United States*. Lexington, Mass.: Heath, 1971. Good source of background information concerning the development of the steel industry, though a bit dated.

Howell, Thomas R., et al. *Steel and the State: Government Intervention and Steel's Structural Crisis*. Boulder, Colo.: Westview Press, 1988. Provides an extensive look at the global steel industry and the development of modern trade practices and policies. Chapters on each of the major steel producing nations, as well as developing countries, are especially informative.

Jones, Kent Albert. *Impasse and Crisis in Steel Trade Policy*. London, England: Trade Policy Research Centre, 1983. An informative discussion of the development and resolution of conflicts in the steel trade. Provides a good look at government trade policy.

Tiffany, Paul A. *The Decline of American Steel: How Management, Labor, and Government Went Wrong*. New York: Oxford University Press, 1988. An informative and detailed report of the factors behind the decline of the U.S. steel industry. Useful because it provides a fairly balanced look at the many different factors contributing to the economic problems of the industry.

U.S. Federal Trade Commission. Bureau of Economics. *The United States Steel Industry and Its International Rivals: Trends and Factors Determining International Competitiveness*. Washington, D.C.: Federal Trade Commission, 1977. This staff report by the Bureau of Economics is a technical, in-depth examination of the economic structure of the U.S. steel industry.

Christopher T. Mark, Jr.

Cross-References

The Federal Trade Commission Is Organized (1914), p. 269; The United States

CARTER SIGNS THE AIRLINE DEREGULATION ACT

Category of event: Transportation
Time: October 24, 1978
Locale: Washington, D.C.

Although deregulation gave managers more flexibility to develop their business strategies, the subsequent shakeout in the airline industry underscored the need to avoid poorly planned rapid expansion

Principal personages:

JIMMY CARTER (1924-   ), the president of the United States who signed the Airline Deregulation Act

DAVID C. GARRETT (1922-   ), the president and chief executive officer of Delta Air Lines at the time of deregulation

ALFRED KAHN (1917-   ), the chairman of the Civil Aeronautics Board in the late 1970's, a chief advocate of deregulation

HARDING L. LAWRENCE (1920-   ), the chief executive officer and chairman of the board of Braniff Airways at the time of deregulation

Summary of Event

The Airline Deregulation Act of 1978 gave the airline trunk carriers more freedom to develop their business strategies by relaxing the constraints imposed by the Civil Aeronautics Board (CAB) under previous legislation. The term "trunk carriers" refers to major airlines that primarily serve large cities and high-density routes. In contrast, local-service carriers link small cities with large traffic centers. In 1978, the United States trunk airline industry consisted of eleven major carriers: American Airlines, Braniff Airways, Continental Air Lines, Delta Air Lines, Eastern Airlines, National Airlines, Northwest Airlines, Pan American World Airways, Trans World Airlines, United Air Lines, and Western Air Lines.

Prior to the Airline Deregulation Act, signed by Jimmy Carter on October 24, 1978, the CAB strictly regulated airline routes, fares, and mergers. For example, before a trunk carrier could provide service on a new route, it had to petition the CAB for approval. Approval was contingent upon the CAB's judgment regarding three issues: need for additional service on the route, which airline should be awarded the route, and whether the route tied into an airline's existing network. Incumbent airlines usually contended that the petitioned route could not support any additional service, so proceedings often dragged on for years.

The CAB regulated air fares by establishing maximums, minimums, or both maximums and minimums. Each carrier was required to obtain permission before introducing a new fare. The CAB ruled on these fare changes to determine whether they were reasonable. Although the CAB designed the fare limits to provide a rate of return on investment equal to 12 percent, this target was rarely reached.

Mergers were a third area in which the CAB exercised control. The airlines used mergers to acquire the route networks and aircraft capacity of other carriers. This strategy was often more expedient than petitioning the CAB for individual routes because the acquiring carrier could receive many new routes simultaneously. The CAB generally approved a merger, however, only if it prevented a carrier from going bankrupt, with the result that a particular geographic area would lose air service.

The CAB regulations effectively prevented trunk carriers from competing on the basis of fares and routes. Although the airlines could offer different in-flight amenities, each aircraft had approximately the same level of comfort. Because their product was undifferentiated, airline managers realized that customers were more concerned with scheduling the most convenient flight than with maintaining brand loyalty. As a result, frequency of service became the most important determinant of market share. The CAB did not regulate flight frequency except to prevent de facto abandonment of routes.

Proponents of deregulation argued that the CAB regulations were responsible for increasing the cost of air transportation. Their argument was based on the premise that as the airlines scheduled more flights to increase market exposure, each flight carried fewer passengers. Costs, and thus fares, rose because the fixed cost of each flight was spread among fewer passengers. They argued that deregulation would permit the airlines to differentiate their product and provide a wider range of fares and services. One anticipated outcome was lower prices.

Advocates of deregulation also argued that the legislation would result in greater efficiency and flexibility. First, by increasing a carrier's flexibility to improve route structures and flight schedules, deregulation would permit better aircraft utilization. Second, assets would not be wasted simply to seek future route awards. Under regulations, some carriers had used artificially low fares to strengthen their bargaining position when seeking future routes. Third, carriers would have more leverage when dealing with labor unions because the U.S. government would not be obligated to aid an ailing airline.

With the exception of United Air Lines, the trunk carriers either vehemently or tacitly opposed deregulation. They argued that the absence of entry restrictions on the more profitable routes would result in duplication and overcapacity. Because more planes would fly these routes, higher rather than lower fares would result. If increased competition resulted in excess capacity, then profitability would decline because each flight would carry more empty seats. In addition, they argued that deregulation would diminish stable and reliable air service. In a deregulated environment, an airline could enter a market on weekends or holidays and carry full flights by offering reduced fares. During periods of reduced traffic demand, however, the carrier could suspend its service. Finally, critics feared that rate wars would develop as airlines offered cut-rate fares to establish themselves in new markets. As incumbent airlines lowered their fares to remain competitive, profits would be reduced. As a result, carriers would have difficulty replacing their fleets.

Opponents of deregulation also argued that smaller cities would suffer reduced or suspended service because the trunk carriers would concentrate their equipment capacity on the lucrative long-haul routes between high-density population centers. This argument was similar to a cross-subsidy issue: The trunk airlines claimed that they used profits from their long-haul routes to negate losses on their shorter, less profitable routes. If deregulation eliminated these profits, then carriers would not be able to offset the losses from their shorter routes and might have to abandon them.

Flights over shorter distances are relatively more expensive in terms of cost per mile because fixed costs, such as passenger and luggage processing, are spread over fewer miles. In addition, slower average aircraft speeds cause higher labor costs per seat mile. Finally, fuel costs per seat mile are proportionately higher because the rate of fuel consumption is greater during takeoff and landing than it is during flight. Because other forms of transportation, such as the automobile, are relatively attractive at shorter distances, demand is highly elastic; that is, customers are very likely to choose a substitute form of transportation if prices go up. As a result, the higher costs of shorter flights cannot be offset by fares that reflect those costs and allow as much profit as earned on longer flights.

These arguments were never substantiated. Several studies were conducted to determine the extent of cross-subsidization, with results indicating that the trunk carriers did not rely heavily on this practice. The Airline Deregulation Act protected small communities by stating that an airline providing the only service on a route had to continue that service until a replacement carrier was found, thus defusing one criticism of deregulation.

Impact of Event

The aftermath of airline deregulation underscored the need for managers to accurately evaluate corporate strategy. For many years, the airlines preferred to pay the costs of CAB regulation rather than face the uncertain environment that would exist without controls. Once the industry was deregulated, however, many carriers were lured by the freedom to expand and increase market share. The result was that many airlines overexpanded, faced overcapacity, sold their product at low prices, and suffered declining profits.

Although airlines earned record profits in 1978, the trunk airline industry exhibited declining performance and reported a net loss in 1980. The loss was incurred because managers did not accurately assess the effects of their strategies on competitors' behavior and profitability. Instead, they engaged in debilitating price wars and provided excess capacity on the more popular routes. Low fares in conjunction with rising fuel and operating costs caused declining profits in the first years of deregulation.

Prior to deregulation, managers were enamored of the concept of flight frequency. Because CAB regulations severely limited the trunk carriers' ability to compete on the basis of fares and routes, flight frequency became the most important determinant of market share. This led to the widespread practice of using long-term debt to finance large aircraft fleets that could provide frequent service. As a result, trunk carriers were highly leveraged, faced large interest charges, and were adversely affected by the 1980-1981 recession that reduced air traffic demand.

A brief description of the corporate strategies implemented by Delta Air Lines and Braniff Airways following deregulation illustrates these points. Delta and Braniff implemented strategies that resulted in good and poor performance, respectively. Both companies used a hub-and-spoke route network prior to deregulation, and both carriers flew the less popular routes to small and medium-sized cities. These flights were then aggregated at a hub city and efficiently scheduled to connect with the carrier's more profitable long-distance flights. This system minimized passenger inconvenience resulting from layovers and made the airlines less dependent on other carriers for their feeder traffic.

A major advantage of this type of network was that each airline was generally a monopoly carrier on its short-haul routes. Consequently, older planes could be used without worrying about flight frequency, competition, or price wars. As a result, these carriers entered the deregulated era in better financial shape than did the larger carriers. Delta had one of the industry's lowest debt ratios, whereas Braniff's leverage was commensurate with the industry average. These two carriers also tended to be more profitable than the larger carriers.

Following deregulation, Braniff changed its strategy and placed more emphasis on adding long-haul routes. In 1979, for example, Braniff added new routes to Europe and the Far East, even though it lacked marketing exposure in these areas. Braniff hoped that the new domestic and international routes would feed each other and increase traffic flow through its domestic hub cities. It also expected that new traffic patterns would help smooth demand over the entire system. This rapid expansion strategy was not compatible with the environment. Braniff tried to expand its operations during a period of rising interest, fuel, and operating costs, but it had to lower prices to remain competitive on existing routes and offer promotional fares to increase its market exposure on the new routes. Braniff ignored the importance of flight frequency and its relationship to market share. In many cases, Braniff initiated only one flight on its new routes, sometimes with an inconvenient arrival or departure time. As a result, Braniff was not able to schedule its system as efficiently as it initially hoped. Braniff also shifted capacity from markets in which it previously held a prominent position, with the result that competitors entered these cities and stole market share.

In contrast to Braniff, Delta maintained its position as one of the trunk industry's most profitable carriers. It did not deplete its resources in price wars on the more popular routes, adding routes only when it perceived a need for additional service. Delta also added routes that could be profitable in the short term. As a result, it initiated service to fast-growing regions in the Pacific Northwest, California, and Texas. Delta did not sacrifice flight frequency in its traditional markets to provide service on these new routes. When Eastern Airlines increased flight frequency to Atlanta, Delta's major hub, Delta countered by simultaneously adding more flights. To combat the tendency toward providing excess capacity, Delta introduced flight complexes at its Atlanta hub. Thirty or forty planes would converge on Atlanta at two-hour intervals, exchange passengers, and fly to different spoke cities. The strategy kept a greater percentage of passengers within the feeder and connector system. Passenger layover was minimized through efficient scheduling which, in turn, reduced the chance that passengers would defect to another airline. Delta became one of the dominant U.S. carriers, and Braniff filed for bankruptcy in 1982.

The Carter Administration made initial progress toward deregulating the truck, railroad, airline, and banking industries. Ronald Reagan also supported deregulation during his two terms in office. As illustrated in the airline industry, success in a deregulated environment would require careful attention to corporate strategy and avoidance of short-term tactics with long-term pitfalls.

Bibliography

Dempsey, Paul Stephen, and Andrew R. Goetz. *Airline Deregulation and Laissez-Faire Mythology*. Westport, Conn.: Quorum Books, 1992. Good retrospective critique of the outcome of deregulation. The authors contend that several key assumptions made by free-market economists were erroneous. The authors advocate some regulatory reform.

Fruhan, William E., Jr. *The Fight for Competitive Advantage: A Study of the United States Trunk Air Carriers*. Boston: Division of Research, Graduate School of Business Administration, Harvard University, 1972. Good resource that analyzes the competitive environment in the trunk airline industry under the auspices of the Civil Aeronautics Board.

Lewis, W. Davis, and Wesley P. Newton. *Delta: The History of an Airline*. Athens: University of Georgia Press, 1979. Comprehensive review of the history of Delta Air Lines from 1929 to 1979. The authors take an easy-to-read historical point of view rather than conducting a rigorous economic or business analysis.

MacAvoy, Paul W., and John W. Snow, eds. *Regulation of Passenger Fares and Competition Among the Airlines*. Washington, D.C.: American Enterprise Institute for Public Policy Research, 1977. Collection of studies conducted by the United States Department of Transportation and other public and private agencies regarding the likely impact of deregulation on airline costs and service.

Saunders, Martha D. *Eastern's Armageddon: Labor Conflict and the Destruction of Eastern Airlines*. Westport, Conn.: Greenwood Press, 1992. An interesting case study that examines the demise of Eastern Airlines from both historical and organizational behavior perspectives. Eastern Airlines was acquired by Texas Air in 1986 and ceased operations in January, 1991. The author analyzes the conflict between Eastern's unions and Texas Air's management, especially Frank Lorenzo. Several airlines failed following deregulation, but Eastern's bankruptcy often is viewed as one of the more tragic.

M. Mark Walker

Cross-References

Congress Centralizes Regulation of U.S. Commercial Air Traffic (1940), p. 815; Amtrak Takes Over Most U.S. Intercity Train Traffic (1970), p. 1431; Carter Orders Deregulation of Oil Prices (1979), p. 1699; Congress Deregulates Banks and Savings and Loans (1980-1982), p. 1757; Air Traffic Controllers of PATCO Declare a Strike (1981), p. 1803; Braniff International Suspends Flight Operations (1982), p. 1826.

THE PREGNANCY DISCRIMINATION ACT EXTENDS EMPLOYMENT RIGHTS

Category of event: Labor
Time: October 31, 1978
Locale: Washington, D.C.

The Pregnancy Discrimination Act expanded employee benefit provisions, clarified the need for nondiscriminatory fetal protection policies, and led to state and federal laws mandating parental leave

Principal personages:
SUSAN C. ROSS (1945-   ), the codirector of the Campaign to End Discrimination Against Women Workers
JIMMY CARTER (1924-   ), the president of the United States, 1977-1981
WENDY WILLIAMS, a coauthor of the Pregnancy Discrimination Act

Summary of Event

The passage of the Pregnancy Discrimination Act in 1978 was the first federal attempt to expand rights and protection for pregnant workers. The Pregnancy Discrimination Act (PDA) is an amendment to Title VII of the Civil Rights Act of 1964 and prohibits discrimination in employment based on pregnancy, childbirth, or related medical conditions. Although women are protected by the act against such practices as being fired or being refused a job or promotion because of pregnancy, the major impact of the PDA relates to employment benefit policies.

The PDA requires employers with fifteen or more employees to provide the same benefits for pregnancy-related conditions as they provide for other medical conditions. For example, a woman unable to work for pregnancy-related reasons is entitled to disability benefits or sick leave on the same basis as an employee unable to work because of physical injuries from an accident. If a firm allows salary continuation for victims of heart attacks, it must do so for pregnant workers as well. It would be illegal, on one hand, to allow eight weeks of unpaid leave for cancer treatment but, on the other hand, to limit maternity leave to four weeks. If employees are entitled to get their jobs back after a leave for surgery or illness, so are women who have been unable to work because of pregnancy. In addition, any health insurance coverage provided must cover expenses of pregnancy-related conditions on the same basis as expenses for other medical conditions. In essence, employers may not differentiate between pregnancy and illness.

Changes in the legal treatment of pregnancy discrimination in the work force have their roots in action begun in the 1960's concerning sex discrimination. The most comprehensive federal law dealing with sex discrimination is Title VII of the Civil Rights Act of 1964. Title VII prohibits discrimination in employment decisions based on race, religion, color, national origin, and sex. Although discrimination in all aspects of employment on the basis of sex was banned, Title VII did not address whether discrimination based on pregnancy was a form of sex discrimination.

Congress established an enforcement agency, the Equal Employment Opportunity Commission (EEOC), to administer and interpret Title VII's provisions. Immediately after the passage of Title VII, the EEOC took the position that denying benefits to pregnant employees would not be discriminatory. Continued congressional debate concerning protection against sex discrimination brought about a reversal of that opinion. In 1972, the EEOC issued its guidelines on discrimination because of sex, which state that work disabilities resulting from pregnancy or pregnancy-related illness are temporary disabilities, and that leave, medical, disability, seniority, and reinstatement rights comparable to those provided to nonpregnant employees must be provided to pregnant employees or those with pregnancy-related disabilities.

Following the issuance of the EEOC guidelines, many states passed legislation requiring employers to offer coverage for pregnancy-related disabilities comparable to that offered for other disabilities. Lower courts consistently ruled that denying benefits to pregnant women that were available to nonpregnant employees violated Title VII. Despite the EEOC guidelines and lower court rulings, many employers tended to treat pregnancy differently from other medical conditions. Frequently, pregnant workers were not allowed to use disability plans, and other benefits such as seniority rights and medical insurance were often discontinued during unpaid maternity leaves. Female employees challenged such policies and charged that they constituted a form of sex discrimination in employment under Title VII of the Civil Rights Act.

Two cases that reached the United States Supreme Court were the catalysts for congressional debate and passage of the PDA. In 1976, the Supreme Court held in *Gilbert v. General Electric Corporation* that employers could exclude pregnancy-related disabilities without creating sex discrimination. The plaintiff in the case had applied for benefits, under the company's temporary disability plan, for pregnancy-related complications while she was on maternity leave. The firm refused her claim because she was on maternity leave. She sued under Title VII, and the lower courts ruled in her favor. The Supreme Court, however, held that the denial of disability benefits for a pregnancy-related condition did not constitute discrimination. The Court concluded that men and women were covered for the same risks except for pregnancy, and the exclusion of a risk affecting only women did not constitute discrimination based on sex. One year later, in *Nashville Gas v. Satty*, the Supreme Court ruled that the denial of sick-leave pay to pregnant employees was not a violation of Title VII.

The reaction to these two cases was immediate and intense. A coalition of women's organizations, civil rights organizations, and labor unions formed in support of legislative reform. Wendy Williams, coauthor of the Pregnancy Discrimination Act, commented at congressional hearings that the Gilbert decision reflected an attitude that women are marginal, temporary workers. To eliminate employers' use of women's role as childbearers as a justification for inequitable treatment, Sue Ross, codirector of the Campaign to End Discrimination Against Pregnant Workers, called for an explicit federal law eradicating discrimination based on pregnancy and childbirth. Congress responded by passing the Pregnancy Discrimination Act.

Impact of Event

The passage of the Pregnancy Discrimination Act was the first attempt at a national policy on maternity that would influence personnel policies related to job security, hiring and promotion, safety standards, and employee benefit plans. Although compliance with the PDA was far from universal, many companies expanded employee benefit plans and initiated innovative programs to help pregnant women in the workplace. The PDA provided employers with the initiative to examine fetal protection policies and laid the foundation for state and federal regulations and laws concerning parental leave.

The primary impact of the PDA related to employee benefits plans. Although some companies provided equal benefits for pregnant and nonpregnant employees prior to the PDA, compliance with the PDA has been far from universal. Subsequent to the passage of the PDA, many companies evaluated their policies and adjusted them in order to comply with the law, while others were unsure as to what was required. Compliance with the PDA is highly correlated with organizational size. Immediately following enactment of the PDA, most large firms had adjusted benefits in order to comply with the law, but noncompliance was common among small organizations. Only about half of the firms with fewer than one hundred employees complied with the PDA by 1981. Small firms that ignored the law claimed that they did not know what was required to comply. A survey of small firms indicated that they were confused as to whether employers were required to provide health insurance, disability insurance, and sick-pay benefits for pregnancy-related conditions or merely to adjust existing benefits to cover pregnancy-related conditions equitably.

Prodded by the PDA, some companies expanded employee benefits and incorporated innovative features into their personnel policies. One new feature was to permit new fathers to take up to six months of unpaid leave to care for a newborn. Another benefit extending beyond the PDA requirements related to unpaid leave. American Telephone and Telegraph (AT&T) provided disability payments to pregnant employees before they gave birth and before they were certified as disabled. In drawing up new plans affecting pregnant employees, AT&T adjusted treatment of other employees as well. Employees who were not pregnant also became eligible for time off in advance of an anticipated disability.

As a result of the Pregnancy Discrimination Act, some companies instituted programs for pregnant workers aimed at holding down the costs of expanding benefits and maintaining employee productivity. Cash incentives or alternative care arrangements, such as in-home nursing care following the birth, were offered to employees who leave the hospital earlier than expected. Such efforts lowered the cost to employers of health insurance and disability insurance premiums.

Numerous companies ran workplace seminars aimed at helping pregnant employees develop good health habits. According to occupational health nurses, these seminars on prenatal health care help reduce absenteeism during pregnancy and reduce the average length of maternity leave.

The issue of pregnancy-related discrimination has been examined by employers in the context of fetal protection policies. Companies concerned about reproductive hazards have instituted policies intended to protect fetal health. Some of these policies excluded women from jobs and occupations involving exposure to risks to the fetus. Johnson Controls, for example, refused to employ women in departments where lead was used because of concern about potential fetal injury.

The courts have ruled that policies that exclude women from jobs that may pose hazards to their reproductive health or the health of a fetus are direct violations of the Civil Rights Act of 1964 as amended by the Pregnancy Discrimination Act of 1978 unless the threat cannot be abated by means of control of the risk or other protection from it. In three separate court cases, stringent tests for fetal protection policies were established. The courts ruled that a fetal protection policy may discriminate against women if persuasive evidence exists that the risk to the fetus is real and likely to occur and that the risk is confined to women or fetuses.

Employers responded to the prohibition of discriminatory fetal protection policies in several ways. Several large companies initiated research studies aimed at identifying potential connections between occupational exposures and adverse reproductive effects. Larger corporations offered protection from reproductive hazards through temporary job transfers of pregnant workers to jobs of comparable work at equal pay and began taking steps to try to minimize reproductive hazards for both female and male employees.

In response to the passage of the PDA, states addressed issues concerning pregnant workers through laws and regulations. Although only a few states had enacted laws pertaining to reproductive hazards by the early 1990's, a majority of states had addressed some aspect of work as it pertained to pregnant women. A number of states enacted laws or promulgated regulations covering pregnancy under disability laws and prohibiting discrimination in hiring and promotion decisions based on pregnancy.

One trend concerns laws governing maternity leave not related to disability. Under the PDA, employers must grant disability leave to pregnant employees to the same extent as offered to other employees for different types of disabilities. The PDA does not require employers to grant leave for child care. Several states passed laws mandating unpaid parental leave or maternity leave. Because the PDA provides for equal treatment, employers must offer the same parental leave to fathers as to mothers.

American companies typically did not offer maternity leaves that extended beyond the period of disability. The Family and Medical Leave Act passed by the Bill Clinton Administration addressed that issue. The primary provisions of the FMLA centered on requiring a fixed number of weeks of unpaid parental leave, continued health benefits, and job security.

Employers are faced with difficulties in setting parameters with respect to pregnancy leave. Under the PDA, employers are prohibited from placing limits on the length of pregnancy leaves unless they also place identical limits on other disability leaves. This restriction has led to substantial state legislation regarding family and medical leaves as well as to the proposal of the federal Family and Medical Leave Act.

Bibliography

Bureau of National Affairs. *Pregnancy and Employment: The Complete Handbook on Discrimination, Maternity Leave, and Health and Safety.* Washington, D.C.: Author, 1987. Provides an overview of legal developments covering pregnancy discrimination and maternity-leave issues. Reviews issues involving reproductive hazards to pregnant workers. Details programs initiated by employers.

Dabrow, Allan, and Gina Ameci. "What You Should Know About Pregnancy and the Law." *Management Review* 80 (August, 1991): 38-40. Examines several lawsuits subsequent to the PDA relating to discrimination in employment. Discusses trends relating to parental leave at the state and federal levels.

Kamerman, Sheila B., Alfred J. Kahn, and Paul Kingston. *Maternity Policies and Working Women.* New York: Columbia University Press, 1983. Discusses why maternity benefits are important and presents the evolution of federal maternity policies for working women. Also discusses the benefits mandated at the state level. Includes examples of maternity benefits from specific companies.

Kohl, John P., and Paul S. Greenlaw. "The Pregnancy Discrimination Act: Compliance Problems." *Personnel* 60 (November/December, 1983): 65-71. Summarizes the origins of the Pregnancy Discrimination Act and reports the results of a study investigating organizational compliance with the PDA.

Zigler, Edward F., and Meryl Frank, eds. *The Parental Leave Crisis.* New Haven, Conn.: Yale University Press, 1988. Provides a history of maternity-leave policies. Discusses why parental leave is important and examines the need for a national parental-leave policy. Useful for understanding the impact of women in the work force on laws and employer policies.

Iris A. Pirozzoli

Cross-References

Congress Passes the Equal Pay Act (1963), p. 1185; The Civil Rights Act Prohibits Discrimination in Employment (1964), p. 1229; Nixon Signs the Occupational Safety and Health Act (1970), p. 1466; The Supreme Court Orders the End of Discrimination in Hiring (1971), p. 1495; The Supreme Court Upholds Quotas as a Remedy for Discrimination (1986), p. 1915.

VISICALC SPREADSHEET SOFTWARE IS MARKETED

Categories of event: New products and business practices
Time: 1979
Locale: Wellesley, Massachusetts

Daniel Bricklin's VisiCalc, the first electronic spreadsheet program, brought the power of the personal computer to businesspeople

Principal personages:
DANIEL BRICKLIN (1952-   ), a Harvard Business School student and VisiCalc's designer
ROBERT FRANKSTON (1950-   ), a Harvard Business School student and VisiCalc's programmer
DANIEL FYLSTRA (1954-   ), a Harvard Business School student and VisiCalc's marketer

Summary of Event

Students often undertake tremendous efforts to avoid doing their homework. The introduction of computers offered the opportunity for them to get computers to do it instead. One student perfected the process, creating a multimillion dollar corporation from his efforts.

That is the story of first-year Harvard Business School student Daniel Bricklin. While struggling in 1978 to solve financial-planning problems on his calculator, he wondered how much easier the task would be with the aid of his Apple II computer. He was one of the first owners of a computer that many people were calling a high-tech toy. He discussed his idea with a longtime friend and expert programmer, Robert Frankston. The program that resulted from their discussions and work would not only make them millions of dollars but also change the way people perceived the personal computer.

At the time, Frankston was a partner in Personal Software, a company he founded with another student, Daniel Fylstra, with an initial investment of $500. In 1978, their only big seller was a chess game. They agreed to implement and market Bricklin's ideas. They called their program VisiCalc, short for "visible calculator." It was their first computer program designed to aid in juggling financial figures.

VisiCalc was an instant success. More than 100,000 copies were sold by late 1979, at a price of $100 to $300 apiece. To better serve customers' needs, they offered several versions. VisiCalc was so successful that it began to outsell other business programs of the day, such as Data Factory and General Ledger. The specialized product even outsold many general-market game programs.

Prior to the advent of VisiCalc, most business managers had to learn a computer programming language such as BASIC or the business-oriented COBOL if they were to have computers help them make decisions. The prospect of learning such languages was daunting, with the payoff uncertain. Programming itself often resulted in hours being wasted in the creation of inefficient or unsatisfactory programs. As a result, sales of personal computers were limited. When VisiCalc came along, requiring no programming knowledge, managers could see for the first time the power of the personal computer. By creating the first electronic spreadsheet, Bricklin gave them an invaluable tool and a good reason to purchase personal computers. Businesspeople could now see the personal computer as more than just a high-tech toy.

Managers using VisiCalc could ask the most important questions concerning business plans, then analyze the impact of decisions before implementing them. Any plan that could be expressed in the format of formulas and columns of numbers was open to testing. Different numerical assumptions could be made and tested quickly, with the computer doing all the necessary recalculation. VisiCalc provided the means to play "what if" games almost effortlessly. Investment, inventory, and budget issues all could be analyzed. For example, before taking any action, a manager could use VisiCalc to help analyze how the company's expenses, sales, profits, and dividends would be affected.

This computer program was useful to people other than business managers. People of all professions seemed to find a use for it. Some used it to track income taxes. Teachers began to use it to keep track of students' grades, as it provided an easy method of recording grades and computing averages. It was even reported that a theater in Massachusetts bought VisiCalc to figure out which pattern of showing times attracted the highest revenues from films.

By 1982, Bricklin, Frankston, and Fylstra had earned fortunes from VisiCalc. Personal Software moved from Massachusetts to the Silicon Valley and was renamed VisiCorp. VisiCalc had sold more than 200,000 copies and inspired a host of competing products, referred to as "visiclones" and "calcalikes." These included packages with names such as SuperCalc, EasyCalc, and UltraCalc. Major software companies also joined the race to create the best clone. Lotus Development Corporation's 1-2-3 and Microsoft's Multiplan were popular contenders. The companies that could afford to do so offered integrated packages combining electronic spreadsheet programs with other applications such as word processors, databases, business graphics, or communications.

In the highly competitive software market that emerged, many companies simply could not keep up with changes. Bricklin learned this the hard way. VisiCorp's expected annual sales were about $35 million. Industry analysts projected that VisiCorp would go public within two years and speculated that its stock market valuation would be as high as $125 million. Bricklin and Frankston decided to market VisiCalc on their own. They founded a new company called Software Arts and went through a costly lawsuit with their marketing partner. VisiCorp continued to market the program under an exclusive agreement until 1984. When the lawsuit between the two companies was resolved, Software Arts began selling VisiCalc under its own name. Unfortunately, the lawsuit had drained company resources. In one year, Software Arts' revenues fell almost 75 percent, to $3 million in 1984. Bricklin and Frankston could not afford to update VisiCalc and keep it competitive with other products on the market. As a result, competing programs began to outperform it.

In 1985, Bricklin sold what little remained of Software Arts to Lotus. A year later, Lotus announced that it would no longer produce the pioneer spreadsheet program VisiCalc, believing that Lotus 1-2-3 was a better product. The original spreadsheet program had a life of only six years and total sales of approximately one million copies.

Impact of Event

In 1978, when personal computers were being introduced to the market by such companies as Apple and Tandy, many people thought of them as high-tech toys. After Bricklin decided to go into business for himself and sell an electronic spreadsheet program, this view changed. His VisiCalc, the first business-oriented program to bring the power of the computer to businesspeople, changed the personal computer from a toy into a powerful business tool, one that would soon be seen as essential.

VisiCalc revolutionized the practice of business. The early users of Apple II computers were mostly hobbyists, scientists, and intellectuals. News of the productivity of the new VisiCalc program spread quickly, and its popularity increased. As a result, the businessperson's perceptions changed in respect to the worth of the personal computer. People began to see that personal computers could be used for serious business work.

VisiCalc's success undoubtedly contributed to the success of the Apple II computer, as it gave an entire new market segment, that of businesspeople, a reason to buy the machine. Most analysts credit the incredible growth rate of Apple Computer in part to VisiCalc's success. Within eight years of the program's release, the personal computer software business was a $5 billion industry with fourteen thousand companies and twenty-seven thousand different products. The release of VisiCalc began this personal computer explosion. VisiCalc quickly climbed to the top of the software best-seller list and stayed there. Programming was evolving and markets for programs were expanding, but Bricklin's insight marked a leap in the development of the software industry and use of personal computers.

Before VisiCalc was released, most managers had to use BASIC or another programming language such as COBOL to get their work done on a computer. Few could even see the value of owning a computer, since the programming that most people could accomplish was limited. VisiCalc presented managers with a complete, versatile program; all they had to do was plug in their own data and formulas. For the price of a few hundred dollars, they could purchase a decision-making tool that they never would have been able to develop on their own and that could save hundreds or thousands of hours of calculating time. Bricklin's success would exceed his dreams: Every future spreadsheet product would be no more than an enhancement of his basic idea. The market became cluttered with hundreds of similar packages.

Although financial modeling and planning programs were available on mainframe computers, none had the potential of VisiCalc. VisiCalc created a breakthrough in personal productivity. Taking advantage of Apple II hardware, VisiCalc let users recalculate the rows and columns of a spreadsheet quickly. The almost instant reworking of calculations involving complex formulas gave users a new sense of power. They experienced how a computer could enhance their own productivity by letting data manipulations keep up with the pace of their own thoughts and ideas. No longer would they have to send an idea and its associated data to the computing department and wait for answers from a mainframe computer: Now they could enter data on their own machines and see results almost instantly. The fact that answers came so quickly encouraged more experimentation and fine-tuning of business plans.

Mainframe financial modeling packages were often slow, on-line systems. VisiCalc created new possibilities beyond improved performance. After users entered values and formulas in their mainframe programs, they had to wait for the computer to recalculate the related parts of the spreadsheet. The typical wait was about three seconds for each edit and about five minutes for each recalculation. Because of VisiCalc's increased speed in comparison to mainframe programs, users felt a sense of freedom to experiment. Before VisiCalc, refining a spreadsheet once the first draft had been formatted often took more time than it was worth. VisiCalc changed that. Users could perform more "what-ifs" per hour than ever before.

VisiCalc also gave the business world a new, affordable accounting system. Prior to its release, some businesses could not afford computerized mainframe record keeping and were forced to keep records manually. Tracking of business matters was prone to inaccuracies, records were sometimes lost, and files were not always readily accessible. Spreadsheets made computerized information storage efficient, fast, and affordable. Furthermore, VisiCalc's ease of use allowed businesses to replace high-priced accounting services with clerical work. The availability of data also helped managers do their jobs more quickly and effectively. The fact that information was available in an easily accessible form encouraged them to use it more frequently.

Bricklin presided over the birth of the personal software industry, with his greatest contribution being the electronic spreadsheet. By 1982, his product had sold 200,000 copies and inspired an industry of competitors; by the end of its life, VisiCalc had sold about a million copies.

By the mid-1980's, industry software sales began to decline for the first time. As Bricklin's competitors captured more of the marketplace by offering more features, integrated packages, and advances in technology, VisiCalc began to lose sales. His own company could not compete. This was a trend that many other small businesses would follow. In 1985 alone, fifty-seven personal computer software companies were bought out, up from twenty-three the year before. The annual growth rate of personal-computer software sales slowed to 15 percent, down from the 64 percent yearly growth over the previous five years. The top fifteen companies creating personal computer software were taking in 72 percent of all sales, up from 37 percent in 1981. The three biggest companies—Lotus, Ashton-Tate, and Microsoft—accounted for 35 percent of all sales. Consequently, Bricklin watched his electronic spreadsheet idea expand and grow in other firms' hands.

With advances in technology, the electronic spreadsheet package of the 1990's became even more powerful and even easier to use. Worksheets were larger, consisting of up to four million cells (16,384 rows by 256 columns). Users could almost instantly convert numerical data into graphs and charts of many styles and colors. With the aid of a computer's "mouse" device, they could sum rows or columns of numbers, format data, and print impressive reports more easily. Laser printers made it possible for them to create high-quality printed products quickly and without leaving their desks. By learning a few simple programming commands built into the programs, they could also create their own operations for the program to perform. Software and hardware thus evolved to complement each other. Bricklin's 1979 marketing of VisiCalc began that evolution.

Bibliography

Fertig, Robert T. "Spreadsheet Calculators." In *The Software Revolution: Trends, Players, Market Dynamics in Personal Computer Software*. New York: North-Holland, 1985. Discusses hardware, markets, and types of applications used on personal computers. Written for anyone interested in learning more about personal computer systems.

Field, Anne R., and Catherine L. Harris. "Software: The Growing Gets Rough." *Business Week*, March 24, 1986, 128-134. Discusses business trends in the personal computer market. Discusses the top fifteen firms in the personal computer hardware and software business in 1986. Also discusses the impact of the explosive growth of the personal computer market and makes several predictions.

Gibney, Frank, Jr. "The Tail That Wags the Dog." *Newsweek* 99 (February 22, 1982): 55. Suggests that Bricklin's brainstorm for VisiCalc came from staring at a blackboard in class one day. Includes a photo of Bricklin and Frankston at a trade show, representing Software Arts.

Langdell, James. "VisiCalc Production Ends." *PC Magazine* 4 (August 6, 1985): 33. Gives the details of a historic moment in the personal computer saga. Filled with quotations from a spokesman for Lotus Development Corporation. Announces other products Lotus acquired from Software Arts, such as Spotlight and TK! Solver.

"Sagas of Five Who Made It." *Time* 119 (February 15, 1982): 42-44. In addition to covering VisiCalc, discusses the success stories of Federal Express, Nike, Pizza Time, and Schwab & Company. Focuses on VisiCorp and Dan Fylstra, including many quotations from him. Credits Fylstra's marketing abilities for VisiCalc's success.

Seymour, Jim. "Who Owns the Standards?" *PC Magazine* 6 (May 26, 1987): 174-176. Discusses how VisiCalc was copied and improved by a number of software companies. Also discusses copyright laws and their general effects on the market and users.

Taylor, Alexander. "The Smash Hit of Software." *Time* 117 (March 2, 1981): 69. A good brief summary of the story of VisiCalc. Taylor draws analogies between the music and computer industries, explaining that software is to a computer what a record album is to a stereo. Offers a creative example of how to use an electronic spreadsheet.

Patrick Bridgemon

Cross-References

The Pocket Calculator Is Marketed (1972), p. 1517; Jobs and Wozniak Found Apple Computer (1976), p. 1611; CAD/CAM Revolutionizes Engineering and Manufacturing (1980's), p. 1721; IBM Introduces Its Personal Computer (1981), p. 1809.

THE THREE MILE ISLAND ACCIDENT PROMPTS REFORMS IN NUCLEAR POWER

Category of event: Consumer affairs
Time: March 28, 1979
Locale: Harrisburg, Pennsylvania

The nuclear power plant accident at Three Mile Island exposed weaknesses and led to new safety measures designed to avoid a repetition elsewhere

Principal personages:
DICK THORNBURGH (1932-), the governor of Pennsylvania, 1979-1987
WILLIAM W. SCRANTON III (1947-), the lieutenant governor of Pennsylvania, 1979-1987
JOSEPH M. HENDRIE (1925-), the chairman of the U.S. Nuclear Regulatory Commission, 1977-1979
JIMMY CARTER (1924-), the president of the United States, 1977-1981

Summary of Event

On March 28, 1979, the Three Mile Island (TMI) nuclear power plant on the Susquehanna River near Harrisburg, Pennsylvania, nearly suffered a catastrophe as its Unit Two malfunctioned, setting into play events that resulted in the most serious accident to that time in the history of the commercial nuclear power industry. Had it not finally been contained, the malfunction would have resulted in devastation similar to that caused by the plant in Chernobyl, Ukraine, in 1986.

The TMI accident exposed many weaknesses in nuclear power plant design, management, and operation. The ineffectiveness of the Nuclear Regulatory Commission (NRC) and inadequacy of emergency preparedness were also exposed, leading to proposal of many changes by the many investigators deployed to study the event, including a presidential commission and congressional committees, the Nuclear Regulatory Commission, Pennsylvania governmental groups, and industrial organizations. In 1980, the comptroller general published a report to Congress that reviewed eight of the other reports and gave its own independent observations.

The Three Mile Island Unit Two, as well as its sister, Unit One, was a pressurized water reactor. It generated electric power by boiling water into steam, which then spun the blades of a turbine generator. The heat to convert the water to steam was produced by chain reaction fission of uranium in the reactor's core. This core was covered with water as its primary coolant and encapsulated in a structure forty feet high with walls of steel eight inches thick. The coolant was radioactive and under pressure, which allowed it to be superheated to 575 degrees Fahrenheit without boiling. It then was pumped to a steam generator, where the coolant heated cooler water in a secondary system. Under less pressure, the water turned to steam and spun turbine blades, propelling a generator. The steam passed through a condenser, changing it back to water. It then began its circuit through to the boiler and back again through this secondary system, also called the "feedwater" circuit.

At 4 A.M. on Wednesday, March 29, 1979, two pumps in this system shut down; the steam turbine followed a few seconds later. Its steam was released. What little coolant was left in the secondary system boiled. The primary coolant could not transfer its heat load and it too began to boil, increasing pressure in the reactor and in the primary system. A relief valve opened, allowing radioactive water and steam to drain into a tank to prevent a primary coolant explosion. This valve should have shut off after thirteen seconds, but it remained open for more than two hours.

Less than a minute later, emergency backup pumps automatically engaged to add water to the secondary system. No water was added, however, because valves controlling the flow had been closed for maintenance two weeks earlier. According to Nuclear Regulatory Commission rules, the plant was to be shut down if these valves were closed for more than seventy-two hours.

Two minutes into the crisis, the emergency core coolant system kicked in to add water to the reactor core. Technicians, however, believed that the reactor was already full of water. They also assumed that the pressurizer relief valve was closed when it was not.

Four minutes later, with pressure in the primary cooling loop high, it was thought that the system was filling with water. Since additional increases in pressure could cause the system to blow, one emergency pump was stopped. Twelve and one-half minutes into the incident, the other was reduced to one-half speed. This was proper procedure, since the attendants believed the system was filling with water. This condition is known as "going solid" and must be avoided to lessen the possibility of the primary system's breakdown. The reactor core in fact was not covered by water, and temperatures began rising toward the meltdown point of 5,000 degrees Fahrenheit. There were no meters that could measure the depth of water in the reactor core, so the operators could only guess about this critical information.

At eight and one-half minutes into the crisis, the closed valves on the feedwater system were opened, filling the secondary system with water, which helped to draw heat from the primary system. The relief valve allowed primary cooling water to drain into a tank that spilled its radioactive water onto the containment building's floor. The water then was pumped into a tank in the nearby auxiliary building. Radioactivity was released in this final procedure at 4:38 A.M.

Pockets of steam collected in two sets of pumps for reactor cooling, resulting in vibrations that caused them to be turned off. With no cooling system in operation, the reactor suffered severe damage. The twelve-foot-tall fuel rods were only half covered with water. The shields around the rods themselves were destroyed by the intense, rising heat, releasing radioactive debris into the primary coolant, which itself was spilling onto the floor. Hydrogen and radioactive gases from the coolant collected in the containment building. Radiation levels rose within the buildings and was released into the atmosphere. At 6:50 A.M., a general emergency was declared.

Early Wednesday afternoon, hydrogen that had accumulated in the containment building exploded. Hydrogen continued to be created by the uncovered core, fueling fears of a catastrophic explosion.

Another scenario envisioned was the so-called "China Syndrome." In the scenario, the core would become so hot (about 5,200 degrees Fahrenheit) that it would melt. This superheated material would bore its way through the bottom of the plant and down through the ground until it hit water. The water would become high-pressure steam and would erupt from the earth, spewing radioactivity into the air all around the plant. A typical nuclear reactor could release about the same radiation as would a thousand bombs of the size used at Hiroshima.

A 1975 study estimated that a plant slightly larger than Three Mile Island could cause thirty-three hundred deaths and forty-five thousand radiation injuries immediately. Forty-five thousand cancer and forty thousand thyroid tumor fatalities would result in the longer term. Fourteen billion (1979) dollars of damage to property would also occur.

Controlled and uncontrolled radiation leaks from the plant continued through Wednesday, March 28, and Thursday, March 29. On Friday, Governor Richard Thornburgh ordered an evacuation of pregnant women and small children within five miles of the facility. A hydrogen bubble began to grow in the reactor vessel. It was thought that it could self-ignite in five to eight days, resulting in a possible meltdown. A general evacuation was considered by Thornburgh and Lieutenant Governor William W. Scranton III but was not ordered. It was thought that it might set off an evacuation panic and result in more injuries than it might prevent.

On Saturday morning, John Herbein, the Metropolitan Edison vice president for generation, said that the bubble had decreased in size by two-thirds and that the danger was over. Harold Denton of the NRC disagreed and said that the bubble actually had increased in size. Lack of information, poor communication among the numerous people from the varied agencies involved, incorrect wire service reports, and alarmist news reports fueled the mounting alarm on the part of the public, both locally and nationally. More than half of the families within a twelve-mile radius of the plant evacuated at least one member.

Later on Saturday, Harold Denton told Thornburgh that the size of the hydrogen bubble had been reduced. Joseph M. Hendrie, a commissioner of the NRC, had a group working on the same problem. They reported that the bubble could be explosive in six or seven days.

On the afternoon of Sunday, April 1, President Jimmy Carter visited the facility. At about the same time, the hydrogen bubble shrank, eliminating the possibility of explosion, and the crisis wound down.

Impact of Event

Numerous changes were made in the operation of nuclear power plants as a result of the Three Mile Island incident. This was a contingency for which there had been no plan, since it was thought to have a negligible probability of happening.

Until TMI, nuclear plants were constructed with three levels of safety built in, known as "defense in depth." The first level involved using quality construction standards and emergency practices to prevent accidents. It is inevitable that mistakes will be made, accidents will happen, and equipment will break down. These factors required another level to prevent or control their effects. These were built into the original design. The last level of safety assumed that special design features would fail. The containment building could mitigate or slow the release of radioactive particles from the plant should that happen.

In a complete meltdown, the core would eat through the floor of the plant, contaminating the groundwater supply. Radiation might also quickly breach the containment building and result in many deaths and injuries. Because it might be impossible to contain a meltdown, design features to delay the release of radioactivity were suggested. They provided more time to evacuate the area. They included core "catchers" to slow the core melting through the floor, a filtering system to provide for filtering and release of gases in the containment building to prevent overpressurization, and hydrogen control systems to prevent or minimize the formation of a hydrogen bubble, which was so potentially dangerous at TMI. Control room design changes were adopted that made controls more recognizable and accessible to operators in emergency situations.

Prior to 1979, nuclear plants were located close to major population areas. It was thought that the probability of radiation exposure to the public was quite small. After the accident, it became apparent that anything made by man was subject to failure. A return to the policy of constructing plants far from populated areas was thought to be prudent.

The inadequate qualifications and training of operators contributed to the severity of the accident. Training programs had been geared toward running the plant under normal conditions rather than under stressful emergencies. Supervisory and management personnel knew little about actual operations and were not able to help the operators mitigate problems.

The Nuclear Regulatory Commission now requires more operators, who are better qualified and have passed a more stringent licensing examination. Supervisors need engineering expertise, training is more rigorous, and simulators are used to prepare operators to deal with emergency situations, sometimes even duplicating the TMI conditions.

Studies found that initial situations similar to that at TMI had occurred at other plants, but operators were able to react before a major emergency developed. There was no system in place at the NRC or within the nuclear power industry to collect or distribute information to other operators about the problems encountered. A system to review and analyze information was implemented to collect data on American and foreign nuclear reactors. The Office for Analysis and Evaluation of Operating Data was created to be the focal point of this effort.

At the time of the TMI accident, the quality assurance programs of both Metropolitan Edison and the NRC were deficient. Standards used in the construction and operation of power plants were to be monitored by an independent department within each utility to ensure compliance. The NRC reviewed the utilities' efforts. These standards did not apply to equipment unrelated to safety or to radiation survey monitors. Equipment not related to safety had a significant involvement in the accident, and many of the radiation monitoring instruments at TMI did not work. An acknowledgment from the NRC that rigid quality assurance standards and their strict implementation were essential was expected to lessen the likelihood of a future similar event.

Emergency procedures on the part of the NRC and state and local governments were found to have been lax or nonexistent. The accident demonstrated that an emergency was possible, prompting emergency and evacuation plans to be implemented or upgraded for existing nuclear power plants. In addition, operating licenses would be granted to new nuclear generating plants only if state and local governments had federally approved emergency plans. The Federal Emergency Management Agency, rather than the NRC, became responsible for evaluating emergency plans.

During the emergency, numerous TMI employees were assigned various emergency response duties. Many had received no training and did not understand what needed to be done. Additionally, half of the radiation dose rate monitors were not operable. The NRC became more rigorous in requiring emergency training and equipment maintenance. Each of the five members of the Nuclear Regulatory Commission had equal responsibility and authority in all decisions in 1979. The chair had vaguely defined administrative and executive functions, but decision-making power lay with joint action of the commissioners and not with the chair. With no one ultimately in command, slow, inefficient management resulted. After reorganization of the NRC in 1980, the chair had more power, although the commission as a whole still set the framework within which the chair could operate. The chair was allowed to act in the name of the commission in an emergency, determining policies, giving orders, and directing all actions concerning the emergency. The chair gained the ultimate responsibility for emergency decision making. This was expected to provide more timely responses instead of the delays involved with management by committee.

Overall, the TMI accident prompted reconsideration of nuclear power as a source of energy. Although relatively inexpensive, nuclear power posed the risk of disasters and the problem of nuclear waste disposal. Regulators had to decide how many costly safety requirements to impose, and the federal government faced choices of which energy sources to promote and even whether to allow construction of new nuclear power plants. The 1986 nuclear disaster at Chernobyl renewed these concerns worldwide.

Bibliography

Cantelon, Philip L., and Robert C. Williams. *Crisis Contained: The Department of Energy at Three Mile Island*. Carbondale: Southern Illinois University Press, 1982. Evaluation of the Department of Energy's performance during the emergency.

Del Tredici, Robert. *The People of Three Mile Island*. San Francisco: Sierra Club

Books, 1980. Interviews with local people and others connected with the event.

Gray, Mike, and Ira Rosen. *The Warning: Accident at Three Mile Island*. New York: W. W. Norton, 1982. A very readable investigative report that dramatically pulls the reader through the complex events of the Three Mile Island disaster itself after reviewing prior problems experienced at other nuclear plants. Less technical than some of the other publications, but fast and informative reading nevertheless.

Sorensen, John H., Jon Soderstrom, Emily Copenhaven, Sam Carnes, and Robert Bolin. *Impacts of Hazardous Technology: The Psycho-Social Effects of Restarting TMI-1*. Albany: State University of New York Press, 1987. Reviews the background of TMI and projects the effects of starting the undamaged sister reactor, TMI-1.

Starr, Philip, and William Pearman. *Three Mile Island Sourcebook: Annotations of a Disaster*. New York: Garland, 1983. This book is divided into three sections. The first provides a chronology of media coverage from TMI's announcement of opening in 1966 until 1981. Three local newspapers, *The New York Times*, and *Newsweek* are surveyed. The next section is annotations of state and federal documents. The last covers books, articles, and other publications written about TMI.

Stephens, Mark. *Three Mile Island*. New York: Random House, 1980. Written by a staff member of the presidential commission. Recounts the immediate events of the incident and offers suggestions to avoid future problems.

U.S. General Accounting Office. *Three Mile Island: The Most Studied Nuclear Accident in History*. Washington, D.C.: Author, 1980. This inquiry was made to determine whether the investigations done up to that time were thorough and accurate in their presentation of the facts and their conclusions as to the causes of the accident. Eight investigative reports, as well as other materials, were reviewed. The General Accounting Office found that although reports varied as to depth and detail, the facts and conclusions were consistent. Equipment breakdowns, insufficient training of operators, poor design, and inadequate emergency and operating procedures were the chief culprits. Blame was also placed on the Nuclear Regulatory Commission with its poor structure, practices, and attitudes.

John R. Tate

Cross-References

The U.S. Government Creates the Tennessee Valley Authority (1933), p. 650; A Soviet Power Plant Begins an Era of Nuclear Energy (1954), p. 1046; GPU Announces Plans for a Commercial Nuclear Reactor (1963), p. 1196; The Environmental Protection Agency Is Created (1970), p. 1460; The United States Plans to Cut Dependence on Foreign Oil (1974), p. 1555; The Alaskan Oil Pipeline Opens (1977), p. 1653; Carter Orders Deregulation of Oil Prices (1979), p. 1699; Toxic Gas Leaks from a Union Carbide Plant in Bhopal, India (1984), p. 1893.

CARTER ORDERS DEREGULATION OF OIL PRICES

Category of event: Government and business
Time: April 5, 1979
Locale: Washington, D.C.

In response to increasing U.S. dependence on foreign oil and the rising costs of deliveries from OPEC producers, President Carter began deregulating the price of domestic oil

Principal personages:
 JIMMY CARTER (1924-   ), the president of the United States, 1977-1981
 HENRY M. JACKSON (1912-1983), a U.S. senator who led the fight against decontrol in Congress
 RICHARD M. NIXON (1913-1994), the president of the United States, 1969-1974

Summary of Event

Price controls on domestically produced oil were inaugurated in the United States in 1971 as part of Richard M. Nixon's efforts to curtail inflation. The inflation rate, or rate of increase in prices, was about 4 percent. That level would soon look benign, but at the time it was deemed to be unacceptably high. Eight years later, the administration of President Jimmy Carter confronted inflation rates, interest rates, and unemployment rates racing toward double-digit figures, largely as a result of international oil prices that had increased more than tenfold between 1973 and 1979. The Carter Administration would free most domestic oil from price controls in an effort to revive domestic production and decrease the country's growing dependence on oil imported from members of the Organization of Petroleum Exporting Countries (OPEC).

During the 1968-1973 period, economies across the developed democratic world began to expand at nearly twice the postwar rate. This rapid expansion caused problems in the economies of many of these countries. In the United States, the economy of which was already under inflationary pressure as a result of the Vietnam War, the rate of inflation climbed to and remained near 4 percent, threatening to undo real economic growth and the steady growth in the standard of living Americans had come to expect. Prior to the 1972 presidential campaign, the Nixon Administration moved aggressively to counteract inflationary pressures by taking the unprecedented peacetime step of imposing direct wage and price controls on broad sectors of the American economy.

Two years later, most of the controls had been removed by the Nixon Administration, but not the controls on petroleum. After October, 1973, when the price of imported oil nearly quadrupled, industry exerted strong political pressure to keep the cost controls on domestically produced oil. At the time, the United States imported about 30 percent of the oil that it consumed, and the quadrupling of its price had put severe cost pressures on American industry. Controls on the price of domestically produced oil remained in place throughout the remainder of the Nixon Administration and the Gerald Ford Administration that followed.

Liberal Democrats in Congress opposed President Ford's attempt to motivate conservation by decontrolling oil prices, thus allowing them to rise. The Democrats, who controlled Congress, argued that decontrol would produce additional financial pressure on consumers, with most of the benefit going to the oil companies. In response to Ford's proposal in 1975 to decontrol oil prices, Congress enacted the 1975 Energy Policy and Conservation Act, which continued mandatory controls on domestic oil prices through June 1, 1979. Thereafter, the president was empowered to extend, modify, or decontrol oil prices by executive action.

In 1979, congressional Democrats representing the energy- importing Northeast and Midwest were no more enthusiastic about decontrolling the price of oil than they had been four years before. By the third year of the Carter Administration, however, the situation facing the United States had altered considerably from that of 1975, when the American economy had seemed to be adjusting to the mix of controlled domestic oil prices and uncontrolled prices for imports from OPEC. Oil dependency had increased to the point at which half of America's oil needs were met by OPEC, which threatened another price hike. It had become apparent that the continued existence of controls on domestic oil was discouraging exploration for new petroleum sources and development of oil fields inside the United States, thus contributing to the country's growing dependence on OPEC suppliers.

On April 5, 1979, in a televised message to the American people, President Carter announced his intention to use his authority under the 1975 Energy Policy and Conservation Act to commence decontrolling domestically produced oil on June 1, with all controls on oil prices to be eliminated by October 1, 1981. Domestic producers were at the time allowed to sell their oil in a price range of $6 to $13 per barrel, depending on when it had been pumped from the ground. Decontrol would open the door to substantial "windfall" profits, since the world market price for oil at the time was approximately $14 per barrel. President Carter called upon Congress to enact a tax on these profits. The tax would enable some of the windfall to be channeled into support for a major government-backed program to research and develop synthetic fuel sources as alternatives to imported oil.

Ultimately, the president would get his way on both counts, but not without a fight. In the House of Representatives, the Commerce Committee on May 5 narrowly rejected a proposal to extend price controls by congressional action. The full House, with Republicans heavily defending decontrol, would in October likewise reject a proposal to retain controls.

Sustaining Carter's decontrol of the price of oil proved much easier for the White House than prying from Congress the proposed windfall profits tax. That tax faced stiff opposition from the Republican minority in both the Senate and the House of Representatives. Carter's original plan envisioned a 50 percent tax on windfall profits until 1981. The tax would be based on the price increase following decontrol and would apply to oil already being produced in the United States or held in storage. The tax would also be linked to all future oil price increases instituted by OPEC, again at the 50 percent rate. The "OPEC tax" part of the program was almost immediately watered down, ostensibly because it would apply to newly discovered oil as well as to already-flowing petroleum and thus might discourage exploration for new oil reserves. Wrangling in Congress, primarily in the Senate, delayed passage of the windfall profits tax until 1980 and reduced its scope by exempting from it income on oil discovered after 1978 and certain categories of costly-to-produce oil. Nevertheless, as passed by Congress, the windfall profits tax was expected to generate nearly $100 billion in revenue in the short term, to be used to find alternative energy sources for the United States. By 1990, the tax revenue was anticipated to be in excess of $200 billion.

Impact of Event

The consequences of the deregulation of the price of domestically produced oil offer good examples both of the impact of partisan change on American public policy and of the degree to which the unintended consequences of policies can ultimately compete with the intended benefits. The 1980 National Energy Security Act redirected revenues from the windfall profits tax to a variety of different energy options. Many "soft" energy options, including conservation programs and research in the solar power field, received subsidies as a result of the coalition-building process in Congress used to ensure a large majority in support of the act. The centerpiece of the program was a plan for loan guarantees and other government subsidies designed to encourage rapid research into, development of, and deployment of a synthetic fuels industry capable of generating more than a million barrels of oil per day from American coal and shale by the mid-1980's. This program of guarantees and subsidies had a projected price tag of nearly $80 billion. The quasi-corporate Synthetic Fuels Corporation (SFC) was chartered to oversee the program and award public contracts. It was immediately capitalized with nearly $20 billion.

Carter lost the 1980 presidential election to Ronald Reagan, who chose to place energy policy in the hands of the market. His campaign platform offered strong opposition to the SFC. The SFC thus had a brief history. Its directors were consumed with their own scandals and often went on record as sworn to shut it down. It was also victimized by the changing times. As the Reagan Administration began to project budgetary deficits, the money earmarked for government-backed energy research and development under the auspices of the SFC posed an all-too-tempting target. None of the money from windfall profits taxes would ever be appropriated to the SFC, and most of the agency's original allocation was rescinded or unspent by the time the SFC finally shut its doors in the mid-1980's. Not a single coal-into-oil or shale-into-oil plant was ever constructed.

Carter's 1979 decontrol of oil had affected 80 percent of all domestically produced oil by the time Reagan took office and affected the remainder several months ahead of schedule. The decontrol of domestic oil prices, combined with the soaring price of OPEC oil throughout 1979 and 1980 and projections that OPEC oil would be selling for at least $60 per barrel by 1990, launched a wave of exploration inside the United States. High-cost wells plunged miles beneath the surface in search of oil in once-fertile areas such as Oklahoma. Lured by the promise of rich returns, banks not only made loans easy to obtain for such ventures but also joined as partners in them. Unfortunately for the banks, many wells came up empty. The most substantial pools of oil already had been found. Even more unfortunately, the country, and in fact the entire Western world, slid into a major recession, and industrial operations were cut back. America's demand for oil plummeted at the very moment when the Alaskan oil pipeline made an additional two million barrels of oil per day available from domestic sources.

OPEC countries were caught in the middle. They desperately produced oil beyond their quotas to pay for their own contracted development schemes. In the face of this overproduction, the organization was unable to prevent the collapse of OPEC prices from a high of $38 per barrel in 1980 to less than $8 per barrel in mid-decade. American banks suffered the fallout from these developments. Some of the largest banks in Oklahoma and Texas collapsed along with the price of oil. Windfall profits had turned to losses.

Bibliography

Arrow, Kenneth J., and Joseph P. Kalt. *Petroleum Price Regulation: Should We Decontrol?* Washington, D.C.: American Enterprise Institute for Public Policy Research, 1979. Written on the eve of the Reagan Administration's decision to lift the last controls on petroleum, this short study contains most of the arguments in favor of decontrol in addition to a valuable discussion of the probable winners and losers inside the U.S. petroleum industry.

Banks, Ferdinand E. *The Political Economy of Oil.* Lexington, Mass.: Lexington Books, 1980. An excellent summary of the micro and macro aspects of increasing oil prices. The price, supply, and consumption of oil are all explored, along with the suppliers. An outstanding overview of the subject.

Bradley, Robert L., Jr. *The Mirage of Oil Protection.* Lanham, Md.: University Press of America, 1989. A solid historical examination of the frequently self-defeating efforts of government to intervene in oil markets. Bradley also offers a valuable analysis of OPEC's weakness.

Glasner, David. *Politics, Prices, and Petroleum: The Political Economy of Energy.* Cambridge, Mass.: Ballinger, 1985. A good, generally easy-to-follow work on energy scarcity, energy use, and the effect of energy policies on the market. Discusses natural gas as well as oil. Includes coverage of such basic topics as windfall profits and the effect of price controls on gasoline prices.

Kalt, Joseph P. *The Economics and Politics of Oil Price Regulation: Federal Policy in the Post-Embargo Era.* Cambridge, Mass.: Massachusetts Institute of Technology Press, 1981. An excellent analysis of the effects of price controls on the

American energy market, wrapped in an analytical framework as much concerned with normative as with positive economics. Extensive documentation.

Kash, Don E., and Robert W. Rycroft. *U.S. Energy Policy: Crisis and Complacency.* Norman: University of Oklahoma Press, 1984. A highly recommended critique of energy policy during the Reagan years and of the radical shift taken by that policy under Reagan, away from the traditional approach to energy policy in America.

Sherrill, Robert. *The Oil Follies of 1970-1980: How the Petroleum Industry Stole the Show (and Much More Besides).* Garden City, N.Y.: Anchor Press/Doubleday, 1983. A readable, argumentative, informative, and often thoughtful examination of oil politics in the 1970's, with a particularly good section on the oil industry's public relations work and a particularly bombastic analysis of the 1979 fight over decontrol.

Uslaner, Eric M. *Shale Barrel Politics.* Stanford, Calif.: Stanford University Press, 1989. Uses U.S. efforts to construct a shale oil industry as a case study. An excellent study of the obstacles to developing a coherent energy policy in the United States.

Yanarella, Ernest J., and William C. Green, eds. *The Unfulfilled Promise of Synthetic Fuels: Technological Failure, Policy Immobilism, or Commercial Illusion.* Westport: Conn.: Greenwood Press, 1987. A solid collection of remarkably jargon-free essays probing the rise and fall of the most recent American and international efforts to develop synthetic fuels as commercial energy sources for the Western world. The chapter on the American Synthetic Fuels Corporation is particularly relevant.

Joseph R. Rudolph, Jr.

Cross-References

The Panama Canal Opens (1914), p. 264; OPEC Meets for the First Time (1960), p. 1154; Atlantic Richfield Discovers Oil at Prudhoe Bay, Alaska (1967), p. 1331; An Offshore Oil Well Blows Out near Santa Barbara, California (1969), p. 1374; Nixon's Anti-Inflation Program Shocks Worldwide Markets (1971-1974), p. 1489; Arab Oil Producers Curtail Oil Shipments to Industrial States (1973), p. 1544; The United States Plans to Cut Dependence on Foreign Oil (1974), p. 1555; The Alaskan Oil Pipeline Opens (1977), p. 1653.

THE SUPREME COURT RULES ON AFFIRMATIVE ACTION PROGRAMS

Category of event: Labor
Time: June 27, 1979
Locale: Washington, D.C.

The Supreme Court upheld the legality of preferential treatment in the Weber case, making it possible for affirmative action programs to continue

Principal personages:
> BRIAN WEBER (1946-   ), a production worker at Kaiser Aluminum, Inc.
> WILLIAM J. BRENNAN, JR. (1906-   ), the Supreme Court justice who wrote the majority opinion
> WILLIAM H. REHNQUIST (1924-   ), the Supreme Court justice who wrote the dissenting opinion

Summary of Event

The passage of Title VII of the Civil Rights Act in 1964 made it illegal for employers to discriminate against anyone on the basis of race, sex, color, religion, or national origin. Title VII was supposed to create an atmosphere of equal opportunity, in which all candidates theoretically had the same chance to secure a job and other employment benefits. It was soon recognized, however, that prohibiting present and future discrimination would not fully remedy the consequences of past discrimination. Members of groups disadvantaged by prior discrimination did not have the experience, credentials, status, or contacts to compete on an equal footing with those who had never been the target of discrimination.

The government therefore imposed on federal contractors the duty to undertake "affirmative action," that is, to engage in special efforts to hire and promote members of groups that were underrepresented in their work forces. The overall goal was to bring groups that had been discriminated against into statistical parity in the work force at a faster than natural rate. Affirmative action required employers to compare the relevant labor market to their present labor force and to identify discrepancies and situations in which minorities and women were underrepresented. They then had to file written affirmative action plans that included goals, timetables, and strategies to correct the deficiencies.

Opponents soon chose to test the validity of affirmative action by questioning the legality of the results the legislation created. Affirmative action has been interpreted in several ways. It was commonly understood that an employer undertaking affirmative action would actively recruit underrepresented groups, eliminate managerial prejudices toward underrepresented groups, and remove employment practices that put victims of previous discrimination at a disadvantage. There has never been a question about the legality of these types of practices. To most employers, however, the safest way to comply with affirmative action involved extending preferential treatment to qualified members of underrepresented groups through the use of hiring quotas. This meant, for example, that if women were underrepresented in a particular company, and a woman and a white man applied for a job and had the same qualifications, the woman would be given preference. At the extreme, quotas might also result in less-qualified women and people of color being preferred over white men. Such practices resulted in what was called reverse discrimination against members of groups that were adequately represented, in particular, white men.

Such a result appeared to be in conflict with Title VII (section 703), which specifically prohibits employment discrimination based on race, gender, color, religion, or national origin. The basic issue was therefore whether an affirmative action plan that classifies people according to their race, gender, and national origin and then makes employment decisions at least partially based on those classifications violated Title VII. Opponents of affirmative action argued that its practical effect mandated preferential treatment for certain groups of people, while Title VII specifically stated that it did not require the granting of preferential treatment. A series of court cases, most of which reached the Supreme Court and culminated in the ruling in *United Steelworkers of America v. Weber*, eventually decided the fate of affirmative action.

The Supreme Court initially seemed to take a position against preferential treatment, in *Griggs v. Duke Power Co.* (1971). This case concerned a company that had unintentionally produced a discriminatory effect against African Americans by requiring tests and educational credentials that were not job related. The decision made it clear that the court considered these practices to be violations of Title VII and that artificial and unnecessary barriers to employment had to be removed. The court also specifically stated, however, that no person or group had a right to preferential treatment simply because of membership in a particular group or because of being the target of prior discrimination.

The arguments against preferential treatment seemed to grow stronger in 1976 with *McDonald v. Santa Fe Trail Transportation Company*. Three men, two white and one black, were charged with the same indiscretion. The company fired the two white men but gave the black man a warning. The two white men charged the company with discrimination, but the company responded that Title VII was meant to protect the disadvantaged and that the two white men therefore had no protection. The Supreme Court disagreed, eventually ruling that the term "race" was all-inclusive and Title VII therefore also prohibited discrimination against whites.

Another 1976 ruling, this time by a lower court, ordered American Telephone and Telegraph (AT&T) to pay damages to a white man who had lost a promotion to a woman with less experience and seniority. The promotion decision had been made in the context of a federal consent decree, in which AT&T had agreed to hire and promote women and people of color into jobs previously dominated by white men. The male employee believed that he was nevertheless the victim of sex discrimination, and the court agreed, contending that "innocent employees" should not be made to pay for a company's past discriminatory practices.

A more direct blow was dealt to affirmative action in *Regents of the University of California v. Bakke* (1978). The university reserved a percentage of its medical school openings for minority students. A white applicant was denied admission to the University of California at Davis Medical School because the white allotment had been filled and the only slots open were those saved for minority candidates. In a narrow and indecisive ruling, the Supreme Court affirmed a lower court order to admit Allan Bakke to the medical school, claiming that the university's admission system violated both the Constitution's equal protection amendment and Title VII. The Court made it clear that quotas based exclusively on race were illegal in a situation in which no previous discrimination had been shown. The justices did not, however, outlaw the use of quotas in situations where previous discrimination had occurred. The Supreme Court further muddied the waters when it also ruled that although race could not be the sole deciding factor, the university could continue to take race into consideration in its selection system.

The net effect of these decisions placed employers in a difficult position and affirmative action in potential jeopardy. In the light of the various rulings, employers believed that they had to find ways to increase the presence and position of underrepresented groups without causing any discrimination against the white majority. Such a balancing act was extremely difficult, if not impossible. The controversy was finally decided in 1979 with *United Steelworkers of America v. Weber*.

In 1974, the United Steelworkers of America and Kaiser Aluminum voluntarily entered into a fifteen-plant collective bargaining agreement that included an affirmative action plan designed to remedy racial imbalances in Kaiser's skilled craft work force. The plan reserved half of the openings to in-house craft training programs for African Americans until the percentage of black craft workers at Kaiser mirrored the local labor force. The litigation arose from a charge at the Gramercy plant in Louisiana, where 1.83 percent of the skilled craft workers were black, while 39 percent of the local work force was black. After the plan was put into operation, seven black and six white workers were selected from the production work force to enter the training program. Brian Weber, a white production worker, bid for admission into the program and was rejected; he had more seniority than all the black workers who were selected. Weber subsequently filed a class action suit, alleging that the plan discriminated against whites and was therefore in violation of Title VII.

The basic issue was whether a private sector employer could voluntarily implement an affirmative action plan that involved preferential treatment when there was no proof of prior discrimination but the work force did demonstrate racial or sexual imbalance. The majority opinion, authored by Justice William J. Brennan, Jr., ruled that any employer or union that was trying to eliminate imbalances in its work force could voluntarily use a plan that involved preferential treatment, even if that plan benefited individuals who had not themselves been the victims of discrimination. In reaching this decision, the justices emphasized that Kaiser's affirmative action plan was the result of negotiation and agreement between the company and the union. The

Supreme Court further stipulated that although Title VII does not require preferential treatment, neither does it prohibit it.

The Weber decision did not legitimize all quota systems. It stated that in order for a quota system to be lawful, it must be part of a permissible affirmative action plan. The court offered the following guidelines as to what constitutes a permissible affirmative action plan: It is designed to break down old patterns of discrimination, it does not needlessly trammel the interests of white employees, it does not create an absolute bar to whites, it is a temporary corrective measure, and it has the goal of eliminating racial imbalance.

There was a strong dissent in the *Weber* case, authored by Justice William H. Rehnquist. The minority quoted convincing evidence from the *Congressional Record* that indicated that some members of Congress, including strong proponents of the bill, did indeed intend that Title VII prohibit all preferential treatment.

Impact of Event

Review of the findings of *Weber* and the previous cases results in a four-faceted scenario. If an employer has been found guilty of employment discrimination, affirmative action involving preferential treatment appears to be sanctioned by Title VII, which allows the courts to impose any relief or affirmative action deemed appropriate. In these cases, the affirmative action is viewed as a remedy for illegal behavior, that is, a way to redress an imbalance created by deliberate discrimination. On the other hand, if an employer has an imbalanced work force but has not been found guilty of discrimination, the courts have no power to order any plan involving preferential treatment. A firm is free, however, to voluntarily adopt measures that result in preferential treatment, provided they are part of a permissible affirmative action plan. Although "permissible" has never been specifically defined, the five criteria laid out in *Weber* are regarded as useful guidelines. Finally, a firm cannot voluntarily adopt preferential treatment tactics that are not part of a permissible affirmative action plan.

The Weber ruling is especially noteworthy because it is one of the few in judicial history in which a court has rejected the actual wording of a statute in favor of what it interprets as the legislative intent. The Court acknowledged that Title VII does indeed prohibit all racial discrimination but contended that the law had to be interpreted in the context of the history and purpose of Title VII. The Court held that the primary concern of Title VII was the plight and position of African Americans, and it was therefore illogical to assume that the act would therefore ban all voluntary and race-conscious efforts to correct the effects of past discrimination. In effect, the Court said that despite the inevitable result of reverse discrimination, preferential treatment is permissible when its goal is the correction of longstanding social problems. Based on this reasoning, and despite subsequent challenges, most major firms in the United States implemented affirmative action, and most plans involved some degree of preferential treatment.

The battle, as of the early 1990's, was probably far from over. From its inception, affirmative action has had its detractors and its defenders. Both proponents and opponents of affirmative action continued to make valid and legitimate points about the evils and the benefits of preferential treatment. Some voiced moral and societal objections; opponents protested that it is unfair to require present generations to pay for the sins of predecessors, that affirmative action causes discrimination against white men, and that all employment decisions should be based solely upon merit. Detractors further argue that any legislation that allows preferential treatment is bound to increase hostility toward the groups it is meant to help. Others point out, however, that to rely on the natural progression of time to correct the effects of past discrimination would take far too long and would perpetuate an untenable situation.

Although the Weber ruling may have settled prominent legal questions about preferential treatment and affirmative action, it by no means ended the controversy. The continuing debate again took center stage in the late 1980's, when a more conservative Supreme Court handed down a series of decisions unfavorable to affirmative action and equal employment opportunity legislation. Congress quickly responded with the Civil Rights Act of 1991, which basically undid all the conservative Court decisions.

Legislative and judicial activity continued to generate uncertainty for businesses, as they did their best to hire and promote women and people of color while still trying to treat individual white men fairly. This balancing act appeared to be producing mixed results. Because of affirmative action, women and people of color gained entry into organizations, but they were not being promoted into higher and more influential positions. Whether affirmative action can be declared a success, therefore, had yet to be determined.

Bibliography

Buchholz, Rogene A. "Equal Employment Opportunity." In *Business Environment and Public Policy*. 4th ed. Englewood Cliffs, N.J.: Prentice-Hall, 1992. Chapter 12 provides a concise and understandable synopsis of affirmative action. Gives insight to both sides of the issue. Excellent summary of major cases dealing with affirmative action.

Dudley, William, ed. "Does Affirmative Action Alleviate Discrimination?" In *Racism in America: Opposing Viewpoints*. San Diego, Calif.: Greenhaven Press, 1991. Presents a series of articles arguing both for and against affirmative action. Provides moral and societal context. Lively style, interesting points.

Eisenberg, Theodore. *Civil Rights Legislation*. 3d ed. Charlottesville, Va.: Michie, 1991. Provides a lengthy reprint of the Weber ruling and other significant affirmative action cases. Written in lawbook fashion. Somewhat difficult to understand for those not versed in the law.

Ledvinka, James, and Vida Scarpello. *Federal Regulation of Personnel and Human Resource Management*. 2d ed. Boston: PWS-Kent, 1991. Provides an excellent history of the controversy surrounding preferential treatment. Easy to read.

Player, Mack. *Federal Law of Employment Discrimination in a Nutshell*. 3d ed. St. Paul, Minn.: West, 1992. A "nutshell" reference guide to employment discrimination law. Contains the latest legal developments. Lays out highlights in a brief, orderly fashion.

Marie McKendall

Cross-References

Congress Passes the Equal Pay Act (1963), p. 1185; The Civil Rights Act Prohibits Discrimination in Employment (1964), p. 1229; The Supreme Court Orders the End of Discrimination in Hiring (1971), p. 1495; The Pregnancy Discrimination Act Extends Employment Rights (1978), p. 1682; *Firefighters v. Stotts* Upholds Seniority Systems (1984), p. 1882; The Supreme Court Upholds Quotas as a Remedy for Discrimination (1986), p. 1915; Bush Signs the Americans with Disabilities Act of 1990 (1990), p. 2028.

SONY INTRODUCES THE WALKMAN

Category of event: New products
Time: July 1, 1979
Locale: Tokyo, Japan

The Sony Walkman provided personal, portable stereo sound and became the most successful audio product of the 1980's

Principal personages:
 AKIO MORITA (1921-   ), a Japanese physicist and engineer, cofounder
  of Sony
 MASARU IBUKA (1908-   ), a Japanese engineer who cofounded Sony
 NORIO OHGA (1930-   ), a Japanese opera singer and businessman who
  ran Sony's tape recorder division before becoming president of the
  company in 1982

Summary of Event

The Sony Walkman was the result of the convergence of two technologies: the transistor, which enabled miniaturization of electronic components, and the compact cassette, a worldwide standard for magnetic recording tape. As the smallest tape player devised, the Walkman was based on a systems approach that made use of advances in several unrelated areas, including improved loudspeaker design and reduced battery size. The Sony company brought them together in an innovative product that found a mass market in a remarkably short time.

Tokyo Telecommunications Engineering, which became Sony, was one of many small entrepreneurial companies that made audio products in the years following World War II. It was formed in the ruins of Tokyo, Japan, in 1946, and got its start manufacturing components for inexpensive radios and record players. They were the ideal products for a company with some expertise in electrical engineering and a limited manufacturing capability.

Akio Morita and Masaru Ibuka formed Tokyo Telecommunications Engineering to make a variety of electrical testing devices and instruments, but their real interests were in sound, and they decided to concentrate on audio products. They introduced a reel-to-reel tape recorder in 1946. Its success ensured that the company would remain in the audio field. The trade name of the magnetic tape they manufactured was "Soni," this was the origin of the company's new name, adopted in 1957. The 1953 acquisition of a license to use Bell Laboratories, transistor technology was a turning point in the fortunes of Sony, for it led the company to the highly popular transistor radio and started it along the path to reducing the size of consumer products. In the 1960's, Sony led the way to smaller and cheaper radios, tape recorders, and television sets, all using transistors instead of vacuum tubes.

The original marketing strategy for manufacturers of mechanical entertainment devices had been to put one into every home. This was the goal for Edison's phonograph, the player piano, the Victrola, and the radio receiver. Sony and other Japanese manufacturers found out that if a product were small enough and cheap enough, two or three might be purchased for home use, or even for outdoors use. This was the marketing lesson of the transistor radio.

The unparalleled sales of transistor radios indicated that consumer durables intended for entertainment were not exclusively used in the home. The appeal of the transistor radio was that it made entertainment portable. Sony applied this concept to televisions and tape recorders, developing small portable units powered by batteries. Sony was first to produce a "personal" television set, with a five-inch screen. To the surprise of many manufacturers who said there would never be a market for such a novelty item, it sold well.

It was impossible to reduce tape recorders to the size of transistor radios because of the problems of handling very small reels of tape and the high power required to turn them. Portable tape recorders required several large flashlight batteries. Although tape had the advantage of recording capability, it could not challenge the popularity of the microgroove 45 revolution-per-minute (rpm) disc because the tape player was much more difficult to operate. In the 1960's, several types of tape cartridge were introduced to overcome this problem, including the eight-track tape cartridge and the Philips compact cassette. Sony and Matsushita were two of the leading Japanese manufacturers that quickly incorporated the compact cassette into their audio products, producing the first cassette players available in the United States.

The portable cassette players of the 1960's and 1970's were based on the transistor radio concept: small loudspeaker, transistorized amplifier, and flashlight batteries all enclosed in a plastic case. The size of transistorized components was being reduced constantly, and new types of batteries, notably the nickel cadmium combination, offered higher power output in smaller sizes. The problem of reducing the size of the loudspeaker without serious deterioration of sound quality blocked the path to very small cassette players. Sony's engineers solved the problem with a very small loudspeaker device using plastic diaphragms and new, lighter materials for the magnets. These devices were incorporated into tiny stereo headphones that set new standards of fidelity.

The first "walkman" was made by Sony engineers for the personal use of Masaru Ibuka. He wanted to be able to listen to high-fidelity recorded sound wherever he went, and the tiny player was small enough to fit inside a pocket. Sony was experienced in reducing the size of machines. At the same time the walkman was being made up, Sony engineers were struggling to produce a video recording cassette that was also small enough to fit into Ibuka's pocket.

Although the portable stereo was part of a long line of successful miniaturized consumer products, it was not immediately recognized as a commercial technology. There were already plenty of cassette players in home units, in automobiles, and in portable players. Marketing experts questioned the need for a tiny version. The board of directors of Sony had to be convinced by Morita that the new product had commercial potential. The Sony Soundabout portable cassette player was introduced to the market in 1979.

Impact of Event

The Soundabout was initially treated as a novelty in the audio equipment industry. At a price of $200, it could not be considered as a product for the mass market. Although it sold well in Japan, where people were used to listening to music on headphones, sales in the United States were not encouraging. Sony's engineers, working under the direction of Kozo Ohsone, reduced the size and cost of the machine. In 1981, the Walkman II was introduced. It was 25 percent smaller than the original version and had 50 percent less moving parts. Its price was considerably lower and continued to fall.

The Walkman opened a huge market for audio equipment that nobody knew existed. Sony had again confounded the marketing experts who doubted the appeal of a new consumer electronics product. It took about two years for Sony's Japanese competitors, including Matsushita, Toshiba, and Aiwa, to bring out portable personal stereos. Such was the popularity of the device that any miniature cassette player was called a "walkman," irrespective of the manufacturer. Sony kept ahead of the competition by constant innovation: Dolby noise reduction circuits were added in 1982, and a rechargeable battery feature was introduced in 1985. The machine became smaller, until it was barely larger than the audio cassette it played.

Sony developed a whole line of personal stereos. Waterproofed Walkmans were marketed to customers who wanted musical accompaniment to water sports. There were special models for tennis players and joggers. The line grew to encompass about forty different types of portable cassette players, priced from about $30 to $500 for a high-fidelity model.

In the ten years following the introduction of the Walkman, Sony sold fifty million units, including twenty-five million in the United States. Its competitors sold millions more. They were manufactured all over the Far East and came in a broad range of sizes and prices, with the cheapest models about $20. Increased competition in the portable tape player market continually forced down prices. Sony had to respond to the huge numbers of cheap copies by redesigning the Walkman to bring down its cost and by automating its production. The playing mechanism became part of the integrated circuit that provided amplification, allowing manufacturing as one unit.

The Walkman did more than revive sales of audio equipment in the sagging market of the late 1970's. It stimulated demand for cassette tapes and helped make the compact cassette the worldwide standard for magnetic tape. At the time the Walkman was introduced, the major form of prerecorded sound was the vinyl microgroove record. In 1983, the ratio of vinyl to cassette sales was 3:2. By the end of the decade, the audio cassette was the bestselling format for recorded sound, outselling vinyl records and compact discs combined by a ratio of 2:1. The compatibility of the audio cassette used in personal players with the home stereo ensured that it would be the most popular tape recording medium.

The market for portable personal players in the United States during the decade of the 1990's was estimated to be more than twenty million units each year. Sony accounted for half of the 1991 American market of fifteen million units selling at an average price of $50. It appeared that there would be more than one in every home. In some parts of Western Europe, there were more cassette players than people, reflecting the level of market penetration achieved by the Walkman.

The ubiquitous Walkman had a noticeable effect on the way that people listen to music. The sound from the headphones of a portable player is more intimate and immediate than the sound coming from the loudspeakers of a home stereo. The listener can hear a wider range of frequencies and more of the lower amplitudes of music, while the reverberation caused by sound bouncing off walls is reduced. The listening public has become accustomed to the Walkman sound and expects it to be duplicated on commercial recordings. Recording studios that once mixed their master recordings to suit the reproduction characteristics of car or transistor radios began to mix them for Walkman headphones. Personal stereos also enable the listener to experience more of the volume of recorded sound because it is injected directly into the ear.

The Walkman established a market for portable tape players that exerted an influence on all subsequent audio products. The introduction of the compact disc (CD) in 1983 marked a completely new technology of recording based on digital transformation of sound. It was jointly developed by the Sony and Philips companies. Despite the enormous technical difficulties of reducing the size of the laser reader and making it portable, Sony's engineers devised the Discman portable compact disc player, which was unveiled in 1984. It followed the Walkman concept exactly and offered higher fidelity than the cassette tape version. The Discman sold for about $300 when it was introduced, but its price soon dropped to less than $100. It did not achieve the volume of sales of the audio cassette version because fewer CDs than audio cassettes were in use. The slow acceptance of the compact disc hindered sales growth. The Discman could not match the portability of the Walkman because vibrations caused the laser reader to skip tracks.

In the competitive market for consumer electronics products, a company must innovate to survive. Sony had watched cheap competition erode the sales of many of its most successful products, particularly the transistor radio and personal television, and was committed to both product improvement and new entertainment technologies. It knew that the personal cassette player had a limited sales potential in the advanced industrial countries, especially after the introduction of digital recording in the 1980's. It therefore sought new technology to apply to the Walkman concept. Throughout the 1980's, Sony and its many competitors searched for a new version of the Walkman.

The next generation of personal players was likely to be based on digital recording. Sony introduced its digital audio tape (DAT) system in 1990. This used the same digital technology as the compact disc but came in tape form. It was incorporated into expensive home players; naturally, Sony engineered a portable version. The tiny DAT

Walkman offered unsurpassed fidelity of reproduction, but its incompatibility with any other tape format and its high price limited its sales to professional musicians and recording engineers.

After the failure of DAT, Sony refocused its digital technology into a format more similar to the Walkman. Its Mini Disc (MD) used the same technology as the compact disc but had the advantage of a recording capability. The 2.5-inch disc was smaller than the CD, and the player was smaller than the Walkman. The play-only version fit in the palm of a hand. A special feature prevented the skipping of tracks that caused problems with the Discman. The Mini Disc followed the path blazed by the Walkman and represented the most advanced technology applied to personal stereo players. At a price of about $500 in 1993, it was still too expensive to compete in the audio cassette Walkman market, but the history of similar products illustrates that rapid reduction of price could be achieved even with a complex technology.

The Walkman had a powerful influence on the development of other digital and optical technologies. The laser readers of compact disc players can access visual and textual information in addition to sound. Sony introduced the Data Discman, a handheld device that displayed text and pictures on a tiny screen. Several other manufacturers marketed electronic books. Whatever the shape of future entertainment and information technologies, the legacy of the Walkman will put a high premium on portability, small size, and the interaction of machine and user.

Bibliography

Armstrong, Larry, and Amy Borrus. "Sony's Challenge." *Business Week*, June 1, 1987, 64-69. A profile of the company at a crossroads in its fortunes. Dwells on unsuccessful products and the problems that Sony faced in the intensely competitive market for electronic products.

Klein, Larry. "Happy Tenth Anniversary, Sony Walkman!" *Radio-Electronics* 60 (October, 1989): 72-73. A short history of the Walkman, written by an audio expert who had covered this product since its introduction.

Lyons, Nick. *The Sony Vision*. New York: Crown Publishers, 1976. A popular history of Sony that outlines the philosophy of its founders. Ends in the 1970's and therefore does not cover the development of the portable stereo.

Morita, Akio, with Edwin Reingold and Mitsuko Shimomura. *Made in Japan: Akio Morita and Sony*. New York: Dutton, 1986. A personal account of the history of the Sony corporation from the end of World War II to the 1980's. Relies heavily on Morita's memory and his own somewhat biased accounts of the development of key products.

Schlender, Brenton R. "How Sony Keeps the Magic Going." *Fortune* 125 (February 24, 1992): 76-79. An overview of the Sony Corporation, with an emphasis on its latest products. Provides information about the corporate culture and the style of research and development. Has a rare interview with Masaru Ibuka.

Andre Millard

Cross-References

Bell Labs Is Formed (1925), p. 470; Morita Licenses Transistor Technology (1953), p. 1009; Sony Introduces the Betamax (1975), p. 1573; Compact Discs Reach the Market (1983), p. 1848; Sony Purchases Columbia Pictures (1989), p. 1996.

AMERICAN FIRMS ADOPT JAPANESE MANUFACTURING TECHNIQUES

Category of event: Manufacturing
Time: The 1980's
Locale: The United States

American firms, in response to gaps in productivity and quality, adopted various techniques developed in Japan

Principal personages:
> TAIICHI OHNO (1912-   ), a vice president of Toyota Motor, inventor of just-in-time concepts
> SHIGEO SHINGO (1909-   ), an engineer and consultant who invented just-in-time inventory practices in collaboration with Ohno
> KIICHIRŌ TOYODA (1925-   ), the president of Toyota Motor

Summary of Event

The adoption of just-in-time inventory practices by American firms in the early 1980's helped American industry to respond to the Japanese challenge. Firms were making vigorous efforts to close gaps in their productivity and quality, which had both fallen behind the performance of Japanese firms. The United States had been directly confronted by the productivity and quality levels achieved by Japanese industry, which seriously threatened the competitiveness of American firms.

The typical Japanese business orientation maintained that a company that allows exploitation, including that of consumers, cannot achieve long-term success. The astonishing results obtained in Japan through focusing on quality, long-range strategic planning, partnership with suppliers, and adoption of the principle that the employees are the company necessitated a rethinking of priorities and a change of outlook on the part of American industry. Many Western managers believed that Japanese techniques could not be applied in Western companies and that matching Japan's successes would be impossible. Evidence refuted notions that these accomplishments resulted from cultural differences, and managers became willing to experiment with the techniques.

Japan's fundamental economic goal since 1945 had been to achieve full employment through industrialization. As a means of attaining this goal, the Japanese employed a strategy to gain dominance in selected product areas. They imported technology, concentrated on achieving high productivity, and embarked on a drive to improve quality and reliability. Two basic concepts behind the drive toward dominance were elimination of waste and respect for people. Elimination of waste involved such tactics as keeping plants small and specialized, using workers in groups to take advantage of teamwork and cooperation, producing with just-in-time methods, and minimizing setup times for jobs. Respect for people involved lifetime employment, unions sponsored by companies, use of automation and robotics to eliminate tedious and dangerous tasks for humans, management by consensus or committee, and quality circles. The Japanese recognized that every worker could make a contribution, often beyond his or her immediate tasks, and that suppliers often could assist in improving a company's productivity or in reducing its costs.

Some of the new Japanese techniques were difficult to translate into the American industrial environment because of cultural factors or resistance on the part of workers. Many, however, were appropriate and practical, such as the just-in-time philosophy, minimized setup time, and concentration on quality. The just-in-time philosophy acted as a framework and organizing principle for other innovations.

Most accounts agree that the just-in-time philosophy was developed in Japan at Toyota Motor Corporation. Until the late 1970's, the technique was limited in use to Toyota and its family of key suppliers. In 1949, Toyota had found itself on the brink of bankruptcy. At that time, the United States was far more productive than Japan in automobile production. Kiichirō Toyoda, president of Toyota Motor Corporation, issued a challenge to his company to catch up with the United States within three years. Responding to the challenge, Taiichi Ohno, a company vice president, pointed out that the lack of success was a result of wastefulness in the production process. Ohno proceeded to organize a production system dedicated to elimination of waste. In collaboration with Shigeo Shingo, an engineer, he invented the just-in-time system. Under that system, parts arrive at the company or at individual workstations just in time for their use, rather than being stockpiled. The company thus saves the costs of carrying large inventories of parts or components. The system also encouraged greater coordination of plans both within the company and with outside suppliers.

Toyota's subsequent success has been attributed to implementation of an integrated production system based on the elements described previously. The system, however, was not a quick solution to management problems. Experts estimated that such a system might take as long as ten years to develop and integrate because it involved such a radical overhaul of management philosophy and worker orientation to jobs.

Ohno realized that managers needed to change their concept of how business was done, at all levels of the company. The secret of success was a never-ending search for improvements in productivity and quality. Ohno was inspired by his observation of an American supermarket, in which items selected from shelves by customers were replaced just in time for the next round of customers. He saw that as a model of efficiency.

The production system developed at Toyota did not receive much attention until the 1970's, when other Japanese firms began to recognize the potential suggested by the system. During the late 1960's, managers in the United States began to realize that systems for production management and scheduling were imposing costs that were larger than necessary. Managers therefore began to concentrate on efficiency in production. At the same time, however, firms were also concerned with diversifying into new fields and improving the quality of their products. Within this context, the emphasis on efficiency was lost.

The financial burden associated with large inventories produced a revolution in production scheduling and resulted in a shift in priority to focusing on reducing inventory costs through such just-in-time systems as materials requirement planning (MRP). The conviction that MRP was the answer to the just-in-time challenge survived until the mid-1970's, when American managers noticed that Japanese firms operating without MRP still obtained better results. As they studied the Japanese approach, American managers noticed that it was considerably simpler. To attain the best results, however, it was necessary to introduce radically new approaches and modes of thinking.

Impact of Event

A survey in 1984 found that American firms that had applied just-in-time methods had obtained extraordinary results. Not uncommon were 90 percent reductions in throughput time, 90 percent reductions of work in process, 10 to 30 percent reductions in manufacturing costs, 75 percent reductions in setup times, and 50 percent reductions in the floor space required for production. Similarly, a study of eighty European plants revealed typical benefits of 50 to 70 percent reductions in throughput time, 50 percent reductions in average inventories, 20 to 50 percent increases in productivity, 50 percent reductions in setup times, and an average payback for investments in just-in-time methods of less than nine months.

In 1976, a Quasar plant in Chicago that manufactured Motorola television sets was purchased by Matsushita. Within two years, with the same full-time work force, Matsushita doubled output, increased product quality twentyfold, and reduced the costs of servicing warranties by more than 90 percent. General Motors began using Japanese techniques in 1980 and soon cut inventory costs by about 75 percent, increasing the turnover of inventories almost fivefold. Other American automobile manufacturers obtained similar results.

General Electric, Westinghouse, and RCA also reported impressive results. The computer system division of Hewlett-Packard increased productivity by 55 percent, decreased welding defects by more than 90 percent and rejected items by 95 percent, and reduced the lead time for production by 90 percent. Other American companies that profitably adopted Japanese production techniques, including just-in-time inventory practices, included Black & Decker (power tools), Deere & Company (heavy machinery and farm equipment), and American Telephone and Telegraph. In Europe, gains were equally impressive. Firms benefiting from the techniques were as diverse as Olivetti (typewriters), Michelin (steel cord), Fiat (aircraft engine parts), Famitalia Carlo Erba (pharmaceuticals), Lever Industriale (detergents), and Europa Metalli (metals).

Just-in-time practices were applied to processing industries such as production of chemicals, pharmaceuticals, and metals as well as to production to order and to more traditional manufacturing. Just-in-time practices proved applicable in service industries as well as in the factory. The successes, however, did not mean that implementation of Japanese production techniques was free of problems or provided the solution to every difficulty. Many problems refused to go away quickly. Resistance to change by both managers and workers, underestimation of education and training needs, shortages of parts or components as production scheduling changed, and lack of commitment were commonly reported.

The 1980's will be remembered as a period of dramatic change in Western manufacturing. Changes for the most part had their source in the overwhelming success of Japanese industry in lowering costs and improving quality, as demonstrated by Toyota, Suzuki, and many manufacturers of electronic components, among other firms. Once they realized that they had fallen behind in the productivity race with Japan, many Western managers thought that they were beaten. Until the end of the 1970's, many of them believed that catching up would be impossible. They had preconceived notions about the sources of Japanese success, including a belief that Japan had unbeatable advantages in labor costs, the number of labor hours per worker, worker attitudes, and punctual suppliers. Western managers did not believe that these conditions could be matched in their environments. Facts soon demolished all of these alibis for poor performance, and Western managers had no choice but to try to understand the Japanese lesson and make serious efforts to close the productivity and quality gaps.

The Japanese successes particularly affected American industry, as the two countries competed in many product lines, but other countries also found themselves challenged. American managers launched their own revolutions in strategy, organization, management, and workplace culture, sometimes modeling efforts on Japanese successes and other times creating new techniques to fit the American environment.

Management philosophy came to accept that quality rather than efficiency was the top priority and that operating horizons had to be expanded beyond the short term to achieve long-term success. Clients were to be satisfied as well as possible, even if that meant spending money in the short term. Suppliers were partners in the production process, and employees were not merely suppliers of labor but instead could make valuable contributions through their ideas and simply through becoming more motivated and more concerned about the welfare of the company. Further developments set in motion by the advent of just-in-time techniques included focusing on rapid development and introduction of new product lines and achieving competitive advantage through flexibility in manufacturing.

Bibliography

Hay, Edward J. *The Just-in-Time Breakthrough*. New York: Wiley, 1988. A dynamic, comprehensive, practical, and clearly written explanation of just-in-time concepts and their relationship to quality, vendors, management, systems, and technology. Written from the perspective of an experienced practitioner. Outlines the process of getting started and cautions against the pitfalls.

Hernandez, Arnaldo. *Just-in-Time Manufacturing: A Practical Approach*. Englewood Cliffs, N.J.: Prentice-Hall, 1989. Explains the fundamental concepts from a theoretical angle, covers critical operational rules, and provides specific instructions for starting a just-in-time system from scratch. Shows how the concepts apply to all levels in the organization, for both workers and management.

Hirano, Hiroyuki. *J.I.T. Factory Revolution: A Pictorial Guide to Factory Design of the Future*. Cambridge, Mass.: Productivity Press, 1989. An encyclopedic picture book of just-in-time practices. Shows how to set up each area of a plant and provides many useful ideas for implementation. Simply, easy-to-read text. Pictures provide a vivid depiction of work in a just-in-time environment.

Japan Management Association, ed. *Kanban and Just-in-Time at Toyota: Management Begins at the Workplace*. Translated by David J. Lu. Rev. ed. Cambridge, Mass.: Productivity Press, 1989. Based on seminars at Toyota, one of the best practical introductions to just-in-time procedures. Explains every aspect in clear and simple terms. Discusses the underlying rationale, system setup, getting everyone involved, and refining the system once in place.

Merli, Giorgio. *Total Manufacturing Management*. Cambridge, Mass.: Productivity Press, 1990. Provides a thorough comparison of Western and Japanese management approaches and cultural distinctions. Develops a model for production organization and integrates the tools and methods that support this model. Lays out the principles and steps for just-in-time practices and offers a powerfully integrated strategy and implementation plan.

Ohno, Taiichi. *Toyota Production System: Beyond Large-Scale Production*. Cambridge, Mass.: Productivity Press, 1988. Written to enable people to understand the system correctly and implement it successfully in their own plants. The emphasis is on concepts, with only a few case studies. Based on the knowledge and experience of one of the originators of just-in-time procedures.

Shingo, Shigeo. *A Study of the Toyota Production System from an Industrial Engineering Viewpoint*. Cambridge, Mass.: Productivity Press, 1989. Written by one of the inventors of the just-in-time system. Explains the philosophy, highlights the system's important aspects, provides additional information, and criticizes weaknesses. Aims to treat the subject in such a way that special features will stand out.

Kambiz Tabibzadeh

Cross-References

Hashimoto Forms the Roots of Nissan Motor Company (1911), p. 185; Ford Implements Assembly Line Production (1913), p. 234; Simon Publishes Administrative Behavior (1947), p. 890; Morita Licenses Transistor Technology (1953), p. 1009; CAD/CAM Revolutionizes Engineering and Manufacturing (1980's), p. 1721; Japan Becomes the World's Largest Automobile Producer (1980), p. 1751.

CAD/CAM REVOLUTIONIZES ENGINEERING AND MANUFACTURING

Category of event: Manufacturing
Time: The 1980's
Locale: The United States

Computer-Aided Design (CAD) and Computer-Aided Manufacturing (CAM) enhanced flexibility in engineering design, leading to higher quality and reduced time for manufacturing

Principal personages:
> PATRICK HANRATTY, a General Motors Research Laboratory worker who developed graphics programs
> JACK ST. CLAIR KILBY (1923-), a Texas Instruments employee who first conceived of the idea of the integrated circuit
> ROBERT NOYCE (1927-), an Intel Corporation employee who developed an improved process of manufacturing integrated circuits on microchips
> DON HALLIDAY, an early user of CAD/CAM who created the Made-in-America car in only four months by using CAD and project management software
> FRED BORSINI, an early user of CAD/CAM who demonstrated its power

Summary of Event

Computer-Aided Design (CAD) is a technique whereby geometrical descriptions of two-dimensional (2-D) or three-dimensional (3-D) objects can be created and stored, in the form of mathematical models, in a computer system. Points, lines, and curves are represented as graphical coordinates. When a drawing is requested from the computer, transformations are performed on the stored data, and the geometry of a part or a full view from either a two- or a three-dimensional perspective is shown. CAD systems replace the tedious process of manual drafting, and computer-aided drawing and redrawing that can be retrieved when needed has improved drafting efficiency. A CAD system is a combination of computer hardware and software that facilitates the construction of geometric models and, in many cases, their analysis. It allows a wide variety of visual representations of those models to be displayed.

Computer-Aided Manufacturing (CAM) refers to the use of computers to control, wholly or partly, manufacturing processes. In practice, the term is most often applied to computer-based developments of numerical control technology; robots and flexible manufacturing systems (FMS) are included in the broader use of CAM systems. A CAD/CAM interface is envisioned as a computerized database that can be accessed and enriched by either design or manufacturing professionals during various stages of the product development and production cycle.

In CAD systems of the early 1990's, the ability to model solid objects became widely available. The use of graphic elements such as lines and arcs and the ability to create a model by adding and subtracting solids such as cubes and cylinders are the basic principles of CAD and of simulating objects within a computer. CAD systems enable computers to simulate both taking things apart (sectioning) and putting things together for assembly. In addition to being able to construct prototypes and store images of different models, CAD systems can be used for simulating the behavior of machines, parts, and components. These abilities enable CAD to construct models that can be subjected to nondestructive testing; that is, even before engineers build a physical prototype, the CAD model can be subjected to testing and the results can be analyzed. As another example, designers of printed circuit boards have the ability to test their circuits on a CAD system by simulating the electrical properties of components.

During the 1950's, the U.S. Air Force recognized the need for reducing the development time for special aircraft equipment. As a result, the Air Force commissioned the Massachusetts Institute of Technology to develop numerically controlled (NC) machines that were programmable. A workable demonstration of NC machines was made in 1952; this began a new era for manufacturing. As the speed of an aircraft increased, the cost of manufacturing also increased because of stricter technical requirements. This higher cost provided a stimulus for the further development of NC technology, which promised to reduce errors in design before the prototype stage.

The early 1960's saw the development of mainframe computers. Many industries valued computing technology for its speed and for its accuracy in lengthy and tedious numerical operations in design, manufacturing, and other business functional areas. Patrick Hanratty, working for General Motors Research Laboratory, saw other potential applications and developed graphics programs for use on mainframe computers. The use of graphics in software aided the development of CAD/CAM, allowing visual representations of models to be presented on computer screens and printers.

The 1970's saw an important development in computer hardware, namely the development and growth of personal computers (PCs). Personal computers became smaller as a result of the development of integrated circuits. Jack St. Clair Kilby, working for Texas Instruments, first conceived of the integrated circuit; later, Robert Noyce, working for Intel Corporation, developed an improved process of manufacturing integrated circuits on microchips. Personal computers using these microchips offered both speed and accuracy at costs much lower than those of mainframe computers.

Five companies offered integrated commercial computer-aided design and computer-aided manufacturing systems by the first half of 1973. Integration meant that both design and manufacturing were contained in one system. Of these five companies—Applicon, Computervision, Gerber Scientific, Manufacturing and Consulting Services (MCS), and United Computing—four offered turnkey systems exclusively. Turnkey systems provide design, development, training, and implementation for each customer (company) based on the contractual agreement; they are meant to be used as delivered, with no need for the purchaser to make significant adjustments or perform programming.

The 1980's saw a proliferation of mini- and microcomputers with a variety of platforms (processors) with increased speed and better graphical resolution. This made the widespread development of computer-aided design and computer-aided manufacturing possible and practical. Major corporations spent large research and development budgets developing CAD/CAM systems that would automate manual drafting and machine tool movements. Don Halliday, working for Truesports Inc., provided an early example of the benefits of CAD/CAM. He created the Made-in-America car in only four months by using CAD and project management software. In the late 1980's, Fred Borsini, the president of Leap Technologies in Michigan, brought various products to market in record time through the use of CAD/CAM.

In the early 1980's, much of the CAD/CAM industry consisted of software companies. The cost for a relatively slow interactive system in 1980 was close to $100,000. The late 1980's saw the demise of minicomputer-based systems in favor of Unix work stations and PCs based on 386 and 486 microchips produced by Intel. By the time of the International Manufacturing Technology show in September, 1992, the industry could show numerous CAD/CAM innovations including tools, CAD/CAM models to evaluate manufacturability in early design phases, and systems that allowed use of the same data for a full range of manufacturing functions.

Impact of Event

In 1990, CAD/CAM hardware sales by U.S. vendors reached $2.68 billion. In software alone, $1.42 billion worth of CAD/CAM products and systems were sold worldwide by U.S. vendors, according to International Data Corporation figures for 1990. CAD/CAM systems were in widespread use throughout the industrial world. Development lagged in advanced software applications, particularly in image processing, and in the communications software and hardware that ties processes together.

A reevaluation of CAD/CAM systems was being driven by the industry trend toward increased functionality of computer-driven numerically controlled machines. Numerical control (NC) software enables users to graphically define the geometry of the parts in a product, develop paths that machine tools will follow, and exchange data among machines on the shop floor. In 1991, NC configuration software represented 86 percent of total CAM sales. In 1992, the market shares of the five largest companies in the CAD/CAM market were 29 percent for International Business Machines, 17 percent for Intergraph, 11 percent for Computervision, 9 percent for Hewlett-Packard, and 6 percent for Mentor Graphics.

General Motors formed a joint venture with Ford and Chrysler to develop a common computer language in order to make the next generation of CAD/CAM systems easier to use. The venture was aimed particularly at problems that posed barriers to speeding up the design of new automobiles. The three car companies all had sophisticated computer systems that allowed engineers to design parts on computers and then electronically transmit specifications to tools that make parts or dies.

CAD/CAM technology was expected to advance on many fronts. As of the early 1990's, different CAD/CAM vendors had developed systems that were often incompatible with one another, making it difficult to transfer data from one system to another. Large corporations, such as the major automakers, developed their own interfaces and network capabilities to allow different systems to communicate. Major users of CAD/CAM saw consolidation in the industry through the establishment of standards as being in their interests.

Resellers of CAD/CAM products also attempted to redefine their markets. These vendors provide technical support and service to users. The sale of CAD/CAM products and systems offered substantial opportunities, since demand remained strong. Resellers worked most effectively with small and medium-sized companies, which often were neglected by the primary sellers of CAD/CAM equipment because they did not generate a large volume of business. Some projections held that by 1995 half of all CAD/CAM systems would be sold through resellers, at a cost of $10,000 or less for each system. The CAD/CAM market thus was in the process of dividing into two markets: large customers (such as aerospace firms and automobile manufacturers) that would be served by primary vendors, and small and medium-sized customers that would be serviced by resellers.

CAD will find future applications in marketing, the construction industry, production planning, and large-scale projects such as shipbuilding and aerospace. Other likely CAD markets include hospitals, the apparel industry, colleges and universities, food product manufacturers, and equipment manufacturers. As the linkage between CAD and CAM is enhanced, systems will become more productive. The geometrical data from CAD will be put to greater use by CAM systems.

CAD/CAM already had proved that it could make a big difference in productivity and quality. Customer orders could be changed much faster and more accurately than in the past, when a change could require a manual redrafting of a design. Computers could do automatically in minutes what once took hours manually. CAD/CAM saved time by reducing, and in some cases eliminating, human error. Many flexible manufacturing systems (FMS) had machining centers equipped with sensing probes to check the accuracy of the machining process. These self-checks can be made part of numerical control (NC) programs. With the technology of the early 1990's, some experts estimated that CAD/CAM systems were in many cases twice as productive as the systems they replaced; in the long run, productivity is likely to improve even more, perhaps up to three times that of older systems or even higher. As costs for CAD/CAM systems concurrently fall, the investment in a system will be recovered more quickly. Some analysts estimated that by the mid-1990's, the recovery time for an average system would be about three years.

Another frontier in the development of CAD/CAM systems is expert (or knowledge-based) systems, which combine data with a human expert's knowledge, expressed in the form of rules that the computer follows. Such a system will analyze data in a manner mimicking intelligence. For example, a 3-D model might be created from standard 2-D drawings. Expert systems will likely play a pivotal role in CAM applications. For example, an expert system could determine the best sequence of machining operations to produce a component.

Continuing improvements in hardware, especially increased speed, will benefit CAD/CAM systems. Software developments, however, may produce greater benefits. Wider use of CAD/CAM systems will depend on the cost savings from improvements in hardware and software as well as on the productivity of the systems and the quality of their product. The construction, apparel, automobile, and aerospace industries have already experienced increases in productivity, quality, and profitability through the use of CAD/CAM. A case in point is Boeing, which used CAD from start to finish in the design of the 757.

Bibliography

Choobineh, Fred, and Suri Rajan, eds. *Flexible Manufacturing Systems*. Norcross, Ga.: Industrial Engineering and Management Press, Institute of Industrial Engineers, 1986. This book begins with a discussion of programmable automation technologies, including CAD/CAM, and covers planning, design, operation, and control issues involved in flexible manufacturing systems.

Groover, Mikell P., and Emory W. Zimmers, Jr. *CAD/CAM: Computer-Aided Design and Manufacturing*. Englewood Cliffs, N.J.: Prentice-Hall, 1984. A textbook for CAD/CAM theory and practice; also a good source for learners of CAD/CAM.

Henderson, Breck W. "CAD/CAM Systems Transform Aerospace Engineering." *Aviation Week and Space Technology* 136 (January 22, 1992): 49-51. Describes use of computer-aided design and computer-aided manufacturing in the aerospace industry, where it is widely accepted. New tools have eliminated costly design steps and made product development faster and cheaper. Data generated by sophisticated CAD/CAM systems have allowed rapid prototyping, allowing conversion of CAD data directly into solid models of complex parts in a matter of hours and for a fraction of the cost of traditional methods.

Jurgen, Ronald K. *Computers and Manufacturing Productivity*. New York: Institute of Electrical and Electronics Engineers, 1987. Devoted exclusively to a discussion of productivity and automation. Full of illustrations, data, and issues, presented in an easy-to-read format.

Machover, Carl, and Robert E. Blauth, eds. *The CAD/CAM Handbook*. Bedford, Mass.: Computervision Corporation, 1980. A fairly comprehensive book on CAD/CAM. Serves both general and advanced readers.

Medland, A. J., and Piers Burnett. *CAD/CAM in Practice*. New York: John Wiley & Sons, 1986. A well-written manager's guide to understanding and using CAD/CAM. Does not assume any knowledge of CAD/CAM on the part of the reader. Illustrations are clear and concise.

Jay Nathan

Cross-References

Firms Begin Replacing Skilled Laborers with Automatic Tools (1960's), p. 1128; Sara Lee Opens an Automated Factory (1964), p. 1202; VisiCalc Spreadsheet Software Is Marketed (1979), p. 1687; American Firms Adopt Japanese Manufacturing Techniques (1980's), p. 1716; IBM Introduces Its Personal Computer (1981), p. 1809.

DEFENSE CUTBACKS DEVASTATE THE U.S. AEROSPACE INDUSTRY

Category of event: Foundings and dissolutions
Time: The 1980's
Locale: The United States

The end of the Cold War and the decline of defense spending led to the demise of the U.S. aerospace industry

Principal personages:
GEORGE BUSH (1924-   ), the president of the United States, 1989-1993
RICHARD CHENEY (1941-   ), the secretary of defense under President George Bush
RONALD REAGAN (1911-   ), the president of the United States, 1981-1989
RICHARD H. TRULY (1937-   ), the administrator of NASA
CASPAR WEINBERGER (1917-   ), the secretary of defense under President Ronald Reagan

Summary of Event

Early in his presidency, Ronald Reagan began an across-the-board rearmament program for the United States, with additional new spending running at $140 billion a year. He had a political more than a military intent, intending to show the Soviet Union that it could not keep up in the economic and technological arms races. Efforts began with the deployment of cruise missiles in Europe and the expansion of numerous weapons programs at home. The expansion program reached a peak of sorts with Reagan's 1983 speech stating his administration's intention to pursue a Strategic Defense Initiative (SDI), popularly known as "Star Wars." After that, the Soviet Union found itself unable to compete, either technologically or economically, in the Cold War. Internal pressures soon forced the Soviet Union to abandon Communism and to renounce goals of world conquest.

In the United States, American politicians quickly started to speak of a "peace dividend," wherein the savings from decreases in previously high levels of defense spending would be transferred to the civilian economy. Quickly, however, the "peace dividend" evaporated as the effects of layoffs worked their way through government contractors. A number of defense contractors found themselves in trouble and issued pink slips to thousands of highly paid, well-trained workers.

The defense budget rose from $81 billion in 1970 to $296 billion in 1990, but as a share of gross national product it actually fell by almost 4 percent during that period. In comparison, the Social Security and Medicare budgets grew from $36 billion to $345 billion. Although every aspect of the defense industry felt distress, the aerospace industry suffered acutely. Not only did orders for new aircraft tail off, but entire planned programs, such as the Navy's AX (Attack Experimental) aircraft, the modifications to Grumman's F-14 Tomcat, the V-22 Osprey, and a number of missile, experimental, and SDI-related projects, were canceled outright, were delayed, or had funding greatly reduced. In addition, the National Aeronautics and Space Administration (NASA), another client of the aerospace firms, saw its budgets constrained. During the late 1980's, virtually all of NASA's budget went for the fleet of existing space shuttles and toward development of the Space Station Freedom. For contractors not involved in those projects, NASA provided little employment.

Competition in the aerospace companies' civilian/commercial market also weakened their position. By the late 1980's, the European Airbus airline had cut deeply into sales of U.S. firms, both domestically and internationally. New planned aircraft, such as the McDonnell Douglas 80, faced delays in entering the highly competitive market.

Defense cuts rather than commercial sluggishness constituted the major problem for many aerospace contractors. Ironically, the 1980's drawdown in defense was the smallest of any in recent history. The difference in defense expenditures between the peak and the low point, as a percentage of gross domestic product, was only 2.9 percent in the post-1986 reductions, compared with 4.8 percent after the Vietnam War, 4.3 percent after the Korean War, and 35.6 percent after World War II. Moreover, the decline was more gradual. After World War II, the reductions averaged 8.9 percent annually, but the post-1986 reductions averaged only .26 percent. At the peak of World War II, annual spending on defense exceeded $885 billion (in 1993 dollars), while the post-1986 annual reductions totaled only $354 billion. Comparisons of this nature showed apparent inconsistency with the relatively serious problems many companies faced.

McDonnell Douglas, for example, was one of the leading aerospace companies, producing military and commercial aircraft as well as space vehicles. The McDonnell and Douglas companies had merged in 1967 to offset swings in the defense industry with swings in the commercial aircraft industry. In the late 1980's, as the world's largest defense contractor, McDonnell Douglas found itself teetering on the brink of unprofitability despite a huge backlog of orders. McDonnell Douglas had orders for the F/A-18 Hornet with the Navy and the F-15 Eagle and C-17 cargo aircraft with the Air Force, in addition to helicopter, space, and missile work. Nevertheless, its corporate investment in programs such as the Advanced Tactical Fighter had proved a drain, and McDonnell Douglas had the next to worst return on assets of any major aerospace contractor, trailing only General Dynamics. Its return on equity was third worst. In 1989, the company announced a radical restructuring to deal with its worst financial quarter since the merger. McDonnell Douglas forced five thousand mid-level managers to resign their titles and compete for half that number of jobs. A year later, McDonnell Douglas laid off twenty-two thousand employees.

General Dynamics (GD) was one of the few companies doing worse than McDonnell Douglas. It took a $639 million loss in 1990 and had the worst return on assets and return on equity of any of the nine major aerospace contractors. Only Grumman had a poorer bond rating. Unlike the relatively healthy Boeing Company, GD had virtually all of its work, 85 percent, in defense. In 1992, GD started to move out of aerospace by selling its fighter production program, mostly focused on production of the F-16 Fighting Falcon, to Lockheed Corporation, another industry giant. Lockheed had only about one-third the sales ($9 billion) of industry leader Boeing, but it had good earnings per share and an acceptable bond rating. It also had a recent success, production of the famous F-117 Stealth fighter, effectively used in the Gulf War of 1990. It maintained a large budget for "black," or secret, programs.

Despite Lockheed's production record, it had severe problems in its Trident D-5 missile production program. That, combined with its inability to break into commercial airline manufacturing (with the exception of the L-1011), made the company vulnerable to Air Force budget cuts. Only Boeing, with its almost $30 billion in sales and its twenty-year backlog in orders, was able to postpone the effects of the defense downturn. Even Boeing, however, found itself feeling the decline in defense production. In 1993, the Washington-based aircraft manufacturer joined the other companies by announcing significant planned layoffs.

Impact of Event

In 1990, Iraq's invasion of Kuwait and the subsequent U.S. military action led many to think that the defense cuts might not be as harsh as expected, or might be slower than expected. The election of Bill Clinton to the presidency in 1992 brought defense policy statements during his early tenure that suggested that the cuts would be worse than expected. At the same time, NASA's fragile budget came under fire because of the ballooning expense of the Space Station Freedom, the failure to develop a reliable follow-on to the expensive space shuttles, and the performance errors of some NASA technology, such as the Hubble Space Telescope. Those events led some experts to predict another round of defense industry mergers, such as those that had occurred in the 1960's and 1970's.

By 1990, world events had caused some policymakers to reevaluate the sensibility of drastically downsizing the Department of Defense and the "military-industrial complex." The Gulf War proved, or at least greatly reinforced, the notion that the United States could build "high-tech" weapons that worked. That was true especially during the first six months after the war, when the claims for success of weapons such as the cruise and Patriot missiles were exaggerated by the media and the military. More significant, the threats posed by the Iraqi-launched Scud missiles on civilian populations greatly boosted the desirability of missile interception systems, which formed the basis of the Strategic Defense Initiative. Thus, one of the most expensive, "high-tech" sectors in the defense budget received an unexpected lift from a Middle Eastern despot with "low-tech" weapons.

After the first round of glowing reports on the Patriot and cruise missiles, however, a revisionist analysis claimed less effective performances from the weapons than once thought. Those criticisms arrived at a time when the budget deficit was growing and legislators were searching for ways to cut government spending. After all, if the weapons did not work, why spend additional money maintaining and improving them? Subsequent studies revised the critics' analysis, showing that most weapons performed at the highest standards ever attained in modern war. For example, American aircraft in the Gulf War flew more than twenty-nine thousand sorties with a loss of only fourteen aircraft, the lowest percentage of losses in any American war and barely half the loss rate as in the Vietnam War. Another measure, the mission capability rates (the rate at which aircraft were maintained) actually exceeded the peacetime rate in eleven major lines of aircraft used in the Gulf. The comparison is blurred because typically under peacetime conditions aircraft might be held out for repair or maintenance for problems that would be repaired overnight under war conditions. Four of the aircraft attained mission capability rates of more than 95 percent.

Excellent performance did not change budget realities, however, and a number of firms by the late 1980's found themselves in the position of being out of business as a result of elimination of a single weapon. Grumman, for example, fought desperately to have the F-14 Tomcat upgraded for attack missions. Without the upgrades, Grumman would close. In the late 1980's, the Navy leaned heavily toward the AX (Attack Experimental) aircraft, but that program was canceled in 1990 after budget overruns and poor management. Grumman hung on. General Dynamics, on the other hand, had to sell its F-16 production line after the elimination of other fighter airplanes.

By 1990, most of the major airframe and propulsion contractors had concluded that the only way to survive was for them to join in consortia or "teams" to bid on expensive projects. That defeated the intent of the competitive bid contracts in some programs, while two or more "teams" competed for other contracts, as in the case of the Advanced Tactical Fighter (ATF, won by a Lockheed-led team and renamed the F-22). Other projects that saw teams either compete for the contracts or be formed in order to receive the entire contract award included the National Aero-Space Plane (General Dynamics, McDonnell Douglas, Rockwell, Rocketdyne, and Pratt & Whitney); the Light Helicopter Experimental (LHX) team of Boeing and Sikorsky, plus the engine team made up of a pairing of Allison and Garrett; and a variety of international teams, each featuring a U.S. contractor, for the new joint service trainer contract. The impetus toward sharing resources and knowledge gained ground in the late 1980's and early 1990's, but the evidence was far from conclusive on which investment and procurement practices were the most effective. A study by Jacques Gansler, a defense industry expert, showed that national and international cooperative efforts have taken longer and cost more than if each country had produced the weapon itself. A 1983 General Accounting Office document reported no teaming efforts that resulted in satisfied participating services and actual savings. If assessed solely on the variable of cost, teaming or joint programs generally resulted in higher costs to the taxpayer. Moreover, a spate of critics of corporate combinations produced work that showed that the most successful industries were the most highly competitive and the least reliant on government support, two traits that characterized few aircraft manufacturers by 1990.

Supporters of the consortia concept argued that the United States had fallen behind Europe with its Airbus airliner, funded in 1969 at a meeting in which Germany and France, as well as the Hawker-Siddeley company, agreed to unite to keep the market from the American aircraft manufacturers. The success of Airbus remains a matter of debate. It captured more than 20 percent of the world market, for the first time taking Boeing's share of the world market below 60 percent. Airbus, however, devoured more than $7 billion in taxpayer's money, and Europe did not create a single net new job from 1970 to 1981, the time during which the Airbus was being built in Europe to keep jobs from going overseas. Other forces certainly were at work regarding employment, but the evidence on Airbus was not unequivocal. Naturally, American aircraft manufacturers clamored for assistance from the U.S. government based on their perception that the Europeans gave their companies an unfair advantage.

The final, most obvious impact of the decline of the American aerospace industry came in the human terms of unemployment. White collar workers, engineers, and high-tech workers all faced unprecedented levels of layoffs, especially in California, where the economy started to stagnate for the first time in the post-World War II period. Defense cutbacks came at a time when Los Angeles had just become the nation's leading manufacturing center as well as one of the top high-tech regions in the United States. The effects on the California economy were felt in the real estate market, where growth in prices slowed to 5 percent per year—virtual stagnation in California terms. In some areas, housing prices fell, and homes stayed on the market far longer than in the past. Outmigration of companies started in earnest in the early 1990's. Neighboring states such as Arizona and Nevada, seeing their opportunity to attract defense giants, offered special tax breaks or other incentives to relocate. Lockheed relocated some of its factories to Georgia in response to an attractive deal offered by that state's government. Smaller defense companies left the Golden State in droves. How far the defense decline would go, and its ultimate effects on the aerospace industry, remained unknown by 1993. Les Aspin, Clinton's secretary of defense, made it clear that he supported still deeper cuts in the defense budget. At the same time, an international economic slowdown had caused many nations to cancel their purchases of American commercial aircraft, exacerbating the troubles from the defense side of the economy.

Bibliography

Gansler, Jacques. *Affording Defense*. Cambridge, Mass.: MIT Press, 1989. A follow-up to his *The Defense Industry* (1980). Ganlser details the problems and pitfalls of weapons procurement in an age in which legislators were determined that contractors would not get away with "fraud and abuse." In reality, as Gansler shows, the system was pregnant with barriers to efficiency that only served to drive up costs. Rules that required competition in all lines of weapons often caused two or more unhealthy companies to limp along, growing increasingly dependent on the military.

Hallion, Richard P. *Storm over Iraq: Air Power and the Gulf War*. Washington, D.C.:

Smithsonian Institution Press, 1992. More than a history of the Gulf War. Hallion provides a synopsis of air power theory, a review of trends in procurement and production, a superior technical appraisal of tactics and technologies, and an overall thorough assessment of the role of aircraft in modern warfare.

Morrocco, John D. "Defense Conversion Panel Urges Dramatic Changes." *Aviation Week and Space Technology* 138 (January 25, 1993): 64-65. Provides a critical comparison of defense drawdowns, those following World War II, the Korean War, and the Vietnam War and that of the 1980's. Invaluable statistics include spending relative to gross domestic product, average change per year, and difference between high points and low points.

Puth, Robert C. *American Economic History*. 3d ed. New York: Dryden Press, 1993. A general survey useful for trends in government, defense, and civilian budgets in the 1980's, as well as a review of employment and investment statistics relevant to the defense industry.

Weinberger, Caspar. *Fighting for Peace: Seven Critical Years in the Pentagon*. New York: Warner Books, 1990. Contains a detailed insider's discussion of the buildup during the Reagan years.

Larry Schweikart

Cross-References

The U.S. Service Economy Emerges (1960's), p. 1138; A European Consortium Plans the Airbus (1967), p. 1303; McDonnell Aircraft and Douglas Aircraft Merge (1967), p. 1314; Congress Begins Hearings on Cost Overruns for the C-5A Galaxy (1969), p. 1384; The Concorde Flies Passengers at Supersonic Speeds (1976), p. 1606; Japan Becomes the World's Largest Automobile Producer (1980), p. 1751.

ELECTRONIC TECHNOLOGY CREATES THE POSSIBILITY OF TELECOMMUTING

Categories of event: Labor and business practices
Time: The 1980's
Locale: The United States and other industrial nations

Developments in electronic office equipment installed in people's homes enabled business employees to work at home as telecommuters

Principal personages:
ALVIN TOFFLER (1928-   ), a futurist who predicted the rise of telecommuting
THOMAS W. MILLER, the director of the National Work at Home Survey
PATRICIA LYON MOKHTARIAN, a researcher who chronicled advances in telecommuting
JACK M. NILLES, a consultant to the California Telecommuting Pilot Project in the late 1980's

Summary of Event

In the early 1980's, key improvements were made in both the power and the affordability of electronic office equipment. These developments enabled many business employees to work all or part of the week at their place of residence. The personal computer was the centerpiece of the modern gadgetry. With a modem, a printer, a fax machine, a telephone with special features, and, a few years later, a small copy machine, a home-based white-collar worker could put together a "virtual office" with links to the company office to enable transfer of information in either direction.

The term "telecommuters" was adopted for home-based workers connected to their employers by electronic equipment. The pioneers of such work practices were a few isolated individuals with unusual levels of specialized technological expertise who set up arrangements of their own design. In the early 1980's, the technology became accessible to large numbers of typical businesspeople. By 1984, about two hundred companies had made some experiments with telecommuting, and about thirty had set up programs.

Companies with employees working at home were initially concerned about productivity. Soon, however, some insurance companies, such as Blue Cross and Blue Shield of South Carolina, were able to report improvements in output when workers stayed at home. Employees were initially interested in flexibility in the ways of combining work and home obligations. Many other advantages of telecommuting were gradually recognized, and futurists surmised that the way work is done in society could be transformed. Some projected that by the middle of the 1990's, there could be twenty million telecommuters.

Technical developments in home-installed electronic equipment connected to equipment at the corporate office offered new possibilities in the flexibility of working arrangements. The developments included portable telephones and other devices that allowed workers to contact employers when on the road, held up in traffic, or on commuter trains. By the early 1990's, fax machines that could be used in cars were on the market.

In most cases, the equipment for telecommuters was provided by employers. There were some individuals, however, whose enthusiasm to set up home-working arrangements led them to buy their own equipment.

With a personal computer at home, a worker can produce letters, reports, budgets, sales projections, forecasts, and other documents in exactly the same way as in the corporate office. Necessary data could come via modem, and finished documents could go back the same way. The machine at home, together with its software, needed to be compatible with that at the office. For some years, there were problems of information exchange between Apple and International Business Machines (IBM) systems and between personal computers and mainframes. Translatability and conversion features were built into the systems as manufacturers recognized that users were increasingly linking machines.

When a modem is used in conjunction with a computer, access to data stored elsewhere becomes possible and a conduit for communication is established. This makes available a whole range of information and business support services, including electronic mail service. These capacities reduce the isolation that would otherwise be the condition of workers at home.

Worker mobility increased with the advent of laptop computers. These small machines are powered by rechargeable batteries. They are light enough to be carried around, but many were nearly as powerful as some personal computers by the early 1990's.

Improvements in computer printer technology also benefited telecommuters. Many printer manufacturers offered several versions of their products, intended for various levels of use and different levels of quality. Printers for home use need not be different from those attached to computers in offices, but cost savings could be realized by using a printer designed for less strenuous or exacting work.

The facsimile machine established itself as an indispensable piece of office equipment. The word "fax" became part of the English language, as both a noun and a verb. A fax machine sends a copy of a document to another machine, using telephone lines. Falling costs and increasing use of the machines made them affordable for home offices and allowed workers to reach a large proportion of the business world without leaving home.

Developments in telephone technology are often mentioned in the context of telecommuting. A worker dealing with routine claims processing for an insurance company, for example, may need nothing more than basic telephone service. Others may need a line separate from their personal telephone, together with a message system or voice mail. Still others may need cellular telephones, which can be taken on the road. Cellular telephones made long commutes more productive and allowed offices to keep in touch with traveling employees.

People who switched to working at home could get some benefits from advanced technology even without purchasing equipment. For documents not suitable for fax or modem delivery, and for people without these devices, improved services of the United States Postal Service, United Parcel Service, and Federal Express were available. Businesses, particularly copy shops, began offering fax service to customers.

For a time, the major weakness in the telecommuter office was the lack of a copier. Home-based workers in the 1980's regularly used the services of local copy centers as a useful supplement to the home office. This was expensive in terms of time, if not in charges for copies. Copy machines were large, heavy, and expensive, and so not suitable for use in the home. Responding to the needs of home-based workers, manufacturers began producing inexpensive desk-top copiers. With this addition, home offices took on the characteristics of corporate offices.

Impact of Event

Telecommuting has had effects on individuals who work at home, their employers, and society as a whole. Telecommuters spend less time, or no time, traveling to and from work. This reduces the unproductive use of time and reduces expenditures for gasoline and vehicle maintenance. Telecommuters also enjoy flexibility in organizing their work, being less constrained by office hours. In the case of parents, the chance to work at home permits combining paid work and child-care responsibilities. Many parents found it possible to look after children while putting in a normal day's work. In some cases, parents from different families shared child-minding duties while maintaining, among themselves, the required attention to computer terminals.

Parents who decide to stay home to provide childcare can ease their transition back to the office by finding employment as telecommuters or in other home-based work. Telecommuting offers a solution to the conflicting pressures of work and family. Telecommuting also enables a gradual return to work for convalescents not yet ready for five-day-a-week rigor. Persons rendered immobile through an injury such as a broken hip or a permanent disability can be productive even though unable to travel to work. Telecommuting thus offered new possibilities for disadvantaged workers.

The disadvantages of telecommuting primarily flow from the isolation of being at home. Many employees who have known the ways of the office become acutely aware of what they are missing when they stay at home: the informal communication and social interaction of the office. Some worry that their reduced visibility will limit their promotion prospects. The value of face-to-face contact as part of the communication that supports work activities is missed when working at home. These concerns are mitigated when the employee goes to the office for part of the working week.

Motivation can be affected in either direction by telecommuting. Those who need the stimulation of rapport with others will be less motivated at home. Others may enjoy the feeling of enhanced competence when they discover that they can find a way to meet a challenge without recourse to the help of the worker at the next desk. Although human oversight is diminished, home-based workers can still be given production goals. Some computer software allows monitoring of the amount of work performed.

The situation for disabled workers is delicate and complex. Special efforts to use home-based technology to bring house-bound people into the workforce can either liberate them from the feeling of being unproductive or reinforce their sense of isolation. Companies may decide that it is less expensive to keep a worker at home than to redesign the office to meet his or her needs.

Regarding the impact on companies, a primary concern is the productivity of employees working at home. Without acceptable productivity, no company is likely to permit telecommuting. The verdict from diverse companies is that responsible and mature employees generally show an increase in productivity when working from home. Companies that had instituted telecommuting programs by the 1990's included those in banking, insurance, publishing, business services, computers, catalog retailing, and stock brokerage. All found that telecommuting had the potential to increase productivity.

There are legitimate concerns whether a person working at home will be distracted by various elements of the home environment and thus deflected from work. The office itself has distractions, however, and many workers find it easier to concentrate and keep on task at home. Although not everyone may be temperamentally suited to working at home, many people are more productive. The company office can maintain links and can telephone or fax a telecommuter to keep a check. At the other extreme, some people increase the length of their workday because there is no longer a point in the day when they leave the work environment. Their work is in their homes and may be difficult to ignore.

Aside from gains in worker productivity, companies benefit through economies in office space, parking, and other overhead expenses. More subtle effects include enhancement of communicative skills of managers, since more precision is needed to convey instructions to people who are not physically present; development of different methods of project management to allow workers who do not physically meet to bring parts of a project together; and development of judicious schemes of goals and rewards for people working outside the office. All these gains can translate into better use of traditional, office-based employees.

Some companies with telecommuting employees are faced with problems of monitoring and security. In most cases, the requirement that work be done to specification and by a certain deadline are the only control criteria necessary. In some cases, a business might be worried about home employees using company equipment for free-lance work or about the use of proprietary information by employees who could undertake work for competitor companies or sell information.

The impact of telecommuting on society as a whole is potentially enormous, as it reduces the distinctions between work and home. Tax law has had to adapt to workers who are neither office-based nor self-employed, or who work part of each week at an office outside the home. At the local level, laws that restrict use of the home for commercial purposes were challenged.

Another consideration for society is the matter of pollution and fuel consumption resulting from the familiar types of commuting. As travel becomes more expensive, inconvenient, and time-consuming, the benefits of telecommuting increase. Telecommuting reduces the burdens on those forced to travel and on society in general by reducing traffic congestion and pollution.

Regarding questions of distributive economics, the impact of telecommuting may well include both bad and good. Organized labor has warned of the increasing use of employees who, because they are dispersed, are unlikely to become part of a collective unit that protects their interests. Labor unions warn of home-based sweatshop labor. On the positive side, there is evidence that in Great Britain, home-based workers' pay is better than average. It is conceivable that the hiring of home-based people in low-income neighborhoods by companies in the suburbs could be encouraged as a public policy for reducing geographic disparities in income.

The technology that supports telecommuting has both liberating and isolating tendencies. Its long-term impact will depend on how business and workers choose to act on the possibilities that the technology creates.

Bibliography

Arden, Lynie. *The Work-at-Home Sourcebook.* 4th ed. Boulder, Colo.: Live Oak, 1992. Gives practical information about many aspects of telecommuting and other home-based work. Indicates the kinds of work that lend themselves to home work and includes directories of companies that have telecommuting programs. Helpful for anyone searching for a telecommuting job or other home-based employment.

Best, Fred. "Technology and the Changing World of Work." *The Futurist* 18 (April, 1984): 61-66. Deals with the many issues associated with working at home, including skill requirements, displacement of workers, and management of decentralized systems. Includes speculation about a future home-based economy.

Hamilton, Carol-Ann. "Telecommuting." *Personnel Journal* 66 (April, 1987): 90-111. A guide for setting up telecommuting programs in a company. Recognizes various factors affecting employees, including security, employee benefits, career development, equipment, and insurance. Useful for companies considering a telecommuting program.

Kanarek, Lisa. *Organizing Your Home Office for Success: Expert Strategies That Can Work for You.* New York: Penguin, 1992. A practical guide to organizing the office at home. Includes material on choosing the location for the office, filing systems, planning, time management, handling information, and choosing printers. Contains useful lists of suppliers of equipment.

Kinsman, Francis. *The Telecommuters.* New York: John Wiley & Sons, 1987. A study of telecommuting in Great Britain. Describes specific company schemes in detail and reports high productivity and good earnings among telecommuters. Interesting and futuristic.

Wolfgram, Tammara H. "Working at Home: The Growth of Cottage Industry." *The Futurist* 18 (June, 1984): 31-34. Offers a perspective about the future of work. The trend toward work at home is noted. States that some issues need to be faced, including the changing of laws that restrict home-based work.

Richard Barrett

Cross-References

Nixon Signs the Occupational Safety and Health Act (1970), p. 1466; Federal Express Begins Operations (1973), p. 1538; AT&T and GTE Install Fiber-Optic Telephone Systems (1977), p. 1647; IBM Introduces Its Personal Computer (1981), p. 1809; A Home Shopping Service Is Offered on Cable Television (1985), p. 1909; Bell Atlantic and TCI Announce Merger Plans (1993), p. 2066.

U.S. REGIONAL BRANCH BANKING IS APPROVED

Category of event: Finance
Time: The 1980's
Locale: The United States

By *authorizing regional banking in the Northeast, Southeast, and West, national banking authorities took a step toward integrating the U.S. banking system through interstate branch banking*

Principal personages:
> AMADEO P. GIANNINI (1870-1949), the longtime president of the Bank of America and an early force in revising branch banking laws
> JOSEPH PINOLA (1925-   ), the head of California's Western Bancorporation, which formed a network of banks in the West
> WALTER B. WRISTON (1919-   ), a longtime chairman of the board of Citibank

Summary of Event

The appearance of what were known as regional compacts among banks in the 1980's marked a point of evolution in the American banking system toward national branch, or interstate, banking. Establishing the exact time that interstate banking became more of a reality than a goal is difficult, as it occurred in incremental steps over the course of two hundred years, and against considerable opposition. Most authorities agree that major shifts occurred in the 1980's thanks to the deregulatory mood that came to Washington with the administration of Ronald Reagan.

Since the creation of the First Bank of the United States in 1791, which permitted branch offices in several states, many financial thinkers have argued that branching constitutes the most efficient and flexible form of bank structure. Branches are offices that have full banking powers. They can take deposits, make loans, and deal in a variety of exchanges, but their assets and liabilities ultimately are consolidated with the parent bank and all other members of the bank's branch system. Rather than appearing as those of a single bank, the assets of the branch will reflect those of the parent and all other branch offices.

States developed their own branching laws, often by default. In California and Arizona, for example, no legislative rulings dealt with branching until it was well developed in those areas. Older southern states, which tended to have more branching than northern states, wrote branch banking permission into the banks' charters. Elsewhere, as in Nebraska, Oklahoma, New York, and other states, branching at times was expressly prohibited.

Independent "unit" banks dominated much of the northern tier of the United States and the Midwestern states. Unit banks feared the competition that branch banks associated with large parent banks might bring and maintained powerful lobbies in the state legislature against any state laws permitting branches. They also lobbied in Washington against any national legislation that would allow branch banks. Prior to the Civil War, only a few northern states ever had branch banks, but North Carolina, South Carolina, Georgia, Tennessee, Alabama, and Georgia all had at one time allowed branches, and many southern states even permitted "agencies," or offices that were less than full-service banks, from out of state to operate within their borders. Georgia banks had several agencies in Florida, for example, and cross-state ownership through corporate façades was not uncommon. George Smith of Wisconsin, for example, performed most of his banking activities through a bank chartered in Atlanta that issued Georgia bank notes that circulated in Illinois.

During the Civil War, the federal government passed laws chartering national banks through the office of the Comptroller of the Currency. Those laws prohibited the newly chartered national banks from branching, constituting yet another victory for the unit bankers. Between 1870 and 1900, however, the national bank system consistently lost members to the more lenient state systems. Because state charters often allowed branches, the national banking system operated at a serious disadvantage in many states.

The most important state in which the national system had to compete with state branching advantages was California, where A. P. Giannini had built a small bank, the Bank of Italy, into a statewide powerhouse. Giannini recognized the inherent virtues of branching: It offered quick transfer of funds among regions of the state, it could collect deposits from dozens of different locations for customer convenience, and it spread the bank's name across large geographical areas. By 1927, Giannini had expanded his Bank of Italy into a holding company network that consisted of 155 branches. Another California competitor, Joseph Sartori, who ran the Security Trust and Savings Bank in Los Angeles, had 50 branches. Whereas Sartori was happy to keep his network inside California for the time being, Giannini wanted to expand nationally and took steps to overturn or circumvent the McFadden Act, which became law in 1927.

The McFadden Act, named for the chairman of the House Banking and Currency Committee, Louis T. McFadden of Pennsylvania, represented a response to the drain of banks out of the national bank system into state charters. In general, state charters were more lenient regarding capital requirements. More important, many states permitted branching, whereas national banks could not branch. McFadden's bill permitted national banks to branch in states that allowed branching and stated that any bank that joined the national system could retain all of its branches in existence when the act went into effect. Some historians have attributed the McFadden Act to a deal worked out with Giannini to bring his massive Bank of Italy into the Federal Reserve System. Giannini did join the national system, bringing three hundred branches into the national network, in 1930. Shortly thereafter, the Los Angeles First Security National Bank and Trust joined the national system with its one hundred branches. If each branch were counted as an independent bank, this would have represented a 20 percent expansion in the number of national banks joining the system in a three-year period.

Giannini had bigger ideas. He wanted to take his bank to a national scale with true interstate branch banking. His anticipated amendment to the McFadden Act, which would have permitted such branch banking, never materialized. Branch banking remained solely a state issue until the 1970's.

Meanwhile, the industry changed dramatically in favor of branching. In 1945, for example, unit banks had 72 percent of all offices. By 1988, banks with at least one branch operated 76 percent of the sixty thousand offices in the nation. The total number of branches had soared, from four thousand in 1945 to more than forty-six thousand by 1988.

With the advent of computers, people found that they could transfer money rapidly to any bank in the nation. To remain competitive, banks had to offer flexibility. At the same time, large banks such as Citicorp, under the leadership of Walter B. Wriston, had located important operations in states other than those of banking headquarters. In the case of Citicorp, the credit card operations center was located in South Dakota. The threat of large banks or nonbank businesses such as Sears or Merrill Lynch buying banks in other states through holding companies forced regional giants to look for ways of expanding their business to other areas while protecting their own territory.

In 1975, Maine offered out-of-state holding companies the opportunity to purchase Maine banks if the home state of the holding company reciprocated by allowing Maine-based companies to acquire businesses in that home state. By 1984, Maine had dropped the reciprocity requirement, but it provided the basis for the first regional compact, by which a group of New England states permitted their banks to invest in one another. That allowed banks in the region to merge with each other but prohibited mergers by the big outsiders, such as Chase Manhattan Bank and Citicorp. It also allowed banks to establish branches in any state in which a bank had merged. A similarly successful regional compact occurred in North Carolina and Georgia, where North Carolina National Bank and Citizens and Southern greatly expanded their operations. Other states simply permitted large out-of-state banks to purchase in-state institutions. In 1980, Joseph Pinola of California's Western Bancorporation formed a network of twenty-one banks in eleven western states under the common name of First Interstate Bank. That represented a franchise arrangement, not true interstate banking under which banks could move funds across state lines at will.

At that point, the momentum toward interstate banking stalled. The large New York banks all had purchased footholds in other states and even had started to unload some of them in the bank recessions of the 1980's. Well-run local banks proved difficult for outsiders to manage, and many of them lost money. By 1993, for example, Chase Manhattan Bank, which had bought the highly profitable Continental Bank in Arizona, was looking to unload its purchase after consistently failing to keep the bank at the levels of profitability it had reached under local management. At the same time, the popularity of reciprocity agreements faded. Thus, by 1993, no burst of legislation had moved the nation's banking structure closer to interstate banking.

Impact of Event

The regional compacts and the reciprocity agreements indicated a realization on the part of local banks that their markets no longer would be protected from out-of-state competitors, even when those competitors specifically could not charter full-service banks in their states. Some states permitted one-function banking activities by banks or other institutions, under which a company could accept deposits but not make loans, or could make loans but not accept deposits. That gave Wall Street giants such as Merrill Lynch and Prudential windows through which they could attract some banking business into money market accounts that paid higher interest rates than did local banks and allowed companies such as Sears to make loans. In any case, local bankers acted out of self-preservation instincts to stymie further encroachment on their territory.

When Citibank opened a credit card processing office in South Dakota, the trend appeared clear: No local region was immune to outside operations, no matter how restricted. The combination of a chain of institutions in the West under the banner of First Interstate Bank was undertaken in anticipation of unrestricted interstate banking. That still had not occurred by 1993, leaving First Interstate essentially as a franchise operation and diminishing the interest in reciprocity agreements among large, national rivals.

Several factors help to explain the lack of progress in interstate branch banking. First, the appearance of Japanese competition in the 1980's absorbed the attention of most large banks. Japanese banks soared into eight of the top ten places among the world's largest banks by the mid-1980's. New York giants such as Citicorp and Chase found themselves less interested in getting into South Carolina and more interested in establishing ties to South Korea.

Second, a financial recession struck the United States in the 1980's, most of it related to real estate and the collapse of the savings and loan system. Large banks of any type that had extensive real estate holdings, particularly in Texas and California, found themselves in trouble. Ironically, those problems came at a time when many lenders to troubled foreign borrowers such as Mexico and Brazil had just written off millions of dollars worth of bad loans. Bank of America, for example, managed to work its way out of disaster and eliminate large blocks of foreign loans even as some critics predicted its impending doom. As the larger banks worked themselves back to health, they did not have the energy to simultaneously pursue changes in regulation and legislation that the deregulatory atmosphere of the Reagan Administration had offered. As a result, they missed a chance to change the laws.

Third, the expansion of bank holding companies in some nonbranching states gave a number of banks control over large amounts of bank assets. In 1987, for example, the forty-nine hundred one-bank holding companies had 21 percent of all bank assets, but about one thousand multiple-bank holding companies controlled forty-three hundred banks and 70 percent of all bank assets. The bank holding company had become the dominant form of banking organization in the United States, somewhat diminishing the advantages of branching.

Finally, computer technology evolved so rapidly that branching became less important than it had been when money moved more slowly. Bank holding companies could move money electronically to virtually anywhere in the world in a matter of minutes, and customers in Ohio and Montana used credit cards from New York-based Citibank or California-based BankAmerica. The only strong advantage that the branches retained was in receiving local deposits, but even that function was dulled somewhat by the appearance of brokerage houses' money market funds, credit unions, and direct deposit payrolls.

Regional compacts opened a window of opportunity for national interstate branch banking. By the time that many banks were in a financial position to take advantage of it, however, the legislative and technological windows made branching less important.

Bibliography

Calomiris, Charles. "Is Deposit Insurance Necessary? *A Historical Perspective.*" *Journal of Economic History* 50 (June, 1990): 283-295. This comprehensive study of state-sponsored deposit insurance schemes examines alternative structures for maintaining bank liquidity and solvency. It concludes that states with branch banking laws were far more resilient than those with any other type of structure, including deposit insurance. Calomiris builds on several other pieces he has written on branching and deposit insurance that, when combined with the data and results in this article, make the case for branching overwhelming.

England, Catherine, and Thomas F. Huertas. *The Financial Services Revolution.* Washington, D.C.: Cato Institute, 1988. Although biased against government regulation, this book details developments in banking and financial services through the appearance of the regional compacts.

Hector, Gary. *Breaking the Bank: The Decline of BankAmerica.* Boston: Little, Brown, 1988. A critical assessment of the Bank of America that lionizes A. P. Giannini. Written just prior to the bank's miraculous comeback, *Breaking the Bank* appears outdated and less than perceptive in its chapters on recent developments.

Klebaner, Benjamin. *American Commercial Banking: A History.* Boston: Twayne, 1990. A thorough and concise treatment of American banking. Klebaner discusses the expansion of branching, bank holding companies, and regional compacts. Although it is an up-to-date history of the banking industry, this book lacks some of the case study and entrepreneurial approaches found in other works.

Schweikart, Larry, ed. *Encyclopedia of American Business History and Biography: Banking and Finance, 1913-1989.* New York: Facts on File, 1990. Includes discussions, in the introduction and in topic headings, of trends in banking, branching, and regional agreements. Especially useful are the biographies of Joseph Pinola, A. P. Giannini, and others involved in the branch/interstate banking movement.

Larry Schweikart

Cross-References

The McFadden Act Regulates Branch Banking (1927), p. 539; The Banking Act of 1933 Reorganizes the American Banking System (1933), p. 656; The Banking Act of 1935 Centralizes U.S. Monetary Control (1935), p. 717; Congress Deregulates Banks and Savings and Loans (1980-1982), p. 1757; Mexico Renegotiates Debt to U.S. Banks (1989), p. 1981; Bush Responds to the Savings and Loan Crisis (1989), p. 1991.

GREAT EVENTS
FROM
HISTORY II

CHRONOLOGICAL LIST OF EVENTS

VOLUME I

VOLUME II

VOLUME III

VOLUME IV

VOLUME V